THE HISTORY OF
THE GREEK AND ROMAN THEATER

Fig. A. Colossal bronze tragic mask (*see Fig. 301*)

THE HISTORY OF
THE GREEK AND ROMAN
THEATER

BY MARGARETE BIEBER

1961

PRINCETON, NEW JERSEY

PRINCETON UNIVERSITY PRESS

LONDON: OXFORD UNIVERSITY PRESS

Publication of this book has been aided by a grant from the
American Council of Learned Societies and by the Ford
Foundation program to support publication, through univer-
sity presses, of works in the humanities and social sciences

Printed in the United States of America
by The Meriden Gravure Company, Meriden, Connecticut

The publishers wish to express their gratitude
for the cooperation of the individuals and
museums named in the List of Illustrations
and Sources, and especially for assistance from
the staffs of The Metropolitan Museum of Art,
New York, The Museum of Fine Arts, Boston,
The Art Museum, Princeton University, and
Yale University Library.

TO MY AMERICAN, GERMAN, AND ITALIAN FRIENDS AND COLLEAGUES

Felix, qui potuit rerum cognoscere causas—VERGIL, *Georgica* II 490

Fig. B. Theater of Taormina (*see Fig. 636*)

CONTENTS

PREFACE

THIS book is an attempt to reconstruct the history of the development of the ancient theater, making use of all the different available literary, epigraphical, architectural, and figurative sources. The completely preserved Greek dramas—32 tragedies, 2 satyrical plays, 15 comedies—and the Latin dramas—10 tragedies and 28 comedies—as well as the fragments of lost plays have been excellently edited, and their development has been well treated in the best histories of ancient literature. The testimony of ancient writers, such as Vitruvius, Pollux, the various grammarians who wrote scholia on the classics, and the many occasional remarks of different authors have been cited and utilized again and again. The inscriptions relating to the performances have been treated by Wilhelm and particularly well used by Pickard-Cambridge. Books on theater buildings with all details have been admirably written by Dörpfeld, Fiechter, von Gerkan, and Stillwell. A number of handbooks, such as those by Albert Müller, Navarre, Flickinger, Allen, and Pickard-Cambridge, give a systematic survey of theatrical antiquities, including monuments, but with the chief emphasis on the philological and literary side. Wieseler was the first to collect and edit systematically, in 1851, the monuments as illustrations of the masks, costumes, and settings. His work was excellent for his time, but the text as well as the illustrations are now out of date. I tried to replace his book in 1920 with my *Die Denkmäler zum Theaterwesen im Altertum*, which is now out of print. In my *History of the Greek and Roman Theater*, which the Princeton University Press published in 1939 and of which this is a second edition, revised and enlarged, I attempted to demonstrate how indispensable are the hitherto neglected figured sources like vases, terracottas, and mural paintings. They are objective and contemporary, in contrast to the literary sources, which are for the most part subjective opinions of individuals, and often of much later writers. My earlier book was built up systematically and analytically according to the subjects. This book is an attempt to construct the story of the rich development of theatrical life in the different periods and places of the ancient world, laying stress on the beginnings and the reasons for changes. My goal is to build out of the various elements a connected whole, a history of the theater of the ancient world.

It is my belief that important problems, such as the presentation of tragedy in the fifth century, the exact place of presentation in the Greek theater, the period and use of the first high stage, the staging of the comedies of Menander and others, can be solved, or at least illuminated, by uniting the literary, architectural, and figurative sources, using each source for its own period and leaving out all modern conceptions of stage production. We must remember how Wilamowitz-Möllendorf tried to stage the plays of Aeschylus with regard to their contents only, as if Aeschylus had had at his disposal the means of the illusionistic stage settings of the nineteenth century. He merely demonstrated the endless possibilities which these earliest tragedies offer, even to a modern stage manager. On the other hand, A. von Gerkan wishes to exclude from the history of the theater the existing plays as if they were purely literary monuments. We must never forget that these plays, including even those of Seneca, were written for presentation, not for reading, and that the theater buildings were erected for presenting these plays. It is necessary to avoid extreme positions taken by men who are primarily philologists or architects. We must, however, never forget that these specialists are the men who, by their research, have done much to promote our knowledge of the ancient theater.

I treat in this book the archaic, classical, and Hellenistic Greek theater, and the Roman republican and imperial theater in chronological sequence, laying emphasis on the origin and the early development of each period. The most important literary evidence is best found in Pickard-Cambridge, *The Theatre of Dionysus in Athens* (1946) and *The Dramatic Festivals of Athens* (1953). The 865 illustrations have been collected over a period of more than thirty years. Many have already been used in the *Denkmäler zum Theaterwesen*, but most of them were taken for me by good photographers during 1930-31, with the help of the International Fellowship granted me by the American Association of University Women. Others have been acquired since 1951 in Italy and in the United States with the help of grants from the American Philosophical Society and the Princeton University Department of Art and Archaeology. All museum photographs have been taken with the permission of those who were directors of the museums at the time. The negatives have been presented by me to the respective museums, to the German Archaeological Institutes in Rome and Athens, or to the Department of Fine Arts and Archaeology of Columbia University.

This revised edition is intended not only to supplant the edition of 1939, but also to supplement it. There are 866 instead of the 566 illustrations of the original edition. I believe that these illustrations

vii

give in themselves a picture of the development of the theater for about 1,000 years, from approximately 600 B.C. to A.D. 400. The text is also enlarged. The author has embodied her own research and that of many scholars in the United States, Britain, Italy, France, and Germany since 1939. New ideas are worked in, particularly on the background to the development of the theater, so that the text gives at the same time a kind of history of the ancient civilization.

In accordance with the modern interest in the representation of ancient plays, as evidenced by productions in colleges and universities and by theater managers and movie producers, illustrations of modern productions have been included in the new Chapter XVI, and indications made for the entries, exits, and groupings of the actors in the productions of the classical periods. The chapters on the Roman theater are much enlarged and mostly completely rewritten to embody the lower-class entertainments, which have many parallels with our "shows" and athletic events.

I want to express my gratitude to the following colleagues who have obliged me by reading and correcting parts of my manuscript: Dr. Jane Henle of the School of General Studies, Columbia University, who read the whole manuscript; Professor W. B. Dinsmoor of Columbia University, who read Chapters V and IX on Greek theater buildings; Professor Richard Stillwell of Princeton University, who read Chapters XIII and XIV on Roman theater buildings; Professor A. D. Trendall of Canberra, Australia, who read Chapter X on Italian popular comedy; and Professor Randolph Goodman of Brooklyn College, who read Chapter XVI on the influence of the ancient on the modern theater and helped me to prepare the Index.

It would require too long a list to name all the colleagues and friends who, through granting me permission or through other aid, have assisted me in accomplishing the task which I have set for myself. I want to mention among my German friends only three, now dead: Georg Loeschcke, Walter Amelung, and Gerhard Rodenwaldt; among my American friends, those who have contributed most to enable me to continue my work in my new country: William Dinsmoor, the late Albert M. Friend, Hetty Goldman, Gisela Richter, the late Baldwin Smith, Richard Stillwell, Emerson Swift, and Kurt Weitzmann.

I owe special gratitude to Herbert S. Bailey, Jr., Director, Benjamin F. Houston, and Helen Van Zandt of Princeton University Press for the careful editing of this book. Mr. Houston deserves much praise for the patience and understanding with which he has discussed with me all the problems involved. We have decided to change the Greek forms of names (which I prefer for Greek persons and places) to the more usual Latin or English forms as they are found in the *Oxford Classical Dictionary.*

M.B.

New York City
Easter 1957

A NOTE TO THE READER

THE transliteration of Greek words used in this book follows the style of *The Oxford Classical Dictionary* (Oxford: The Clarendon Press, 1949), which is in turn based upon the *Journal of Hellenic Studies*. With the permission of the publishers of the *OCD*, we quote here from the "Note to the Reader" in that volume (p. xx):

"In the spelling of Greek and Latin words the rules for transliteration adopted in the *Journal of Hellenic Studies* have been in general followed; but no attempt has been made to achieve a pedantic uniformity. Where there is an accepted form of an ancient name, such as Hecuba, Clytemnestra, Phidias, Pisistratus, that form has been used. Similarly, such established forms of common nouns as *choregus, didascaliae, palaestra, scolia, strategus* have been thus spelt, while the Greek spelling has been retained for less familiar words such as *ephetai, hektemoroi, nauarchos.* . . . The whole subject is one on which scholars differ, and it has been found necessary to impose a measure of uniformity in face of some disagreement."

CHRONOLOGY

I. GREECE

ca. 600 B.C.	Chorus of satyrs (tragoi, goats) in dithyramb or tragic chorus at Corinth and Sicyon
ca. 550	Thespis introduces the first speaker. Archaic orchestra in the Agora in Athens. Sacred precinct of Dionysus
534	Pisistratus introduces drama into the state festivals of Athens
525-456	Aeschylus
510	Introduction of dithyramb into the Dionysiac festivals at Athens
ca. 500	Drama presentations transferred from the Agora to the precinct of Dionysus
496-406	Sophocles
490	Aeschylus fights in the Battle of Marathon
487/86	Comedy admitted to the great City Dionysia
484-406	Euripides
476/75	Phrynichus, *Phoenician Women*
472	Aeschylus, *Persians*. Comedy by Magnes. Second actor
468	Sophocles' first victory over Aeschylus
467	Aeschylus, *Seven against Thebes*. Satyr drama *The Sphinx*
ca. 465	Classical orchestra in Athens
458	Aeschylus, *Oresteia*. Third actor. Ornate background
455	First presentation of Euripides
449	Tragic actors chosen by the state and given own contest
446-442	Odeion erected by Pericles
ca. 445	Sophocles' satyr drama *The Hunting Dogs*
442	Contest for comic actors introduced
ca. 442	Sophocles, *Antigone*
441	First victory of Euripides
ca. 440	Euripides' satyr drama *The Cyclops*
438	Euripides, *Alcestis*. Sophocles' victory over Euripides
431	Euripides, *Medea*
ca. 429	Sophocles, *Oedipus the King*
428	Euripides, *Hippolytus*
425-388	Aristophanes active
425	Aristophanes, *Acharnians*
424	Aristophanes, *Knights*
423	Aristophanes, *Clouds*
422	Aristophanes, *Wasps*
421	Aristophanes, *Peace*
421-415	Oldest stone skene in Athens, time of Peace of Nicias
415	Euripides, *The Trojan Women*
415-410	Euripides, *Iphigenia in Tauris*
414	Aristophanes, *Birds*
413	Euripides, *Electra*
411	Aristophanes, *Lysistrata* and *Thesmophoriazousae*
409	Sophocles, *Philoctetes*
405	Aristophanes, *Frogs*
ca. 400-330	Middle Comedy
ca. 392	Aristophanes, *Ecclesiazousae*
388	Aristophanes, *Plutus*
ca. 350-330	Stone skene, stoa, and auditorium in Athens finished by Lycurgus
343/2-292/1	Menander
335-325	Aristotle, *Poetics*
334	Lysicrates erects his monument for the victory with a chorus of boys
ca. 330	Beginning of New Comedy
ca. 320	Theophrastus, *Characters*
316	Menander, *Dyskolos*
316/5	Menander wins his first victory with his *Anger*
4th and 3rd centuries	Height of the art of acting
3rd century	Guilds of Dionysiac artists are formed
ca. 300	The theater of Priene with proskenion
300-279	Theater of Delos built in wood according to inscriptions
274-250	Stone skene built in Delos
ca. 270	Theocritus, *Mimes*
ca. 250	Theater of Ephesus
219	Thyromata stage in Oiniadae
200-150	Thyromata stage in Oropus
180	Thyromata stage in Delos
ca. 180-160	Hellenistic proskenion stage in Pergamon
ca. 150-80	Hellenistic proskenion stage in Athens

II. ITALY, ROME, AND THE PROVINCES

ca. 500-460	Epicharmus of Syracuse writes travesties of myths and of daily life
ca. 460	Democopus builds the theater of Syracuse. Phormio invents the coulisses
4th century	Many Greek tragedies and farces performed in Magna Graecia
364	Ludi Etrusci in Rome
ca. 350	Assteas of Paestum and other vase painters depict scenes from the Italian farce
ca. 300	Rhinthon's hilarious tragedies performed in Magna Graecia
ca. 250	Theater of Syracuse rebuilt
ca. 250-184	Plautus
240-204	Livius Andronicus translates Greek tragedies and comedies into Latin and presents them at the Ludi Romani in Rome
235-201	Naevius presents translations of Greek tragedies and comedies and also Roman historical plays at Rome
ca. 220-130	Pacuvius
from 220	Ludi Plebeii at Rome
before 215	Plautus, *The Twin Brothers Menaechmi*
from 212	Ludi Apollinaris at Rome
206-204	Plautus, *Miles Gloriosus*
200	Plautus' *Stichus* performed at the Ludi Plebeii in the Circus Flaminius
ca. 200	Large theater built at Pompeii
after 194	Plautus, *Aulularia* and *Amphitryon*
191	Plautus, *Pseudolus*
ca. 190-159	Terence
after 190	Plautus, *Bacchides* and *Casina*
179	First wooden theater at Rome torn down again
from 173	Mimes at Rome at the Floralia
ca. 170-ca. 90	Accius
166-160	Presentations of comedies by Terence

154	First stone theater in Rome torn down again		61/2	Theater of Dionysus at Athens remodelled in the Roman form and dedicated to Nero
105	Gladiatorial fights at Rome become a national celebration		66	Roman scaenae frons added to the stage in Ephesus
ca. 100	Theaters at Segesta and Tyndaris are rebuilt		after 68	The *Octavia*, although attributed to Seneca, published after his and Nero's death
1st century	Height of the art of acting. Roscius			
99	Stage building of Claudius Pulcher		69-96	The Flavian emperors build the Colosseum
ca. 89	The Atellan farce of Novius and Pomponius		69-79	Vespasian builds the lower part of the Colosseum
ca. 75	Small roofed theater in Pompeii			
ca. 70	Amphitheater in Pompeii		80	Titus dedicates the amphitheater
58	The luxurious theater of Aemilius Scaurus torn down again		81-96	Domitian finishes the upper part of the amphitheater
55	Theater of Pompey in Rome		117-138	The Emperor Hadrian. Theater in Palmyra built. Merida rebuilt. Circus added to the theater in Aezani
50	Theater of Corinth rebuilt			
40-30	Frescoes in Boscoreale imitate scene painting			
31 B.C.-A.D. 14	The Emperor Augustus. 70 festival days of which 40 are devoted to plays. The architect M. Artorius rebuilds the large theater at Pompeii for the Holconii. The architect Numerius builds the theater in Herculaneum		138-192	The Antonine Emperors. Many theaters built in North Africa: Timgad, Djemila, Dugga
			140-144	The orchestra in Ephesus remodelled for gladitorial shows and animal baiting
			161-180	The architect Zeno, son of Theodorus, builds the theater in Aspendus
ca. 30	Theater in Arles		ca. 162	Herodes Atticus builds the "odeum" on the slope of the Acropolis at Athens
29	L. Varius Rufus, *Thyestes*			
22	Pantomime introduced in Rome		2nd century	Julius Pollux, *Onomasticon*
16-13	Vitruvius, *De Architectura*		193-211	Septimius Severus emperor. Theater of Sabratha in Tripolitania
12 B.C.	Agrippa died. He built the theater at Ostia and perhaps the one at Merida, and the Odea on the Agora of Athens and in Corinth			
			211-217	Caracalla emperor. The theater at Corinth made into a hunting theater
11 B.C.	Theater of Marcellus in Rome finished by Augustus		3rd century	Cake moulds in Ostia and sarcophagi testify to continuation of theatrical plays. New theaters in Bosra and Philippopolis in Arabia and Eš-Šuhba in Palestine
CA. 30 B.C.-A.D. 79	Many wall paintings and reliefs in Pompeii testify to the lively interest in the theater			
A.D. 10-20	Theater of Minturnae		ca. 270	The archon Phaedrus remodels the stage of the theater of Dionysus at Athens
39-65	Lucanus writes fabulae salticae for pantomimes			
			354	175 festival days, 101 devoted to theater plays
41	The robber Laureolus is nailed to the cross in a mime		ca. 400	Comedy *Querolus*
41-62	The tragedies of Seneca (died A.D. 65)		5th-6th centuries	Ivory tablets testify to continuation of all types of spectacles at Constantinople (Byzantium)
44	Theater of Ephesus remodelled on the Roman plan			
			568	End of spectacles at Rome
45-96	Statius writes fabulae salticae for pantomimes		692	End of spectacles at Constantinople
60-68	The Emperor Nero appears on the stage			

III. INFLUENCE OF THE ANCIENT THEATER ON THE MODERN THEATER

Tenth century	Moral comedies by Roswitha of Gandersheim		1585	Teatro Olimpico opened with Sophocles' *Oedipus the King*
Twelfth century	Vital de Blois, *Aulularia* and *Geta*		1586	Kyd, *Spanish Tragedy*
			1591	Shakespeare, *Comedy of Errors*
1314	Mussaro's *Ecerina* in Senecan style		1594-1600	Camerata in Florence creates opera in imitation of Greek tragedy
1470	Printed edition of Terence			
1472	Printed edition of Plautus		1605	Inigo Jones' turning devices based on Vitruvius
1484	Printed edition of Vitruvius. Plautus' *Aulularia* presented in Rome, Quirinal			
			1606-1671	Corneille writes tragedies in Senecan style
1502	Printed edition of Sophocles. Plautus' *Menaechmi* presented in the Vatican. Five comedies of Plautus presented in Ferrara		1640/41	Furttenbach builds a theater at Ulm based on Vitruvius
			1653-1671	Molière imitates Plautus and Terence
			18th century	Height of acting and opera singing
1503	Printed edition of Euripides		1760	The Japanese reconstruct the revolving stage after Vitruvius
1518	Printed edition of Aeschylus			
1536	Aristophanes' *Plutus* presented in Cambridge		1762	Gluck, *Orfeo ed Euridice*
1555	Hans Sachs, *Alcestis*		1776-1790	Alfieri, *Oreste* (1776), *Antigone* (1783), and *Alceste seconda* (1790)
from 1560	Seneca's tragedies performed in London			
from 1574	Plautus and Terence performed at the Universities of London and Oxford		1779 and 1787	Goethe, *Iphigenia in Tauris*
			1803	Schiller, *Bride of Messina*
1576-1599	Theaters in London used by Shakespeare resemble the "Assteas" stage		1816	Shelley, *Prometheus Unbound*
1580-1584	Teatro Olimpico in Vicenza by Palladio		1872	Nietzsche, *Die Geburt der Tragödie*
1581	First English translation of Seneca's tragedies			

1876   Festival theater for Wagner's operas in Bayreuth

1896   Lautenschläger builds revolving stage in the Residenz-Theater at Munich

20th century   Many imitations of Greek tragedies and an ever-growing number of representations of the original Greek tragedies in translations in Europe and America

1903   Hugo von Hofmannsthal, *Electra*

1908   Menander's *Arbitrants* presented in Lauchstedt, Germany

1909   Gabriele d'Annunzio, *Hippolyte*

from 1909   Randolph-Macon College, Virginia, presents tragedies in the Greek language

1910   *Oedipus the King* presented by Reinhardt in the Schumann Circus

1914   Franz Werfel, *Trojan Women*

from 1914   Presentations of Greek tragedy in the theater of Syracuse

1917   Walter Hasenclever, *Antigone*

1919   *Oedipus the King* presented by Max Reinhardt in the Grosse Schauspielhaus

1920   Euripides' *Hippolytus* presented in Oxford

1921   Sophocles' *Antigone* presented in the Deutsche Volksbühne, Berlin, with Mary Dietrich

1922   Euripides' *Hippolytus* presented in Giessen

from 1927   Presentations of Greek tragedies in Delphi and Ostia

from 1928   Presentations of Greek tragedies at Wellesley College

1929   Presentations of Menander's *Arbitrants* at Bryn Mawr College and Haverford College

1930   Aeschylus' *Persians*, Plautus and Terence presented in Cassel and Frankfurt a.M.

1931   Eugene O'Neill, *Mourning Becomes Electra*
Euripides' *Hippolytus* presented at Vassar College

1934   Aeschylus' *Agamemnon* presented in Bradford, England

1935   Aristophanes' *Birds* presented in Berlin, painted by Heckel

1936, 1937, 1942, 1950   Presentations of tragedies of Euripides by Milton Smith at Columbia University

1937   Maxwell Anderson, *Wingless Victory*

1937-38   Jean Giraudoux, *Amphitryon 38*

1938   Euripides' *Iphigenia in Tauris* presented at Sabratha

1940   Aristophanes' *Frogs* performed at Reed College, Oregon

1942   Jean Anouilh, *Antigone*

1943   Jean-Paul Sartre, *The Flies*, based on Aeschylus' *Eumenides*

1946   Anouilh, *Medea*. *Oedipus the King* presented on Broadway with Lawrence Olivier

1947-49, 1951   Anouilh's *Medea*, translated by Robinson Jeffers, presented on Broadway with Judith Anderson

1948   Menander's *Arbitrants* presented in Berkeley, California. Euripides' *Alcestis* presented at Barnard College and at Riverdale Country Day School

1949   Gerhart Hauptmann, *Die Atriden, Eine Tetralogie*

1950   Cole Porter, *Out of this World*

from 1951   The Greek National Theater presents Greek tragedies in New York, Athens and Delphi

1954-55   *Oedipus the King* presented in Stratford, Ontario, by Tyrone Guthrie. Menander's *The Girl from Samos* presented in New York by Ida Ehrlich

from 1955   Presentations of tragedies in Epidaurus

1955   Sophocles' *Antigone* presented at Wheaton College

1956   Euripides' *Trojan Women* presented at Wheaton College. Sophocles' *Electra* presented at Cedar Crest College

1956-57   Milton Miltiades presents a *Theban Trilogy* in New York

1957   Wayne Richardson presents a *Trojan Trilogy* in New York

1959   *Oresteia* presented on television in New York
Oedipus the King, adapted by Leo Brady, performed in Carnegie Hall, New York

Fig. C. Aristophanes' *The Birds*, performed in Berlin, 1935.
(*see Fig. 843a*)

GLOSSARY OF TECHNICAL TERMS

ACROTERION (*pl.* acroteria): Figures and ornaments on the apex and lower angles of a pediment

ADDITUS MAXIMUS: Main entrance to the orchestra or arena

AEDICULA: A decorated niche in a wall or a small chapel

AGON: Contest

AGONIST: Contestant

AGONOTHETES: Chairman, president, or judge at contests

AMPHITHEATER: A building with seats all around the arena, for gladiatorial shows

AMPHORA: Large vase with two handles

ANAGNORISIS: Recognition, identification

ANALEMMA (*pl.* analemmata): Sustaining walls at the side of an auditorium

ARCHITRAVE: Lowest member of the entablature, a lintel carried from the top of one column to another

ATELLAN FARCE: Oscan popular plays, taken over by the Romans

ATLANTES (Gr.), telamones (Lat.): Male figures forming support of an entablature in place of columns; cf. caryatids

ATTIC: The low story above the entablature of the main story

AULAEUM: Stage curtain, dropped at the beginning, lifted at the end of a performance

AULOI: Double pipes, similar to the oboe or recorder but always used in pairs

BALUSTRADE: Row of short pillars with rail or ornamental parapet

BEMA: Platform

BOULEUTERION: Assembly hall for the magistrates or members of the council; town hall

CAPITAL: The topmost member of the columns which are the most distinctive members of the architectural orders

CARYATIDS: Female figures supporting an entablature in place of columns; cf. atlantes

CAVEA: The auditorium of a theater, so called because originally excavated in a hillside

CELLA: The interior, enclosed main room of a temple

CHARONIAN STEPS: A staircase leading up from a subterranean tunnel to the center or to the edge of the orchestra; used for ghostly apparitions

CHITON: The main Greek dress, worn long by women and short by men

CHLAINA: Loincloth worn by satyrs, made of goatskin

CHLAMYS: The mantle worn by men, pinned on the right shoulder

CHOREGI: Rich citizens who provided money for performances

CHOREUTAE: Members of a chorus who performed songs and dances

CHORODIDASKALOS: The teacher of the chorus

CITHARA: Musical instrument with strings, similar to the guitar; used in public performances

COLONNADE: A row of columns supporting a roof

COMEDY (Gr. komoidia): Song of the gay parade in honor of Dionysus; comic drama

CORINTHIAN ORDER: A capital decorated with acanthus leaves and volutes, said to have been invented in Corinth

CORNICE: Uppermost member of the entablature

CORYPHAEUS (koryphaios): The leader of the chorus

COTHURNUS: High boot originated by Aeschylus for tragic actors

COULISSE: Movable scenery, screens serving as background or side decorations

CRATER: Vessel for mixing wine and water, with wide open mouth

CREPIDA (*pl.* crepidae): Buskins, used by the Romans like the Greek cothurnus but with thick block-like soles or stilts; same as ocribas (q.v.)

CUNEI (Lat.): Wedge-shaped sections of the auditorium

DEUS EX MACHINA: The god who flies in on a machine and often brings the solution of difficulties

DEUTERAGONIST: The second actor, who played several roles

DIAZOMA (Gr. girdle): Horizontal passage between the several rows of seats

DIDASCALIA: List of presentations of dramas with indication of authors, dates, and success

DISTEGIA (Gr. double roof): Building with two stories

DITHYRAMB: The hymn sung in honor of Dionysus; the name alludes to the double birth from Semele and from the thigh of Zeus

DORIC ORDER: Simple capitals, developed in Dorian countries; frieze consists of metopes and triglyphs (q.v.)

ECCLESIASTERION: Assembly hall

ECCYCLEMA: A rolling machine or movable platform, used to show interior scenes

EIDOLON: Image, ghost of a dead person, phantom

EMBATES: Boots for travellers

EMMELEIA: Solemn chorus dance in tragedy

ENGAGED COLUMN: A semi-detached column

ENTABLATURE: The superstructure carried by columns; it consists of architrave, frieze, and cornice

EPHEBUS: Young man of or over the age of eighteen

EPISKENION: Upper story of the scene building

EPISODION: Episode, part which was originally interpolated between two choric songs (odes); the portion of dialogue in tragedy

EXARCHON, exarchos: Leader of the chorus singing the dithyramb in honor of Dionysus

EXODOS: Exit, departure of players from place of action; passage to go out by; final song sung when the chorus is marching out

EXOMIS: A narrow tunic covering only one shoulder, worn by slaves and artisans

FABULA CREPIDATA: Roman tragedy imitated from the Greek and played in the Greek tragic costume

FABULA PALLIATA: Roman comedy in which the actors wear the pallium, a mantle similar to the Greek himation; imitated from Greek plays

FABULA PRAETEXTA: Roman tragedy with subject-matter taken from upper-class life; played in the toga praetexta

FABULA TOGATA: Play in which the Roman toga is worn, with Roman subjects

HEMICYCLE: Semicircular recess

HERÖON: Sanctuary for a hero, small shrine or chapel

HILAROTRAGODIA: A play which mixes serious and gay elements, particularly a parody of a mythological subject

HIMATION: Greek mantle, freely draped, for men and women

HOSPITALIA: The side doors, sometimes leading to the guest rooms of the Roman stage

HYDRIA: A water jar with three handles

HYPOKRITES: An answerer, one who answers the questions of a chorus and becomes the first actor; one who represents somebody other than himself

HYPOSKENION: The room below the platform of the stage

INTERCOLUMNIATION: The space between the columns of a colonnade

IONIC ORDER: Capital decorated with volutes and continuous frieze; developed in eastern Greece

ITINERA VERSURARUM: Entrances from the side buildings (versurae)

KALPIS: A hydria with rounded forms

KANTHAROS: The wine cup with two high-curving handles used by Dionysus

KATABLEMATA: Backdrops thrown over a permanent frame

KATATOME (Gr. cutting): The cutting away of the rock on the slope of the Acropolis above the theater of Dionysus

KERKIS (*pl.* kerkides): Wedge-shaped sections of the theatron, divided by radiating staircases

KERYKEION: A herald's staff

KOMAST: Member of a gay parade (komos, comus), often singing and dancing after a symposium

KORDAX: Gay dance in Old Comedy

KYLIX: Flat wine cup or bowl

LEKYTHOS: A slender vase for oil and perfume

LOGEION: (Gr. speaking place): The podium or platform of the Hellenistic stage

LYRE: Small string instrument for accompanying single voice

MAENADS: The female followers of Dionysus

MAENIANUM: A gallery in the circus and amphitheater: ima, the lowest; medium, the middle one; summum, the uppermost

METOPE: Rectangular panel between triglyphs in the Doric frieze

MIME; MIMUS: Play given without masks, imitating real life; the performer in this simple drama

NARTHEX: Tall reed with firm stem, used as sacred wand (thyrsus) for Dionysus and his followers

NEBRIS: Fur of a deer, used by Dionysus and his followers as a scarf

NYMPHAEUM: A place dedicated to the nymphs with a fountain or running water

OCRIBAS: Buskin with heavy wooden, block-like soles or stilts; same as crepidae (*q.v.*)

ODEION (Gr.), odeum (Lat.): A roofed music hall

OINOCHOE: Wine jug

ONKOS: A hairdress with the hair built up high above the forehead of masks used in tragedy, imitating an archaic hairdress

ORCHESTRA (Gr. dancing place): Place of action for the chorus and the actors in the classical period, mostly circular

ORDER: The architectural system composed of the columns and entablature (Doric, Ionic, Corinthian)

OSCAN PLAYS: Popular farces performed by the Oscans in Campania, later also in Rome

OSCANS: The inhabitants of Campania, also of Pompeii

PALUDAMENTUM: The Roman mantle worn over the shoulders, pinned at the right shoulder like the Greek chlamys

PANTOMIME: Play given by a single actor who performs all roles with intense gesticulation and with different masks

PALLIUM: Roman mantle: name for the himation taken over by the Romans from the Greeks; palla when worn by women

PAPPOSILENUS: The old father of the satyrs

PARABASIS: Part of Old Comedy, when the chorus turned to the audience and addressed it in the name of the poet

PARACHOREGEMA: A supernumerary, often playing a small or mute role

PARAPET: Low balustrade; a protective wall

PARAPETASMA (Gr.), siparium (Lat.): A curtain hung before the decorations or openings on the stage

PARASKENION (Gr.), parascenium (Lat.): Side wings of the theater building

PARODOS (*pl.* paradoi): Lateral entrances to the orchestra of the theater; songs of the chorus sung while entering

PEDESTAL: Base supporting a column or statue

PEDIMENT: Triangular termination of a roof with slanting sides

PEPLOS: Woolen dress with overfold, worn by women only

PERIACTI: Triangular revolving structures with different painted scenery attached to their three sides, serving as side decorations

PERSPECTIVE: Art of reproducing objects on plane surface so as to give the impression of the real shape, scale, relative position, and distance of the actual objects

PERSONA: Player's mask; character in a play

PETASUS: A wide-brimmed hat

PHLYAX (Gr. gossip): Player in popular farce

PHORTIKA: Coarse and vulgar jokes of a porter

PIER: Free-standing rectangular support or short wall having the function of a column or pilaster but mostly of heavier mass

PILASTER: Rectangular column, free-standing or engaged or semi-detached in a wall

PILLAR: Pilaster or column

PINAX (*pl.* pinakes): Decorated panel filling the intercolumniations of the proskenion or the thyromata (*q.v.*) at the back of the stage

PLECTRON: A rod used to play the strings of a cithara or lyre

PLINTH: Bottom of a column base or podium

PODIUM: Low wall or continuous pedestal for columns or wall; a raised platform

PORCH: Entrance, vestibule

PORTICUS (Lat.), stoa (Gr.): A hall with its roof supported by columns, or a colonnaded porch

POSTSCAENIUM: The rooms behind the scene building

PRECINCTIO: The rounded corridor separating the galleries from each other; corresponds to the Greek diazoma (*q.v.*)

PROAGON: Preparation for a contest, assembly of all contestants on the first day of the great city Dionysia

PROSCAENIUM (Lat.): The Romans used the word for the whole stage as well as for the front of the stage and of the stage building

PROSKENION (Gr.): Building before the skene; the oldest high Hellenistic stage; later the front of the stage

PROTAGONIST: The first or leading actor

PROTHYRON: A porch in front of the main door

PROTOME: Upper part of human or animal body, a half-figure

PSYKTER: A vase for keeping wine cool

PULPITUM: Roman stage; podium or platform for the actors

REGIA: The royal door; the central door of the Roman stage, leading into the palace of the main hero

SATYRS: The male followers of Dionysus, with animal tails and ears

SCAENA DUCTILIS: Movable screen serving as background

SCAENA VERSILIS: Turning prisms, decorated differently on the three sides, serving as side wings; cf. periacti

SCAENAE FRONS: The richly decorated front of the scene building

SIKINNIS: Dance in satyric drama

SILENUS: An old satyr

SIPARIUM: A curtain used on the stage

SKENE (Gr.), scaena (Lat.): Temporary building, booth for the players; later the permanent back building of the theater

SKENOGRAPHIA: Stage painting

SKENOTHEKE: Storeroom for the properties in the skene

SKYPHOS: Deep wine cup with two handles

SOCCUS: A shoe worn in Roman comedy

SOCLE: Projecting footing of a wall or pedestal

SOMATIA: Tights stuffed with pillows, used in comedy

SPARSIONES: Sprinkling to refresh the audience in the Roman theater

SPEIRA: Rolled arrangement of the hair, used in comedy particularly for older slaves instead of the stephane for more dignified men

SPHENOPOGON: Old man with wedge-shaped beard in comedy

STASIMON: Song of the chorus performed in the orchestra between the dialogues

STEPHANE: A wreath of hair; a hair roll above the forehead, worn in New Comedy instead of the onkos in tragedy

STOA (Gr.), porticus (Lat.): Building with its roof supported by rows of columns, parallel to the rear wall

SYRMA: Dress with long train, worn by tragic actors

TABERNACLE: Niche with a canopy or roof-like projection over it

TECHNITAE: Professional actors and musicians in the guilds of the Hellenistic period

TELAMONES (Lat.), atlantes (Gr., *q.v.*): Male figures used as supports

TELARI: Linen decorations fixed on triagonal side wings, in imitation of the Greek periacti and the Roman scaena versilis

TELESTERION: Hall of initiation for the mysteries of Eleusis

TETRALOGY: A set of three tragedies and one satyr play, performed on the same day

THEATRON (Gr. seeing place): The auditorium (Lat. hearing place) of the theater; later used for the whole building

THEOLOGEION: Speaking place for the gods; a high platform or roof of a building on which the gods and heroes appear

THERSILION: Assembly hall in Megalopolis, named from the dedicator

THIASOTE: Members of the sacred herd (thiasus), followers of Dionysus

THIASUS: The followers of Dionysus, consisting of satyrs and maenads

THYMELE: The sacrificial step of the altar; the altar itself; and later the whole orchestra in which the thymele stood

THYROMA (*pl.* thyromata): Great doorway; wide opening in the second story of the theater, forming the background and sometimes the rear stage of the Hellenistic theater

THYRSUS: The sacred wand of Dionysus, made from narthex, wreathed with ivy and vine leaves, often with pine cone on top

TOGA: The official dress of the Roman upper classes; stiff and uniform in contrast to the freely-draped himation and pallium (*q.v.*)

TOGA PRAETEXTA: The ceremonial dress of the Roman emperors and higher magistrates, decorated with purple stripes

TRAGEDY (Gr. tragodia): Song of the followers of Dionysus which developed into serious drama in Greece

TRIBUNALIA: The boxes for the magistrates who were in charge of the games and who often were tribunes; situated above the side entrances

TRIGLYPH: Member of the Doric frieze, with three vertical grooves alternating with the metopes (*q.v.*)

TRILOGY: A set of three tragedies performed consecutively on the same day

TRIPOD: Kettle or cauldron standing on three legs, given as prize in contest and often consecrated to a god, particularly Apollo or Dionysus

TRITAGONIST: The third actor, who was the least regarded; sometimes designation of a bad actor

TUNIC: The main dress of the Romans, same as the Greek chiton (*q.v.*)

TYMPANON: The triangular interior of a pediment

VELUM: The canvas roof, used as a sunshade over the auditorium in the Roman theater

VENATIONES: Baiting of wild animals in the amphitheater

VERSURAE: The side buildings of the Roman theater, corresponding to the Greek paraskenia

VESTIBULE: Anteroom next to the outer door of a house

VOMITORIA: The entrances from the covered passages leading to the different sections of the auditorium, with wide openings which "vomit" or spit out the numerous visitors

XOANON: The primitive image of a deity

THE HISTORY OF
THE GREEK AND ROMAN THEATER

Fig. D. Actors celebrating (*see Fig. 538*)

CHAPTER I

THE RISE OF THE SATYR PLAY AND OF TRAGEDY

See Fig. 32

THE performance of a Greek tragedy is apt to make a markedly deep impression on an educated audience. It may almost be described as miraculous that the works of Aeschylus, Sophocles, and Euripides, belonging as they do to the very beginning of the drama in the fifth century B.C., should be works of art so lofty as to retain their heroic greatness and eternal life even today. We shall never be able to explain this miracle fully, but we can try to arrive at some understanding of it, first by observing the elementary conditions which the tragic poets found, and then by considering which additional factors were needed for the creation, from these roots and origins, of Attic tragedy.

The religion of Dionysus is the only one in antiquity in which dramatic plays could have developed. There were, of course, other cults in which events from the life of the gods were represented in mimic scenes, as in Egypt, Eleusis, and Delphi. The death of Osiris, the rape and return of Persephone, the fight of Apollo with the dragon, were repeated in definite forms in hymns and rituals. There was, however, no development to a living literary form.

The difference between the religion of Dionysus and any other religion which anthropologists, historians of religion and of the theater, and some philologists have considered as sources of the drama is this: All other religions, primitive as well as highly-developed, have *rituals* or *liturgies*, repeating the same story every year, while only the Greek worshippers of Dionysus developed *myths* and with them the material for the highest form of literature, the drama.

The Dionysiac cult took over from the older cults several factors. The performances were given, like the others, on definite days. They were, like the others, performed as contests; they were freely accessible for all. They were, like the others, connected with sacrifices, processions, and music. Yet the Dionysiac religion had peculiarities which distinguished it from all the other religions of the ancient world. There are particularly four facts which explain at least partly why dramatic plays could develop only in this cult.

1. The religion of Dionysus entered Greece much later than the cults of the other gods—Zeus, Hera, Athena, Demeter, Apollo—which already had roots in the Mycenaean period. It came from the north via Thrace and Boeotia or, according to other sources, from the east via the Peloponnesus and Attica, where it received definite cult forms not before the sixth century. Thus, not only the epic poetry, which gave the subject-matter to drama, but also the lyric poetry, which gave it its rhythm, were already mature and could transmit their forms to the new dramatic poetry. On this base, a new, free, and versatile form could develop.

2. The story of the life of Dionysus is much more variegated than those of the other gods. His miraculous birth, his fights, sufferings, struggle for acknowledgment, and other events in his life gave a much richer content to the Dionysiac songs and games than the events in the lives of the other gods. Thus his special hymn, the dithyramb, probably had from the beginning a much more diversified content than the hymns for the other gods. We may assume that the earliest hymn celebrated the god Dionysus, particularly as the name of the hymn means double birth, alluding to the miraculous birth first from Semele, then from the thigh of Zeus. But then other subjects were also used. The tyrant Cleisthenes transferred to Dionysus the chorus originally sung for the hero Adrastus (Herodotus, v 67). Theseus, the Attic national hero, is the subject of the Dithyramb XVII of Bacchylides.

3. The Dionysiac religion is an ecstatic religion. The wine, the gift of the god, and religious rapture changed the mortal followers of the god in their frenzy into members of the Dionysiac thiasus, the sacred herd of the god. They danced originally in the mountains, particularly near Delphi and near Thebes, to the sound of flutes, clappers, and tympana. In their exalted feeling the men believed themselves to be satyrs, the followers of the god; the women believed themselves to be maenads, called bacchae in Thebes, thyiades in Delphi, and lenae in Athens. The singer Arion is said to have given to the singers of the dithyramb—which he produced in the beginning of the sixth century at the time of the tyrant Periander in Corinth—the costume of the satyrs (Herodotus, I 23f; Suidas *s.v.* Arion). This dress was taken over into the satyr drama, when the dithyramb became too often alien to the Dionysiac stories. The original sacred chorus had to be preserved in another form. The practice of representing someone other than oneself grew out of the ecstasy and led to the development of the mimic art of the actors.

4. The Dionysiac religion was from the beginning inclined to disguise individual personality in favor of a transformation into a higher being. There is no better aid in representing somebody else than to take his costume. Thus the chorus singing in honor of the god becomes a satyr chorus. The Greek word *tragos* means one who dresses up and performs as a follower of Dionysus. Therefore, tragedy is a song in honor of Dionysus. At the Attic rural Dionysia the members of the gay parade dressed up as animals, and from their song during the gay *Komos*

comedy developed. In the Peloponnesus the participants in the Dionysiac cult imitated the demons which they believed to be his followers.

Thus the Dionysiac cult contains all the elements which are necessary for the development of a serious drama or a gay comedy by disguised human beings.

The drama is the latest of the three most important literary forms—epic, lyric, and drama—created by the Greeks and still fully active today. The earliest is the epic, represented for us as it was for the Greeks by Homer. The artist Archelaus of Priene of the second century B.C. expressed well the view that from Homer all other forms are derived (Fig. 1).[1] His relief represents in the upper three registers Zeus, Mnemosyne, and their children, the nine Muses. Two of them, Melpomene and Clio, the Muses of Tragedy and History, flank Apollo in a cave, beside which stands the statue of a victorious poet. In the lowest register (Fig. 2) Homer is enthroned in his sanctuary like a god, with personifications of his two epics, the *Iliad* and the *Odyssey*, kneeling beside him. Chronos, the God of Time, and Oikoumene, the personification of the inhabited world, stand behind him, Chronos with a scroll containing his poems, Oikoumene holding a wreath over his head. The idea is that the fame of Homer is unbounded in time and space. Before the poet stands a boy named Mythos, with a sacrificial bowl and jug, who functions as an attendant at the altar, for the stories of the gods and heroes have been given by Homer a form valid for all ages. Behind the altar stands the bull to be immolated as a sacrifice to Homer. History scatters incense on the altar, for the myths had already become history, being the stories of the great legendary period, which were therefore incorporated as the first part into the history of the later times. Then follow Poiesis, lyric poetry; Tragoidia, tragedy; and Komoidia,

Figs. 1, 2. The Muses with Zeus and Apollo; Glorification of Homer. Relief of Archelaus of Priene, British Museum.
(See List of Illustrations and Sources)

Fig. 3. Citharist. Attic vase, Vatican

comedy. The last two are in stage costume. This
sequence corresponds to the historical development.
The final form was given to the Homeric poems in
the eighth century; lyric poetry developed in the
seventh and sixth centuries, its material being borrowed frequently from myth, that is, from prehistoric times; tragedy came at the end of the sixth
century; and artistic comedy came last, in the course
of the fifth century. At the end of the lowest register
behind these figures stand the Virtues: Good Memory, Trustworthiness, Fortitude, and Wisdom, surrounding a small child named Physis, or human
nature, who is educated by Homer in these achieve-
ments.

Drama, then, derives its material from the epic,
that is, from heroic saga, which remained always,
with few exceptions, the subject-matter of Greek
and Roman tragedy. Its form, however, comes from
the kind of poetry that was second in point of time,
namely, lyric poetry. Lyric means song to the accompaniment of the lyre. The Greek poem was
never read or spoken, but intoned. Nietzsche[2] rightly
identifies the ancient lyric poet with the musician;
compared with the Greek, our modern lyric poets
appear as incomplete as the image of a god without
a head. Song in the public life of the Greeks was
accompanied by the large, richly-ornamented cithara. It was "invented," as the Greek said, in 675 by
Terpander of Lesbos.[3] It was, however, already in
use in the Orient, in Egypt, and in Crete in the third
and second millennia. It is shown on the arm of
Apollo in the relief of Archelaus (Fig. 1) and in
many vases on his arm or on the arm of citharists

Fig. 4. Citharist and Victory. Attic vase, Athens

or citharoedi, sometimes standing on a platform, a
bema, or the thymele, and rewarded by Nikai bringing fillets and vases, as on a vase of about 430 in
the Vatican and one in Athens (Figs. 3, 4).[4]

A smaller, slender lyre was used in private life,
particularly by poets. Anakreon, on a lekythos from

3

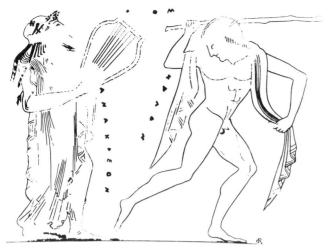

Fig. 5. Anacreon. Drawing from Attic lekythos, Gela

The auloi or double pipes were used since the seventh century particularly for accompanying sacrifices, processions, chorus singing, and dancing. This wind instrument is often called a flute. It is, however, rather to be compared to the modern recorder or to the oboe, as it is played not from a blow hole in the side but from one at the upper end. It has the peculiarity that always two pipes are connected. The auloi became the favorite instrument for the followers and worshippers of Dionysus. Flute and cithara players wore long floating festival robes (see Figs. 9, 14, 15, 27, 28b).[7]

Figs. 6, 7. Alcaeus and Sappho, Attic vase, Munich

Fig. 8. Youth with lyre. Attic vase, Metropolitan Museum

Gela in Syracuse (Fig. 5), and Alcaeus and Sappho on the Munich vase (Figs. 6, 7)[5] carry their instruments on their left arms and the plectron, the rod to play the strings, in their right hands. It was of great importance, not only for lyric poetry but also for the growth of the drama, that all children were taught to sing to the lyre. On several vases of the cycle of Epictetus and other vase painters, belonging to the period when the drama was taking shape, young men appear (Fig. 8), but also older men and women with the lyre.[6]

On the charming school vase of Duris (Figs. 10, 11),[8] dating from the youth of Sophocles, we see boys learning to read, to write, and to recite poetry, but at the same time to sing to the flute and to play the lyre. We understand then what it means when, after the battle of Salamis in 480 B.C., Sophocles, according to his biography, led the dance of victory, stepping with his lyre at the head of the chorus of boys. Poetry and music had become bone of his bone.

Fig. 9. Fluteplayer. Attic vase, British Museum

10. Instruction in poetry and music

Figs. 10, 11. School vase by Duris, Berlin Museum

11. Instruction in reciting and writing

Fig. 12. Choral dance. Early Attic vase, Athens

Fig. 13. Choral dance of girls. Attic vase, Villa Giulia, Rome

The victory of Salamis was celebrated not only by song, but by ordered steps, that is, by dance. The poem was woven into the music by rhythm. The choral dance was a widespread phenomenon of Greek culture, and a much earlier one than the drama.[9] On the geometric and early Attic vases of the eighth and the seventh centuries B.C. young men and maidens holding one another by the hand move in the dance (Fig. 12), as does the chorus of maidens on the fifth-century vase by the Villa Giulia master (Fig. 13).[10] Occasionally prizes of victory, particularly tripods, are represented on the vases, when the chorus singing was performed in the form of a contest, an agon. This practice, usual in most festive institutions, contributed considerably to the growth of all arts—musical, gymnastic, and dramatic. A youth always stepped at the head of the chorus, as the leader or exarchos. Such a one is Theseus in festival dress on the François vase (Fig. 14),[11] leading the victory dance in Delos with the chorus of Athenian boys and girls whom he had rescued from the minotaur in the labyrinth in Crete.

Tragedy, according to Aristotle, developed from the exarchontes, the leaders of the dithyramb.[12] The dithyramb was a song of rejoicing and a chorus dance in honor of Dionysus. Such a one the poet Archilochus was said to have produced and led when he was drunk with wine, the gift of the god.[13] Arion, the famous citharoedus, was said to be the first to compose a dithyramb, to give it a name, and to have these poems performed in Corinth (Herodotus I 23f). About the same time the tyrant Cleisthenes instituted chorus singing in Sicyon in honor of Dionysus, by transferring to him the choruses formerly sung in honor of the hero Adrastus (Herodotus v 67). Arion let men in the guise of satyrs sing his verses (Suidas, *s.v.* Arion).[14]

Thus the song in honor of Dionysus was originally performed by men in the disguise of the demonic followers of the god, the satyrs with equine ears and tails, as represented on so many vase paintings (see Figs. 19, 21, 39, 43). But the extant examples of the dithyramb—such as the song to Theseus by Bacchylides (No. XVII) and those presented in the Athenian theater—were performed in festive dress and not in this disguise of horse-like or goat-like creatures. (Each of the ten Attic tribes sent a chorus of fifty boys or fifty men to the festival.) It was the satyr play, the final form of which developed from the dithyramb at the end of the sixth century, which retained the satyr chorus and its costume. The themes of the later dithyrambs were borrowed, as were those of the satyr drama and of tragedy, not only from the Dionysus saga, but from a large variety of subject-matter of heroic saga in general, such as the stories of Heracles, Jason, Prometheus, and others (see below, Figs. 30-32, 39-43). Occasionally, however, episodes from the life of Dionysus were used. This is evidenced by the chorus of satyrs on a red-figured kalpis in the Museum of Fine Arts in Boston, who dance wildly to the tune of a bearded fluteplayer, swinging parts of a couch which they are probably trying to assemble (Fig. 15).[15] A vase of about 450 found in Altamura, with the decking of Pandora, has four Panes in loincloths and a fluteplayer (Fig. 16).[16] The three old satyrs on a vase by Polion in the Metropolitan Museum of Art face a young fluteplayer with his two flutes in his hands (Fig. 17).[17] The satyrs hold large concert citharas; one is plucking the strings with his plectron. They thus remind one of the chorus of Arion, but they, like the Panes (Fig. 16), also might be taken from a comedy like Cratinus' *Satyroi*, performed in 424 B.C. —that is, about the time when this vase was painted by Polion—and might be a parody of the Dionysiac festivals, like the *Frogs* of Aristophanes. Certainly the subject of a prize-winning dithyramb is illustrated in the frieze of the monument of Lysicrates, the

Fig. 14. Theseus leading a choral dance at Delos. Detail of the François vase, Florence

Fig. 15. Satyrs with parts of a couch. Attic kalpis, Boston

Fig. 16. Fluteplayers and Panes; Gods bringing gifts to Pandora (above). Crater, British Museum

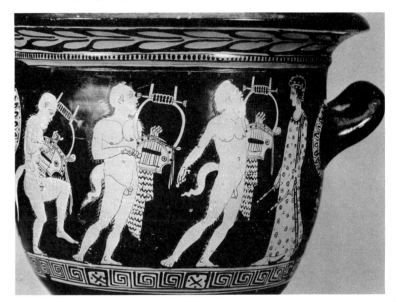

Fig. 17. Satyrs and fluteplayer. Vase by Polion

choregus who had won the victory with a chorus of boys in the year 334 B.C. (Fig. 18). He erected the monument in the form of a small round temple to support the tripod awarded as prize.[18] The subject corresponds in some degree to the Homeric Hymn No. VII to Dionysus. When going over the sea (see Fig. 59), Dionysus had been taken prisoner by pirates. These, however, were punished by the satyrs, beaten and thrown into the sea, where they were changed into dolphins. The dithyramb, therefore, had as its primary subject the doings and adventures of the god, and as secondary themes—which became more and more frequent—tales of the heroes taken over from Homer and other sources. The original form of the dithyramb with cithara or flute accompaniment was preserved side by side with the other forms which developed from it, that is, side by side with the satyr play and tragedy.

Fig. 18. Dionysus, satyrs, and pirates. Frieze from the Monument of Lysicrates, Athens

7

Fig. 19. Dionysus, maenads, satyrs. Vase by the Methyse Painter, Metropolitan Museum

Fig. 20. Maenad in ecstasy. Cup by the Brygus Painter, Metropolitan Museum

Figs. 21-24. Maenads. Vase by the Cleophrades Painter, Munich

Satyric drama probably developed first from the singing of men who were disguised as satyrs in a chorus in honor of Dionysus introduced by Arion. These demonic followers of the god, with equine ears and tails—the models for the satyr chorus in the dithyramb and in the satyr drama—are represented on innumerable vase paintings of the sixth and fifth centuries B.C. They dance in frenzy around their lord Dionysus, to the music of the flute, lyre or cithara, for example on the Brygus cup in Paris.[19] Often they are not alone, but accompanied by maenads (Fig. 19), who as a rule dance much more wildly than the satyrs (Figs. 20-24).[20] Often, notably on the Lenaea vases collected by Frickenhaus (Fig. 25a-b),[21] the maenads are alone, reveling in honor of their lord and dancing in ecstasy to the sound of cymbals, flutes, or tympana, waving torches about the image and altar of the god, on which offerings of big jars filled with wine (stamnoi) and cakes are placed. Through all Greek art there moves a procession of inspired, dancing women (Figs. 20-24 and 45).[22] Literature also bears witness to women as

Fig. 25a-b. Dance in the sanctuary of Dionysus. Lenaea vase, Naples

special vehicles of the Dionysiac ecstasy. This ecstasy is another of the essential factors in the growth of the drama.[23] Although Aristotle speaks of a dithyramb intoned by men when he says that tragedy was developed from the leaders of the dithyramb, a chorus of women occurs in many tragedies. In the archaizing *Bacchae* of Euripides, the chorus consists of maenads, and nowhere is the cult of Dionysus so rapturously described as in this work of the poet's old age. The religion of Dionysus, studied in its original form and at its fountainhead in Macedonia, is made to live again for us by the genius of Euripides. The human being becomes, through spiritual surrender, the demon, the sacred animal of the thiasus, the divine herd of the god. The man represents a satyr, the woman a maenad, but they feel as if they are real demons in their ecstasy, and thus can make visible also for others the ecstasy which they have experienced at the festival of their god. Comprehension of female ecstasy is essential if we want to understand the sincere emotion which underlies the dithyramb and tragedy. Dramatic art requires the actor to lay aside

the personality with which he was endowed by birth and to feel himself as one who has abandoned the limitation of his own personality. He must lose his own identity and become a changed being, a demon, a god, or a hero.

The participants in the dithyramb, the satyr drama, and the tragedy were always men, for Attic morality banished women from public life. Thus the parts of the maenads and of other women were always played by men. They needed, however, for these parts the comprehension of religious emotion, which women experience more deeply than men.

As the first disguise of the singers of the dithyramb was that of the satyr, so perhaps the first form of the drama was the satyr play, although it received its final literary form only later under the influence of tragedy. The initial step towards mimesis was taken when the dancer-singer was changed, through ecstasy and a corresponding disguise, into a mime, one who represents someone other than himself. Many vases depict the satyr, dressed with a loincloth to which a tail is attached, in the presence of a maenad or a fluteplayer (Figs. 26-29).[24]

26   27

Figs. 26-29. Satyrs wearing loin cloths with tails

28a-c

29

9

Fig. 30. Odysseus with companions about to blind Cyclops, satyrs singing at right. Vase, formerly Richmond, now in the British Museum

31

The perfected satyr drama is known to us in literature from the *Hunting Dogs* or *Trackers* (Ichneutai, Ἰχνευταί) of Sophocles presented about 445 B.C. and the *Cyclops* of Euripides presented

32

Figs. 31-33. Satyr play with Dionysus, actors, chorus, poet Demetrius, fluteplayer Pronomos. Vase, Naples

about 440 B.C. and reflected in an early Italian crater of the Cook Collection at Richmond (Fig. 30).[25] The famous vase in Naples, called the satyr play vase or the Pronomos vase from the satyr chorus and its fluteplayer named Pronomos, shows how these dramas were performed in the second half of the fifth century (Figs. 31-33).[26] Dionysus and Ariadne recline on a couch beneath a spreading vine, the plant of the god, which grows wherever he rests (see Fig. 59). Next to the divine couple is a woman seated on the couch holding the mask of a maiden with an oriental headdress, toward which Eros, holding a garland, extends his arms. Near to

Dionysus an actor is standing, holding the mask of an oriental king. On the other side of the couch an actor with the mask and the costume of Heracles is standing. The two actors have elegant boots, the cothurni, and dresses with rich patterns which are also found on the chiton of the woman on the couch and on the mantle of Ariadne. The woman holding the mask may be the personification of the plays, Paidia (see Fig. 113). The title of the play may have been *Hesione*. This is the name of the oriental princess beloved by Heracles and denied to him by her father Laomedon, the king of Troy, despite the father's promise to marry her to the hero after he

10

had killed a sea monster. Whereupon Heracles came back with an army and destroyed Troy for the first time. He then gave Hesione in marriage to his friend Telamon. This could be a good subject for a satyr drama, in which the chorus of satyrs interfered in the action. The chorus on the vase consists of twelve members, a number retained in the satyr drama, after Sophocles had raised the number to fifteen in tragedy. There are ten young men in goatskin loincloths, one—probably the leader of the half chorus—with a short chiton and small mantle of woven fabric, and one older man in the dress of the old Papposilenus (cf. Figs. 36-38), made of shaggy goatskin. He holds the mask of an old man, and a panther skin is laid over his left shoulder. The young choristers hold their masks at all possible angles, so that we can study them from all sides and even from the inside. Only one has already put the mask over his head and is practising the dance of the satyr drama, the sikinnis. He has his right hand on his hip, his left arm extended horizontally with the hand bent upward, dancing on the toes of his right foot and

decorated robe, surrounded by tragic actors holding their masks, can be seen on fragments of a vase similar to the Pronomos vase (Figs. 34, 35).[27] It was painted around 400 in Tarentum, was formerly in the possession of Curtius and is now in Würzburg.

The true and definite form of the satyr play in which the mischievous satyrs take liberties with venerable figures from Greek mythology is shown not only in the satyr play vase, but also on the Hel-

33

Figs. 34a-b, 35. Chorus of tragedy. Fragments of vase from Tarentum, Würzburg

throwing his left leg upward with bent knee. He dances for the inspection of the poet Demetrius, who is seated holding a scroll. The two musicians are in the center of the lower row; Pronomos, seated, is playing the double flute, in a richly decorated sleeved robe, and the lyre player, standing, is holding his lyre, dressed only in a cloak, a chlamys, fastened around his neck and hanging in the back. As in tragedy, the fluteplayer had to be in the orchestra all the time with the chorus, and therefore he is dressed similarly to the actors, while the lyre or cithara player accompanied only single songs of the actors, and might even stay inside the scene building. Such a fluteplayer in a sleeved and richly

lenistic mosaic from the house of the tragic poet in Pompeii, now in Naples (Fig. 36).[28] The two young men in goatskin loincloths, one with the mask pushed back on his head, practice the dance movements for a performance of a satyr play. Their leader, the Papposilenus, will be acted by a young man, who is in the act of drawing a goatskin chiton with sleeves over his head with the help of an attendant. The fluteplayer in a richly decorated robe and with a large wreath on his head stands in front view, behind him an attendant reads from a scroll. The poet or teacher of the chorus (chorodidaskalos) is seated holding the mask of a heroine. This female mask lies on a low footstool before him together with the mask for the old Papposilenus. Behind him on a table is the mask of the hero. We thus have a similar group of personalities—hero, heroine, and old Silenus—and the same type of masks as on the Pronomos vase. The poet or teacher may be Aeschylus who was both (cf. p. 20).

If the poet on the Naples mosaic is Aeschylus, then the Papposilenus, who appears as father of the satyrs in the plays of Sophocles and Euripides, may have already been used by Aeschylus. This has indeed been assumed by Crusius and Robert for a satyr play in the *Sphinx* of Aeschylus produced in 467, because a southern Italian vase in Naples, attributed to Python, depicts the old Silenus standing in his shaggy dress before the Sphinx (Fig. 37). He has the Dionysiac soft boots, the thyrsus, and the nebris. In his right open hand he holds a bird, which does not fly away, thus probably is dead. The

Fig. 36. Chorus teacher and satyr chorus. Mosaic, Naples

Fig. 37. Silenus and the sphinx. Southern Italian vase

story must have been similar to the one told about a man going to the Apollo of Delphi asking him whether the bird in his hand was dead or alive. If Apollo had said dead, he would have quickly choked him; if Apollo had said alive, he would let him fly away. This story is satirized on a vase, also by Python, in Mannheim. Silenus holding a bird is standing before the seated Apollo.[29] On the Naples vase Papposilenus must have played the role of Oedipus, but instead of answering the question of the Sphinx, he has given her a riddle. We must, however, realize that this vase is about a hundred years later than Aeschylus' play, and therefore it proves nothing as to the original performance but only as to the dress at the time of the painting of the vase.

The question as to how much can be traced back to an earlier age—when we consider the form of the satyr play as evidenced by Sophocles, Euripides, and the monuments—is of the utmost significance for the origin of tragedy and for the relation of tragedy to the satyr drama. The greatest problem is why the word tragedy contains tragos ($\tau\rho\acute{\alpha}\gamma o\varsigma$), meaning goat, which has nothing whatever to do with serious tragedy. Many authors assume that the tragos is simply the satyr who appears at first only in the dithyramb and later solely in the satyr play.[30] Why then has the word satyr passed over into that one of the three kinds of Dionysiac plays which has nothing whatever to do with serious tragedy, while on the other hand the word tragos, meaning goat, came to denote the serious form of the drama?

Frickenhaus[31] tried to solve the puzzle by the ingenious hypothesis that the tragos was not the satyr of the chorus but Papposilenus who, in the perfected satyr play, is the exarchos, the leader of the satyr chorus. He bases his opinion on that of Aristotle who stated that the exarchos of the chorus was the first tragoidos. Frickenhaus cites also the *Ichneutae* of Sophocles (v. 358), where Papposi-

Fig. 38. Papposilenus playing flute

Fig. 39. Prometheus and satyr chorus. Bell crater, Gotha

lenus is addressed as tragos and wears a robe made of goatskin. Frickenhaus errs, however, for this speech by Kyllene is addressed not to the old father but to one of his sons, a satyr. The nymph expressly calls her interlocutor a young man, whose hair, it

many satyr play vases of the earlier fifth century (Figs. 40-43),[34] except on the late Naples vase (Fig. 31), can we find Papposilenus in goatskin. Only on such later vases as the one in the Jatta Collection at Ruvo (Fig. 38) and the one from Tarentum in Am-

Figs. 40, 41. Jason and dragon. Cup by Duris, Vatican; Attic vase, Metropolitan Museum

is true, is growing thin on top and who has a goatee, the beard of a goat. The second piece of evidence brought forward by Frickenhaus from *Prometheus the Fire-Bringer* of Aeschylus (Fragment 207): "Thou goat shalt singe thy beard," is also addressed to a satyr of the chorus, one who, it is expressly stated, wished to embrace the fire.[32] The same fact is proved by a group of vases collected by Beazley, where satyrs surround Prometheus (Fig. 39).[33] They have lit their torches at the flame in a narthex, in which the hero has brought down the fire from heaven to men (cf. Fig. 42).

Neither on these Prometheus vases nor on the

Fig. 42. Jason, played by a satyr, and Dionysus holding a narthex. Crater, Bologna

Fig. 43. Heracles as Atlas with satyrs. Vase, South Italy

44

sterdam, formerly in the Arndt Collection (Fig. 44), or on fourth-century Apulian, Attic, and Boeotian vases (Fig. 45) and in later statues (Figs. 46, 47) is old Silenus depicted in his goatskin.[35] On all others, satyrs with only loincloths or without any covering consort directly with the heroes (Figs. 39 and 43).

The stories of the strong man Heracles (Fig. 43) and of the fight of Jason with the dragon (Figs. 40-42) lend themselves particularly well to satyr play use. The vase in the Metropolitan Museum (Fig. 41) depicts Jason as a frightened human being protected by Athena while he takes the golden fleece from the fierce dragon. In the fine cup by Duris the hero hangs helplessly in the jaws of the dragon (Fig. 40).[36] The presence of Athena assures us that he will be saved. The painter of the crater in Bologna (Fig. 42) has put a satyr in the place of Jason, protected by his god Dionysus. This lets us understand how the writer of the satyr play which the vase painter had seen could turn this serious myth into a satyric drama.

Particularly important is the kylix, a wine-cup, in the British Museum by the Brygus painter (Fig. 48a-b),[37] which goes back to the time of Pratinas, the older contemporary of Aeschylus. Here the satyrs caper in an unbridled riot of noise around the thymele or low sacrificial platform, near which stand the altar and the image of Dionysus. On one side of the vase they attack Iris, who has come to take the sacrifices from the altar, and jump over thymele and altar to catch her. She will, however, escape, for she can fly. On the other side they attack even Hera, the queen of heaven. She also will escape, for she is not only protected by Hermes, the male messenger of the gods, who was probably the exarchos of the chorus, but more efficiently by Heracles, dressed as an Athenian archer. The situation is similar to the dancing song of Pratinas: "What noise, what dances, what riot has come to the thymele of Dionysus!"[38]

Figs. 44-47. Papposileni wearing goatskin

45

46

47

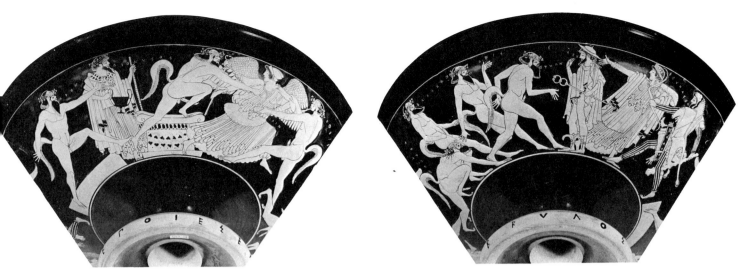

Fig. 48a-b. Satyrs attacking Hera and Iris. Kylix by the Brygus Painter, British Museum

Hermes as exarchos of a satyr chorus, with petasos, kerykeion, high boots, and a richly-patterned cloak stands in the middle of a frivolous and wanton satyr chorus also on the well-known psykter, a cooling vase for wine, by Duris, in the British Museum (Fig. 49).[39] The satyrs drink in difficult positions. Two kneeling on the ground are fed by two of their companions, each from two different containers. Two try to drink standing on their hands from a cup standing on the ground, one of which is upset by a companion. When we look closely at the face of the chorus leader, it is not that of the youthful Olympian god, but that of a satyr. We may, therefore, conclude that the first exarchos of a satyr chorus was one of the satyrs themselves, but in different disguise. Thus a first step toward the adoption of the heroic saga, and thereby toward tragedy, was taken by dressing one of the satyrs as Hermes, as Heracles, as Perseus, as Prometheus, as Jason, or even as Dionysus, whichever the needs of the individual play demanded. A second step toward the development of tragedy came when the mask of the leading satyr was replaced by that of a god or hero, the exarchos appearing in the dress

of such a figure and impersonating him with an appropriate mask and no longer the satyr mask. A third step came when the exarchos as an actor was entirely separated from the satyr chorus. Not until then could old Papposilenus, as an established figure, step into the place of the leader as an intermediary between chorus and heroes. Papposilenus thus cannot help us to define the name and the origin of tragedy.

Another explanation, although coming from antiquity—in the Parian chronicle of the third century B.C.—is likewise fallacious. According to this account, tragedy is named from the goat which was the prize of victory and the sacrificial victim of Dionysus. The first prize, however, was never a goat, but usually a tripod, and if an animal, a bull. In the time of Arion a goat was the third award, the second was an amphora full of wine, and the first a bull.[40]

Although none of the former explanations of the name of tragedy are satisfactory, they all contain a germ of the truth. The goat is the sacred animal of Dionysus. In many primitive religions the believer, by eating the sacred animal or by wearing

Fig. 49. Satyr chorus led by Hermes. Psykter by Duris, British Museum

15

its skin, becomes himself the animal.[41] The worshipers of Dionysus danced around the sacred goat, singing the dithyramb. They then sacrificed it, ate its flesh, part of which they gave to the gods. Then they made themselves a dress out of its skin, a full dress for Papposilenus (Figs. 36-38, 44-47),[42] a loincloth for the satyrs (Figs. 26-29, 31-32, 36),[43] and a chlaina, a small mantle for satyrs (Euripides, *Cyclops*, v. 80) and maenads, who threw it around their shoulders (Figs. 20, 22, 24-26). Nourished and dressed by the sacred animal, they felt themselves to be goats (tragoi), just as worshipers of Poseidon were horses (hippoi), the devotees of Artemis she-bears (arktoi), or bees (melissai). The change of dress, taking the goatskin as a costume, endowed the worshipers of Dionysus with goat nature whether they were old or young, men or women.[44] The shaggy fur of Papposilenus (χορταῖος χιτών) imitates the natural fur of forest demons.

Parallels from other non-dramatic Greek cults show that all these factors are still insufficient to explain the rise of tragedy. In Delphi the story of the killing of the dragon by Apollo, in Eleusis the story of the rape of Persephone and her return to her mother Demeter as a symbol of death and resurrection, were repeated in the same form every year. The same is the case in dramatic performances of provincial tribes in the New Hebrides, as I was told by Professor Paul Wingert of Columbia University. These are cruder, and the Eleusinian mysteries are more refined, than the religion of Dionysus. The Dionysiac religion produced also mysteries which were more efficacious and spread out in much wider regions than the Eleusinian, for its prophets went about the land to instruct and convert mankind. This is reflected in the stories of the wanderings and struggles of the god. The shrines of Dionysus were scattered over the mainland of Hellas, the islands of the Greek sea, the coasts of Asia Minor and Southern Italy, from which they later reached Rome.[45]

Like all mystery religions the Dionysiac mysteries promised purification, teaching, and the vision of godhead. They differed, however, from all others, particularly from the Egyptian and Oriental ones of Isis and Mithras, in that here the purification from earthly things was not external, but through spiritual ecstasy; an ecstasy furthered through the noble gift of the god, wine, by means of which the disguised human being feels not only an outward, but an inward change. The teaching came not from priests, but through revelation. The vision of the godhead was attained not through the guidance of any official hierarchy but through direct union with

the divine. The mortal men and women became members of the holy thiasus of Dionysus, animals of his holy herd (the thiasus), a goat, a tragos: "I fell, a small goat, into the milk; I, who was a man, became a god"; "Happy and blessed one, thou shalt be a god instead of a mortal"—so the Orphic-Dionysiac tablets of gold found in South Italy are inscribed. Perhaps such a goat, who had been a man, is represented on the black-figured lekythos of the early fifth century in Berlin (Fig. 50). A goat with a human face is surrounded by sileni. One holds his horn, while the other seated on a rock is holding a writing tablet and a stylus.[46]

Thus everyone who dances for the god, sings, plays a musical instrument, appears in a satyr drama, a tragedy, or a comedy at the festivals for Dionysus is a thiasote or a tragos. The maenads, the satyrs, their leader—whether Papposilenus or Hermes or Dionysus himself, or any one of the other heroes or gods—all are tragoi. Tragedy, the most elevated form of the cult of the god, also presupposes ecstasy and has retained the name for the followers of the god Dionysus. Tragedy, then, is the *song of the holy thiasus in honor of the god.* Hence it was only in the religion of Dionysus that the drama could be fashioned, for only by god-given intoxication could a man be changed into a thiasote,

Fig. 50. Goat with human face. Lekythos, Berlin Museum

an actor. Tragedy, then, remains always, in this sense, a goat-song (tragic ode, tragodia). But the satyr drama with its revelling and capering of the satyr chorus, and even comedy, with its often burlesqued and absurd jokes, are not mere expressions of pleasure. They always remain grave, sacred, and religious events.

An interesting parallel not only to the dance-drama in ecstasy, but also to the interplay of jest and earnest in religious festivals, is found in the plays performed by the inhabitants of the island of Bali (Figs. 51-52).[47] These people living in a hot climate wear very light clothing, but for their dance-drama they dress fully, from head to foot, and fall into ecstasy by means of wine.

The many factors already discussed—epic, lyric, music, dance, dithyramb, satyr play, ecstasy, and mimesis (histrionic impersonation)—require, however, something more to make the rise of drama possible. Out of them there could have developed settled liturgies and mimetic performances, as in the cults of Delphi, Eleusis, Egypt, the New Hebrides, and Bali, actions (dromena) with fixed and prescribed text, formulae, and vestments. None of these has produced a living drama as the Dionysiac religion has. It was improvised at first, as Aristotle says,[48] and then brought into artistic and literary form. The enkindling spark which turned the dithy-

ramb and the satyr play of the northern Peloponnesus into great tragedy was the genius of the Attic poets. The history of the Greek theater in classical times is therefore the history of the development of a religious idea into a national, literary, and artistic event.

Figs. 51, 52. Dancers on the Island of Bali

CHAPTER II

ATTIC TRAGEDY

See Fig. 121

The Oldest Attic Tragic Poets

ACCORDING to the Attic conception of the religion of Dionysus, the most important event in the life of the god was his visit to Icarius in Icaria, situated north of Athens on the slope of Mount Pentelikon. This incident, with two others, the miraculous birth of Dionysus from the thigh of Zeus and the reception of Dionysus among the gods of Athens, is represented on reliefs, which, having been transferred from their original position, probably an altar, are today on the late bema of Phaedrus in the theater of Dionysus Eleuthereus of Athens (Figs. 53-55).[1] Dionysus has caused the vine to spring up, and the satyr who follows him snatches greedily at the grapes. Icarius grasps a branch with his left hand as a sign of ownership and with his right leads the goat (tragos), which has nibbled the tender shoots and is now to be slaughtered in honor of the god. Erigone, the daughter of Icarius, serves at the altar, holding the sacrificial dish. In the background behind Icarius appears the dog Maera. This dog later went with Erigone in search of her father, who, when teaching peasants to cultivate the vine, was struck down by drunken men and thus became a martyr to the holy cause of Dionysus. The last two slabs show Dionysus enthroned among the other gods of Athens in his sanctuary below the Acropolis, on which the columns of the Parthenon appear.

The district, whose eponymous hero Icarius became, was the birthplace of Thespis, the true founder of Attic tragedy.[2] It was Thespis who invented the first actor, that is to say, he put a hypokrites ($\dot{v}\pi o\kappa \rho \iota \tau \acute{\eta} s$), an answer- and response-giver, opposite the exarchos ($\dot{\epsilon}\xi \acute{a}\rho \chi \omega v$ or $\ddot{\epsilon}\xi a\rho \chi o s$) of the chorus, both leader and chorus now appearing in the most widely differing costumes. The spoken dialogue between the actor and exarchos was developed by interpolations between the songs of the chorus, and therefore is called Epeisodion, an epi-

Figs. 53-55. The life of Dionysus. Reliefs built into the front of the Roman stage, Theater of Dionysus at Athens

Fig. 54. Visit of Dionysus to Icarius

Fig. 55. Dionysus enthroned in his sanctuary in Athens

sode. The subject-matter was taken from the heroic saga in the form made familiar by epic. The chorus maintained the lyric form, although its members, including the exarchos, were changed, according to the themes of the dialogue parts, into citizens, either male or female, of the mythical age. This form of dramatic art was brought by Thespis to Athens, where in the year 534 B.C. the first performance was given under Pisistratus.[3] According to a later tradition Thespis "drove his tragedies on wagons."[4] This car is perhaps the car in the form of a ship on which, according to the testimony of black-figured vases, Dionysus, represented no doubt by his priest, was driven in company with his flute-playing satyrs and drawn perhaps by men dressed as satyrs into his holy precinct at the festival of the great City Dionysia (Figs. 56-58; see below, Chapter IV, pp. 52-53).[5] It is quite probable that Thespis with his chorus, a wandering troupe, drove his wagon about Attica until he found in Athens a permanent habitation. In any case, the ship-car, as carrus navalis, had a long life. It passed by way of Rome into the Roman provinces, and makes its appearance as "floats" in carnivals (carrus navale, reinterpreted as carne vale by the Italians) at Nice, Cologne, and New Orleans even today. In New York one can see on Columbus Day, October 12, a ship on wheels, a model of the Santa Maria, in which Columbus landed in America at one of the Bahama Islands in 1492. The origin of all these usages is the ship in which Dionysus was thought to have come to Attica every spring, as it is painted on a cup by Exekias in the time of Thespis (Fig. 59),[6] and described in Homeric Hymn No. VII.

Thespis is said to have first treated the face of his actors with white lead, then covered it with cinnabar or rubbed it with wine lees, and finally introduced masks of unpainted linen. But neither faces painted vermillion nor the later pure white linen masks could have other than a grotesque effect (cf. below, Figs. 66-71). Therefore Choerilus, the successor of Thespis, made further experiments with masks, and Phrynichus, the pupil of Thespis, introduced women's masks.[7] These were probably uniformly light in contrast to the men's, which were kept dark, as is true of the women's faces in contrast to the men's on vases of the sixth century (Fig. 14). It may also mean that Phrynichus was the first to allow the chorus to appear as women.

Phrynichus made the first attempt to bring historic events into tragedy in his *Capture of Miletus*, presented soon after the destruction of Miletus by the Persians in 494, which led to the Persian invasion of Greece in 490. Phrynichus also dramatized the defeat of the Persians in the second invasion of 480/79, in his *Phoenician Women*, performed in

Figs. 56-58. "Thespis car" in procession. Black-figured Attic vases

Fig. 59. Dionysus sailing over the sea. Cup by Exekias, Munich

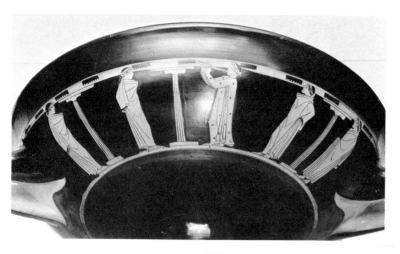

Figs. 60, 61. Fluteplayer accompanying chorus; Chorus teacher.
Cup by the Briseis Master, Metropolitan Museum

Fig. 62. Chorus teacher and satyr chorus. Detail from Fig. 36

476/5 under the archon Adeimantus, with Themistocles as choregus (Plutarch, *Life of Themistocles*, 114C). In both, as well as in Aeschylus' *Persians*, performed four years later, the scene is laid in Persian territory. Thus remoteness of time in the legendary tragedies is replaced by remoteness of place in the contemporaneous plays.

Phrynichus boasted that he had invented more figures in dancing than there are waves in a stormy sea (Plutarch, *Symp. Quaest.*, VIII,9,3, pp. 732f). This means that the chorus still played a leading role, as it does in Aeschylus' *Hiketides*. The chorus, therefore, had to be trained very carefully—probably in groups—by several fluteplayers. The members had not only to memorize the words but also the music and the dance steps. A late archaic vase by the Briseis Master in the Metropolitan Museum of Art in New York City (Figs. 60, 61)[8] shows on each side a fluteplayer in a long-sleeved robe accompanying four young men who are singing. This may be a group of four at the time when the chorus, consisting of twelve members, entered in four files of three ranks or three files of four ranks. Later choruses consisting of fifteen members could enter in five files of three ranks or three files of five ranks. In the center of the cup (Fig. 61) a chorus teacher, with a rod in his hand, looks at a contrivance for twelve oblong tickets, as they were probably handed out to the members of the chorus to check their attendance. The rehearsal takes place in a colonnade, a rare feature at the time (480-470), when the Briseis painter produced this vase. It may be that the Stoa Basilica is depicted, the first public building to be erected after the destruction of Athens in 480 by the Persians. It was the seat of the highest magistrates, the archons eponymos and basileus, who were in charge of the Dionysiac festivals (Aristotle, *Ath. Pol.*, 56f). The beautiful vase, therefore, might be connected with a victory celebration of the period of Phrynichus and Aeschylus.

Aeschylus

The literary and dramatic efforts of the earliest Attic tragedians were completed and perfected by Aeschylus (c.525-456 B.C.). He appeared first in 499-496 at the same time with Choerilus and Pratinas. The latter, from Phlius near Sicyon, introduced satyric drama as well as tragedy. He wrote 32 satyr plays among 50 dramas.[9] Since a later age considered Aeschylus the principal representative of satyric drama, it is probably he who appears as chorus-teacher (chorodidaskalos, χοροδιδάσκαλος) on the mosaic in Naples (Fig. 62, detail of Fig. 36). A head in the Capitoline Museum of the same type, with a pointed beard cut in the old-fashioned

Fig. 63a-b. Marble herm of Aeschylus.
Capitoline Museum

Fig. 65. Bronze head of Aeschylus.
Museo Archeologico, Florence

wedge-shape and with a bald pate, is also supposed to represent Aeschylus (Fig. 63a-b).[10] A gem in Homs near Leptis Magna represents Aeschylus in the same way. It is certainly the opposite to the portrait of the younger, modern, sophisticated Euripides (Figs. 106-107), as the two are also described in Aristophanes' *Frogs*. That Aeschylus was bald is testified by the story that an eagle mistook his bald head for a rock and threw a tortoise on it to break the shell.

If satyric drama was already introduced by the older contemporaries of Aeschylus, it was certainly influenced by Attic tragedy. The form known to us through Sophocles and Euripides goes back to Pratinas and Aeschylus, and not to a different earlier form of tragedy. We have, then, the peculiar sequence that tragedy, the latest form of Dionysiac poetry, was the first to be adopted (534 B.C.) in Athens for the Dionysiac festivals. The next form, satyric drama, was the second, and the dithyramb, the earliest form, was the last, for it was introduced only after the founding of democracy (510). The earlier forms were not admitted until they had taken a definite artistic and literary character, acquired by the imitation of the latest form of tragedy. Comedy, which in itself consists of the earliest elements (see Ch. III), secured its established form only at the beginning of the fifth century, and was correspondingly inserted last in the program of the Dionysiac festivals.

Aeschylus introduced the second actor, according to Aristotle (*Ars Poet.*, IV, pp. 1449a, 15f). As a consequence the dialogue could develop far more freely than when it existed only between the representative of the chorus and one actor. It marked also the first stage in the withdrawal of the chorus, whose dwindling importance in the later periods had the most far-reaching literary and dramatic consequences. The development from pure chorus-drama to actor-drama can easily be traced in the seven plays by Aeschylus which are extant of his original seventy to ninety plays. In the earliest, the *Suppliants* (Hiketides) the fifty Danaids are the protagonists throughout, and they sustain a most vivid action.[11] Mrs. Sikelianos has shown this very successfully in her presentation on the occasion of the Delphic Festival in 1930 (see Ch. XVI, Figs. 847 and 850). Only one player confronts the chorus, never more. There is no prologue, that is, no spoken entrance scene. In the *Persians* (472) there were two actors, but their employment was so awkward

Fig. 64. Aeschylus. Copy of statue erected by
Lycurgus (?), Vatican

21

and unskilful that Xerxes, the Persian king, and his mother Atossa never meet. In the *Seven Against Thebes* (467) and in the *Prometheus* the dialogue becomes more fluent, but is still hampered by being limited to two players. Then Aeschylus takes over the third actor from his younger rival Sophocles. Now a more and more elaborate dialogue develops, which begins at once with an artistic prologue. The *Oresteia*, performed in 458, was played for the first time before a rich background (see Ch. XVI, Fig. 854, performance in Reading, England), whereas the earlier dramas worked only with movable scenery using the full round of the orchestra. The biographer of Aeschylus says rightly: "Whoever holds the view that Sophocles was the more finished tragic poet, is right. He should, however, consider that it was much more difficult after Thespis, Phrynichus, and Choerilus to bring tragedy to so great a height, than it was, once Aeschylus had spoken, to reach the perfection of Sophocles."

As to the scenic innovations of Aeschylus, the *Vita* informs us that he decorated the theater magnificently, bringing into requisition paintings and mechanical devices, tombs and altars, trumpets, ghostly apparitions and furies. Moreover, he introduced a definite actor's costume. He gave the players sleeves, a long robe with train, and he increased their height by means of taller cothurni (κόθορνοι), buskins, and by a high hairdress (onkos ὄγκος). The ancient history of Music (Μουσικὴ ἱστορία) adds that he introduced large and dignified masks.[12] It is supposed, therefore, that a statue in the Vatican, carrying the mask of Heracles, incorrectly restored with the head of Euripides, is a copy of the statue of Aeschylus, erected together with those of the other two great tragic poets in the Athenian theater in the time of Alexander the Great by Lycurgus (Fig. 64).[13] The head of this type seems to be preserved in a bronze head (Fig. 65), found together with a head of Sophocles, now in the Museo Archeologico of Florence, of which marble copies—the best in Naples and Copenhagen—also exist.[14]

What Aeschylus did was not so much to introduce and discover new things as to improve fixed cult usages and establish them in the theater. The three essentials of the tragic costume—mask, sleeved robe, and tall buskins—all originated in the worship of Dionysus, and therefore remain obligatory, although with certain formal changes, until the end of antiquity. Greek tragedy was always a sacred ceremony in honor of the god, and therefore the mask, the sleeved robe, and the cothurnus, borrowed from the Dionysiac religion and its ritual, had to stay as a symbol of the devotion of his followers to the god. Even the Romans kept the form of the costume,

although they often distorted and exaggerated it.

This development is seen most clearly in the mask. Thespis used it unpainted, and hence it must have looked grotesque. Such grotesque masks are found still today among the American Indians, on the South Pacific islands, among the Negroes of Central Africa, and were used also in archaic times among the Punic inhabitants of Tunis (Figs. 66-69).[15] In Greece itself there were grotesque masks in several cults of the early periods, as for instance in Sparta at the shrine of Artemis Orthia in the first half of the sixth century, and in Lycosura at the shrine of Demeter.[16] In Mycenean religion an important part must have been played by animal-headed demons imitated by masked men; for this we have the evidence of Mycenean gems (Fig. 70),[17] and of a Mycenean fresco (Fig. 71),[18] on which such demons, often engaged in ritual, are represented. These animal-headed and distorted demons, growing as they did out of the theriomorphic conceptions as demons in animal form, retreat more and more under the clear sky of the Olympic religion. The Medusa head becomes a terror mask, although the Corfu pediment of about 590-580 B.C. proves that the Gorgon Medusa was originally a great goddess.[19]

The only masks to retain a general significance in historic times are those of the Dionysiac demons,

Figs. 66-69. Punic masks. Musée du Bardo, Carthage

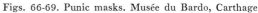

Figs. 70, 71. Animal-headed demons.
Gem; fresco, Mycenae

the satyrs, which were worn by young men as early
as about 600 B.C., since they sang the dithyramb of
Arion in satyr's costume. On the satyr play vase
in Naples the satyr masks in the hands of the members of the chorus (Figs. 31, 32) are exactly like
those of the satyrs of the Bacchic thiasus on the
other side of the vase (Fig. 33).[20] When the exarchos was given a part differing from those of the
satyrs, when the chorus played the role of men and
women of prehistoric times, when the actor confronted the exarchos in the role of a god or a hero—
then we have these masks of heroic characters in
use as well as those of the satyrs. Yet the mask never
loses its religious significance. On the satyr play
vase the Muse holds the mask of the heroine. A
number of monuments show us the mask in the hand
of the god himself, as the female mask—probably
of a maenad—on a crater in Bari (Fig. 72),[21] and
on a wall painting from Pompeii.[22] Dionysus may
be displaying it to his thiasus or putting it on an
actor. A votive relief with tragic masks has been
found in the theater of Dionysus. Devotees can be
seen consecrating a mask to him, or it may be
shown hanging or deposited in his shrine. On a
wine jug of the Eretria master the mask of Dionysus, lying in a winnowing basket decorated with
ivy, is venerated by two women who bring wine and
fruit.[23] On many Lenaean vases a mask on a post
decorated with dresses represents the god himself
(Figs. 73 and 25 above). Hence the thiasote who
dances or plays in honor of Dionysus must at all
times wear the mask. Aeschylus, by giving it a
dignified form, raised the mask as far above the
grotesque of the archaic age as he elevated tragedy

Fig. 73. Masks on post. Black-figured lekythos, Athens

Fig. 72. Dionysus holding mask, with thiasus. Crater, Bari

itself above its "satyrlike" origin. The earliest (about
470 B.C.) example of a serious mask in the time of
Aeschylus can be seen on the fragment of a wine-
jug found on the market place of Athens (Fig. 74).[24]

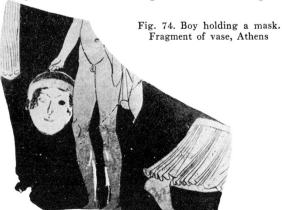

Fig. 74. Boy holding a mask.
Fragment of vase, Athens

Figs. 75-78. Archaic and archaistic hairdresses

A special way of dressing the hair about 500 B.C. survives in the onkos, the high coiffure of the tragic mask. It is simply an imitation of the archaic hairdressing, which brought forward the ends of the long twisted tresses and built them up over the brow. Good examples are the terracotta in Olympia (Fig. 75), the marble archaistic head from Delos in Athens (Fig. 76), the copies of the Hermes of Alcamenes from Pergamon in Istanbul, its replica on the double herm in the stadium of Athens (Fig. 77), and the archaistic head from Pompeii in Naples (Fig. 78).[25] The pointed beard cut in the form of a wedge in the period of the Persian war also survives in several masks, particularly in comedy (Figs. 135-140, 143, 147-150). Aeschylus, according to his portraits (Figs. 62, 63), certainly wore this form of beard himself.

It is more difficult to prove that the long, floating, sleeved robe also came from the Dionysiac worship. We know it as belonging to the Eleusinian cult, worn by Iacchus, who is related to Dionysus, by the priest, and by the dadouchos, the torch-bearing boy. Hence the former belief, that Aeschylus, who was born at Eleusis, borrowed it from the Mysteries.[26] The monuments which show the hierophant, Iacchus, or the dadouchos in the sleeved robe, are all, however, the products of later periods. Good examples are the Eleusinian vases, one in Leningrad and another in Lyons (Fig. 79a-b),[27] the Ninnion

pinax[28] of the fourth century, or the urns[29] and the sarcophagus from Torre Nova[30] of Roman times. It was, therefore, not the actors who copied their dress from the Eleusinian priests, but rather the Eleusinian priests who borrowed this costume from the

Fig. 80. Dionysus in sleeved robe. Black-figured vase, Bonn

Fig. 79a-b. Sleeved robe in Eleusinian cult. Late Attic vase, Lyons

Figs. 81-84. Dionysus in sleeved robe

actors. This fact was already known in antiquity (Athenaeus, I, p. 21c).[31] Pringsheim assumed that both derived their costume independently of each other from the festival robes of the Pisistratid age.[32] This is correct in regard to the elaborately woven-in figure and vegetable patterns of sixth-century dress depicted on the François vase (Fig. 14) and other black-figured vases of the sixth century.[33] They were certainly also influenced by oriental dresses at the time of the Persian wars. Although they were no longer in use in the fifth century, the satyr play vase (Fig. 32), the Andromeda vase (below, Figs. 110-111), and other vases are evidence of the survival of the rich patterns in the theater of the fifth and the fourth centuries (see Figs. 121-122). The long-sleeved robe with train (syrma, σύρμα), moreover, on Greek monuments occurs only for Iacchus, who is almost identical with Dionysus (see Fig. 79). The Eleusinian priests wear it only on Roman monuments.[34] At the Dionysiac festivals the richly-patterned dresses reminded one of the heroic age, from which the poets took their material.

An especially noteworthy fact, on the other hand, is that frequently on Greek monuments the sleeved robe is found to be worn by Dionysus. The series of Greek monuments which depict Dionysus wearing the sleeved robe begins with a black-figured vase in Bonn (Fig. 80),[35] dating from the period when Attic tragedy was taking form. The later archaistic monuments which show Dionysus in this type of robe, particularly neo-Attic marble vases and bases (Figs. 81, 82)[36] certainly are adaptations of figures of the same early age. A pedestal in the style of Praxiteles at Athens, upon which originally a tripod won as a prize of victory for a dithyramb was set, shows Dionysus with wine cup and thyrsus in the sleeved, long floating robe (Fig. 83). Another base in the Museo Nazionale Romano in Rome has either Dionysus or his priest, holding a dish with cake, in this dress (Fig. 84).[37] On a fourth-century vase from Thebes in Athens Dionysus in a short, sleeved robe is riding a panther (Fig. 85).[38] On the relief with the visit of Dionysus to a mortal in the Louvre, he also wears the short, sleeved dress (Fig. 86).[39]

Fig. 85. Dionysus in sleeved robe riding a panther

Fig. 86. Dionysus in sleeved robe visits a mortal. Relief, Louvre

Figs. 87-89. Dionysus in sleeved robe. Wall paintings from Pompeii; mosaic, Naples

In addition, there are wall paintings from Pompeii, one showing a bronze-colored statue of Dionysus to whom a woman makes a sacrifice, another the god in a green dress covered with grapes before Mount Vesuvius (where a good wine, lacrimae Christi, is still made), both figures in the sleeved robe (Figs. 87, 88).[40] A mosaic which is probably based on the *Lycurgus* of Aeschylus, shows Dionysus in this dress behind Ampela, the personification of the vine, or Ambrosia, a nymph, whom the mad Lycurgus tries to kill (Fig. 89).[41] When, therefore, the deeds and adventures of Dionysus were celebrated in the tragedies, the god must have appeared in this garment. In the same way in any play given in his honor, the other gods and the heroes were obliged to wear the long floating robe, or at least the sleeves, which were never a part of everyday dress of men. The youthful Dionysus (Figs. 85, 86), Heracles (Fig. 31), other wandering heroes (Fig. 306), and the Furies (Figs. 96-97) put on a short dress with long sleeves.

The cothurnus, the third feature of the actor's dress,[42] is proved by the *Frogs* of Aristophanes (ll. 45ff.) to be typical of the effeminate Dionysus, as contrasted with the club of Heracles adopted from this more masculine god. It was originally a woman's footwear. On a vase in Boston (Fig. 90),[43] one of the two young men who dress for the part of women, probably in a tragedy, wears the female high soft buskins and the mask. Holding the mantle rolled together in his left hand, he recites his part. The other actor is putting on the buskins, while the female mask with the hair bound up with a kerchief lies on the ground before him. The fillet around his short hair is to help hold the mask in place without hurting his skull. The vase belongs to the Periclean period. The cothurnus was so characteristic for Dionysus that Pausanias (VIII, 31, 4) recognized a statue as that of Dionysus by the cothurnus alone. The *Vita* expressly states that Aeschylus enlarged the earlier cothurnus and thereby gave additional height to the actors.[44] That means, he put a sole under the original cothurnus, which was a soft buskin.[45] This sole was continually heightened or added to in the course of centuries, in accordance with the development of the stage (see below, Figs. 307, 785, 797-799). The original form of soft leather without a separate sole is worn by several figures of Dionysus (Figs. 85-87, 91),[46] for like the mask and the sleeved robe, it was his lasting characteristic. On a Roman sarcophagus in Rome with a replica in Princeton, a satyr puts the boots

Fig. 90. Actors dressing

Fig. 91. Dionysus wearing cothurni

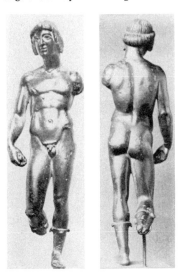

Figs. 92, 93. Satyr putting cothurnus on infant Dionysus. Sarcophagi, Capitoline; Princeton

on the child Dionysus (Figs. 92-93).[47] Therefore, among his followers it is particularly the old Silenus who wears the high buskin together with the chiton of shaggy goatskin (Figs. 38, 47, 94), or even when naked (Fig. 95).[48] The younger satyrs also wear the cothurnus occasionally, and so do the Erinyes on vases inspired by Aeschylus' *Eumenides.* For these Aeschylus had special masks and dresses made[49]; the *Vita* (59) mentions these expressly and vases of the fourth century give us a vague idea how they appeared (Figs. 96-97).[50] They retain the pattern of the dresses and the high boots. The fifth-century Erinyes were undoubtedly more terrifying to look upon than the fourth-century representations, as is proved by the account we have of the horror of the spectators.

The actor's costume introduced by Aeschylus appeared strange and absurd to the Romans,[51] and so it appears to us in late Roman examples (below, Figs. 797-799, 832). There are two contributory causes for its persistence through the whole of antiquity. The sleeved robe and the high boots are the

costume of Asia Minor and the Orient as well as of Thrace and North Hellas. The religion of Dionysus entered the Greek mainland by two routes, over the sea from the east, and through Macedonia and Boeotia from the north. From both directions it brought with it an outlandish costume which to the lightly-clad Greeks appeared solemn, and which was soon indissolubly bound up with the sacred plays of Dionysiac worship. Yet this dress may not be described as barbaric and oriental because of its foreign character, any more than the cult of Dionysus and the Attic tragedy may be. Like all other cultural advantages borrowed from abroad, the dress and the plays were perfected as something purely and nationally Greek.

A second reason why this dress should appear as peculiarly suitable for the actors is the fact that it covered the whole person from head to foot, with the exception of the hands which were used for gesticulation. This complete covering made the wearer unrecognizable. The individual actor must give up his identity in order to represent the char-

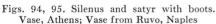

Figs. 94, 95. Silenus and satyr with boots.
Vase, Athens; Vase from Ruvo, Naples

Figs. 96, 97. Scenes from the *Eumenides*, Aeschylus.
Southern Italian crater, Louvre; Vase, British Museum

acters of a higher life. It is easy to see how appropriate this floating garment is to the spirit of a
redemptive religion and of Aeschylean tragedy. The
solemn robe which completely enfolded the body
must have been a great help to the actor when he
tried to forget his own personality and daily life
and to be absorbed completely in his sacred task. He
must have felt as a priest feels when, garbed in the
vestments of liturgy, he fulfills some holy rite. It
is inconceivable that he should undertake a task
of this kind in the dress of everyday life.

Sophocles

As the *Vita* of Aeschylus indicates, Sophocles
(496-406), the favorite of his own and of a later
age, was able to build further upon the creations
of Aeschylus. Success came to Sophocles more easily

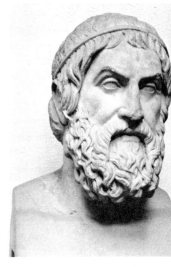

98

99

100

101a-b

Figs. 98-103. Sophocles. 98, Museo Archeologico, Florence; 99, 100, British Museum;
101, Head of 102 before restoration; 102, Lateran; 103, Bibliothèque Nationale

102

103

than to his predecessor Aeschylus and to his successor Euripides. He learned from both and surpassed both. He received an excellent education.
When sixteen years of age he was chosen to lead as
an exarchos the victory dance for the defeat of the
Persians at Salamis. We know his portrait from several heads showing him as a mature and as an old
man (Figs. 98-100).[52] In the celebrated standing
statue in the Lateran (Figs. 101-102)[53] the author
of the *Antigone* is depicted the perfect man, the
καλὸς κ'ἀγαθός, as the Greek artists of the fourth
century and the Attic people saw him. In the
relief statuette in the Cabinet des Médailles of the
Bibliothèque Nationale in Paris (Fig. 103)[54] the old
Sophocles, the author of the *Oedipus at Colonus*, is
conceived as he appeared as the defendant before

the judges of Athens, when he convinced them by reading his praise of Athens from his last masterpiece that he was unjustly accused of incompetence by his son.

Sophocles first produced tragedies in 471, and by 468 he had gained victory over the older master and thirty years later, in 438, over the younger. We know seven of his 123 dramas, exactly the number we know of Aeschylus. Unlike those of the latter, however, they show great uniformity of style.

Probably Sophocles matured early. His introduction of the third actor is characteristic. Only the earliest preserved play, the *Ajax*, has an imperfect dialogue between three persons. In all other plays it is fine and smooth, whether for two actors or for three. The single drama is rounded off in a way that differs widely from the treatment of Aeschylus. It is instructive to compare the *Electra* of Sophocles with the *Oresteia* of Aeschylus, who presents the same material in a trilogy. Sophocles, in consequence of his austere dramatic construction, offers no less material in a single play than Aeschylus in his three dramas. Epic narrative and lyric song give place more and more to the dialogue. The chorus sustains the mood of the whole, reflecting it in lovely songs. The hero carries the action and the ethos. His attitude in the face of god-determined destiny, his character in the light of this destiny, is the subject of the action. His *Oedipus the King* was considered by Aristotle as the model drama and Oedipus the model hero.[55]

We are told of Sophocles that he invented skenographia or scene painting. He was thus the first to put behind the actors a defined background as skene. This fact belongs to the innermost essence of his poetry. He is, with Pericles and Phidias, the representative of true classic art, in which the seen and unseen blend with one another in peculiar clarity. *Ajax, Antigone, Electra, Oedipus, Philoctetes* appear before the mind's eye when we think of

Sophocles as characteristic, detached figures, as they appear on contemporary vases. The figures of Sophocles must have appeared against the skene in sharply defined silhouettes, unlike the figures of Aeschylus, which were seen in the round. The entrances and exits of his actors and chorus also were finely balanced (see p. 59, Fig. 238).

Sophocles appeared himself as an actor only in his youth, taking parts in which his skill as an ephebos trained in music and gymnastics could come to the fore. Thus he was brilliant in the role of Nausicaa as a skilful ball player, and in that of Thamyras as a lyre player and singer. Perhaps the vase painting showing Thamyras blinded by a Muse (Fig. 104)[56] in the Ashmolean Museum reflects a votive pinax painted for the young genius in honor of a victory with this early drama. An impression of placid, serene beauty must have been left by the plays of Sophocles, despite the frequent cruelty of their subject-matter. A vase fragment in Dresden (Fig. 105)[57] may reflect the lost *Tereus* of Sophocles. Tereus, in richly decorated sleeved dress, pursues Procne and Philomela, the two sisters whom he has wronged and who as a revenge have slaughtered his son and given him the flesh of the boy to eat. This was the scene before a messenger told how all three were changed into birds.

With Sophocles began the differentiation of the offices of poet, actor, musician, and chorus leader, all of which Aeschylus had combined in his great, many-sided personality. The drama now has a definite construction: first prologue, or the exposition; then parodos or entrance song of the chorus; then first, second, third, fourth epeisodion alternating with first, second, third, fourth stasimon or song (that is, the dialogue parts or histrionic scenes alternate with songs of the chorus); last comes the exodos, the final song, the recessional of the chorus. When the chorus was omitted in the later periods, this led to the five-act play.

Fig. 104. Thamyras. Attic hydria, Oxford

Fig. 105. *Tereus*. Fragment of vase, Dresden

Figs. 106a,b-108. Euripides. Head, Mantua; Herm found in Rieti, Copenhagen; Drawing from lost statue

Euripides

When Euripides (c.484-406) appeared, the external and internal structure of tragedy had been completed. It would, however, never have attained the significance for the world's history, literature, and civilization had not this philosopher among the poets entirely altered it once again.[58] He succeeded only after tremendous struggle and suffering. The marks of his difficulties and disappointments may be seen on his face in a portrait made in his old age (Figs. 106a-b) and the one (Fig. 107) belonging to the Lycurgean statue now lost (Fig. 108).[59] Euripides first studied painting and then philosophy, before he became a dramatist. He appeared in a dramatic contest for the first time in 455, when he was almost thirty years old, but it was not until 441, when he was over forty, that he carried off the first prize. The extant tragedy, *Hippolytus*, won him his second victory in the year 428, and the fifth did not come until after his death, with the representation of the *Bacchae*. What his contemporaries denied him, posterity accorded in full measure. A relief of about the second century B.C. in Istanbul depicts him as the representative of tragedy in a sanctuary of Dionysus, conversing with the personification of Skene, that is, the stage (Fig. 109).[60] Euripides and Skene hold between them the mask of Heracles, probably from Euripides' *Mad Heracles*. Behind Skene is a female mask, probably the wife of Heracles, Megara, and behind Euripides the mask of an older man, probably the bad king Lycus. Of the ninety-two dramas of Euripides, seventeen tragedies and one satyr play are extant, more than survive of Aeschylus and Sophocles together.

Euripides changed the form of the drama by altering the beginning and the end. The prologue no longer gives the opening of the action, but deals with preceding events, often in a single speech by a god. The conclusion brings the much decried *deus ex machina* ($\theta\epsilon\grave{o}s$ $\mathring{a}\pi\grave{o}$ $\mu\eta\chi\alpha\nu\hat{\eta}s$), the god on the machine who appears in order to cut the knot. Both these changes are the result of Euripides' fundamental innovations. Educated as a freethinker and a sophist, he handled the traditional myths as so much raw material, to be changed and shaped at will. He could not, however, do away with certain fixed and established features of the heroic saga. Hence he was obliged, by means of the prologue, to indicate the alterations to his audience, and at the end, by supernatural intervention, to bring into harmony with tradition the action which had run along different lines. This artificial device was adopted by Sophocles in his old age from Euripides. In the *Philoctetes* of Sophocles, for instance, the hero, owing to the nobility of Neoptolemus, is placed in the position of being able to refuse to return to Troy with his deadly enemy Odysseus. But, as the myth insisted that Troy was to be overthrown by the bow of Philoctetes, the hero must, at the end of the play, be induced to go to Troy of his own free will. This is done in Sophocles' *Philoctetes* by the intervention of Heracles, in Euripides' *Philoctetes* by that of Athena, as vase paintings prove (Fig. 119). This literary innovation resulted

Fig. 109. Euripides and Skene. Relief, Istanbul

in scenic changes. Mechanical devices had to be invented by which the gods could appear and disappear speedily. These devices (see Chapter VI) were as much the butt of comedy as were the enlightened philosophical, religious, and social ideas of Euripides.

The setting for a tragedy of Euripides may be studied from the Andromeda crater in Berlin (Figs. 110-111).[61] The painter of this vase must have done his work when recently impressed by the play, performed in 412 B.C. It was parodied by Aristophanes as early as 411 in his *Thesmophoriazousai* (lines 1110ff.). In the *Frogs* (lines 52-54) Dionysus reads the *Andromeda* of Euripides, and thereby conceives such a longing for the poet, who had died in the year 406, that he goes down to Hades to bring him back to the world above. Bethe has reconstructed the famous play from the vase (Figs. 110-111) and the extant fragments.[62] It began with the monologue of Andromeda, who is chained to the rock, and who informs us of past events. The maiden has been left a victim of the sea monster in atonement for her mother's crime. The vase shows her in the center, with arms outstretched, chained to the rock (Fig. 111b). She wears a straight flowing, sleeved robe with rich pattern similar to those on the satyr play vase (Fig. 32). A cloak hangs at her back. She is distinguished by the tiara as an Oriental princess, as is the Hesione of the satyr play vase. Her father Cepheus, sitting at her feet, also wears this headdress. Small chests containing marriage gifts lie about the bride of Hades. Perseus comes to her, attired as a traveler, in his hand the sickle with which he has killed Medusa (Fig. 111c). He offers to fight with the sea monster on condition that Andromeda will go with him as his wife. Having obtained the promise he rushed into the combat with a prayer to Eros. On the vase Aphrodite is crowning

Fig. 110. Performance of *Andromeda*. Crater, Berlin

him because he has subjected himself to the power of love, and for love's sake has undertaken the deadly struggle. Hermes withdraws, after having accompanied Perseus on his adventure against Medusa and brought him to Ethiopia and Andromeda. The country of Ethiopia and its people are indicated by a member of the chorus who is wearing a tight jersey and a short, richly patterned chiton, with a face of Negro type (Fig. 111a). This must be a mask, and the chorus, be it male or female, indicated the inhabitants of the country in which the play was laid. Here it is the foreign race of the Ethiopians, whereas the actors have Greek features. The chorus serves, so to speak, as a frame, suggesting the place of action and the people of this place. It has become in Euripides a sympathetic, but passive spectator, from being an important part of the action in Aeschylus and an intensively feeling companion of the hero in Sophocles. In Euripides the actors alone sustain the action, but the chorus continued to exist as sympathizer from Euripides to Seneca and more modern imitators. The role of *deus ex machina* was played, as the vase testifies, by Aphrodite, whose chiton also has the rich patterns (Fig. 111c). She was obliged to intervene because the parents of Andromeda did not wish to keep their promise to marry their daughter to the rescuer. Only those who fail to consider the monuments can suppose that it was Athena who appeared on the machine.[63]

Fig. 111a-c. Details of the Andromeda crater

Fig. 112. Later version of *Andromeda*. Vase, British Museum

Fig. 113a-b. Actors with tragic masks before Dionysus. Relief from the Piraeus, Athens

Fig. 114. Agave with the head of Pentheus, and Bacchae. Stucco relief, Subterranean Basilica, Rome

Vase painting does not, of course, give a picture of any definite moment in the performances. The Andromeda vase, however, is so strongly under the influence of the theatrical presentation, that the very grouping of the figures suggests how the actors must have appeared in the orchestra where the tragedy was performed, when seen from the auditorium above.[64] Even the altar, which always stood in the orchestra, is reproduced (Fig. 110). On the other hand, Cepheus, Perseus, and Hermes would hardly have appeared in the theater so lightly clad. Art here retains its freedom to combine the realistic with the ideal picture. Against this may be set a fourth-century painting strongly influenced by a later performance, with the heroine bound to two columns of the theater (Fig. 112).[65]

The male parts were also played in the long sleeved robe, as is proved by the relief from the Piraeus (Fig. 113a).[66] The three actors who come into the presence of their god Dionysus wear the long syrma with sleeves. The foremost actor, who is somewhat shorter than the others, appears to hold in his hand a youthful mask, either that of a woman or of the young Dionysus, in the opinion of the author, while other scholars see the mask of an old man, perhaps Tiresias (Fig. 113b). Certainly an elderly bearded mask is in the hand of the middle actor, while the mask of the third actor is lost with his head. The first actor salutes the god, while the two others carry tympana in their left hands. We are certainly dealing with a Dionysiac drama, perhaps with the *Bacchae* of Euripides, for the relief belongs to the time when this play was performed. The deep impression which this late drama of Euripides made may be gathered also from later representations: the painting in the house of the Vettii[67] and the stucco relief in the Subterranean Basilica in Rome, depicting Agave dancing with the head of her slain son, whom she has mistaken for a lion, accompanied by the dance of one sister and the tympanon playing of the other (Fig. 114).[68]

Countless vase paintings from the fourth century B.C. bear witness to the growing popularity of Euripides. Scenes from his tragedies, both lost and extant, are represented.[69] They testify how his plays were performed and repeated endlessly, not only in Athens but also throughout the educated Greek world, particularly in Sicily and Southern Italy, the so-called Magna Graecia. From here the tragedies of Euripides reached the Romans, for whom they were presented both in the original and in translation. Numerous works of art of the Roman period illustrate the subjects of Euripides' dramas (see below, Chapter XV).

A theme greatly favored for representation was

Figs. 115, 116. Orestes and Iphigenia in Tauris, according to Euripides. Southern Italian vases, Louvre; Naples (from Ruvo)

that of *Iphigenia in Tauris*. Different scenes of this tragedy, the subject-matter of which Euripides had freely invented, as he often did, were illustrated. The scene of the anagnorisis, the recognition between brother and sister, was treated with great frequency (Figs. 115, 116, and 774).[70] From the theatrical production only two things were, as a rule, taken: the dress of the heroine, here Iphigenia, which is always more ornamented than in daily life, and the temple in the background. On many fourth-century vases occurs a central building, which indicates either a temple (Figs. 116, 117) or a palace (Figs. 121 and 122a). The form of this structure is certainly based on a definite conventional design, but we may assume that the type was taken from a form of temporary building which was in common use as a background in the theater of the classical times.[71] The vase painters, of course, drew only the general scheme of the real buildings.

The successful comparison of the Iphigenia pictures with the extant tragedy allows us to reconstruct from the paintings the lost tragedies of Euripides and those which survive only in fragments. The effort has been particularly successful in the case of the *Antigone*. The name suggests to us the familiar Sophoclean drama, but in antiquity the more pathetic drama of Euripides was preferred. One vase painting (Fig. 117)[72] which gives its subject-matter agrees with the fragments and with the 72nd *Fable* of Hyginus. Heracles stands in a temple or heroön, speaking with Creon, who wears the richly ornamented sleeved robe and the large royal cloak of the theatrical costume. Leaning on his scepter and bending forward, he listens to the words of the god. Behind him stands a boy whose cloak has patterns similar to those of the king's dress. There follows an old woman, who can only be the wife of Creon, Eurydice. Above sits Ismene,

sister of Antigone, holding an open box. On the opposite side Antigone, her hands bound behind her back, is brought in by a young man with spears. Haemon, the son of Creon, stands behind this group in an attitude of deep mourning. At his feet lies a second open box. Neither this situation nor the figures of Heracles and of the boy occur in Sophocles' *Antigone*. Everything, on the other hand, fits in with Euripides' version. Antigone was to be killed by Haemon, who, however, falls in love with her, saves her, and hides her. From their union a son is born. He, when older, comes into the town, takes part in the games, and is of course victorious. His grandfather acknowledges him as a true Spartan, from physical signs. The contents of the two boxes prove him to be the son of Haemon and Antigone, and thus the grandson of Creon. Antigone is imprisoned and is now once more to die. Then Heracles appears as *deus ex machina* (see Chapter VI) and causes Creon to recognize the union of his son. Heracles, through his marriage with Megara, is Creon's son-in-law, and like the son of Haemon and Antigone, is illegitimate. Heracles, therefore, is the right person to give the tragedy a happy ending. Clearly the sublime tragedy has been brought down to the level of mortals. We see here better than from any of the extant plays how easy it was for the New Comedy of Menander, with its themes taken from the life of the Athenian citizens, to grow out of tragedy in this Euripidean form.

Fig. 117. *Antigone* according to Euripides. Southern Italian vase, Ruvo

Figs. 118, 119. *Philoctetes* according to Sophocles and Euripides. Lekythos, Metropolitan Museum; Vase in Syracuse

Fig. 120. Death of Dirce, according to the *Antiope* of Euripides. Crater from Polazzuolo, Berlin

Instead of a temple or a palace, some tragedies had a cave as background. Examples are the plays *Philoctetes* of Sophocles as well as that of Euripides. Vase paintings based upon stage setting for Sophocles' *Philoctetes* (Fig. 118) have only a large rock and a single tree as a setting, while those for Euripides' *Philoctetes* represent a large cave around the hero (Fig. 119).[73] The vases testify that Euripides had a chorus of women and used Athena as *deus ex machina*, instead of Heracles who was used by Sophocles. The *Antiope* of Euripides, like the *Antigone*, has been reconstructed from literary fragments and from monuments.[74] Most important is a painting on a vase in Berlin (Fig. 120)[75] which represents the concluding scene. Dirce is being dragged by the bull, while Antiope rushes terrified from the sight. This was certainly not acted in the orchestra, but was narrated by a messenger. The final scene represented dealt rather with the attempt of the two sons of Antiope to kill the husband of Dirce, the wicked Lycus. These three men and Antiope are shown inside a large cave. Lycus wears the long chiton with patterned sleeves, decorated belt and crossbands, a mantle, scepter, and high boots (the cothurni). The young men force him to his knees. The conspicuously large cave is only to be explained as a stage background, since the scenery on vase paintings is elsewhere extremely scanty and slight. The panther skin on the upper edge of the cave indicates the Dionysiac festival which brought Dirce to the mountains. It reminds us at the same time of the actual festival in honor of which the play was performed. It ended certainly with Hermes, holding his herald's staff, appearing as *deus ex machina* above the cave. He commands the brothers to let the king live according to the tradition of the myth, from which Euripides had tried to deviate.

Post-Euripidean Tragedy

With Euripides the living growth of Attic Tragedy came to an end. It was bound to do so, for Euripides had destroyed the religious meaning of tragedy without being able to cast off the fetters of the cult. Post-Euripidean tragedy continued his tradition, but became still more pathetic, sometimes indeed sentimental. This later Greek tragedy is lost to literature, except for the insignificant *Rhesus*, sometimes wrongly attributed to Euripides. Hence the Medea vase in Munich is a monument of singular importance, both from the literary and the dramatic points of view (Figs. 121-122).[76] By means of it we come to know a play which is closely connected with the *Medea* of Euripides, which drama took only second place in the contest of 431. But posterity rated it higher, and Euripides' modern conception of Medea as the murderess of her children belongs to the literature of the world. He probably used the flying machine for the first time in this play.

The *Medea* as represented on the Munich vase, though post-Euripidean, nevertheless follows closely the story as told by Euripides. The killing of Jason's bride by the poisoned robe and the burning head-dress, the murder of the children, the escape in the dragon car, all these are repeated. Many of the details, however, are altered. Not only the father, but the brother also perish with the bride, so that the royal house of Corinth dies out. As a consequence, only the sons of Medea could become rulers of Corinth, and one of the boys is indeed saved by an attendant (Fig. 122c). It is not Medea herself who drives the serpent car, but Oistros, the personification of Frenzy. At the edge of the picture stands Aeetes, the father of Medea (Fig. 122b). He appears as an eidolon, a ghost, out of the depths to reproach his daughter and to prophesy an evil destiny for her evil deeds. The orchestra of the theater

Figs. 121, 122a-c. *Medea* according to a post-Euripidean tragedy. Southern Italian vase, Munich

is indicated as the scene of action, first by tripods on pillars, as on the satyr play vase (Fig. 31) and as they still stand above the theater in the precinct of Dionysus (Fig. 251), and second, by an altar, as on the Andromeda vase (Fig. 110) and as it always stood in the orchestra (see Figs. 228-229, 260, 273-274). The palace is the same, but bigger and more richly decorated than on Euripidean vases (Fig. 117). King Creon, Aeetes, and Medea wear the tragic dress with differently patterned sleeves. The king has belt and crossbands like Lycus (Fig. 120). Aeetes and Medea wear the tiara, like other kings and princesses (Figs. 32, 111b). Both have an

ornamented vertical middle stripe, like Iphigenia (Fig. 116). Externally, then, as internally, this fourth-century tragedy, to which the vase testifies, is in direct continuity with the art of Euripides, who was the last great poet of the Greek tragic drama.

The tragedies of Euripides underlie most Roman tragedies down to Seneca (see Chs. XI and XV). The same is true for French tragedies by Corneille and Racine; German tragedies by Schiller and Goethe; and many others down to the Broadway production of *Medea*, played by Judith Anderson, which is a modern free adaptation of Euripides' play by Robinson Jeffers (see Ch. XVI, Fig. 842).

CHAPTER III

OLD COMEDY AND MIDDLE COMEDY

ARISTOPHANES

See Fig. 166

TEARS and laughter, solemnity and jest, are closely interrelated in the childhood of individuals and of people. The Greeks of the archaic and of the classical period had deep and sincere religious feelings, but they also had a good sense of humor. Although comedy developed later in literature than the other dramatic forms, its elements are as old as theirs.

Comedy comes from Komos, as tragedy comes from Tragos. Comedy thus means the song of the komasts, the gay revellers, as tragedy means the song of the goats, the followers of Dionysus. According to Aristotle (*Poetics*, 1449a, 9-11), comedy developed from improvisations, originating from the leaders of the phallic ceremonies and the reciters of phallic songs.[1] How such a komos looked during the recitation may be gathered from Aristophanes' *Acharnians* (lines 273ff.), the earliest of his extant

comedies, produced in the year 425 B.C. Dikaiopolis is celebrating the Rural Dionysia, the festival at which the komos evolved. He organizes a ritual procession and sings a licentious song to Phales, the companion of Dionysus. The Komos (ὁ κῶμος), also according to Aristotle, sang derisive songs abusing unpopular persons in town. Assuming that the villagers came to town and delivered their mock orations at bedtime, the name comedy has wrongly been derived from kome, a village (ἡ κώμη), or from koma, deep sleep (τὸ κῶμα). The only correct interpretation is that the revellers, the members of the Komos, teased and made fools of the spectators. The komasts, not wishing to be recognized, adopted masks among which animal masks were especially popular. Such animal masks are used by Aristophanes for the chorus of several comedies: the

Figs. 123, 124. Dancers dressed as birds; Men in the masks of cocks. Black-figured vases, British Museum; Berlin Museum

Fig. 125a-b. Warriors riding on dolphins, and on ostriches. Black-figured vase, Boston

Fig. 126. Knights riding on men disguised as horses. Black-figured vase, Berlin Museum

Wasps (422), the *Birds* (414), and the *Frogs* (405). The birds play an important part in the action, with manifold masks for the different kinds of birds which the text mentions. The wasps play only a small part. The frogs disappear with Charon altogether, after having probably pushed the boat of the ferryman in and out of the orchestra and after having amused the audience with their grotesque hops, their "Brekekekex-koax-koax," and their jeers at the god of the festival (lines 290ff.). Aristophanes himself tells in the parabasis of the *Knights* (lines 520ff.), produced in 424 B.C., that his predecessor Magnes had used choruses of birds, stinging wasps, and frogs. Magnes appeared in 472 with a comedy at the same festival at which Aeschylus produced his *Persians*.²

We are taken still further back from the fifth, to the sixth century by black-figured vase paintings on which there are choruses of men dressed as animals, dancing and singing to the sound of a flute, played by a musician in everyday dress, a long chiton, and a freely draped mantle (Figs. 123-125). Thus men move rhythmically dressed as birds with wings and feathers on the head and body on a vase in the British Museum (Fig. 123) and men wrapped in mantles but with masks of cocks on a vase in the Berlin Museum (Fig. 124).³ A deep drinking cup, a skyphos, in the Boston Museum of Fine Arts, depicts on one side six helmeted warriors riding on dolphins (Fig. 125a), perhaps a parody of Arion who is said to have been rescued by a dolphin; on the other side six young knights wearing the chlamys are riding upon ostriches (Fig. 125b).⁴ Facing the ostrich riders with the flute player is a dancing dwarf, like the crabs—the sons of Carcinus—at the end of the *Wasps*. Another forerunner of Aristophanes had a chorus of knights riding on horses, de-

picted on a Berlin vase (Fig. 126).⁵ They are seated on companions dressed as horses with protomes and tails of horses. This illustrates the adventure related by the chorus in Aristophanes' *Knights* (lines 595ff.) and the praise of the horses who behave like soldiers. This can only be understood if one imagines that one-half of the choreutai is mounted on the other half, disguised as horses with masks and tails. This praise of the horses as well as the reference to Magnes are in the parabasis of the *Knights*. This is an interlude, named from parabainein ($\pi\alpha\rho\alpha\beta\alpha\acute{\iota}\nu\epsilon\iota\nu$), to step across, to come forward, to turn around to the spectators instead of to the actors, and address the audience. This has rightly been recognized as the earliest element of comedy, developed from the original komos. Personal mockery and direct address of the dressed up revellers to the audience develops in the literary comedy to scurrilous and often political attacks upon contemporary personalities.⁶ Similar revels in animal masks at a religious festival could be seen on the island of Bali, where the masks of parrots (Fig. 127), frogs (Fig. 128), and bulls (Fig. 129) were used.⁷

Figs. 127-129. Actors as parrots, frogs, and bull. Island of Bali

Fig. 130. Return of Hephaestus.
Corinthian vase, Athens

Fig. 131. Corinthian dancers. Kylix, Metropolitan Museum

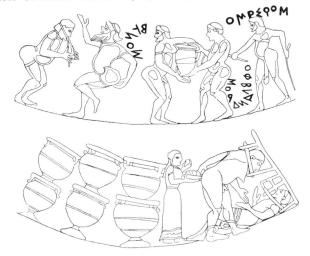

Fig. 132. Punishment of wine thieves. Corinthian vase, Louvre

to make the evolution of comedy possible, dialogue parts were required in addition to the merry chorus of the Rural Dionysia in Attica. The first dialogue parts must be imagined as a series of loose farcical scenes.[8] Corresponding to these in the comedies of Aristophanes are the scenes following the parabasis. Often, as for example in the *Acharnians* and in the *Birds*, the leading hero is brought into contact with a number of characters, for whom he proves himself more than a match, like the Merry Andrew in a puppet play.

These farcical scenes were first developed not in Attica, but in the Peloponnesus. Aristophanes in the *Wasps* (lines 57 ff.) calls the stale, hackneyed jests "Megarian."[9] From Megara then, the nearest neighboring Doric state, farce came to Attica. The appearance of this ancient Doric farce may be learned from Corinthian vase paintings of the early sixth century B.C. On one of these in Athens (Fig. 130)[10] Dionysus and his followers are bringing Hephaestus, drunk and mounted on a mule, to Olympus. Zeus stretches out his hands in welcome, pleased that the wine god has succeeded in leading the wicked son to Hera, his mother, whom he had fettered and will now liberate. All the characters wear a burlesque, indeed an indecent, costume. The garment is too short and thickly padded, the phallus is huge. The faces are grotesque, with bulging eyes and bristling hair and beard. As nobody but Dionysus may carry the vine branch, his followers must be the demons, who in the Peloponnesus take the place of the Ionic sileni and the Attic satyrs. They appear on a series of Corinthian vases and some Attic imitations as gay revellers without their god (Fig. 131).[11] The evolution of Doric farce from these performances may be seen on a vase with the capture and punishment of wine thieves (Fig. 132).[12] Two men are carrying a wine jar. Two others, gay and drunk, are dancing to the flute with burlesque movements, which may be the source of the kordax used in Attic comedy (see below, Figs. 180-181). Punishment draws near in the shape of an overseer with two sticks. The thieves are put into the stocks by the head, so that the one can lie only on his back, the other stand only in a stooping position. The latter, whose feet are also in the stocks, is reaching out backward with difficulty toward the dumplings which a pitying maid brings. The punishment is perceptibly aggravated in that the prison is a wine cellar, full of the fragrance of the longed-for but unattainable wine. Sosibius in Athenaeus (XIV, 15, 621) refers to a theme closely akin to this as a subject of Doric comedy, namely, the capture of fruit thieves. The three characters bear the names Eunous, Omrikos, and Ophelandros, that mean the

In the remaining comedies of Aristophanes the chorus consists simply of men or women: charcoal burners in the *Acharnians*; Athenian citizens and farmers in the *Peace* (421); half-choruses of old men and of old women in the *Lysistrata* (411); women celebrants of the festival in the *Thesmophororiazousae* (410); women citizens of Athens in the *Ecclesiazousae* (about 390). In the *Clouds* (423) the chorus consists of women with big noses, meant to be fantastically adorned personifications of the Sophistic philosophy, which is compared to the clouds, as these also often assume fanciful shapes (lines 340-344).

Just as neither satyric drama nor tragedy could evolve from the chorus of satyrs until a real actor had been added to the exarchon and his chorus, so,

Figs. 133, 134. Angry old man and drunkards of Old Comedy. Terracotta statuettes, Berlin

of the earlier comedies numbered only a few hundred, while the comedies of Aristophanes had over a thousand. This development must have taken place when comic plays were admitted to the festival of the great City Dionysia in 486 B.C.

Doric farce brought with it its costumes and typical characters. They are represented in many terracotta and some bronze statuettes. The majority of these belong to the first half of the fourth century, as testified by finds of Hetty Goldman in Halae, David Robinson in Olynthus, Homer and Dorothy Thompson in the Agora of Athens, and Agnes Stillwell in Corinth.[15] The Periclean age did not like grotesque forms and extravagant features, and thus these statuettes begin probably around 400 B.C. But Aristophanes' later plays certainly belong to the same period as some of these statuettes, and he, as well as his predecessors, used a corresponding costume. Thus in the *Lysistrata* (lines 661 f. and 686 f.) it is clear that when the cloak is discarded, bare paunches and buttocks must have appeared, reproduced by flesh-colored tights (*somatia*). These, stuffed out with cushions in front and behind, are intended to represent the nude body. The delightful figures of an angry old man (Fig. 133) and of two drunkards (Fig. 134)[16] show such a padded jerkin, the phallus, and the grotesque grinning faces of the Peloponnesian goblins. They wear over the tights, stuffed out with pads, a belted tunic, often as an exomis, leaving one shoulder bare. Others wear only the mantle, as in the *Lysistrata*, thus a fat old man, crowned with a wreath and a broad fillet, the ends of which hang on the shoulders; and thin men who have drawn the mantle over the head (Figs. 135-138).[17] They all have the pointed or wedge-shaped archaic beard (the goatee) worn during the time of the Persian war (see above, Ch. II, p. 20). Some (Fig. 138) have red on hair and beard. One of these sphenopogons (σφηνοπώγων) comes from Megara Hyblaea, now preserved in the collection of the University of Rostock (Fig. 136). He places both hands on his hips with a provocative gesture.

Benevolent, the Rainbringer, and the Beneficent, names therefore of kindly vegetable spirits, after whom they are modelled. Besides the names, they have kept, or rather imitated, the appearance of the demonic followers of the wine god. Hence they and their imitators retained through Old and Middle comedy the short padded jerkin, the visible phallus, and the cunning masks.

These roughly improvised farces were given a literary form by Epicharmus of Syracuse (about 530-440).[13] His plays, however, cannot be described as comedies, since they lack the chorus, which originated in the Komos. They were called dramas in antiquity. They must have resembled the loose episodes at the end of Attic comedy. Epicharmus developed the agon, the scene of conflict between two parties, which is likewise found in Attic comedy. Epicharmus' themes were, on the one hand, travesties of heroic saga, on the other hand, portrayals of daily life which he held up to ridicule. In his plays, and in Doric farce in general, the most popular characters are Heracles and Odysseus,[14] who are also depicted in Attic comedy as the gourmand and the coward (see Figs. 170-173). A few of the stock characters of Doric comedy were also established in Attic comedy and lived on through antiquity: the parasite, the boastful soldier, and the cook (see below, Figs. 368-383).

All these elements, then, came to Attica and were here bound up with the Komos, the gay chorus of revellers. This union of Doric and Attic elements was never so close in comedy as the union of the Peloponnesian chorus with Attic dialogue was in tragedy. The combination was not an organic one, but was made externally under the influence of tragedy. The first part of Aristophanes' comedies, with prologue, parodos, epeisodia, and stasima, is indeed nothing other than an imitation of the first part of tragedy. Hence we understand why the lines

Figs. 135-138. Old Comedy characters wearing mantles

From Sicilian comedy came the figures of the warriors, with old-fashioned beards, wearing the pilos, the peaked hat of the traveller, carrying their luggage, water flask, shield, and sword (Figs. 153-154).[26] The cook also comes from Doric comedy. Statuettes are found in Doric Tarentum (Fig. 155) and in Megara (Fig. 156).[27] He has a shopping

139   140   141   142   143

144   145   146   147   148   149   15

Figs. 139-168. Statuettes of characters of Old Comedy. (See List of Illustrations and Sources)

As eating and drinking play a great part in comedy, baskets with food are carried on the head (Figs. 139-141) or in the hand (Figs. 142-143).[18] Herdsmen with a lamb or a calf over the shoulders (Figs. 144-146)[19] have the wreath of the symposion, thus are looking forward to their part of the banquet. The wandering pedlar or a slave is heavily burdened with a pack on his back and a basket in front (Fig. 147).[20] He certainly is making the stupid and vulgar jokes of the porter (phortika, φορτικά). When at the beginning of the *Frogs* Xanthias makes them, complaining about the heavy load he has to carry, Dionysus dismisses them as played out, banal, and overdone. Thus this pedlar originates in the Doric farce.

Seated men, often also with the wedge-shaped beard, may mostly be slaves, who have taken refuge on an altar to evade punishment. Several are holding a hand against an ear, which may have been boxed (Fig. 148).[21] In a fragmentary statuette in the Louvre an old man has his hands bound behind his back. He wears the coarse jerkin of the slave (Fig. 149).[22] Another holds a purse which he may have stolen (Fig. 150).[23] Another with a bald pate reclines with his right hand on the crown of his head (Fig. 151).[24] His left eye is half closed as if he is beginning to sleep. A man with a baby in his arms (152) recalls the motif of the lost and found baby, popular in New Comedy (Figs. 400, 401, 507).[25]

basket, with a calf's head or an eel, a delicacy mentioned in Aristophanes' *Acharnians* as bought by Dikaiopolis and coveted in vain by Lamachos (lines 877-886 and 958-970). Good and abundant food, and with it the cooks, are, of course, of paramount importance in comedy. The cooks, therefore, are conceited and vainglorious. Their representations show round red faces, bald pates, and huge openings for the prating, inquisitive, and boastful mouths. This type is named after a Megarian actor, Maison, and under this name it has passed on into the New Comedy (see Figs. 378-383). To the cooks belong the delightful kitchen slaves, who rejoice in copying the pompous bearing of their masters (Figs. 157-158). The bronze statuette of such a kitchen slave has been found in Olynthus (Fig. 159).[28]

Ancient comedy had, moreover, perfected a series of female characters whose images were considered formerly, on account of their figure, to be caricatures of pregnant women (Figs. 160-165). But not only

152

153   154

151

155   156   157   158   159

160   161   162   163   164   165

young women are depicted with a fat paunch, like the red-haired laughing girl in Boston (Fig. 160), the weeping girl in the British Museum (Fig. 161), and the wailing young woman in Athens (Fig. 162), but also an old woman with a face as yellow as a quince, and probably a character just as sour, in Berlin (Fig. 163), and the old harridan in the Metropolitan Museum of Art in New York (Fig. 164) who might play the role of the old vixen attacking the young man in the last episode of the *Ecclesiazousae*. Even an old nurse with a baby on her arm in Rostock has this padded body (Fig. 165).[29] Furthermore, a fat middle-aged woman of this kind appears on one base together with a comic actor in Würzburg (Figs. 166a-c), sweetly whispering to the man who clasps his hands in astonishment; it recalls the scene when in the same *Ecclesiazousae* (lines 606 ff.) Praxagora explains the advantages of her communistic state to her husband Blepyros. In another such pair on a common base in the Louvre a fat woman embraces a smaller man with a wedge-

shaped beard (Fig. 167). This may be a wedding scene (a gamos) as we find it at the ends of the comedies like Aristophanes' *Peace* and *Birds*.[30]

It is clear that the women of ancient comedy were obliged to follow the sacred tradition of the padded bodice. There are evidently two reasons for this. The fat paunch pertained to the Dionysiac demons, who were imitated by the comic actors. Just as the horsetail was compulsory for the actors in satyric drama, who imitated the Attic followers of Dionysus, so the fat body was compulsory for the comic actors. Moreover, all the parts were played by men who, since the number of actors was limited, were often obliged to change their masks. It would hardly have been possible to put on or take off the padded body every time they changed their sex.[31] That only the mask and dress are changed is alluded to in a statuette in Vienna (Fig. 168).[32] An old woman with a grinning mouth holds the laughing mask of a young man before her padded body. The transfer of dress from one sex to another is a popular motif

166a-c   167   168

Fig. 169a-b. Parody of a tragic hero, from Dodona

in comedy. We need only to think of Charley's Aunt. In the *Ecclesiazousae* the women take the garments of their sleeping husbands. In the *Thesmophoriazousae* the brother-in-law of Euripides dresses as one of the women participating in the festival. This idea was not far-fetched, because all female roles were played by men.

Just as the typical characters of daily life were taken over from Doric farce, but with endless variations and enrichments, so also were the characters from the heroic saga. The model for these is no longer the mythos, as shaped by the epic, but the form created by tragedy; for tragic poetry has by now supplanted epic as teacher of the people. There is a delightful bronze statuette from Dodona in Athens, showing a "tragic hero" in a padded jersey, with a genuine goblin face framed humorously by the high onkos or tragic style of hairdress (Fig. 169).[33] His actual costume, over the jersey which clings tightly to his body, is a tunic of rough ma-

terial with edges left open at the side, one drawn over the other. He is pulling himself up by his hands and jumping in undisguised terror over some obstacle. He is obviously a coward running away from an imaginary danger, after a lot of high-flown talk; just as Dionysus himself in the *Frogs* (lines 280 ff.) takes refuge with his priest from the supposed Empusa. Heracles is represented with his bow and club (Figs. 170-171), Odysseus with his pilos (Figs. 172-173), Cadmus with his travelling bag and pail or pitcher, with which he goes to the watering place where he meets the dragon (Figs. 174-175, cf. Fig. 207). One hero with a pestle (Fig. 176) looks like Ares in the *Peace* by Aristophanes, who is described by Hermes as wanting to pound up all Greek cities into a huge mortar. The hero in the Louvre (Fig. 177) is a spirited caricature of a tragic king in a green mantle and a red crown. All these figures appear in Attic statuettes as they do in Attic Old Comedy.[34] There is also Telephus the hero wounded in the thigh by Achilles, who came to Greece to be healed by the spear which had wounded him; in order to be secure from his enemies, he kidnapped the little Orestes and flew with him to an altar, threatening to kill him if the boy's father Agamemnon would not cure him. The wretchedness of this hero is well rendered by the statuette in Munich (Fig. 178).[35] Euripides brought him to the orchestra in rags. Therefore Aristophanes makes fun of this miserable hero in the *Acharnians* (line 326), where he is parodied by Dicaeopolis

170   171   172   173   174   175

Figs. 170-178. Parodies of tragic heroes in Attic Old Comedy

176   177   178

Figs. 179, 180. Tympanist and kordax dancers

Fig. 181a-d. Comic chorus.
Relief found on the Agora, Athens

with a coal basket instead of a child, and in the *Thesmophoriazousae* (lines 689ff.), where Mnesilochus, the brother-in-law of Euripides, snatches a wineskin dressed as a baby.

Cithara and flutes were used in comedy as in tragedy and satyr play. There were, in addition, clappers and tympana (Fig. 179).³⁶ The typical dance of comedy was the kordax, which is licentious in contrast to the solemn emmeleia of tragedy and the gay but less wanton sikinnis of the satyric drama (see above, Fig. 32).³⁷ A good description of the kordax is at the end of Aristophanes' *Wasps*. A vase painting in Corneto (Fig. 180)³⁸ depicts the kordax. Three men with grotesque faces, two with bald heads, asses' ears, and protruding tongues tilt forward on the tips of their toes, kick their legs to an exaggerated height, and turn in a whirling dance. They thereby drag their clothes tightly around their unwieldy padded bodies. A chorus dancing a kordax seems to be represented on fragments found on the Athenian Agora (Fig. 181a-d),³⁹ perhaps from a choregic monument or the dedication of an agonothetes. The flute player seems to be a woman. The men, eight of which are preserved in parts, have stuffed-out bodies, short tunics, a small round hair ornament on the apex of their heads; a small mantle is hanging over the left shoulder and back, and they are shouldering a long thin staff. They all lift the right leg, so that the knee is at the height of the buttock. It looks as if on Fragment c the buttock of the second is bumping against the knee of the third man—unless this man was turned in the other direction so that the two buttocks clash. Such a movement, the lifting of the thigh into a horizontal position, so that the lower leg from knee to foot is on a level with the buttock, is already represented on the late black-figured vase in the Museo artistico industriale in Rome, with eight young men dancing

Fig. 182. Chorus with fluteplayer

to the rhythm of a flute player (Fig. 182).⁴⁰ Five of the youths have small heads on the apex of their skulls. We thus have here, probably, some popular entertainment.

If we wish to understand the extant comedies of

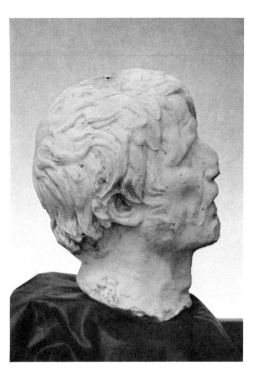
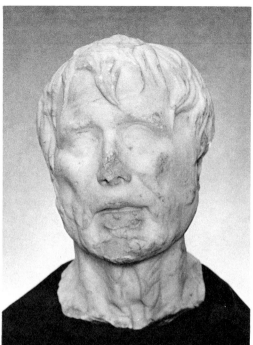

Fig. 183. Aristophanes. Collection David Robinson, University of Mississippi

Aristophanes which cover the years 425 to 388,[41] we must keep all these rollicking figures before our eyes, remembering that the dialogue scenes came from the inartistic Dorian farce, and the chorus scenes from the lighthearted mumming and revelries of the Rural Dionysia. The origin of the different elements explains the faults of Aristophanes' work: the uncouth character, the indecency of many of his jokes, and the loose way in which the different parts hang together.

Despite these faults, however, the comedy of Aristophanes is one of the greatest gifts which Greek culture has bestowed upon us. Despite seams and fissures in the masonry, the structure rises as a uniform whole, with a definite idea running through it, and with gems of poetry in the place of the inartistic chorus songs of an earlier age. Side by side with the old, rough-and-tumble buffoonery of the farce and the bantering of ordinary individuals by the ancient komoi, we have parodies and often serious attacks upon statesmen, generals, philosophers, and poets, who, in the opinion of Aristophanes, were doing harm to the people. Thus Pericles, Lamachus, Nicias, and Demosthenes could be seen by the Athenian audience during the fifth century. But Cleon in the *Knights* was not masked because maskmakers and actors refused to portray him. Aristophanes, therefore, took the part himself and daubed his face with red color in the old fashion. Otherwise we must assume that the masks gave caricatured likenesses of the heads of the celebrated men. We know this of Socrates, who is said to have stood up during the presentation of the *Clouds*, to

let the people see the likeness. The tragic poets Euripides in the *Acharnians*, Euripides and Agathon in the *Thesmophoriazousae*, Aeschylus and Euripides in the *Frogs* must have been recognizable to the audience who knew them so well. It can be assumed that the shaping of masks of definite personalities in the theater furthered the development of portraiture during the later part of the fifth century.

Aristophanes attacked not only the outstanding personalities of public life, but he confronted the whole population, described as Demos in the *Knights*, with its sin. He denounced it as being quarrelsome, credulous, and fickle. There are political, national, literary, and social tendencies in the plays of Aristophanes and his predecessors. Aristophanes was a champion of the Peace Party. When, however, peace had finally come, it was too late. With the downfall of democracy, Attic comedy also lost ground. In the *Ecclesiazousae* (the Women in Council, or the Women's Assembly, ca. 392 or 390 B.C.), Aristophanes renounced political and personal themes, and seized upon the ideas of communism and women's rights, which were taken up soon afterwards by Plato in his *Republic*. In the *Ecclesiazousae* the women dress in the garments of their sleeping husbands and go to the council meeting on the Areopagus, with the result that the state power is handed over to them. In this play the chorus still takes part in the action, but it has already less importance, and the parabasis, formerly its principal function, is omitted. In the *Plutus*, the feeble work of Aristophanes' old age, the chorus is entirely lacking. Only the instruction "chorou" (χοροῦ), the chorus part, points to the interpolation of songs and dances. Here comedy approaches its predecessor, the Doric farce, which had no chorus. Middle Comedy avoided individual resemblances. Platonius states that the comedy masks exaggerated the features of the face so as to resemble nobody. The supposition that the so-called megaphone masks with exaggerated wide mouths were invented when the theater of Lycurgus with a larger auditorium was erected, is attractive,[42] but, considering the excellent acoustics of the Greek theaters, unlikely.

Aristophanes amused his public, but not the leading and influential persons, whom he lampooned. His type of comedy was early supplanted by new forms or even by the return to more primitive forms, from which he had evolved his masterpieces. The poet, therefore, never received an honorary statue, as did the tragic poets and the poets of New Comedy. We possess no contemporary portrait of Aristophanes. Many scholars including myself believe, however, that we have an excellent imaginary portrait of the poet (Fig. 183).[43] It was created in the Hellenistic period, probably as a companion piece to the portrait of Menander, with whom some Roman double herms couple him. Aristophanes is depicted as an older man, whose beginning baldness is hidden by some strands of hair falling irregularly onto his forehead. He looks coarse and unkempt. The beard has only irregular tufts, brow and cheeks are furrowed, the skin of the neck is crumpled and sacks of flesh hang below the deeply sunk eyes. The Hellenistic inventor of this portrait knew, however, how to express in these masterly rendered outer forms the intelligence and fiery expression, indicating the sincere striving of Aristophanes for high social and political ideals, and the disappointment in his failure to accomplish his goals.

An Attic vase painting of the early fourth century (Fig. 184)[44] shows actors who might just as well have appeared in a Doric farce. Zeus is depicted with a follower who sits on his luggage, about which he may have made phortika or low, vulgar, tiresome jokes. There are also represented a grotesque servant, a woman with a mask in her hand, and a flute-player, at whose feet another mask is lying. We thus have five actors and seven characters. Comedy with its abundance of gay characters had to have a greater number of players than tragedy and satyr drama.

Seven characters are also found in each of the two groups of statuettes of comic actors in the possession of the Metropolitan Museum of Art (Figs. 185-198).[45] They were all found together in one grave in Athens. This is very important, for though we have many single figures of comic actors, this is the first instance in which such a large group has been found as a series. The second important fact about these statuettes is that they belong to Middle Comedy, of which we have only scanty fragments in literature. This fact limits the dating. The statuettes cannot belong to the last third of the fourth century, for Middle Comedy ended around 330, when the New Comedy of Menander, Philemon, and others replaced it and the costume of the too-short chiton over the stuffed-out tights was discarded. Several parallels have been found in Olynthus, destroyed by Philip of Macedonia in 348,[46] while on the other hand the types, though similar, do not agree with those of Aristophanes. Therefore, the right date seems to me to be 380-350, after the *Ecclesiazousae* and *Plutus* of Aristophanes, which belong to the beginning of the fourth century.

It is unlikely that all fourteen of the statuettes in the Metropolitan Museum belong to one comedy. Aristophanes has more than fourteen dramatis personae only in his earlier plays, the *Acharnians* and the *Birds*. In most plays he has fewer, and in all plays the number of characters of sufficient im-

Fig. 184. Actors of Middle Comedy. Attic vase, Leningrad

| 185 | 186 | 187 | 188 | 189 | 190 | 191 |

Figs. 185-191. Seven actors of Middle Comedy found together in one tomb. Yellow terracotta statuettes from Athens, Metropolitan Museum

portance to have been copied in art, are never more than five to seven. The same is true of New Comedy, where in no case is a total of fourteen attained for the dramatis personae. In addition, the series is divided into two even halves by the color of the clay: seven statuettes (Figs. 185-191) are of yellow and seven (Figs. 192-198) of red clay. We thus have two groups. The execution in both is good, but the yellow series is superior. The backs (Figs. 187b, 189b, 196b, 197b, 198b) are as finely executed as the fronts.

In each series we have an old woman, a young woman, and five men. In the yellow series, the old woman (Fig. 185) holds a child dressed in swaddling clothes and a pointed cap. The young woman (Fig. 186) is giggling—more likely than weeping— behind her himation. Among the men, Heracles is easily recognizable (Fig. 187). He wears his lion's skin over his head, has a club in his left arm and a bow hanging at his left side from a strap over his breast. He puts his finger into his mouth. This is not the ordinary type of Heracles found in statuettes of old comedy, where he stands with his legs crossed, leaning on his club as on a walking stick, holding his bow in his hand (Figs. 170-171). This lion's skin

is drawn over his head so that the ears stand out at the top and the claws are knotted on his breast. In the New York statuette there are really two lions' skins, or at least two lions' heads. One is made into a cap for the hero's head, the other hangs down next to the bow and beside a claw on the left side. This is a two-fold Heracles, and may be a parallel to Dionysus dressed up as Heracles in the *Frogs* of Aristophanes. In this comedy Heracles laughs at Dionysus (v. 47) because he combines buskins and the lion's skin. Later the slave Xanthias has to dress as Heracles in order to receive Heracles' punishment, with which Dionysus is threatened. Here the joke may be that some braggart soldier has dressed as Heracles. We know that Nicostratus of Argos dressed with club and lion's skin for the battle (Diodorus, xvi,44) and that the use of the lion's skin for a mortal hero was common for Alexander and the Diadochi. The braggart soldier and the mocking of his false bravery is common in both Old Comedy (for example, Lamachus in *Acharnians*) and New Comedy. Therefore it is possible in Middle Comedy, during which Anaxandrides wrote a comedy entitled *Heracles*. The false Heracles (Fig. 187) is not thinking of fighting, but of some good

| 187b | 189b | 196b | 197b | 198b | | Figs. 199, 200. Replicas of 188, 190 |

46

192   193   194   195   196   197   198

Figs. 192-198. Seven actors of Middle Comedy found together in one tomb. Red terracotta statuettes from Athens, Metropolitan Museum

meal. He is hungry. That is why he puts his finger in his mouth. Heracles is represented as a loose character and a gluttonous gormandizer in many farces and comedies. Hence the young woman (Fig. 186) may be his paramour and the baby on the arm of the nurse or grandmother (Fig. 185) their child. It may even be the story of Heracles, Auge and little Telephus.

The weeping man with the traveller's cap (Fig. 188, cf. Fig. 199 from Olynthus) is probably the one who has to pay the expenses of Heracles' greed. The other two men bring food (Fig. 189) and drink (Fig. 190) for the banquet, which Heracles, or the braggart soldier dressed as Heracles, will enjoy with his girl. On the head of one was an amphora or hydria, as in the statuette in Palermo (Fig. 200)[47] from which steam arises, indicating that it contains a hot punch in which probably more wine than water is mixed. The other man carries a basket, probably filled with delicacies (cf. above, Figs. 142-143). The banquet was probably at the end of the play as in Aristophanes' *Acharnians* and *Wasps*. The slave in a fur or rough woolen jersey (Fig. 191) is nursing his knee and looking forward to his part of the banquet.

The other series in the Metropolitan Museum, in red clay (Figs. 192-198), again has an old and a young woman. The old woman (Fig. 193) seems to imitate the young one (Fig. 192) in drawing the himation coquettishly to one side; she is probably the nurse of the young one. She reminds us of the old women in the *Ecclesiazousae* of Aristophanes, who try to take the lover away from the young woman.[48] Besides this contrasting pair of women, we have two contrasting pairs of men, one standing (Figs. 194-195) and one seated (Figs. 196-197). Standing are a slim (Fig. 194) and a fat man (Fig. 195), probably mocked in the manner of Middle Comedy, which ridiculed physical imperfections, bad behavior, shamelessness, covetousness, and old age. The mood of the two is also contrasting. The slim man is serious, wrapped up in his himation in

a meditative position. He may be a philosopher, like the cynic Crates of Thebes, whose pupil Zeno was said by Philemon (Fragment 85) to teach one how to be hungry. Philemon began in the time of Middle Comedy, but belongs, with Menander, to New Comedy. The fat man is laughingly baring his flabby breast and fat belly.[49] The two seated men (Figs. 196-197) also show contrasting moods. The one holding a full purse (Fig. 196, cf. above, Fig. 150) is rightly joyous. He seems to sit on an altar, because probably he has stolen the purse and seeks refuge. He may later change to sadness, when he is caught. He has contorted eyebrows, giving to the two sides of his face a different expression. Quintilian (xi,3,74) tells us that fathers of families in comedy wore a mask showing on one side a raised, on the other side a lowered brow. He could thus, by showing different sides of his head, appear to the audience either in a violent or in a mild mood without having to change the mask. Several masks, the most beautiful of which is one in marble from the Kerameikos in Athens (see below, Ch. VIII, Figs. 335-337 and Ch. XV, Fig. 810), illustrate this literary evidence. Perhaps the other seated man, who seems dejected and puts his finger greedily into his mouth (Fig. 197) will later get the money. He may be the original owner of the purse, which has been stolen. He is a traveller, as is evidenced by his cap and heavy cloak. The slave, seated in a pensive posture (Fig. 198), his head on his hand and his elbow on his knee, will probably find a means of taking the money away by intrigue. He is thus the forerunner of the leading slave in New Comedy.

The single figures of the two series of statuettes in the Metropolitan Museum are already known from other replicas (Figs. 199-200),[50] with the exception of the two seated slaves, one of the yellow and one of the red series (Figs. 191 and 198), though nearly related figures are extant. It may be due to accident that exact replicas are missing.

These statuettes indicate two examples of comedy in the middle period, showing relationships to the

Fig. 201. Poet with two comic masks. Relief, Lyme Park

Fig. 202. Actor dancing as Perseus. Oinochoe, Athens

masks of an older and a younger man on a relief in Lyme Park, found in Athens, must be one of the Middle Comedy. It might even be Aristophanes, as its date is ca. 380 B.C. (Fig. 201).[52]

Farce, on the other hand, lived on unaltered. For instance, on a vase in Athens Perseus dances on a small stage before two spectators (Fig. 202).[53] On Boeotian vases of the fourth century there are trivial scenes from daily life, such as a fight between cooks and geese (Fig. 203).[54] On Kabeiric vases travesties of the saga are represented by fat-paunched heroes (Figs. 204-207). Odysseus in the costume of a goblin receives the magic drink from Circe on a vase in the British Museum (Fig. 204), but then he threatens the witch-like Circe on a vase in Oxford (Fig. 205). The other side of the same vase depicts him sailing over the waves on wine jars, which provide him with drink, and using the trident he has stolen from his enemy Poseidon in order to calm the waves and procure fish as food (Fig. 206).[55] A vase in Berlin shows Cadmus, who is to fight the

older and the newer form. They still have the costume of Old Comedy, but already the individual characterization of New Comedy has begun. Middle Comedy, as it was already called in antiquity, is only a feeble reflection of Attic Old Comedy. It still ridicules stories told by the poets,[51] just as tragedy of the fourth century uses the same stories as that of the fifth, but is also feeble compared with that of the fifth. At the same time, Middle Comedy is a forerunner of the Hellenistic Comedy depicting courtesans, old men, and young prodigals. The development of Old Comedy ends at the same time as the development of tragedy. A poet with two

Fig. 203. Cooks attacked by geese. Corinthian vase, Athens

Fig. 204. Odysseus and Circe. Vase from the Kabeirion, British Museum

dragon, as a coward[56] (Fig. 207, cf. the statuettes, Figs. 174-175). Instead of fighting he falls backward, loosing his pail and behaving like Dionysus in the *Frogs* (lines 484-493). To us it seems strange indeed, that the Thebans should laugh at Cadmus, their greatest hero, just as the Dorians laughed at Heracles, and the Athenians even at Dionysus, the Lord of the Festival given in his sacred precincts. The juxtaposition of solemn tragedy and uncouth farce, in which the same gods and heroes appear at the same festival, testifies, however, to the sound vigor and sense of humor of a people who can play with their ideals and yet not lose them.

The Perseus vase, the Fight between Cooks and Geese, and the Kabeirion vases (Figs. 202-207) attest the continuation of the old farce of the archaic period. Other popular entertainments which lived through all times are dances. An Attic red-figured bell crater of the early fourth century in Heidelberg (Fig. 208)[57] shows a youth and a woman dancing with masks. It can hardly be the kordax, as one actor has raised his mask. One is dressed as we may suppose the chorus to have been in the *Ecclesiazousae*. It was supposed that the scene represented actors at a rehearsal, as on the mosaic (Fig. 36), where one of the actors also has pushed up his mask. A more likely interpretation, however, is that of a dance during a procession (pompe) at a Dionysiac festival. This need not be the great City Dionysia, but could well be the Anthesteria, when there were no dramatic performances, but some gay entertainments.

The same festival has been supposed to be the occasion for selling unglazed pots with polychrome comic figures, five of which have been found on the Athenian Agora (Figs. 209-210).[58] Grotesque men are dancing, one named Dionysus, the god of the festival opposite a man named Phor . . . ; one carrying a staff and an oinochoe, two carrying a large white object on a spit (Fig. 209) supposed to be a large loaf of cake baked on a spit, named obelias (ὀβελίας) by Photius and carried in procession in honor of Dionysus according to Athenaeus (III, 111b) and Pollux (VI,75). A man rowing a fish with long oars (Fig. 210) may be a caricature of Arion rescued by a dolphin, or of Theseus carried by a dolphin when he visits his father Poseidon on the bottom of the sea. I believe that these burlesques were performed by revellers at the Anthesteria, and

Fig. 207. Cadmus and the dragon. Kabeirion vase, Berlin

Figs. 205, 206. Odysseus and Circe; Odysseus on raft. Vase from Thebes, Oxford

Fig. 208. Dancing couple. Crater, Heidelberg

Figs. 209, 210. Two men dancing, carrying an object on a spit; Man rowing a fish. Glazed vases, from the Agora of Athens

perhaps at the Rural Dionysia, where such gay parades originated in the archaic period (see Ch. IV).

Some of these gay scenes may also have been presented at private festivals. This may be true for the Perseus vase (Fig. 202), where only two spectators are present. It certainly is true for the acrobats, usually female, such as described by Xenophon (*Symposion* II and VII). Similar feats are performed on a table, which serves as a stage, by a man in oriental dress whose lively dance is accompanied by two women playing the auloi and a tympanon, on a vase in Athens (Fig. 211) and by a nude girl on an Attic hydria from Nola in Naples (Fig. 212).[59] The girl is resting on her arms and tries to drink from a kylix which is standing near her feet. Another nude girl dances between swords planted in the ground and is accompanied by a flutist. Still another dances a pyrriche, a war dance, wearing a helmet and a shield, but otherwise is also nude. Her movements are accompanied by clappers shaken by a girl musician. Similar feats appear on Italian vases[60] (see Ch. XI, Fig. 579) and, according to Xenophon, they may have been brought to Athens from Syracuse. They were certainly not admitted to the Greek theater of the classical period.

Bearded men dressed as women—with kerchief, wide chiton, mantle, and umbrella—on vases in the Robinson Collection at the University of Mississippi and in Cleveland (Figs. 213 and 214) and accompanied by a flute-playing girl on an amphora in Delos[61] also represent private entertainment, perhaps in some cult, but have nothing to do with the theater.

Fig. 211. Oriental dancer on table

Fig. 212. Nude girl performing on table. Attic hydria, Naples

Figs. 213, 214. Men in women's dresses. Vases, Robinson; Cleveland

CHAPTER IV

THE DIONYSIAC FESTIVALS

See Fig. 12

PERFORMANCES of dithyrambs, tragedies, satyr plays, and comedies, were acts of religion. Therefore they took place at the festivals of Dionysus, within the holy precincts of the god. In Attica there were four Dionysiac festivals, celebrated in order from midwinter to spring.[1]

I. The lesser or *Rural Dionysia* took place in the month of Poseideon, December, and the beginning of January. At this festival the komoi or revelries were performed in honor of Dionysus and the phallic chant was recited. From the leaders of this revelry, according to Aristotle,[2] comedy was evolved. Sacrifice and drinking of wine, the gift of the god, also belonged to it. An idea of the festival is given by Aristophanes in his reduced imitation of the procession in the *Acharnians* (vv. 237 ff.). In later years repetitions were given, in the country, of tragic and comic plays which had found favor in the city. Several of these festivals in the larger districts of Attica came to have a certain importance. In the Piraeus, the harbor town of Athens, for instance, plays by Euripides were produced, which attracted Socrates (Aelian, *Var. Hist.*, II,13). Plato's *Symposium* has as its background a feast of Agathon, the tragic poet, in honor of a victory won in the Piraeus. Sophocles and Aristophanes were performed in Eleusis.[3] Icaria, associated with the ad-

Fig. 215. Masks of comedy, and satyr before Dionysus

vent of Dionysus and the beginning of tragedy, had regularly organized dramatic festivals.[4] Aixone, a small community in Attica, celebrated during the fourth century the Dionysia with chorus singing and particularly with comedies. An honorary monument for two choregi, dated either 340 or 313 according

Fig. 216. Plan of Lenaion sanctuary and theater, Athens

Fig. 217. Reconstruction of the Lenaion theater, Athens

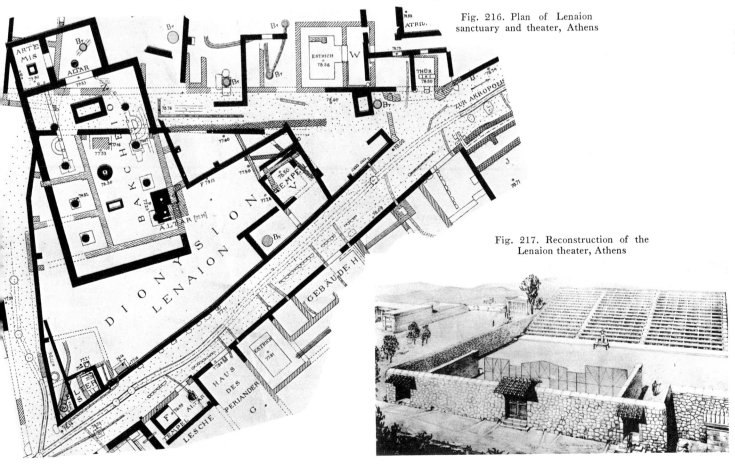

to the inscription, has in its upper part a seated Dionysus and a satyr standing before him, alluding either to the dithyrambs in honor of Dionysus or perhaps to a satyr drama (Fig. 215).[5] In the entablature five masks, probably of the Middle Comedy, are represented: an old man, an oldish woman, a slave, a youth, and a girl.

II. The *Lenaea* occurred in Gamelion, the marriage month, also called Lenaion, January and beginning of February. The name of the festival comes from Lenai (Λῆναι), maenads, and the name of the month from the common ceremonies which took place for engaged women, who were initiated into the Dionysiac mysteries in the Lenaion. On the last day of this month, in the night of the dark moon between this and the following month and festival, the marriage was consummated.[6] It was at the Lenaean festival that comedy was first improvised at Athens. After it had acquired literary and artistic form, it was produced by the state at the Lenaea from the first half of the fifth century on. Tragedy appeared about fifty years later, around 442 B.C., but the comic plays seem always to have been the more important at this festival.[7] The archon basileus had the direction of the performances in the shrine of Dionysus Lenaeus (Aristotle, *Pol. Ath.*, LVIII), which has been located in the marshy hollow between the Acropolis, Pnyx, and Areopagus, therefore called Dionysion in Limnais, in the marshes (Figs. 216-217).[8] The Lenaion plays were transferred to the permanent theater after it had been built in the precinct of Dionysus Eleuthereus on the southern slope of the Acropolis.[9] As they took place in winter when the sea was closed for ancient shipping, their importance was only local.

III. The *Anthesteria* took place in Anthesterion, the month of flowers, February to the beginning of March, which corresponds to our spring. This festival consisted of three parts: first, the new wine in the caskets was broached at the Pithoegia; then the newly-wed and all citizens celebrated the Choes, or feast of jugs, in which they drank the new wine; the last day was the feast of pots, Chytroi. At the Choes

the children received little pots as presents, of which many examples have been found.[10] They are decorated with pictures of children playing. One (Fig. 218)[11] imitates the wedding procession of the archon basileus, who with the attributes of Dionysus, thyrsus and cantharus, is seated on the wedding car, while his wife, the basilinna, is helped into the car. Behind them three boys carry the symbol of marriage, the plough. The newly-wed came to the sanctuary of Dionysus, where the marriage of the basileus and the basilinna was the imitation of the marriage of Dionysus and Ariadne, a promise of happiness. It is not the Thespis car, as has been assumed, but this wedding car, which was used at the Anthesteria. A similar representation of the carrying of a bride on a car is on a black-figured lekythos in Giessen (Fig. 219). The bridegroom drives, the bride is seated in the rear.[12] On the last day at the feast of pots, Chytroi, food was set out in pots for the souls of the departed. Such festivals, whether for brides, children, or for the dead are not suitable for dramatic performances, which have been falsely supposed to have taken place at the Anthesteria. Perhaps there was a contest between the actors of comedy to be chosen for the City Dionysia (Plutarch, *Vitae decem Oratorum*, 841f.) and some gay processions and dancing (see Figs. 209-210 in Ch. III).

IV. The great or *City Dionysia*, celebrated in Elaphebolion, the month of stags, March to the beginning of April, is the principal festival. It was celebrated not only by the city and the ten counties

Fig. 219. Wedding car. Black-figured lekythos, Giessen Museum

Fig. 218. Wedding of Dionysus and Ariadne. Children's oinochoe, Metropolitan Museum

of Attica, but by the members of the Attic federal state and by many strangers, as at this time of the year the sea was navigable. The direction was in the hands of the highest state official, the archon eponymos (ἄρχων ἐπώνυμος), whose name was written at the head of each theatrical record, the so-called Didascalia. To him were sent the plays which were to be produced. He made a selection from them and gave to each poet a chorus and a choregus, a wealthy citizen, who had to bear, as a state tax, the costs of the presentation, the rehearsals under a chorus-trainer, the costumes and other equipment.[13] The costs were considerable and even higher than for tragedy for the dithyrambs sung by fifty men of five tribes, less for comedies and for dithyrambs sung by fifty boys of the other five tribes. The ten dithyrambs were performed on the first day of the festival. Then followed, beginning 487/6, five comedies on a day of their own, with five poets competing with one play each. At the time of the Peloponnesian war, however, the number was limited to three, and the day for comedy was cancelled. One comedy was played on each of the following three days after each tetralogy, a set of three tragedies (called a trilogy) and followed by a satyr play.[14] The tragic performances began at sunrise. This follows from the fact that several tragedies begin with a scene at dawn, for example the *Agamemnon* (vv. 4ff.) of Aeschylus and the *Andromeda* of Euripides (Fragment 114, ed. Nauck). The comedies, in contrast, were given in the evening. This follows from the passage in Aristophanes' *Birds* (vv. 785ff.), where the advantages of flying are extolled. Among them is the possibility that the spectators would have to escape from the long-winded tirades of tragedy, flying home to dinner and flying back to the theater for the comic performances.[15]

Since Pericles had erected the odeum, a roofed music hall, in 446-442 (see Figs. 237 and 258),[16] a proagon, an introduction of the whole personnel active in the contests, was held here. The poets, the choregi, the actors, the musicians and the chorus members paraded in rich dresses with golden crowns or wreaths on their heads, but the actors did not wear their masks or costumes. This was a kind of advance announcement instead of a playbill. On the first day of the festival proper there was a procession (Pompe, πομπή) with the Thespis car, a trumpeter at the head, maidens with sacrificial implements and priests leading the bull which was to be sacrificed in the sacred precinct (see above Figs. 56-58).[17] After the plays there was an assembly (ekklesia, ἐκκλησία) of the people, at which the prizes and awards were distributed and everything

unseemly which had occurred during the festival was rebuked and punished.

The program at the great City Dionysia in the time of Pericles must have been as follows:

First day, Elaphebolion 8: Proagon
Second day, Elaphebolion 9: Procession, sacrifices, ten dithyrambs
Third day, Elaphebolion 10: Five comedies
Fourth, fifth, and sixth days, Elaphebolion 11-13: Three tetralogies; each day three tragedies and one satyr play
Seventh day, Elaphebolion 14: Assembly

During the Peloponnesian War the third day was cancelled, and the then third, fourth, and fifth days were lengthened by one comedy each in the evening; as evidenced by Aristophanes' *Birds* (vv. 786-89), people came to see the comedies after dinner. In the Hellenistic period, as evidenced by inscriptions dating from 306-117 B.C., the second day, Elaphebolion 9, was an intermission and a day of stated meetings. The assembly may have been postponed to Elaphebolion 18 and 19, after the feast of the Pandia, which took place on Elaphebolion 15.[18]

The aspect of the festival must have been dazzling. First the festival robes, which were sometimes of purple and gold as described by Demosthenes (*Oration against Meidias*, 22). Then the burlesque costume of comedy. Then the solemn costume given by Aeschylus to the tragic actors, followed by the gay satyrs. The number of the participants was also astonishing. The dithyrambs alone needed 500 choreutai, with at least ten flute players. In each comedy there were about five actors and 24 choreutai with their flute players and sometimes citharists. In each tragedy, of which nine were presented, there were three actors, fifteen chorus members, and probably at least two musicians. In each of the three satyr dramas there were three actors, and twelve chorus members with their flute player. There must have been about 700-800 choreutai, 30-50 actors, 20-40 musicians. If we add the mute characters, choregi, chorus teachers, magistrates, judges, and stage hands, the number of active participants must have been not much less than one thousand. The fact that all performances were competitions and that there was a great variety to be seen, explains the fact that the Attic audience stayed in the theater for several days from morning until night.

In order to explain the little that remains of the archaic and classical theater building, all the various purposes for which it was intended must be kept in mind. The development of the theater building to meet all these requirements will be shown in the following chapter.

CHAPTER V

THE DEVELOPMENT OF THE THEATER BUILDING

IN THE CLASSICAL PERIOD

THE performance of dithyrambs and of tragic, satyric, and comic plays took place during the classical period in Athens at the City Dionysia and at the Lenaea in honor of Dionysus and therefore always in his sacred precincts. During the earliest period, the time of Pisistratus and his sons, when Thespis had come to Athens in 534 with his troupe on wagons, the performances were given in an orchestra in the Agora, which was probably situated where, later, Agrippa built his odeum (see Ch. XIII, Figs. 617-619). The spectators sat on wooden stands (ikria, ἴκρια) until they broke down in the 70th Olympiad (499-496 B.C. Photius s.v. ikria and Suidas s.v. Pratinas). The original primitive wooden form on the market place may be seen on a vase by Sophilus (Fig. 220).[1] The lively gesticulations and movements of the enthusiastic spectators make us understand why these bleachers collapsed in 498 B.C., and why the seats in the theater were excavated on a hillside and later executed in stone.

The smooth surface and the circular shape of the Greek orchestra have recently been explained from the form of the threshing floor, which has remained the same in Greece since antiquity.[2] It is possible that gay dances at religious festivals and particularly at harvest time were performed at the same place where the oxen had trodden out the grain (*Iliad* 20,495f.) or the grapes had been dried. The "ox-driving dithyramb" (Pindar, *Olym.* 13,25f.) may have received its name from this usage.

The oldest comedies were given in the Lenaion precinct, which Dörpfeld has located in the Dionysion in Limnais, the marshy hollow between the west slope of the Acropolis, the Areopagus, and the Pnyx (Fig. 216).[3] Most of the state performances of comedy after 487/6 during the fifth and the first

half of the fourth centuries also took place in the Lenaion, thus the *Frogs* by Aristophanes (see Fig. 221). Here, beginning about 442 the contests of comic actors took place, and after about 432 tragedies were also occasionally performed; but no permanent theater was ever built. After the completion of the theater of Dionysus Eleuthereus on the southern slope of the Acropolis, the Lenaean plays were transferred to this sanctuary.

The sacred precinct on the south slope of the Acropolis was probably dedicated to Dionysus about the middle of the sixth century, when the little temple in soft poros stone was erected and decorated perhaps with a pediment relief representing a bacchic dance of satyrs and maenads (Fig. 222), which, however, might have decorated a still earlier monument in the sanctuary.[4] There certainly was also an altar and sacred grove, with an enclosing wall. As the oldest form of the Dionysiac service was the dancing and singing of a chorus, there must have been from the beginning a chorus (χορός) or an orchestra (from orcheisthai, ὀρχεῖσθαι, to dance), that is, a dancing place for the chorus, named after its purpose. We call an orchestra a body of people playing instruments, and we also apply the term to the ground floor of the modern theater. These modern definitions are, however, derived from the term describing the nuclear center of the theater building, the arena, where originally music was produced and dances performed. The orchestra lay on a terrace above the earliest temple on the slope of the Acropolis. The oldest orchestra was reconstructed by Dörpfeld (Fig. 223) as a circle with a diameter of about 85 feet (27 meters), while Dinsmoor gives it 83½ feet. Fiechter is of the opinion that the wall used by Dörpfeld for his reconstruction is only a

Fig. 220. Spectators on temporary stands. From a vase by Sophilus, Athens

Fig. 221. Plan for presentation of Aristophanes' *Frogs*, Bieber

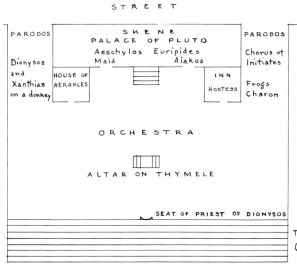

Fig. 222. Bacchic dance. Poros relief, found in the sanctuary of Dionysus Eleuthereus at Athens

retaining wall for a road leading up to the orchestra terrace, and thus the orchestra would have been not much larger than the later dancing place (Fig. 224).[5] Anti believes that the earliest orchestra was rectangular, as it certainly was in the Lenaion precinct (Fig. 217). But this is unlikely, as in most theaters it is circular. It suffices in any case for very artistic dances given by big choruses. It may well have been also the goal of the procession, to which the black-figured vases (Ch. II, Figs. 56-58) bear witness. In the center stood a thymele or a bema with the altar on sacrificial steps and close by the holy image which was borne out of the temple on festival days, so that the god might enjoy the plays (see Fig. 48, in Chapter I).

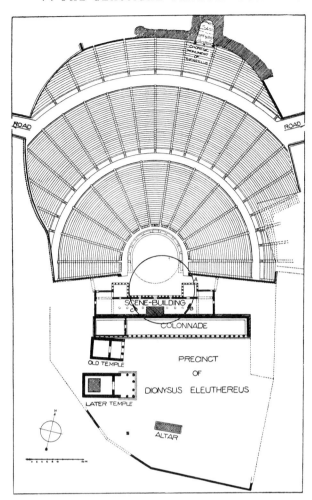

Fig. 223. Plan of the precinct of Dionysus Eleuthereus by Dörpfeld

Fig. 224. Oldest period of precinct of Dionysus Eleuthereus. Plan, Fiechter

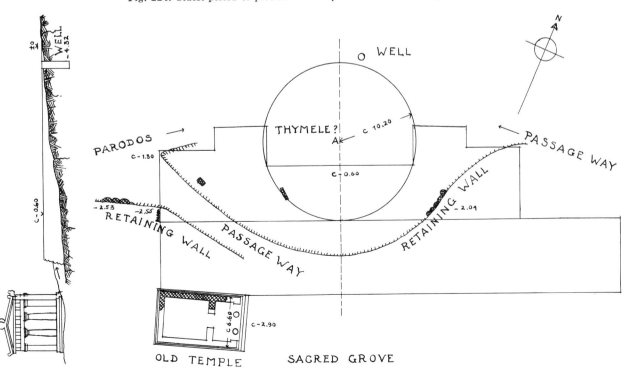

Fig. 225. Theater of Syracuse

226  227

Figs. 226-230. Oldest temple and orchestra in precinct of Dionysus Eleuthereus. Reconstructions

228   229

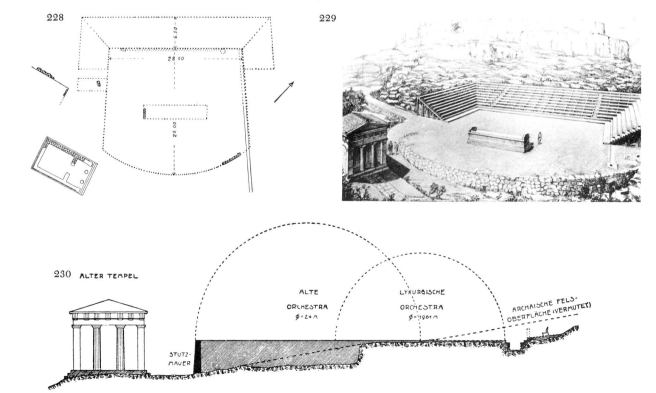

230 ALTER TEMPEL

ALTE ORCHESTRA Ø=24 M

LYKURGISCHE ORCHESTRA Ø=19.61 M

ARCHAISCHE FELS-OBERFLÄCHE (VERMUTET)

STÜTZ-MAUER

56

The spectators found better accommodations on the slope of the Acropolis than they had had in the Agora. The wooden scaffolding or bleachers could not as easily collapse as on the level market place. They could, however, not be cut out of the rock, as was done in Syracuse (Fig. 225), where a perfectly rounded theatron, a hollow auditorium, has been preserved.[6] The name theatron, seeing place or reviewing place, is characteristic of the fact that the Greeks wanted to see as well as hear, while the Romans, like us moderns, emphasized hearing in calling their seating place an auditorium. The name theater (from theasthai, $\theta\epsilon\hat{\alpha}\sigma\theta\alpha\iota$, to see) was only later extended to the whole building.

The earliest tragedies and satyr plays of Phrynichus, Pratinas, and Aeschylus and the few comedies given in the precinct of Dionysus Eleuthereus after 487/6 did not have a background building. The actors probably dressed in a small hut or booth (skene), perhaps hidden in the sacred grove which we must suppose grew in the southern part of the precinct. The chorus and the first actor then entered the orchestra through the main parodos, or approach, which led up a somewhat steep incline from the southwest to the terrace of the dancing place. After Aeschylus had introduced the second actor, he also entered here. The long chorus songs in the earlier tragedies, between which the dialogue parts of the actors were but episodes, gave the actors plenty of time for a change of costume. The great orchestra, the steep approach, and the small temple were, then, the only buildings in the precinct until about 460 B.C. (Figs. 226-229).[7]

The simple properties which the earliest works of Aeschylus require, such as altars, rocks, and tombs, could be set up easily at the edge of the terrace. Indeed, the fact that this terrace is raised some two meters, or some six and a half feet, above the level on which the earliest temple stands (Fig. 230)[8] makes it seem probable that ghostly apparitions like the phantom of Darius in the *Persians*, or the descent of Prometheus, could be produced with greater effect here than later, when a skene or provisional playhouse was erected at the edge of the orchestra.

The tiny provincial theater of Thorikos in Attica had, like the auditorium in Athens, a boundary wall following the contour of the ground (Fig. 231).[9] It has kept the flat form of the auditorium and the steep slope of the orchestra terrace, where a skene could never have been erected. It gives us, therefore, the best idea of the way the Athenian theater must have appeared in an early period. The orchestra forms a rectangular space with rounded corners, and the ends of the parallel rows of seats in the

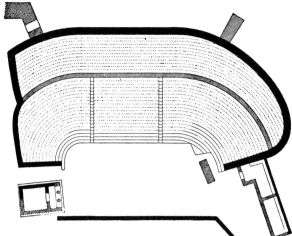

Fig. 231. Theater of Thorikos

theatron curve to enclose the orchestra. A small archaic temple and a small house for dressing and stage properties, a skenotheke or hall, were built at the sides of the orchestra.

The first extant drama for which large buildings, a temple and a palace were necessary is the *Oresteia* of Aeschylus, produced in the year 458 B.C. It was for a long time a matter of controversy whether this earliest skene, which means a booth or a hut or a tent, was set up inside a segment of the orchestra-circle or outside at the southern edge of the orchestra (Fig. 232).[10] Both views involved difficulties which seemed to be insoluble, for the dancing ground could not be obstructed, and the erection of a temple or a palace at the steep southern slope would have necessitated large unsightly scaffolding, substructures, and retaining walls.

The problem may be solved if we assume that the part of the orchestra which was used for the performances was smaller than was formerly believed, with a diameter of only some 65 feet (about 20 meters). This dancing ground was more than large enough for a dithyramb of fifty men and even for the liveliest movements of a chorus consisting, for tragedy, of fifteen and, for comedy, of twenty-four performers. There was enough space, about 20 feet, left at the southern part of the orchestra terrace for the erection of any temporary buildings

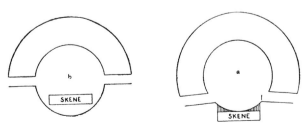

Fig. 232. Possible positions of earliest skene, Allen

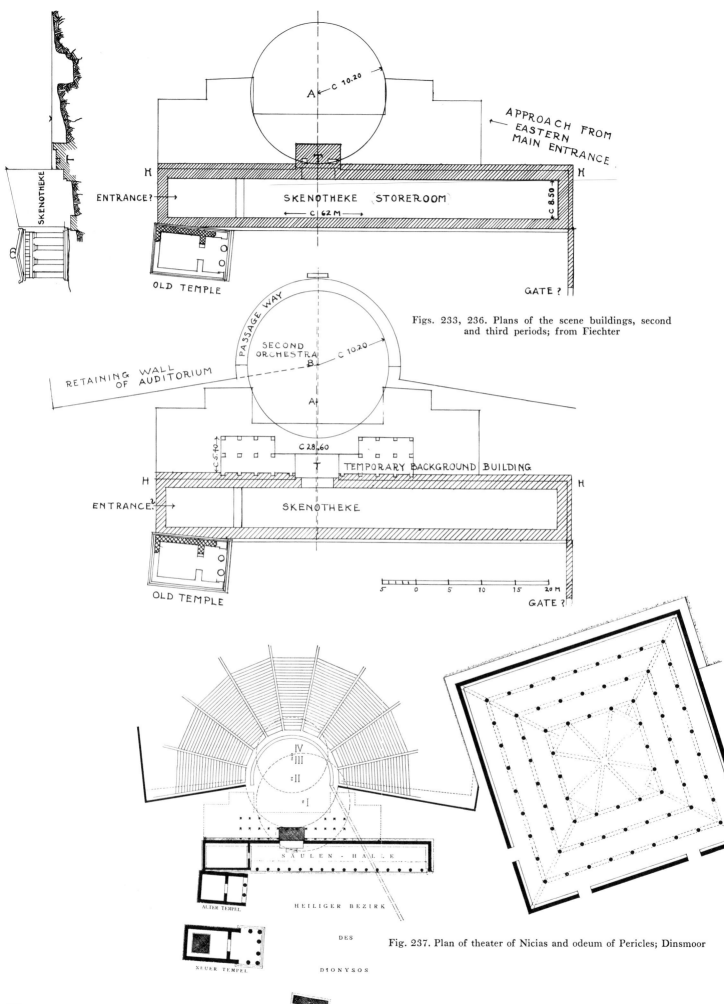

SKENOTHEKE

APPROACH FROM EASTERN MAIN ENTRANCE

A ← C 10.20

H   H

ENTRANCE? →   SKENOTHEKE   STOREROOM   C 8.50

← C 62 M →

OLD TEMPLE   GATE ?

Figs. 233, 236. Plans of the scene buildings, second and third periods; from Fiechter

PASSAGE WAY

SECOND ORCHESTRA
B ← C 10.20

RETAINING WALL OF AUDITORIUM

A

C 5.40   C 28.60

H   H
                 T   TEMPORARY BACKGROUND BUILDING

ENTRANCE? →   SKENOTHEKE

OLD TEMPLE

5   0   5   10   15   20 M

GATE ?

IV
III
II
I

SÄULEN-HALLE

ALTER TEMPEL

HEILIGER BEZIRK

DES

NEUER TEMPEL

DIONYSOS

ALTAR

Fig. 237. Plan of theater of Nicias and odeum of Pericles; Dinsmoor

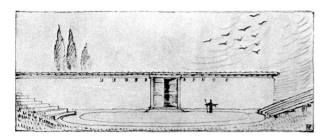

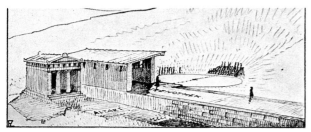

Figs. 234, 235. Front and rear views of the reconstructed scene building, Athens; Fiechter

which could be constructed before the festival began, in elaborate or simple forms, according to the expenditures which the choregi were willing to afford. It was probably mostly a simple long building, used as a storeroom (skenotheke) and as dressing room for the actors, who, in the *Oresteia* and in the dramas of Sophocles, were obliged to return to the scene of action much more quickly than in the earlier days, when the chief part was taken by the chorus. They now could change their costumes in a dressing room close to the scene of performance (Figs. 233-236).[11]

It was easy to change the scenery by slight alterations during the intermissions between the four plays of a tetralogy or during the night between two of the festival days. Painting doubtless bore a part in this, as is proved by the report that Sophocles invented the art of skenographia or scene painting (Aristotle, *Poetics*, 1449a, 18), and that Agatharchus had painted a scene for Aeschylus, upon which the philosophers Democritus and Anaxagoras had based their doctrine of linear perspective (Vitruvius, VII, praef. 11).[12] How far we can infer from the plays the appearance of the scenery is a question that remains unanswered. It is a sound rule that the theatrical scenery cannot have differed in principle from the actual buildings of the same period.[13] But if we consider the wealth of development of Greek art in the fifth century—its architecture, painting, sculpture, craftsmanship, decoration—and the equally extensive development of the drama, we shall not readily assume that before the last quarter of the fifth century any definite form of theater building had been permanently established. Such a form can only have evolved gradually at the end

of the fifth and in the course of the fourth centuries, when literature and art also struck a slower tempo in their unfolding.

Pericles built the odeum, the music hall for concerts, in 446-442 as a square with the roof supported by many columns, similar to the telesterion in Eleusis, and the Thersilion in Megalopolis (below, Fig. 276), arranged like a checkerboard, so that anybody standing in the center, for example the musicians and actors who in the proagon presented themselves to the public, could be seen equally well from every side. This odeum was erected east of the theater, and is probably the reason why the theater axis was shifted westward (Fig. 237).[14] As the construction of the odeum prevented an eastward expansion, the orchestra was shifted to the north-northwest, that is, it cut deeper into the slope of the Acropolis than before. The theatron or auditorium became steeper. The ends of the auditorium were supported on earth and the fill was held in by stone retaining walls (analemmata). Outside these analemmata the parodoi or entrances led from both sides into the orchestra. The eastern approach, coming from the odeum, probably sloped more gently upward than the western one. Through both, the spectators came to the theater early in the morning and took their seats on benches that were still wooden and straight. The chorus and many actors also came during the festival days through these entrances.

Thus in Sophocles' *King Oedipus*, while the audience assembled for this first tragedy of a tetralogy in the early morning, the people of Thebes at the same time may have assembled around the altar in the center of the orchestra, the women and children perhaps sitting down on the thymele, the sacrificial steps of the altar. Then Oedipus stepped out of the palace and talked with the priest in the orchestra. Creon and later the stranger from Corinth came through the left or eastern parodos, from outside, while the chorus and Teiresias, living in the city, came from the right or western parodos. All came into the orchestra and were there met by Oedipus and later Jocasta, who stepped out of the skene, decorated as a palace, to meet them there (see my

Fig. 238. Possible entrances for actors in Sophocles' *Oedipus*, Bieber

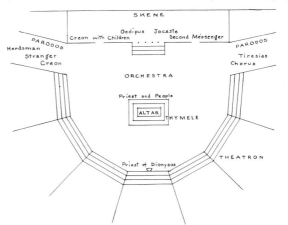

Fig. 239. Early classical structure of the scene building;
Dörpfeld

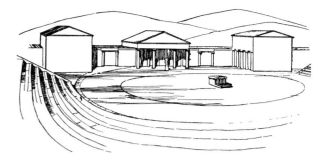

Fig 240. Possible background buildings of the fifth
century, Mahr

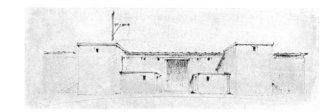

Figs. 241, 242. Possible background buildings of the fifth
century, Fiechter

attempt to show the first entrances of the actors for this play, Fig. 238). The reconstruction by Dörpfeld (Fig. 239) agrees with this arrangement.[15]

One thing is absolutely sure: players and chorus appeared through the whole of the classical period, at one and the same place, that is, in the orchestral area. Almost all extant dramas and all the comedies contain scenes in which the players and the chorus act together, sometimes even mingling freely, coming to close quarters, or returning together.[16] As the importance of the actor's parts increased, the action centered more and more at the skene, the temporary scene building, often decorated as a palace, the abode of the main actor, outside the dancing ground (Figs. 239-240). In the beginning this skene was a mere adjunct to the area of action. But it became more and more important when the importance of the chorus parts diminished.

The skene, therefore, was transformed in time from a temporary building, a tent or log cabin, to a permanent stone building, beginning in the period of the peace of Nicias (421-415). First a hall was built, named skenotheke by Fiechter, Säulenhalle by Dörpfeld (Figs. 233, 236, 250), but rightly named hall by Pickard-Cambridge and stoa by Dinsmoor who follows Vitruvius (v,9,1), (see Fig. 237).[17] The stoa was of considerable length, and was built on a breccia foundation, a material not used before the later fifth century. On the north and east sides it cut into the rock of the Acropolis slope. To the west it impinges upon the old temple. Its north wall served as background to the plays while it faced south toward the precinct. From its interior, steps ascended north about seven feet to reach the higher level of the orchestra. They led the main actors out through a wide door to a platform (T on Figs. 233 and 236) which could be decorated as a movable porch, a temple façade, a stairway, an altar, or whatever the poets needed for their plays. This large massive foundation was erected in breccia in the time of Nicias, but may have had a predecessor.

Figs. 243, 244. Pergamon, views of theater, terrace, and orchestra

Figs. 245, 246. Pergamon, terrace and pavement with stone sockets for timber

It projects about 10¾ feet before the central door. On either side were five vertical slots in the masonry for a skeleton of upright timbers. In front of them we must assume several rows of corresponding stone sockets set in the earth floor to the right and left of the orchestra, so that various combinations, including side buildings, paraskenia, were possible. The name skene was kept on, indicating the continuous custom of erecting a new background building, leaning against the front of the stoa, every year during the classical period. Fiechter has shown some of the possibilities for adjustable structures, which the incisions in the front wall of the stoa, combined with the holes to be assumed in the orchestra soil, offered to the theater manager (Figs. 241-242). Another has been attempted by Mahr (Fig. 240).[18] There are, of course, many more possibilities. Broneer, for example, believes that the model for the oldest skene was the tent of Xerxes, a suitable background for many dramas and probably resembling Persian palace architecture.[19]

Local need was the reason for keeping up this custom of temporary construction as late as the Hellenistic period in Pergamon (Figs. 243-247).[20]

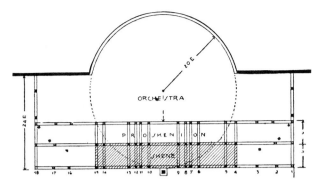

Fig. 247. Pergamon, plan of orchestra and stage building

but seldom that the full circle, which tends to form on a level ground—as may have been the case in the sixth century in the Agora—could be executed on a slope. Anti believes that the original orchestra in the sanctuary of Dionysus Eleuthereus was square or trapezoidal (Figs. 228-229). Dinsmoor and Caputo believe that it was polygonal, but essentially circular (Fig. 237).[21] The way a half- or three-quarter circle forms of itself on a rising hillside is illustrated in the village communities of Switzerland which assemble in a ring, or in the circle of spectators around the choral dance of Roumanian peasants (Fig. 248). This is an old national dance called the "Hora" (Chora, Choros? which is more likely than dance of the seasons or hours). A similar dance, also called Hora, is danced in Israel, where it might have been brought by immigrant Roumanian Jews. It is even performed in a Jewish orphan asylum in New York. The dance performance on the island of Bali is watched by spectators in a polygonal figure which is tangential to a circle and thus essentially circular (Fig. 249).[22] Dinsmoor (Fig. 237) has given this form to the auditorium of the time of Nicias. The spectators sat on wooden benches which, of course, had to be straight, but could be arranged as a polygon. The seats of honor (proedria) were of stone, as slabs with inscriptions assigning them to the priests and vertical demarcation lines prove.[23] The upper rows were benches of movable planks supported by separate stones embedded in the earth. The single wedge-shaped divisions (kerkides) were separated from each other by

Beneath the theater, built by Eumenes II (197-159 B.C.) in a steep and shallow hollow, ran a terrace leading from the market place to the temple of Dionysus. It was impossible to build a permanent stage house here over this terrace. Provision was made, therefore, for erecting temporary buildings with wooden timbers, for the insertion of which three rows of quadrangular holes were cut into the pavement of the terrace (Figs. 243, 246). They were sunk in pieces of light-colored, hard stones, in contrast to the dark pavement of the rest of the terrace. The plan (Fig. 247) shows that in the front of the middle portion three wide openings were left for doors. Diagonally arranged holes at the sides indicate side entrances or side decorations, perhaps periaktoi (see Ch. VI, p. 75). Although the theatron was much larger, the orchestra itself was not greater than that in Athens.

The theatron in Athens also developed slowly to a more durable and better form. The spectators originally stood or sat on the slope of the Acropolis, as will always happen when there is anything to be seen in an open space overlooked by a height. It is

Fig. 248. Dance "Hora" of Roumanian peasants and spectators

Fig. 249. Sacred dance and spectators, Bali

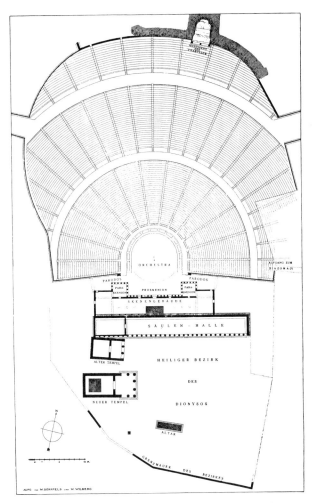

Fig. 250. Plan of the sacred precinct of Dionysus Eleuthereus in Athens, fourth century. Dörpfeld

radiating aisles. Thus the majority of the people still sat on wooden benches, the ikria mentioned in 411 by Aristophanes (*Thesmophoriazousae*, v. 395).

Most of the boundary wall is the only part of the Athenian theatron of the fifth century which is built in stone, and for this reason it has survived. It is determined in some places by the contour of the ground, in others by older buildings. At the east it made a right-angle turn, for here it was in contact with the odeum of Pericles (see Figs. 237, 250 and 258). The enclosing wall at the west cut off the precinct of Dionysus from that of Asclepius. Toward the north a wide ancient pathway, leading along the south slope of the Acropolis, was probably the uppermost boundary of the theatron in the fifth century. Later it became a diazoma, girdle or rounded passage separating the third from the second gallery. The third gallery was probably added between this road and the steep cliff above, when this, containing a grotto, was cut back and became the so-called katatome or cutting, later adorned by

Thrasyllus with a choregic monument (Fig. 250).[24] This upper part (Fig. 251)[25] was merely a segment of a circle.

The southern boundary of the theater of Athens, facing the actual precinct, was the above-mentioned hall or stoa (see above, pp. 55ff., Figs. 223, 233, 236, 237, 250). It was impossible to build the hall further to the south, for even in the present position its most westerly part is already in contact with the small archaic temple (see Figs. 226-230), which was allowed to remain, although another temple was built simultaneously with the stoa farther south. Alcamenes, the pupil of Phidias and the leading sculptor during the Peloponnesian war, worked the cult statue of Dionysus in gold and ivory for this later temple. Either this temple or more probably the long and spacious hall contained wall paintings, mentioned by Pausanias (1,20,3), between the temples of the precinct of Dionysus Eleuthereus and the odeum. Vase paintings of the late fifth century, like the one on the back of the satyr-play vase in Naples (Fig. 33) with the wedding of Dionysus and Ariadne, or the one on a vase in Bologna with Dionysus leading Hephaestus back to Olympus to liberate his fettered mother Hera (Fig. 252) may have been copied from—or at least inspired by—these murals.[26] They prove that the scenes from the life of Dionysus were huge compositions with many figures from the thiasus, for which there would not have been enough room in the little vestibule or in the cella of the temple.

The northern wall (H in Figs. 233 and 236) of the hall, in the time when most of the preserved plays by Sophocles, Euripides, and Aristophanes were performed, was used as the back of the wooden skene and as supporting wall of the orchestra terrace. Here the temporary playhouses were built in varying forms, and as this is the time of the greatest interest to the drama student, we have naturally a great interest in reconstructing these changing forms (see above, p. 60, Figs. 239-242). We have three aids for the reconstruction of the wooden playhouses of the fifth century: (1) inferences from extant plays; (2) inferences from vase paintings with scenes from the fifth- and fourth-century plays; (3) inferences from the form of the later stone skene.

All three sources must be used with caution:

(1) The extant plays, with the exception of the feeble *Rhesus* and the weak works of Aristophanes' late period, belong to the fifth century. Every drama can be staged in the most diverse ways. The conditions for the diverse plays are manifold. In many cases no background building whatever was needed as in the earlier dramas of Aeschylus, or in the *Oedipus Coloneus*, the work of Sophocles' old age,

Fig. 251. Theater of Dionysus, Athens

when only a sacred grove was to be indicated. Often only one building was used, for example, a temple in the *Ion* of Euripides; a palace in the *Agamemnon* and in the *Choephoroe* of Aeschylus, in the *Antigone* and in *Oedipus the King* of Sophocles, and in the *Medea* and the *Antigone* of Euripides, as evidenced by vase paintings (see above, Ch. II, Figs. 117, 121, 122a); a tent in the *Ajax* of Sophocles and in the *Trojan Women* of Euripides; a cave in both the *Philoctetes* of Sophocles and of Euripides (cf. Fig. 119), and in the *Birds* of Aristophanes. In all these cases a simple skene with the prothyron set up before the central door and on podium T (Figs. 233 and 236) in the shape of a temple façade (Figs. 240, 241) a columned porch, a tent, or a cave would suffice. Dörpfeld has reconstructed, with the help of numerous vase paintings, theater palaces of this kind (Fig. 239).[27]

The extant tragedies and comedies, however, also show a series of cases in which two buildings were necessary. Thus Aeschylus' *Eumenides* needs the temple of Apollo in Delphi and the temple of Athena in Athens. The *Iphigenia in Tauris* needs the temple of Artemis and the dwelling of the priestess Iphigenia. The *Clouds* of Aristophanes needs the houses of Strepsiades and of Socrates. Moreover, some plays need three buildings. Thus Aristophanes' *Acharnians* has the houses of Dicaeopolis, of Euripides, and of Lamachus; his *Frogs* needs the house of Heracles, the tavern and the palace of Pluto (see Fig. 221).

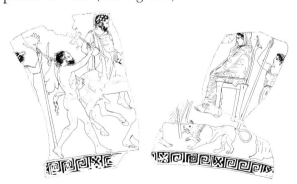

Fig. 252. Return of Hephaestus. Vase, Bologna

65

(2) Many vases show one palace or one temple or one cave (see Ch. II, Figs. 115-122); a few others have two side buildings, like the Campanian vase with Iphigenia and Orestes in Tauris, well interpreted by Lehmann-Hartleben (Fig. 253).[28] It represents the scene from Euripides' *Iphigenia in Tauris* (vv. 936ff.), in which brother and sister are consulting about the theft of the image of Artemis and their flight. Orestes and Pylades stand on the level of the orchestra, indicated as soil, in front of the dark wall of the skene, which represents a house with a tiled roof. To the left is the temple of Artemis, marked by the image of the goddess which has been painted as if standing outside; to the right the priestess' dwelling, from which Iphigenia steps.

This vase, however, and many other vases with undoubted stage buildings, belong to the fourth century, while most of our plays belong to the fifth century. We must, therefore, ask how far the vase paintings may be taken as evidence not only for their own age, the fourth century, but possibly also for an earlier time. We also must remember that the vases often give only the illustration of the subject matter of the drama, and in many cases prefer scenes which are only narrated by a messenger and not played.[29] We can therefore come to a tenable conclusion only when the vases agree not only—like the Iphigenia vase (Fig. 253)—with the extant plays but also with the stone skene which was developed from the temporary wooden skene.

Fig. 253. Iphigenia and Orestes in Tauris.
Campanian vase, Louvre

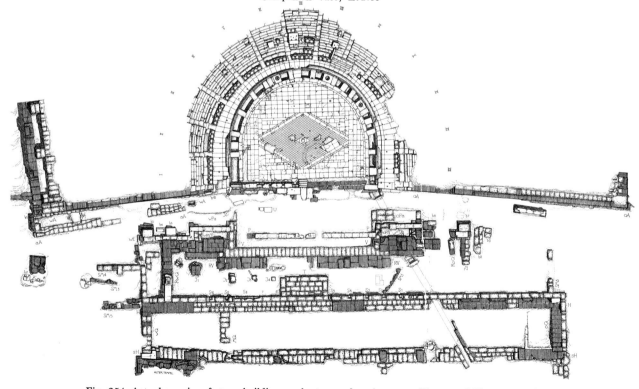

Fig. 254. Actual remains of stage building, orchestra, and analemmata. Theater of Dionysus, Athens

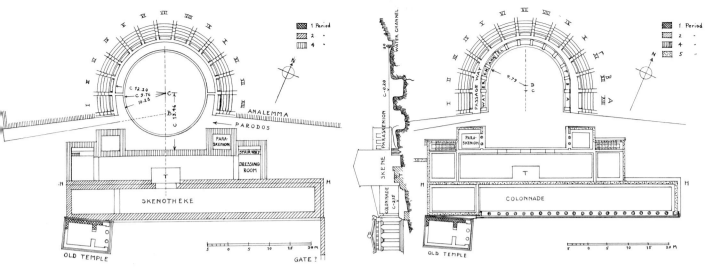

Figs. 255, 256. Plans of theaters of Pericles and of Lycurgus; Fiechter

(3) The earliest stone skene, of which remains have been preserved, is that of the Athenian theater of Dionysus Eleuthereus. It went, however, through numerous changes and developments. The breccia foundations for a skene with side wings, paraskenia (παρασκήνια), were built before the wall H, which had served as a background for the temporary play-houses and as a northern wall of the stoa. It thus

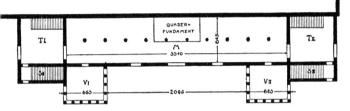

Fig. 257. Plan of Lycurgean skene; Dörpfeld and Frickenhaus

became the southern wall of the stone skene (Figs. 254-256).[30] The great rectangular base of stone (T), which had been used for front decorations in the fifth century was now in the interior of the skene, and may have been used for mechanical devices, perhaps the crane of the flying machine (see Ch. VI, Figs. 281-283). The holes for posts along the former front wall, now the interior back wall, may have been used for the occasional erection of an episkenion, a building on the roof, or of a distegia, an upper story.[31] Dressing rooms for the actors and the chorus were attached at the sides, and from these staircases led to the upper level. The rectangular rooms, projecting in front on both sides, facing the corner between the parodos and the passage around the orchestra, seem to have been correctly named paraskenia, side buildings of the skene.[32] They are for the first time mentioned by Demos-

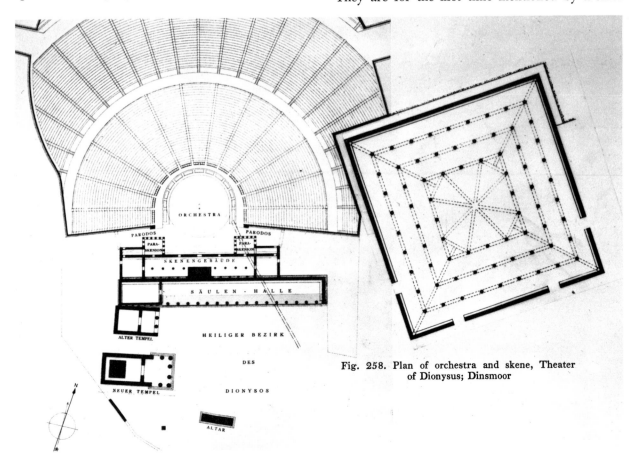

Fig. 258. Plan of orchestra and skene, Theater of Dionysus; Dinsmoor

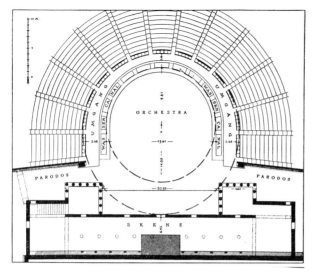

Figs. 259, 260. Ground plan and structure of the Lycurgean theater; Mahr

thenes (*Oration against Meidias*, xxi,17). Dörpfeld, followed by Dinsmoor and Mahr, assumed that they were colonnaded in front and at the sides (Figs. 257-259).[33] Fiechter thought first that they were closed at the sides and colonnaded in front (Fig. 256).[34] He, as well as Bulle and Mahr, give interesting reconstructions, but with too heavy side wings (Figs. 260-261). Lehmann-Hartleben and Bulle believe that the front and side walls of the paraskenia were closed and perhaps broken only by doors, as they appear on the Iphigenia vase (Fig. 253).[35] Frickenhaus and Fiechter in their reconstructions of the scene building of the fourth century assume that

Fig. 261. Reconstruction of the paraskenion theater; Fiechter

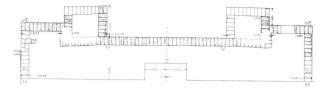

Fig. 262. Breccia foundation for the stone skene

the paraskenia were lower than the skene between them.[36] Their strong substructures, however, suggest an original height equal to that of the main building. Therefore, Fiechter reconstructed the skene with two-storied paraskenia (Fig. 261).[37] This view is supported by a third-century inscription in Delos, which mentions lower paraskenia. This indicates paraskenia having two stories.[38] It seems to me, however, that as long as the skene was erected in wood and with the scenery painted on canvas it had usually only one story, which served as a background to the plays, as is to be seen on the Iphigenia vase. This vase corresponds not only to the recognizable outline of the earliest stone skene in Athens (Fig. 262) but also to the earliest foundations for the skene buildings in Eretria (Figs. 263-265),[39] in Syracuse (Fig. 595),[40] in Segesta with very strong substructures for the paraskenia (below, Ch. XIII, Figs. 596-598),[41] in Tyndaris (Fig. 599),[42] and in Pompeii (Figs. 607, A in 608).[43] It is proved by the Iphigenia vase in Paris (Fig. 253) that plays were acted in the fourth century not on a proskenion, a stage between the paraskenia, but in front of the skene and between the paraskenia on the ground floor in the orchestra. A stage was not erected in the same place before Hellenistic and Roman times. The picture of a wooden paraskenion-theater with slender columns, rich entablature, and acroteria is depicted on a fragment found in Tarentum and now in Würzburg (Figs. 266a-b).[44]

May we now accept this form of the skene with side wings and of the plays represented on vases of the fourth century for the presentations in the fifth century? I think we may, at least for the period after 458 when Aeschylus produced the *Oresteia*. The drawings of the earlier Athenian stage buildings made by Fiechter and Mahr without the knowledge of the vases (Figs. 253, 266), and based on the requirements of the plays, have the projecting paraskenia (Figs. 255-256, 260-261).[45] The requirements of a play of the fifth century and those of the fourth century, when the first stone skene was laid out and finished under Lycurgus, did not differ from each other, since the development of tragedy and of Old Comedy came to a standstill about 400 B.C. We may suppose that the stone skene was designed and executed in a form which had repeatedly proved itself, during the fifth century, practical and useful

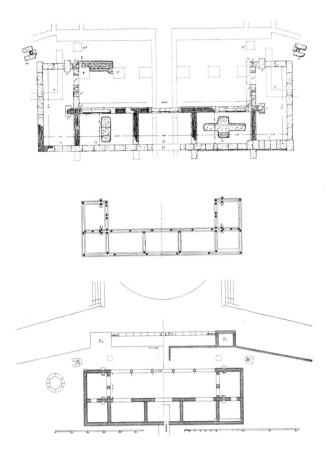

Fig. 266. Wooden skene. Vase, Würzburg;
reconstruction, Bulle

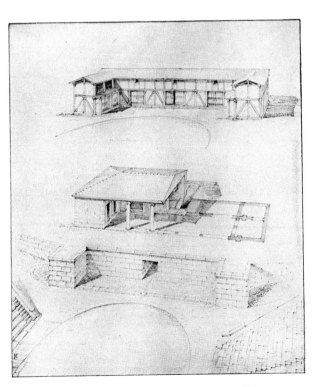

Figs. 263-265. Eretria, oldest stone building,
reconstructed plans and buildings; Fiechter

for a number of performances. The skene of the
classical period thus advanced steadily from south
to north in the direction of the slope of the Acropolis, that is, in the direction of the auditorium.

Even when three buildings were necessary, the
playhouse with two paraskenia and the orchestra
between could fulfill all conditions of the *mise en
scène* by using the buildings one after the other like
the simultaneous stage of the Middle Ages. In the
precinct of Dionysus Eleuthereus there was space
for acting in the orchestra of about 20 meters or
65 feet in breadth and depth, extensive enough to
exclude from consciousness for the moment the part
of the skene not in use. Besides, one of the paraskenia or the middle part of the skene could easily
be hidden temporarily by planks or by curtains.[46]
The paraskenia have their origin in the fact that
Euripides and Aristophanes needed more possibilities for entrances than their predecessors.

Even in smaller theaters, like the Lenaean theater
situated in the sanctuary of Dionysus in Limnais
(in the swamps), a similar wooden background
building could be erected. Here the frogs, the

animals which live in the marshes, were one of the two choruses in the comedy by Aristophanes, produced in 405 B.C. My attempt to show the entrances of the actors and the two choruses (Fig. 221) is based on the investigations of Anti.[47] A street leading from the market place to the Acropolis separated the theater from the sanctuary with temple and altar (see above Figs. 216-217). Dionysus and Xanthias riding on a donkey probably entered at the beginning of the play from this street through a straight parodos into the square orchestra. They first came to the house of Heracles, probably laid into the left paraskenion, for Dionysus as a foreigner enters from the left. Then Charon and the chorus of frogs enter from the right, as they are at home in the region. I believe that the frogs drew and shoved the boat of Charon, which is a kind of parody on the Thespis car (see above, Figs. 56-58). The assumption that they sang behind the scene takes the humor out of their duet with the god, whom they surround while he is rowing in the boat.[48] When Charon has let Dionysus out near the palace of Pluto, imaginary monsters send the god of the festival fleeing to his priest, who certainly here, as in the large theater, sat in the center of the front row. The chorus of the initiates of the mysteries comes from the right. The second paraskenion was probably the tavern out of which the hostess steps, to threaten Dionysus whom she believes to be Heracles. Then the maid comes out of one of the side doors of the palace, represented in the main building, and invites Xanthias, who has been dressed as Heracles, to a meal. Then Aeacus comes out of the other side door and beats both, until he takes them into the palace. In the last scene Pluto, Dionysus, Aeschylus, and Euripides come out of the main door in the center of the palace for the celebrated literary contest in the orchestra. Finally Dionysus goes out with Aeschylus through the left parodos, the chorus goes out through the right parodos, while Pluto and Euripides re-enter the palace.

While the auditorium in the small Lenaean theater consisted only of straight wooden benches, and the skene always remained a temporary building, the theatron in the theater of Dionysus Eleuthereus and its skene were finished in stone in 338-326 B.C. by the orator Lycurgus. The hall opened now with a colonnade to the south into the sacred precinct. It became a kind of foyer for the visitors during the intermissions and a refuge in case of rain. These colonnades remained a regular extension and ornament to the rear of the Greek and Roman theaters (cf. Ephesus, Ch. IX, Fig. 448; Theater of Pompey and Marcellus theater, Ch. XIII, Figs. 632, 640; Ostia, Ch. XIV, Fig. 647; Merida, Fig. 684; Sabratha, Fig. 694). Lycurgus probably erected statues of the great poets of the fifth century near the entrance (see Ch. II, Figs. 64, 101, 102, 107, 108).

The auditorium was truly democratically conceived, with provision for equally good places everywhere; at the same time it was practically arranged for the purpose of easy filling and emptying. The public entered through the parodoi between the skene and the retaining wall of the auditorium and then entered a passageway behind the water channel which separates the orchestra from the theatron. This channel and the passageway form a half circle with straight continuations opposite the paraskenia (Figs. 255-256, 258-259).[49] The same U, or horseshoe, form is given to the thirteen wedge-shaped sectors (kerkides, cunei) in which the seats rise stairwise. The lowest gallery is carried out with absolute regularity. Twelve staircases lead the spectators to their sections. The seats are delicate in outline (Fig. 251). Each has a hollow which allows plenty of room for the feet. The seats are so low as to imply the need of cushions. The second gallery was probably separated from the first by a rounded passageway (diazoma, girdle). It did not have a full and even horseshoe form, as it was narrowed in the east by the odeum of Pericles, in the west by the sanctuary of Asclepius (Fig. 258). The highest gallery above the ancient path became part of the theater only in the period of Lycurgus or later. There was room for only a narrow segment between this road and the cliff, which was cut back, the so-called katatome or cutting, which exposed a grotto with a spring, now dedicated to the Virgin Mary under the name of Panagia Spiliotissa. Thrasyllus erected his monument here in 319 B.C., and his son Thrasycles added as his victory monument in 270 B.C. a statue of Dionysus, now in the British Museum.[50]

In the front row are the seats of honor for the priests and officials of the city. Originally benches, they were later replaced by individual thrones. Exactly in the center of the middle section there remains today the chair of honor for the priest of the Lord of the play, Dionysus Eleuthereus, the Liberator. Before it stood a footstool. Holes in the ground prove this seat to have been distinguished by a canopy. On the back of the throne are carved satyrs and a vine; on the front Arimaspeans and griffins. At the side, a winged boy, Agon, the personification of the contest, is represented with fighting cocks (Figs. 267-269).[51] This throne seems to date from the first century B.C., but it is imitated from classical models, perhaps one of them the older Lycurgean throne. We may assume that a still older throne was put up here as well as in the Lenaean precinct. In front of a similar throne must have been played the gay scene in the *Frogs* of Aristophanes

Figs. 267-269. Throne of priest of Dionysus

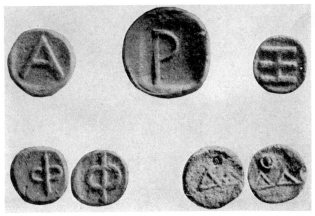

Fig. 270. Greek theater tickets

(vv. 297ff.), in which Dionysus takes refuge with his priest from the supposed terrors of the underworld (see Fig. 221).

It is likely that the central section behind the seat of the priest of Dionysus was reserved for guests of honor, while the five sections on both sides of it may have been assigned to the ten Attic tribes, which contested with the ten dithyrambs. The two outermost sections on each side may have been reserved for foreigners and late-comers. A woman in the Fragment (41K) of a comedy by Alexis of Thurioi complains that she had to sit in the outermost wedge like a foreigner, when she wanted to see the spectacles. A theater ticket has the name of the tribe Erechtheus.[52] These tickets are of bronze or lead, decorated with heads of Athena and other symbols, and often have letters according to the wedge in which the holder of the ticket was to sit (Fig. 270).[53] There is one letter for the first; there are two letters, one on each side, for the second; and two on each side for the third gallery. The latter are rare, as there were only ten short wedges, while the second gallery had fourteen full sections plus several outside sections curtailed by other structures, and the first gallery thirteen full-length sections. The ideal form would be such that each upper gallery would have twice as many wedges as the lower one.

This is the case in the theater of Epidaurus, which even in antiquity was considered to be the most harmonious and beautiful of all (Figs. 271-274).[54]

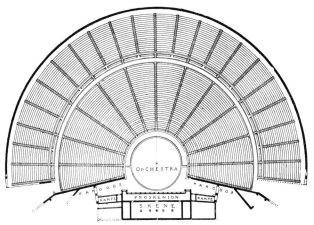

Fig. 271. Theater of Epidaurus. Plan

Fig. 272. Epidaurus, general view

Pausanias (ɪɪ,27,5) attributes this building to the architect Polycleitus. To his theater belongs the symmetrically-rounded auditorium with twelve sections and thirteen radiating staircases in the first gallery, twenty-two sections with twenty-three staircases in the second gallery. The orchestra is clearly marked as a complete circle by a limestone threshold laid around it. Its center is designated by a circular stone, probably the setting of a small altar. The passageway between the orchestra and the auditorium is deepened in its inner half 7½ inches to

Fig. 273. Theater of Epidaurus

form the water channel. The two outermost wedges of the auditorium are at the outer half of the passageway and are designed with a somewhat greater radius, so that they are not parallel to the curve of the orchestra circle. By this means the rows of seats in the outermost wedges are removed somewhat from the edge of the orchestra, and the passage widens out—a very important factor for the rapid emptying of the theater through the parodoi. Yet these outer sections are still turned to the orchestra, not to the skene, since they were constructed only for plays acted in the orchestra. The first row of seats around the orchestra and above the rounded passageway between the two galleries are the seats of honor. The earliest skene touched only the tangent of the circle formed by the lowest row of seats in the first gallery. Thus the early skene of Polycleitus served as no more than a background for the play. The foundations for the side rooms, the paraskenia, were later made into ramps for the Hellenistic proskenion. The fine doorways (Fig. 275) which loosely connect the corners of the skene with the retaining walls (the analemmata) of the auditorium may also belong to the fourth-century building.

Fig. 274. Epidaurus, orchestra and auditorium

The theater of Epidaurus shows in every respect the perfection of the architectural and dramatic ideas of the classical age. Every seat had an equally good view of the performance going on in the orchestra. It is a truly democratic theater with equal accommodation for every visitor.

Fig. 275. Epidaurus, Parodos Gate

The classical theater thus has four main periods of development. (1) In the time of Pisistratus and his sons an orchestra was built in the Agora, a temple and an altar in the sacred precinct of Dionysus. (2) In the time of Aeschylus and the early period of Sophocles an orchestra, wooden seats, and temporary decorations were erected in this precinct. Pericles built the odeum and the sustaining wall around the auditorium. (3) In the time of the peace of Nicias, during the Peloponnesian war, a stone hall and provision for a wooden paraskenion theater were erected. (4) In the later fourth century Lycurgus built the stone theatron and a stone paraskenion theater in Athens and Polycleitus the same in Epidaurus. With them the theatron achieved its final perfection. The scene building, on the other hand, found its first typical form only in the late classical period, while its development belongs to the Hellenistic period (see Ch. IX). The three component elements of the Greek theater: orchestra, skene, and theatron did not form a single architectural unit.

The most important thing to bear in mind when reading Greek plays is that in the classical age there was no such thing as a raised stage.

CHAPTER VI

SCENERY AND MECHANICAL DEVICES

DETAILED literary accounts of stage settings and scenery in the ancient theater are given by Vitruvius (*De Architectura*, v,6,8-9) and by Pollux (*Onomasticon*, IV,123-132). The latter writes, in addition, on the machinery of the theater. Since Vitruvius lived in the time of Julius Caesar and the emperor Augustus and had published his book on architecture about 16-13 B.C., while Pollux belongs to the period of the Emperor Commodus (A.D. 180-192), who made him teacher of rhetoric in Athens, there is the question as to how much of each account refers to its own period and how much goes back to the classical Greek period. The early Roman theater of the time of Vitruvius differed, of course, from the theater known to Pollux some two hundred years later. But both authors use earlier sources, and where both agree, they may refer to the classical theater. This is particularly true for such devices when referred to also in extant plays of the fifth century, or when their description agrees with classical buildings, vase paintings, or some of the scanty remains in the theaters themselves. I, therefore, have less doubt that these accounts may be traced back to the classical period than most of the authors who have used Vitruvius and Pollux for the problems regarding the decoration in the classical theater.[1]

Both authors speak of one main and two side doors (Pollux, IV,124; Vitruvius, v,6,8).[2] This is the largest number which can be inferred from the plays (see above, Ch. V, p. 66) and these, when the permanent skene had been put up in stone, proved to be the most generally useful. The middle door, representing the most distinguished and important building, was, of course, always richly decorated. The fact that the Periclean age is the time of a climax in art leads us to believe that the settings in this period must have had artistic value. Anti may be right when he uses the palace of Larissa on the Orontes for his reconstruction of the skene in Syracuse.[3] For a temple, Euripides in his *Ion* (vv. 184-218) gives an excellent description of the temple of Apollo at Delphi. It is, of course, always a question whether objects described by a poet were left to the imagination of the audience or also set before their eyes.

The background decoration was not set up as substantial architecture before the time of Lycurgus (see above, Ch. V, p. 60). Until then it consisted of a temporary structure leaning against the front wall of the stoa. A wooden structure served as a skeleton framework which was covered with movable scenery. Such coulisses are said to have been invented by Phormis or Phormus of Syracuse in the period of Gelo (485-478). These screens were, however, only skins, scraped, dried, and tinted red, thus a kind of parchment without pictures.[4] Pinakes, panels or tablets or canvasses in wooden frames, painted according to the requirements of the plays, are first mentioned for Aeschylus. They were painted by Agatharchus (Vitruvius, VII, praef. 11), and the research into perspective by Democritus and Anaxagoras was based on them.[5] The invention of scene-painting, skenographia, is credited to Sophocles (see Ch. II, p. 29). We may conceive of this scenery, on the evidence of the painting and drawing of the time, as being quite simple and showing no more than just the beginning of perspective and illusion. Nevertheless, it was of great importance for the development of perspective, for skenographia (σκηνογραφία) became identical with perspective. The backdrops or screens are called katablemata (καταβλήματα), throw-overs, wrappers, by Pollux (IV,131). As they could be thrown over the more permanent frame very quickly, the change of decoration which had to take place in the relatively short intermissions between the four plays on each festival day could be easily accomplished.[6] Vitruvius distinguishes among tragic, comic, and satyric settings according to the three forms of dramatic plays.

Sometimes the whole setting may have been painted on one large screen and placed before the wall of the skene. This was the scaena ductilis (Vitruvius, v,6,8), perhaps called proskenion (προσκήνιον) in the classical period. Antiphon (in Athenaeus, XIII,587b) compares the courtesan Nannion with a proskenion because she had a lovely face, much gold and expensive clothing, but when naked she was unusually ugly. In this case only a coulisse or movable screen, a scaena ductilis, can be intended, which, when drawn away, left the bare skeleton wall in view.[7] The reconstruction of the palace of Larissa may give an idea of such a painted scaena ductilis.[8] Several movable painted screens could be put up one behind the other, so that when the front one was pulled away, the one immediately behind appeared. This simple procedure might well go back to an earlier period. It is testified for the fourth century in the theater of Megalopolis (Fig. 276).[9] This theater of three tiers of regular shape, for about 21,000 spectators, is the largest theater on the Greek mainland. It has tracks coming out of a storeroom at the side, not only for one scaena ductilis, but for a whole wooden scene building which could be rolled out and in on wheels.

The katablemata could also be attached to the wing settings of the skene. These side scenes were called periaktoi (περίακτοι) and, like the scaena ductilis, certainly belong to the classical period.[10] Vitruvius (v,6,8), and Pollux (iv,126f, 130f) describe them as prisms, differently decorated on each of the three sides. Turning them indicated a change of scene. To indicate a different locality in the same town, it became a convention to turn only the right periaktos; to change the entire scene of the play, both were turned. The side entrances of the theater, the parodoi, which were near, either beside or in front of the periaktoi (see Fig. 281), had the same sort of symbolical significance. At the right or western one, the characters entered as if coming from the city or harbor; from the left or eastern one, as if coming from the country.[11]

No indubitable architectural trace of these periaktoi is actually found until the Hellenistic period. In the theater of Elis, at each of the points where we should expect the periaktoi, there is indeed a stone with a hole in the middle for a beam (Fig. 277).[12] In Pergamon, where contrivances for a wooden scene building were retained during the Hellenistic period on account of local conditions (see Ch. V, pp. 62f., Figs. 243-247),[13] there are similar holes for timbers arranged diagonally to the side. The periaktoi must have revolved around such beams, which were firmly fixed. Two large stones with a rounded hole for the inserting and turning of a pole, found in the theater of Dionysus in Athens, may be contrivances for periaktoi (Figs. 278-279).[14] A mental picture of these periaktoi may be reconstructed with the help of the Renaissance Telari stage (Ch. XVI, Fig. 840).[15] If the scenery of the three consecutive tragedies and of the satyr play were different, or even if a change of scene was required during a single drama, these side wings could be turned conveniently and quickly in the intervals between, and even during, the plays, since they were attached to revolving prisms. If more than three changes were required, as at the time of the Peloponnesian war, when a comedy also was produced in the same series, the pictures on the back face of the periaktoi could be changed without difficulty before the fourth alteration of the scene of the action. This seems to me so simple an arrangement and so suitable for an open-air theater, that I see no difficulty in placing its origin in the classical period.

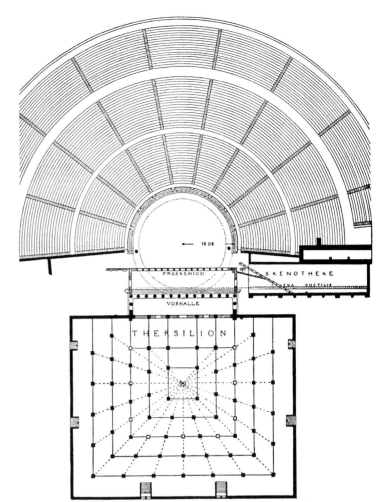

Fig. 276. Megalopolis; Plan with skenotheke for scaena ductillis

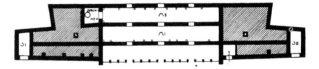

Fig. 277. Elis, plan of stage building with periaktoi

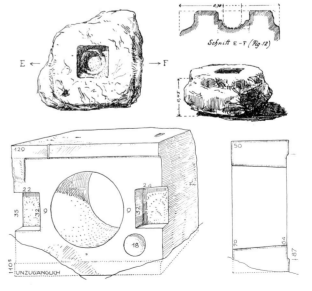

Figs. 278, 279. Stone sockets for poles

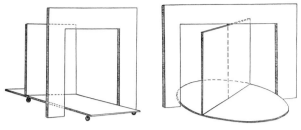

Fig. 280a-b. Possible forms of the eccyclema; Mahr

No device is better attested as belonging to the fifth century than the eccyclema (ἐκκύκλημα), the rolling machine, or movable platform; and none is more important for the *mise en scène* of Euripides' tragedies (Figs. 280a-b).[16] It is described in detail by Pollux (IV,128). According to the parodies of it in Aristophanes' *Acharnians* (vv. 395ff.), where Euripides himself is rolled out of his house, and the *Thesmophoriazousai* (vv. 95f. and 265), where Euripides induces the poet Agathon to be rolled out, it was a favorite device of Euripides for revealing an interior scene. It also could be used to show the results of actions in the interior of the house, when murdered people were wheeled out. It was, like the turning of the periaktoi, an expedient for the open-air theater. Since, owing to the tiered seats of the auditorium, a realistic picture of an indoor scene under a roof could not be given, it was necessary to resort to makeshifts. For instance, a throne on which a person sat, or a couch on which one lay, like Phaedra in Euripides' *Hippolytus* (see Fig. 281), was pushed or wheeled out on a podium and then represented the interior of a palace. The platform was circular or probably mostly semicircular, and perhaps sometimes square. It may well have been manipulated by moving on a pivot in somewhat the same way as the modern revolving stage, of which the eccyclema is a modest forerunner. In any case, the doors opened as the setting was wheeled out, and closed as it disappeared again. For this purpose flat screens which could be shifted to the side, in other words, the scaena ductilis in combination with the eccyclema, would have been particularly useful.[17]

Evidence for the use of the flying machine in the fifth century B.C. is given in the parodies of Aristophanes' *Peace* (performed 421 B.C.), and *Thesmophoriazousae* (411 B.C.).[18] Trygaios in the *Peace* (vv. 174ff.) flies to heaven on a dung-beetle and appeals to the scene shifter or mechanician not to let him fall. Euripides appears on the flying machine in the *Thesmophoriazousae* (vv. 1098ff.) to free his father-in-law or brother-in-law, who is held prisoner by the women. The first passage is a parody of Euripides' *Bellerophon*, the second of Perseus in Euripides' *Andromeda*. Both these heroes are mentioned in Pollux (IV,128) as using the flying machine, a proof that this and some others of the mechanical contrivances named by Pollux may actually be ascribed to the fifth century. The extensive use of the flying machine is testified by the comic poet Antiphanes (Fragment 191, 13-16 K), who says that the tragic poets lift up a machine as readily as they lift a finger, when they haven't anything more to say.

Euripides certainly made ample use of the flying machine for his *deus ex machina* (θεὸς ἀπὸ μηχανῆς) who often appeared over the scene building at the close of the play. He seems to have used the flying machine first in the *Medea* (produced 431 B.C.), which gave him an effective exodus for his heroine. Then he used the flying machine for the *deus ex machina* probably for the first time in the *Hippolytus* (performed 428 B.C.), and here he has even two appearances, Aphrodite in the beginning and Artemis at the end (Figs. 281-282).[19] I think it possible that the large base T, used originally for entrance porches (see above, Figs. 238-239), but later inside the wooden scene building (see Figs. 254-259), could be used as a base for the crane which lifted the goddesses and deposited them on the roof, either of the palace, sometimes called theologeion, or of their shrines. These shrines were probably the paraskenia, the side-buildings, opening up with columns, which were lower than the main skene. The shrine of Artemis must have been to the left, as

Figs. 281, 282. Plan and sections of scenery and machinery for Euripides' *Hippolytus*, according to Bieber

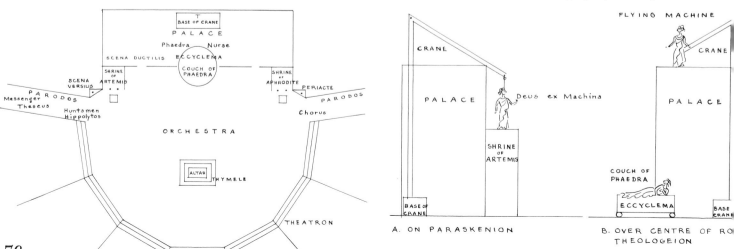

Hippolytus coming with his huntsmen from the country, through the left parodos, offers wreath and prayer to Artemis before going into the palace. Probably there were painted periaktoi between the shrines and the entrances of the parodoi, which had the same significance as these. The left one may have shown the countryside, in which Hippolytus has been hunting and of which Phaedra raves; while the right suggested the city from which the chorus, living in town, enters. Euripides probably also used the eccyclema in this play, for Phaedra lies on a couch when first seen, probably pushed or wheeled out by the nurse and a maid. The same couch may have been used at the end of the play to carry the body of Hippolytus indoors. Perhaps the scaena ductilis was used at the same time to open the central door, when the couch was moved through it. Euripides won one of his rare victories with the *Hippolytus*, and it may be due partly to these many innovations used here for the first time. They certainly contributed to the new plan of a scene building executed soon afterwards during the peace with Sparta under Nicias (Fig. 237).[20]

An early Apulian vase in the Metropolitan Museum of Art in New York (Fig. 283),[21] may be a reminiscence of the impressive use of the flying machine for carrying a body through the air. Here it is the body of Sarpedon whom Sleep (Hypnos) and Death (Thanatos) have lifted from the battlefield and bring home to his mother Europa. Europa, in the long-sleeved tragic robe and oriental cap, such as Andromeda and Medea wear (see Figs. 110, 111b, 121, 122a), sits under a porch, surrounded by younger children or servants who, like her, look up at the apparition. Perhaps this is a recollection of the representation of an Euripidean drama, treating the story of the death of Sarpedon. Aeschylus

Fig. 283. Europa's son Sarpedon, carried through the air by Hypnos and Thanatos. Apulian vase, Metropolitan Museum

had already used the subject in his *Kares* or *Europa*. The other side of the vase shows Thetis standing before Hephaestus, who is seated beside Aphrodite on a couch inside his workshop. The presence of Eros alluding to the infidelity of Aphrodite and the pathetic gesture of the woman to the right, again bring to mind a Euripidean drama, while the subject had already been treated by Aeschylus in his *Nereids*, the second play in his trilogy *Myrmidons*, *Nereids*, and *Phryges*, also in the *Redeeming of Hector*.

While the base T might have been used for the crane of the flying machine, tracks for a flying machine might have been preserved over the arched passage in the scene house of Eretria (Figs. 284-288).[22] Unfortunately, however, the marble blocks containing these tracks have long since disappeared, and the architectural remains belong with the proskenion (logeion) to the Hellenistic age. In any

Fig. 284. Eretria, view of orchestra with Charonian staircase

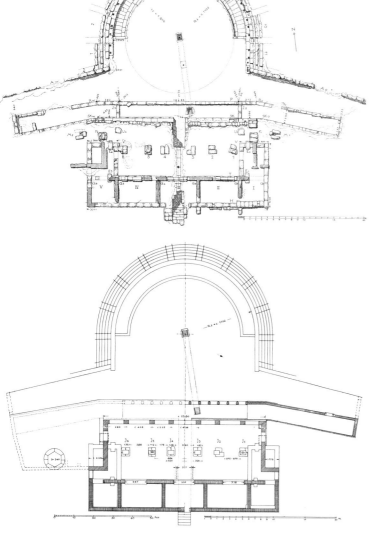

situated farther back and on a much higher level, but it is now destroyed. We, therefore, have no proof that the arrangement was originally there.[23] We have, however, abundant evidence for phantoms even in Aeschylus: the ghost of Darius in the *Persians* and the ghost of Clytemnestra in the *Eumenides*, as well as the assertion in his *Vita* (§14) and in Pollux (IV,132) that he astonished his spectators by magnificent fittings, paintings, mechanical devices, and ghostly apparitions.[24] For the fourth century we have the ghost of Aeetes in the post-Euripidean tragedy *Medea*, as testified by the Munich vase (Fig. 289; cf. Fig. 121). The Charonian staircase thus certainly goes back to a classical tradition. The earlier ghosts may have appeared not in the center but at the edge of the classical orchestra, as seems to be indicated by the Medea vase. The theater of Corinth had two Charonian staircases at each end of the front of the Hellenistic proskenion, with which they are contemporary (Fig. 728a-b).[25] Sometimes only the heads or the upper part of persons emerged from the ground.[26]

During all of the classical period the most diverse architectural features had to be built of wood according to the demands of the plays—different walls, turrets, and watch towers (see Figs. 240-242, 261). The distegia (διστεγία), the upper story, is mentioned by Pollux (IV,129) as being used in Euripides' *Phoenicians* (vv. 90ff.), whence Antigone looks down on the army. The houses in Aristophanes' *Ecclesiazousae* (v. 698 and v. 961) also had upper stories, from the windows of which the women look down.[27]

Figs. 285, 286. Eretria, plan of remains, and restoration; Fiechter

case the position of the grooves, above and in the center, corresponds to the spot where, at the end of Euripides' plays, the *deus ex machina* was bound to appear. This speaking place for the gods (theologeion, θεολογεῖον) may have been occasionally a high platform built of wood, as for the *Psychostasia*, the "Weighing of Souls" by Aeschylus mentioned by Pollux (IV,130). The *deus ex machina* could, however, also appear over a side building (see Fig. 282 for the *Hippolytus*).

An underground passage ending in a staircase served, according to Pollux (IV,132), as Charonian steps (Χαρώνιοι κλίμακες), a subterranean staircase for ghostly apparitions. Such an arrangement was discovered well preserved, but belonging with the proskenion to the Hellenistic period, in the theater of Eretria (Figs. 284-288). This passage starts at the Hellenistic proskenion, continues underground, and opens up in the center of the orchestra of the same Hellenistic period. The fourth-century orchestra was

Figs. 287, 288. Eretria, plan and section of earlier and later theater; Flickinger

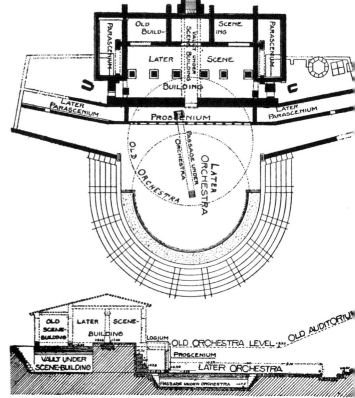

In addition to the backgrounds, side decorations, and mechanical devices, a number of properties such as altars, tombs, statues of gods, hills, rocks and cliffs were needed and were used even before the erection of the wooden skene. They were sometimes so large that there was room for the entire chorus on or about them (Figs. 228-229). This, however, does not mean, as Wilamowitz and Noack believed, that there was constructed an Aeschylean permanent "Chorpodium" or stage for the chorus.[28] The plays of Aeschylus are so far from being conventionalized in any way that I cannot conceive of stereotyped arrangements for his theater. It is also not feasible to assume typical forms for Sophocles, Euripides, and Aristophanes.[29]

Not until the drama after Euripides had received an established form did the background and the equipment with its manipulations become conventional. The evolution of the scenery follows slowly that of the background building, which itself follows only gradually the requirements of the plays.

Fig. 289. The Ghost of Aeetes. From the Medea vase (Fig. 121)

CHAPTER VII

THE EVOLUTION OF THE ART OF ACTING

See Figs. 310, 297

THE function of the actor was differentiated from that of the poet late in the history of the ancient theater. Acting reached its peak among the Greeks in the fourth century B.C. and among the Romans in the first century B.C. When Thespis, disguised as a god or a hero according to the role he had to play, stepped forward to answer (ὑποκρίνεσθαι) the chorus, he became a hypocrite (ὑποκριτής), an answerer, and thus created the first actor simultaneously with the first tragedy around the middle of the sixth century. In the oldest cyclic lyrical chorus for Dionysus, the dithyramb, the poet himself was the leader of the chorus, the exarchos (ἔξαρχος). At the time of Bacchylides, in the early fifth century, the leader of the chorus, the coryphaeus (κορυφαῖος) still answered the questions of the chorus, for example, in the dithyramb concerned with the character and deeds of the Attic national hero Theseus.[1]

Aeschylus, too, was his own chief actor, but he had to train a second actor, since he replaced the interchange of question and answer between actor and chorus with a dialogue between two characters. The old usage of a dialogue between chorus and actor, however, lived on for a long time. In the *Suppliants* and in the *Persians* of Aeschylus one actor addresses the chorus more frequently than he does the other actor. When an actor entered through the parodos he always met the chorus first, and thus, following the old habit, he addressed the chorus first.[2] Then the importance of the actor steadily increased, after Sophocles had introduced the third actor whom Aeschylus at once adopted. Sophocles appeared in a few roles of his earlier plays only in his youth, until about 460 B.C. Then a complete separation of the activities of the poet and of the actor was achieved. The poets, beginning with Sophocles, strove to have regard for the in-dividuality of the professional actors in their plays.[3] Aeschylus first employed Kleandros and later Mynniskos. Sophocles preferred Tlepolemos. The choice in the early period lay chiefly in the hands of the poets.[4] The acting was done with free and expressive gesticulations and movements of the whole body[5] (see Figs. 291-294).

In 449 B.C. the actor became independent of the poet, and his choice, like that of the tragedies, depended upon the state. The archon selected three actors and apportioned them to the three poets. Each of the chief actors or protagonists (πρωταγωνισταί) engaged the two subordinate, supporting actors under him, who later were called the second and third agonists, contestants (συναγωνισταί) or the deuteragonists (δευτεραγωνισταί) and the tritagonists (τριταγωνισταί). In the fifth century each group of three actors played for one poet; for example, in 418 B.C. Callippides acted in all three tragedies of Callistratus, and Lysicrates in all three tragedies of another poet.[6] The three protagonists, however, became independent of the prize-winning tragedies and competed for their own prizes. This contest of actors was introduced in addition to the contest of poets in the year 449 B.C. at the festival of the great City Dionysia, and about 432 B.C. at the festival of the Lenaea for tragic actors, while it was introduced for comic actors at the Lenaea in 442 B.C.[7] Since the allotment of good actors increased the chances of the poet and *vice versa*, this system was changed in the fourth century. Each actor played in one drama of each poet. Thereby the strength of the actor was spared, since it was certainly a great strain for the same actor to hold the principal roles in three tragedies all on the same day on which he might possibly appear in a satyr drama as well. It is not improbable, however, that in this last play he gave

Figs. 290-294. Tragic actors. Terracotta statuettes. 290, Heracles, from Amisus (Samsun), Louvre; 291, 292a-b, Youths in tragedy, from Myrina, Vienna, and from Asia Minor, Athens; 293, 294; Messengers of tragedy, from Rheneia, Mykonos, and from (probably) Pergamon, Berlin

the more difficult roles to his supporting fellows. The art of acting gained variety through this assignment of the great actors to the several representations. We know for example, that in the year 341, at the Lenaean festival, three noted actors played for Astydamas: Thettalus acted in *Achilles*, the first tragedy; Neoptolemus in *Athamas*, the second; and Athenodorus in *Antigone*, the third drama. These same actors had parts in the three plays of the two other dramatists.[8] Neoptolemus was the victor in 341, Thettalus in 340 B.C.

The protagonist probably dealt out the different roles in collaboration with the trainer of the chorus (chorodidaskalos, χοροδιδάσκαλος), who was in earlier times the poet himself. While the number of actors was limited to three, the ever-increasing number of characters must have made the assignments of the roles difficult. Sometimes they could not be made satisfactorily, and the state or the choregus had to add at their own expense a fourth actor to the three regularly furnished by the state. This fourth actor was a supernumerary (parachoregema, παραχορήγημα).[9] Sometimes the latter had a speaking part, sometimes he sang, but more often he played only a mute role. Children were also sometimes necessary, as for example in Euripides, Astyanax in *The Trojan Women* and the children of *Alcestis*, the daughters of *Oedipus the King* in Sophocles, and the children of Trygaios in Aristophanes' *Peace*.[10] Animals were also sometimes necessary, such as the horses drawing the car which brings in Agamemnon in Aeschylus' *Agamemnon* or the donkey on which Xanthias rides in Aristophanes' *Frogs*. Often the same role had to be enacted by several actors. In such cases the costume, enveloping the whole figure, was of great assistance in concealing the change of actor.[11]

Since comedy was played at first voluntarily by nonprofessional actors, the number of actors in the beginning was in no way limited. Here, too, the dramatist was at the same time an actor; for example, the comedian Crates, when a young man, played in a production of Cratinus.[12] In the older

comedies, just as in the tragedies, the chorus held a place of importance, and probably held it for a longer time. The members of the chorus, however, were not looked upon as actors, either in the comedies or in the tragedies, since they were citizens supplied by the tribes, costumed according to the needs of the play. They were paid by the choregus and coached by the chorus trainer. Not until 486 B.C. did the state concern itself with comedy. A contest between the comic actors at the Lenaea occurred perhaps for the first time about 442, and certainly was in existence after about 422, but at the festival of the great City Dionysia it did not occur until after about 325 B.C.[13] After this time the number of comic actors decreased, though previously their number had usually been greater than in the tragedies. In the *Lysistrata* (vv. 78ff), four speaking actors are needed on the scene of action at the same time. Since single comedies, and not trilogies, were presented, it was easier to find actors for comedy than for tragedy.

The religious, impersonal costume enveloping the entire figure was a hindrance to the unfolding of the personality in tragedy even more than in comedy. Facial expression, especially, was hidden by the mask. Since the representational art of the fifth century, however, with few exceptions—the pediment figures from the temple of Zeus in Olympia, the wall paintings by Polygnotus, and the vase by Pistoxenus—did not express feelings and passions by the play of the features, but rather through the posture and movements of the whole body, we may conclude that the art of acting in the fifth and in the following centuries also laid the greatest emphasis on these methods. In addition, the actor had not only to master the art of speaking, but he had to be able to declaim and sing to music. Singing and reciting were accompanied by the flute. The lyre was reserved for special odes or solos, as when Sophocles sang the role of Thamyras (see above, Fig. 104). Aeschylus and Euripides in the *Frogs* of Aristophanes also sang to the lyre. Clearness of voice and correct enunciation were more important than a

Figs. 295-299. Comic Actors. Terracotta statuettes (295, bronze). 296, excited; 297, running; 298, angry; 299, running

Fig. 300a-b. Actors of tragedy, studying their masks. Wall painting, Naples; Marble relief, Vienna

strong voice, as the splendid acoustics in the Greek theater let spoken word and song reach the uppermost rows. Usually each actor had to play more than one part, especially if he was a second or third actor, since all plays had a larger number of dramatis personae than the number of actors available. The actor, therefore, had to adapt and change to the personality and mood of the different characters which he represented, not only his mask, costume and movements, but also his voice, to suit the different male and female roles. Occasionally he had even to dance or rave in ecstasy or madness, for example, Agave in Euripides' *Bacchae* and Heracles in his *Madness of Heracles* (Figs. 114 and 479). Voice and gesture had to fit the size of the theater. One can expect strong and simple motions in tragedy (Figs. 290-294)[14] and lively exaggerated motions in comedy (Figs. 295-299).[15] Running and violent gesticulation with the arm are the rule.[16]

The mask facilitated the submergence of the individual personality of the actor in that of the character represented. The actors are sometimes represented studying the mask, which had to express the outstanding features of the personality represented. This may be seen in a wall painting in

Naples (Fig. 300a), in the relief from Athens in Lyme Park, Stockport, dated ca. 380 B.C. (Fig. 201), and in reliefs in Vienna (Fig. 300b) and Naples.[17] The mask (Fig. 301),[17a] being the most important part of the actor's costume, was dedicated in sanctuaries of Dionysus (Fig. 302).[18] The onlooker of the fifth century B.C. certainly saw only the images created by the dramatists, the personalities of the heroes, and not the tragic actors presenting their roles. A good example of a tragic mask copied probably from the fifth-century type is the mask of a bearded hero in the hand of a muse at Mantua, which is copied from a late fifth-century type (Figs. 303-304).[19] The tragic masks remained dignified in the fourth century and even in the Hellenistic times, as can be seen from the mask of Heracles held by the muse Melpomene in the Vatican (Fig. 305).[20] The

Fig. 302. Actor of tragedy. Wall painting, Naples

Fig. 301. Colossal tragic mask, found in the Piraeus. Bronze, Hellenistic, found in a warehouse probably burnt during Sulla's attack of 86 B.C.

actors appeared even through the mask. Famed actors were held in the highest honor. They were granted privileges and were even selected for diplomatic embassies. They received the help and protection of sovereigns and leading personalities of states, just as the poets in other periods received them. Aristodemus, for example, was invited to the court of Philip of Macedon, and Thettalus to the court of Alexander the Great; and they were sent on important political missions.[24]

Of course, only highly distinguished actors of the first rank were treated with such honor. The mediocre actor, such as the rhetor Aeschines had been in his youth, was a laughing stock and, as was common in all ages, his morals were under suspicion (Demosthenes, *De Corona*, 262).[25] Only a few attained real fame and received high salaries, after they had won in one of the prize contests, which are recorded on inscriptions along with the victories of the poets. It was probably through the influence of prominent

Figs. 303, 305. Muse of Tragedy. Mantua; Vatican

Fig. 304. Mask of 303   Fig. 306a-b. Actor holding tragic mask. Vase fragment from Tarentum, Würzburg

mask on the fragment of a crater found in Tarentum and now in Würzburg, held by an actor garbed in a short chiton, is that of a strong and handsome hero in the prime of life, with blond hair and beard (Fig. 306a-b).[21] The mask in the hand of an actor on a relief in Copenhagen is that of a young and serious woman.[22]

In the fourth century the high level of dramatic writing was slowly lowered to be succeeded by the elevation of the art of acting. Aristotle (*Ars Rhetorica*, III,1,4, p. 1403b33, cf. *De Arte Poetica* XIX,1456b) states that in his time the actor counts for more in the contests than the dramatist.[23] This is due to the development of interest in the individual which characterized the fourth century, in contrast to the fifth, when the emphasis was laid on the general and the typical. In this period for the first time the personality of the dramatists and their

leading actors that performances of the old tragedies of Aeschylus, Sophocles, and Euripides, which offered opportunities for effective characterization, took a definite place beside the new tragedies in the annual program of the festival of the great City Dionysia. Euripides was particularly popular.[26] Neoptolemus revived and acted in the *Iphigenia in Tauris* of Euripides in 341, and in the *Orestes* of the same poet in 340 B.C.[27] Polus played the role of Electra in the tragedy of Sophocles just after the death and cremation of his son. During the scene in which Electra bewails the supposed death of her brother Orestes (*Electra*, vv. 1126ff.), Polus carried the urn containing the ashes of his son in his arms and played the scene with such a depth of feeling that his audience was deeply stirred (Plutarch, *Demosthenes*, 28,p.848B; Gellius, *Noctes atticae*, VI-VII,5). His rendering of *Oedipus the King* and of

Oedipus at Colonus is also praised as impressive (Plutarch, *De Amicitia*, VII). Polus played in 306 for Demetrius Poliorcetes after his victory at Salamis.[28] The great actors began to modify the plays of the classical dramatists in order to create more effective and striking roles. The statesman Lycurgus, who had finished the theater in marble and set up the statues of the three great tragic poets, put an end to this abuse by depositing in the archives state copies of the classical tragedies. Failure to conform with these was punished by severe penalties. It is said that Alexander the Great himself paid the fine for the actor Lycon (Plutarch, *Alexander*, 29,3).[29]

Beginning with the early third century B.C., the actors were organized into guilds, called the union of the Dionysiac artists (οἱ περὶ τὸν Διόνυσον τεχνῖται σύνοδος or κοινόν).[30] A protagonist, a leading actor, or a musician, often a flutist who was at the same time a priest of Dionysus, was at their head. Such a leader of the troupe is probably the one on the wall painting found in Herculaneum, now in Naples (Fig. 302), who dedicates his mask inside a folding frame, while a kneeling woman is writing, probably a dedicatory inscription, on the pillar carrying the dedication.[31] This protagonist must have played some young hero in a white-sleeved robe with a broad golden belt, a purple mantle, and white shoes with red laces. He has double soles instead of the single sole given by Aeschylus to his actors, and thus the original votive tablet, from which this wall painting is copied, must belong to the Hellenistic period. The onkos on the mask is also higher than it used to be in the classical period (Figs. 32, 34, 74, 90, 304, 306). Long brown locks fall from the onkos onto the forehead and the shoulders. The complexion is light brown. One can see distinctly that the mask comprises also the rear part of a head. The actor must have just taken it off, for his own hair is disheveled. Another such leader of a guild who wears the costume of Dionysus is on a relief in

Fig. 307. A leader of an actor's guild in sacred precinct. Marble relief, Dresden

Dresden, which is dated in the later Hellenistic period (Fig. 307).[32] He wears the nebris, the skin of a doe, and has a wreath of ivy, the sacred plant of the god. His soles have four layers, as the cothurnus was continuously added to during the Hellenistic and Roman periods. An old drawing shows still more clearly a curtain, rocky soil, a pillar, altar, and cult-statue indicating that this actor-priest is seated in a closed sacred precinct. He is enthroned on an elegant chair, such as were set up in the theater of Lycurgus (see above, Figs. 267-269). He looks up to a woman whose movement cannot be explained, as her upper part is lost. On the other side stands a small flute-playing boy.

To the union belonged the actors of tragedy, comedy, and satyr play as well as dramatic, epic, and lyric poets, teachers (didascali, διδάσκαλοι) of actors and of the chorus, stage managers, costumers, trumpeters, heralds, members of the chorus, dancers, and musicians of every kind: soloists and accompanists, such as singers, rhapsodes, citharodes, citharists, and flute-players. The troupe of performers presented plays which had been tried out in the great Athenian festivals of Dionysus. They produced epic, dramatic, and lyric plays, old as well as new tragedies and comedies, and even purely musical presentations and declamations to music. An inscription dated 254 B.C., found in the market place of Athens, shows that the actors competed in a contest of old plays, old tragedy, old comedy, and old satyr play. The continuation of satyr play even in the later Hellenistic period is evidenced by literary sources and by a relief of which six copies exist. Two satyrs are led by a leader, while a muse seated under a tree in a sacred precinct holds on her knees a mask of a serious character (Fig. 308).[33]

The guilds were called to the residences of the Hellenistic rulers and to the great sanctuaries, particularly Delphi, but Pythian and Olympian festivals were introduced in many places. However versatile they were, the guilds always remained religious organizations, and as such were respected and protected even in times of war. The actors were exempt from military service and from taxes.[34] As they were allowed to emigrate to all parts, they took the classical masterpieces of Athens to the entire ancient world. They thus contributed much toward the circulation and preservation of classical drama in the east as well as in Italy. The most important guilds were those of Athens, of Thebes, the Isthmian and Nemean guild, the Ionian guild whose center was at Teos, and the guild of artists of Egypt, at Ptolemais in Egypt.[35]

In Hellenistic times the art of acting took on ever more lifelike and human forms, paralleling the de-

Fig. 308. Muse and satyr chorus in a sacred precinct. Marble relief, Naples

(Fig. 293) represents a traveller in distress and exasperation. Another statuette from Pergamon (Fig. 294) with a large tragic onkos, lifts his head and gesticulates with tensely outstretched arm. He may be a messenger bringing some important and exciting news. The gesticulations of the Old as well as of New Hellenistic comedy are even more lively and unrestrained than in tragedy (Figs. 295-299).[38] The two literary forms of comedy and tragedy were thus sharply separated from each other also by the different modes of acting.[39]

The tragic masks in the Hellenistic period have a more lively expression than those of the classical period (Figs. 32, 34, 74, 90, 113b, 304-306). Thus the terracotta mask in Berlin (Fig. 309) of an old bald man with wrinkled forehead, heavy eyebrows, and bent nose shows vigor and intense thinking, while that of King Priam, said to have been found in Thebes, now also in Berlin, with a bluish Phrygian cap, reddish brown hair and beard, and blue iris, exhibits in his raised eyebrows and emaciated cheeks excruciating torment and terror (Fig. 310).[40] On a marble frieze found in Pergamon masks of tragedy and comedy are inserted in a dionysiac ivy garland (Figs. 311-313, cf. Ch. VIII, Fig. 380).[41] The mask of Heracles (Fig. 311) with many curls and savage expression is contrasted to that of an old woman with similar curls, but with a wrinkled face, crumpled skin, and meagre cheeks, from which the cheekbones stand out (Fig. 312). She looks fearful and terrorized. A young woman with slightly waved, parted hair ending in twisted locks looks astonished and apprehensive (Fig. 313). The over-life-size mask in the Piraeus (Frontispiece and Fig. 301) has the grandiose style of the Pergamon frieze.

velopment of literature, in which New Comedy became most important. Characteristic is the story of the actor Apollogenes, who in the third century B.C. impersonated Heracles, Achilles, Antaeus, and Alexander in tragedy, but won, in addition, a boxing victory in Alexandria. We can, therefore, understand why he preferred roles in which he could display his bodily strength and perfect physical training.[36] The contest for actors furthered the perfection of professional skill and virtuosity. Terracotta statuettes from the Hellenistic period of tragic actors wearing masks depict the lively gesticulations of the actors.[37] The bearded actor with the mask and club of Heracles, a high Hellenistic belt, and high soles (Fig. 290) has restrained motion. The statuettes of the youth in tragedy, from Asia Minor (Figs. 291-292), represent him as inclining his head to the side as if in the greatest consternation and grief. The way his hand grasps the folds of the mantle from the inside depicts emotional turmoil. He also has high soles below his sandals. A statuette from Delos

Figs. 309, 310. Tragic masks of old man, Priam. Terracotta

Figs. 311-313. Masks of Heracles, old woman, young woman. Marble frieze, Pergamon

The lively expression of the masks in the Hellenistic period is a parallel to the evolution of realistic portraiture, which arose in the fourth century and created psychological masterpieces in the Hellenistic age. This can be seen in the features of the faces of the actors (Figs. 290, 300, 302, 306-307) which are very expressive, although during the play they were hidden under the mask and the movements alone transmitted the emotions. Particularly the graying actor on the fragment in Würzburg (Fig. 306b) is in contrast to the mask which he holds, a fine psychological study of an older man with disheveled hair and closely-cropped beard, gazing intensively on the mask of the handsome hero he has to personify.

The interest in the mask was displaced by the interest in the individual actor. Therefore the players probably appeared at the end of the performance without masks as we see in the Würzburg fragment. The chorus of the dithyramb was always sung without masks. It was no longer a tribal contest of amateurs, but was taken over in the Hellenistic period by professional technitae ($\tau\epsilon\chi\nu\hat{\iota}\tau\alpha\iota$). The tendency to show the actual features and not a mask found a desired field of activity in a new Hellenistic type of drama, the mime, which was played without masks and this made facial expression possible.[42] In the mime women for the first time were allowed to appear upon the stage. Their mimetic art is usually especially expressive.

CHAPTER VIII

NEW COMEDY · MENANDER

See Figs.
336, 366

NEW COMEDY[1] replaced Middle Comedy about 330 B.C., that is, approximately at the time of Alexander the Great. Middle Comedy had already shown an increasing tendency to turn from political themes to those of daily life. The courtesan, especially, seems to have played an important role, just as she did in life. The chorus declined more and more in importance[2] as testified by the *Plutus*, a late work of Aristophanes which belongs to Middle Comedy. The chorus developed to an interlude, sung and danced by a group of men without a written chorus song, announced only by "chorou" (χοροῦ), part of the chorus. All these traits are found in New Comedy with added force. The cause of these changes was the greatly altered political situation. Athens was no longer an independent democracy, but was a province under the domination of Macedonia. Accordingly, the freedom of speech, of which Aristophanes had availed himself so liberally, no longer existed. Athens had become a small university town. In comparison with the large new capitals of the successors of Alexander, it was of no political importance whatever. It remained to the end of antiquity the center of art, science, philosophy, and rhetoric, but life became comfortable, commonplace, and even Philistine. The sorrows, joys, manners, and peculiarities of individual citizens took the foreground. As more attention was paid to personal character in life, it therefore played a more prominent role in comedy also. The mode of living was, however, also influenced by the new Stoic and Epicurean philosophies, and they, too, influenced the poets of New Comedy.

It is hardly surprising that tragedy developed no further but continued in its old course. The works of the famous poets of the fifth century had become classics, which, it was supposed, could not be improved upon. They were chosen by great actors to be played in Athens and in many other places at festivals, where the actors gained praise for their revivals (see Ch. VII, Figs. 306-307). The many tragedies which were still written and presented each year were not permitted to vary from the accustomed pattern. Old Comedy, on the other hand, had waned and died together with political freedom, and was never resuscitated. In its stead a new comedy was created which was just as characteristic of the Hellenistic period as tragedy had been of the fifth century. It represents in endless variety the conditions existing among the higher, wealthy bourgeoisie, with delicate shades and nuances in the character sketches.

The most important poet of New Comedy is Menander (343/2-292/1).[3] The tradition of Middle Comedy was handed down to him by his uncle Alexis. He had enjoyed the benefit of an excellent education. He attended the lectures of Theophrastus, whose book of *Characters* with its sharply etched presentations of human types probably appeared about 320 B.C. and undoubtedly influenced the psychological descriptions, observations, and analyses of character by Menander and other writers of New Comedy. Menander put in his required year of military service as an ephebus (that is, a citizen between eighteen and twenty years of age) with his friend Epicurus, who was of the same age (συνέφηβος). The new philosophy founded by Epicurus left deep marks on the comedies of Menander. It has nothing in common with the later interpretation of merely deriving all possible pleasure from life; instead it preached an ideal of freedom from pain and imperturbable serenity and tranquility in suffering. Menander in his later years may have known Zeno, the founder of the philosophy of the Stoa. From him he learned to bear calamities and difficulties courageously. Menander became also a friend of another pupil of Theophrastus, Demetrius of Phaleron, who later became the ruler of Athens. This friendship became a source of danger to Menander after the fall of Demetrius. Ptolemy I tried to draw Menander to his court in Alexandria, but the poet refused to leave Athens, and he is said to have declined also an invitation to Macedonia. He lived all his life in Athens and died while bathing in the sea at the Piraeus.

Menander wrote more than one hundred comedies over a period of about thirty-three years. His first work was the *Self-Tormentor* (ʽΕαυτὸν τιμωρούμενος), which he wrote around 322 B.C., at about the age of twenty. His first victory, so the Parian marble chronicle informs us, was won with the *Anger* (ʼΟργή) in 316/5. Only eight victories are said to have been won by Menander in his lifetime. The recently discovered *The Sullen Man* (Dyskolos, Δύσκολος) was presented in 316. The best of the plays partially preserved today is the *Arbitrants* (Epitrepontes, ʼΕπιτρέποντες), which shows unusually refined character portrayal. The fate of the person is depicted as depending, both theoretically and practically, upon his character (see lines 880-887). Other surviving scenes come from the *Girl from Samos* (Samia, Σαμία), the *Girl Who Gets her Hair Cut* (Perikeiromene, Περικειρο-μένη) *The Hated Man* (Misoumenos, Μισούμενος) and the *Hero* (Ἥρως). We may add meager fragments of some sixty comedies by Menander and fragments from Menander's contemporaries and followers, such as Philemon, Diphilus, Posidippus, and Apollodorus, but also the translations and adaptations of Greek New Comedy for which we are indebted to Latin writers (see Ch. XI, pp. 148-156). We have twenty-one comedies by Plautus, who began to write some fifty years after Menander's death (Plautus died in 184 B.C.). He was, however, strongly influenced also by local Italian farces. Terence (died 159) approximates more nearly the original Greek Comedy, and, in fact, he is called a "half Menander" by Caesar ("O dimidiate Menander," Suetonius, *Vita Terenti*, v). Of the six surviving comedies of Terence, performed 166-160 B.C., four are based on Menander. These are: the *Lady of Andros* (Andria, Ἀνδρία) combined with *Girl of Perinthos* (Perinthia, Περινθία); the *Self-Tormentor* (Heauton Timoroumenos, Ἑαυτὸν τιμωρούμενος); the *Eunuch* from the *Eunuch* (Ἐννοῦχος) combined with the *Flatterer* (the Kolax, Κόλαξ) of Menander; and the *Brothers* (Adelphi, Ἀδελφοί). The remaining two plays of Terence are copied from plays by Apollodorus of Carystus: *Phormio* from the *Plaintiff* (Epidikazomenos, Ἐπιδικαζόμενος) and the *Mother-in-Law* from *Hecyra* (Ἑκυρά).

The works of Menander show the influence of Euripides in their dramatic action, the substance of which this tragic poet had humanized and brought down to earth. Menander presented for the first time real individuals in ordinary situations taken from life as he observed them in the contemporary life of the rich middle class of Athens. One main motif is the love of the rich youth for a poor girl, who in many cases has been abandoned as a baby, has been reared in modest circumstances, has remained a decent girl, and is at the end reunited with her long lost parents, and in a happy ending is married to her lover. This situation is not quite as strange as it seems to us today, for in Athens abandonment of unwanted children was allowed. Yet the plots are by no means monotonous. They are varied according to the qualities of the persons involved. The characters are differentiated with vivid individual traits. Whereas Aristophanes often changes the character of an individual arbitrarily, Menander sticks to the pattern he has created for each of his characters. He never paints them black or white but with fine nuances, and he recognizes their right to assume different attitudes in different situations. He shows tolerance for feminine guilt as well as for weakness and ridiculous habits of men. He likes people as they are with all their faults and stupidities.

This human attitude and the refinement of his art hampered the success of Menander during his lifetime. Later, however, he was highly estimated. The grammarian Aristophanes placed him second only to Homer, as reported in the epigram on a herm in Turin (Fig. 314): "Not without reason have I placed you, dear Menander, alongside and opposite the gaze of the head of Homer, inasmuch as the wise grammarian Aristophanes, excellent judge of your writings, gave you second place immediately after that great genius."[4] Plutarch preferred him to Aristophanes ("Comparison of Aristophanes and Menander," in *Moralia*, 853A-854D). In the imperial period, however, interest in his work was confined mostly to his clever philosophical sayings, which were collected in anthologies as gnomai, sentences. In later Roman times Aristophanes was preferred to Menander, because of his purer and more classical Attic. Among the Latin imitations of Menander there is unfortunately no play whose Greek model has come down to us. Nevertheless it is possible, from the remains of the plays of Menander, to see how much more refined Menander is than Plautus and how much more powerful than Terence. The best point of comparison lies in the characters of Menander's soldiers, parasites, courtesans, and slaves, all of whom have much better characters and are more amiable than those of his Latin followers.

While Menander and his colleagues wrote mostly plays dealing with the life of Athenian citizens, they also composed some travesties of the heroic saga. Thus Diphilus wrote four, Philemon wrote two parodies of tragedy; one, named the *Myrmidons*, certainly dealt with Achilles whose Thracian subjects were called by this name. The same hero probably played the main role in the *Achaeans* by Menander. This play is known only through the emblema of a mosaic found at Ulpia Oescus in Thrace, now Bulgaria (Fig. 315).[5] Above the

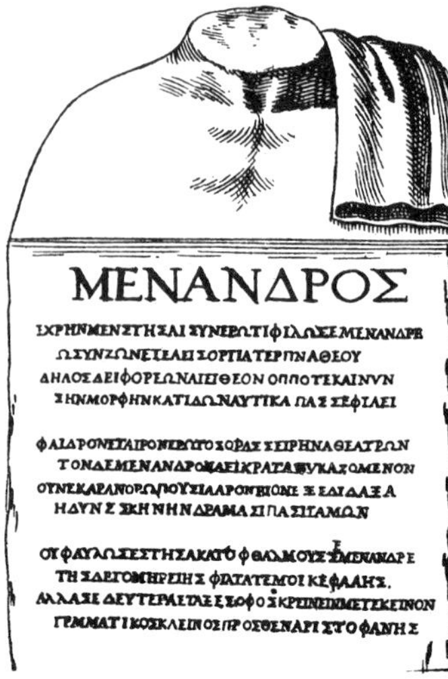

Fig. 314. Epigram on Menander by the grammarian Aristophanes. Herm, Turin

heads of four masked men the inscription MENAN-
DROU ACHAIOI appears. At the left Agamemnon, holding a scepter, and at the right Achilles, accompanied
by his friend Patroklos, are separated by a seated
gray-haired man, who could be the wise Nestor or
Phoenix, the old tutor of Achilles. The subject must
have been the quarrel of the Achaian heroes over
the girl Chryseis, whom Achilles claimed as a booty
and Agamemnon took away from him, as described
in the first book of the *Iliad*. Perhaps this story was
treated in a lost tragedy by Euripides and gave a
welcome subject for a caricature. Sophocles also
wrote an *Assembly of the Achaeans* ('Αχαιῶν σύλλογος)
which contained speeches by Achilles and Odysseus.[6] This may have been a satyr play. The mask
of Patroklos has a closed mouth, and one of the jokes
may have been that Patroklos never opened his
mouth. In tragedy there often were mutes because
only three speaking actors were allowed. A door to
the left and an altar to the right indicate the scene
of action. The trapeze below the feet of the actors
may be an indication of the stage. The dresses are
the long chiton and the chlamys of the warrior
heroes. It is conceivable that this play by Menander
remained alive in the homeland of Achilles. Menander was still presented in the time of Plutarch (*De
Iside et Osiride* 70).

Menander is described by Phaedrus (Fables,
Fabulae Aesopiae, v,12) as "approaching in wide
garment with delicate and languid step" (cf. Athenaeus, 248d and 364d). Pausanias (I,21,1) mentions
a statue of Menander in the theater of Dionysus at
Athens. This was a seated figure, the base of which
has been preserved with the inscriptions of the
names of the poet and of the artists, Cephisodotus
and Timarchus, the sons of Praxiteles.[7] This statue
is probably used in the Hellenistic reliefs in Princeton, formerly Collection Stroganoff in Rome, and in

the Museum of the Lateran (Figs. 316-317).[8] They
show Menander sitting at a table. He is surrounded
by the three characteristic masks of his comedies: in
his hand he holds the mask of a youth, on the table
lie the masks of a young woman and the mask of
a man, evidently the father of the youth. Perhaps
these reliefs are based on a votive relief for the
victory with the *Girl from Samos*, for the youth
could be Moschion, the woman Chrysis, and the
older man Demeas, the father of Moschion, who
considers Chrysis as his common-law wife. The
standing woman on the Lateran relief is either
Menander's beloved Glycera or, as in the relief of
Euripides (Fig. 109), the personification of Skene.
The Princeton relief (Fig. 316) does not have this

Figs. 316, 317a. Menander and masks of New Comedy.
Marble reliefs, Princeton; Lateran

Fig. 315. Menander, *Achaioi*. Mosaic, Bulgaria

Figs. 318, 319. Menander. Boston; Collection Robinson

Fig. 320. Theater ticket with head of Menander. Alexandria

Fig. 317b-c. Head from 317a, Lateran

figure. It is, therefore, probably an addition of the Augustan age, when the Lateran copy was made. Glycera was the model for the decent and amiable courtesans in the plays of Menander. Alciphron (IV,9,5) tells how Glycera prepared the masks for Menander.

The head of the Lateran relief (Fig. 317b-c) agrees with a type of portrait of which over forty copies are known. The best are in Boston, (Fig. 318), in the collection of David Robinson, University of Mississippi, (Figs. 319a-b), Corcyra (Corfu), Ince Blundel Hall (with restored nose), and Copenhagen, where an excellent reconstruction of the bronze original head has been made.[9] The features show traces of physical suffering patiently borne and of a nervous constitution coupled with sensitivity and refinement. Menander appears to be between forty and fifty years of age. The same head is sometimes, as in Bonn and in the Museo Nazionale Romano, combined with a bearded head, which has a thick fillet, probably a sign that the older man was deceased. This head has been named Hesiod or Homer, but I believe that it is meant to be an imaginary portrait of Aristophanes (Fig. 183a-c).[10] The herms thus combine the greatest representatives of Old and New Comedy.

There probably was a second portrait of Menander, which gave him a wreath and drapery over the shoulder. The wreath appears on a replica of the head in Oxford;[11] on theater tickets from Pergamon and Alexandria (Fig. 320),[12] on which the poet holds a mask, while his name is inscribed on the reverse; on the mosaic of Monnus in Trier and on a mosaic found in Daphne, the harbor of Antioch-on-the-Orontes, now in Princeton (Fig. 321).[13] This latter reflects the late Roman conception of Menan-

der. The connection with Glycera, already found on the relief in the Lateran (Fig. 317) has now become of major interest. She occupies the center of the picture, probably standing behind the couch on which Menander reclines. The personification of Comedy is standing at the end of the couch. The courtesan and the personified Comedy are on equal footing. Beside the couch stands a banquet table. The poet enjoys life and love like an Epicurean or a young man out of his comedies.

The wreath appears also on another pictorial representation of Menander showing him seated on a finely-curved Attic chair, in the House of Menan-

Fig. 321. Muse of Comedy and Glycera with Menander. Mosaic from Antioch-on-the-Orontes, Princeton

Fig. 323. Menander. Bust, Venice

der in Pompeii (Figs. 322a-c).[14] It belongs to the period of Nero, but may be copied from a painted portrait which Craterus executed for the Pompeium in Athens (Pliny, xxxv,140). The name is twice inscribed, and on the scroll in his left hand part of the title reads: "Menander was the first to write New Comedy in four books" (Menander. Hic primus [novam?]) Comediam scripsit . . . Lib. quattuor (Fig. 322c).

Perhaps there was a second sculptured portrait of Menander in Athens, which was draped. Chiton and mantle are on busts in Venice (Fig. 323), Verona, and Kenya[15] and on a medallion at Marbury Hall, with a scroll in the background and the name on the lower part of the frame, agreeing in general features with a lost medallion designed in 1578 by Galle (named Theodorus Gallaeus), formerly in the possession of Orsini.[16] It may have been a contemporary portrait by the sons of Praxiteles, who after the death of the poet were commissioned to represent him for the theater with nude upper body.

Without iconographic value, but of great interest is the fact that Menander, together with Sophocles, Euripides, Epicurus, and Zeno, was among the outstanding personalities whose likenesses were chosen to adorn the skeleton goblets of Boscoreale.[17] Menander is holding a torch and the mask of a courtesan. He is accompanied by a skeleton flute player and by the poet Archilochus of Myrina, playing the lyre. Next to Menander are the inscriptions: "Menandros of Athens" and "live," conveying as early as the Augustan period the conception which Aristophanes of Byzantium has expressed in his lines: "Menander! Life! I wonder which of you has copied which?"

Since the New Comedy had stripped off all fantastic and improper elements and had become a moral drama and a mirror of the daily life of the rich bourgeoisie, it also discarded the indecent

Fig. 322a-c, Menander.
Wall painting, Pompeii

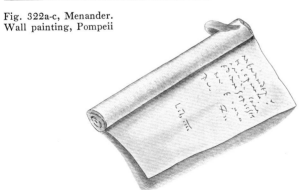

costume borrowed from the Dionysiac goblins, and in essential features assumed the garb of every day. Only the tights with sleeves and long trousers were preserved under the main dress. The stuffing of the body and grotesque masks were preserved for some lower-class characters like some of the slaves, cooks, soldiers, and parasites—characters which had been taken over from Old and Middle Comedy.

As the same characters continued in Latin comedy, it often is difficult to decide whether the reliefs, wall paintings, mosaics, statuettes, and masks in marble, bronze, and terracotta illustrate the Greek originals or the Latin imitations. As a general principle it may be right to consider the more grotesque figures as Roman, the more refined and variegated ones as Greek, just as the personalities in the Greek originals are more refined and more variegated than the personalities in Plautus. Terence is nearer to the Greeks than Plautus but, being less popular, has been illustrated only in the late Roman period. As the cultivated Romans beginning in the second century B.C. read and spoke Greek, many Greek plays were performed in Rome, and certainly they were performed in Magna Graecia. I, therefore, feel justified in having included in this chapter most of the comedy illustrations preserved since the Hellenistic period.

The costume does not help to distinguish Greek and Latin figures, as it was taken over with the subject matter from the Greek originals. This is particularly true for the himation, called a pallium for men and palla for women. As the most characteristic part of the costume for comedy it has given its name to the fabula palliata (see below, Ch. XI, p. 154). The masks can be grouped with the help of the list of sets, described in the catalogue of Pollux (*Onomasticon*, IV,143-154), which, like his list for tragic masks (IV,133-142), probably is based on a Hellenistic source.[18] It seems to me, however, certain that this source described the wardrobe and usual stock of masks possessed by a traveling guild of actors, and thus does not apply to the original plays of Menander and other writers of Greek New Comedy. The masks of the early Hellenistic period certainly were much more individual and variegated, just as the personalities were. There are very few repetitions in those monuments which by inscriptions or finding places are certainly Greek. One can, indeed, stage all of the preserved New Comedies with Pollux' assortment of masks and with the preserved masks. The majority of the masks suit the bourgeois types created by New Comedy, and they reveal the same refined variety and differentiation as the types of comedy themselves.

Fig. 324. Scene from New Comedy. Marble relief, Naples

Beside these, however, some masks are reminiscent of tragedy, which corresponds to the fact that the tragedy of Euripides had a strong influence on New Comedy. Stronger still is the grotesque element taken over from Old Comedy and Doric farce. Just as in Roman translations and contaminations of comedies so also in the later Roman comedy masks the coarser elements are preferred and even increased.

The comedy scene on a relief in Naples (Fig. 324)[19] shows masks and costumes which might have been worn in Menander's comedies, although the subject matter is quite different. An enraged father hurries out of his mansion, indicated by a richly decorated door, swinging his cane as if to beat his son, who comes home drunk, swinging a hypothymis, the fillet worn at banquets. Another man restrains the furious father, holding his right hand and arm. A flute girl and a slave accompany the youth, the latter supporting his young master, but seemingly also trying to hide behind him. All wear tights. The two men and the youth wear a chiton and a large, carefully draped mantle. The father, who carries a staff with a bent handle in his left hand, wears a mantle which is fringed, a sign of elegant dress in Hellenistic times. The slave has only a short chiton and a scanty cloak hanging from his right shoulder. The little flute player is dressed in a chiton reaching to her feet, with a mantle knotted in front so that her hands are free to play the flute. The costumes of the old men could be given to Smicrines in the *Arbitrants*, to Demeas and Niceratus in the *Samia*; that of the youth to Chaerestratus and Charisius in the *Arbitrants*, to Moschion in the *Samia*; that of the flute girl to Habrotonon; and that of the slave to Onesimus in the *Arbitrants*, and to Parmenon in the *Samia*.

Figs. 325, 326. Fathers of New Comedy. Terracotta, Paris

The masks would also fit the characters of Menander. The two men offer excellent contrasting masks of bourgeois men: a choleric and a phlegmatic, an irritable and a conciliatory type. Two large terracotta statuettes, formerly in the Collection Janzé and now in the Bibliothèque nationale at Paris, repeat the two types of the two old men on the comedy relief (Figs. 325-326).[20] The one with the long curled beard seems to plead, the other to argue with his right hand made into a fist, his left gesticulating excitedly. A wall painting from the Casa dei Dioscuri in Pompeii, now in the Akademische Kunstmuseum in Bonn (Fig. 327)[21], represents another enraged old man who is speaking to a woman. He wears the same fringed mantle and carries a similar crooked staff as the father in the Naples relief. The situation seems to be similar if not identical to the last scene preserved of the *Arbitrants*:

Fig. 327. Old man and woman, last scene of **Menander's** *Arbitrants* (?) Wall painting, from Pompeii, Bonn

Fig. 328. Old man spying on slave and fluteplayer. Wall painting, Naples

Fig. 329. Masks of girl fluteplayer and slave. Mosaic, Rome

the grandfather Smicrines scolds the old nurse, but is mocked by her and the slave, who appears in the background. A similar old man in the same costume, leaning on a staff, spies on a slave and a fluteplayer in a wall painting from Herculaneum in Naples (Fig. 328).[22] He seems to have a pointed beard, a wedge-shaped goatee, and thus is a sphenopogon (σφηνοπώγων), wearing one of the masks inherited from Old Comedy, for this is an archaic fashion (see above, Ch. III, p. 39). The scene represented may be a famous one, for the two masks of slave and flute girl reappear on a mosaic in the Capitoline Museum (Fig. 329).[23] The flute girls on the comedy relief, the wall-painting, and the mosaic (Figs. 324 and 328-329) are certainly what Pollux (iv,153) calls the little courtesan (ἑταιρίδιον) who wears only a simple ribbon in her hair.

330, 331   332   333, 335   334   336, 337

Figs. 330-337. Masks of fathers from New Comedy (See List of Illustrations and Sources)

Among the single masks for the father there are many variations. A marble mask in Dresden (Fig. 330)[24] has the same hair roll over the forehead (stephane) as the actors on the comedy relief and the same beard with carefully rolled corkscrew strands reminiscent of a tragic hero as the conciliatory father there. Another in Athens (Fig. 331)[25] of terracotta, probably from Myrina, has a bald forehead and a rather ironic expression, reminding one somewhat of Socrates. Similar is the mask worn by an old man comfortably wrapped in a himation in Vienna (Fig. 332).[26] A small mask from Pergamon, formerly in the possession of the author, has in contrast an angry expression (Fig. 333)[27] like the enraged father on the comedy relief. Both eyebrows are drawn up in the outer part. This type of mask, being the most characteristic one, is held by Thalia, the Muse of Comedy (Fig. 334). Pollux mentions several times that the eyebrows are drawn up, but several times he says also that only one eyebrow was drawn upward (IV,144-45). The reason for this differentiation is given by Quintilian (XI,3,74): "pater interim concitatus interim lenis est, altero erecto altero composito est supercilio, atque id ostendere maxime latus actoribus moris est, quod iis quas agunt partibus congruat.—The father is sometimes angry, sometimes mild. One of his eyebrows is drawn up, the other is smooth. The actors used to show that side which agrees with the role they have to play." Such changes are more frequent in Greek comedy and in Terence (for example, Cnemon in the

last part of the *Dyskolos* of Menander, and Demea in the last part of *Adelphoi*) than in Plautus, and therefore they certainly go back to New Comedy. The possibility of turning a mild and an angry face alternately to the public was a substitute for the missing facial expression. A relief with the mask of a man in Mantua shows well this peculiarity (Fig. 335).[28] The two sides of the face are certainly quite different from each other. The right half is cheerful, the other looks angry. The two different eyebrows are connected by a sharp curve. Five marble masks on a red-stuccoed ground from the Stoa of Attalus in Athens have the brows sharply divided (Figs. 336-337).[29] The right one is strongly lifted, the left one is less attenuated. These seem to be fathers, but the contrivance is transferred also to the servant, who has in Latin comedy more reason for change from joy to fear and anger than in the Greek comedy where, as Menander and the comedy relief show, he has only secondary roles.

The young men play the largest roles in New Comedy. They can be divided roughly into the serious and the gay type. The one is represented in Menander by Charisius, the young husband in the *Arbitrants*, the other by Moschion in the *Samia* and the *Perikeiromene*. The first is represented in a terracotta in Athens, probably from Myrina (Fig. 338).[30]

Figs. 341, 342. Youth playing the cithara; Musician playing the cymbala

Figs. 338-340. Serious youths of New Comedy

Figs. 343a-b-345. Masks of gay youths of New Comedy

onkos (Fig. 340).[32] Its counterpart is the girl with mitra or sphendone (Fig. 363).

While these masks have a stephane without any adornment, the gay youths often have a fillet wound around a metal ring, showing that they are coming home from a banquet. The young man on the comedy relief in Naples (Fig. 324) has this fillet (hypothymis) in his hand. A statuette of a young man from Myrina, in Berlin, originally playing a cithara, has the ring with the fillet hanging deeply over his forehead (Fig. 341).[33] His hair seems to be fluttering to both sides. He corresponds to the description of the second youth with blowy hair (Pollux, IV,147, ἐπίσειστος). As the cithara player needs both hands for the instrument and the plectrum, with which he touches the strings, his mantle is knotted in front. The same arrangement of the mantle and the metal ring with a fillet, which hangs down on the shoulders, reappears in another statuette of a musician in Athens (Fig. 342).[34] He is a cymbalist, who is bending forward in the act of striking together the two concave bronze plates in his two hands. The metal ring with a broad fillet wound around it is also laid deep into the forehead of a youthful mask in Munich, found in Samsun (Amisus) (Fig. 343).[35] Another mask from the same place, now in the Louvre, has a thick wreath instead of the ring (Fig. 344).[36] The same is true of a fine mask of a young man with a slender face from Myrina in Boston (Fig. 345), and a marble mask in the British Museum, corresponding to the delicate youth of Pollux (IV,147, ἁπαλός).[37]

Music did not play the same important role in

He corresponds closely to the youth of serious tragedy (above, Figs. 291-292), and to the oldest, most excellent youth of Pollux (IV,146). He is tightly wrapped in his mantle, the himation, his right hand laid on the folds before his chest, his left grasping the folds hanging at the side. His mask, like all the masks of young people, has well-modulated and realistic features, but with a slight frown and some wrinkles on his forehead. The same is true of a mask from Agrigentum in the collection of Dr. Vollmer in New York (Fig. 339).[31] A youth with an onkos of corkscrew locks arranged radially and hanging down at each side, on a terracotta disk found in Selembria, northern Greece, is certainly a serious youth of New Comedy who is imitating the tragic

Figs. 346, 347. Musicians and women in scenes of New Comedy. Mosaics by Dioscurides, Naples

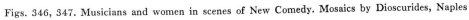

348   349   350   351   352

Figs. 348-352. Old women of New Comedy (See List of Illustrations and Sources)

New Comedy as it did in Old Comedy and tragedy where the musician had to remain in the orchestra to accompany the chorus. Since Middle Comedy the regular chorus was replaced by an improvised dance indicated by "chorou" (χοροῦ), part of the chorus. While they perform, the actors retire to their houses, as is shown in the *Arbitrants*, vv. 33-35: "Let's go, for, see, there is coming here a mob of young bloods and it seems to me not the time to interfere with them." Such musicians, similar to the statuettes (Figs. 341 and 342), are depicted on one of the two mosaics copied from paintings by Dioscurides of Samos, found in the so-called Villa of Cicero in Pompeii and now in Naples.[38] They are of particularly fine technique with many differently colored stones, which imitate a finely shaded tempera painting. The scene with the musicians appears to be a chorus interlude of New Comedy (Fig. 346). A woman, followed by a miserable dwarf, accompanies on her flute the clumsy dancing of two men, both adorned with wreath and fillets, wearing tights with long sleeves, a chiton, and a white mantle knotted loosely in front. The cymbalist agrees almost perfectly with the statuette (Fig. 342), while the other beats a tympanon instead of playing a cithara (cf. Fig. 341). That this is the copy of some celebrated painting is testified by a painted copy found in Stabiae, now also in Naples.[39] The figures are the same, only the execution is much coarser, and the dwarf is separated from the fluteplayer.

The companion piece of the mosaic with an interlude by Dioscurides, the one with four women (Fig. 347),[40] also brings something new in comedy: an interior scene. One old and two young women are seated around a table, on which an incense stand and a laurel wreath may indicate that a love charm is being prepared. The two young women seem to consult the old woman in some affair of the heart. The woman in the center is talking with lively gesticulation. The one to the left, seated on a chair covered with an elegant rug and cushion, seems to wring her hands as if in fear and despair. The old witch has fortified herself with a drink of wine from the silver cup in her right hand, while with the left hand she seems to emphasize some point in her advice. Behind her is a servant girl standing in modest attitude. The four women correspond to the four categories into which Pollux (IV,150-154) has divided his seventeen women: three old women, five bourgeois women, seven courtesans, and two young maid servants. In Menander's *Arbitrants* we have the old Sophrona, the bourgeois woman Pamphila and the young courtesan Habrotonon; in his *Perikeiromene* Doris is a maid of Glycera. The women of the Dioscurides mosaic could therefore be used to visualize the appearance of the women in Menander and his successors. If, on the other hand, we want to compare them with the list of Pollux, the old witch may be the wolfish old woman, the woman to the left a false maiden, the one in the center a full-grown courtesan, and the little girl standing, the delicate little servant with bobbed hair. There are, however, other possibilities, and it is more important to compare here and elsewhere the original plays than the much later catalogue of the lexicographer.

There are many variations in the four groups of masks in the preserved monuments as well as in the preserved Latin plays. It seems that the masks of the old women could be used for free women as well as for slaves. The oldest thin, wolfish woman with squinting eyes, whose face is covered by many fine wrinkles, is worn not only by the old sorceress on the mosaic of Dioscurides, but is also rendered in a terracotta mask in Berlin (Fig. 348).[41] The wreath indicates that she loves wine and banquets. Her opposite is the fat old woman with thick wrinkles, certainly often a procuress and perhaps sometimes the friend and mother of false virgins and courtesans. A terracotta statuette in Munich seems to represent such an old procuress. She has a fat and short figure and is dressed in a chiton that is much too long (Fig. 349).[42] For this reason a pouch, which is also much too long, bulging from the lower belt at the waist, adds greatly to her grotesque appearance, which may be borrowed from Attic Old Comedy. Her right hand is protruding and she seems to offer four small elongated objects, which may be cakes or small fishes. She seems to talk and offer some food to a person larger than herself. Her broad face is framed by a large stephane around which is laid a band decorated with rosettes. Pollux (IV,151) mentions that the procuress and mother of courtesans wore such a fillet (ταινίδιον τὰς τρίχας περιλαμβάνον). A similar mask of a fat woman is in Bonn (Fig. 350). As a third type, Pollux mentions the homely little old woman with a snub nose and only two teeth remaining in each jaw (ἐν ἑκατέρᾳ τῇ σιαγόνι ἀνὰ δύο ἔχει γομφίους). This mask surely belongs to the old nurse of the unknown, freeborn daughter of a worthy citizen, who has been mistaken for a courtesan, and therefore is living in a humble condition until an old nurse of this type reveals her true birth. A terracotta relief in Florence (Fig. 351)[43] and a small mask in Berlin (Fig. 352)[44] with its wrinkled skin and toothless (or almost toothless) mouth correspond to the description offered by Pollux.

The terracotta statuette of an elderly lady in Berlin (Fig. 353)[45] found in Capua, has the mantle drawn over her head like the old witch on the Dioscurides mosaic. She has her head bent to the side and both arms wrapped in the mantle, with only her hands free, which were probably gesticulating accompanying a lively speech. Thus we may suppose appeared Myrrhina, the rich Corinthian matron in the *Perikeiromene* of Menander. In the list of Pollux, she would be the garrulous woman (λεκτική) with smooth hair, straight eyebrows, and white complexion, the sheltered bourgeois woman. Another old woman in a terracotta in the British Museum (Fig. 354)[46] is clenching her fists inside her himation and seems to be in a furious mood.

A terracotta statuette in Berlin (Fig. 355)[47] represents a young bourgeois woman, who has both shoulders and arms, including hands, tightly wrapped in her himation. Her right hand is laid on her breast. She may be a young freeborn daughter of citizens, who has become involved in affairs of the heart, like the ones on the mosaic of women by Dioscurides. She lifts her head as if complaining. Her hair is parted and bound up to a bow on the crown of her head. Her body looks padded, and this device of farce and Old Comedy may here have been used to indicate that the young lady is pregnant. This would be suitable for the false virgin

Figs. 353-355. Bourgeois women

(ψευδοκόρη) in Pollux, who has her hair bound up on the upper head and looks like a newly-wed bride. Similar is the girl in pitiable attitude on a mural painting from the Casa del Centenario,[48] and a mask, slightly over life size, from Pompeii in Naples, also with parted hair and a bow made out of her hair above the front part of her skull (Fig. 356).[49]

There are more representations of courtesans than of bourgeois women, quite understandably, because they play a much greater role in New Comedy than the respectable women. Some, however, rose to become concubines or common law wives. A statuette in Munich seems to represent such a woman, who is seated comfortably on a housewife's chair (Fig. 357)[50] from which she directs the members of the household. She lifts her right hand, has her head inclined to her left and turned slightly to the right and upward, as if gaily talking to some standing figure. Her face is surrounded by a huge frame of curly locks. She thus corresponds to the concubine of Pollux (IV,153, παλλακή . . . περίκομος). She is an older woman. Still older seems to be the courtesan represented in a mask from Corneto in Berlin (Fig. 358).[51] She has a wrinkled face and probably greying hair, which she tries to conceal by a bonnet. She thus may represent Pollux' oldest courtesan with

Fig. 356. False virgin
Fig. 358. Courtesan

Fig. 357. Concubine.
Terracotta, Munich

Figs. 359, 360. Young courtesans   Figs. 361-364. Courtesans

grey hair scattered through her dark hair, who is described as garrulous (σπαρτοπόλιος λεκτική). A younger courtesan is represented in a statuette in Munich (Fig. 359).[52] She is wrapped from head to feet in a large himation, tinted violet with broad white borders. She has her hands inside the mantle, the right hand before the breast, the left placed upon the hip. She wears red shoes, and her right foot is placed on a small footstool. The white border of the mantle effectively frames her fiery red face. Her slightly waved hair is parted and she is smirking impudently. She probably is the type of impertinent, shameless, and greedy courtesan, one of the thoroughly artful little hussies who plunder their lovers. She corresponds to the perfect little courtesan of Pollux (IV,153) with red complexion and hair laid over the ears (τέλειον ἑταιρικόν). A still younger and less disagreeable courtesan is represented in a statuette in Athens (Fig. 360) that probably was found in Myrina.[53] She wears a peplos, the dress worn in the Hellenistic period by quite young girls only. The same peplos with long overfold is worn by the girl embraced by a youth (Fig. 368). The left hand is lightly placed upon the hip, the right hand is protruded in a lively gesticulation. Her head is inclined to her left shoulder. She seems to talk to somebody who stands at her right side. In the list of Pollux she might be the courtesan with a broad fillet, a mitra (IV,154), διάμιτρος) who has a colored hairband around her head. The mitra is here combined with a hair bow. A bow tied on the fillet is worn on a marble mask of a girl in Naples (Fig. 361),[54] who has a rather innocent expression. The same is true of another mask in Naples which combines the bow with a kerchief, laid deeply into the forehead (Fig. 362).[55] The folded cloth looks almost like a turban. Both these masks have stiffly twisted corkscrew locks hanging at the sides. The mask on a terracotta disk from Selembria in Berlin has a mitra or sphendone over her parted hair (Fig. 363). She is the counterpart to the youth (Fig. 340).[56] A broad fillet alone confines the parted hair of a mask found in Myrina, in the Boston Museum (Fig. 364).[57] Her

hair is yellow, thus blond. The mitra is violet with white borders. Her face shows a shy smile. Most courtesans love to array themselves with ornaments. A marble mask from Tivoli, now in the Vatican (Fig. 365a-b)[58] has a broad fillet and thick cords between the forehead and the hairband, all of which seem to be of gold. This may be the golden courtesan of Pollux (IV,153), whose hair was adorned with much gold (διάχρυσος). A female mask from Amisus in the Louvre (Fig. 366),[59] found together with a youth (above, Fig. 344), has the ends of her hair gathered in a bunch which stands up on the crown of her head like a flame. She has very youthful features and a rather frightened expression. In the list of Pollux (IV,154), she would be the little lamp or torch (λαμπάδιον) who is the last of the courtesans enumerated, and therefore the youngest, as Pollux arranges his lists according to age.

Still younger than the young courtesans are the slave girls, like Doris, the maid of Glycera in the *Perikeiromene*. Such a one in modest attitude and with bobbed hair is represented on the mosaic with women by Dioscurides (Fig. 347). Two masks from Apulia in Munich (Fig. 367a-b)[60] have childish features, pert little noses (σιμοί) and parted hair. Pollux distinguishes between the delicate slave girl employed in a citizen's home (ἄβρα περίκουρος) and the coarse pug-nosed little servant who belongs to a courtesan. The little lady's maid of the citizen's house is clothed in white and has bobbed hair evenly arranged around her face. As short hair is the sign of slavery, it is the greatest offense for Glycera to get her hair cut like a slave girl. The little slave of the courtesan has her hair parted and laid smoothly to the sides (παράψηστον) and she has a snub nose curving upward (ὑπόσιμον). She wears scarlet robes.

Lower-class bourgeois types which already belong to the older comedy, but have found their development only in New Comedy, are the soldier, the parasite, and the cook. The soldier is well characterized in Menander's *Perikeiromene*. Polemon is blustering and impulsive, but is repentant. He tries to reconcile his beloved Glycera and earnestly seeks

Fig. 367. Masks of maidservants

Fig. 365. Mask of "Golden Courtesan." Marble; Vatican

Fig. 366. Lampadion

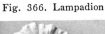

her forgiveness for having cut her hair. She comes back to him and is given to him in marriage by her father. Such a soldier is represented in a statuette in Munich, found together with a pair of lovers with their arms around each other (Fig. 368).[61] This results in a situation similar to the one in the

Fig. 368. Soldier and pair of lovers

369a-b. Soldier. Bronze statuette   Fig. 370. Soldier with flat cap

Perikeiromene, where Polemon sees Glycera kiss a man, who is her brother, but whom he suspects to be her lover. The youth is wrapped in his mantle, the girl is characterized as very young by the peplos (see above, Fig. 360). The soldier wears a short chiton and a chlamys, the dress of soldiers and travelers. He carries his sword inside the sheath on the right (that is, the wrong) side. He sadly leans his head toward his right shoulder. An older bearded soldier in a corselet (Fig. 369) found in the Agora of Athens seems to be boasting with outstretched arms.[62] Long locks fall on his shoulders. Another statuette in the British Museum is wearing a chlamys pinned before the breast and a plate-like flat cap (Fig. 370).[63] The soldier with a lance in the lost wall painting found in the Casa della grande Fontana in Pompeii (Fig. 371)[64] also wears a flat cap, a short chiton, and a chlamys which, with the pinned part originally on the right shoulder, is shifted to the left shoulder. His right hand grasping a lance, his left proudly placed upon his hip, a flat cap on his head, his hair falling over his ears, he looks grim and stupid. He conforms to Pollux' (IV,147) long-haired braggart soldier (ἐπίσειστος στρατιώτης ἀλαζών). Behind him is a smaller man also with a chlamys, thus probably one of his hired soldiers. His parasite approaching with wide stride looks up to the great man like a devoted dog. He probably repeats the stories of the great feats of his bread-giver with exaggerations. Behind him are two other smaller men, perhaps also hired soldiers or servants, for the officers in the time of the Diadochi became rich and could afford luxurious domestic establishments. The lost *Kolax*, the Flatterer, by Menander may have

Fig. 371. Soldier and parasite

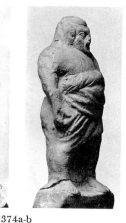

372a-b

374a-b

376

Figs. 372-377. Parasite flatterers. Terracotta (See List of Illustrations and Sources)

373a-b

375a-b

377

had a similar scene. The two seated men in the foreground probably have nothing to do with the comedy. They seem to be portrait statues of Aeschylus and Sophocles. A more refined flatterer appears in a statuette from Myrina in Athens (Fig. 372)[65] and in a mask in Berlin (Fig. 373).[66] Both have serious expressions, a high, bald smooth forehead like fawning dogs, and a hooked nose (ἐπίγρυπος); this, according to Pseudo-Aristotle (*Physiognomica*, 811a,II,61), signifies impertinence and is compared to the beaks of greedy ravens. Some parasites are of good extraction, but have become poor by laziness and thus have to live from the good will of more fortunate friends. They try to make themselves agreeable by flatteries and jokes, indulge the whims of their benefactors and patiently run errands for them. They cannot afford servants, and therefore the statuette (Fig. 372) carries an oil flask and strigil, attributes of the parasite mentioned by Pollux (IV,120), which as a rule are carried by slaves for their masters. The left hand sustains the right elbow and the right hand is lifted in lively gesticulation. He seems to be angry and seriously scolding for some small mistake, in order to make the praise of more important things more effective. Much coarser is a statuette from Capua in Berlin (Fig. 374a-b),[67] of which there are replicas in Munich, the Louvre, and elsewhere.[68] This low-class flatterer emphasizes his fat belly by draping his himation tightly around

his waist with a roll and an overfall. He stands in a clumsy position, holding the folds of his mantle loosely with both hands, has drawn his head between his shoulders and is looking down. His mask has stupid and coarse features. A variation in Berlin[69] emphasizes the fat paunch through the folded hands. A mask, formerly in Rome, seen in 1926 at the gallery of the dealer Jandolo, has a bald forehead, eyebrows drawn upward, and a very marked squint (Fig. 375).[70] A statuette in Lebanon (Fig. 376) has a similar head on a lean body. The hands are folded and the parasite seems to look up imploringly to his bread-giver. A mask in Tarentum has the bald forehead and large ears of the coarse parasite and an enormous crooked nose knocked out of shape (Fig. 377).[71] Thus there are three types of the parasite, which we also find in later literature: the polished flatterer with the hooked nose, the common parasite in the company of the braggart self-asserting officer, and the particularly coarse Sicilian parasite (Pollux, IV,148). In Latin comedy the coarse type, originating in the comedies of Epicharmus of Sicily, was favored as we see him in the parasite Peniculus in Plautus' *Menaechmi*. The great Roman actor Roscius in the first century B.C. played the role of the parasite without a mask because he squinted, and he may have resembled the mask (Fig. 375).

The most grotesque lower-class free men are the cooks, who are public caterers and are called in

378   379   382

380

Figs. 378-382. Cooks   381

Fig. 383. Lady and cook. Wall painting, Palermo

when there is a banquet or a wedding feast to be prepared. In the *Girl from Samos* Parmenon brings the cook and his assistants home from the market, so that he may prepare the dinner on the occasion of the wedding of Moschion and Plangon. He is described as curious and as such a chatterer that his tongue could make hash without knives. His type and mask are derived from the Doric farce and are used in Old and Middle Comedy (see Ch. III, Figs. 155-156 and 200). The Maison type is said to have been invented by a man of this name in Megara, a fact which calls to mind the Megarian farce. From the old type is derived the wedge-shaped beard of the statuette in Tarentum of a bald cook (Fig. 378). He carries a huge fish in his right hand, while his left hand rests on his hip under his cloak. A statuette found in Myrina, now in Berlin (Fig. 379),[72] seems to be preparing some dish. He has a kind of long apron tied around him, of the kind still worn today by chefs. He has put the wreath of the symposion on his head. He probably has a sweet-tooth and thus likes to enjoy his own creations. His grinning face expresses conceit and noisy cheerfulness. The wreath may hide baldness, as it appears on two masks: one (Fig. 380)[73] with a face similar to that of the statuette in Berlin comes from the marble frieze found in the gymnasium of Pergamon, together with tragic masks set into an ivy garland (see above, Figs. 311-313); the other, of terracotta, said to have been found also in Pergamon, now in Berlin (Fig. 381)[74], is much more individual and grotesque, his enormously broad mouth showing his teeth. Both have a tuft of hair in

the center of the high forehead. While the relief mask has wavy strands, the terracotta one has tufts of short hair at the sides. This seems to be the loquacious Tettix, a cook from a foreign land, forever chattering and perhaps jumping like a cicada (τέττιξ). He also has a small number of solitary curls forming a beard on his chin. The description of the Maison and the Tettix in Pollux (IV,150) agrees with the two main types of these cooks.

The bald-headed cook represented in a terracotta statuette in Munich carries a large basket (Fig. 382). A wall painting in Palermo, copied from a framed picture (Fig. 383),[75] seems to represent a cook holding a similar shopping basket. He is speaking with a tall lady, who might be a bourgeois woman, or possibly a courtesan. She is accompanied by a little maid, wrapped in her himation, similar to the maid on the mosaic of Dioscurides (Fig. 347), but she has drawn the mantle over her head. The scene reminds one of Plautus's *Menaechmi* (I,4, vv. 219-25). Erotium tells her cook Cylindrus to shop for a dinner for three, of which she herself, Menaechmus, and his parasite will partake. The cook protests because the parasite will eat enough for eight.

Other low-class, but freeborn men are the peasants, as described in Menander's *Farmer* (Georgos, Ἀγροικος, Fragment 97K): "I am a country boor, even I will not deny it. . . . " A mask found in Kyme (Fig. 384),[76] in the Collection Lecuyer, depicts such a farmer with badly shaven cheeks, a broad mouth showing his strong and healthy teeth, and a stupid expression. Another such mask of a stupid rustic with short cropped hair is in Leipzig (Fig. 385).[77]

Figs. 384, 385. Masks of peasants. Terracotta

101

Figs. 386, 387. Procurers

Another low-class citizen is the slave-dealer, the leno or pornoboskos (πορνοβοσκός) with whom the young men and their slaves are always fighting, because he sells the courtesans to the highest bidder. A terracotta statuette from Myrina in the Louvre and an impressive mask found in Priene, now in Berlin (Figs. 386 and 387),[78] probably represent this procurer. He has contracted brows, and a disagreeable grin, his baldness hidden by a ring around which a broad fillet is wound, the ends of it hanging on his shoulders. He seems to greet some rich customer with outstretched hands. He appeared in Menander's *Kolax* and is described in Pollux (IV,145) as being bald and similar to the Lykomedeios, who has a long beard.

Coarsest of all, naturally, are the masks of the slaves, which were borrowed from Old Comedy and therefore often display a hairdress of the early fifth century, the rolled arrangement of the hair which is known as speira (σπεῖρα). Examples are a terracotta disk from Myrina in Boston (Fig. 388),[79] a masked small head found in Pergamon, in the Collection Humann, and a mask from the island of Melos, both in Berlin (Figs. 389 and 390),[80] a terracotta mask from Naples, formerly in the possession of the author (Fig. 391),[81] one formerly in the Collection Vogell, last seen in Kassel (Fig. 392), and the marble mask in Rome, Museo Nazionale Romano delle Terme, found on the Via Salaria near the Porta Salaria in the tomb of the Calpurnii (Fig. 393).[82] They all have distorted eyebrows and broad, flat noses with wide nostrils; the mouth is surrounded by a kind of megaphone, on which the hairs of a short beard are indicated. This trumpet-like arrangement may have helped when the voice of the actors had to fill the large Hellenistic and Roman theaters, but considering the excellent acoustics of the auditoria this seems hardly necessary.

The expressions in these masks are much diversified, from great seriousness to gay laughter, just as the role of the servants is much diversified in New Comedy. In Menander the slaves are human individuals with fine gradations of character just like the free persons. In the *Hero* the slave Davus is in love and his companion Geta is a helpful fellow. In the *Perikeiromene* the slaves are much devoted to their masters, Sosias to the soldier Polemon and Davus to the young Moschion. The slaves are not, however, the leaders of the intrigue and not clowns as sometimes in Latin Comedy. Onesimus in the *Arbitrants* is officious and philosophically inclined, but unimportant; his plot is superseded by the much better one of the harp player Habrotonon. The goatherd Davus and the charcoal burner Syriscus in the same play certainly had peculiar masks and dresses adapted to their professions. The servants are neither as impudent nor as important as in the Latin Comedies.

This agrees with the scenes in which slaves appear in the company of bourgeois characters in monuments. On the marble relief with a Comedy scene (Fig. 324) the slave sustains his young master and tries to hide behind him. In the wallpainting in Naples, his master finds the slave carousing with a flute player (Fig. 328), just as Onesimus in the *Arbitrants* is a friend of the music girl. His and her mask together appear again in the mosaic (Fig. 329). In both cases he has a red face and exaggerated lifted brows, which, according to Pseudo-Aristotle (*Physiognomica*, 67, 811b and 812a), signifies impertinence because red hair and a red complexion signify a foxy rascal. In this case the scoundrel dares to celebrate a banquet with the slave girl who was hired for the master, not for the servant. The festival wreath worn by both these slaves is also found in a good mask in Berlin (Fig. 394).[83] In the scene where "Smikrines" scolds "Sophrona" (Fig. 327) the slave stands in the background. In the picture with the braggart soldier the servants stand modestly behind the captain and the parasite (Fig. 371). The stupidity of some slaves is well expressed in the mask formerly in the Collection Vogell (Fig. 392).

The slave probably rose in time to a more important position. In a mural painting from Herculaneum in Naples and a replica in the Atrium of the Casa di Casca Longo, where it is set into a fine

388

Figs. 388-394. Masks for the leading slave of New Comedy

389

390

391

392

393

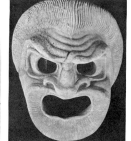

394

Fig. 395. Leading slave and pair of lovers. Wall painting, Pompeii

wall decoration of the third style (Fig. 395),[84] the slave mocks a young couple by making the gesture of horns (corna) which still today in Italy means an attempt to avert evil. The young woman and her lover seem dismayed, he puts his arm protectingly over her shoulder. The slave has grey hair and wears a wide mantle draped in the same manner as it is worn by bourgeois older men, decorated with fringes, a sign of luxury. He therefore is probably a freed man. In the list of Pollux (IV,149) he would be the Pappos, the only slave with grey hair. As the two pictures have been painted in the two cities destroyed by Vesuvius, they must be copies of a celebrated Greek painting. There is also a similar figure of a Pappos, moving with a wide stride and lively gestures and wearing a white speira and fringed mantle, represented in a terracotta from Myrina in Athens (Fig. 396).[85]

Other slaves, one with a wineskin from Myrina in Boston and one from Smyrna in Vienna, seem to be running at high speed (Figs. 297 and 299).[86] Both have the speira. A running slave in Athens, formerly in the Collection Misthos, probably from Smyrna (Fig. 397),[87] has, on the contrary, a bald pate, with only a few straight hairstrands at the sides. His eyebrows are drawn together and swing high out

in the outer part. He wears a cushion to pad his body, held by two belts above and below, similar to the actor tearing his side hair strands in the bronze statuette at Florence (above, Fig. 295). Over his chiton he wears a chlamys pinned at the right shoulder. According to Pollux he would be the slave with hair on the lower part only (κάτω τριχίας), who is bald and has his eyebrows lifted (ἐπηρμένος τὰς ὀφρῦς). Such a one is also shown in the statuette of a slave carrying a traveling bedsack on his back from Megara in Berlin (Fig. 398).[88] He is wearing a chlamys so that it covers his front also, although it hangs longer in the back. This traveling cloak indicates that these slaves are sent on errands and have to accompany their masters on trips. They certainly will not fail to complain about the too much running and too heavy burdens imposed on them, that is, they will make phortika, the jokes of the porter, as in Old Comedy. They are derived—like the cook—from the Maison of Old Comedy. In a statuette in Athens, probably from Myrina (Fig. 399),[89] such a servant dressed in a chlamys seems to have fulfilled successfully his mission or journey, for he has put on the wreath and broad fillets of the symposium and is dancing a jig. He spreads out both arms, lifting his left arm and his head to his left. His hair is curled at the sides of his pate. He thus conforms to the curly-haired slave of Pollux (IV,149, οὖλος). The Greek slaves were allowed to celebrate banquets in contrast to the Roman slaves, as explained in Plautus (Stichus, vv. 446ff.). Another slave, whose mission may have failed, is in another statuette at Athens; in contrast, he is very angry and clenches his fists, grasping the small mantle laid on his left shoulder (Fig. 298).[90]

As the child who is exposed and later found and recognized is a main subject in New Comedy, it is to be expected that the servants would be found in association with babies. Thus the charcoal burner Syriscus in Menander's Arbitrants asks his wife to hand him the foundling (vv. 85f.). A statuette from Tarentum, found together with the cook (Fig. 155), holds a child in swaddling clothes in his left arm and lays his right hand on his breast as if pleading (Fig. 400).[91] In the list of Pollux he would be the leading servant (ἡγεμὼν θεράπων). On a mosaic, for-

Figs. 396, 397. Slaves running; 398, Slave with bedsack; 399a-b, Slave dancing; 400, Slave with baby

Fig. 401. Slave discovering a baby. Mosaic, Naples

merly in the Collection Sant'Angelo, now in the National Museum of Naples (Fig. 401),[92] the same leading servant seems to have found a baby in a basket from which he is lifting the covering. A figure to his right, lost for the most part, lifts his left hand as if in astonishment, while a boy looks on at the other side. As the leader of an intrigue, he is standing in a pensive posture with his hands folded. His himation is drawn tightly around his body, and he lifts his head proudly in a statuette in Munich (Fig. 402).[93] His eyebrows are particularly distorted, giving an expression of sharp deliberation and a feeling of superiority. A bronze statuette in the Museo alla Scala in Milano (Fig. 403)[94] grasps his left wrist with his right hand and has deep furrows on his forehead as a result of deep reflections. The same gesture is shown in a statuette in the possession of Professor Seyrig in Beirut (Fig. 404) and in one from Myrina in the Louvre (Fig. 405).[95]

This leader and other slaves often appear seated. Thus a leader is represented in a bronze statuette in the British Museum with crossed feet, his lifted head sustained by his right hand and his left hand supporting the elbow of his right arm (Fig. 406).[96] A small bronze in the Museo archeologico in

Florence[97] also supports his head with his right hand, which is supported by the elbow on his right thigh; his left hand is laid on the seat and his legs are crossed above the knees. A terracotta statuette in the Louvre shows the leader much excited (Fig. 407). Both his hands in the Louvre statuette, and his left hand in the one in Vienna, grasp the little mantle hanging from his left shoulder. His left shoulder is drawn up higher than his ear and his head is bent down. He obviously is emotionally upset. He and the following five figurines have the legs crossed like Figs. 406 and 407. A quieter and more dignified man represented in a statuette found in Vulci, now in Berlin (Fig. 408),[98] is wrapped in a large himation with both hands inside the mantle, in a manner similar to the older youth above (Fig. 338). He thus might be a bourgeois, but could also be a Pappos, as his mask is too grotesque for a dignified man. He wears a wreath with a long fillet for a banquet, as does the mask of the curly-haired slave above (Fig. 394). A wreath is also shown on the seated slave in a terracotta in the Louvre (Fig. 409).[99] He has laid his clasped hands between his knees. The bronze statuette of a slave in Princeton found in Egypt (Fig. 410)[100] grasps his left wrist with his right hand like the standing bronze figurine in Milan (Fig. 403). He wears a mantle over both shoulders, a ring around his lower neck, perhaps to mark him as a fugitive slave, and stretches his big head forward as if looking fearfully for an aggressor. A statuette vase in the British Museum also seems to represent a fearful slave who has taken refuge on an altar. He wears a wreath with a long fillet (Fig. 411).[101] Much more at ease is the curly seated slave in chlamys represented in a statuette from the Collection Misthos, thus probably from Myrina, in Athens.[102] He gesticulates gaily with his right arm, leaning his head, which is adorned with a wreath and fillet, on his right shoulder. He is seated on a small rounded bench, while others (Figs. 407 and 409) are seated on a simple square seat and still others (Figs. 406, 410-412) are probably seated on an altar. A round altar is certainly used as refuge by the bronze actor in Hartford, Connecticut (Fig. 412).[103] He has thrown himself backward on a round altar decorated with garlands and masks, turning

Figs. 402-405. Slaves with folded hands

402

403

404a-c

405

Figs. 406, 407. Seated slaves

his head to his right, waving his right arm with a fist against his persecutors, and dangling his legs with crossed knees in the air. We might restore a similar altar to the much corroded bronze figurine from Egypt in Berlin (Fig. 413).[104] This actor also has his knees crossed with his feet hanging free, both arms spread out in lively gesticulation, the right forward, the left to the side, the head turned to the right. This motif of a flight to an altar is frequent in Latin Comedy and Roman marble statuettes and reliefs (see Ch. XI, Figs. 556-558; Ch. XII, Fig. 587).

The often mentioned catalogue of Pollux's *Onomasticon* (IV, 143-154) includes 44 comic masks, 9 being those of old matured men, 11 those of youths, 7 those of slaves, and 17 those of women. In each division the arrangement is essentially according to age. In addition, the coiffure, the color of the hair, the manner of wearing the beard, the complexion, the shape of the eyebrows, and, in fewer instances, the characteristics of other parts of the face or the facial expression are taken into consideration in the classification. C. Robert has shown that one can actually stage all Latin comedies, which are mostly based on Greek New Comedy, with this assortment of masks. This author and O. Navarre, A.K.H. Simon, T.B.L. Webster, Pickard-Cambridge, Gisela Krien, and occasionally other scholars, have partly accepted, partly rejected, partly supplemented the attributions of Robert.[105] Pickard-Cambridge, instead of assigning the right masks out of Pollux's list to each character in the scanty remains of Greek New Comedy, tries to illustrate the catalogue given by Pollux with the figurative representations of scenes, statuettes, and masks. This author, on the other hand, has realized that Pollux wrote almost half a millennium later than Menander. Even if his catalogue is based on Aristophanes of Byzantium (ca. 257-180 B.C.), and more likely on the wardrobe of Hellenistic actors' guilds, he certainly reflects more the usage at his own time than the earlier periods. There are more shades of forms and expressions in the Hellenistic monuments than are listed in Pollux, and the masks in the time of Menander were not of normal or standardized types. They were probably only a little more standardized in Terence, while Plautus may have been on the way to definite types (see Ch. XI). Pollux is at the end of this develop-

ment with the tendency to standardize typical masks. For earlier works it is more important to explain the masks from the valuable remains of Menander and other Greek comic writers than from Pollux.[106]

The figurative monuments together with the texts teach us much not only of the numerous situations and amusing individuals of the New Comedy, but also of the lively, refined, and varied gestures (see Ch. VII, p. 81, Figs. 295-299 and this chapter, Figs. 395-413). The fathers are much more self-controlled than their light-headed sons, and if a father sometimes becomes violent, a prudent friend restrains him, as on the comedy relief in Naples (Fig. 324; cf. Figs. 325-328). The servants, on the contrary, are often uncontrolled and unduly lively. This is the case with the slave on the comedy relief who tries to hide behind his young master while supporting him. Other examples are the old freedman on the mural paintings in Naples (Fig. 395) who stands with his legs wide apart and mocks the lovers. The slaves in the statuettes are shown running, dancing, or alertly poised on an altar (Figs. 396-413; cf. Ch. VII, Figs. 297-299). Their pose often expresses deep thought, or in other cases mistrust and a readiness to jump up and run away upon the advent of danger. It is interesting to compare the statuette of a seated bourgeois or freedman, who is talking and yet keeps his hands inside his large mantle (Fig. 408) with that of a seated younger slave, both of whose hands are outside his chlamys and who talks with lively gesticulation (Fig. 413).

Among the women we find all varieties of poses depicting everything from the deepest emotion to the greatest joy: a sad girl (Fig. 355; cf. Figs. 161-162); an excited chattering courtesan (Fig. 360); obstrusive, indiscreet garrulity in the statuette of a stout matchmaker (Fig. 349); cunning laughter of the courtesan, mocked by the old freedman on the wall painting (Fig. 395) and in the statuette of an impudent lassie (Fig. 359); and boisterous laughter in the seated concubine (Fig. 357). The three women on the mosaic of Dioscurides (Fig. 347) form an expressive group: the old one reckons aloud, the young woman in the center, probably a courtesan, demonstrates with her hand, while the other

Figs. 410-413. Slaves taking refuge on altars

410   411   412   413

s. 408, 409. Seated man and slave

young woman, probably a bourgeoise, listens fearfully with lowered head. The clumsy dance movement of the two musicians on the other mosaic of Dioscurides (Fig. 346); the abandon evident in the music of the flute player (Fig. 328) and of the merry cithara player (Fig. 341); the eager preparation of a dish by the gossiping and curiously spying cook (Fig. 379), who is adorned with the floral wreath of the symposium; the coarseness of the parasite (Figs. 372-377); the sad pose of the officer punished for his bragging words (Fig. 368); the false friendliness of the procurer (Figs. 386-387)—all these let us guess how these plays of Attic New Comedy, coupled with the highly developed art of staging and acting during the Hellenistic period, attained their highest, most subtle, and most inspiring presentations, which were in perfect accord with the content and meaning of the plays.

We must, of course, always take into consideration that Greek art, despite the tendency to truth to nature in the Hellenistic period, never copied exactly from nature, and still less so from theatrical performances. The terracotta, bronze, and marble masks certainly differed considerably from the original masks, most of which were probably made of linen covered with stucco and painted in individual manners. Cork or wood might also have occasionally been used. The interest in portraiture might have induced the artists to give more facial expression to the imitated masks than the originals had.

This same interest led to the development of the mime, the last form of performance which invaded the Greek theater in the late Hellenistic period. It developed in Syracuse, from which it later came to Greece as well as to Rome (see Ch. XI, p. 160). It was given in rustic and religious festivals. Sophron composed the first literary mimes in prose.[107] Costumes and characters were taken from daily life of the middle and lower classes. There were monologues, dialogues, little scenes, and dances.

The mimes were sometimes serious, but mostly jocular (μῖμοι σπουδαῖοι and γελοῖοι). They were played by men and women without masks, and were also divided into male and female scenes (μῖμοι ἀνδρεῖοι and γυναικεῖοι). Subjects among the male mimes were the peasant and the tuna fishers. This might be illustrated by a southern Italian vase found in Lipari, now in the Collection Mandralisca at Cefalù, showing a fish vendor selling half a tuna fish, which he has cut with a big knife, to a customer with a large head and bald forehead on a meager body (Fig. 414).[108] Among the female mimes

Fig. 414. Tuna fisherman and customer. Southern Italian vase from Lipari

subjects were the needlewoman and the sorceress. This is related to the subject of the mosaic of Dioscurides showing women (above Fig. 347).

The Sicilian mime came to Athens in the early fourth century. Plato liked Sophron and is said to have imitated the form of the mime for his dialogues. Xenophon in his *Symposion*, II and VII, portrays a wandering troupe from Syracuse, in which a boy and girl accompanied by a flute player present, at the house of the wealthy Callias, dances and acrobatic feats, such as somersaults in which the girl tumbles in and out of a circle of knives stuck point upward in the floor. Similar tricks are pictured on vase paintings from Southern Italy (see Ch. XI, Fig. 579). In conclusion, the boy and the girl give a ballet, the theme of which is the love of Dionysus and Ariadne. The banquet depicted is assumed to have been given in the year 421 B.C. Not much later than this ballet is an Attic vase painting in the Collection Vlastos at Athens. It depicts the dance of a mime who makes a caricature of the hero Perseus (Fig. 202).[109] The dance is acted on a small stage, such as the popular entertainers carried with them for the farce (see Ch. X). The patron is probably a wealthy Athenian represented seated on an elegant Attic chair together with a handsome young man.

In the Hellenistic period the mime was given a

poetic form by Theocritus, whose *Adoniazusae* or Women at the Adonis Festival (No. 15) is considered to be the best ancient mime. The *Pharmaceutriae* (No. 2) are related in subject to the Dioscurides mosaic (Fig. 346). Herondas is coarser but probably more effective for recitation. The fragment of a mime with the lament of a forsaken girl before the door of her lover has been found in Egypt.[110] A late Hellenistic lamp in Athens (Fig. 415)[111] gives us the three actors (mimologoi, μιμολόγοι) of such a literary mimus and the name of the plot (hypothesis, ὑπόθεσις): The *Mother-in-Law* (Hekyra, Ἑκυρά). In the center is a bald, stupid-looking man with enormous ears, broad nose, and a fat belly. He is flanked by an older man and a youth, probably the husband and the son-in-law of the principal character. They could, however, also represent a youth and an older citizen quarreling with a slave dealer or panderer (pornoboskos, πορνοβοσκός), a situation similar to Herondas, *Mime* No. 2.[112] Both of them walk away apparently in violent discussion, and they look back upon the man in the center while they leave. The mime may be responsible for the popular jokes at the expense of mothers-in-law. Terence in his *Hecyra* certainly treats her very respectfully. None of the mime players wears a mask. In addition to the normal types like the youth, abnormally ugly and even deformed persons performed in the mime. This form of entertainment had great popularity in Rome (cf. Ch. XI, p. 160; and Ch. XV, Figs. 775, 786, 825-829). The mimes probably did not enter the Greek theater before the Roman period but were played in private houses.

Fig. 415. Actors of the mime *Hekyra*. Terracotta lamp, Athens

In the clever preface to his play *Great Catherine*, Shaw says: "No sane and skilled author writes plays that present impossibilities to the actor or to the stage engineer. If, as occasionally happens, he asks them to do things that they have never done before and cannot conceive as presentable or possible (as Wagner and Thomas Hardy have done, for example), it is always found that the difficulties are not really insuperable, the author having foreseen unsuspected possibilities both in the actor and in the audience, whose will-to-make-believe can perform the quaintest miracles. Thus may authors advance the art of acting and of staging plays. But the actor also may enlarge the scope of the drama by displaying powers not previously discovered by the author."[1] Not only Hardy, and not only Wagner, whose wishes in regard to stage settings were first carried out fifty years after his death by his son,[2] but all the great dramatists were ahead of their day in this respect. Succeeding generations are the ones who, with conscientious investigation and admiration for the greatness of creative geniuses, have exhausted the possibilities of staging and setting contained in the plays of the masters. The best example of this is the history of the production of Shakespearean drama, from its simplest to its most complicated forms, with the eventual return to the original form of presentation.

It is consequently explicable that, for the great tragedians, an effective framing of the scene of performance by means of the paraskenia did not take place before the last part of the fifth century. Furthermore, the stone skene at the edge of the orchestra was not planned in a durable and practical form before the time of Pericles; it was begun for the first time during the peace of Nicias (421-415) (Fig. 237) and was not finished before the age of Alexander the Great (Figs. 257-260). The newly-constructed building had not long been in use when new ideas in staging arose. The high development of the art of acting in the fourth century (see Ch. VII) demanded, for the most esteemed artists, as distinguished a place as possible. The chorus, on the other hand, was neglected to such an extent in tragedy as well as in comedy that the classical orchestra became too large for it in the dramatic plays, although at the same time, of course, the lyrical choruses in all periods required this space. The favorite drama of the Hellenistic audience, however, was no longer tragedy but New Comedy (see Ch. VIII). In this the aim of the poet was not, as in Old Comedy, the ridiculous and grotesque situation but the portrayal and clear delineation of the individual characters. It was, therefore, of prime importance to make these individual figures visible to the audience with relief-like precision. This led to a raised stage for the first time in Greece.

The theater of Priene[3] (Figs. 416-425) is the

Fig. 416. Priene

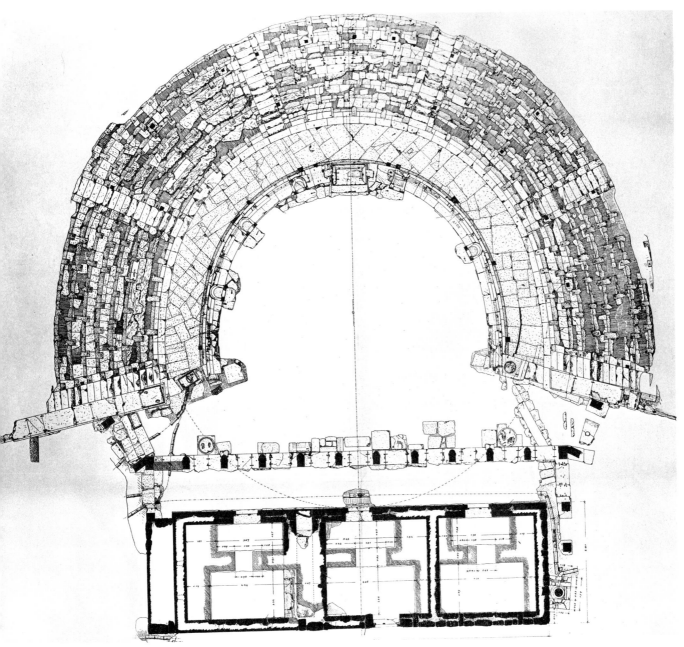

Figs. 417, 418. Theater of Priene. Plan of actual remains;
Plan of earlier theater reconstructed; von Gerkan

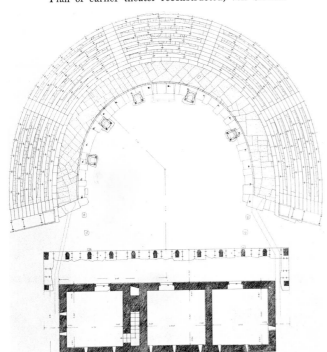

earliest and, since it is well preserved (Figs. 416-417) although small, it is for us the most important among the new theaters which were erected in Hellenistic times. Only in such a new building, and not in older remodelled ones, could new ideas find clear and unquestionable expression. In his careful and constructive researches A. von Gerkan has worked out in a reliable way the oldest form of this theater (Figs. 418-419), and also the later remodelling (Figs. 420-421) with their dates. The theater was included in the general building plan of the whole city, and the auditorium was probably laid out at once about 340 B.C., as were all the other public buildings. It was designed in the classic form of a horseshoe, and built by digging out the earth at the slope of the hill and erecting supporting walls

109

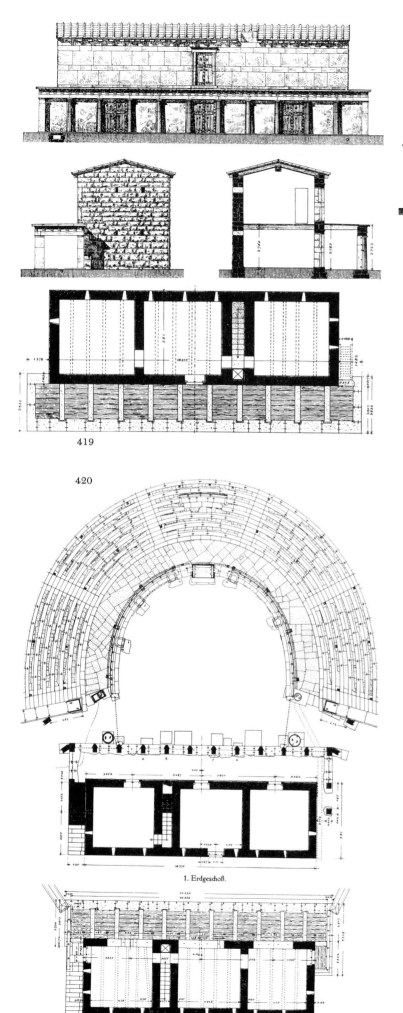

419

420

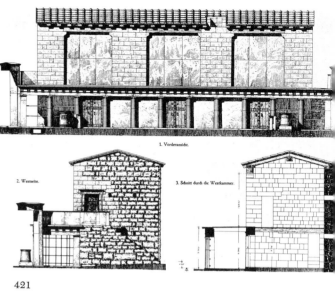

1. Vorderansicht.

2. Westseite.　　3. Schnitt durch die Westkammer.

421

Figs. 419-421. Theater of Priene. Earlier and later scene buildings, reconstructed

1. Erdgeschoß.

(Figs. 416, 425). In about 300 B.C. the seats of honor were already granted. The erection of the stone skene, however, did not come until the beginning of the third century. Its form is perfectly clear: a two-story structure with a one-story forebuilding facing the orchestra (Figs. 420-421). The flat roof of this lower building was made of wooden planks set between stone beams (Figs. 416 and 419). The front wall consisted of engaged half-columns of stone set against rectangular stone pillars (Fig. 422a-b). Since there were holes for bolts on the sides of the pillars, wooden panels must have been fastened to them by bolts. We thus have the pillars as a stone framework and a permanent support (Fig. 422b),[4] the attached stone columns as a permanent decoration (Fig. 422a), and interchangeable painted decorations on wooden panels between the supporting posts (Figs. 419 and 421). According to von Gerkan,[5] the top story, above the flat roof, was at first completely closed except for one door (Figs. 419 and 423). Bulle,[6] on the contrary, is of the opinion that it had from the beginning three doors facing the orchestra, corresponding to the doors of the lower story. For the later period there is no doubt that in Priene, as in most of the other theaters, narrow piers were constructed so as to form three wide openings (Figs. 420-421, 424-425).

The names for the different parts of this Hellenistic stage building are given in the inscriptions from Delos,[7] which begin in 305 B.C. and describe the progress of the work on a wooden theater consisting of a skene and a proskenion, mentioned in

Fig. 422a-b. Priene, pilasters of proskenion

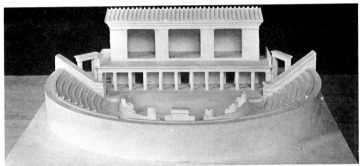

an inscription of 280 B.C. Stone construction of the auditorium began in 297, of the skene in 274. There can be no doubt that the skene is the two-story main building. The proskenion is the porch, veranda, or colonnade which is laid before it at the same height as the lower story. Its roof is at the same level as the floor of the upper story. The inscriptions of 282/81 and 280/79 B.C. mention the pinakes, which are, of course, the panels fastened between the pillars; the inscriptions furnish the additional information that these panels were painted. When, in 279 B.C., a wooden beam eleven cubits long was needed for the logeion, the speaking-place or platform, only the flat roof or terrace of the proskenion can be meant.[8] When in the same year the roof of the skene was painted, the building must have been completed. When the skene was rebuilt in stone beginning 274 B.C., at the same time stone foundations for the side wings (paraskenia) were laid. These side wings must have been two stories high, for they are specifically called upper and lower paraskenia, to correspond with the upper and lower skene. The upper story (episkenion) was at that time still made of wood. Some of the pinakes were constructed anew, others were repaired and used again.[9] From 269 to 250 B.C. the whole skene was gradually transformed into stone, and the tiers of seats in the auditorium (theatron) were still being erected as late as 246 B.C.[10] In the year 180 B.C. a commission was given for wooden pinakes above the logeion.[11] Consequently, the large openings above the logeion, such as were found in the later theater of Priene (Figs. 421, 424-425), probably date from that time. According to an inscription of Oropus (Figs. 426-429),[12] these large openings were called thyromata ($\theta\nu\rho\acute{\omega}\mu\alpha\tau\alpha$, large openings for pinakes or backdrops) and belonged to the upper skene, the episcenium (episkenion), just as the small pinakes belonged to the columns of the proskenion. Since the theater at Oropus is well preserved, it confirms the names for the parts of the Hellenistic theater derived from the associa-

Figs. 423-425. Priene, earlier and later scene buildings, with pinakes

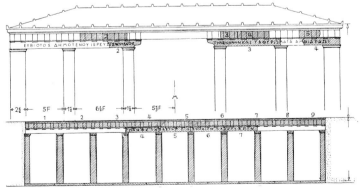

Fig. 426. Theater of Oropus, thyromata

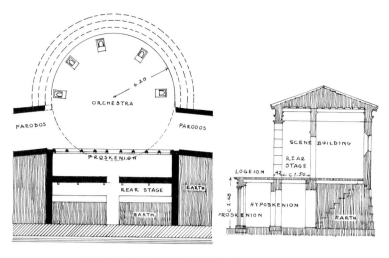

Figs. 430-431. Terracotta altars in the shape of houses. Vorderasiatischen Museum, Berlin

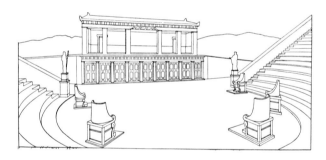

Figs. 427-429. Theater of Oropus, reconstructions

little terracotta altars belonging to the Vorderasiatischen Museum in Berlin (Figs. 430-431),[14] taken from the cult room of the archaic temple of Ishtar in Assur, which was destroyed about 2700 B.C., have the form of a two-story house. Each has a projecting lower story, with a flat terrace at the level of the floor of the second story extending the width of the entire building. At the front of the forebuilding of the one house (Fig. 430) is a wide door, and at its side there are triangular windows, while the back wing has a square window on the upper floor. Two doors open out on the terrace. The other house (Fig. 431) has four doors in the forebuilding and four triangular windows in front. Above the terrace are four doors and above them four windows. On the side there is a door below, a large window above, and two small ones on the second floor. It is a light structure, a kind of arbor for the hot season. It is built with the help of a scaffolding of vertical wooden posts and horizontal beams. It is thus a real "skene," a temporary building.

This type of broad house with a colonnade in front of the main room, often framed by two side wings in the form of paraskenia, is frequent in Asia Minor in all periods for temples (Fig. 432b, c, d) as well as for palaces (Fig. 432e, f, g).[15] Often there is an open terrace on the roof of the portico between the side buildings, with a door leading out from the upper floor to the terrace. The fact that this form is used for temples as well as for palaces makes it useful for stage performances, since the scene in the tragedies—which continued in the classical form and with the classical mythical material—is almost always either the one or the other. This type of house is still used today in Iran and Iraq.[16]

In Egypt the so-called soul houses, dating from the Eleventh to the Twelfth Dynasties, have a fore-

tion of inscriptions from Delos with the marble building at Priene.

As Priene was only a small, though an educated and highly cultivated city, we can not conclude that this type of Hellenistic proskenion theater originated in Priene itself. Bulle, indeed, has presumed that the new form originated in Alexandria.[13] One must also consider the other capitals of the East, to which the cultural leadership of the Greek world had now been transferred. This presumption is supported by the scheme of design of the proskenion theater: a house with a forebuilding equal in height to the first story occurs in Asia Minor as well as in Egypt, as a very old form which was probably always popular. Two

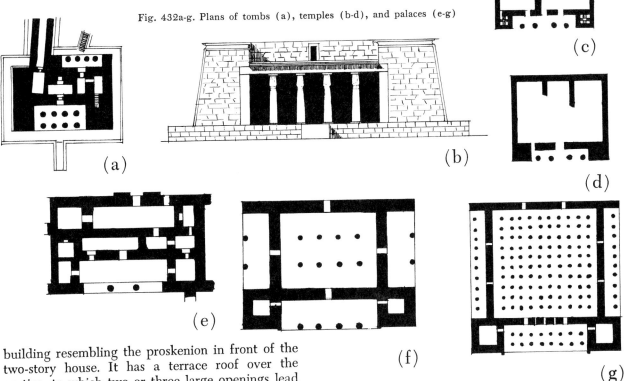

Fig. 432a-g. Plans of tombs (a), temples (b-d), and palaces (e-g)

(a)

(b)

(c)

(d)

(e)

(f)

(g)

building resembling the proskenion in front of the two-story house. It has a terrace roof over the portico, to which two or three large openings lead from the upper story. There are some 150 models preserved (Figs. 433-434).[17] Similar porticos are found in the rock tombs from the Fifth to the Twelfth Dynasties (Fig. 432a).[18]

Several examples of this form of flat-roofed portico, attached as a porch to a higher main building, are known in Greece also, dating from the fourth century B.C. on. The earliest example is the Leonidaeum in Olympia,[19] in which a one-story peristyle was erected around the two-story building, so that the terrace on the portico could serve to connect the single guest rooms and the stairs leading up from below. The southeast building of Olympia[20] also has a portico surrounding it as a porch on three sides.

In Hellenized Southern Italy, the first exterior portico, as far as I can see, is that in the Villa of Mysteries at Pompeii. The first building, dated by Maiuri in the third century B.C., was surrounded on three sides by a portico.[21] Later this colonnade was transformed into a roofed corridor with windows, but, in front of the room with the famed mystery frescoes, the columns were allowed to stand unaltered (Fig. 435). Above them a terrace for the newly-built upper story was constructed; thus this part of the building conforms entirely to the type of the Hellenistic proskenion. From the first century B.C. on, such terraces above the rows of columns of a portico, attached in front or running around the building, were common in villas. The terrace before the part of the Villa of Diomedes built on a higher level and the promenade above the colonnade around the garden situated on a lower level are

Figs. 433, 434. Egyptian soul houses. Terracotta; Boston; Metropolitan Museum

Fig. 435. Villa of Mysteries. Pompeii

Fig. 436. Villa of Diomedes, section

113

Fig. 437. Roman villa surrounded by porticos. Wall painting from Stabiae, Naples

good examples (Fig. 436). We find them also in the reproductions of such Roman villas on the wall paintings.[22] In one case even people are depicted walking on the roof of the lower portico (Fig. 437).[23] I am convinced that the Roman villas had such open terraces level with the upper story much more often than the ruins and their modern reconstructions allow us to realize. They are also frequently found in American colonial houses.

These parallels show that the Hellenistic proskenion building was meant to reproduce a house and its forebuilding with a terraced roof. The forebuilding has the form of a colonnade attached as a porch or veranda to the main building. It often has paraskenia, which are connected with each other by the colonnade. The question is, how this Hellenistic type of theater was used. Three main views concerning the scene of performance in the Hellenistic theater are held:

1) The skene and proskenion always served merely as a decorative background for the plays in the Hellenistic as in the classical era. The chief champion of this view is Dörpfeld.[24]

2) The proskenion was first built to serve as a decorative background, but in the second century B.C. the scene of performance was transferred to the roof of the colonnade which was now used as a platform for the actors (logeion). The chief advocate here is A. von Gerkan.[25]

3) The proskenion from the beginning possessed

a stage terrace (logeion) in the form of a platform above the columns. The place of performance was upon this platform, at first in front of a solid wall with doors, and, beginning with the second century B.C., in front of wide openings (thyromata) into which backdrops and other decorations were set, or which, when left open, served to exhibit interior scenes. Chief advocates of this view are Bethe, Fiechter, Bulle, Dinsmoor, and this author.[26]

Dörpfeld founded his opinion chiefly on the fact that the tragedies in Hellenistic times had not changed; and, this being the case, it would not be necessary to change the scene of the performance. Only rarely did an actor appear on the roof of the house or on the theologeion identified with it by Dörpfeld. The wall of the proskenion could be characterized with the help of the painted pinakes as three different buildings, corresponding to its three doors. According to Dörpfeld, the row of columns of the proskenion is only a decoration serving as background to the actors in the orchestra, parts of which could be transformed to represent a temple, a palace, or a citizen's house by placing gables upon the colonnade. Dörpfeld consequently considers the forewall as the most important part of the proskenion. The platform—that is, the roof supported by the columns—was rarely used, only occasionally in the plays and once in a while for a single speaker appearing before assemblies of the people.

Von Gerkan accepts this theory of Dörpfeld for the early Hellenistic period, because in his opinion the proskenion of Priene, thoroughly investigated by him, actually had only one possible entrance from which the individual actor could make his appearance, i.e., from the central door of the upper story of the skene. The gods appeared upon the roof of the main building by means of an elevator which was discovered by von Gerkan (Figs. 419-421, 425). The theater at New Pleuron (Figs. 438-439), according to this author, also had only one door leading out to the platform above the proskenion. The pinakes at the front of the proskenion carried the scenery, before which the actors appeared in the orchestra. The platform was transformed for the first time into a stage not before the middle of the second century in Priene, and at about the same time or only a short time before this in Oropus (Figs. 426-429) and other theaters. Side entrances and parapets were added, the rear wall (that is, the front wall of the second story) was opened into broad thyromata (Figs. 424-429), in which decorations were placed and in which scenes of interiors could be represented. Because of the raised stage a new proedria—that is, a section for seats of honor

Figs. 438-439. New Pleuron, theater. Plan and reconstruction

—was constructed at the same level as the stage in Priene.

The breaking up of the front wall of the upper story behind the podium in order to form large openings between piers—three of them in Priene (Figs. 424-425), five of them in Oropus (Figs. 426-429) and seven in Ephesus (Figs. 443-447)—was first recognized by Fiechter as an attempt to increase the space on the podium; in other words, these thyromata formed a rear stage, thereby proving that the platform was the actual stage. Here palaces, landscapes, and houses could be much more effectively represented than upon the small pinakes between the columns of the front porch wall (cf. Figs. 421-425). Fiechter does not doubt that the proskenion was built to serve as a stage from the very beginning. The New Comedy and the decline of the chorus necessarily demanded a high stage as the scene of performance. The long proskenion sufficed for all staging demands.

Fiechter's theories were carried farther by Bulle. New Comedy, consisting only of dialogue, demanded a new kind of stage and therefore produced one. The type of play depicting the rich bourgeoisie, with few characters, required a narrow space in which to concentrate the actors so as to produce the effect of a relief (Fig. 346). Bulle and Dinsmoor

believe that already in the fourth century Middle Comedy was presented on a raised logeion and that the oldest temporary wooden logeion in Athens was erected, at the very latest, at the time when Menander flourished. The architectural decoration of the front of the proskenion was necessary for non-scenic uses. Bulle further believes that in the middle of the fourth century the new ideas for constructing the stage were tried out with temporary buildings. As an example of a Middle Comedy needing the new form of logeion construction, he gives the *Amphitruo* of Plautus (see Ch. XI, p. 151). He therefore holds the opinion that Lycurgus had erected a stage of the new type in Athens about 330 B.C., and that this example was followed in Epidaurus at the end of the fourth century.

I myself think that the development of the logeion followed slowly upon the new literary ideas. The theater of Lycurgus was certainly the realization of a purely classical tradition, and the new type took shape not in Athens, but in the East about 300 B.C. I consider the combination of the skene with a proskenion, equal in height to the first story, to be a compromise which met the needs of the lyrical choruses and the old classical tragedies with a rich background building, as well as the needs of New Comedy with the raised stage. For the thymelic artists the row of columns in the proskenion was the background, comparable to the colonnades in the Hellenistic market places. For the scenic artists the forewall was changed by the pinakes from a colonnade into a panelled front wall or a basement for the stage without special significance. Above these the actors appeared before a solid housewall, pierced by three doors, paralleling in all respects the closed fronts of most Greek private houses. For a background the standard height of the proskenion hall was a little too low; for a stage it was somewhat too high. However, it made it possible, on the one hand, for the actors on it to be well seen, and, on the other, for the musicians to pass in the customary manner from the lower story of the skene, through the hyposkenion, into the orchestra. The combination of wood and stone in terrace and forewall of the proskenion gave excellent acoustics for both kinds of presentations.[27]

I agree with Dörpfeld that in Athens at the time of Lycurgus, when the stone skene was being completed, a change in the place of action would be unthinkable, considering the strong classical tradition. That the proskenion was not yet used as a stage at the time of Middle Comedy is proved by the joke of the comic poet Antiphanes.[28] The courtesan Nannion is compared with a proskenion because she had a lovely face, much gold, and expensive

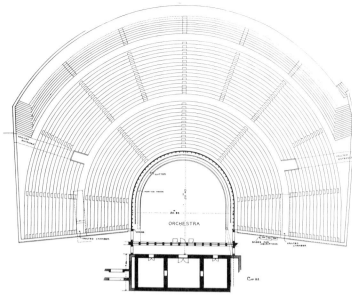

Fig. 440. Assos, theater, plan

clothes, but when naked she was unusually ugly. In this case only a coulisse or movable screen, a scaena ductilis, can be intended, which, when drawn away, left the bare skeleton wall in view. If a proskenion of a later type had been meant, only the brightly painted pinakes could have been removed, but a row of columns would have remained. Plautus, who is sometimes quoted as needing a two-story stage for his *Amphitruo*, did not play upon a Hellenistic, but upon a South Italian stage (see Ch. X, Figs. 479-484 and Ch. XI, p. 151).

I further agree with von Gerkan that the first proskenion in Priene was poorly equipped for presentations. A single door (Figs. 419 and 423)[29] was totally inadequate, because the actors of New Comedy were often required to enter many times from different directions.

The Hellenistic proskenion, however, was created neither in Athens nor in Priene. With the Peloponnesian War, Athens lost not only the political but also gradually the cultural leadership and it must be remembered that the Lycurgean theater marks the end of the classical period and not the beginning of the Hellenistic era. Priene, in turn, may have been an educated and cultivated city, but, because of its small size, modified the creations of the large cities to suit its needs. Even if we had the good fortune to possess early Hellenistic theaters from Alexandria, Antioch, or one of the other residences of the Diadochi, we should probably find them inadequate in regard to stage equipment. The long narrow scene of performance was probably the same everywhere. We must, however, remember that we have at Priene the oldest instance of a stage on Greek soil. It is certainly not as practical as the stage of the phlyakes, which appeared somewhat earlier in Southern Italy (see Ch. X); but, in recompense, it is more beautiful and more monumental with its decorative wall in front.

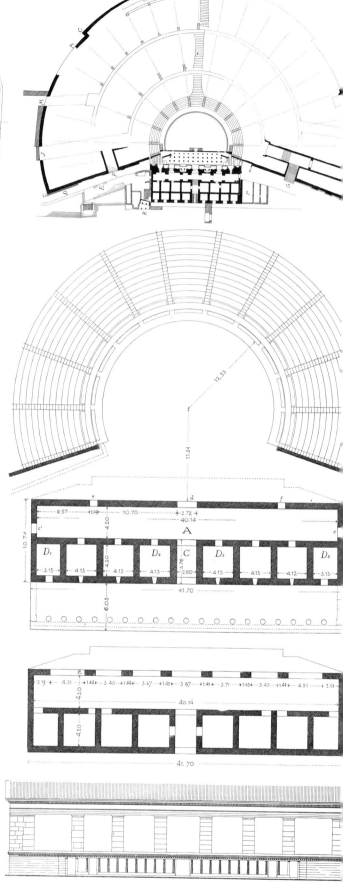

Figs. 441-444. Theater in Ephesus. Actual remains; Hellenistic theater and stage; Upper story; Elevation of the stage

116

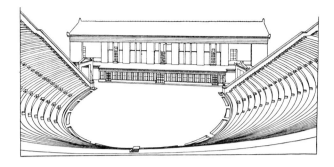

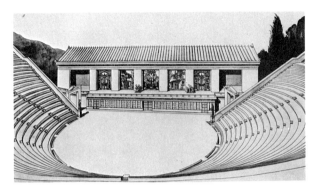

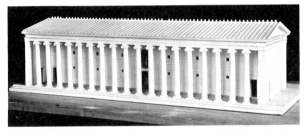

Figs. 445-448. Ephesus. Reconstructions of Hellenistic theater, Fiechter; Bulle; Model in Stuttgart, Fiechter

The new Hellenistic ideas, developing in combination with native forms, and already realized in the large eastern residences, came to Delos and Priene, as well as to Assos (Fig. 440),[30] Ephesus (Figs. 441-448),[31] and elsewhere in Asia Minor in not yet perfected form. This form has been designated by Bulle as "the type of the flat wall."[32] All four theaters mentioned above were probably completed in the first half of the third century, and the theater of Assos (Fig. 440) is closely related to that of Priene (cf. Fig. 418). The theater in Ephesus must have been planned about 274, at the time of the foundation of the whole Hellenistic city. In dis-

agreement with von Gerkan, Bulle makes the assertion for Priene (Figs. 416-421) that probably from the very beginning the long narrow stage had three doors leading onto it. With the passing of time, however, additional entrances were created in Priene and Assos. At both these theaters, where from the very beginning the proskenion extended on both sides beyond the skene, extensions were now added at both ends of the skene. On the west side the extension reached as far as a door leading to the upper story; on the east side it led to a flight of stairs, the first step of which was at the rear corner of the stage building.[33] An actor could thus reach the podium from below as well as directly from the upper story without using the upper door from the inside, so that there were three possibilities of entrance even if there was only one central door. The edges of the terraces were protected by parapets. In Delos the terrace seems to have extended around the whole building (Figs. 449-451).[34] In this case it is—like the stage building with a colonnade in front—the imitation of a house surrounded by a covered

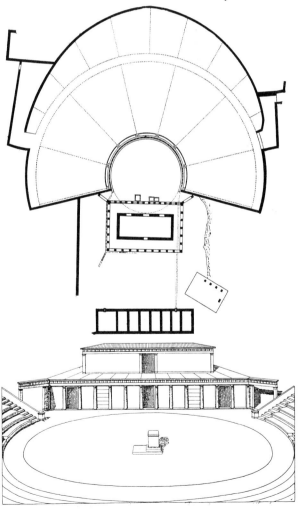

Figs. 449, 450. Theater of Delos. Plan; reconstruction, Dörpfeld

Fig. 451. Theater of Delos. View of the ruins

colonnade on all sides. Such a one is the Leonidaeum, named for its builder, in Olympia. It is a hotel for distinguished visitors. The terraces formed by the roofs permit communication between all rooms in the upper story. The luxurious symposium tent of Ptolemy II and the villa on a ship of Ptolemy IV had such an outer peristasis.[35]

This eastern type with a long and narrow stage invaded the Greek mainland during the third and second centuries B.C. Instead of the stairways leading up to the proskenion most theaters have, however, ramps. These are sometimes laid out horizontally, as in Eretria (Figs. 452-454).[36] The reason here is that the scene building which had been erected in the fourth century on a higher level and with paraskenia, was probably extended forward in the middle of the third century and, together with the orchestra, sunk below the natural surface of the ground (see Figs. 284-288). The logeion was on the older level, while the columns of the proskenion stood on the new lower level of the orchestra. The ramps are slightly inclined, for they run parallel to the slanting analemmata, the supporting walls of the auditorium.

In most cases the ramps ascended along the parodoi to the floor of the logeion, the stage on the height of the proskenion. In the theater of Sicyon, built in the first half of the third century, these sloping paths are cut out of the living rock, which also fills a great part of the lower story (Fig. 455).[37]

Figs. 452-454a-b. Theater of Eretria. Plan of actual remains; Reconstruction of the third scene building;
Section and reconstruction of the Hellenistic building

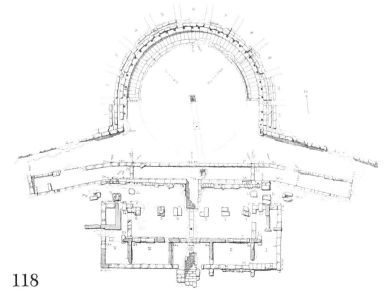

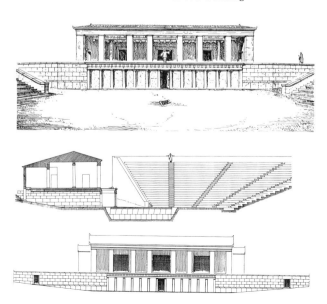

118

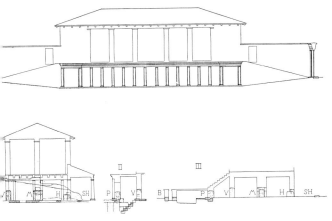

Fig. 455. Theater of Sicyon. Elevation and sections of scene building

Fig. 456. Theater of Epidaurus. Reconstruction of stage building, Puchstein

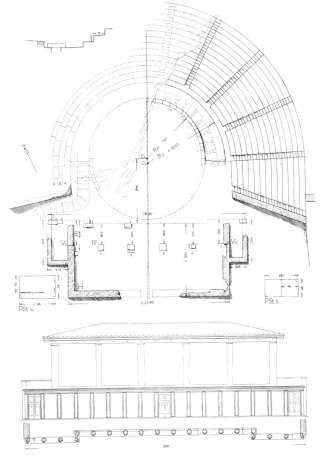

Figs. 457-459. Theater of Oeniadae. Plan and elevation of stage building, Fiechter; stage building and orchestra, Bulle

As a consequence, the ramps are well preserved, and together with the unusable lower story testify that the terrace of the proskenion was used quite early as a stage. A proskenion with ascending ramps as side entrances was built at Epidauros in the second century, replacing the paraskenia of the fourth century. The ramps begin at the outer and smaller opening of the entrance porches. They end on the top of the former paraskenia, which now form only flat decorative projections of the proskenion (see above, Figs. 271-274 and Fig. 456). The reconstruction by Puchstein in Fig. 456[38] shows Medea preparing the murder of her children and a messenger coming up on one ramp. Puchstein has wrongly added a Roman stage roof supported by walls which open with doors to the stage. The rim of limestone enclosing the orchestra circle (see above, Fig. 274) was probably laid at the same time when the proskenion and the ramp were built. The stone circle marked off definitely the place where the lyric chorus performed, in contrast to the stage for the scenic plays.

The same is true for Oeniadae in Acarnania. A stone circle was laid around the orchestra at the same time that a proskenion was set before a simple rustic paraskenion theater of the fourth century, at the instigation of Philip V of Macedonia about 219 B.C. (Figs. 457-459).[39] The old and new portions of the paraskenion- and the proskenion-theater were connected by pillars set in the corners between the old paraskenia and the new proskenion. In the interior there is a row of pillars which may have taken the place of the old front wall of the classical skene, for this row of pillars touches the ground circle of the lower seats, while the new reduced orchestra, enclosed by the lightly-colored, round limestone threshold, almost touches upon the proskenion, being only as far distant from it as the paraskenia project. The orchestra, no longer needed for tragedies with big choruses, thus diminished continually, while the stage was continually being made more practical through the opening of the

119

thyromata in the upper story. Oeniadae seems to be the first theater on the mainland in which the upper wall was opened by five thyromata, designed as a background, with painted backdrops to be inserted for the plays. This late form thus came very early from the East to Macedonia. In Oeniadae there are no ramps, but, in agreement with the Eastern form, as in Priene (Figs. 416-421), the proskenion was broader than the main skene, so that the actors could enter through side doors from the upper floor. The prosperity of Oeniadae was short, for in 167 B.C. it fell under Roman rule, and the theater was later remodelled in the Roman form.

In most theaters, however, there are ramps rising upward as side entrances from the parodos entrances, as in Oropus, Sicyon, Epidaurus (above, Figs. 428-429, 455-456), and in Corinth (Fig. 460).[40]

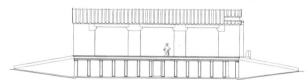

Fig. 460. Hellenistic theater of Corinth

The transformation of the paraskenia into walks leading upward was more practical than the retention of the paraskenia, which in classical times often were of only one story; and if they had a second story, they probably had no openings at all on the upper floor, or at best only windows, since as yet no high stage lay between them. The rising ramps of the mainland and the corresponding terraces, platforms, and staircases in the eastern cities plainly show that the shifting of the scene of performance in the majority of the theaters actually took place in the third century B.C.

The typical form of the late Hellenistic Greek stage thus was the thyromata stage with wide openings separated by rectangular piers. The idea of this building design is most clearly seen in the small theater in the sanctuary of Amphiaraus at Oropus (Figs. 426-429).[41] The proskenion, together with its pinakes, was dedicated, according to an inscription, by a stage manager about 200 B.C. The upper story of the main building, however, was constructed out of stone, probably not before about 150 B.C., according to another inscription, dedicated by a priest. This inscription gives the name thyromata, big doors, for the wide openings in the front of the upper skene building. This wall rises above the logeion—that is, behind the platform of the proskenion—with five wide openings separated by rectangular piers or broad pillars. Behind this front with the piers lies a second wall, which forms, on the inside of the skene, a corridor-like space. This space could serve

as rear stage to increase the depth of the logeion; or the wide openings could be hidden or closed temporarily by curtains or screens or movable painted scenery; or they could be decorated as the interior of a room. By these means numerous possibilities for entrances and scenes were gained. The side entrances by stairs, ramps, side corridors, and paraskenia had now become superfluous, since they could be replaced by entrances from the outer thyromata. Smaller theaters, like Priene with only three thyromata (Figs. 420-421, 424-425) or Oeniadae with five (Figs. 457-459), retained the outer side entrances; but large theaters, like Ephesus (Figs. 443-447) with seven thyromata, used the outermost openings as side entrances. Sometimes the central opening seems to have been wider than those on the sides, thus creating a rhythmical symmetry with the emphasis on the center, which was much better suited for a background than the regular row of half-columns at the front wall of the proskenion. In Oeniadae the cornice above the pillars ends with corbels above the central opening. A comparison of the upper and lower façades shows clearly the character of the colonnade of the proskenion as merely serving to support the platform (see below and Figs. 421 and 424). The lesser use of the orchestra in Oropus as well as in Priene is testified by the five marble thrones for guests of honor on the circumference.

In the theater of Pergamon the Hellenistic proskenion, built under Eumenes II (197-159 B.C.), cuts deeply into the orchestra, because it had to be erected on the narrow terrace which leads from the market place to the temple of Dionysus and which could not be fully used. To keep this street open only temporary structures with a skeleton of upright timbers could be built, as had been done in the classical period at Athens. The timbers are arranged in three rows, so as to allow a proskenion in front and three thyromata in the middle row (Figs. 461-462; cf. Ch. V, Figs. 243-247).[42]

Theaters having paraskenia were seldom built new in the Hellenistic period, and then only for special reasons. The theater in Babylon, which probably goes back to the one erected in honor of Alexander the Great, is built of unbaked clay bricks. This poor and inept material explains the retaining of the strong and solid side buildings.[43] In the small theater in New Pleuron in western Greece, erected soon after the construction of the city wall in 234 B.C., the building of the paraskenia was necessary to afford side entrances to the stage, for the only other entrance was through a door from the tower of the city wall (Figs. 438-439).[44] The latest theater having paraskenia is the theater at the Piraeus, the

Figs. 461, 462. Theater of Pergamon, orchestra and terrace

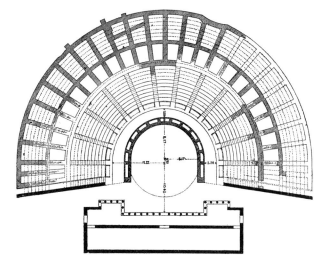

Fig. 463. Plan of theater in the Piraeus

harbor town of Athens (Fig. 463).[45] It is dated about 150 B.C. and was probably erected under the influence of Athens, but with the difference, that a proskenion was included from the beginning.

Wooden constructions may often have preceded the stone buildings. This was certainly the case in Megalopolis and Sparta. Megalopolis—the largest theater on the Greek mainland, with a capacity of about 21,000 spectators in three tiers—is connected with the assembly room for the ten thousand Arcadians, which was named Thersilion after its dedicator (Fig. 276).[46] Between the theatron and the assembly hall a permanent stone skene could not be erected. Therefore a large wooden scene building with a proskenion was constructed in the third century. It ran on wheels and was stored in the skenotheke, a shed erected in the left parodos. It was replaced by a stone proskenion after the destruction of the Thersilion in 222 B.C.

At Sparta a similar rolling stage was erected in the Augustan period. Heretofore, only non-scenic plays were presented at the Gymnopaidia and Hyakinthia in honor of the Spartan heroes, with choruses, parades of horsemen, ball games, and so on, and therefore no stage was needed. The main building moved on rollers and the proskenion on wheels in three rows of stone sills, and it was stored in a skenotheke at the right parodos. Sparta received a permanent Roman scaenae frons not before A.D. 78 in the time of the Emperor Vespasian, when a fire had destroyed the movable scene building. But even then only a temporary stage was erected.[47] Tragedies, comedies, and dithyrambs were given regularly, the latter at least until A.D. 100. The dithyrambs outside Athens were, however, not given by tribes but by the guilds (see Ch. VII).

The wide deep thyromata sheltered by the roof of the back stage give proof of the baroque taste of the late Hellenistic era, which aimed at strange effects. This was the cause of one last change in the Hellenistic theater, namely the transformation of the pillared proskenion, which had half columns and painted pinakes set between them, into a portico composed of completely circular columns without panels. The deeply-overshadowed hall under the podium corresponds now to the deeply-receding thyromata over the podium. It is the same taste which also created the high Ionic colonnade at the rear façade of the theater in Ephesus (Fig. 448). Also at Priene the pinakes disappeared in the later period somewhere around 150 B.C.[48] Good examples

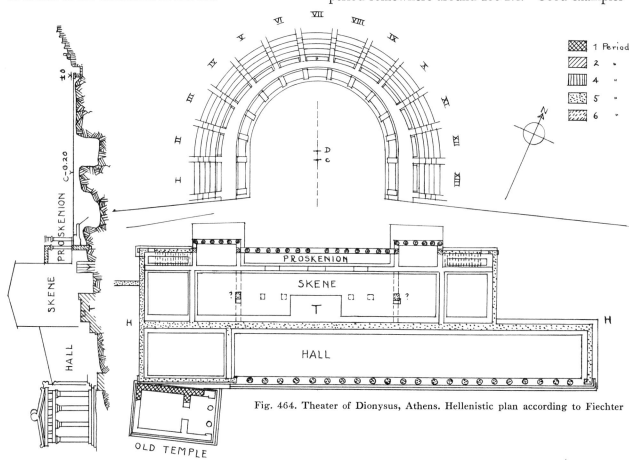

Fig. 464. Theater of Dionysus, Athens. Hellenistic plan according to Fiechter

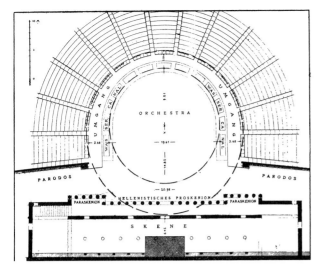

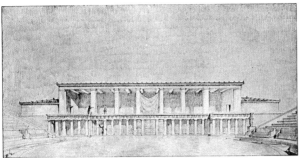

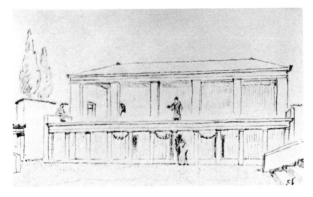

Figs. 465-467. Theater of Dionysus. Hellenistic plan, stages;
Fiechter

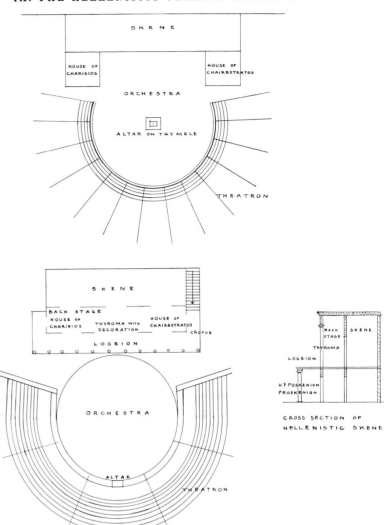

Figs. 468, 469. Plans and section for Menander's *The Arbitrants*; Athenian style of 300 B.C., Asiatic style 200 B.C., Bieber

are the theaters in Thasos[49] and in the Piraeus (Fig. 463).[50]

I do not doubt that it was this latest form of the Hellenistic theater which came to Athens not earlier than the second century B.C. and perhaps only after the destruction of Athens by Sulla in 86 B.C. A marble proskenion with 14 columns was set in between the Lycurgean paraskenia which were levelled and remodelled, but kept a front with six columns (Figs. 464-467).[51] The proedria with the beautiful seats of honor in the first row were executed in the style of the fourth century (above Figs. 267-269).[52] Athens, the center of classical culture, although it had become at this time only a Roman province, stuck obstinately to its conservative cult system, religious organization, and art

forms. The dramas of the writers of New Comedy were certainly played in Athens in the orchestra, while in the East they were performed on the high stage. This is certainly true for Menander, the founder of this new drama (Figs. 468-469).[53]

Thus the painted decorations of the stage building moved upward during the Hellenistic period. It is hard to say what the small pinakes below, and later the large screens above, looked like, but in any case they must always have been related to the contemporary monumental paintings. We may assume that the earlier pinakes below were plainer and more soberly painted than the later panels between the thyromata. The Roman pinax in Priene, built of cement and painted to represent the woodwork of a door,[54] serves as such a suitable filling for the supporting wall to justify the conclusion that similar simple paintings on pinakes were often used. We hear, however, also about figures painted on the

123

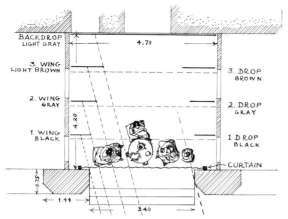

Fig. 470. Stage setting inside a thyroma, after Bulle

proskenion. Thus the figure of Demetrius carried by Oikoumene on the proskenion of Athens is described by Athenaeus (XII,536a) who quotes from Duris. As this must have occurred during the time of Demetrius (306-295), we must assume that a wooden stage was erected occasionally in Athens, or that Athenaeus uses proskenion in the sense of scaenae frons. It is too bad that we possess none of the tablets painted on wood or canvas from the Hellenistic times. We can only conclude that the decorations inside the thyromata were more realistically and more artistically executed than the small pinakes below. The painting of two tablets in Delos in the year 282 B.C. was paid for with 200 drachmas, which means that they must have been covered with valuable real paintings.[55]

A certain suggestion about these painted decorations is given by contemporary reliefs, mosaics, and wall paintings. The name thyroma, big door, leads to the supposition that these openings could be closed with a monumental door. This is indeed the case in the comedy relief from Naples (Fig. 324), where this entrance portal probably indicates the mansion of the rich bourgeois whose son comes home intoxicated. In the other half of the relief is a city view, indicating the place from which the youth returns. It is partly hidden by a curtain, parapetasma ($\pi\alpha\rho\alpha\pi\acute{\epsilon}\tau\alpha\sigma\mu\alpha$).[56] Before the thyromata were opened, a wall with only one large door could be in the background. This is the case in the mosaic of Dioscurides with musicians performing on the narrow stage (Fig. 346). The other mosaic of Dioscurides with four women depicts an interior scene within the frame of a thyroma (Fig. 347). An interesting sketch showing an attempt at the setting of this women's scene inside a thyroma has been made by Bulle[57] and has been redrawn by Elisabeth Wadhams (Fig. 470). The scene with the braggart soldier and his parasite (Fig. 371) on a wall painting, known only in a drawing, is also set in an interior between two piers, as the attempt of Bulle (Fig. 459) shows. The two dignified men seated against these piers seem to be statues of Aeschylus and Sophocles.

The wall paintings of the second style, that is, of the first century B.C., contain many Hellenistic motifs with many theatrical features.[58] The most important ones are those now in the Metropolitan Museum of New York (Figs. 471-474).[59] They are in the

Figs. 471, 472. Scenery for tragedy. Wall paintings from Boscoreale, Metropolitan Museum

cubiculum of the villa from Boscoreale, dated about 40-30 B.C. and decorated in the second style. They are not exact copies of the theatrical backdrops, but eclectic combinations in the Roman taste of the essence of decoration used for tragic (Figs. 471-472), comic (Fig. 473), and satyric (Fig. 474) settings. The same three kinds of scenery are mentioned by Vitruvius, *De architectura*, v,6,9: "genera autem sunt scaenarum tria: unum quod dicitur tragicum, alterum comicum, tertium satyricum. horum autem ornatus sunt inter se dissimili disparique ratione, quod tragicae deformantur columnis et fastigiis et signis reliquisque regalibus rebus; comicae autem aedificiorum privatorum et maenianorum habent speciem prospectusque fenestris dispositos imitatione, communium aedificiorum rationibus; satyricae vero ornantur arboribus speluncis montibus reliquisque agrestibus rebus in topiarii speciem deformati"; vii,5,2: "patentibus autem locis uti exhedris propter amplitudines parietum scaenarum frontes tragico more aut comico seu satyrico designarent." ("There are three kinds of scenes, one, called tragic; second, the comic; third, the satyric. Their decorations are different and unlike each other in scheme. Tragic scenes are delineated with columns, pediments, statues, and other objects suited to kings; comic scenes exhibit private dwellings, with balconies and views representing rows of windows, after the manner of ordinary dwellings; satyric scenes are decorated with trees, caverns, mountains, and other rustic objects delineated in landscape style." "In their open rooms, such as exedrae, on account of

the size, they depicted the façades of scenes in the tragic, comic, or satyric styles.")[60]

These three kinds of scenery mentioned by Vitruvius could never be combined in one set, as they are in Boscoreale and in the reconstruction of Ephesus by Bulle (Fig. 446), who has set all three decorations incorrectly side by side in the frames between the piers.[61] It would be better if variations of a single style were set in, either of the tragic (royal palaces, temples, shrines with columns, pediments, and statues), or of the comic (private buildings, houses with balconies and windows, views of a city), or of satyric (landscape settings, a country district with trees, caves, gardens, mountains, or a seashore). The piers likewise had to be adorned. That the Boscoreale frescoes are inspired by theatrical settings is clear from the fact that many of their motifs agree with those mentioned by Vitruvius. The fact that no human beings are represented also makes it likely that actors were to supply this human element. The monumental doors dominating the foreground of four panels (Fig. 473) are too large in comparison with the window in the wall and the high buildings behind it. They are thyromata agreeing with the elegant door on the relief with a comedy scene in Naples (Fig. 324), while the buildings behind have their nearest parallel in the city view of the same relief. The masks are not theatrical masks, although some remind one of comic masks of an old father or a leading servant, (Fig. 472), but whether theatrical or purely dionysiac, like satyrs or Pans (Fig. 473), they were and still are

Figs. 473, 474. Scenery for comedy and satyr play. Wall paintings from Boscoreale, Metropolitan Museum

characteristic decorations of the theater, because the plays were sacred performances in honor of Dionysus. The spatial composition in the Boscoreale frescoes testifies to a high development of illusionistic backdrops in the late Hellenistic theater.

The proskenion is, then, the stage of the Hellenistic period, which with the passing of time became more and more practically and richly equipped. As formerly, the musicians—that is, the old lyrical choruses singing the dithyrambs, as well as the now numerous popular soloists, rhapsodes, cithara players, citharodes, and later even magicians—appeared and performed in the orchestra before the two-story building. The dithyramb, sung in the Athenian theater by the tribes, was also executed by choruses of boys and men every year at the Dionysiac festivals by the Arcadians, who sang the compositions of Philoxenus and Timotheus (Polybius, IV,20).[62] In other places the professional technitae replaced the tribes in the performance of the dithyrambs, as they did for the scenic plays. As, therefore, the orchestra continued to be used, the proskenion was always built partially of wood, to afford better acoustics. The few actors of the new tragedy without a chorus, of New Comedy, and of the mime—if it entered the theater—made their appearance upon the stage.

The differentiation in use between the logeion and orchestra is also given by Vitruvius (*De architectura*, v,7,2) for his time, that is, 16-13 B.C., the time of the appearance of his books on architecture, thus for the late Hellenistic theater: "ampliorem habent orchestram Graeci et scaenam recessiorum minoreque latitudine pulpitum, quod λογεῖον (logeion) appellant, ideo quod apud eos tragici et comici actores in scaena peragunt, reliqui autem artifices suas per orchestram praestant actiones; itaque ex eo scaenici et thymelici graece separatim nominantur." ("The Greeks have a roomier orchestra and a scaena set further back, as well as a stage of less depth. They call this λογεῖον [logeion], for the reason that there the tragic and comic actors perform on the stage, while other artists give their performances in the entire orchestra; hence, from this fact they are given in Greek the distinct names "Scenic" and "Thymelic.")[63] Pollux (IV,123), on the basis of older sources, also differentiates between scenic and thymelic artists, that is, stage players and chorus: "ἡ μὲν σκηνὴ τῶν ὑποκριτῶν ἴδιον, ἡ δ' ὀρχήστρα τοῦ χοροῦ, ἐν ᾗ καὶ ἡ θυμέλη." ("The Skene belongs to the actors, the orchestra in which the thymele stands, to the chorus.")[64] The division of the two classes of presentation in these theaters thus corresponds to the division of the scene of performance in the Hellenistic theaters into two parts.

The forms of the late Roman Hellenistic theaters are indeed in full agreement with the rules for the plan given by Vitruvius, v,7,1: "In Graecorum theatris . . . primum in ima circinatione . . . quadratorum trium anguli circinationis lineam tangunt, et cuius quadrati latus est proximum scaenae praeciditque curvaturam circinationis, ea regione designatur finitio proscaenii. Et ab ea regione ad extremam circinationem curvaturae parallelos linea designatur in qua constituitur frons scaenae. Per centrumque orchestrae proscaenii regioni parallelos linea describitur et qua secat circinationis lineas dextra ac sinistra in cornibus hemicyclii centra signantur; et circino conlocato in dextra ab intervallo sinistro circumagitur circinatio ad proscaenii sinistram partem; item . . . ad proscaenii dextram partem." ("In the theaters of the Greeks . . . first in the circle at the bottom . . . the Greeks have three squares with their angles touching the line of circumference. The square whose side is nearest to the scaena and cuts off a segment of the circle, determines by this line the limits of the proscaenium. Parallel to this line and tangent to the outer circumference of the segment, a line is drawn which fixes the front of the scaena. Through the center of the orchestra and parallel to the direction of the proscaenium a line is laid off, and centers are marked where it cuts the circumference to the right and left at the ends of the half circle. Then, with the compasses fixed at the right, an arc is described from the horizontal distance at the left to the left hand side of the proscaenium; again . . . to the right hand side of the proscaenium.") The Eastern type of the proskenion comes especially close to the rules of Vitruvius, as we know it in Priene, Ephesus, and Delos (Figs. 475-476).[65] In the ground circle, which corresponds to the line of the lowermost circle of seats, a square is inscribed; the side of this square which is nearest to the place of the skene and opposite the middle of the auditorium is the front line of the proskenion. The front line of the skene, being the rear boundary wall of the proskenion, is formed by a line drawn parallel to the first at the extremity of the circle, that is, a tangent to the orchestral circle. The proskenion, therefore, intrudes upon the basic orchestra circle by the full amount of its projection before the main scene-building.

The pulpitum, the stage, being at the height of the upper story of the main building, should be from ten to twelve feet high, that is, 2.95 to 3.53 m. The theaters of Assos (Fig. 440), Sicyon (Fig. 455), Eretria (Figs. 452-454), and Epidaurus (Figs. 271-274 in Ch. V, and Fig. 456) have these measurements. The theaters of New Pleuron (Figs. 438-439), Oeniadai (Figs. 457-459), Oropus (Figs. 426-429),

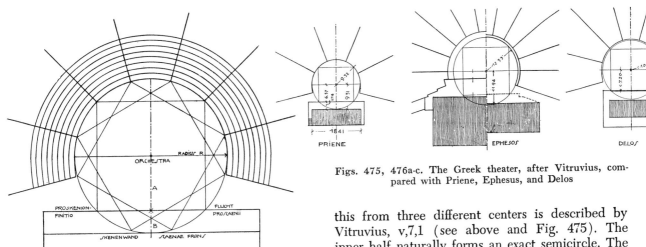

Figs. 475, 476a-c. The Greek theater, after Vitruvius, compared with Priene, Ephesus, and Delos

and Priene (Figs. 416-425) are under this size; Athens (Figs. 464-468) and the Zea theater in the Piraeus (Fig. 463) exceed it somewhat. The reason for these differences is that the former theaters are very small and the latter very large. Naturally, with the greater distance of the tiers of seats, the height of the stage increases proportionally. The depth of the stage also depends on the ground circle, since it must occupy about three-tenths of the radius of the orchestra. This is the case in Priene (Fig. 476a) and in Delos (Fig. 476c). The individual parts of the Greek proskenion-theater are organically and harmoniously correlated in their proportions. Since, however, even in its latest forms the high shallow stage was not very practical, it was replaced even on Greek soil at the time of the Roman emperors by the low and deep Italo-Roman stage (see Chs. XIII and XIV).

In its last form the Greek theater consists of three parts, each one of which originated in a different period. The orchestra is a creation of the archaic, the auditorium of the classical, and the stage of the Hellenistic period. The preserved ruins and the description of Vitruvius show that these three parts had not really fused in the Hellenistic era, but were only loosely held together by the laws of rhythm and harmony. With the passing of time the orchestra continually decreased in size and the stage building advanced in the direction of the auditorium. In the end the lyrical chorus no longer occupied the place defined by the circle of the lowest row of seats, but only the circle defined by the inner side of the lowest gangway and the water channel, where, at the edge of the orchestra, in Oropos (Figs. 428-429) and Priene (Figs. 416-418; 424-425) the seats of honor were placed. The stage now cuts into the larger circle while it touches upon the smaller circle as a tangent, just as formerly the stageless skene touched on the large circle.

The auditorium forms a horseshoe or a U-shape at the level of its lowest tiers. The construction of

this from three different centers is described by Vitruvius, v,7,1 (see above and Fig. 475). The inner half naturally forms an exact semicircle. The outermost sections may continue the circular arc for a little more and bend inwards. This results in a horseshoe plan for the orchestra, as in Ephesus and Delos (Fig. 476b-c). In most cases, however, the lower rows of seats are constructed with double their radius, using as centers the opposite end of the median diameter of the orchestra, at the points where this line touches the circumference of the circle on the right and left. This results in a straight prolongation of the semicircle, which looks stilted and gives a U-shape plan to the orchestra.

Vitruvius (v,3,7) praises the advantageous plan and perfect construction of the classical auditorium, whose rising tiers of seats bring out to their fullest effect the harmonious sounds of the human voice as well as of the music: "veteres architecti naturae vestigia persecuti indagationibus vocis scandentis theatrorum perfecerunt gradationes, et quaesierunt per canonicam mathematicorum et musicam rationem, ut, quaecumque vox esset in scaena, clarior et suavior ad spectatorum pervenerit aures . . . theatrorum per harmonicen ad augendam vocem ratiocinationes ab antiquis sunt constitutae." (". . . the ancient architects, following in the footsteps of nature, perfected the ascending rows of seats in the theaters from their investigations of the ascending voice and, by means of the canonical theory of the mathematicians and that of the musicians, endeavored to make every voice uttered on the stage come with greater clearness and sweetness to the ears of the audience . . . the ancients devised methods of increasing the power of the voice in theaters through the application of harmonics.") See also Vitruvius (v,8) on acoustics of the site of a theater.

According to Vitruvius (v,7,1-2) the stairs dividing the auditorium into sections must lead up from the angles of the three inscribed squares at the points where they touch the circumference of the circle. The number of stairways is doubled in each upper tier: "gradationes scalarum inter cuneos et sedes contra quadratorum angulos dirigantur ad primam praecinctionem, a praecinctione inter eas iterum mediae dirigantur, et ad summam quotiens praecinguntur, altero tanto semper amplificantur." ("Let

Fig. 477. The auditorium at Delphi

the ascending flights of steps between the wedges of seats, as far up as the first curved cross-aisle [see auditorium of theater in Delphi, Fig. 477], be laid out on lines directly opposite to the angles of the squares. Above the cross-aisle, let other flights be laid out in the middle between the first; and at the top, as often as there is a new cross aisle, the number of flights of steps is always increased to the same extent.") Accordingly, the lowest tier in each theater ought to have eight flights of stairs, which applies to Delos (Fig. 476c); smaller theaters, such as that in Priene (Figs. 417-418, 476a) have only six, and larger ones, such as those in Sparta and Ephesus (Fig. 475b) have ten and twelve respectively.[66]

Vitruvius, as he himself states, does not lay down any set rules, but only makes suggestions for the best method of designing and erecting theaters with the greatest perfection. He says (v,8,2): "his praescriptionibus qui voluerit uti, emandatas efficiet theatrorum perfectiones." ("Whoever is willing to follow these directions, will be able to construct perfectly correct theaters.") The rules for the stage house—that is, the part which in Vitruvius' time was still in the process of evolution—are not given as stable and binding, but are meant as fluid and dynamic guides to the best form which would coordinate the different parts according to the laws of harmonic proportions and good rhythm. The rules of Vitruvius for the Greek theaters were applied only rarely after his time, since theaters of purely Greek type were built seldom thereafter. The Hellenistic theaters were rebuilt on a Roman plan (see Figs. 441 and below 717-736) or new Roman buildings were erected (see Chs. XIII and XIV). In these theaters of the Roman period, however, entirely different and more practical rules and laws were employed. It is the stage and not the orchestra which gives to the Roman theater a unity more complete than the Greek theater ever attained.

CHAPTER X

ITALIAN POPULAR COMEDY

(THE PHLYAKES)

See Figs.
522, 513

THE theater played a great role in the Greek settlements of Southern Italy during the classical period. Tragedy was introduced from Attica. Under Hieron I (478-467) *The Women of Aetna* by Aeschylus was presented in the theater of Syracuse (*Vita Aeschyli*, §9).[1] The theater was known as the oldest and most beautiful in Sicily. It was built by Damocopus and dedicated in about 460 B.C. There for the first time movable colored walls, the coulisses—perhaps an invention of Phormis or Phormos—were used (Aristotle, *Eth. Nic.*, IV,1123a,21, cum scholion; Athenaeus, XIV,652a; Themistion, *Oratio* 27,337b; Suidas, *s.v.* Φόρμος Συρακούσιος).[2] Euripides was especially popular, so that Greek captives after the unlucky Sicilian expedition could win their freedom by reciting parts from his dramas. The vases of Southern Italy dating from the fourth century give proof of a growing preference for Euripidean and post-Euripidean tragedies (see Ch. II, Figs. 110-112, 115-122).[3] The production of tragedy was the same as in Athens, that is, in the orchestra before a central hall which in most dramas could represent a palace or a temple, and often between or before two paraskenia, which could represent different buildings (see Ch. V, Figs. 253-266).[4]

Comedy in Italy, however, differed greatly from that of Athens. The merry dramas of Syracuse, Tarentum, and other cities of Magna Graecia (as the southern part of Italy settled by the Greeks was named), had no komos, no chorus, and therefore one ought not use the name comedy for them. They were mimes, first given literary form in the fifth century by Epicharmus. They used the same main themes which the old Doric comedy in the Peloponnesus had dealt with in the sixth century B.C.: travesty of mythology in some plays and travesty of daily life in others (see Ch. III, pp. 38f.). Gradually, however, they evolved to the point where the subject of mythological burlesque was no longer the myths themselves, but rather the form of the mythical material which had been established by the well-known and popular tragedies.

The parody of tragedy was given its literary form in Magna Graecia by Rhinthon of Syracuse about 300 B.C. It was called hilarious tragedy (hilarotragodia). The actors of this informal farce were called phlyakes (φλύακες), or gossips, and were compared with the mimes and the deikelists of the Doric farce (Sosibius in Athenaeus, XIV,621 f). We know this farce partly from scanty fragments of the plays,[5] partly—and much better—from a great number of vase paintings.[6] From these pictures we learn to know not only the contents and the plot of numerous plays, but also the costumes and the way in which they were acted. The dates given to these vases vary from the end of the fifth to the last decades of the fourth centuries. The date for the best vases of Asteas from Paestum seems to be between 350 and 330 B.C. Therefore, all these vases are older than the literary farce of Rhinthon. On the other hand, they are contemporary with the Athenian Middle Comedy. Their value is augmented by the fact that they throw light on a period of which we have so few literary remains. We can see how many motifs have wandered from the Greek mainland to Southern Italy. Stock characters like Odysseus, Heracles, the bustling slave, the thief, old men, and old women are found here and there.

Thus an early Italian crater shows a parody of the story of Dolon caught in a tragi-comical manner by Odysseus and Diomedes between theatrical trees (Fig. 478).[7] There is no such hilarotragodia mentioned in literature, but other pictures agree in subject matter with the titles attested for Rhinthon. Among them was a *Heracles*. This Doric hero was presented several times also by Epicharmus.[8]

Fig. 478. Dolon caught by Odysseus and Diomedes. Early South Italian crater, British Museum

Fig. 479a. *The Madness of Heracles*. Vase by Assteas, Madrid

The famous vase of the Paestum painter Assteas in Madrid, dated soon after 350 B.C., represents the murder of the children of Heracles by the mad hero in a manner which might correspond to the *Heracles* by Rhinthon or one of his forerunners, since the style can best be interpreted as hilarious tragedy (Figs. 479a-b).⁹ The appearance of the hero with enormous plumes attached to his helmet may have been similar to the one of Lamachus as he must have appeared in Aristophanes' *Acharnians* (see lines 1103, "Bring me the plumes for my helmet"; 1105, "How white and beautiful are these ostrich feathers"; 1109, "Bring me the case for my plumes"; 1111, "Alas! the moths have eaten the hair of my

Fig. 479b.

crest.") The same impression of tragicomoedia was given by an Italian representation of Verdi's *Trovatore* in the Lewisohn Stadium in New York in 1936. In this open-air performance, sung in a foreign language, the hero wore a costume similar to that of Heracles on the Assteas vase, with enormous plumes on his helmet. Gay tragedy is also indicated when Heracles throws his child into a burning funeral pyre, which is composed in part of unburnable metal articles and all sorts of household utensils, such as the wool basket of the housewife, all thrown together in a disorderly heap. The gesture of Iolaus, depicting idle astonishment, that of Mania, who beats her breast, and the wrinkled features of the mother Alcmene—all suggest the same interpretation. These three last-named figures appear in a sort of loggia or open gallery, while the wife, Megara, tearing her hair and beating her breast, flees through a door instead of snatching the child away from the father.

The scene building is covered by a roof, resting upon two tall Ionic columns, while the loggia in the background is supported by Doric columns. Whether this setting represents a stage or the inside of a house is a matter of dispute. I believe that it is a stage building, for a terracotta relief in Naples, dated in the late fourth or early third century, has the same open gallery, columns in the background and slender turrets at the sides instead of the tall Ionic columns (Fig. 480).¹⁰ Three doors between the background columns lead to the low pulpitum in front, where the actors stood; the marks for their figures are still visible. The stage which Shakespeare used was also similar.¹¹ It is a form of stage building peculiar to Southern Italy.¹² The mosaic found in Pompeii depicting the rehearsal of a satyr chorus shows a similar style of architecture, certainly borrowed from the theater (see Ch. I, Fig. 36).¹³ The form was developed in a monumental way in

Fig. 480. Model of a stage. Terracotta, Naples

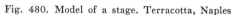

Segesta (see Ch. XIII, Figs. 596-598, 600-601). Python, the younger contemporary of Assteas, shows sometimes a similar arrangement of figures looking down from above, for example, in the picture of Alcmene on the funeral pile.[14] Although he does not indicate a gallery, he may have received the inspiration from the hilarotragodia. The whole structure on the Assteas vase in Madrid is apparently built of wood, not of stone; it thus is a form of provisional theater set up for the farce or hilarious tragedy, wherever the plays were given. In Syracuse and Corinth provision for the footings of such a provisional theater has been discovered (Figs. 595, 726-728).[15]

This pretty and practical form seems to have been used by Plautus also. In the *Amphitruo* (v. 863) Jupiter says that he lives here in the upper story (in superiore cenaculo).[16] From inscriptions in Pompeii we know that such cenacula were rented separately. The new excavations have shown that these upper stories opened not only upon the atrium with a gallery, which seems to have been the older style,[17] but also upon the street.[18] The "Assteas stage," like the eastern Greek Hellenistic proskenion theater, thus imitates the actual construction of a house. This explains the differing opinions as to whether a stage or a form of architecture taken from daily life is depicted on the vase in Madrid. It represents an actual house form copied for theatrical purposes. The framing at the sides with columns on the vase, and with slightly projecting turrets on the terracotta relief, reminds one of the paraskenion theater in the Hellenistic form, such as we have in New Pleuron and the Piraeus (Ch. IX, Figs. 438-439, 463). The theaters in Segesta and Tyndaris, as reconstructed by Bulle[19] may be a special late Hellenistic type evolved from the paraskenion theater on Italian soil. Perhaps this took place in Tarentum in Apulia,

but it could have occurred also in some other city in Campania or in Paestum in Lucania, the native city of Assteas.

This Assteas stage, is, however, not the predominant form of stage in Southern Italy, for most of the other vases representing farces, including those of Assteas, show a much simpler form. These farces represented on the vases have a wealth of humorous and ridiculous situations. The plots were taken partly from mythology, partly from daily life, as they were in the old Doric farce (Ch. III, Figs. 130-132). Gods and heroes on the one side, popular subjects on the other side, are found in about even proportions in the Southern Italian farce, while in the developed comedies of Plautus—as formerly in the comedies of Aristophanes—the subject matter taken from actual life prevails.

Heracles is a favorite hero of the phlyakes, as he is in the plays of Rhinthon and in every other farce. A vase in Leningrad (Fig. 481)[20] gives a parody of the story of how he came to Delphi to be purified after he had killed his teacher Linos. As Apollo refused to absolve him, he stole the tripod, and Athena had to reconcile him with the god. The vase based on the farce depicts him as having jumped on the holy tripod, holding his club, with which he has threatened Apollo. The god has fled to the roof of his temple, holding the bow with which he kills evil-doers and the laurel with which he purifies repentant sinners. Heracles tries to bring him down by tempting him with a basket full of fruit and cake. He holds the club in his right hand, ready to strike as soon as Apollo reaches for the gifts. The god, realizing the ruse, moves more and more to the edge of the roof and holds his attributes away from Heracles, while he looks greedily at the offerings. In the next moment he will reach for them, the club will whiz down on his hand, and he will fall down from the roof to the edge of which he has moved. He will not fall to the ground but into the basin containing the holy water, to take a cold bath in it and to lose his bow to Iolaus, who is standing ready to snatch it. This involuntary bath certainly gave great pleasure to the public of the farce. On the wall is a wreath and the mask of a stupid-looking old man. The four masks are excellently drawn and finely differentiated. They are the forerunners of the four main masks which the Oscan Atellan farce later transmitted to the Roman farce: Maccus, the greedy blockhead, here Apollo; Dossenus, the clever hunch-back, here Heracles, who indeed has a high back; Bucco, the braggart, here Iolaus, who will certainly boast that he has captured the bow of Apollo; and Pappos, the stupid old man. These are types which can be used in any doltish farce. They were revived in the Italian Commedia dell'Arte.[21]

Fig. 481. Heracles angers Apollo. Phlyakes vase, Leningrad

Fig. 482. Heracles angers Zeus. Phlyakes vase from Ruvo, Leningrad

Fig. 483a-b. Visitors to Zeus Ammon. Phlyakes vase, Bari

Heracles and Iolaus also visit a sanctuary of Zeus, the highest god, in order to offer a sacrifice, on a vase from Ruvo in Leningrad (Fig. 482).[22] While Iolaus, or some old man, prays piously and pours a libation of wine from a jug on the altar, Heracles, supposed to offer a dish with offerings to be laid on the altar, turns around and eats the food. He is just stuffing the last tidbit into his mouth, under the very nose of Zeus. The highest god, seated on a throne too high for him, tries to kick the greedy hero—his son as a result of the love affair with Alcmene—and he threatens in vain to send down his thunderbolt. His sacred bird, the eagle, has become a small decoration of his scepter.

The visit of travellers to Zeus Ammon in the Libyan oasis, on a vase in Bari (Fig. 483a-b),[23] is also anticipated with fear by the god. The Libyan Zeus sits beside a palm tree indicating the place of the event, holding his eagle around the neck, and he fearfully observes the visitors. One ascends the stage for the purpose of consulting the oracle. The other, certainly the servant of the first, heavily loaded with bedsack and provision basket, makes eyes at the sacrificial gifts in the basket, entrusted to his care. This may be meant as a parody of the visit of a Greek, similar to the one of Alexander the Great to Zeus Ammon, who acknowledged him as his son. As this took place in 330 B.C., the vase, dated in the first half of the fourth century, is earlier than this event.

Heracles is the son of Zeus and Alcmene. On a vase in the Vatican, bought in Naples by Raphael Mengs, probably painted by Assteas, Zeus steals to a mistress identified as Alcmene by Winckelmann (Fig. 484).[24] The loved one looks down from a window. Hermes holds a lighted lamp for his father Zeus,

so that he can see where he has to place the ladder which he is carrying over his shoulders with his head between two rungs. He wears a too-small crown, while Alcmene has an elaborate hairdress and much jewelry. Hermes can be recognized by his herald's staff, the kerykeion, and his wide-brimmed hat. In the *Amphitruo* of Plautus, Mercury, the Roman Hermes, also helps Zeus in his love affair with Alcmene (v. 993: amanti subparasitor.) He takes there, however, the form of the slave Sosias, and Zeus that of the husband of Alcmene, Amphitruo. Here, on the contrary, they appear as gods, and Alcmene is not the modest wife who can be seduced only when she believes that the visitor is her own husband. Perhaps the vase agrees with the *Amphitruo* of Rhinthon, which play may also have influenced Plautus, for he names his play a tragicomoedia (see Ch. XI, p. 151, Plautus, *Amphitruo*, v.63).

Fig. 484. Zeus visits Alcmene (*Amphitryon*). Phlyakes vase, Va

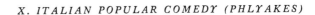

Fig. 485. Ares and Hephaestus fight before Hera.
Phlyakes vase, British Museum

The Queen of heaven, the wife of Zeus, was equally mocked. The amusing story of the revenge of Hephaestus on his mother Hera was certainly very popular. It appears in the Doric farce (see above Fig. 130), on the François vase, and was

Figs. 486-487. Heracles bringing monkeys to Eurystheus; Heracles knocking at a door

treated by Epicharmus in his comedy *The Comasts and Hephaestus.* Hera had thrown her ugly son out of Olympus as a child so that he became lame from the fall. In revenge he sent her a throne, from which she could not rise again. Zeus promised to give Aphrodite in marriage to whoever would release her from the fetters. A vase in the British Museum (Fig. 485)[25] shows Ares, who loves Aphrodite, and Hephaestus fighting before Hera, a picture of misfortune, seated on her son's fatal gift. Ares has a helmet with full plumes like those of Lamachus in the *Acharnians* of Aristophanes and of Heracles on the Assteas vase (Fig. 479). Hephaestus, in contrast, wears a kind of night cap with a tassel. He will certainly be the victor, for Ares is already ·retreating. Hephaestus will not be compelled by force to give way and will not release his mother until he has received Aphrodite as his bride. Her later love affair with Ares may have been alluded to in the farce.

One of the twelve deeds of Heracles is alluded to in the picture from Camarina, in the Museo Civico of Catania, in which the hero walks in to Eurystheus, his employer, using his club as a walking stick (Fig. 486).[26] The lion skin is reduced to a head cap. He brings the captured ape-like Kerkopes in reed cages, attached to the ends of his bow, which he—like the slaves in Attic comedy (see above Fig. 147)—carries over his shoulder. The king, wearing a small crown and holding a scepter in his arm, greets the hero with outstretched arm. The altar between the two shows that the performance was not only an entertainment but also a sacred play. Comedies with the title "Kerkopes" were written by Hermippus, Eubulus, and Plato. On a crater formerly in the Hope Collection, the feasting Heracles is served by two phlyakes.[27]

Heracles uses his club to knock at a door, on a vase in Berlin (Fig. 487).[28] He is holding a bow in his left hand, and the lion skin hung over his left arm flutters out behind him. The servant, seated on a mule, looks on with interest, as the gate is probably about to give way. He carries an enormous bundle on a dung-fork (see the agricultural implement behind the farmer in Fig. 514 below). He is probably making *phortika*, porters' jokes, like Xanthias in Aristophanes' *Frogs.* As the entrance scene in this comedy is similar to the vase in Berlin, it was formerly used as an illustration of Aristophanes. But here the real Heracles, not Dionysus disguised as Heracles, knocks at the door of a palace or a shrine, in which we may imagine a god or hero dwelling; or he tries to force his entrance into Hades or Olympus. There is again a sacred altar between the two figures.

Fig. 488a-b. Heracles abducts a woman
from a shrine. Phlyakes vase, Lentini

Two vases found in Sicily depict Heracles as a libertine. On one, in Lentini (Figs. 488a-b)[29] he has forced his way into a shrine and tries to abduct a woman praying before an altar. Behind the altar a small statuette is set upon a high pillar. The woman is perhaps Auge, later the mother of Telephus, the founder of Pergamon. An old matchmaking pair—or perhaps the old nurse and the

father Aleus—looks on smirkingly. On the other vase, from Centuripe in Milan (Fig. 489),[30] Hermes has led his brother to a woman. The latter, however, unveiling herself, illustrates the adage: "Behind the Lyceum, in front the Museum." As a consequence, the hero is so frightened that the club falls out of his hand; Hermes also seems to lose his herald's staff from his outstretched right hand. A less likely interpretation is the story of Alcestis brought back from Hades by Heracles.

The famous deed of Antigone, who, contrary to the command of Creon, buried her brother Polynices, is ridiculed in a picture in which a man has disguised himself in women's clothes (Fig. 490),[31] like the brother- or father-in-law of Euripides in the *Thesmophoriazousai* of Aristophanes. As the watchman leads the supposed Antigone before Creon (Sophocles, *Antigone*, vv. 376ff), he takes off the woman's mask and reveals himself as a bearded, baldheaded man. The hydria in his arm may allude to the fact that he has already buried Polynices and has brought his ashes in the urn, for which this form of vase was occasionally used. Thus it may be that this vase painting is based on another version of the

Fig. 489. Heracles pursues a woman, guided by Hermes. Phlyakes vase from Centuripe

Fig. 490. Parody of *Antigone*

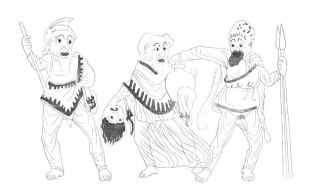

Antigone saga than the one employed by Sophocles.

The Trojan saga was popular in the Italian farce, as it was later in Latin literature. Achilles as a student of the wise Cheiron is depicted on a vase, found in Apulia, now in the British Museum (Fig. 491).[32] He is a modest and gentle youth wrapped in his himation, as he follows his old tutor who journeys to a watering place seeking a cure among the nymphs for his gout or arthritis. The old man is hampered by his disease and clambers painfully up the small flights of steps to the stage. A servant named Xanthias pulls him onto the stage by the head, while another servant pushes him forcibly from behind. This servant and Cheiron assume the form of a centaur, as two actors in a Disney movie assume the form of a moose, and two actors in Bali the form of a bull (see above, Ch. III, Fig. 129). The nymphs looking on from above are ugly old ladies in lively conversation. Cheiron is said to have taken a cure with the nymphs of Anigrus in Elis (Pausanias, v,5,10). Epicharmus in *Heracles et Pholus* described a knee ailment of Cheiron. Cratinos and Pherecrates wrote comedies with the title *Cheiron*. The cure may have been laughed at as the cures in the sanctuaries of Asclepius in Aristophanes' *Plutus*.

The birth of the beautiful Helen—later the cause of the Trojan war, in which Achilles and many other heroes died—is depicted on a vase in Bari (Fig. 492).[33] Zeus had approached Leda, the wife of Tyndareus of Sparta, as a swan. As a consequence Leda has laid an egg and has hidden it in her wool basket. When the right time for the birth is near, Zeus sends Hephaestus—who has once before cleaved the head of the god so that Athena could be born—to cleave the egg for the birth of his daughter Helen. But before he can strike his axe down Helen rises out of the egg and greets her mother, who spies through the door, while the step-father Tyndareus throws up his arm in astonishment. Helen, like the young hero Achilles, is represented as a heroine of normal beauty. Leda and Tyndareus are in contrast all the uglier.

The death of the aged king Priam of Troy who was killed by Neoptolemus, the son of Achilles, is the subject of a vase in Berlin (Fig. 493).[34] The king, wearing a caricature of a royal oriental head-dress, has fled to an altar, and lifts his left hand imploringly to his murderer. He apparently delivers a tragic oration in a parody of such speeches in tragedy. Neoptolemus has his sword drawn to kill him, but has first to let him finish his stirring and endless tirade. The young hero wears a caricatured traveller's hat and chlamys.

Another scene which took place after the taking of Troy is on the vase painted by Assteas, found at

Figs. 491-493. Servants helping Cheiron up steps; Birth of Helen; Priam and Neoptolemus. Phlyakes vases

Fig. 494. Ajax and
Cassandra in sanctuary
of Athena. Rome

Fig. 497. Warriors and dog. Naples

Fig. 495. Odysseus with Queen and King of the Phaiakes

Buccino (ancient Volcei in the Basilicata of Lucania), now in the Museo di Villa Guilia at Rome
(Fig. 494).[35] Ajax has threatened to rape the
prophetess Cassandra, the daughter of Priam. He
has followed her into the sanctuary of Athena,
whose cult statue stands in the center of the picture.
But the two change roles in the farce, and the
maiden in turn threatens the great hero, who des-
perately clings to the idol. The energetic princess
grasps his high helmet and pushes her knee into
the nape of his neck and her foot into his back. The
old priestess with a much too large temple-key
recoils in horror. This picture is one of the funniest
and cleverest of the popular farce.

From the *Odyssey* comes the story of the arrival
of the shipwrecked Odysseus at the court of the
king and queen of the Phaeacians. On a Campanian
vase in the Louvre (Fig. 495)[36] Odysseus in the

guise of a poor modest traveller appears before the
king and queen, both decked with their white
crowns. Arete is the active one of the couple. She
lifts her hand and rushes forward to greet the distinguished guest, who may perhaps be a suitor for
their daughter Nausicaa. The king Alcinous stands
with bowed head, his left hand on his hip, his right
on a large staff, and waits patiently for his turn.
He is thin in contrast to the stout and pompous
queen. The shipwreck of Odysseus was also treated
by Epicharmus (Athenaeus, XIV,619b; Pollux, X,134).

A local story gave the subject for a lost vase in
which a figure appears fearfully balancing on a
tuna fish (Fig. 496).[37] This favorite food in Southern
Italy takes the place of the dolphin in the legend of
Taras, who rode a dolphin according to coins from
Tarentum. Arion, the master of musical art, was
saved by a dolphin when thrown into the sea. It
is, however, more likely a representation of Taras,
the founder of Tarentum. Rhinthon and the Phlyakes
farce were connected with this rich commercial

Fig. 498. Sappho and Alcaeus. Bari

Fig. 496. Phlyax riding a tuna fish

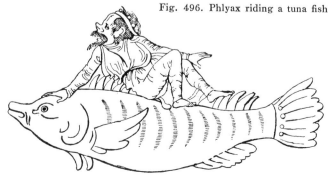

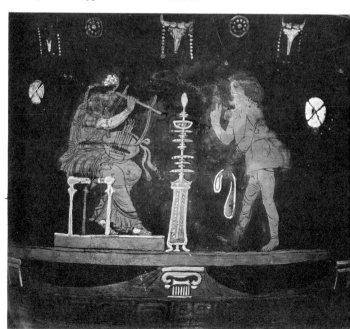

city. The theater was so popular that Pyrrhus closed it in order to obtain hired soldiers from this important city (Zonaras, VIII, Ch. 2, p. 370). When the Romans entered the port of Tarentum in 282 B.C. the people did not fight against the fleet, because everybody was in the theater enjoying the hilarotragodia (Cassius Dio, Fragm. 39,5; Dionysius of Halicarnassus, XIX,4).[38]

The vases and certainly the plays which they illustrate thus make fun of a whole series of heroic characters. Many more Southern Italian vases, however, depict scenes from that type of farce which takes its motifs from the daily life of the people.

Some military adventure seems to be mocked at on a vase in Naples (Fig. 497).[39] An older man holding a shield and a bow is seated on rocky ground. Opposite him a soldier with a lance and a helmet seems to receive instruction. Between them a man standing with his foot on a rocky elevation and holding his left arm with his right hand points to a dog who must play a role in this unexplained story.

The motif of love and other relations between the sexes played an ever larger part in farce, as it did in comedy. A proposal of marriage is certainly meant on the vase in Bari (Fig. 498).[40] The woman is seated with a cithara in her arm. The man approaches with a full purse in his left hand, greeting her with his right. Between them is a thymiaterium. These are probably the lyric poets Sappho and Alcaeus, the same as on the fine vase in Munich (Figs. 6-7). There Alcaeus seems to have proposed to Sappho, but she turns away from him and he hangs his head in distress over her refusal. The comic actor with his well-filled purse will certainly be more fortunate.

Love in the balance may be the subject of a vase in Syracuse (Fig. 499a-b).[41] A man and a woman play on a seesaw, the woman standing and the man kneeling. An old Silenus stands in the center on the support for the long board. The woman, holding a tympanon, wearing a peplos and a mantle which is wrapped around her head and shoulders, seems to

Fig. 499a-b. "Love in the Balance." Syracuse

be jumping up and down, for she touches the board only with her toes. She has made such a violent movement that the man on the other end of the board has been thrown into the air. He makes a gesture of dismay with both hands. The woman is certainly the winner in the game. A merry-go-round with a seated phlyax playing the flute and two phlyakes standing face to face are on a vase found near Tarentum,[42] now in the University of Syracuse Museum.

A lover whispers to a woman hiding behind an ornate door on a vase in the British Museum (Fig. 500).[43] She seems to lend a willing ear. Also willing, like Alcmene (Fig. 484), is the woman, richly dressed, who looks out of a window (Fig. 501).[44]

Fig. 501. A lover climbing a ladder. British Museum

Fig. 500. Lovers at a door. British Museum

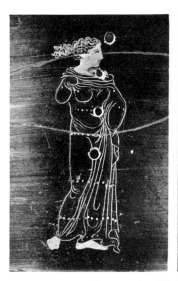

Fig. 502a-b. Old lover bringing apples to a young woman.
Gnathia vase, Boston

Fig. 503. Heads of lovers. Terracotta fragment, Tarentum

Fig. 504. Father and son fight over a woman. Ruvo

The lover is a step ahead of Zeus on the other vase. He is already climbing up the ladder to his beloved, while Zeus is still carrying the ladder around his neck. The man offers her apples, which means a declaration of love, and he holds as a second present a fillet serving as a headband or belt. A slave provides light with a torch and also carries a pail of wine. He serves his master in his love affair as does Hermes in the adventure of Zeus.

Fig. 505. Two slaves leading a girl. Moscow

Apples are the present which an older man has gathered in the pouch of his mantle for the lovely young woman who expects him on the other side of a crater in Boston (Fig. 502a-b).[45] In his eagerness he runs so quickly that most of the apples will have fallen out of his cloak before he has reached his beloved. An old bald man and a comely young girl are embracing, she leaning her head against his cheek, in a fragmentary terracotta group in Tarentum (Fig. 503).[46] The jovial old man has a wedge-shaped beard and his brows are unevenly drawn, as if his mood is going to change (see Figs. 196-198, 335-337, 810). The woman wearing a headband is probably a fickle courtesan, who caters to whoever brings her presents, like one of the sisters in the last scene of the *Bacchides* of Plautus.

Generally, however, it is the young man who wins in love. When age and youth, probably even father and son, fight over a woman, as on a crater in Ruvo (Fig. 504),[47] the woman will naturally fall to the young man. Both men, wielding swords in their right hands, have grasped the woman with their left hands. The youth, however, has a firm grip on her wrist and also has put his foot on her foot. The old man has only her shawl in his hand. Thus, in the next moment the youth will pull up the woman and run off with her while the father will be left standing with the empty mantle. Fights over a woman occur also in Plautus in the *Casina*, the *Mercator*, and in the *Asinaria*, but these are fights with words, not with swords. The love theme took on much coarser forms in the popular farces than in the literary comedy.

A crater in the Moscow Museum (Fig. 505)[48] depicts two slaves, who instead of quarreling over a woman as the masters do, are satisfied with one big girl for the two of them. They lead her along carrying big bolsters in richly-ornamented covers of the kind used for the couches at banquets. The *Stichus* of Plautus closes with a similar scene, and the departure for a gay banquet is a popular and fitting conclusion for any comedy or farce.

Fig. 506. Woman feeding a man from a bottle. Göttingen

Fig. 507. Slave and young couple with baby. Crater, Naples

When married couples are shown, the wife is depicted as domineering, as in the rulers of the Phaeacians (Fig. 495). On a vase in Vienna,[49] an old long-snouted shrew is talking in a lively and domineering manner to a man who leans on his cane as he listens, astonished and overawed. Contrast of husband and wife is a favorite subject of farce and comedy. It is probably a wife who forces a man to drink from a milk bottle on a vase in Göttingen (Fig. 506).[50] He may have enjoyed too much wine. She pulls his head down, and while he grasps her wrist and lifts his right hand in anxiety she pushes the feeding bottle into his mouth. The explanation, as

Fig. 508. Old miser Charinus with thieves and slave. Vase by Assteas, Berlin

an attempt of the man to vomit, may only give part of the story.

A young couple on a crater in Naples seems to be concerned with a baby (Fig. 507).[51] At least it seems that a child in swaddling clothes is the object which the young man passes to a woman standing before a richly-decorated door. An old slave looks back fearfully at the scene. Certainly the child belongs to the young pair and was, as in the *Arbitrants* (Epitrepontes) of Menander, deserted and found again. Other less likely explanations are: Hermes and Apollo giving Ion to the Pythia, or Lichas receiving the raiment of Heracles from Deianeira.

Theft, such as that of fruit and wine, had already been a theme in the old Doric Peloponnesian farce (see Ch. III, Fig. 132). Money, cake, wine, and meat are stolen in the Italian farce. The most delightful and realistic scene is presented to us by the crater of Assteas, probably found in Nola, in Berlin (Fig. 508).[52] The old man Charinus has thrown himself upon his money chest, a strongbox of a form which can be seen even today in many Pompeian houses.[53] Two thieves try to tear him away. The one, named Cosilus, has taken hold of his left arm and the mantle on which the old miser is lying. The other, named Gymnilos, pulls with both hands at his left foot and thigh. Between them they will roll him off the chest and get the money. The servant named Carion stands with trembling knees, his hands stretched forward with a fearful gesture, but he does not even try to help his master. The theme is related to the *Aulularia* (the Comedy of Pots) by Plautus, who knew and made use of the native farce (see Ch. XI, p. 150f.). In the comedy by Plautus the gold was hidden in a pot; here it is in the strongbox. But in both cases the miser by his fear betrays the place where the treasure is hidden.

Petty thieving and nibbling of dainties on the sly are represented on other vases. On a vase from Ruvo in a private collection in Southern Italy (Fig. 509)[54] the couple Honorable (Philotimides) and Grace (Charis) hold between them a dish of mixed delicate foods which they have taken from a small dining table. He lifts a string of figs, while she is about to push a big cake into her large mouth.

Fig. 509. Pilfering of dainties. From Ruvo, Milan

As they are so engrossed in their enjoyment of the food, they overlook the fact that their slave, Xanthias, is sliding into the pouch of his garment the best piece—a large cake in the shape of a heart. He is just about to leave. Another slave has stolen a whole jug of wine and a cake, from which he has already taken a bite, from an old woman, on a vase in Berlin, also from Ruvo (Fig. 510).[55] The old woman pursues him with outstretched arms and wide stride. Her carefully bound up hair is in ridiculous contrast to her witch-like face with protruding chin. On a vase in Leningrad (Fig. 511)[56] two merry slaves carry off a pail of wine and a roast, while dancing to the tunes of a little flute player preceding them. The meat and drink were certainly pilfered, and the flute player was surely not originally engaged for the banquet of the slaves. In the last scene of the *Stichus* of Plautus the fact that slaves can also have festivals is explained as a Greek custom.

Fig. 512. Policeman, thief, and old woman

Fig. 513. Thrashing of a slave. Berlin

Fig. 510. Thief with wine jar pursued by old woman. Berlin

Fig. 511. Two slaves with pail of wine and roast on spit, led by fluteplayer

When thieves are caught they are harshly punished. On a vase in New York (Fig. 512),[57] dated about 400 B.C., a thief is forced to throw both arms up—because he has his hands bound together above his head—so that he can be beaten without hindrance. He complains: "He has tied both my hands aloft" ($\kappa\alpha\tau\epsilon\delta\eta\sigma'$ $\ddot{\alpha}\nu\omega$ $\tau\dot{\omega}$ $\chi\epsilon\hat{\iota}\rho\epsilon$). An overseer or policeman stands behind him with a stick. He is a barbarian, for he murmurs incomprehensible words, perhaps meaning: "I shall give you enough blows" ($\nu o\rho\alpha\rho\epsilon\tau\tau\epsilon\beta\lambda o$). An old market woman stands on the stage before a richly-ornamented door and scolds him, threatening to provide more blows or to hand him over: "I shall grant" or "provide" ($\dot{\epsilon}\gamma\dot{\omega}$ $\pi\alpha\rho\dot{\epsilon}\xi\omega$). Thus the poor man will probably receive one beating from the overseer or policeman, and a second from his wife or whoever is the owner of the loot recovered, which consists of a goose, a basket with a small animal in it, and a mantle. To the left stands a young man on higher ground called tragedian ($\tau\rho\alpha\gamma o\iota\delta\delta s$), and before him hangs the mask of a

Fig. 514. Farmer, clerk, learned lady. Leningrad

bearded comedian. We thus certainly have here a tragicomoedia in the manner of Rhinthon.

A harsh thrashing is meted out to a slave on a vase in Berlin (Fig. 513).[58] The overseer, with a stick bent in a sharp zigzag, holds the end of a rope which is wound around the neck of the culprit, who bends his knees deeply and lays his hands on his knees, to make himself as small as possible. Another slave mocks him from above by thumbing his nose. Blows are of course very popular in coarse farce, as they are in Attic Comedy and later in the comedies of Plautus. In the parabasis of Aristophanes' *Pax* (vv. 734ff) the chorus praises the poet because, among other things, he no longer permitted slaves to be beaten and mocked at by their comrades as the other comic poets did. Yet in the *Frogs* (vv. 616ff) Dionysus, the god himself, and his slave Xanthias are beaten alternately by Aiakos.

Deceiving and snubbing of an ignorant farmer seems to be the subject of a vase from Ruvo in Leningrad (Fig. 514).[59] The countryman has put his luggage on a pitchfork and leans forward on his cane. He seems to plead with the haughty overseer who has written out a bill for him on a large writing tablet. A seated lady holding another tablet

digs with the stylus, the writing pencil, at her teeth. The farmer is not prepared for the mass of knowledge exhibited by the learned lady and her steward. He will certainly be snubbed and outwitted. Another bad bargain awaits the man who tries to sell a bird in a cage to a shrewd-faced and pompously gesticulating man on a vase in the Louvre (Fig. 515).[60]

Boxing was a popular sport in Italy, beginning in the sixth century in Etruria, from where it was probably introduced into Campania when the Etruscans occupied this province. On a Campanian hydria in the Boston Museum of Fine Arts, of excellent execution and preservation, blows are exchanged between two "nude" men (Fig. 516).[61] The costume simulates a nude body with the breasts painted on the tights. Buttons are used for the navel, the one of the left fighter is hung loosely from a thread. The masks have a ring at the apex so that they can be hung on a wall when not used. A boxing match is imitated and parodied. Both champions balance on their left feet and extend their right feet forward, at the same time drawing backward, away from each other. The man on the right has both hands made into fists, as if he were about to strike; the other boxer holds his right hand ready but extends his left hand beseechingly. Both seem to be afraid of each other's blows and may run away to different sides at the end. Perhaps a parody on the fight of Amykos and Pollux is meant, a subject treated in a play by Epicharmus.

Contrasts of two related characters are popular themes and have created delightful types. Old age and youth are contrasted in the fight for a woman (Fig. 504), as well as in the nocturnal scene where a white-haired father leads his drunken son home from a banquet, indicated by the pail of wine in his hand, on a crater found at Capua, now in the British Museum (Fig. 517).[62] He prevents the son from falling down on a goose. A wise and sanguine old man is engaged in discussion with a blackhaired,

Fig. 515. Seller of birds. Louvre

Fig. 516. Caricature of two boxers. Campanian hydria, Boston

Fig. 517. Father leading his drunken son. British Museum

Fig. 518. Old man and
excited friend. Fragment
from Tarentum, Heidelberg

Fig. 520. Two women
gossiping. Phlyakes
vase, Heidelberg

himation listens placidly, while the other gesticulates vividly, telling the latest gossip.

Single figures also appear, painting many different and individual characters of the farce: the jovial but timid old man (Fig. 521),[66] an ancient Milquetoast, found in Lecce, now in Vienna; a white-haired father of comedy, leaning against a column, from Tarentum, in Würzburg (Fig. 522)[67]; the caricature of an augur, with the curved staff, big horns from which fillets hang, behind him a bird who seems just to have laid an egg, from Paestum in Naples (Fig. 523)[68]; a fat glutton and carouser, wearing a small crown, carrying a torch in his arm for some nocturnal festival (Fig. 524),[69] in Tarentum. Then there are the running slaves: one on a calyx crater, with a torch and a large purple-red mantle hanging over his left arm—formerly in the Collection Matsch in Vienna, now in the Metropolitan Museum of Art in New York City (Fig. 525)[70]—has a wreath with some kind of horns, as if imitating an augur. Another on a jug in Boston seems to be a thief who runs with his left leg high in the air, while he tries to hide something in his exomis (Fig. 526).[71] Another slave, on a vase from Egnazia in the British Museum dated around 350 B.C., is running, carrying a little table on which a high pyramidical cake seems to indicate a religious festival (Fig. 527).[72] Such a cake appears also in the large basket which a slave on a vase in the Louvre (Fig. 528)[73] carries on his head. The other offerings which he brings to an altar are fruits, round cakes, and nuts. As he carries a torch, it seems to be a nocturnal festival. The little duck probably played her part as the goose in Fig. 517. Many of these figures appear on the so-called Gnathia vases —that is, mostly Apulian Vases, the best from Tarentum—dated from the middle of the fourth to the early third centuries, on which we can also find many single masks.[74]

Single figures in terracotta are rarer than on vases. The best come from Syracuse (Figs. 529-530),[75] the home city of Epicharmus and Rhinthon. Fragments of similar figures have been found in Tarentum. The three slaves (Fig. 530) come from the workshop of a Syracusan potter on the island of Ortygia. They form a series in dress as well as in movement: nude, exomis, full tunic.

Figs. 523-525. Augur, Naples; Fat torchbearer, Tarentum; Augur, Metropolitan Museum

Fig. 519. Master and slave. Phlyakes vase, Bari

excited friend on a fragment from Tarentum in Heidelberg (Fig. 518).[63] A placid old man is walking with his crooked cane, while his slave, leaning on a rough stick and heavily laden with travelling bag and provision basket, follows him and calls him to turn around, making the gesture of horns (corni) to avert some imaginary evil, on a vase in Bari (Fig. 519).[64] Two women are contrasted on a vase in Heidelberg (Fig. 520).[65] One wrapped in her large

Figs. 521, 522. Old men.
Gnathia vase, from Lecce, Vienna;
Fragment from
Tarentum, Würzburg

Fig. 526. Running slave.
Jug, Boston

Fig. 527. Slave carrying a table with cakes.
Gnathia vase, British Museum

Fig. 528. Slave carrying a basket
to an altar

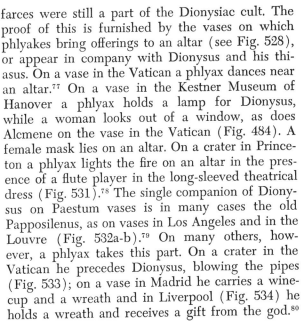

Figs. 529, 530. Female and male phlyakes; Three slaves of farce.

Fig. 531. Phlyax lighting fire on an altar

The costume of these phlyakes of Southern Italy is still the old costume of the farce, which had also been adopted in the Attic comedy and was still used by Aristophanes and by Middle Comedy of the fourth century.[76] All characters wore tights, stuffed out in front and behind, covering body, arms, and legs. The men exhibit the phallus and too-short vest, the slaves and lower classes at times an exomis, leaving one shoulder bare. Some are depicted as naked with the breast and the navel painted on the tights, or the navel is indicated by a button (see the boxers, Fig. 516). Everything is more grotesque and more realistic in this low-class Italian popular farce than in Attic comedy. The tights often fit badly, with creases and seams evident. The chlamys or, generally, a small himation serves as a mantle for the men. The women wear the chiton and usually a large cloak.

The reason for retaining this costume, and, above all, the masks is that the phlyakes, like all actors, were the servants of Dionysus. Even these late farces were still a part of the Dionysiac cult. The proof of this is furnished by the vases on which phlyakes bring offerings to an altar (see Fig. 528), or appear in company with Dionysus and his thiasus. On a vase in the Vatican a phlyax dances near an altar.[77] On a vase in the Kestner Museum of Hanover a phlyax holds a lamp for Dionysus, while a woman looks out of a window, as does Alcmene on the vase in the Vatican (Fig. 484). A female mask lies on an altar. On a crater in Princeton a phlyax lights the fire on an altar in the presence of a flute player in the long-sleeved theatrical dress (Fig. 531).[78] The single companion of Dionysus on Paestum vases is in many cases the old Papposilenus, as on vases in Los Angeles and in the Louvre (Fig. 532a-b).[79] On many others, however, a phlyax takes this part. On a crater in the Vatican he precedes Dionysus, blowing the pipes (Fig. 533); on a vase in Madrid he carries a wine-cup and a wreath and in Liverpool (Fig. 534) he holds a wreath and receives a gift from the god.[80]

Fig. 532a-b. Silenus and Dionysus. Paestan vases

Figs. 533, 534. Phlyax and Dionysus. Paestan vases

Fig. 535. Dionysus and phlyakes watching a female tumbler. Paestan vase attributed to Assteas, Lipari

The excellent crater in the Museo Eoliano of Lipari (Fig. 535)[80a] shows the seated Dionysus and two phlyakes watching a female acrobat performing on a table. Above are two windows from which two women look down. The scene is laid on a low stage, supported by columns and decorated with drapery. The style is that of the Paestan painter Assteas, and the vase is dated about 350 B.C.

The phlyax on a Paestan vase in the British Mu-

seum dances before Dionysus with a large basket on his head (Fig. 536).[81] On a vase from Tarentum a phlyax dances between Dionysus and a maenad; on an askos in Ruvo he dances between a satyr and a maenad (Fig. 537).[82] On some vases there is a Dionysiac scene on one side and a phlyakes scene on the other.[83] These players of the popular farce thus are certainly members of the thiasus of Dionysus.

Fig. 536. Phlyax dancing before Dionysus. Paestan vase, British Museum

Fig. 537. Phlyax dancing between a satyr and a maenad. Phlyakes askos, Ruvo

538. Banquet of three actors. Vase by Python, Vatican. See p. xvi

On the crater by Python in the Vatican (Fig. 538)[84] three young men are characterized as actors of the farce by the masks above them, one mask of a black-haired man with grotesque features, one of a woman, and one of an old man. The youths play a game of cottabus, in which the dregs of their wine cups are thrown on a metal disk above a candelabrum. They may be celebrating a victory at a Dionysiac festival, for they are being served wine by a young satyr, while Papposilenus is lying in a drunken sleep on the floor, and on the reverse Dionysus is seated in the midst of his thiasus. Another such scene in a simpler form is on a Campanian crater in Cambridge.[85] These vases may already have been inspired by the Atellan, the Campanian equivalent of the phlyakes farce.[86] The gifted Oscans adapted the Southern Italian farce and conventionalized the four main types of the farce: Bucco, Maccus, Dossenus, and Pappus. The last they named in their language Casnar (Varro, *Lingua Latina*, VII,20). The plays were named Atellana from Atella, a town in Campania. In this Oscan form the Atellan farce came to Rome.

Certainly the Oscan, no longer the Greek form, is illustrated on a wine jug in the British Museum (Fig. 539),[87] for its inscription has the Oscan form Santia instead of the Greek name Xanthias. The bald actor with pointed beard, who is a freedman to judge from his fringed mantle, stands beside a statuette of Heracles. He probably claims to be as great a hero as the popular Heracles, a boast which the great bowl beside him confirms. His feat will, however, only be in drinking. He could be a Bucco, the big-mouthed, voracious, and boisterous braggart. On the vase with the symposion, the white-haired mask could be the Pappos-Casnar, the comical old man, and the black-haired mask that of Maccus, the glutton or buffoon, from which Plautus later took his middle name. The types were origi-

Fig. 539. Actor as Santia. Oscan vase, British Museum

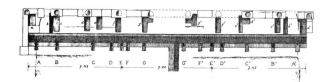

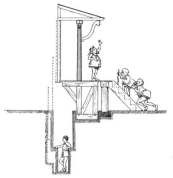

Fig. 540. Plan and reconstructed section of a phlyakes stage

nally individual and varied, as they are in Attic comedy. But when the farce wandered from the south towards the north, from Syracuse, the home of Epicharmus, to Tarentum, where Rhinthon lived and the hero Taras was mocked (Fig. 496); then to Lucania, where, in Paestum, Assteas painted; and then to Campania, where the highly cultured Oscans —who were also the inhabitants of Pompeii—lived, and who may have played the Atellana in their theaters; then the types developed which finally came to Rome.[88] If we can trust the vase with the Santia inscription, the Oscans discarded the phallus.

With the Atellana not only the types and jokes but also their temporary stage buildings came to Rome. We can reconstruct the form of the Southern Italian stage very well from the vase scenes, as about one-quarter include their setting. The stage has three main forms[89] which, however, overlap:

1) Primitive low stage, rough platform with wooden floor upon three or four rectangular posts (Figs. 489, 491, 504, 514, 515, 519).
2) Stage supported by fairly low posts, covered by drapery (Figs. 483, 492, 498, 507, 511, 518, 535) or tablets (Figs. 485, 488). Sometimes steps lead up to the platform and a door is indicated.
3) A higher stage supported by columns without steps but mostly with a back wall (Figs. 508, 509, 517).

The stages often have a short flight of five to seven steps in the center, leading up to the podium (Figs. 483, 485, 488, 489, 491, 507, 518). The forewall is adorned with drapery, and is often decorated with fillets (Fig. 517), wool strands (Fig. 488), wreaths (Fig. 485), branches (Fig. 517), and candelabra or incense stands (Fig. 498). The narrow high posts at the front corners (Fig. 508), which in one case (Fig. 517) carry a garland between them, correspond to the thin columns supporting the roof on the vase with the mad Heracles by Assteas in Madrid (Fig. 479). Such columns are more often found at the back corners, where they frame the rear wall (Fig. 489). This background wall is usually distinguished only by the objects hung upon them. These include masks (Figs. 481, 508, 512, 538), bucrania (Figs. 485, 486, 498, 507, 522), bowls Figs. 485, 489, 539), jugs (Fig. 509), fillets (Figs. 483, 504, 510, 519), and wreaths (Figs. 481, 584, 520). In one case a tympanon hangs near Zeus Ammon (Fig. 483).

The rear wall sometimes has other columns beside the ones set at the corners (479, 522), often doors (Figs. 479, 487, 491, 492, 500, 507, 509, 512), and in several cases windows, indicating an upper story (Figs. 484, 492, 501, 535). The door is often a richly-ornamented porch. It has a sloping or gable roof supported by beams and cross-struts or corbels. In the triangle between the horizontal and ascending parts, which is probably meant to be half a tympanon, there are tendrils, and on the corners of the gables acroteria (Figs. 480, 491, 507, 512). This richly-ornamented porch is the vestibulum, often mentioned by Plautus, for instance in *Mostellaria* (v. 817).

Among the settings, trees are rather common (Figs. 488, 489, 493, 506, 520, 527), including the palm tree for Zeus Ammon (Fig. 483). In addition, there are used: altars (Figs. 482, 486-488, 493, 528, 531), chairs and thrones (Figs. 482, 483, 485, 498, 535), a dining table (Figs. 509, 527, 538), a money chest (Fig. 508), a wool basket (Fig. 492), a ladder (Figs. 484, 501), a basin for holy water, and the tripod of Apollo (Fig. 481) and a thymiaterium (Fig. 498).

The description shows that the requisites of the popular farce were really of the simplest sort, so that they could be carried easily by the troupe when it wandered around. The stage was set up on the market place or in any available place in the smaller cities. In larger cities the wandering actors may have played in the Greek theaters, where they could conveniently erect their little podium in the large orchestra. This was probably the case in Syracuse, where provisions have been made in the rocky ground for the footings of such a temporary stage with a backwall (Fig. 540).[90] A similar temporary stage seems to have been installed in the theater of Corinth, which the Romans conquered in 146 B.C., and rehabilitated not long after 54 B.C.[91]

This simple stage had a world-wide historical significance.[92] It migrated together with the farce— now become the Oscan Atellana—to Rome. Here it became the stage of Plautus, and it combined in the first century B.C. with the Greek theatron to produce the Roman theater structure which, in the main, is still the form of our theater today.

CHAPTER XI

THE ROMAN PLAYS AT THE TIME OF THE REPUBLIC[1]

I. *The Early Republican Period*

WHILE Greek Southern Italy enjoyed tragedy, and comedy in the form of the farce, Rome, as yet uncivilized, remained content in the first centuries of the Republic with very primitive plays. These were called versus Fescennini, after Fescennium in the territory of the Falisci between Latium and Etruria (Horace, *Epist.*, II,1, vv. 145ff).[2] Coarse improvised jokes and personal satire were popular at the harvest festivals in honor of Silvanus and Tellus. The pleasantries gradually became so overdone and immoral that these plays had to be kept in bounds by law. All later Roman plays were taken over from foreign peoples and adapted to the Roman taste.

In Etruria music and dance flourished from the sixth to the fourth centuries B.C. They were used at funerals and at the festivals of the gods. We know of these dances—which evidently alternated with athletic contests such as boxing, wrestling, and chariot races—from representations on Etruscan wall paintings (Fig. 541) and on funeral urns.[3] The dancer was called *ister* from which the Latin *histrio*, actor, is derived. Among the dancers is found a masked harlequin, in the Tomba degli Auguri (tomb of the Augurs) and in the Tomba del Pulcinella (tomb of the buffoon), with the pointed headdress later used for clowns, and a short dress often composed of multicolored pieces like the one later used for harlequins (Figs. 542 and 543).[4] His name is Phersu, which became the Roman *persona*, meaning mask. Another Etruscan figure is Charun, a demon with hammer and grotesque features, found in the Tomba del Orco (the netherworld) in Tarquinii (Fig. 544) and the Tomba François in Vulci; he is also represented in terracotta heads (Fig. 545).[5] He became the model for the servants who burned the defeated gladiators with a hot iron

See Figs. 548, 552

Fig. 541. Etruscan dancers and musicians

Figs. 542, 543. Phersu, the masked dancer

Figs. 544, 545. Charun, the demon with a hammer

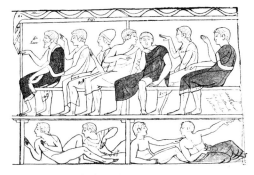

Fig. 546. Spectators on temporary stands. Wall painting, Corneto

to make sure that they were dead and who removed the dead gladiators in the Roman amphitheater. Charun later also became the model for the medieval devil. Etruscan dancers and flute players first came to Rome in 364 B.C., when they were invited on the occasion of a ceremony of expiation to ward off a pestilence. From then on dance and flute playing were part of the public life in Rome. The Etruscan mimetic dancers (histriones) accompanied by the double pipes (tibia) were blended with the Fescennine verses to form the Satura or Fabulae Saturae (Livy, VII,2), a medley of dance and crude scenes.[6] The Satura is, of course, not equivalent to the Greek satyric drama, but as the name implies, consists of a mixture of various elements out of which little dramatic sketches without continuity of content were composed.

For these primitive presentations straight tribunes were erected for the spectators, below which the slaves lay (Fig. 546).[7] These crude entertainments did not need a stage (pulpitum). Such a one, however, came to Rome with the popular farces of Southern Italy, which we know as phlyakes in their Greek form. These farces came to Rome as Fabulae Atellanae,[8] that is, in the form which the Oscans in Campania had given them. The name is taken from Atella, near Capua, the Campanian "Abdera," "Gotham," or "Schildburg," the city of queerness, where the people were supposed to do inept and absurd things. Some of the so-called phlyakes vases represent this younger third-century form. This is certainly the case in the vase which gives the slave beside the statue of Heracles not the Greek name Xanthias, but its Oscan form: Santia (Fig. 539.)[9] The Greek Pappos became the Oscan Casnar (Varro, *Lingua Latina*, VII, 29), and later the Latin Senex, the old man or the grandfather (cf. Figs. 488, 517-519, 521, 538). Also taken over were the Bucco, the stupidus, the dunce or braggart; Maccus, the greedy glutton; and Dossenus, the sly and mischievous hunchback, often acting as schoolmaster, learned man, or doctor. All these types can already be found in the phlyakes farce,[10] and have their origin in the old Doric farce (see Ch. III). These Oscan plays (ludi Osci) were first given by Campanian citizens in the Oscan language, then by

Roman citizens, and they persisted until the time of Cicero (Cicero, *Epistle ad Fam.*, VII,1,3), of Augustus (Strabo, V, 233), and even into the Empire (Tacitus, *Annales*, IV, 14). They were later rewritten in the Latin language (see below, p. 247) and replaced the old Roman satura and the Greek satyr play as a concluding piece. They were perhaps, therefore, later called fabulae satyricae.

II. *The Last Centuries of the Republic (ca. 250-30 B.C.)*

The crude forms of entertainment were replaced in the second half of the third century B.C. by translations and adaptations of Greek tragedies and comedies. From the wealthy and theater-loving Greek city of Tarentum, which was taken by the Romans in 272 B.C., Livius Andronicus came as a child to Rome. He became a slave and later a freedman and tutor in the house of a certain Livius. Having command of both Greek and Latin, he became the first translator in the world's literature. From 240 to 207 B.C. he translated into Latin the tragedies of Sophocles and Euripides as well as Greek New Comedies. The first presentation of a tragedy and a comedy was instituted by Livius Andronicus in the year 240 B.C. on the occasion of the Ludi Romani. Among the titles of his tragedies, which alone are preserved, are: *Achilles*, *Ajax*, *Aegisthus*, *Andromeda*, *Danae*, *Tereus*, and *The Trojan Horse*—all well-known legendary subjects from the Trojan and other heroic cycles. Titles of three comedies are *Gladiolus*, *Ludius*, and *Verpus*. These titles sound more like the farce of southern Italy than like Attic New Comedy. Certainly the farce had from the beginning a great influence on the development of Latin comedy. The Verpus, that is the male counterpart to a virgo, may be represented in the terracotta statuette of a seated old slave at Berlin (Fig. 547).[11] He has his legs and hands crossed and miserably anticipates dressing up as a young maiden whose mask is beside him on the seat. The influence of the popular farce on Latin comedy was however combined with that of Attic Comedy. This was certainly true in the case of Naevius, the younger contemporary of Livius Andronicus. Naevius was born in Campania, the home of the Atellana. He was a Roman citizen and gave his first presentation at Rome in the year 235 B.C. and flourished until 204 B.C. During this time he wrote nine tragedies, probably all of which were taken from Euripides. Among the titles are *Danae, The Trojan Horse, Hector, Hesione,* and *Iphigenia.* The tragedies of Naevius were still played in Rome in the time of Cicero. His comedies were also partly translated from Greek New Comedy, as, for example, the *Colax,* the Flatterer, from Menander. But beside the comedies from Attic citizen life, Naevius also used Italian motifs and blended them with the Greek models. For instance, the heroine of his comedy *Tarentilla* must have been a courtesan from the gay city of Tarentum. A large statuette, found together with that of a youth in a large mantle in the Oscan Pompeii (Figs. 548a-b), may represent such a person.[12] She has red hair and red lips and wears a chiton, colored light blue, in the Hellenistic form, and a palla, a mantle, colored light rose-violet, with fringes, a sign of elegance. The pallium for men, the palla for women are the Latin names for the Greek himation, which was taken over with the subject matter from Greek New Comedy. The Greek type of drama therefore was named Fabula Palliata, after this mantle. The mask of a gay youth with broad fillet and heavy garland of flowers and leaves, from Tarentum (Fig. 549), is representative of the palliata.

Naevius, however, used also native Roman subjects for tragedy as well as for comedy. He is the creator of the Roman national drama, named Fabula Praetexta after the toga of the patricians, which was ornamented with purple stripes (Fig. 550).[13] This form of tragedy had native Roman subjects, taken either from older history or legend, like *Romulus,* dealing with the founding of Rome, or contemporary events, like *Clastidium,* in which the victory of Claudius Marcellus over the Gauls in 222 B.C. is described. Perhaps these patriotic plays were given without masks and were composed for such special occasions as triumphs and funeral games. Since at these events scenic plays took place, the result was a constantly increased demand for the new dramas with a regular plot, which had been unknown in earlier Rome.

Naevius used motifs from native farce and the life of the lower classes in Italy for many of his comedies. The titles *Agitatoria* (the politician), *Ariolus* (the seer or soothsayer), *Carbonaria* (the charcoal-burner), *Corollaria* (the dealer in flowers), *Tunicularia* (the man in the small tunic), and *Figulus* (the potter) describe everyday life in Italian towns. Such types as may have appeared in these native comedies are portrayed in terracotta

Fig. 547. Verpus

Fig. 549. Mask of youth

Fig. 548a-b. Youth and courtesan   Fig. 550. Actor Fundilius Doctus

statuettes from Southern Italy (Figs. 551-553).[14] They all wear short tunics and above them they have oddly draped mantles. The one with a vase and a ham in his hand, who may be a potter, wears the Roman mantle called sagula; the one with the money bag, who may be a moneylender or a dealer, wears the Roman paenula; and the stupid looking man with the hanging arms, who may be an outwitted politician, wears the early form of the Roman toga.[15] They thus are all wearing Roman cloaks. These comedies with Italian plots were called togatae in contrast to the palliatae because they were played in the Roman toga or other local forms of the mantle in contrast to the Greek himation (pallium). Naevius was a many-sided man, and he

Figs. 551-553. Potter; Moneylender; Politician(?) of Italian comedy. Terracotta statuettes, British Museum

was considered the third greatest writer of comedy after the later poets Plautus and Caecilius.[16]

The importance of the Oscan farce becomes evident from the fact that Plautus named himself Maccius after one of its figures.[17] In the prologue of the *Asinaria* (The Comedy of Asses, or the Donkey Play, v. 11) he says that he as Maccus has translated this play into the barbaric language (Maccus vortit barbare). The word barbaric shows that he rightly considered his native language unpolished, and he indeed contributed much to refining it for literary use. Born around 254 B.C. in Sarsina in Umbria, he is the first poet to come to Rome from Northern Italy. His comedies were written in the late third and the early second centuries. From his one hundred and thirty comedies Varro chose twenty-one, all of which, twenty complete and one fragment (the *Vidularia*), have been preserved. The *Twin Brothers Menaechmi* can be dated before 215 B.C. and probably belongs to his earlier plays. The *Miles Gloriosus* (The Braggart Warrior) appeared about 206 B.C.; the *Cistellaria* (The Casket Comedy) about 202 B.C. The *Stichus* was presented in 200 B.C. at the Ludi Plebeii in the Circus Flaminius. The date of the *Pseudolus* is given as 191 B.C. The *Bacchides*, the *Truculentus*, and the *Casina* are probably among his latest pieces presented after 190 B.C. Plautus died in 184 B.C.

We must distinguish three elements in the comedies of Plautus: New Comedy, Italian Farce, and his own contribution. His plots and his characters are taken from the Attic New Comedy of Menander, Philemon, and Diphilus (see above, Ch. VIII, pp. 87ff). The influence of these models is seen in his chief theme: the love of an extravagant or gentle youth for a courtesan or for a freeborn, but not yet recognized, daughter of a citizen and the tricks and deceptions of the slave used to help him. His chief personages are the enamoured, lighthearted, and reckless young man, the courtesan, the worthy mother, and the impudent, lying, and scheming slave. Masks and figurines found in Italy illustrate these characters. The mask of a gay young man from Tarentum (Fig. 549) and statuettes of the youth and the courtesan found in Pompeii (Fig. 548) represent the lovers. The father of comedy wrapped in his large pallium (Fig. 554b) and the slave in his coarse tunic and small mantle, his right hand laid on his back (Fig. 554a) are represented in bronze statuettes found in Rome, now in the Metropolitan Museum of Art. Another bronze statuette of a slave in pensive attitude, as if preparing an intrigue, is in the Museum of Cassel, and another in the Walters Art Gallery in Baltimore seems to expect, or has received, a beating (Fig. 555).[18]

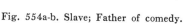

Fig. 554a-b. Slave; Father of comedy.   Fig. 555. Slave

Figs. 556-558 Slaves seeking refuge on altars

Slaves fearing punishment flee to an altar when their intrigue has misfired, as does Syrus in the *Heauton Timoroumenos* of Terence (v,975). Marble statuettes in the Vatican (Figs. 556-557) and in the British Museum (Fig. 558) represent slaves with the wreath of a banquet, which they may have celebrated too early, and they are now fearfully clutching the edge of their seats.[19] Tranio in the *Mostellaria* (The Haunted House, v. 1064ff) is seated on the altar to evade punishment, after his intrigue has been found out by his old master (cf. below, Fig. 587). The *Pseudolus* glorifies the lying slave. Other characters from New Comedy are the brutal and stingy pimp, slave dealer and moneylender, the parasite, the cook, and the bragging soldier, who in the *Miles Gloriosus* is ridiculed as boasting, vainglorious, and mercenary. In the comedies of Plautus as in the statuettes everything is much coarser and more farcical than in the Greek models. (Cf. the Greek statuettes Ch. VIII, Figs. 396-413, with the Roman ones in Ch. XII, Figs. 580-585).

The reason for this is that Plautus was strongly under the influence of the native farce and remodelled the Greek motifs in its direction. He used the stock characters of the Atellana. He may have played the greedy glutton Maccus when he was an actor before becoming a writer, and therefore named himself Maccius. He seems to have used the clever Dossenus for his parasites, such as Saturio in the *Persa* (the Persian), who sells his daughter to a procurer knowing that he can claim her again because she is freeborn. Horace (*Epist.* ii,1,170-174) says that Plautus was a Dossenus among the voracious parasites (adspice Plautus . . . quantus sit Dossenus edacibus in parasitis). Manducus, who in the Latin farce was developed from the big-mouthed Bucco, is mentioned in *Rudens* (vv. 535-536): the procurer Labrax when rescued from the sea after a shipwreck thinks of offering himself as a candidate for the role of a Manducus, because he is chattering aloud with his teeth. This mask with the enormous teeth lived on in the imperial time (see Ch. XV, Figs. 821-822). The senex, developed from the Oscan Casnar as a stupid old man, can be found in several comedies of Plautus. Thus Nicobulus is easily deceived by his own slave in the *Bacchides*, who makes him pay a sum of money for which the son can redeem his mistress. Periphanes in the *Epidicus* is even twice persuaded to give large sums of money extracted under false pretenses. Theopropides in the *Mostellaria* believes the unlikely story of his slave Tranio, who pretends that his house is haunted and that, therefore, his son has sold it and purchased a new house. In the *Casina* the old Lysidamus is deceived by the stratagem of his wife when he tries to get possession of Casina, the beloved of his son. The old man and the young man fight for the favor of the girl. Father and son both wish to marry her to their own slaves, for they believe her to be a slave. The father wants to give her to his old overseer, the son to his own personal attendant. Each hopes that in this way he will be able to enjoy her favor. The father is, of course, cheated: an old bearded slave Chalinus, dressed as a girl, takes the place of the bride (see the statuette in Fig. 547). The father and the overseer are soundly beaten by the attendant, and Casina is finally given in marriage to the son. In the *Mercator* (the Merchant) the father also falls in love with the sweetheart of his son, without suspecting that the boy loves her. The two engage in a battle for the possession of the beloved (vv. 380ff) and each, in order to be able to enjoy her, pretends that he wants to sell her to a friend. The stupid old man makes the mistake of entrusting the girl to a neighbor, and it is of course the son who will get her, as it is in the farce (see Fig. 504).[20] But in Plautus it is a battle of words instead of swords as in the farce. In the *Asinaria* and the *Bacchides* father and son share the favor of a courtesan in a friendly fashion, instead of fighting over her.

While most plays of Plautus have themes which are similar to those in the popular farce dealing with everyday life, only one play, the *Amphitruo*, is influenced by the hilarious tragedy (hilarotragodia) of Rhinthon, as reflected in the vase in Fig. 484.[21] Plautus himself calls it a tragicomoedia (v. 63). It is, of course, on a higher level than the farce. While Jupiter in the farce visits Alcmene in his own form, in Plautus he has to take the likeness of her husband Amphitryon, in order to win the noble and faithful woman, whose innocent affection belongs to her husband.

Plautus thus is by no means just a translator of Greek New Comedy. He has more effective wit and rollicking humor, suitable for stage use, than the more refined Greek comic writers. In addition to their subject matter and to the motifs of the farce, he has entirely unique themes, sentimental and romantic situations, which distinguish his pieces from all other ancient comedies.[22] The *Aulularia* (The Hidden Pot of Gold) and the *Trinummus* (The Threepenny Piece) have a psychological interest in spite of the motifs borrowed from farces. An unusually emotional and noble play is the *Captivi* (The Captives or Prisoners of War). It has popular magnanimity, reward for virtue after hard trials, and punishment of wickedness. Part of the popularity of the comedies by Plautus is due to the role that music plays in them. There was no chorus, but many songs, cantica, and many integral parts of the action were declaimed or chanted to the accompaniment of the flute or double pipe (tibia) with a great variety of musical meters, indicating the changing melodies. This is a peculiarly Italian feature. The importance of the music is shown in the fact that the musician who was in charge of the musical accompaniment, and who may have also composed the music, is sometimes named in the prefatory note, as is Marcipor, the slave of Oppius—together with the actor Pellio—in the *Stichus*. In this play when the slaves hold a drinking party they give a drink to the musician (vv. 762-768). In the *Pseudolus*, the slave from which the comedy takes its name, when he has to leave the stage, promises entertainment by the fluteplayer. In the *Casina* the musician is asked to play the wedding song, the Hymenaeus. Thus music was used not only in some parts, as in the chorus of the Greek plays, but a musical element seems to have pervaded the whole presentation.[23] This interweaving of music is an old inheritance from the Ludi Etrusci and thus genuinely Italian. Many other Italian elements, flavor, and local color are found in Plautus in his introduction of Italian topics and descriptions of Roman places, as, for example, the Forum Romanum in *Curculio*, vv. 467-482. The prologues preserved in twelve of the comedies of Plautus are also unique. They are spoken by an actor, by the personified Prologus, or by a god, such as Mercury in *Amphitruo*; the Lar familiaris in *Aulularia*, the star *Arcturus* in *Rudens*, Luxuria and Inopia in *Trinummus*. The end is often a gay parade, similar to the Komos in Old Comedy.

Plautus is always original and amusing. He has true theatrical instinct and wit. It is not to be wondered at that he was popular in antiquity and still remains beloved today. His popularity certainly contributed to the fact that scenic plays were more and more added to festivals, which at first had only athletic events, races, and gladiatorial fights. These games had come originally from Etruria, then from Campania, earlier than the Oscan farce and the Greek scenic plays and always remained more popular than the latter.

The number of ludi, that is official holidays on which plays were presented, increased steadily. All festivals were associated with the state religion and were given in honor of the gods, under the supervision of the state, with magistrates—mostly aediles—presiding. The presentation of the plays was in the hands of a theater director (dominus gregis). The oldest and most important festivals, the Ludi Romani, in honor of Jupiter, were celebrated in the Circus Maximus, the oldest building for games in Rome, where Livius Andronicus presented his tragedies beginning in 240. From 220 on the Ludi Plebeii or popular games were also given in honor of Jupiter, but in the Circus Flaminius on the Campus Martius. From 212 on the Ludi Apollinares were given in honor of Apollo, and from 194 on the Ludi Megalenses or the Megalesian festival in honor of the Magna Mater or Cybele. A pulpitum, a platform or temporary stage, which had come with the Southern Italian farces to Rome, was erected for these plays on public ground before the temples or in the buildings destined for athletic events. From 214 on theatrical representations of four days' duration took place at the Ludi Romani before the circus races and gladiatorial fights began (Livy, xxix,43). In about 200 B.C. Rome had only eleven to seventeen, in the Augustan period forty to forty-eight days for official scenic representations. To these must be added the scenic Ludi Funebres or funeral games and the Ludi Votivi, plays presented at dedications and triumphs.

In the second century B.C. Greek-Hellenistic influence on Rome was at its height (cf. Livy, xxxix,22, and Polybius, xxx,13). Tragedy and Comedy were Hellenized more and more and were presented even in their original form in the Greek language.[24] This was, of course, only possible for the highly cultivated and educated aristocratic Roman circles such as the families of the Scipios, of Aemilius Paullus, and of Titus Quinctius Flamininus, who were the victors over the Greeks. The dramatic plays spread along with Greek culture and religion. Under the Greek influence the Roman republican literature reached its greatest period during the second century, with its comic poets Caecilius and Terence, and its tragic poets Ennius, Pacuvius, and Accius.

Caecilius Statius (ca. 219-168) wrote forty-two comedies of which we know the titles and about 300 verses. The titles are related to Attic New Comedy, especially to Menander, such as *Andria*, *Synephebi*, the *Substituted Child* and the *Money-Lender*. His Hellenistic style stands midway between Plautus and Terence.

Terence (P. Terentius Afer) was born in Africa about 190-185 B.C. He came to Rome as the slave of Terentius Lucanus, who set him free. He frequented the house of Scipio Africanus and composed for his highly-cultured circle imitations of Greek New Comedies, particularly those of Menander. He is so similar to the Attic poets that he really belongs in the history of the Hellenistic literature, and has always been treated therein (see Ch. VIII, p. 88). He, like Naevius, Plautus, and Ennius before him, sometimes combined plots and characters taken from several Greek originals (see Prologue to *Andria*, vv. 9ff). His six plays, which are all preserved, belong to the period 166-160 B.C.: *Andria* (The *Woman* of Andros) to 166; *Heauton Timorumenos* (The Self-tormentor) to 163; *Eunuchus* and *Phormio* to 161; *Adelphi* (The Brothers) to 160 B.C. *Hecyra* (The Mother-in-Law) had two unsuccessful performances in 165 and 160, before it became a success in the fall of the latter year. The first *Hecyra* and the first three comedies named were presented at the Ludi Megalenses; the second *Hecyra* and the *Adelphi* at the funeral games (Ludi Funerales) of Aemilius Paullus, the victor over Greece; and the third *Hecyra* as well as the *Phormio* were performed at the Ludi Romani. Terence died in 159 in Greece, where he had gone to find more original material for his plays.

Terence was not, like Plautus, a strong and jocose humorist but a refined, subtle, cultured, and morally eminent poet. With the exception of *Phormio*—which is modelled after Apollodorus of Carystus' *Epidicazomenos* (the Claimant)—the plays of Menander are imitated in style and character in the other five comedies of Terence. In *Adelphi* a play by Menander is enriched with a scene from the *Synapothnescontes* (Linked in Death) by Diphilus. This play, with its opposing theories of education of two fathers, one indulgent and one

tainly contributed much to the education of the undeveloped taste of the Roman public.[25]

Through Plautus and Terence, the New Comedy, the last artistic and literary form of ancient drama with purely human content, endured in its Roman form until the end of antiquity. The imperial Roman period, the Middle Ages, and the Renaissance were especially interested in Terence. We, therefore, have illustrated Terence manuscripts, originating probably in the fourth or fifth century A.D., which were copied again and again.[26] On the title pages of *Heauton Timoroumenos* and *Hecyra* the speaker of the prologue, probably meant to be Ambivius Turpio, appears in the pallium, the Greek mantle from which the Roman Comedy takes its name (Fig. 559).[27] At the beginning of each play there is painted an aedicula with the masks of all characters in the order in which they will appear on the stage (Fig. 560). Then a picture of the action of each

Fig. 559. Speaker of Prologue to *Hecyra* (Ambivius Turpio). Miniature from a manuscript of Terence, Vatican

stern, and the counterbalance of the different principles of education, is conceived in an absolutely Greek spirit. His *Hecyra* shows a deep understanding of psychology. An emotional play by Plautus such as the *Captivi* looks like a farce in contrast; and indeed we saw that Plautus was influenced by the farce, while Terence was not. Terence did not hold his public as spellbound as Plautus. The audience twice walked out of the performances of the *Hecyra*, the first time to see rope dancers and the second time to watch a gladiatorial game (Prologues to *Hecyra*, I, vv. 1ff, II, vv. 27ff). Terence uses his prologues not as other playwrights do to explain the plot, but to plead, or let his theater director plead, with the public to give him a fair hearing and not to believe malignant rumors and unfair criticism which said that he was assisted by men of high rank in his writings, and that he spoiled his Greek plays by combining two into one (Prologues to *Andria* and *Heauton Timoroumenos*). In the prologue to this last named play (vv. 36ff), Terence enumerates as the typical figures, which he has taken over from Greek New Comedy, the running slave, the angry man, the greedy parasite, the impertinent informer, and the covetous panderer. He concedes that he has sometimes changed from a single to a double plot (*ibid.*, vv. 16ff). The speaker of the prologues is the theater director Ambivius Turpio, who produced the plays of Caecilius as well as those of Terence and cer-

Fig. 560. Shrine with masks. Miniature from a manuscript of Terence, Vatican

This is a mantle which is folded in two, covers both shoulders, and is pinned on the right shoulder, so that the right arm is left free (Figs. 399 and 561b). When Charinus in *Mercator* plans to go travelling in order to find his beloved girl, he wears a chlamys, but changes back to a pallium when he hears that she is in Athens; but when he is not admitted to her directly, he again puts on the chlamys in order to start on his journey (Plautus, *Mercator*, vv. 851ff, 910ff, 921ff). The chlamys can be thrown back over the shoulders and then hangs only in the back; see

Fig. 561a-c. Scenes from Terence's *Adelphi*. Scenes II,1; II,4; III,2. Miniatures from a manuscript of Terence, Vatican

scene follows (Figs. 561a-c). Our examples illustrate *Adelphi* (vv. 155ff, 260ff, 288ff). Costumes, masks, and gestures correspond remarkably to the older monuments (cf. Figs. 547-548 and 554-558), and show the continuation of a living tradition until the very end of antiquity. For example: Ergasilus in Plautus' *Captivi* says: "I will throw my cloak over my shoulder just as slaves in comedies usually do." This agrees with the slaves in the Terence miniatures who grasp a small mantle hanging from their left shoulder with their left hands. (Compare also *Epidicus* 194f and *Phormio* 844f.)

The costume in Roman Comedy was, as the name palliata tells us, based on the Greek.[28] The pallium worn by men and the palla worn by women is the Greek himation, draped freely and in the most diverse way. Beginning at the left shoulder, it is wrapped around the back and the right side and finally brought back to the left side. It can leave the right arm free (Figs. 548 and 556-558), but it can also cover both arms and shoulders as we see it on the bronze statuette of a father (Fig. 554b) and on the man, probably Ambivius Turpio, who speaks the prologue for Terence's *Hecyra* (Fig. 559). The slaves wear a small scarf-like mantle (pallium collectum) which they gather up when they walk or run (see *Captivi*, 778f, and Figs. 554a and 561b). The chlamys is worn by young men, soldiers, travellers, and also by slaves when they are sent on errands.

the relief in Verona (Ch. XII, Fig. 586). On this same relief the drunken slave is supported by a second slave who wears the exomis, the narrow tunic which covers only one shoulder (cf. Fig. 555). The Greek chiton as well as the Roman tunic cover, as a rule, both shoulders and sometimes form a small sleeve over the upper arm (Figs. 548 and 561). The tights with long sleeves and leggings of Greek comedy are often retained, while the padded body is seen only in lower-class people like slaves (Figs. 554a, 561). The women wear the long tunic, which is also sometimes given to older, more dignified men (Figs. 561a-c).

The footwear in comedy is the soccus, a slipper. Periphanes in Plautus' *Epidicus* promises to his slave soccus, tunica, and pallium. Travellers wear the wide-brimmed petasos. The different classes were distinguished by attributes: the soldier by the sword, the slave dealer by a money bag and straight staff, the master of the house by a curved staff, the cook by a spoon or a receptacle with provisions.

It was formerly believed that the players did not wear masks in the earlier period at Rome, that they wore only wigs, and that for this reason, in contrast to the Greek masked drama, the number of actors was unlimited. But it is more likely that the wigs— white for old men, black for young men, and red for slaves—were attached to the masks, which in Italian as in Greek representations covered the

whole head (see Figs. 339b, 547, 551-553).²⁹ The introduction of the mask by Minucius Prothrymus and Cincius Faliscus in tragedy and comedy (Diomedes, *De Arte Grammatica*, III, 9,7; Donatus in *Praefatio to Adelphoe*, I, 6 and *Eunuchus*, I, 6), which has been dated between 130 and 91 B.C., could have occurred much earlier, as we know nothing else about them. Naevius' *Personata* was certainly presented by masked actors. Early masks are testified by Festus (p. 238 L). How could a comedy of errors like *The Twin Brothers Menaechmi* be presented without masks and without a stereotyped costume which was the same for the same age group and the same for each member of a definite social class? How could it otherwise be explained that, when Menaechmus of Syracuse comes for the first time to Epidamnus, wife, girlfriend, parasite, servant, maid, father-in-law, and physician all mistake him for his twin brother living in Epidamnus, since they had been separated as small boys?

The execution of masks and costumes is much coarser in the Latin than in the Greek representations, just as the Latin plays themselves are coarser than their Greek originals. High reliefs from Pompeii, in Naples, and another relief in the Vatican, which probably came from Ostia, show groups of masks as they were used in the Latin as well as in the Greek New Comedy (Figs. 562-564).³⁰ On a relief set up on a pillar in the garden-peristyle of the Casa degli Amorini Dorati at Pompeii the mask of the slave lies opposite to those of a stern old father and a girl. Slave and father have the speira; the slave also has a fillet and wreath for a banquet. The father has a long beard. The girl has long strands of hair falling to her shoulder; the hair is parted in the center and covered with a mitra. The masks are set against a drapery which is attached to thin columns, a forerunner of the aediculae in the Terence manuscripts (Fig. 560). Father and son reappear in the two reliefs from Pompeii in Naples (Figs. 562-563) as well as in the one in Rome (Fig. 564). In two of the reliefs (Figs. 562, 564) father and slave both have thick wreaths around which fillets are wound. Next to the father is a delicate young son with his hair laid over a speira. In one (Fig. 562) these two masks are laid on a drapery. Beside them and above the slave is a temple. On the reverse are two tragic masks. On the other relief from Pompeii (Fig. 563) there is a rocky background. The father is lying below, the slave above. Opposite the slave is a youth, and below them is a drapery. Beside the son is the mask of a satyr, indicating that satyr plays were still performed. On the reverse of this plaque are the masks

Figs. 562-564. Groups of masks. Marble reliefs from Pompeii and Ostia

Fig. 565. Mask of girl. Mosaic from Pompeii

of an old Silenus and a young satyr in low relief. On the relief in the Vatican (Fig. 564) the mask of another young man is added. The one next to the father, who like the slave wears a wreath with fillets, is that of a delicate, gentle, and serene looking youth. The other on the ground opposite the slave has a serious and angry expression. The hair is in short curls, except for some rather long twisted strands behind the ear. To the right seems to be a stele on two steps. The left corner which contains a similar stepped object is a modern restoration. These may be the masks for a double plot with contrasting characters, as Terence liked to present them. In the *Andria*, for example, Charinus is probably added from the *Lady of Perinthos* by Menander to make a counterpart to Pamphilus, who belongs to the *Lady of Andros* by the same Greek poet.[31] On the back of the relief in the Vatican are a male and a female tragic mask near a rustic altar.

A relief in Cassel shows the masks of an older man and a girl next to each other on some rocks.[32] Below the girl is a torch, below the man a curved staff. He has his hair laid over a speira and over that, hanging deeply over the forehead, a wreath with a fillet around it. He is similar to the father on the reliefs in Naples (Fig. 562) and in the Vatican (Fig. 564). The girl with a broad fillet (mitra) bound in a bow over her forehead is similar to the mask in the garland from the border of the mosaic of the "genius of autumn riding on a lion" in Naples (Fig. 565).[33] These masks are frequent types taken from Latin comedy.

On a round marble medallion from Pompeii in

Fig. 566. Two masks of men. Relief on marble medallion

Naples the mask of a bald man with a long floating beard is grouped with the mask of a man with a short beard, below whom is a lyre (Fig. 566).[34] He thus may be a musician. On the reverse are a Pan and a maenad, again pointing to the bacchic origin of the masks.

We know much less about tragedy in the Republican period than of comedy, because not one whole tragedy has been preserved for us.

Ennius (239-169), a Messapian from the region east of Tarentum, spoke Greek, Oscan, and Latin. Of his twenty tragedies we know only the titles and about 400 lines. The subjects are mostly borrowed from Euripides and the Iliad: *Achilles, Ajax, Alexander, Andromache Aichmalotis, Hectoris Lytra, Hecuba, Iphigenia, Medea exul, Thyestes.* The fragments show a decided tendency to rhetorical effects. Ennius wrote also two Roman historical plays: *Sabinae* (The Sabine Women) and *Ambracia*.

Pacuvius (ca. 220- ca. 130 B.C.) was a nephew of Ennius, born in Brundisium, and he spoke Oscan. He wrote some twelve tragedies, most of them again modelled after Euripides, such as *Dulorestes* (Orestes as Slave) and *Antiope*. Again we have only some 400 lines preserved. Pacuvius also wrote a Fabula Praetexta, *Paullus*, probably in honor of L. Aemilius Paullus after his victory at Pydna (168 B.C.).

Accius (170- ca. 86 B.C.) was fifty years younger than Pacuvius, but a contest between the two is recorded for the year 140 B.C. He is considered the most important among the Roman writers of tragedy, and his plays were still performed in the time of the Empire. Besides Euripides, whom he imitated in the *Medea*, Aeschylus and Sophocles also served as authoritative models. Thus his first drama *Atreus* was probably inspired by Aeschylus and his *Ajax* by Sophocles. The titles of over forty tragedies and of two Fabulae Praetextae with about 700 lines are preserved. In the *Brutus*, Tarquinius Superbus appeared on the stage. Accius is a forerunner of Seneca in using horrific and melodramatic themes, majestic rhetoric, and flamboyant character portrayal.

In the early Augustan age L. Varius Rufus presented a tragedy, *Thyestes*, in 29 B.C. on the occasion of the triumph of Augustus, for the victory at Actium in 31 B.C. Quintilian (*Inst. Or.*, X, 1,98) praised it as equal to any Greek drama (Vari Thyestes cuilibet Graecarum comparari potest), which shows that the Hellenizing of Rome continued. Ovid wrote a *Medea*, which, however, was not presented on the stage.

The exaggerations which we find in the fragments of the tragic poets correspond to the monuments with actors in tragic costume of the Roman period. In principle this tragic costume is still the same as

Figs. 567, 568. Heroine and hero of tragedy. Marble masks

Fig. 569. Heracles, Deianeira, Iole. Masks on marble relief

Figs. 570, 571. Perseus and Andromeda

that which Aeschylus had given to his actors and which Sophocles as well as Euripides had accepted. The long-sleeved robe was probably made more colorful. The greatest change is the lengthening of the whole figure of the Roman actors by higher soles and higher onkos, the hairdress above the mask. The tragic boot, the cothurnus, was originally a soft and elegant footwear, under which Aeschylus had added a sole to make it a firmer support for the actors (see Ch. II, p. 26). In the Hellenistic period the soles were doubled (see Ch. VII, Figs. 290 and 307, actors of tragedy). In the Roman period the sole became a high, wooden, bulky block (Figs. 785, 788-792, 799). A good example is offered by the scene from a tragedy on the terracotta relief (Fig. 588) in the cothurni of Odysseus and Andromache. This may be a representation of the *Astyanax* or the *Hecuba* of Accius. Both man and woman are decidedly padded, a contrivance taken over from comedy, because the figures would otherwise appear too thin compared with their height. Thus the whole figure was made taller and broader, inflated, just as the characters in Latin tragedy departed from the simplicity and grandeur of the classical Greek models to a more weighty and exaggerated rhetorical style.

The Roman tragic masks have wide openings for mouth and eyes and abundant, even luxurious, growths of hair and of the beards of men (Figs. 567-568).[35] There is often a very artificial arrangement of twisted locks. Thus the hero from Pompeii

in Naples (Fig. 568) has two rows of short curls in his beard and corkscrew locks hanging from his half-circle onkos deep over his forehead and on the shoulders. A broad fillet with symmetrical loops at both sides hangs in a bowline over the onkos and down on the shoulders in front of the sidelocks.

Masks of tragedy, like those of comedy, are combined in high relief on decorative plaques in Pompeii, to give the dramatis personae of one play. One represents Heracles and two women, probably Deianeira and Iole (Fig. 569).[36] Between them is an altar with votive offerings of fruit. In the background right and left are towers, probably indicating the city Oechalia, which Heracles has conquered and where he took Iole prisoner. Deianeira, fearing that she might lose the love of her husband Heracles to the captured girl, sent him the shirt of Nessos, believing it to be a love charm. While sacrificing at an altar, Heracles was killed by the poisoned shirt. Perhaps we have here the masks for a Latin adaptation of Sophocles' *Trachinian Women*.

A marble relief in Naples (Fig. 570)[37] and a wall painting in Pompeii found in a house in the Via Stabiana near the theaters (Fig. 571),[38] belonging to the Augustan age, both show the masks of Perseus and Andromeda opposite each other. They are certainly based on the romantic story of how the maiden was left a prey to a sea monster to atone for her mother's sin, and how she was rescued by Perseus, as told in the *Andromeda* of Euripides (see Ch. II, Fig. 110). The monster comes out of the water; the sickle sword or harpe of Perseus is near

157

his mask, and the head of the Medusa, which he has chopped off, is below his mask. In the painting there are also the masks of the parents of Andromeda with high onkoi, below the mask of their daughter. In both monuments the girl has delicate features and parted hair. On the relief she has long twisted strands hanging on her shoulders and back. She and Perseus have narrow fillets. Perseus has short strands standing up over his forehead, long hair falling on his shoulders, and sideburns. In the painting he has a very high onkos with a narrow fillet, and above it there are the head and wings of a griffin. This is the cap of Hades which makes him invisible. Both monuments may be based on a Latin adaptation of Euripides' *Andromeda*. The title *Andromeda* is attested for plays by Livius Andronicus, Ennius, and Accius. It was thus a favorite of the Latin tragic writers. These masks grouped together from a definite play are the forerunners of the aediculae in the Terence manuscripts (Fig. 560).

A male and a female mask with very elaborate and artificial hairdress are laid opposite each other on some rocks on two reliefs from Pompeii in Naples (Fig. 572).[39] On the one illustrated there is a flam-

Fig. 572. Archaistic masks and flaming altar

ing altar between the two masks, decorated with a garland. The same altar stands between masks laid on rocks on a relief found in 1902 under the Quirinal hill in Rome, brought to the Antiquario Comunale on the Celio, now in the Museo Nuovo, formerly Museo Mussolini (Fig. 573a).[40] The hero to the right, at whose side a sword is standing, has a high onkos with twisted locks, broad fillet, and a curled beard similar to one of the mask in Naples (Fig. 568). Opposite is a woman with hair hanging deeply into her forehead as in Fig. 567. Behind her is a bearded man wearing an onkos with corkscrew locks but without fillet. His beard has natural tresses. The companion relief (Fig. 573b) seems to be composed of Dionysiac masks on rocks: to the left the bearded Dionysus with a wreath, to the right a maenad with a double row of knotted wool fillets, behind her a young satyr. Below is a basket with fruit to the right and a drinking horn to the left.

On the reverse of the relief with comic masks and a temple (Fig. 562) in Naples are two tragic masks in flat relief, opposite each other, laid on rocks, with lofty onkoi. The hero has curly ends on his long hair and beard and there is a sword under him; the woman has a kerchief which completely covers her high onkos and side locks.

That the onkos was already worn very high in the later republican period and decorated with luxuriant hair streaming down over the ears, is proved by monuments belonging to the last two centuries B.C. The mosaic threshold of the Casa del Fauno (Fig. 574) in Pompeii is part of the decoration of this fine patrician Oscan house in the second century B.C.[41] It was laid at the entrance to the main atrium at the end of the hall. Two masks are inserted into a luxuriant garland, a female and a male one. The male (Fig. 574) has a reddish-brown face and long brown wavy hairstrands hanging from his onkos

Fig. 573a-b. Group of masks. Marble reliefs from the Quirinal

Fig. 574. Tragic mask. Mosaic threshold, Pompeii

Figs. 575, 576. Tragic masks. Medallions from Pompeii

Fig. 577. Male mask with waved hair and beard. Marble

down to his eyebrows and shoulders. There are enormous openings for the eyes and the mouth. Similar are the colossal masks set up on a cornice or shelf in the Villa of Boscoreale, belonging to the second style of the first century B.C.[42] The medallion from Pompeii in Naples (Fig. 575) probably belongs to the Augustan age.[43] The mask has corkscrew locks hanging over the forehead and on the shoulder, while a kind of pony tail comes out on the crown of the head. Another medallion from Pompeii in Naples (Fig. 576)[44] has, in contrast, a female mask with natural hair parted in the center and a mask of an older man with furrowed forehead, into which the hair falls with soft short strands, while the beard has natural waved long strands. A similar mask with furrowed brow and softly waved hair and beard is in the Metropolitan Museum (Fig. 577).

Several of these monuments show a connection with the Dionysiac cult (see Figs. 572-573), and on a relief in the British Museum (Fig. 578)[45] a group of purely Dionysiac masks is assembled: two maenads above, one with a fillet, the other with a kerchief and mitra; below Dionysus, behind him a thyrsus, and opposite a satyr crowned with ivy. This connection, which we found also in the phlyakes and Atellan farce, explains the continued use of masks in the serious plays.

Eventually, however, the forms of stage entertainment which did not need masks became more popular than the masked presentations. The mime is an old and primitive form of entertainment, which originated in Sicily. Strolling troupes of male and female acrobats and dancers travelled through Greek lands and performed even in Athens, as described by Xenophon in his *Symposion*.[46] Similar dances and acrobatic feats are performed by girls on vase paintings from Southern Italy (Fig. 579).[47] A girl tumbles in and out of a circle of knives stuck in the ground; another shoots arrows with her feet, while her arms support her on the ground; and one dances with swords in her hand. The first mimetic dancer in Rome, Pompilius, is mentioned for 212 B.C. (*Macrobius*, II, 7,2). At the Ludi Apollinares this

old mime continued to dance while the army of the Carthaginians was being defeated outside the Porta Capena. From 173 B.C. on, the mimes became the most important part of the Floralia. The facts that they were played without masks, that women appeared in them, and that the plots were short and often indecent or lighthearted burlesques taken from the lower class of the city life, with adultery a favorite subject, made them very popular among the Romans. The mime was given its first literary form by the knight Decimus Laberius (106-43 B.C.). His rival was a former slave of Julius Caesar, Publilius Syrus, from Syria. Because Laberius had mocked Caesar in one of his mimes, Caesar forced him to act in his own mime against the Syrian slave who won the victory. This was a great affront to the sixty-

Fig. 578. Masks of Dionysus, a satyr, and two maenads. Marble relief

year-old Laberius, who lost his rank of knight through the acting, which was considered undignified without a mask. But the Romans liked to see the facial expressions of the actors. The mime, therefore, gradually replaced in public favor the Atellan farce with its set character masks, and forced the latter out of its position as the concluding piece (exodium) of the tragedies. Beside conclusions, it served also as a play for the intermissions (interludes) of more serious drama, as Cicero (*Epist. ad Fam.*, ix, 16,7) tells us in the year 46 B.C. The mimes wore a motley dress of patchwork (centunculus) and no shoes, or only light sandals or soles. They therefore were called planipedes, flat feet, and it is assumed that the name Plautus comes from his playing with bare feet in the mime, as he did in the Atellana.

The Atellan farce was given literary form in Latin about 89 B.C. by C. Novius (quoted by Cicero, *De Oratore*, ii, 255, 279, 285, in 55 B.C.), and by L. Pomponius, who was active in 89 B.C.[48] Both used the four old Atellan types. We have such titles as *Maccus the Soldier, The Twin Macci, Bucco the Gladiator, Pappus the Farmer, The Two Dossenni.* To these old figures were added motifs, modes of speech, and dresses copied from the Latin farmers. The titles *Rusticus, Agricola, Vacca, Asina, Maialis* —the Rustic, the Farmer, the Cow, the She-donkey, the Pig—give proof of its rustic milieu, which was certainly portrayed with correspondingly coarse and rustic humor, in contrast to the more urban burlesques of the mime. Other themes were taken from civic and family life: *Patruus, Heres-Petitor, Gemini, Nuptuae*—the Uncle, the Legacy Hunter, the Twins, the Wedding. Various social classes, professions, and tradesfolk, moreover, were pictured: *Aruspex, Augur, Medicus, Citharista, Pictores, Piscatores, Fullones*—the Fortune Teller, the Augur, the Doctor, the Cithara Player, the Painters, the Fishers, the Fullers. The last-named, a very respected and truly Italian profession, was treated by both Novius and Pomponius. The scene seems to have often been laid in small towns and villages. Later the same material also passed over to the mime, which temporarily replaced the Atellan farce. The latter bloomed anew, however, under the Empire, and then was sometimes called the exodium because it often followed the serious tragedies as concluding play. The actors were correspondingly called exodiarii and they were always masked.

From the Fabula Togata, the native comedy played in the Roman toga and other Italian dress (see above, Figs. 550-553), arose during the first century B.C. a form which depicted the humble life in country towns of artisans and poor folk living in small private houses, the so-called tabernae. It is therefore named Fabula Tabernaria.[49] Provincials such as the Oscans and Volscians appeared on the stage in their native dress and spoke their own language, because they did not know Latin. The originators of this variety of play are T. Quinctius Atta, who died in 77 B.C., and L. Afranius, whose *Simulans*, the Dissembler, was presented in 57 B.C. and repeated in the time of Nero (Suetonius, *Nero*, xi,2).

Thus at the end of the Republic one could see in Rome many kinds of plays, from sublime tragedy to the coarsest farces and parodies of daily life. The costumes were different for each kind and therefore of the greatest variety.

Fig. 579a-c. Acrobatic entertainers. Gnathia vases from southern Italy

CHAPTER XII

THE ART OF ACTING IN ROME

THE art of acting was highly developed among the Romans.[1] The Italian natives have always had a special gift for mimicry. They are born improvisators, having lively gestures and great skill in the use of language. To this was added in Roman times a strict training which is described by Cicero (*De Orat.*, III,22,83, and 59,220). He says that the actor needs the physical training of an athlete and of a dancer. Quintilian (*Inst. Orat.*, XI,3,86,111,181) recommends to public speakers that they imitate the art of the actors for their gestures. The Romans also had the advantage of inheriting along with the Greek plays the Greek art of acting, which had been developed for centuries. A further circumstance which may have fostered the growth of acting was the fact that Livius Andronicus in the second half of the third century had already separated song and recitation from mimetic art in the numerous cantica of the Latin dramas and comedies. As Livy (VII,2) tells us, one actor sang or declaimed, while another went through the appropriate gestures. This proves that the actor in tragedy must from the beginning of the Roman drama have worn the costume once introduced by Aeschylus, which covered his whole body with mask, long-sleeved robe, and high boots. The attitudes and gestures had to correspond exactly with the spoken word or with the music. Clarity of voice and of expression were demanded. In the popular mimes, which did not use masks, the Roman actors, in contrast to the Greek, were able also to develop facial expression. But in the other plays—tragedy, comedy, and farce—the actors had to express their changing moods by movement and gesture, as the masks prevented facial expression. As the actors were often slaves, they could be made subject to strict discipline and were even beaten if they did not perform satisfactorily (see Plautus, *Cistellaria*, v. 785).[2] The gesticulation in the different kinds of plays was sharply differentiated. Each age and each profession had its peculiar attitudes.

Comedy also adopted, together with the themes of Attic New Comedy, the dress of everyday life, which was often worn over the obligatory tights taken over from Old Comedy.[3] The movements in comedy had to be quick and lively, particularly for slaves. Plautus in the *Miles gloriosus* (vv. 201ff, 901ff) and elsewhere gives delightful portrayals of the expressive attitudes and gestures of slaves planning some intrigue or stratagem. The attitudes described in Plautus' plays correspond with many Hellenistic and Roman statuettes of comic actors. A bronze statuette in Boston (Fig. 580) wearing a Roman tunic with a low belt has its right hand lifted in salutation.[4] The proud attitude of the head thrown back and the left hand on the hip reminds one of public orators like the late Mussolini. A small statuette, formerly in Rome (Fig. 581), demonstrates with his lifted right hand, leans his head forward, and with his left hand holds the small mantle, which, like "Mussolini," he wears over his left shoulder.[5] His tights are of a coarse material, indicated by crossed lines. The same is true of the tights of the slave, shown on a lamp in Rome with a woman (Fig. 582).[6] The crossed lines can be seen on her sleeves and on his legs. The woman, probably a courtesan, is in a pensive mood, supporting her right elbow with her left hand and her head with her right hand. The slave is leaning forward with crossed legs, his right hand before his breast, and he is holding his small mantle with his left hand, as if in an emotional turmoil. The running slave, so frequent in Latin comedy, is represented in a marble statuette in the Villa Albani (Fig. 583).[7] Since he is wearing a large fringed pallium, he is probably a freedman. The slave, deeply absorbed in thought—as described in Plautus' *Miles gloriosus* (vv. 901f) where he is called an architect—may be depicted in a marble statuette in Istanbul (Fig. 584).[8] Leaning against a pillar, he crosses feet and hands, holding his left wrist tightly with his right hand. There are many similar attitudes in Hellenistic

See Figs. 549, 568

Figs. 580-584. Roman actors; Slave and courtesan; Running slave; Pensive slave

Figs. 585, 586. Pairs of comic actors

Fig. 587. Scene of comedy. Terracotta relief, reconstructed

representations of comic actors, like the comedy relief in Naples (Ch. VIII, Fig. 324) and in many statuettes (Ch. VIII, Figs. 332, 338, 402-405). These gestures, therefore, must have been adopted with the comedies, but were developed further by the Romans.

The grouping of two or more persons provides expressive and lively scenes. The two actors on the cover of a Praenestine cista in the British Museum (Fig. 585)[9]—found in the Latin territory of Praeneste and probably belonging to the late third century B.C.—show contrasting emotions. The one carrying a lantern lays his right hand soothingly on the shoulder of the second, who holds in his left hand a lekythos and a strigil (a skin-scraper) and lifts his right hand to his mouth as if stifling an outcry. Both have their heads thrown back. The group makes a good handle for the cista, as the fingers can close firmly around the arm to lift the cover. But the motif must have been observed in the theater of this period which is probably the same as that of Plautus.

Much more lively is a group on a fragment of a so-called Hellenistic relief in Verona (Fig. 586).[10] Two slaves throw themselves violently forward. The one wearing a chlamys and a wreath around his shoulders, who may be drunk, falls around the neck of the other, who is dressed in an exomis, a scanty tunic. Behind the two is a door with a ring as knocker hanging from the mouth of a lion's head. Above is part of a garland. Between the legs of the two appear two steps of an altar.

Three figures are combined in the reconstruction of a terracotta relief preserved in various fragmentary replicas (Fig. 587).[11] A slave has sought refuge at an altar in front of a house and clings with his right hand to its edge, as do the marble figures of seated slaves in the Vatican and British Museum (Figs. 556-558).[12] An excited man, plainly enraged at him, rushes in from the right with a long cane to beat him. But a man standing in the center, obviously good-tempered, tries to quiet him. This is a situation similar to the final scene of the *Mostellaria* by

Plautus (vv. 1093ff). The slave Tranio has prevented his old master Theopropides from entering his own house, pretending that it is haunted. When found out to be a liar, he is to be beaten but takes refuge at an altar; young Callidamates, the friend of the young master, prevents the punishment. The background, a rich scaenae frons, proves in any case that this is a scene from a Latin Palliata.

The same background as on the comedy relief—a rich scaenae frons of an early Roman type (see Figs. 634-637 in Ch. XIII) with three doors—is used for the tragic scene on a terracotta relief of the "Campana" type which adorned the tomb monument of P. Numitorius Hilarus, found on the Via Salaria and now in the Museo Nazionale Romano delle Terme in Rome (Fig. 588).[13] It probably illustrates a performance presented at his funeral and therefore was used in his tomb monument. Before the rich background of an early scaenae frons stands Andromache, the wife of Hector. She grasps the left arm of her and Hector's son Astyanax, who is wear-

Fig. 588. Scene of tragedy. Terracotta relief, Rome

Fig. 589. Tragic scene. Wall painting, from columbarium in Villa Doria-Pamphili, Rome

ing the oriental headdress, the Phrygian cap with the tip hanging forward. Odysseus wears the pointed pilos, under which the onkos is distinguishable, and reddish strands of hair emerge, covering the cheeks. He wears the chlamys of a warrior, and he holds the scabbard of his sword in his left hand. He clearly demands the surrender of the child with the lively gesticulation of his outstretched right hand. Andromache refuses and thrusts the boy to the side, away from the outstretched hand of Odysseus. The masks of the hero and heroine are large. Their sleeved robes have broad belts and fall in deep folds. The soles below their closed shoes are high. The child also has sleeves on his short garment. He wears little high boots, but not high soles. The adolescent boy and girl, who huddle close together, represent the servants whom the queen has to have even in captivity, just as Hecuba in the *Trojan Women* of Euripides has maids. They are much smaller, thinner, and less noticeable than the heroine, whose followers they are; and their gestures indicate that they bewail the fate of the royal house in which they have served. They are probably supernumeraries, and they wear the garb of everyday life. They have taken the place of the old chorus, sympathetically accompanying the fate and action of the main characters with their gestures. The relief probably illustrates a scene from the *Astyanax* of Accius, based on Sophocles. The tragedies of Accius, just as those of Pacuvius, were still given in the first century B.C. Somewhat later Seneca, who knew Accius, has a similar scene in his *Troades* (vv. 705ff).

The fact that tragedies were performed at funerals explains the fact that tragic scenes are found on tomb monuments, not only on that of Numitorius Hilarus, but also on others from Rome and Ostia. A painting in a columbarium discovered in the Villa Doria Pamphili at Rome and transferred to the Museo Nazionale Romano delle Terme (Fig. 589)[14] seems to portray a quarrel between two parties who have been brought before a king-like judge seated on the left. He carries a long scepter, wears a green tunic and a violet mantle, and he has an exceedingly high onkos on his mask. A staff is lying at his feet.

He stretches out his right arm with a commanding gesture. A man holding a lantern, dressed in an exomis, seems to protest with outstretched fingers. A bearded man in a yellow tunic and green mantle with a yellow cap on his onkos, leaning on a long staff, turns to face the judge. At his feet is a basket which seems to contain three little children. Next to it is a slender girl, also in a yellow chiton and green mantle. She and the bearded man seem to point at each other. A woman in a blue tunic and a violet mantle is running toward them, her right hand stretched forward, her left hand lifted to her head which is turned back. She has a gray kerchief laid over her onkos. The last two persons lift their right arms pointing excitedly toward the center. A man shouldering a tool, a pole with a crosspiece— perhaps a plow or a yoke—and dressed in gray tunic and grayish-blue mantle, turns to a running woman whose mantle flies behind her back, emphasizing the quick movement. She holds a staff over her left shoulder, and wears garments of grayish-green. All persons except the lantern-bearer, who is a subordinate person and probably a servant, have the high onkos and long sleeves.

Another tragic scene has been found in a tomb chamber at Ostia and is now in the Lateran Museum at Rome (Fig. 590).[15] A child seems to be the subject of the drama—probably a recognition scene similar to that in the *Ion* of Euripides, only the child here is younger and naked. It seems to flee to a seated king with a high onkos, who lays his hand soothingly on the head of the boy and grasps his right hand, while the boy throws his left arm high up into the air. The queen, seated on the same bench with the king, is the only quiet person. From the left a woman with a high onkos comes running

Fig. 590. Tragic scene. Wall painting from Ostia, Lateran

with wide strides, holding a yellow object which looks like a garment or piece of cloth. This might furnish proof for the identification of the boy, like the dresses and trinkets which the Pythia brings to Creusa so that she can recognize Ion as her own child. A bearded man running forward out of the background with his right hand lifted may be an old pedagogue contributing to the identification of the boy. All figures wear the sleeved stage dress. All these pictures show violent motion and emotions.

The picture painted on white marble, from Herculaneum and now in Naples, of Phaedra, her nurse, and another woman is one of the few preserved ancient tablet paintings (Fig. 591).[16] It may represent a Latin adaptation of Euripides' *Hippolytus*. Phaedra, with a wig of red curls on her huge mask, is made especially prominent by means of stuffing and by shoes on high stilts which are covered by her dress. We can notice here the beginning of the exaggeration which transformed the costume, once so grandiose in fifth-century Athens, at the time of the emperors, into something which excited derision in some regions and even horror in others (see Ch. XV, pp. 239-243). Phaedra wears a long white-sleeved chiton, a white mantle with yellow border, and a yellow veil on her onkos. Her arms are too short compared to the lengthened body. She points to something outside the painting toward which she walks, but she looks back to the old woman behind her whom she seems to chide. This second figure is much smaller, has a hooked nose, and wears a kerchief on her head. She must be the nurse who has betrayed the love of Phaedra to Hippolytus. The old woman hangs her head and left arm and pulls her mantle forward as if in great embarrassment. A third woman who listens in a mourning attitude may be a representative of the chorus. Some time later Seneca adapted the same story in his *Phaedra*, although in a different manner.

The terracotta reliefs and the paintings (Figs. 587-591) were created in the first century B.C. The gestures in all of them are extremely vivacious, in accord with what literary sources tell us. In this period the art of acting reached its height in Rome. It followed upon the highest development of Roman dramatic poetry in the third and second centuries B.C., just as formerly in Athens and in Greek Tarentum the peak of acting was reached in the fourth century following upon the culmination of classical tragedy and old comedy, which preceded it in the fifth century. The most famous actors in Rome were Aesopus in tragedy and Roscius in comedy. The latter, deviating from Greek usage, acted both in tragedy and comedy, both of which he played in masks except when he assumed the role of a parasite. Because he squinted, he played the role of the

Fig. 591. Phaedra and nurse. Painting on marble

sponger without a mask, for the parasite squinted at invitations to fat meals. He may, therefore, have looked like the mask formerly in Rome (Ch. VIII, Fig. 375), which has a pronounced squint. Bulle believes that the actor on the Dresden relief (Ch. VII, Fig. 307) is Roscius, but his physiognomy appears to be Hellenistic Greek.[17] Roscius is said to have acted on the stage one hundred and twenty-five times in one year. His great art is described in the oration of Cicero in defense of Roscius. When Quintilian (*Institutiones oratoriae*, XI,3,71,73-4,89, 91,103,111-12,123,125) gives rules for the gestures of a public speaker, he has partly borrowed them from Roscius or from the admirer of Roscius, Cicero (*De orat.*, III,59,221). The gestures had to correspond not with the single words, but with the meaning of the whole sentence. They had to depict character, which was expressed not only with the head but with the whole body. In the masked plays more attention had to be paid to the other parts of the body by the actors. Whereas the Greeks placed more weight on the ensemble—that is, the effect of the presentation viewed as a whole—the Romans emphasized the stars—that is, the principal and prominent actors—and they placed high value on brilliant and individual accomplishment. Each actor specialized in a particular type of role, so that there were specialists, for example, for the parts of women, gods, youths, and parasites (Roscius). The actors are now no longer only slaves but citizens as well, as was the case with Roscius, who later played without a fee. Decimus Laberius, the knight and writer of mimes, was forced by Caesar to act on the stage against his will (see Ch. XI, p. 159). The chief actors were surrounded by supernumeraries, who probably were then, as formerly and later, slaves.

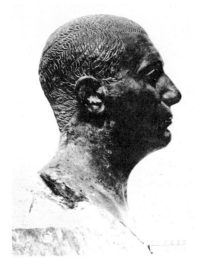

Fig. 592a-b. Portrait of the mime player Norbanus Sorix, from Pompeii, Naples

The art of the mime, which took its name from the imitation of real life, was of course especially well developed and included the art of expressions through the movement of the facial muscles. In this type of play women were allowed for the first time to appear on the stage. The mime never adopted the mask and was played not in stereotyped costumes but in the variegated forms of the dress of daily life. It enjoyed from the first century B.C. a much greater popularity than the masked plays. The archimime Sorix was especially famous, and he was a protégé and friend of Sulla (Plutarch, *Sulla*, 36, 2). Such an archimime was at the same time the director of a troupe of mimic actors and actresses. Beside the archimime stood the deuteragonist (actor secundarium partium) who played the secondary parts. He had often to repeat, emphasize, and distort the jokes of the chief actors. His jests may have been as coarse as those of the clowns in our circus, who imitate the feats of the main performers. Such an actor of secondary roles was C. Norbanus Sorix whose portraits, in the form of a marble pillar with a bronze head, were placed as a sign of high reputation in the temple of Isis and in the cloth market of Eumachia on the Forum at Pompeii (Fig. 592).[18] Perhaps he appeared as actor in mimes and other sacred performances in honor of the Egyptian goddess Isis. It has been assumed that this was the same Sorix who was a friend of Sulla. But Sulla had died in 78 B.C. in Puteoli, two years after he had established a colony of veterans in 80 B.C. in Pompeii. The portrait of Norbanus Sorix is not earlier than the early Augustan period, as is indicated not only by the style but also because the actor was made—probably in his old age—magister of the suburb Pagus Augustus Felix, which was founded under Augustus. He may have been a son or nephew of the older Sorix, whose family perhaps took part in the Roman colonization of the Oscan Pompeii. The honors given to Sorix, particularly the portrait herms, prove that the mime actors were highly respected in this period. The portrait head of Norbanus Sorix has cropped hair groomed carefully in rows of short strands. His physiognomy is expressive, and he looks very self-contented.

Love of the art of acting and boredom with the endlessly repeated subjects of tragedy led to the development of a last type of dramatic performance and of acting: the pantomime.[19] This consists of acting and dancing in dumb show. It was an outgrowth of the separation of declamation, recitation, or song from the mimetic art, for which Livius Andronicus had already paved the way. Later, the cantica, the singing parts, were developed as solo declamation, recitation, or song in tragedy and comedy. Such declamation is portrayed in two small pictures from the Roman Villa near the Farnesina in Rome, now in the Museo Nazionale Romano. One shows an actor with a tragic mask, the other (Fig. 593) an actor reciting while a seated man holds a comic mask.[20] They are dated in the early period of Augustus, to which the first pantomimes also belong. Bathyllus, a freedman and favorite of Maecenas, was born in Alexandria and died in 2 B.C. He introduced, in 22 B.C., the comic pantomime, dealing for example with Pan and Echo or Satyr and Amor. This type was not of long duration. On the other hand, Pylades, a freedman of Augustus, introduced at the same time the tragic pantomime, with subjects taken from Greek mythology. This type lived on through all antiquity (see Ch. XV, Figs. 776 and 783). One actor performed the most diverse roles with changing masks while either a chorus or one interpreter sang or declaimed the content of the story (Quintilian, *Inst. Orat.*, IV,3,63). These actors had to use a very refined gesticulation and had to be very versatile in order to express such diverse actions and characters. They also must have had a good knowledge of mythology and a higher education. This cultivated solo performance was very

Fig. 593. Reciter declaiming a comic subject. Wall painting

Fig. 594. Victorious poet or monologuist. Wall painting, from Pompeii, Naples

logues were now taken out of their context and presented on the stage—or even at funerals and other occasions—by a single actor in tragic costume, with mask, expressive gestures, and finely-differentiated movements. At the funeral of Caesar (44 B.C.) songs from the *Contest for the Arms of Achilles* by Pacuvius and scenes from the *Electra* by Atilius were presented (Suetonius, Caesar, 84). Such solo performances became the pantomimes which had a great vogue in the time of the emperors.

A victorious poet or reciter of a tragic monologue seems to be represented on the fragment of a wall painting from Pompeii (Fig. 594).[21] The dignified man, crowned with a wreath, holding a scroll, comes out of an open door above a small staircase leading to the stage. A tragic mask on the top of the wooden screen through which the door leads alludes to the tragic content of his recital.

The Greek forerunner of this type of entertainment is the lyrical solo declamation, as testified by the *Persians* of Timotheus which describes the battle of Marathon. It was recited with cithara accompaniment by a rhapsode, probably for the first time by the poet himself at the Panionian Festival in 397 B.C., and it was performed again in 207/6 B.C.[22] A comparison between these two related types of public performances shows the same characteristic differences which we can find between the Greek and Roman theater buildings. It is a difference between creative art and elevated spirit on the one side, and of show business and lavish use and adaptation of inherited forms on the other.

popular among the higher classes, while the mime which needed a troupe was more popular among the masses. Sometimes the pantomime was taken from the comedies or tragedies. The portrayal of the battle with the Teloboae in the *Amphitruo* of Plautus would be a good literary example. Such effective monologues, other single parts, or even dia-

CHAPTER XIII

THE DEVELOPMENT OF THE ROMAN THEATER BUILDING DURING THE REPUBLICAN PERIOD

THE development of the theater building always follows the development of dramatic literature. Both were slower in Rome than in Athens. For a long period chariot and horse races, athletic contests, and gladiatorial fights were the main entertainments in Rome. The circus therefore was the first public permanent building for spectacles. Gladiatorial fights were first given on the Forum Boarium by the consuls Appius Claudius and Quintus Fulvius. When the Etruscan dancers and musicians were introduced in 364 B.C., their performances were given in the circus or in public places such as the forum, or in the sanctuaries before the temples (see Polybius apud Athenaeus XIV,4, p. 615; Livy XL,52; XLII,10). The Etruscan players brought with them temporary wooden stands which could be erected everywhere for the spectators. They are portrayed on the wall painting from the tomb at Corneto named after Stackelberg (Fig. 546).[1] These scaffoldings developed later into the Roman auditorium built up freely from the level ground, instead of against a hillside as did the Greek theatron, although occasionally the Greek method was also used by the Romans.

When the popular comedies of Southern Italy came to Rome as Atellan or Oscan farce, they brought with them the phlyakes stage (see Ch. X, p. 146). The many different forms in which this wooden podium could be erected, are depicted on the vases (Ch. X, p. 130ff.)—from the most primitive wooden floor on crude posts (Figs. 489, 491, 504, 514, 515, 159) to the most elaborate "Assteas" stage (Fig. 479).

When, beginning in 240 B.C., the first tragedies and comedies were brought to Rome as translations and adaptations from the Greek, they were presented on such temporary wooden stages. Plautus' *Stichus* was performed in 200 B.C. at the Ludi Plebeii, which took place in the Circus Flaminius. Because other more popular activities such as races and athletic contests were also held here, the stage had to be removed for the days set aside for the circus games. Plautus certainly needed the most elaborate "Assteas" stage (above, Fig. 479) for his *Amphitruo*. He used an upper story, which he calls *cenaculum* (v. 863), apartments used as dining rooms or rented out with a separate entrance and with a gallery opening on the atrium or on the street (see Ch. X, p. 130f.). Windows also indicate

sometimes an upper story (Figs. 484, 492, 501, 535).

The stage for the farce was in this period already blended with the Hellenistic proskenion stage, just as the comedies of Plautus are blends of farce and Greek New Comedy. Therefore the simple posts are sometimes replaced as supports by elegant Greek columns (cf. Figs. 508, 509, 517). As these temporary stages were set up in public places without a building behind them, little staircases led up to the pulpitum from the public place, the sacred precinct, the arena of the circus, or wherever the performances took place. These were retained in the Roman stage as late as the second century A.D. (below, Figs. 680, 686-690, 717, 718). The back walls, however, often had a door, to which perhaps movable stairs could lead up. Sometimes these doors are framed with columns and protected by a gabled roof (cf. Figs. 491, 507, 512). They were called vestibula in comedies, and these are the forerunners of the richly-framed royal doors of the Roman stage. The podium always remained floored with planks to insure good acoustics. Thus these modest phlyakes and Plautus stages are in all respects the forerunners of the elaborate Roman scaenae frons.

There was no provision for a change of scenery in these open-air and curtainless theaters. The podium with its back wall represented whatever the poet wished it to be. "Hoc oppidum Ephesust," this town is Ephesus, says Palaestrio in the *Miles Gloriosus* (v. 88) and "Athenis . . . hoc est proscaenium," this stage represents Athens, the prologue of *Truculentus* (v. 10) informs us. Plautus names the stage with the Greek word proscaenium also in *Amphitruo* (v. 91) and *Poenulus* (vv. 17 and 57). It was not so beautifully executed, however, as the Greek proskenion, and it had to be torn down again at the end of the festivals.

While the stage had to be removed, the wooden seats for the spectators could remain to be used for the following games. Plautus calls the auditorium *cavea* (*Amphitruo*, 66 and 68). There can be no doubt that his audience was seated. "Qui autem auscultare nolet, exsurgat foras—Ut sit ubi sedeat ille qui auscultare volt—Nunc qua adsedistis causa in festivo loco. . . ." ("Whoever does not want to listen may get up and out, so that he who wishes to listen may sit. Now that you are seated in a festive place. . . ." *Miles gloriosus*, vv. 81-83). In the *Amphitruo* (65), *Poenulus* (5, 17-35, 1224), and

Truculentus (968) a seated audience is also addressed.[2] Special seats near the stage were assigned to the senators by Scipio Africanus in 195/4 B.C. on the occasion of the Ludi Romani (Livy, XXXIV,44 and 54), just as they were in the circus near the arena. In the circus there were of course always seats, called by Livy (I,35) "furca spectacula alta sustinentes," high supports for the spectacles. In 179 B.C. the censor M. Antonius Lepidus built an auditorium and a stage (theatrum et proscaenium, Livy, XL,51) near the temple of Apollo—at the place where the theater of Marcellus was later erected—and the censors A. Posthumius Albinus and Q. Fulvius Flaccus built a scaena without a cavea in the circus, where there were already wooden stands (Livy, XLI,27). In 167 L. Anicius gave a spectacle with musicians on a large stage erected in the circus, which Polybius, who describes the performance in Athenaeus (XIV,4, p. 165), called scaena and proscaenium.

A stone auditorium begun by the censors Valerius Messala and Cassius Longinus in 154 B.C. was prohibited by the consul Publius Cornelius Scipio Nasica (Livy, *Epitome*, XLVIII). The senate objected to permanent auditoria because the people spent too much time at the theatrical presentations (Valerius Maximus, *Factorum et Dictorum Memorabilia*, II, 4,2). Seating was allowed, however, in the theaters built more than a mile from Rome. In 145 Mummius again erected subitarii gradus, hastily built steps, for the audience to see his triumphal plays, for which he invited Greek actors (Tacitus, *Annales*, XIV,20).

One reason for destroying the wooden temporary buildings after they had been used for a short time only may have been the hazard of fire in the densely-populated center of Rome. There was indeed hardly any necessity for a permanent theater beside the circus for the scattered festivals and triumphal games. Thus even the richly-decorated theaters of the first half of the first century B.C. were only temporary buildings. The stage wall erected by Claudius Pulcher in 99 B.C. may have been painted in imitation of the thyromata panels of the late Hellenistic stage, and it may have been similar to the frescoes of Boscoreale (see Ch. IX, Figs. 471-474). The paintings in the theater of Claudius Pulcher are described as exceedingly realistic (Pliny, *Nat. Hist.* XXXV,23; Valerius Maximus, *Factorum et Dictorum Memorabilia*, II,4,6). Birds were lured to perch on the painted brick roof. The fragmentary remains of such a painting have been preserved in the small theater at Pompeii (below, Figs. 613-614), built soon after 80 B.C. A scaenae frons painted by Apaturius of Alabanda for the ecclesiasterion at Tralles, an assembly hall built in the guise of a tiny theater, is mentioned by Vitruvius (VII,5,5). The painted scenery pleased the public but not the mathematician Licymnius, who considered it too fantastic. Apaturius yielded to this verdict and was obliged to remove the scenery and to remodel it in a semblance of reality. These seem to be the last examples of merely painted backgrounds.

The Roman scaenae frons, the front wall of the stage house—now erected behind the podium instead of the earlier simple wall of the phlyakes stage—was no longer painted in the Greek manner but tended toward plastic and architectural decorations combined with great ornamental luxury. Thus in 62 B.C. Antonius is said to have used silver, Petreius gold, and Q. Catulus ivory for covering the rear wall of the stage (Valerius Maximus, II,4,6). This is certainly an exaggerated statement. Equally fantastic is the report that the aedile M. Aemilius Scaurus in the year 58 B.C. built a wooden theater, the auditorium of which held 80,000 persons, and the stage of which was decorated with 360 columns in three stories. The lowest story was of marble, the middle one of glass, perhaps mosaic, the uppermost one of gilded wood. Three thousand bronze statues were erected between the columns (Pliny, *Nat. Hist.*, XXXIV,36; XXXVI,5,50,113-115,189). The whole report may have been exaggerated as time went on; it could not be verified, because this expensive theater, too, was soon torn down. It shows, however, that the modest "Assteas" stage had in this period developed to several stories decorated with columns.

Such a monumental development of the popular comedy stage—for which we have evidence in Rome for the period down to the middle of the first century from literary sources about temporary buildings—had in the meantime, however, already taken place in the stone theaters built in Southern Italy and Sicily. There were many stone theaters of the classical as well as of the Hellenistic period, of which those in Syracuse, Segesta, Tyndaris, and Pompeii are the best preserved. The development in these parts was, however, different from that found in the eastern Greek world, and it still offers many unsolved problems.

The theater built by Hieron I in Syracuse was rebuilt by Hieron II (270-216 B.C.) about 230 B.C. At that time it was probably given a wooden proskenion in line with the paraskenia. At the same time provision was made for the erection of a temporary phlyakes stage (Fig. 595; cf. Ch. V, Fig. 225 and Ch. X, Fig. 540).[3] In this region the stage needs were different from those of the Greek mainland and in the east because comedy and farce played a larger part than elsewhere. As a consequence, other forms of the stage evolved.

The stage houses in Segesta (Figs. 596-598, 600-601)[4] and Tyndaris (Figs. 599, 602)[5] were originally

Fig. 595. Theater of Syracuse. Area of the stage building

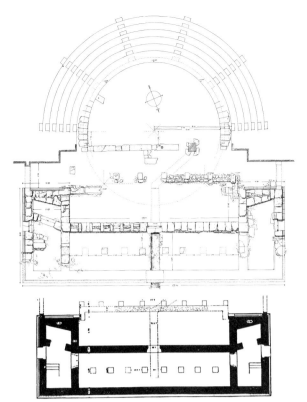

Figs. 597, 598. Theater of Segesta. Plan of the actual remains and stage building

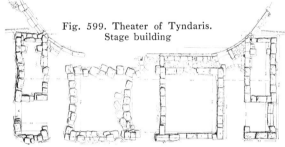

Fig. 599. Theater of Tyndaris. Stage building

paraskenion-theaters with the peculiarity that the inner sides of the paraskenia run obliquely toward the rear in order to give to the onlookers seated at the sides a full view of the place of action before the stage house (Figs. 596-598, 600). A. von Gerkan believes that there never was any proskenion, and that the plays were given in the Hellenistic as in the classical period in the orchestra until a Roman

Fig. 596. Segesta, view of the theater

stage was built. In Tyndaris there are, however, engaged half columns on the front wall of the high stage below the platform (Fig. 602). The two-storied scaenae frons reconstructed by Bulle (Figs. 600-602) is dated by inscriptions which belong not before the second century B.C. according to Marconi, and probably later according to Meritt; while R. Herzog dated them in the first century B.C.[6] The gable, which according to Bulle served as a theologeion, would be an effective finial and would match the gables over the two-storied side buildings, which had open galleries in Segesta (Fig. 601), but only a door in the first story and a window in the second story in Tyndaris (Fig. 602). The existence of the central gable is, however, doubted by von Gerkan, as no remains of it are preserved.[7] The idea that gods appeared inside the pediment is attractive, but it can hardly be proved. The gods must have appeared above a flat roof. It would have been unnatural if they had made their appearance from a door in the pediment as Bulle assumes. Temples in Syria have such doors in the pediments, but they were probably used for cleaning or perhaps oracular purposes, and appearances of gods.

I consider Segesta and Tyndaris, in any case, a transitional form of about 100 B.C.—best named Hellenistic-Italic or Graeco-Roman, or Roman Republican—designed for local plays, as was the wooden forerunner, the "Assteas" stage. The front wall of the podium is not, as in the Hellenistic proskenion, treated as a colonnade but as a solid wall with pilasters in Segesta and engaged columns in Tyndaris. The main story of the scaenae frons is decorated below with Doric columns and their entablature, above with Ionic columns in Segesta and with only flat pilasters in Tyndaris. This rich decoration reminds us of the stage wall of Scaurus built in Rome in 58 B.C. We have here an eclectic mixture of older and newer forms, which is characteristically Roman.

The auditoria in Segesta and Tyndaris have the Greek horseshoe form (Figs. 596 and 597). They probably never developed the vaulted parodoi of the Roman theater (see below, pp. 172ff.). The temporary theaters in Rome must certainly have had the horseshoe form of the auditorium. In the time of Caesar, C. Scribonius Curio built two wooden theaters back to back, which could be turned around. In the morning scenic plays were given, in the afternoon gladiatorial fights. For the latter the theaters were turned and made into an amphitheater (Pliny, *Nat. Hist.*, XXXVI,117). As the amphitheater is an ellipse, the two orchestras which formed the arena must have had the horseshoe or U-shaped form which is similar to one half of an ellipse.

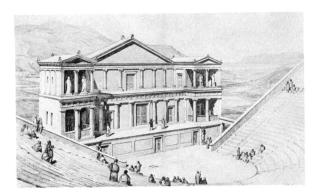

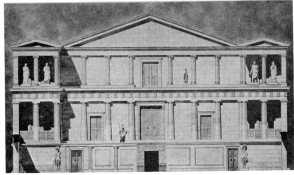

Figs. 600, 601. Theater of Segesta. Reconstructions

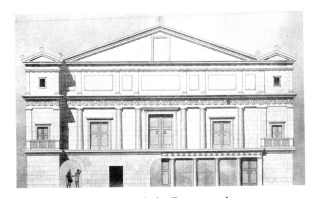

Fig. 602. Theater of Tyndaris. Reconstruction

In Segesta the front faces of the paraskenia are decorated on the ground floor with engaged statues of Pan (Figs. 601, 603). Their lower parts, which alone are preserved, are similar to two statues of Pan in Rome, said to come from the theater built by Pompey in 55 B.C. These are well preserved, together with the pilasters behind them. (Figs. 604a-b; see below, Figs. 630-632.)[8]

In Pompeii the gifted Oscan inhabitants had accepted the Greek civilization from their Greek neighbors much earlier than the Roman conquerors of Magna Graecia, that is, Southern Italy and Sicily. They had built themselves a stone theater in the Hellenistic form around 200 B.C. (Figs. 605-607).[9] It was laid out in horseshoe form on the natural

Fig. 603. Segesta, remains of Pan at the paraskenion

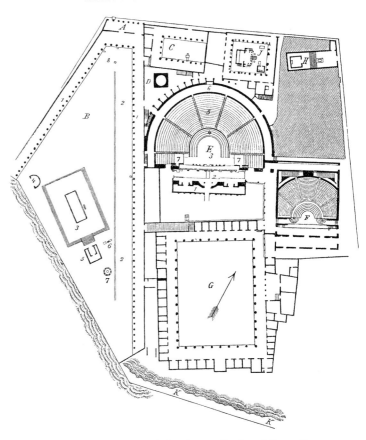

Fig. 604a-b. Two Pans from the Theater of Pompey, Rome

Fig. 605. Plan of the theater district of Pompeii

Fig. 606. Large theater at Pompeii

171

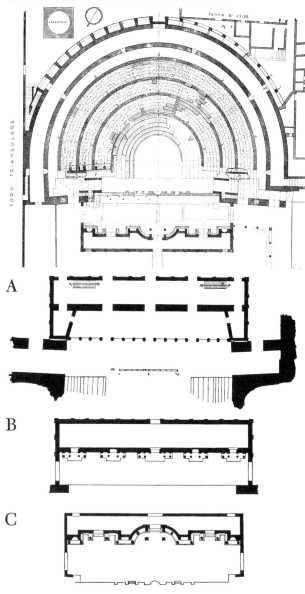

Figs. 607, 608. Large theater at Pompeii. Plan, Maiuri; Successive plans of the stage building, Bieber, *Denkmäler*

slope of the hillside which descended east of the triangular forum (B in Fig. 605) from the north to the south. Above it on higher ground was a palaestra (C in Fig. 605) and later a temple of Isis (J in Fig. 605). Strong stone rings were laid against the slope as a base for the seats which afforded room for about 5,000 persons. The rings end with robust pilasters at the analemmata (Fig. 607). The oldest stage building (A in Fig. 608) was probably erected during the second century B.C. in a form similar to that of Segesta. It was provided with paraskenia flanking a proskenion supported by a colonnade. The inner side walls of the paraskenia were slanted as they are in Segesta. Five doors gave access to the

stage, three from the back wall and one from each side. Open parodoi led into the orchestra which was extended tangentially beyond the half circle in such a way that a full circle could be inscribed (E in Fig. 605 and Fig. 610).

We can study in this theater—even better than in Segesta and Tyndaris—the transformation from a Greek to a Roman theater building. It took place after Sulla had established a colony of Roman veterans in 80 B.C. in the Oscan city. They built the small covered theater (F in Fig. 605; below, Figs. 613-615) in the Roman manner, and this now influenced also the remodelling of the large theater. In order to give it more unity the paraskenia were removed and the parodoi were vaulted. The vaulted side approaches were now called itinera versurarum, the entrances of the projecting wings of the stage building. These afforded side entrances to the stage, while five doors opened from the back wall (B in Fig. 608). The stage was lowered and every door was probably flanked by two pairs of columns on pedestals, which would make twenty columns in all arranged in a straight line in one row.

In the period of the emperor Augustus the duumviri M. Holconius Rufus and M. Holconius Celer built, according to their inscription (Fig. 609) "cryptam, tribunalia, theatrum," a covered corridor, boxes for the tribunes, and the auditorium. The crypta, a covered corridor, is situated between the second and third gallery (E6 in Fig. 605) and from it six doors (vomitoria) lead to the six staircases which divide the main middle gallery (media cavea) (E5 in Fig. 605) into five sections (cunei). The third, uppermost gallery (summa cavea) is above this covered corridor and is reached by four outside doors. One of them leads in from the triangular forum (Fig. 606). It seems to me possible that the Holconii are also responsible for the enlargement of

Fig. 609. Pompeii, inscription of the Holconii

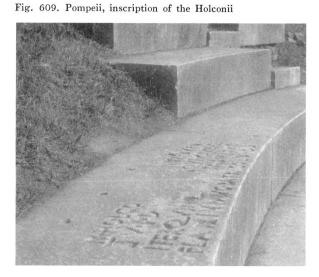

Figs. 610, 611. Large theater at Pompeii. Views of the scaenae frons and stage

the auditorium by an uppermost gallery with the help of this crypta above and the low marble steps in the orchestra below (E4 in Fig. 605 and Fig. 606). These narrowed the orchestra and gave space for the bisellia, the broad honorary seats for magistrates. Thus the space for the plays was decreased, that for the audience increased. The classical place of action has been transmuted into seats of honor for members of the governing bodies. The auditorium has encroached into the orchestra. Holconius Rufus,

the older and more important of the two rebuilders, may be credited with this change. He was given recognition in a lost monument, the inscription for which is preserved on the broad step below the main gallery (Fig. 609). The architect of this re-modelled building, a freedman, M. Artorius Marci libertus Primus architectus, has signed his name outside the eastern parodos on the wall of the auditorium. Above the vaulted entrances are the tribunalia, the balconies or boxes for the magistrates who provided the plays (E7 in Fig. 605). Below these boxes the guests of honor could reach their bisellia in the orchestra. Thus, Artorius with the money of the duumviri has created a building which provided for better means of filling and emptying a large auditorium than any Greek theater had ever achieved. The scene building was given an early Roman straight scaenae frons—probably during the time of the emperor Augustus (B in Fig. 608).

Finally, after the earthquake in A.D. 63—perhaps between 63 and 68, in the time of the emperor Nero—the scene building in Pompeii received its final form, probably imitating those in Rome. A deep, low stage with a varied and richly-decorated wall in the background was built (E2 in Fig. 605, C in Fig. 608, and Figs. 610-611). This scaenae frons has a large semi-circular niche in the center and a rectangular niche on each side. In these niches are the three doors of the Roman theater which Vitruvius (v,6,8) calls aula regia and hospitalia, the doors of the royal palace and of the guest chambers. The curves of the rear wall are emphasized by accompanying columns set upon pedestals. The dressing room is considerably narrowed by the depth of the niches (E1 in Fig. 605 and Fig. 612). Its floor lies somewhat higher than the stage, so that short stairs led from the dressing room down to the stage floor, providing effective entrances for actors, as we see them appear on the wall paintings (above, Fig. 594 and below, Figs. 774-778). The front wall of the stage (proscaenium) below the platform is likewise broken by a rounded niche in the center and flat rectangular niches at the side (Fig. 610). Small flights of steps lead down to the orchestra between the two flat niches at each side. This is carried over from the Atellan farce, which needed these stairs because it did not have a scene building (cf. Figs. 488b, 489, 491). The theaters in Rome certainly had such stairs leading from the stage to the orchestra, for they are mentioned in stories of Suetonius (*Divus Julius*, 39 and *Nero*, 12) of the first centuries B.C. and A.D. The knight D. Laberius descended such steps to reach his seat after the presentation of his mime, and Nero also used these stairs.

Fig. 612. Large theater at Pompeii. View of the stage building from the outside

Rich temporary decoration of this stage on play days is testified by the wall paintings of the fourth style which agree with the architectural late forms of the stage (Figs. 775-778). We find here once more in the scaenae frons the central niche flanked by rectangular niches, the columns or pilasters set upon bases, the three elevated doors from which stairs led down to the stage, and in the front wall of the pulpitum the small rounded and rectangular niches. Added on the painted walls are an abundant number of statuettes, bronze ornaments, carved parapets between the columns, painted prospects, masks, and garlands. Even if these were more easily executed in paint than in solid material, we can be sure that curtains, painted tablets, and plastic figures were profusely used in Rome still more than in Pompeii. The wall paintings inform us that at Pompeii in the time of the Empire mimes, panto-mimes, and athletes were allowed on the stage of the large theater.

While the large theater at Pompeii was the trans-formation of a Greek theater into a Roman one, the small theater, built soon after the foundation of a Sullan colony at Pompeii in 80 B.C. and thus to be dated about 75 B.C., is a purely Roman theater. It is, indeed, the oldest purely Roman theater which has been preserved. It was erected by the duumviri Quinctius Valgus and Marcus Porcius southeast of

the large theater, and it has a capacity of only about 1,500 spectators (F in Fig. 605 and Figs. 613-615).[10] Two inscriptions inform us that it was a roofed theater (theatrum tectum), or an odeum, a music hall, for musical contests, declamations, and recita-tions.[11] The orchestra and the auditorium have a semicircular form, and the orchestra is filled to a large extent with the broad steps for the movable seats provided for the members of the city council (decuriones) and for guests of honor. The low deep stage corresponds to the one described by Vitruvius (see below, Fig. 645). The scaenae frons, or front of the stage house, had an architectural painting in the so-called second style of the first century B.C. The parts of the cavea, which would project beyond the limits of the stage, are cut short so that a solid roof covering both auditorium and stage could be carried by the outer wall. We thus have here a compromise between a rectangular and a curvilinear theater. In the gaps which the curves of the uppermost seats leave at the upper two back corners, staircases lead to a vaulted corridor (crypta) from which doors open onto the cavea. The roof was possible only on smaller buildings. We must assume such a wooden roof for the odeum in Taormina (Fig. 616)[12] and the one mentioned in Naples.[13] Both were, like the one in Pompeii, connected with a large open theater. In Greece odea in the Roman form were built by

Figs. 613-615. Small theater at Pompeii. General view; Orchestra; Telamon

Fig. 616. Odeum at Taormina

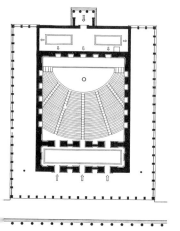

617a. Plan of ground level,
b. Plan of level at the top
of the cavea

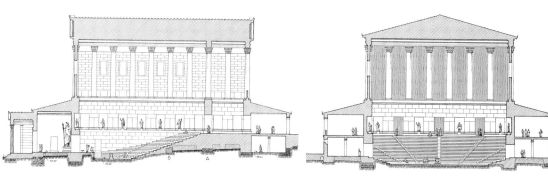

618a-b. Restored sections

Figs. 617-619. Odeum of Agrippa on the Agora of Athens

619a-b. Reconstructions

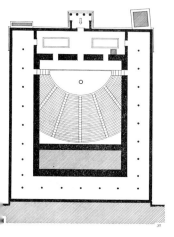

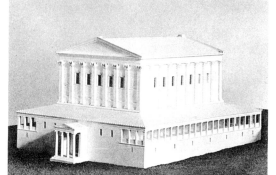

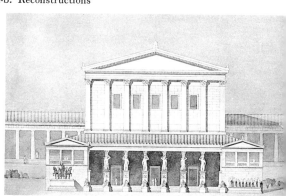

Agrippa, the general and son-in-law of Augustus, on the market place in Athens (Fig. 617-619)[14] and in the Roman colony of Corinth (Figs. 748-749).[15] Small odea or lecture halls were also built in the Greek gymnasia, as in Syracuse (Fig. 620) and in Epidaurus (Fig. 621).[16] The roof gave an architectural unity which no Greek theater ever had attained.

A purely Roman feature is also the parapet, which in the small theater at Pompeii separates the chairs of the magistrates and honored guests from the semicircular passageway running in front of the lowest row of seats. Into this passageway in the small theater of Pompeii some semicircular steps led up, upon which the visitors first mounted to the curved gangway (praecinctio, aisle) (Fig. 614). Thus they reached the six radiating stairways which brought them to their seats, while the magistrates reached their bisellia through the vaulted passageway and along the stage. The kneeling giants as telamons (Fig. 615) supporting the ends of the analemmata above the entrances to the gangway and the winged griffin's feet below are of excellent workmanship.

The same duumviri who had commissioned the little roofed theater at Pompeii erected there soon afterwards, probably around 70 B.C., at their own expense, an amphitheater, the oldest of its kind, for

Fig. 620, 621. Odea, in Syracuse and in Epidaurus

Fig. 622. Amphitheater of Pompeii, interior

Fig. 623. Amphitheater of Pompeii, entrance staircases

gladiatorial games and animal baitings, which as many inscriptions prove were very popular in Pompeii as they were elsewhere (Figs. 622-624).[17] The arena is sunk into the ground so that vaulted passages lead down to it. The lowest tier is separated from the arena as well as from the second tier by parapets. It also is still below ground level. It is entered through a vaulted curved passageway (crypta), which leads around below the second tier. The upper tier is reached by outside stairs built over high arches (Fig. 623). They end at a broad terrace, above which there were boxes for the women. We have here, for the entrances and exits of the public, the beginning of a well-planned structure added to the auditorium from below and from the outside. This structure later developed into that

Fig. 624. Amphitheater of Pompeii and the riot of A.D. 59. Wall painting from Pompeii, Naples

Figs. 625, 626. Amphitheaters of Pozzuoli and Capua

grandiose system of corridors, stairs, and entrance doors which distinguishes the Flavian amphitheater (Colosseum) and other amphitheaters of the time of the Empire (Ch. XIV, Figs. 662-670).

The amphitheater of Pompeii still lacks the subterranean passages, rooms, and elevators for beasts and decorations which we find not only in the Colosseum, but also in the other Campanian amphitheaters and at Puteoli (now Pozzuoli) (Fig. 625) and Capua (Figs. 626-627).[18]

A wall painting from Pompeii in Naples (Fig. 624)[19] shows the outside staircases going up to the terrace above the cavea, the arched boxes for the women, and the city wall against which the amphitheater is built. It also depicts a large palaestra with a swimming pool in the center, built near the amphitheater, which has recently been excavated.[20] The same painting also illustrates a story told for the year A.D. 59 by Tacitus (Annales, XIV,17). The large building, accommodating more than 12,000 persons, was not only used by the inhabitants of Pompeii but also by those of the neighboring cities. When Livineius Regulus, a scoundrel who had been thrown out of the Senate in Rome, tried to gain power in the province by promoting gladiatorial fights, a bloody fight as represented on the painting brought death to many visitors. As a consequence the Senate forbade the use of the amphitheater for ten years.

The Pompeians, however, did not want to renounce their beloved gladiatorial spectacles. They allowed them to take place in the large theater side by side with the mimes, pantomimes, tragedies, and comedies (see Ch. XV, Figs. 775-778). The beautiful colonnaded square behind the theater (G in Fig. 605) was given over to the gladiators. Behind the portico a kind of military barracks was erected, in which elegant weapons, helmets—one (Fig. 628) richly decorated with reliefs—shields, shoulder protectors, greaves, and swords have been found.

The painting (Fig. 624) informs us in addition about the use of a Campanian invention, the velum or velarium, an awning or linen roof credited to Quintus Lutatius Catulus in about 70 B.C. (Pliny, XIX,23; Valerius Maximus, II,4,6). It is represented above the ladies' boxes hanging between two towers of the city wall. The large theater has two rows of corbels in which masts were fixed, which held the velum firm.[21] The Greek name for these awnings, as testified by an inscription in Ephesus, is petasos, a broad brimmed hat,[22] a good description, for it served like a hat to protect the spectators from rain and sunburn. Sometimes, to add a decorative touch to its practical nature, it was painted as well (Lucretius, IV,75-83). A purple awning was stretched

over the theater of Pompey in Rome in A.D. 66 in honor of the visit of Tiridates, the king of Armenia (Pliny, XXXIII,54; cf. Martial, XI,21,6). Nero was painted on such an awning as the sun god in a chariot among stars (Cassius Dio, LXIII,6,2). The awnings were manipulated by sailors who stood on the roof of the colonnade surrounding the uppermost row of seats in the auditorium, and probably also on the roof of the side wings (versurae) of the stage house.

Another Roman detail which we can observe in the large theater of Pompeii is the trench behind the front of the stage for lowering the aulaeum, the curtain (Fig. 611).[23] In the soil of the trench are holes lined with lava stones, which lead to similar holes in a vaulted subterranean trench below. These holes held the poles for the curtain. Such a trench has also been observed in Syracuse (Fig. 595)[24] and in many other theaters—Fiesole, Arles, Lyon, Vai-

Fig. 627. Amphitheater of Capua. Subterranean passages

Fig. 628. Gladiatorial helmet, Pompeii

Fig. 629. Marble relief from Castel San Elia showing scenic plays and circus races

son, Orange, Timgad, Dugga, and Athens—of the time of the Empire (below, Ch. XIV, Figs. 656, 671-673, 676, 687, 724). The curtain was lowered at the beginning of each play and raised again at the end, probably with the help of levers and pulleys. See Horace, *Epistle*, ii,1,189: quattuor aut plures aulaea premuntur in horas. When it was dropped at the beginning of the performance, first the heads and last the feet of the actors could be seen. When it was raised at the end, first the heads and last the feet of figures painted on the curtain would appear (Ovid, *Metamorph.* iii,111ff).[25]

The siparia were smaller curtains to be distinguished from the aulaeum. They were hung from above, before parts of the scaenae frons, and they could be folded and drawn upward or to the side (Apuleius, *Metamorph.* i,8: aulaeum tragicum dimoveto et siparium scaenicum complicato . . . ; cf. X, 29: aulaeo subducto et complicitis sipariis, scaena disponitur). These siparia were already in use on the Hellenistic stage, to cover the decoration of a thyroma, when it was not used. A siparium is hung before a city view in the comedy relief in

Naples (Ch. VIII, Fig. 324). The siparia are represented neatly folded above a Roman scaenae frons on the relief from Castel S. Elia (Fig. 629).[26] Elegant hangings were brought from Pergamon to Rome and were used on the stage even in later periods (Donatus, *De comoedia*, 12,3). Probably good material was used for these curtains, which were lowered with cords from a shelf below the stage roof. They fell down in elegant festoons like the velum over the amphitheater in the painting (Fig. 624).

A roof over the stage is indicated—although worn away—on the relief from S. Elia (Fig. 629). Such a stage roof is already shown on some of the phlyakes stages (Ch. X, Figs. 491 and 540), but in Rome became probably a permanent feature only after permanent theaters were built. The purpose of the stage roof was to serve as a sound reflector and also to protect not only the siparia, but also the statues and other expensive decorations of the scaenae frons. In addition to the architectural ornaments and the permanently erected statues, the stage certainly received on festival days, when plays were presented, special decorations such as paintings, bronze ornaments, hangings, masks, garlands, and wreaths—all of which are found on Pompeian wall paintings (see Figs. 594, 775-778).

Fig. 630. Theater built by Pompey, Rome. Ancient plan

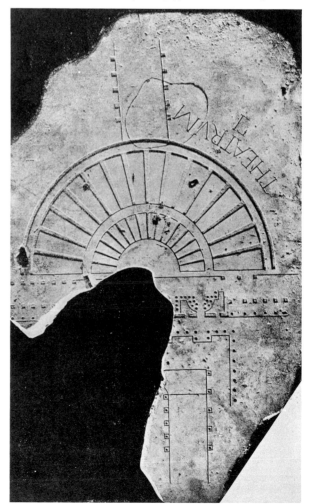

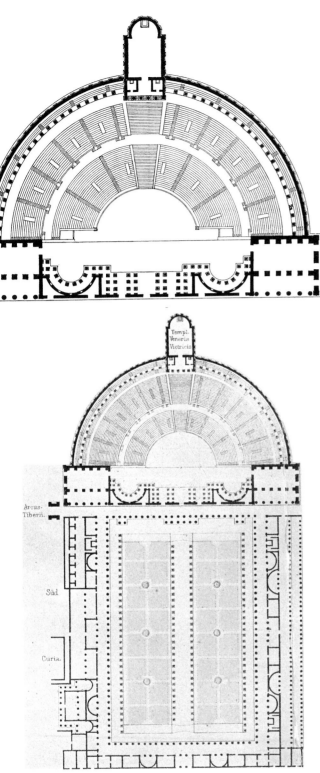

Figs. 631, 632. Theater built by Pompey, Rome. Plan, Renaissance reconstruction; Plan with colonnades behind the scene building

The many details which we learn from the buildings and wall paintings at Pompeii for the early Roman theater are all the more valuable because the first stone theaters in Rome are insufficiently known to us. The first permanent one was built by Pompey in the year 55 B.C. below the temple of Venus Victrix, with which it was intimately related.

It was dedicated in 52 B.C. with a variety of shows. Musical and gymnastic competitions were given in the theater, while in the hippodrome horse races and animal battles with lions and elephants were presented (Cassius Dio, *Historia Romana*, XXXIX,38). The theater was so constructed that the central wedge (cuneus) of the auditorium formed a monumental flight of steps leading up to the temple (Figs. 630-632).[27] We have the plan of this theater only in the late Severian map of Rome. We know that under Septimius Severus in 209-211 there was still building activity on the theater, and that restorations had been made under the emperor Augustus (*Mon. Anc.*, 49) and under Nero in A.D. 66 after a fire in the time of Tiberius. It may be assumed that the general ground plan does not differ from the first building. It thus had a semicircular orchestra and corresponding auditorium as well as the intimate connection of the auditorium with the stage house. We have found such a unity twenty years earlier in the small theater in Pompeii (F in Fig. 605 and Fig. 613). There, however, the plan for a unified theater building is still incomplete, for it is forced into a rectangle. In the theater of Pompey, in contrast, for the first time a completely semicircular form was given to the tiers of seats as well as to the outer façade of the auditorium.

Pompey is said to have used as a model for his theater the theater of Mytilene, which he had visited in 62 B.C. Plutarch (*Vita Pompei*, 42) tells us that Pompey had a design made of this theater, but had it executed larger and more holy (sacred, solemn?) in Rome (περιεγράψατο τὸ εἶδος αὐτοῦ καὶ τὸν τύπον, ὡς ὅμοιον ἀπεργασόμενος τὸ ἐν Ῥώμῃ, μεῖζον δὲ καὶ σεμνότερον). The theater of Mytilene is unfortunately unknown to us, and it is therefore uncertain how much Pompey borrowed from it. It was formerly assumed that he took from it the rounded form of the auditorium with the division into tiers by means of semicircular passageways and into wedge-shaped sections by means of the radially ascending stairs. Such auditoria, however, Pompey could see not only in Southern Italy and Sicily, but also at Rome in the circus and in the temporary theaters. It was rather, as Rumpf has shown,[28] the general plan of a building in which stage house, orchestra, and auditorium were intimately connected with each other with the help of side buildings (versurae) which took the place of the paraskenia of the Greek theater. The open air theater in Mytilene could, however, hardly have been such a unified theater. Mytilene, the large city on the island of Lesbos, probably had as large a theater as that which Pompey built in Rome, and therefore there was no necessity to enlarge it. Mytilene, however, also had a bouleuterion, mentioned in an inscription (*IG*, XII,2,67). Such a

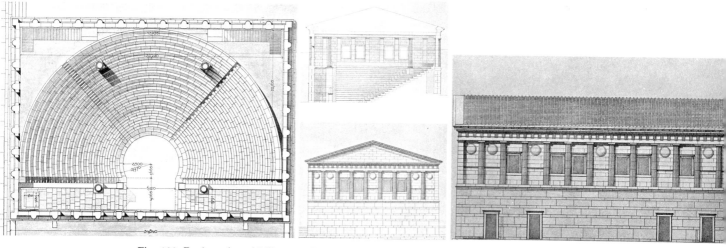

Fig. 633. Bouleuterion of Miletus. a, Plan of assembly hall; b, section and south elevation; c, east elevation

bouleuterion is named a little theater or ecclesiasterion by Vitruvius (VII,5,5), and the podium for the speaker is named scaena. The bouleuterion of Mytilene has not yet been excavated, but other such semicircular auditoria inside a square, as in the small theater of Pompeii, are preserved in Priene, Notium, Miletus (Figs. 633a-c). The latter was erected in the time of Antiochus IV (175-164), who, according to the inscription in Miletus, built a similar one in Antioch.[29] As we have seen, Plutarch says that Pompey had his theater building executed not only in larger size, but also more solemn or lofty (semnos). This may refer to the connection with a temple and also to the more luxurious decoration. Among the sumptuous additions was the colonnaded gallery at the top of the rows of seats, which is level with the top of the back wall of the stage, and was connected with its side buildings (versurae). This covered colonnade could not only be used by the spectators in case of rain and in the intermissions, but belongs to the temple of Venus Victrix. Caputo[30] believes that this connection with a sanctuary and a portico on top of the auditorium was also taken from Mytilene. There was, further, a colonnaded square, like the one behind the large theater at Pompeii (G in Fig. 605) and at Corinth, after the Greek manner, behind the stage building. That in any case the unity of the whole layout is the new feature, appears also from the fact that the older references to temporary buildings either mention only a stage or only an auditorium, or, if both, they are separately named.

The scaenae frons in the theater of Pompey was certainly not so richly and plastically organized in the first layout as it was later, as shown in the Severian plan (Fig. 630). In this late form there were fifty columns set in front of a very large rectangular central niche and two semicircular side niches. This may have been arranged at the time of the remodelling under Nero, for it was at his period that the large theater at Pompeii received a similar

architectural remodelling (C in Fig. 608 and Figs. 610-612). There, as here, the deep scaenae frons had invaded the space originally taken by larger dressing rooms. We may conclude that the theater of Pompey originally had a straight scaenae frons like the large theater at Pompeii (B in Fig. 608) and perhaps similar to the early Roman theaters at Segesta and Tyndaris (Figs. 598-602). Such a straight front decorated with columns on the same plane is best known to us from the terracotta relief of Numitorius with a tragic scene (Ch. XII, Fig. 588), and those with comedy scenes (Fig. 587). They have columns on high bases in the same plane with entablature and small pediments. The same arrangement in a still simpler form with engaged columns existed in Segesta and Tyndaris (Figs. 601-602), and we may assume that such a simple form existed also in the earlier period in the large theater at Pompeii (B in Fig. 608). The same kind of scaenae frons with columns on square bases in a straight line is represented on a marble relief with the model of a stage in the Museo Nazionale Romano delle Terme at Rome (Fig. 634).[31] The main door (regia) lies in a deep rounded niche, while the side doors (hospitalia) are placed in smaller and flatter rounded niches. Flanking the doors are spaces with rectangular sinkings, probably for the insertion of paintings. The columns carry on each side a triangular gable between two rounded ones. Behind them is a closed wall. At the sides are pilasters which carry a stage roof, which is decorated at the edge with cupids carrying garlands. The roof slants upward toward the spectators and has on the ceiling rows of carved rosettes as decoration.

Fig. 634. Marble model of a Roman stage

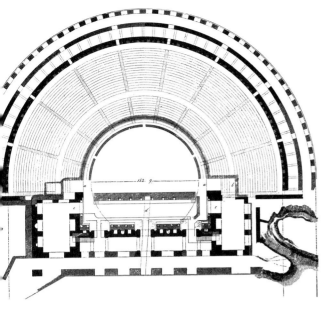

The theater of Taormina in Sicily has the best-preserved scaenae frons in Italy (Figs. 635-637),[32] and it agrees in the general plan (Fig. 635) with the theater built by Pompey. Groups of four columns on a high podium in a straight line separate the regia from the hospitalia, while two large columns on a lower base decorate the main entrance and the side doors, and two columns on a podium stand outside the side doors. Eight niches for statues are behind the columns (Figs. 636-637). The versurae connect the stage building with the auditorium. This is laid out in the Greek manner on a hillside, probably in the late third century, as Philistis, queen of Hieron II, is mentioned in an inscription. In the Roman period it was crowned

Figs. 635-637. Theater of Taormina. Plan, and views of scenae frons

Figs. 638, 639. Theater of Taormina, auditorium and corridor behind the stage

with two concentric vaulted porticoes, the inner of which opened into the cavea with forty-five granite columns on a high parapet (Fig. 638). Eight doors led down through this parapet to the eight stairs of the cavea which separate the nine sections, down which the visitors could walk to take their seats. There are thirty-six niches in the parapet on the inside of this balustrade, probably also intended for statues. Thus the Roman remodelling brought richer decoration but also great improvement for filling and emptying to this originally Greek theater. The room behind the scaenae frons has become, as in the large theater at Pompeii and the theater of Pompey in Rome, a kind of corridor which connects the outer entrances to the large side buildings with each other (Fig. 639).

For a long time the theater built by Pompey remained Rome's only theater. When the emperor Augustus gave the secular plays in 17 B.C., Greek thymelic plays were presented in this theater, while Greek scenic plays were presented in the Circus Flaminius, and the last wooden temporary theater recorded for the capital was erected near the river Tiber for Latin plays.[33]

Soon after, in 13 B.C., Balbus built a second gorgeous stone theater in the Campus Martius, in which four onyx columns are recorded (Suetonius, *Augustus*, 29; Pliny, *Nat. Hist.*, xxxvi,60).[34] Caesar had begun a new theater which was completed by Augustus in 11 B.C. and dedicated to the memory of his nephew and son-in-law, Marcellus. The ancient marble plan of Rome (forma urbis Romae) sketches a part of this theater, and old drawings of Peruzzi published by Serlio show that the general plan was not unlike that of the theater of Pompey (Figs. 640-643).[35] Behind the scene building were colonnaded walks flanked by two small buildings resembling basilicas, from which doors led into the versurae. These high-sided buildings provided, in several

stories, storerooms, side entrances to the stage building (scaena), and side entrances to the stage proper (pulpitum). The public, in order to reach the orchestra and the radiating staircases of the lower gallery, had to enter through vaulted passages laid below the outermost sections; above these were the tribunalia, the boxes, provided for the magistrates who gave the plays. A crypta below the passageway (praecinctio) which separated the two galleries contained small staircases leading to the

Fig. 640. Theaters of Pompey and of Marcellus. Ancient plans

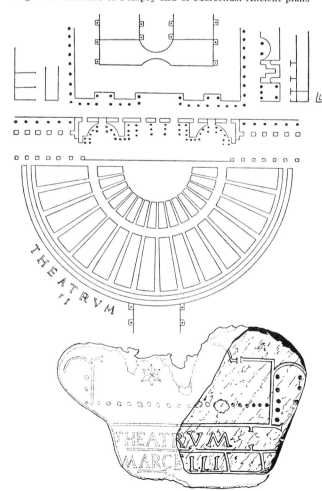

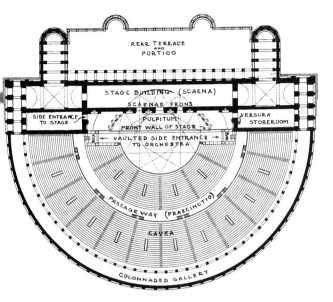

Fig. 641. Theater of Marcellus. Reconstructed plan

cades, between the openings of which are engaged columns with their entablature. They are of the Doric order in the lowest story, with their entablature of metopes and triglyphs, and of the Ionic order in the second story with a continuous frieze and dentals. The Corinthian engaged columns of the third story are not preserved, but some traces remain.

radiating staircases of the upper gallery. Inner staircases also led to the doors in the center of the sections which were called vomitoria, because they spit out (vomit) the masses of spectators. Above the uppermost tier of seats was a colonnaded gallery which at both its ends connected with the upper stories of the versurae.

The whole stage building, the interior and the uppermost façade of the cavea of the Marcellus theater were lost when the castle of the Pierleoni, the Palazzo Savelli, and finally the Palazzo Orsini were built into it. Only the lower outer façade was preserved, and in the lower story artisans practiced their trades (Fig. 642), until it was excavated and restored at the instigation of Mussolini (Fig. 643). The magnificent remains of this outer curvilinear wall of the auditorium correspond to the first and second inner tiers. They open in vaulted ar-

Figs. 642, 643. Theater of Marcellus. Outside façade of the auditorium before and after restoration

185

Fig. 644. Theater of Herculaneum, model

The theater of Herculaneum had a similar although smaller form than the theater built by Pompey at Rome and the remodelled large theater at Pompeii. The cavea seated about half of the number of persons accommodated in Pompeii. The theater was built by the architect Publius Numisius in the time of Augustus, but it was redecorated in the time of Claudius and Nero from A.D. 41 on. Since it was excavated in the eighteenth century with the help of shafts and tunnels like a coal mine, it can hardly be visualized on the spot. Good reconstructions, however, have been made by Mazois, which prove that this provincial theater was, like the Roman one, constructed and sustained by vaulted arches and pilasters (Fig. 644).[36] Staircases led to the passageway between the two galleries and smaller stairs to the uppermost tier. On the top of the cavea, where in Rome the temple of Venus stood, were small shrines (aedicula) for statues, flanked by equestrian statues, while between columns of precious polychrome marble many other statues stood in the niches of the scaenae frons. Among them were the celebrated statues of mother and daughter, called the Herculaneum women, now in Dresden. The proscenium had small niches similar to those in the large theater at Pompeii. The orchestra had low steps for the seats of the magistrates and outstanding citizens; boxes for the magistrates who provided the plays were above the vaulted side entrances. The model demonstrates the importance of the versurae for the unification of cavea and stage building. They have doors at the sides which lead to the stage and others facing the cavea which lead to the praecinctio and to the uppermost gallery with the shrines.

The exterior of the theater of Marcellus and of Herculaneum was imitated by many other theaters of the Roman Empire and by several later amphitheaters (see Ch. XIV, Figs. 663-670). These in turn influenced the façades of later palaces, especially those of the Renaissance. The exterior wall, however, is not merely decorative but expressive of the inner construction, which certainly developed gradually from the high substructures of the wooden theaters. The carefully planned system of radial and concentric walls, stairs, roofed corridors (crypta), vaulted passages, ambulatories (praecinctiones), and doors (vomitoria) served as means of entry and exit for the many thousands of Roman theatergoers, thus enabling them to reach their seats without crowding by separate and uninterrupted approaches leading to each section in each tier. There was no necessity to rush and compete for good seats. All seats afforded an equally good view, because those extending beyond the semicircle were cut off and the stage was low. The spectators were also guided unfailingly to their seats by the Roman tickets, many of which have been found in Pompeii, at Rome, and in the Roman provinces (see Ch. XV, Figs. 811-816). They designate the seats in the different sections by means of Roman numerals and often by additional Greek letters as an aid to a bilingual public. Sometimes buildings or part of a building, probably some entrance to the theater or some part of it, or landmarks, statues, or names designating the sections are shown (see Figs. 813d-e, 814a, 815a).

The form of the theaters built in the late republican and Augustan periods must be the one which Vitruvius Pollio (De architectura, v,3-9) knew when he described, in about 16-13 B.C., the Roman theater (Fig. 645) and recommended it for imitation.[37] He gives (v,6) clear and simple rules for the construction of the Roman theater which he then contrasts (in v,7) with the Greek theater of which he gives a less clear description (cf. Fig. 475). In

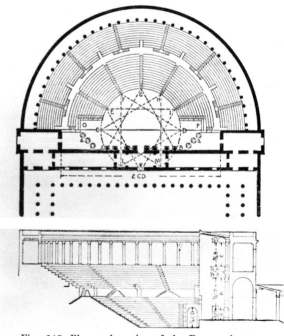

Fig. 645. Plan and section of the Roman theater according to Vitruvius

the orchestra circle, which in both theaters forms the center of the layout, four equilateral triangles are inscribed at equal distances apart, the points of which touch the boundary line of the circle in twelve places. The base of the triangle, the point of which touches the middle of the auditorium, forms the front wall of the stage house, which the Romans richly equipped as the scaenae frons. The line parallel to this, which runs through the center of the circle and thus divides the orchestra into two halves, forms the front wall (proscaenium) of the platform of the stage (pulpitum). In this way the stage has the depth of half of the radius of the orchestra (see Fig. 641 and 645). From this we may conclude—even if we did not know it—that the Roman theater had a semicircular orchestra and a much deeper stage than the Greek. Vitruvius explains this on the basis that all the actors performed on the stage of the Roman theater, while in the Greek theater only the scenic artists made their appearance there, the lyric and other artists (thymelici) appearing in the orchestra.

Vitruvius gives five feet as the maximum height of the stage, in contrast to the twelve feet of the Greek stage. He accounts for this by pointing out that in the orchestra, no longer used for plays, spectators of high rank, like senators, were seated. From this place they would not have been able to see the performances on a high stage. This statement of Vitruvius is confirmed by the broad flat steps for the chairs in the orchestra of the large theater at Pompeii and of other theaters (Figs. 607, 613-614, 656, 696).

Of the twelve corners of the four triangles, seven point in the direction of the ascending stairs in the auditorium which articulate the wedge-shaped sections (cunei) in the lowest circle and lead the visitors to their seats. In the second tier above the first curved cross-aisle (praecinctio) more stairs are added midway between those of the lower sections. The principle of this arrangement is borrowed from the Greek theater, but it was seldom carried out there with perfect regularity. The Roman theater naturally also had variations, since the large theaters have more flights of stairs, and the small theaters fewer. Yet we often find seven stairs, as for example in the theater of Marcellus (Fig. 641) and in Herculaneum (Fig. 644), both being of the time of Augustus and contemporary with Vitruvius. In later theaters we sometimes also have seven stairs (see Figs. 658-659, 680, 685, 689, 694, 726-727), sometimes more (Figs. 700, 710, 733-734), and sometimes fewer (see Figs. 647-650, 655-656, 675, 711-712).

The five remaining angles determine the entrances to the stage. The door opposite the middle angle was the king's, or royal, door (valva or aula regia),

those on either side of it were the guest doors (hospitalia), and the two outermost angles designated the side entrances from the wings to the stage (itinera versurarum). These correspond to the entrances from the paraskenia in the Greek theater, which frame the stage (see Figs. 261-266 and 463-468). In the Roman theater these projecting wings support at the same time the sides of the auditorium.

The open parodoi, which in the Greek theater led into the orchestra between the paraskenia and the analemmata, have in the Roman theater become vaulted passages, which remain the main entrance (aditus maximus) to the orchestra and the lower part of the auditorium. Vitruvius (v,6,6) gives as measurement for the most practical construction of these vaulted passageways one-sixth of the diameter or one third of the radius of the orchestra. This results in rather low side approaches, probably because the tribunalia, or boxes for the officials who gave the plays, are situated on top of these entrances (see Figs. 606, 646, 655-657, 690).

Vitruvius gives several additional measurements in relation to the diameter of the orchestra; thus, the length of the scene building is set at double the diameter of the ground circle (v,6,6), while it was shorter, sometimes only one diameter, in the Greek theater. The height of the podium is to be one-twelfth of the diameter. The columns in the scaenae frons are to diminish in height according to a definite ratio in the upper stories. Vitruvius, being a practical architect, adds that his rules of symmetry must of course be modified to suit the nature of the site or the size of the theater. Some parts, such as steps, cross-aisles, and passages must be made of the same size in a small and in a large theater.

The unity of the Roman theater building is assured by the specification that a roofed colonnade must surround the uppermost rim of the cavea at the top of the rows of seats, and that this must be level with the top of the stage building (Figs. 635, 638, 645, 650, 700-703). Vitruvius (v,6,4) gives as the reason that the voice thereby resounds evenly throughout the theater. He also gives additional specifications for the acoustics (v,3,4-8 and v,8,1-2). He praises the plan of the Greek auditorium, which served as a model for the Roman because of its excellent acoustics.[38] Vitruvius also dedicates a whole chapter to harmonics (v,4) and another (v,5) to sounding vessels, which, although not used in Rome itself, produced advantageous results in districts of Italy and in many Greek states. The acoustics were also improved by the fact that wood continued to be employed for the floor of the stage, also for the doors, barriers, and painted panels set into the stone scaenae frons. The wooden roof over the stage, slanting down toward the scaenae frons and away from the spectators, also served as a kind of sounding board (see Figs. 629, 634, 715). The floor was paved instead of being of earth (Figs. 614, 717) and thus reflected better the sounds coming from the stage.

Dörpfeld[39] tried to derive the Roman theater directly from the Greek by insisting that the inner half of the circular orchestra, towards the spectators, was set deeper into the ground, while the outer half remained at the original Greek level, and that consequently the low Roman stage was at the same level where formerly in the Greek theater the main scene of action also took place. The earlier Greek row of columns in the front wall supporting the platform of the proskenion, in Dörpfeld's opinion, became the scaenae frons behind the platform of the Roman pulpitum. His drawings (Fig. 646), however, which are meant to illustrate this development, succeed only in showing the great differences between the two types of stage.

Fiechter,[40] followed by Bulle,[41] tries on the other hand to develop the scaenae frons from the thyromata, with their inset painted decorations of the late Hellenistic stage. Here again I can perceive only differences. Decorations which were merely painted, tried out by Claudius Pulcher and Apaturius (see p. 168), did not please the Romans. They were therefore replaced by rich plastic and architectural forms totally different in character and mass. Although we do not possess stages from the first century B.C. preserved in Rome, we know that the scaenae frons of Scaurus was decorated with many columns, and such plastic columns are also found in the purely Roman terracotta reliefs with tragic and comic scenes (Ch. XII, Figs. 587-588). The scaenae frons takes the place of the thyromata wall, and the low closed front of the pulpitum, the proscenium, replaces the high engaged columns of the Hellenistic proskenion.

The architects who built the Roman theaters were of Roman nationality, like M. Artorius Primus in Pompeii and Numisius in Herculaneum. This is in contrast to the Greek sculptors, who provided their Roman masters with copies and adaptations of Greek masterpieces, many of which decorated the Roman theaters.

The individual and special creations of the Romans in theater construction seem to me to consist of the following elements: Out of the primitive wooden stage, which had migrated to Rome with the Atellan farce, and out of the rounded auditorium copied from the Greeks, the Romans in the first century B.C. created an architectural unit which was both beautiful and practical. The division of the auditorium, borrowed from the Greeks, is carried

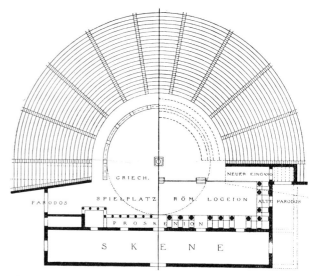

Fig. 646. Differences between the plans of the Greek and Roman theaters, Dörpfeld

out much more systematically and uniformly than in the Greek theaters. This is accomplished by the high substructures, which make the auditorium independent of the formation of the ground used as its site. The construction of large and complex arches and vaulted passages was made possible by the copious use of concrete, seldom used by the Greeks. The Roman architects with this help built tier over tier of corridors, with staircases leading separately to the various parts of the theater. The outside was decorated with the different orders of the Greeks, which the eclectic taste of the Romans liked to combine in the same building. The arched openings between the columns in the ground floor formed the entrances to the rounded passages; in the upper stories they gave light to the rounded corridors and to the stairs. A roofed portico crowned the cavea, which terminated directly at the side buildings of the stage, built as high versurae, with stairs and doors leading to the cavea as well as to the stage. The Roman love of law and organization created a well-planned whole. The Roman materialistic spirit, their love of pomp and luxury, created the splendid display of architectural triumphs of the scaenae frons which exerted their influence into the Renaissance. The Romans needed a permanent decoration striking to the eye in its splendor. It is the same in other fields—such as dress, particularly the Roman toga, which needs a definite form in an effective arrangement. The counterpart to the scaenae frons is found in superimposed orders on the exterior wall of the auditorium. The rear outer wall of the stage building is also richly ornamented, but it is kept flatter and more simple than the scaenae frons facing the auditorium. Thus, the Roman theaters are undoubtedly among the greatest and most masterful creations of Roman architecture.

The main differences between the Greek-Hellenistic and the Roman theater are:

HELLENISTIC	ROMAN
The orchestra is a full circle.	The orchestra is a half circle.
Stage house and orchestra are separated.	Stage house and orchestra are brought into an architectural whole.
The stage is high and shallow.	The stage is low and deep.
The proskenion is decorated with columns and painted pinakes.	The proscenium has a closed front decorated with niches and sometimes small pilasters.
The background of the stage has wide openings (thyromata) with painted scenery.	The background is a sumptuous architectural scaenae frons.
The entrances to the orchestra are open parodoi.	The side entrances are vaulted.
The seats of honor for the priests are in the lowest tier of seats.	Boxes (tribunalia) are above the vaulted entrances for the providers of the plays. Senators, members of the city council, and other distinguished spectators are seated in the orchestra.
The different tribes are separated in sections in the same gallery.	The different classes are seated in different galleries, separated by parapets (barriers).
Entrance for all spectators is through the parodoi and the orchestra leading to the radiating staircases.	Entrance for the public is through different outer vaulted entrances, staircases, vaulted and open passageways.
The auditorium is built against a hillside, and therefore has no outside façade.	The auditorium occasionally is also laid on a hillside (Vitruvius, v,3,3), but mostly built on high substructions from level ground with a rich façade, a colonnaded gallery, and sometimes shrines on top.
No colonnade on top.	
The theater is built in sanctuaries.	The theater can be built anywhere in a healthy place (Vitruvius, v,3,1). It sometimes has a shrine above its cavea.
The Greek theater is a religious and democratic building with equally good seats for everybody.	The Roman theater is a class theater. It has more seats for officials and less space for the performances. It has different seats for the different ranks of society.
The Greek performances are literary events.	The Roman performances are shows catering to the taste of the public (see Ch. XV).

CHAPTER XIV

ROMAN THEATER BUILDINGS IN ITALY AND THE PROVINCES DURING THE EMPIRE

THE Roman theater builders developed during the last century of the Republic a definite method of design for their plans as well as for their elevations. This is described by Vitruvius and evidenced by the remains of the theaters in Rome. The Marcellus theater and the theater of Pompey were, however, rebuilt and redecorated during the Empire in a richer and more luxurious form developed in Rome. The same thing happened to the earlier Greek theaters in Southern Italy and Sicily, such as the large theater in Pompeii (B and C in Fig. 608 and Figs. 610-612) and the theater of Taormina (Figs. 635-637), as well as to many Greek theaters in Greek lands, Asia Minor, and the Greek mainland. The tendency of the Empire was to make everything bigger and better, more luxurious and more pretentious, but also more practical than the Greeks had made it. The peak of this tendency is in the Antonine period. Then a tendency to simplification sets in, although the tendency toward large scale is continued. The theaters all over the Empire became very numerous in agreement with the recommendation of Vitruvius, *The Ten Books on Architecture* (v,3,1): "After the forum has been arranged, next, for the purpose of seeing plays or festivals of the immortal gods, a site as healthy as possible should be selected for the theater." Vitruvius recommends following the principles of healthfulness, which he has given in Book I. He warns (*Ibid.*, v,3,2) particularly against southern exposure: "The air, being shut up in the curved enclosure and unable to circulate, stays there and becomes heated." This and other practical rules given by Vitruvius are followed in new theater buildings which are erected on level ground with the help of arches, rarely used by the Greeks. As they are erected on level ground they are oriented to the north, northwest, and occasionally west (Timgad). The Greek in contrast, and those Roman theaters which use natural slopes, follow different exposures, including southern, for example, in the theaters of Athens; the theater of Dionysus as well as the Roman theater of Herodes Atticus, laid on the south slope of the Acropolis, have southern exposures.

Another characteristic difference is that the Greek theaters were built in sanctuaries, particularly of Dionysus (Athens) and Apollo (Delphi, Delos). The Romans built their theaters anywhere on a "healthy site." However, they sometimes built sanctuaries above the uppermost gallery, as in the temple of Venus Victrix above the theater of Pompey (Figs. 630-632) and the shrine for Ceres in Leptis Magna (Fig. 696). Like the Greeks, they had colonnaded courts behind the scene building for the use of the spectators during intermissions, but they also had covered porticos on top of the cavea, which served as approaches to the uppermost gallery as well as to the sanctuary, and together with the vaulted corridors below the upper galleries served as refuge in case of rain. The comfort of the spectators was augmented by the velum (see Ch. XIII, Fig. 624) and by sparsiones, sprinkling with perfumed water, to offset the heat of the sun (Martial, v,25,7, ix,38,5. Lucretius, ii,416; Pliny, *Nat. Hist.*, xxi,33; Apuleius, *Metamorph.*, x,35; Lucan, *Pharsalia*, ix,808-810).

We must distinguish, therefore, for the time of the Empire, between (1) the purely Roman theaters and (2) the older Greek theaters transformed into Roman ones, which may be called Graeco-Roman. We find the first kind mostly in places which previously had not possessed theaters. New theaters in the purely Roman form were erected particularly in those places and countries which developed a progressive Roman civilization only after they had been conquered and settled by the Romans. These are Northern Italy, Germany, Britain, France, Spain, North Africa, and Arabia. The second kind is mostly found in the Greek lands, Southern Italy, Asia Minor, and the Greek mainland—although single examples of the purely Roman kind are also found in those parts which had become Roman provinces. Another difference between the non-Greek and the Greek provinces is that amphitheaters and circus buildings were erected in a great number in the non-Greek provinces together with purely Roman theaters, while there are very few in Greek lands.[1] The Roman soldiers and veterans who settled in the conquered lands wanted to see their beloved popular entertainments. Therefore in the Greek lands, where no amphitheaters were built, many theaters were remodelled in such a way that gladiatorial fights, animal baitings, and aquacades could be shown to the Roman masters.

Our main sources for the different types of buildings are many well-preserved ruins and inscriptions which often give the dates of the first layout or its remodelling in a later period.

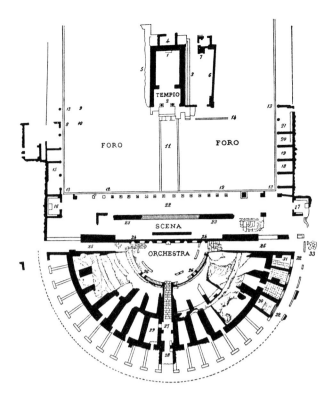

Fig. 647. Ostia. Plan of theater and square

Figs. 648-650. Theater of Ostia. Interior view; Exterior; Reconstruction

Purely Roman Theaters

The oldest purely Roman open-air theater outside Rome is probably the theater in Ostia, the harbor town of Rome, which was built by M. Agrippa, the son-in-law and general of Augustus, in the beginning of the Empire (Figs. 647-650).[2] It is organically connected with the piazza delle corporazione, a large square with a temple, probably of Ceres, in the center. Around the square are the offices for corporations of the ship owners, who imported the grain, oil, and other commodities necessary for the capital. The colonnade around this square served at its smaller end as the foyer of the theater behind the scene building (Fig. 647). The cavea is built against the slope coming down from the main street, the decumanus maximus. The Emperor Septimius Severus and Caracalla as Caesar in A.D. 195 restored and enlarged the theater in brick. A third gallery was built up so that the cavea became higher than the decumanus. Originally there were only two galleries and two side entrances through vaulted corridors. The reconstruction added not only a large central vaulted entrance leading down from the decumanus directly into the orchestra (see Fig. 648), but now outside entrances led through arches between engaged pilasters to the upper gallery (see Fig. 649). In the orchestra low steps were laid for the movable chairs of the dignitaries. The pulpitum was, as always, floored with wooden planks. The proscenium, the front of the stage, was decorated alternately with five half-circle and four rectangular exedrae or niches (Fig. 648). The straight scaenae frons behind the stage was richly decorated with columns, niches, and statues, as the reconstruction (Fig. 650) implies. Several such statues, for example the so-called Venus Marina, have been found here. A stage roof and contrivances for holding the poles for the velum are likely. An elegant altar, now in the Museo Nazionale Romano delle Terme was found in the theater and is dated in the period of Hadrian.[3] Scenic plays are testified for Ostia by inscriptions (CIL, XIV, 353) and by the cake moulds with scenes from tragedy and comedy (Ch. XV, Figs. 793-794). The reconstruction bears witness to the unified plan of the theater.

Figs. 653, 654. Theater of Minturnae. Orchestra and scene building; Cavea, entrances, and stage building

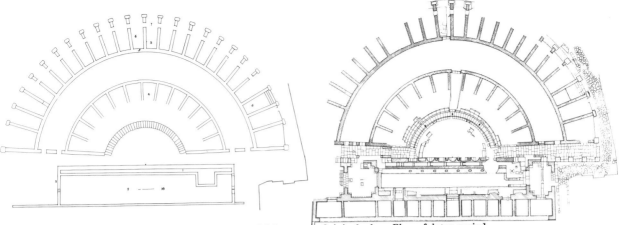

Figs. 651, 652. Theater of Minturnae. Original plan; Plan of later period

Not much later than the theater of Ostia, and similar in its layout, is the one excavated at Minturnae, in Latium, south of Rome near the Campanian border (Figs. 651-654).[4] It was erected in about the second decade of the first century, in the last Augustan period or in the reign of Tiberius. It was connected with the north portico of the forum, whose north wall served as the rear wall of the scene building. The stoa became an appendix to the theater, and the colonnades of this stoa could be used as shelter for the audience in accordance with Vitruvius (v,9,1). In the second century the scene building was rebuilt in a more elaborate form at the expense of the stoa, which was cut up into fourteen compartments as dressing and property rooms (Fig. 652). At the two ends passages were left from the cavea to the forum. The proscenium has three rounded and two rectangular niches. In the orchestra flat steps were laid for the bisellia (Figs. 653-654).

A relief found in Castel S. Elia north of Rome in Southern Etruria is dated in the time of the Emperor Claudius (41-54) (Fig. 629).[5] The scaenae frons, in the earlier straight type, has eight columns in pairs at the sides of the (originally painted) regia and hospitalia. Above them are seven niches corresponding to the three doors and the four pairs of columns, filled with the statue of Apollo in the center and with six muses at the sides. The niches are treated like small shrines framed by columns which support gables. Above is a contrivance for five siparia (see Ch. XIII, p. 180). Below the theatrical scene is a circus race (Fig. 629), indicating that in the province as in Rome and Ostia circus games and scenic plays were given at the same festivals.

Fiesole, ancient Faesulae, near Florence, in Northern Etruria, has an early provincial small theater of the Roman form prescribed by Vitruvius (Figs. 655-657).[6] It has radiating staircases dividing

Fig. 655. Theater of Fiesole. View of cavea and orchestra

193

Figs. 656, 657. Theater of Fiesole. Front of pulpitum and
orchestra; Side entrances to stage and orchestra

the lowest cavea (maenianum imum) into four sections. Vomitoria lead from a vaulted corridor into the upper tiers. It is situated behind the praecinctio between the first and second galleries. The entrance to the uppermost cavea (maenianum summum) was from above, from an upper colonnaded terrace. In the orchestra are four low steps for the movable chairs of the officials. Tribunalia, for the providers of the plays, are above the vaulted entrances which lead into the orchestra alongside the proscenium. This front wall of the pulpitum had a rounded niche in the center and two rectangular niches at each side. A trench for a curtain is behind it. To the original wooden pulpitum vaulted side entrances (itinera versurarum) lead in from the side buildings (versurae) of the stage (Fig. 657). Columns on high pedestals stood before these side doors and before the doors in the background (scaenae frons) leading into the rear scene, which seems to be of a later period.

The theater in Verona (Figs. 658-661)[7] has been drawn and reconstructed by Carotta, Palladio, and others, but their plans are not reliable. The central part of the cavea is built against the slope of a hill above the Adige river, where the church S. Libera now stands (Fig. 658), perhaps in the place of an ancient temple. The two outer portions were erected on high substructures and arches, which afford vaulted entrances to the lower gallery (maenianum primum) and staircases to the upper gallery (Figs. 659-660), which were built of heavy stones. The half-circle orchestra is surrounded by a water channel and had low steps for the bisellia, the

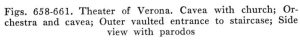

Figs. 658-661. Theater of Verona. Cavea with church; Orchestra and cavea; Outer vaulted entrance to staircase; Side view with parodos

movable chairs of honored guests. The orchestra and the parodoi (Fig. 661) are paved with marble. The scaenae frons had colossal columns with Corinthian capitals, revetments of marble, statues, and architectural decorations of which many fragments have been found. Among them are herms of Dionysus and a satyr.

661

Figs. 662, 664. Amphitheater of Verona. Interior and exterior

Fig. 663. Amphitheater of Verona

Like many other cities, Verona had an amphitheater. It is among the best preserved in Italy, although many of the seats have had to be restored (Figs. 662-665).[8] Pliny (*Epist.* VI,34) attests gladiatorial fights and animal baitings in this amphitheater, so that it must have been finished before 114, the year when the younger Pliny died, but it is probably still earlier. It agrees well with the description of an amphitheater by Ovid (*Metamorph.*, XI,25): "structum utrimque theatrum," a building with an auditorium all around. It gives us a complete picture of the two lower galleries (maeniana) around the elliptical arena (Figs. 662-663). The two large entrances in the main axis have above them the tribunalia, the boxes for the magistrates who gave the plays. The lowest seats are above a high balustrade which protects the visitors against the wild beasts in the arena. Vomitoria lead out in regular distribution to the seats from covered corridors, hidden below the seats. The outside arches (Fig. 664) lead to these vaulted corridors and to the staircases which go up to the upper galleries. The elliptical corridor between the outermost and the second elliptical wall is built in two stories, while of the third floor corridor only a few arches of the outer wall are preserved (Fig. 665). The building

Fig. 665. Verona. Vaulted corridors

idea of this north Italian amphitheater in Gallia Transpadana is the same as in the Flavian amphitheater in Rome.

The Colosseum in Rome was built in the place of a lake which had belonged to the Golden House of Nero by the three Flavian emperors, and, therefore, is called the Flavian amphitheater. Its popular name

Fig. 666. Colosseum, Rome

animals and about 4,000 tame animals were used for the venationes, the hunting of animals and their fights with each other. Domitian (81-96) finished the upper part of this grandiose building. It still represents the consummation of the idea of grouping a big mass of spectators around a central arena.

The Colosseum is 48½ meters high, 188 long, and 156 broad. It has a circumference of 527 meters and a capacity of about 45,000 spectators (Figs. 666-669).[9] It is built in travertine in four stories. The lower three stories open up in arcades, each with eighty arches, flanked by the Tuscan Doric order in the first, the Ionic order in the second, and by the Corinthian order in the third story, while the fourth story has engaged Corinthian pilasters and windows. The arches in the arcades of the second and third stories were probably filled with statues (see Fig. 670). The outside is a reflection of the inside. All eighty arcades on the ground floor are entrances to the arena and the cavea. The two in the long axis lead into the arena, and it was here that the procession of the gladiators entered. The two in the short axis led to the podium in the center above the arena, where the emperor and his retinue had a special box, while around him and on the opposite side the vestal virgins, consuls, praetors, ambassadors, priests, other dignitaries, and honored guests were seated. The seats in the first maenianum were above a low wall which had at its top a fence as a protection against the wild animals. In this first gallery (maenianum primum) persons of senatorial and equestrian rank were seated. They entered through about 38 of the 76 arches of the lowest arcade which were indicated by numbers, agreeing with the tickets indicating the cunea, the wedge-shaped sections in the auditorium. Nineteen of the other arches led to staircases ascending to the second and nineteen to those ascending directly to the third maenianum. The staircase to the second gallery began in the second parallel arcaded gallery, and the one to the third gallery in the third elliptical, concentric vaulted corridor, built between the arcaded walls, which follow the outer one like the layers of an onion (Fig. 669). The number of the arcaded walls and the vaulted corridors decreases in the upper stories, while the cavea spreads out to accommodate more and more people in the middle gallery (maenianum medium), where the patrician citizens wearing togas were seated, and in the upper gallery where the plebeians sat or stood. The galleries were separated from each other by elliptical corridors (praecinctiones) corresponding to the outer vaulted corridors, along side walls (baltei) which were about 5 meters high. Sixty doors (vomitoria) led out from the inner corridors to the different

Figs. 667-669. Colosseum, Rome. Plan; Section; Interior of vaulted corridor

it received from a colossal statue erected next to it originally to represent Nero, but changed by Vespasian to represent the sun god. Vespasian (69-79) built most of this first stone amphitheater in Rome. Titus dedicated it A.D. 80 with games which lasted one hundred days, at which occasion about 5,000 wild

sections. Staircases parallel to the outer wall led up to the fourth, uppermost, gallery, where women were seated in boxes. Thus the space between the outer wall and the slanting tiers of seats was filled with vaulted passages and staircases, which went in all directions and provided direct and easy access to all parts of the cavea. At the top of the wall was a broad walk for the sailors, who pulled the velum, the sunshade, back and forward (see Ch. XIII, p. 179). All these details are well represented on coins of Titus and Gordian (Fig. 670).[10] Many of the brackets for the poles holding the velum are preserved (Fig. 666). Most of the seats are destroyed, but the radiating substructures and vaults between them, which carried the seats rising from the arena inside to the uppermost story of the outside wall, are well preserved.

The arena, named from the sand with which it was covered, is under-tunneled with more elliptical walls, which comprise corridors, cages for the animals, and elevators and machinery needed for lifting the beasts, the scenery and properties, and occasionally also for watering the arena. Here the manifold and cruel spectacles which delighted the Roman public were performed. Whoever survived the fight was tried with burning irons by a servant dressed as Mercury, the messenger of the gods. Another servant dressed as Charun with a hammer, like the Etruscan demon of death (Ch. XI, Figs. 544-545), drew the bodies and the wounded into the death chamber, where the surviving were killed. The amphitheater thus is a monument not only of the cruelty of the Roman people and of the class character of the Roman society, but also of the genius of the Roman architects. In the eighteenth century Maffei described the amphitheater in the following way:[11]

> . . . whoever . . . will take pleasure to examine well the nature of this structure thoroughly, will be forced to acknowledge that nothing more per-

fect, more admirable could be conceived, so as to render the whole really magnificent, and a masterpiece of art . . . that it is practicable to build a fabric which . . . might accommodate so many thousand spectators in such a way that none should incommode another, and with so many distinctions and separate entries, and convenience of entering and coming out in a very short time, and with such nice divisions of stairs and outlets on the higher steps, and with so much convenience of places for various uses, . . .

In Northern Italy there are many purely Roman buildings. Besides Verona, Pola in Istria also has a well-preserved amphitheater of three stories, with a hall of three naves under the arena. While Verona had one theater, Pola had two Roman theaters in addition to the amphitheater.[12]

Both buildings and sometimes a circus are also found in France, because the originally Celtic Gaul had been conquered by Caesar. Many veterans of the Roman army who settled there wanted their amusement. Paris (Lutetia) had an amphitheater combined with a theater and later a second theater. Most Roman buildings are found in the Provence, the original Roman province (provincia Romana), in the valley of the Rhone. The best preserved amphitheater is in Nîmes (Nemausus), already built in the Augustan period according to the inscription of the architect: "T. Crispius Reburnus fecit." It has Doric pillars in the first, and Doric engaged columns in the second story.[13] This amphitheater has been restored to accommodate bull fighting, as has also been the amphitheater in Arles (Arelate) with a capacity of 26,000.[14] These fights are certainly a survival or a revival of the animal huntings (venationes) of the Romans, who introduced them to their provinces in France and Spain. The Spaniards have transmitted them to Mexico.

Arles also had in addition to the amphitheater a circus and a large theater which accommodated

Fig. 670. Coin of Titus, showing the Colosseum

Fig. 671. Theater of Arles

Fig. 672. Theater of Vaison

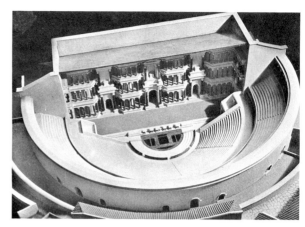

Fig. 673. Large and small theaters of Lyon   Fig. 674. Large theater of Lyon. Model

12,000. The latter was erected probably as early as the founding of the colony in 46 B.C. It is well preserved in its lower part, so that the plan could be reconstructed (Fig. 671).[15] The scaenae frons has a large rounded niche for the regia, with four columns before the staircase on which the actor could make an effective entrance. The postscaenium has only small dressing rooms which open on a portico, from which one could enter the large versurae. There is a trench and shafts for the working of the curtain. Broad entrances lead to the orchestra which was reserved for the seats of honor. If the altar in

Arles with swans in the style of the Ara Pacis came from the theater, it would prove the original building to have been finished in the period of Augustus,[16] but the columns of Carrara marble and the African marble used seem to testify to a remodeling during the second century. The largest theater in Gaul is the one in Autun (Augustodunum), built for 13,000 spectators. It was also used for gladiatorial fights and animal baitings; therefore, the lowest seats are placed on top of a high podium.

The theater at Vienne is almost as large as the one at Autun.[17] Above its two galleries it has an

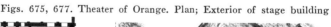

Figs. 675, 677. Theater of Orange. Plan; Exterior of stage building

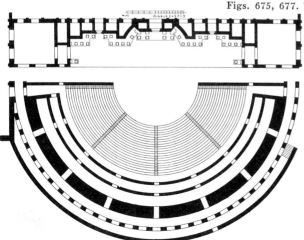

Fig. 676. Theater of Orange. Interior

upper portico and again the substructure for a temple connected with the theater. It was dedicated to Apollo. Two vaulted galleries open up with vomitoria to the cavea, which accommodated about 10,000 spectators. The orchestra has four low steps in white marble and one in violet breccia for the seats of honor. A balustrade of green cipolin marble separated it from the cavea. The proscaenium was decorated with niches and pilasters. Reliefs, one with animals, and a caryatid probably decorated the scaenae frons. Other important theaters are in Vaison-la Romaine (Vasio) (Fig. 672)[18] and in Lyon (Lugdunum) with a smaller theater next to it (Fig. 673).[19] The large theater is well preserved. A model was made and exhibited in Frankfurt-am-Main in 1937 (Fig. 674). Both these theaters have trenches for the curtain.

At Orange (Arausio) the amphitheater has disappeared, but the theater is the best preserved in France (Figs. 675-679).[20] It is a unified building with a high impressive outside, as well as inside façade. The cavea is built on a hillside, and beside it is the rounded end of a circus which stretches along and beyond its west side (Fig. 678)[21]—a combination which occurs in a different manner also at Aezani and Pessinus (see below, Fig. 743). The outer uppermost parts of the cavea are built up freely on arches, and a covered colonnade runs around it at the upper rim. An outside staircase ascends the hill to the uppermost seats. The free standing parts of the auditorium are provided with staircases and roofed galleries leading to the dif-

ferent sections. The high tower-like sidebuildings, the versurae, corresponding to the Greek paraskenia, open with arcades in two stories and provide staircases leading to doors for the upper galleries. They were certainly used for dressing rooms, rehearsals, and the preparation of movable properties, for behind the scaenae frons there are only some small recesses. These open on a long corridor-like room, which in turn opens to the outside with an arcade. In the upper stories there are blind arcades. This outer façade fronted a peristyle whose north portico was connected with the scene building. The colonnaded court thus served as a foyer as at Minturnae (above, p. 192f.) and in accordance with Vitruvius (v,9,1) provided shelter and recreation in case of rain. Above the blind arcades are two rows of brackets or corbels, the lower ones with round sinkings, the upper pierced with circular holes to fix the masts which carried the roof over the stage (Fig. 677). The square slots for the cantilevers of the stage roof are seen above the scaenae frons (Fig. 676). This inner façade has two stories of decoration above the regia, three over the hospitalia. In the center above the deep rounded exedra for the regia is a large niche in which stood the statue of an emperor, the torso of which has been found. The sides were ornamented with statues, friezes—one with centaurs—and mosaic pictures. Columns of granite, green, yellow, and white marble stood before the niches. This scaenae frons is 36 meters high and 103 broad (Fig. 679).[22] There are arrangements for raising and lowering a curtain.[23]

Figs. 678-679. Theater of Orange. Theater combined with circus: Scaenae frons

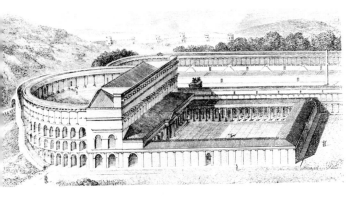

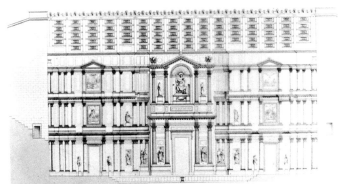

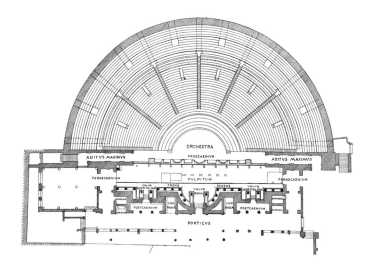

Figs. 680-684. Theater of Merida. Plan; Orchestra; Scaenae frons; Arched outer entrance to staircase; Colonnaded court behind stage building

In Belgium (Belgica), western Germany (Germania Romana), and southwestern England (Britannia), which had been only partly occupied by the Roman armies, there also are many amphitheaters, for example in Trèves (Trier, Augusta Treverorum), Mayence (Mainz, Mogontiacum), and Cologne (Köln on the Rhine, Colonia Agrippinensis). They are, however, more modest than those in France and were often built wholly or partly of wood. Sometimes they were intended for both amphitheatrical and theatrical use, and such mixed buildings are also found in northern France (demi-amphithéâtres or théâtres mixtes).[24] Only a few real theaters for scenic plays are found in these and the northern Roman provinces, for example in Augst (Augusta Rauricorum).[25]

It is different in Spain (Hispania) which, like Gaul, had become a Roman province in the first century B.C. Thus the grandiose theater of Merida (Emerita) in Lusitania (western Spain) was built and completed in 18 B.C. by Agrippa, but was renewed and redecorated by Hadrian (117-138) in A.D. 135 (Figs. 680-684).[26] The orchestra with the steps for the bisellia is paved with marble (Figs. 680-681). Long vaulted entrances (aditus maximus) lead from outer arches (Fig. 683) into the orchestra and to the precinctio behind the parapet separating the seats of honor from the cavea; fifteen other exterior entrances lead to the staircases and vomitoria. The proscaenium has three rounded and four rectangular niches and, at the ends, two little staircases leading up to the (originally wooden) pulpitum. The scaenae frons (Figs. 680-682) has a deep, rounded niche for the regia and flat rectangular niches for the hospitalia. Staircases lead down to the pulpitum, framed by columns following the curves of the niches. All the columns stand on a high podium; and they are so far removed from the wall that statues on high pedestals could be set up between the columns and before the wall (Fig. 682).

Twelve little shaft-holes in line with the proscaenium testify to a drop curtain. The postscaenium is reduced to two rooms behind the hospitalia, opening, like the regia, on the rear portico. This colonnade connects the two parascaenia at the sides and is part of the colonnaded peristyle which served as a pleasant walk during intermissions or as a refuge during rainstorms (Fig. 684). That tragedies were given in Spain is also testified by Philostratus (*Apollonios of Tyana*, v,9; cf. Ch. XV, p. 243). He tells how the inhabitants of Sevilla (Hispalis in Baetica) were so frightened by the gaping masks, the stuffed-out bodies, and the high stilts of the actors that they fled out of the theater. In Merida there were also an amphitheater and a circus; a large amphitheater is preserved in Italica; and a large theater and a circus are in Saguntum.[27]

The northern coastland of Africa became a Roman province in 146 B.C. when Carthage, the Punic capital, was captured and destroyed by Scipio Africanus. More and more land was won for Roman civilization after the wild beasts had been captured for the venationes in the amphitheaters, and after the Sahara desert had been pushed back by irrigation—both done on a large scale. Amphitheaters were then built in Carthage, Leptis Magna, and other cities. The best preserved amphitheater is in El-Djem (Thysdrus).[28] The preserved Roman buildings belong mostly to the second century A.D. when the Antonines (138-192) and particularly Septimius Severus (193-211), who was born in Africa, took interest in this province. The plays kept their religious character, for they were given mostly by the highest priests of the provinces; and some have chapels on top of the uppermost rim, as in the theater of Pompey. There are well-preserved theaters in Timgad, Djemila, and Dugga in Algiers—excavated by the French—and in Sabratha and Leptis Magna—excavated and admirably restored by Italian scholars.

Timgad (Thamugadi) in Numidia (Algiers) has been well preserved—together with the whole city—by the sand of the Sahara (Figs. 685-687).[29] It is a good example of a Roman class theater which gives separate seats to the different classes of Roman society. High parapets separate the orchestra with its shallow steps from the lower gallery, and another parapet separates this from the higher gallery. Entrances are through the colonnade on the top of the cavea, which is partly built on a hillside, and through vaulted corridors, which begin at the side entrances. The front of the pulpitum is deco-

Fig. 686. Theater of Timgad

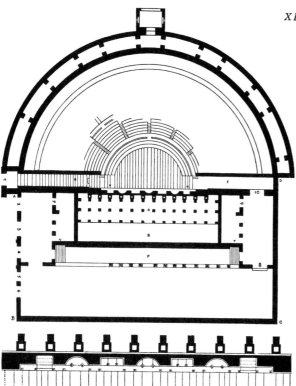

Figs. 685, 687. Plan of theater of Timgad and provision for curtain

The theater in Djemila (Gemila) also has a high terrace behind the scaenae frons, from which the actors could make an effective entrance down to the pulpitum, or they could reach it through the large side buildings. The front of the podium (proscaenium) has, like Timgad, three rounded and two rectangular niches, while at the sides are the little "phlyakes" staircases (Fig. 688).[30] The wall of the proscaenium is decorated with Corinthian engaged pilasters, opposite which originally stood small free-standing columns.

Figs. 689, 690. Theater of Dugga. Plan, and view of the stage from the cavea

rated with three rounded and two rectangular niches and—as often—two "phlyakes" staircases lead up to the stage at the sides. As the staircases are, of course, also in rectangular niches, this results in four rectangular and three round niches, an arrangement which is also found in the large theater of Pompeii, in Vienne (France), Djemila, and in Dugga. The wooden floor was supported by two rows of rectangular pillars. Behind the proscaenium are holes for the poles to which the curtain was attached (Fig. 687). The scaenae frons is lost. The large side buildings open onto the stage and, to the rear, onto a colonnade, which is higher than the stage and has to be reached by stairs. From this portico the actors reached the door of the scaenae frons and descended by other stairs to the platform.

Fig. 688. Theater of Djemila, proscaenium

Figs. 691, 693. Theater of Dugga. Scaenae frons, reconstructions of scaenae frons and stage

Fig. 692. Theater of Dugga, stage (scaenae frons, hyposcaenium, proscaenium)

Dugga (Thugga) in Tunis was built by P. Marcius Quadratus, a priest of the deified emperor Augustus (flamen divi Augusti) in the time of the emperors Antoninus Pius (138-161) and Marcus Aurelius (161-180). It is well preserved and was recently restored (Figs. 689-693).[31] The priest built "scaenam cum sipariis, et ornamentis omnibus, theatrum cum basilicis et porticis et xystis." That is, he erected "the stage building with the curtains and all ornaments, the auditorium including the basilicas or halls, colonnades and walks." We therefore must credit to him the whole building. The ornaments must be the thirty-four Corinthian columns which stand before the back wall on bases over five feet in height, and which follow the lines of the three niches, the semi-circular one for the regia and the rectangular ones for the hospitalia. Before each door two larger columns support a stretch of entablature, above which statues were probably set up in aediculae. At the top was the contrivance for the siparii, as we see them on the relief from San Elia (Fig. 629). In the central niche stood the statue of an emperor, probably one of the Antonines. Behind the scaenae frons four irregular rooms lead to the portico, from which the actors reached the doors. It also connects the two side halls, which are probably the basilicas of the inscription. Thus this portico connected all parts of the theater with each other. The large exedra on the outside may belong to the xystos. From the side buildings, which served for preparation rooms, wardrobes, and dressing rooms,

the stage was reached by side doors. Small staircases led down to the lower level, and up to the tribunalia and to the covered interior corridors, which opened up through vomitoria to the radiating staircases. Most spectators entered through the vaulted side passages; a few went below the tribunalia to the seats of honor. The others went through the passageway behind the lowest parapet and thus came to a broad stairway with fifty-two steps. This stairway led up to the principal one of the five entrances leading in from the outside through a semicircular wall, which was the back wall of an arcade and opened to the uppermost gallery in thirty-one arches. The parapet behind the five shallow steps in the orchestra for the seats of honor had a bronze gate in the center, so that the guests of honor could also come down the central stairs and reach their chairs from above. The pulpitum, like those in other African theaters, had in the front three semicircular and two rectangular niches flanked by small flights of stairs (Fig. 692). Under the wooden floor of the stage, supported on small pillars, was a lower floor, from which a trap door opened in the center of the stage for the appearance of ghosts. There was also scenic machinery and a curtain which could be manipulated from the side (see Fig. 693). In a cubicle at the side was a peephole at eye level and an opening large enough to allow a man to crawl through to the hyposcaenium or whisper to the actors or direct the stagehands when it was time to move the curtains or let ghostly apparitions arise from the trapdoor

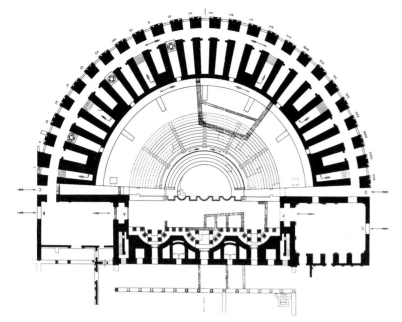

Figs. 694, 695. Theater of Sabratha. Plan; Stage with scaenae frons reconstructed

built by Septimius Severus in Rome[33] and to other nymphaea in Asia Minor (see below, p. 210). It certainly provided the actors with most effective entries, particularly through the regia. The actors came from the portico behind the scene building, from which they mounted a few steps, could pause on the platform in the doorway, where they would appear tall and dignified, and then step slowly down to the stage between the colorful columns. The front of the stage (the front wall of the hyposcenium or the proscenium) had again, like the other African theaters, three rounded and two rectangular niches, while little staircases led up from the sides. Reliefs on the front depict the plays given there, tragedy and mime (see Ch. XV, Figs. 785-786), and figures of the three Graces, Paris and Venus, Muses, Tyche-Fortuna, and personifications of Roma and Sabratha clasping hands, surrounded by warriors. Behind the proscenium is the provision for a curtain. Behind the deep scaenae frons are four small irregular rooms opening on the same portico as the entrances to the stage. The side buildings are large halls which can be entered from the portico, serving as a foyer. They can be reached also from the outside, and from the stage. Inner staircases of these side buildings lead up to the corridor between the first and second galleries. The twenty-four arches of the outer façade of the cavea lead to six ramps with steps to the upper cavea, while five passages go directly to the inner covered corridor. From here doors lead to the open corridor, from which one ascended to the middle gallery. Other ramps lead to the vomitoria in the different sections. The lowest corridor is behind the parapet which separates the shallow steps of the magistrates from the lower gallery, to the seats of which one ascended on the outer radiating staircases. The marble parapet ended in dolphins. The small orchestra is paved with white marble. Orchestra and lowest corridor were reached through the long passages leading in from the outermost arcades or from the side buildings. Sabratha thus had a perfect system of radiating vaulted passages between radiating walls, outer and inner semicircular corridors, ramps, and staircases for use of the audience.

Leptis Magna in Tripoli also has been excavated and excellently restored by Italian scholars, and it will soon be published in full by Caputo (Figs. 696-699).[34] It was built in the time of the emperor Augustus, but it received many refinements and decorative and practical additions under the later emperors. The original theater was probably similar to the theater of Pompey in Rome (Figs. 630-631), for it also had a temple on the uppermost rim of the cavea. This temple was broader than it was deep

Sabratha in Tripolitana was built in the period of Septimius Severus about A.D. 200, and it is the largest theater found in Africa. It was excavated by Giacomo Guidi and splendidly restored by Giuseppe Caputo. It has the most effective scaenae frons of any Roman theater preserved in three stories (Figs. 694-695).[32] There are ninety-six columns arranged before the high back wall, decreasing in height in each upper story. Larger columns on separate bases and with separate entablature stand before the three large niches, through which the actors passed from the regia and the hospitalia. Between and outside the doors the columns are placed on a common podium. Larger columns flank the side entrances from the versurae (parascenia), and smaller columns stand before the niches in the back wall. The material used for the columns is white marble, violet pavonazzetto, green cipollino, and black granite. The façade with its seven divisions is similar to the Septizonium

Figs. 696-699. Theater of Leptis Magna. Orchestra and auditorium; Additus maximus and tribunal; Scaenae frons; Regia

because it had to be adapted to the upper colonnade. The theater was dedicated in A.D. 1-2 by the proconsul Rubellius Blandus. In A.D. 35/6 a native Punic woman, Suphunibal Ornatrix, the daughter of Hannibal Rufus, gave the money for the accompanying temple which was dedicated to Ceres Augusta. Another temple, dedicated to Caesar, Augustus, and Livia was built, probably in the Claudian period, in the portico behind the scene building. This portico served as a foyer and, as in Corinth, included a fountain. An altar, perhaps for Bacchus, was dedicated by a flamen Titus Claudius Sextus. The orchestra has flat steps and a pavement of painted stucco. A broad paved entrance leads to it from the outside between the cavea and the versurae (Figs. 696-697). Above the inner end is the box for the magistrate who provided for the plays. An inscription at this place informs us that this box was built in A.D. 10-14.

The scaenae frons of the theater of Leptis Magna was originally in stone. The new façade in marble (Figs. 698-699) was dedicated by L. Hedius Rufus Lollianus Avitus, who was proconsul about 159-160 in the time of Antoninus Pius. There were originally three stories as in Sabratha (Fig. 695), but only the proscenium and the lower order have been reconstructed. The columns are of white marble, red breccia, green cipollino, and for the epistyle a bluish marble is used, which resembles Hymettus marble. The columns stand on a high podium, following the retreating curves of the niches for the regia and the hospitalia. Single larger columns frame the staircases, on which the actors descended to the pulpitum (Fig. 699). Large statues stood between the columns on the podium; small statues stood in the six rounded niches of the front wall of the pulpitum.

Thus all the scaenae frontes of the African theaters erected in the later second century, when this coastland to the south of the Mediterranean sea flourished, are almost identical (Figs. 685-699). They are all enriched by colorful columns, and large exedrae and rectangular recesses. With their movements, projecting forward and receding backward, they make contrasts of deep shadows and sharp lights, which almost dissolve the wall. Behind the scaenae frons lie colonnades connecting the deep side buildings. These have become large rooms or halls, sometimes called basilicas. They have taken over the functions of the scaena for dressing rooms, wardrobes, and rooms for preparation of the shows. The postscaenium, the rooms behind the scaenae frons, decreases and the space for the decoration increases. Roman love of luxury and ostentatious display created architectural masterpieces in these African provinces.

While the Romans brought a new civilization to northern Africa, western Asia had long been colonized by the Greeks and had a Greek Hellenistic culture, which the Roman conquerors had also accepted. There were many Hellenistic theaters but no amphitheaters built by the Greeks. Many amphitheaters were, therefore, erected by the Romans; the first was the one in Caesarea in Palestine built by Herod, in which he celebrated contests in honor of Augustus in 8 B.C. (Josephus, *Ant. Jud.*, xv,9,6), and in which Titus in A.D. 70, only eighty years later, had many Jewish prisoners killed in gladiatorial fights and in combats with wild beasts (Josephus, *Ant. Jud.*, xvi,5,1).[35] The best preserved amphitheater is in Pergamon. Purely Roman theater buildings, were, however, erected only in remote places where the Greek influence had not reached or was weak. Thus we find theaters newly built in the Roman imperial period in southern Asia Minor (Aspendus), in the interior (Palmyra) and in Semitic Arabia (Bosra and Philippopolis) and Palestine (Amman and Eš-Šuhba).

The best preserved purely Roman theater in Asia is the one erected at Aspendus in Pamphylia in southern Asia Minor. It is perhaps the most important Roman building of the province of Pamphylia (Figs. 700-706).[36] It was designed by the architect Zeno, son of Theodorus, during the reign of Marcus Aurelius (161-180), and it was dedicated to the gods and to the imperial house. This theater by Zeno shows the final culmination of the practical as well as representative ideas of Roman theater architecture. Although part of the semicircular cavea is built against the east slope of the Acropolis of Aspendus, the upper part stands up freely and a portico supported by fifty arches runs around the top. The cavea is broader than the scene building, so that the vaulted side entrances, beginning at the

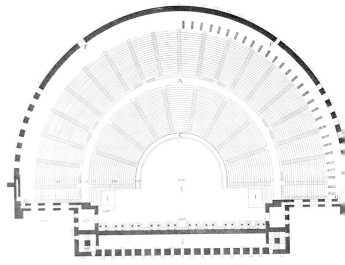

Fig. 700. Theater of Aspendus. Plan

end of the outer wall of the cavea, are long walks leading into the side buildings which open with the lower doors on the pulpitum (Figs. 700-702). Above the entrances are the boxes for the magistrates which could be reached only from the side buildings by a staircase. Other staircases in the versurae led to doors opening on the praecinctio between the first and second gallery and at the upper story on the arcaded portico. The building is thus a perfect unit (see Fig. 701). The scaenae frons is luxuriously decorated with about forty free-standing columns (see the reconstruction, Fig. 705; cf. Fig. 706). They are nearly all lost, but the parts which were bound into the wall are well preserved (Fig. 704). The columns stood on a high podium in groups of two each between the five doors of the rear wall. The wall, in contrast to the African and many other theaters (see Figs. 673-676, 679-682, 689-691, 694-695, 698-699, 707), has no receding niches cutting into it, but is straight. The common socles of the columns as well as the entablature above them and in the second story run back to the wall. The entablature is richly decorated with cymatia, scrolls, and garlands carried by ox skulls. The upper story is crowned by gables over each of the ten groups of two columns, but in the center is a large pediment above two pairs of columns, decorated with the figure of Dionysus between scrolls. Thus there are only nine smaller pediments which alternate in curved and triangular forms. They form a kind of aedicula or tabernacle. Smaller aediculae of the same form are between the groups of columns in the back wall, like tabernacles for statues. That there was a wooden roof above this luxurious façade is shown by sinkings in the back wall and traces for cantilever trusses at the side buildings, which rose from the back wall toward the front (Figs. 701-705). They were held by poles, for which two rows of corbels are set in the outer façade of the scene building (Fig. 702), like those for the velum at the

Figs. 705, 706. Aspendus. Pulpitum with scaenae frons and stage roof, reconstruction; Detail of entablature

Figs. 701, 702. Theater of Aspendus. General view; exterior

Fig. 703. Aspendus. Sections

Fig. 704. Actual state of scaenae frons

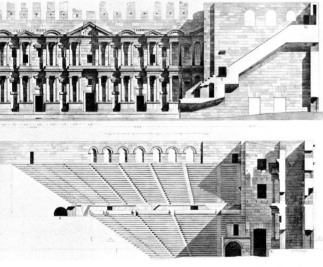

outside of auditoria. The upper ones have circular holes, the lower round sinkings for the poles. This outer wall is that of a high and shallow corridor, which, instead of a postscaenium, connects the two side buildings. One enters it through five doors decreasing in size toward the sides, opposite to the five doors which lead to the pulpitum. Above are small square windows, and still smaller ones lighten up the staircases in the versurae. In the second story are windows in arched openings corresponding to the upper story of the scaenae frons, and then again two rows of small rectangular windows. The exterior view (Fig. 702) shows best the complete fusion of auditorium and stage building (Fig. 703).

In contrast to Aspendus and in agreement with the western and African theaters, most Roman theaters in Asia have a large central niche for the regia and smaller niches for the side doors, which cut deeply into the sustaining wall. A good example is

209

Fig. 707. Theater of Palmyra. Elevation of scaenae frons and plan of stage

Palmyra (Fig. 707).[37] It was built in the Hadrianic period, with columns on a high common pedestal following the rounded central and the rectangular side niches, for the main doors. Other doors lead on to the pulpitum at the ends of the back wall and from the side buildings. Larger columns standing on their own pedestals before the regia carry a pediment and frame a niche above the door. The theater in Antioch, the capital of Syria founded by Seleucus Nicator about 300 B.C., must have been similar to the one in Palmyra. Trajan rebuilt the scaenae frons after the earthquake of 114/5 and Malalas (*Chronographia*, ed. Dindorf, 1831, p. 276) says that the emperor set up a copy of the celebrated Tyche of Antioch "on top of four columns in the middle of the nymphaeum of the proscaenium."[38] This use of the word nymphaeum indicates the great central hemicycle deep enough to contain the four columns. The nymphaea in Asia Minor—for example that in Aspendus[39]—rival indeed the scaenae frontes in luxur-

ious decoration. Perhaps the same architects built both, and it could well be that the basins before the nymphaea as well as the basins in the theaters were occasionally used for the popular aquacades in the late Roman period, with similar baroque backgrounds used as real or as imitated nymphaea (see Ch. XV, p. 237).

Another theater of the same type was in Amman, the Greek Philadelphia, named originally from the Ammonites in Palestine, later captured and renamed by Ptolemy II Philadelphus. Situated near the Dead Sea, it is now the capital of Transjordan. It has a very well preserved auditorium (Figs. 708-709).[40] A few very imposing columns of the scaenae frons with their Corinthian capitals are preserved (Fig. 709).

Figs. 708, 709. Theater of Amman. Auditorium; View through scaenae frons

The theater at Daphne, the suburb of Antioch-on-the-Orontes, was built in the time of Vespasian in a bowl formed by the encircling hillside.[41] The pulpitum has a straight front without niches which prolongs the walls of the parodoi. The orchestra is separated from the cavea by a stone barrier. In the center of the orchestra is a circular slab, with a depression for an altar, or for a fountainhead, to which water channels lead. A gutter around the orchestra may have been used to convert it into a water basin for aquacades. The Corinthian architecture of the scaenae frons is of good workmanship.

To the third century belong the theaters in Bosra (Fig. 710)[42] with three broad flat rounded niches in the scaenae frons, and those in Philippopolis in Arabia and Eš-Šuhba in Israel, with a flat background wall (Fig. 711).[43] The decoration is much simpler than in the second-century examples. The postscaenium is no longer an open, but a closed corridor behind the scaenae frons, connecting the two small parascenia with staircases and the cavea up to the portico above the uppermost row of seats.

All parts communicate with each other and make the auditorium easily accessible from all sides.

The Greeks of the mainland had their roots in classical civilization. After the country had become a Macedonian and later a Roman province, Athens still remained the spiritual capital of the Greek world. The Greeks kept to their classical forms of performances and accepted only late the Hellenistic type of the theater building (see above, Ch. IX). They did not build amphitheaters, with the exception of the one in the Roman colony in Corinth, built there on the ruins of the Greek Corinth.

Athens itself was reached by the Roman form of the theater in the Antonine period when the rich sophist Herodes Atticus honored the memory of his wife, Regilla, who died A.D. 161, with the erection of a theater on the southwest slope of the Acropolis, as a counterpart to the theater of Dionysus on the southeast slope. The cavea is laid on the slope of the Acropolis, but is crowned by a Roman semicircular surrounding portico (Figs. 712-716).[44] The scene

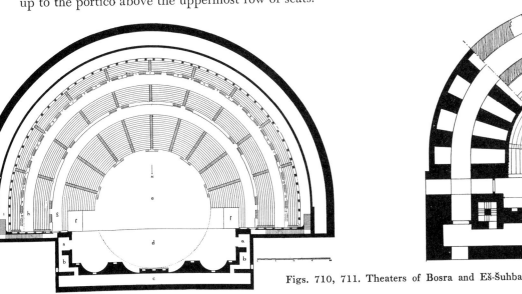

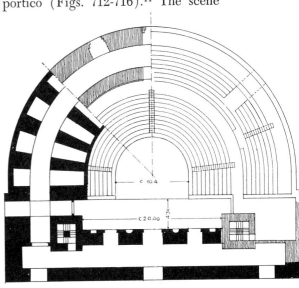

Figs. 710, 711. Theaters of Bosra and Eš-Šuhba

Figs. 712. Theater built by Herodes Atticus, Athens. Plan

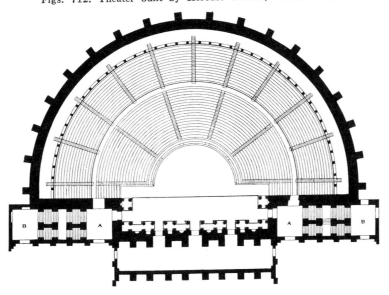

Fig. 713. Theater of Herodes Atticus. Exterior

Fig. 714a. Theater of Herodes Atticus, Athens

building opens up with arches set upon pilasters in the Roman manner (Fig. 713). The postscaenium is a hall entered from the sides. The sidebuildings extend the full length of the parodoi. They open below on the stage; to the cavea over staircases to the praecinctio, the semicircular passageway, which separates the two galleries; and farther up to the portico (Fig. 714). Thus the theater is a unit in the Roman style. The scaenae frons is decorated with one row of pilasters opposite which stand columns raised on high pedestals. The entablature was crowned with triangular and curved pediments. Between the doors and above the regia are niches for statues. In the upper story are arched openings. It is doubtful whether a roof of cedarwood, mentioned by Philostratus (*Vitae Sophistarum*, II,1,5 [p. 551] and II,5,8 [p. 571]) belonged to this theater rather than to the odeion on the market place, which Herodes Atticus probably renewed (see Ch. XIII,

Fig. 714b. Theater of Herodes Atticus. Stage and versura

Fig. 715. Theater of Herodes Atticus. Reconstruction, Fiechter

Fig. 716. Theater of Herodes Atticus. Reconstruction, Versakis

p. 174-177 and Figs. 617-619 and below p. 221). It is likely that this theater of Herodes had only the ordinary wooden roof over the pulpitum (Figs. 715-716). It is well equipped for scenic plays, which were at that time displaced by gladiatorial shows in the theater of Dionysus (see below, p. 215).

Graeco-Roman Theaters

Many of the Greek theaters on the mainland and in Asia Minor were modernized in the Roman period. The first to be reconstructed in the Roman style was the sacred theater of Dionysus Eleuthereus in Athens (Figs. 717-725).[45] It was dedicated to the Emperor Nero, probably in 61/2, or at the earliest in 54/5, by Claudius Novius, a Romanized Greek. The inscription with the dedication to Nero and Dionysus was engraved on the architrave over the central aedicula of the scaenae frons (Figs. 721-722).[46] Dionysus had to share the possession of the theater with Nero also in Lisbon (*CIL*, II,183) and in Aspendos with the imperial house (see above, p. 208). At Athens the large marble scaenae frons

Fig. 717. Theater of Dionysus, Athens. View of orchestra

Fig. 718. Theater of Dionysus, Athens. Orchestra and stage

in two stories has been best reconstructed by Fiechter with some improvements by von Gerkan (Figs. 721-723). The new stage was brought forward and cut off a large part of the orchestra, which was paved with white, bluish, and reddish marble in a geometric pattern (Figs. 717-718). In the center is a large stone with a round depression for an altar. The proscaenium wall was probably smooth. Behind it are shafts for the curtain (Figs. 724a-b). The low Hellenistic colonnaded parascenia flanked the high versurae, which, however, were not connected with the auditorium. The parodoi always

remained open (Figs. 719-720). The Athenian theater, therefore, never attained the unity of a genuine Roman building.

When Hadrian visited Athens in A.D. 126, each tribe dedicated to him his portrait statue in their allotted sections. A box was erected for him in the auditorium, and new seats of honor were set up above the older ones at the edge of the orchestra. These seats in the lowermost part of the auditorium were no longer the best ones, because a parapet was erected closely in front of them (Figs. 717-719, 725). The orchestra had become a conistra or

Figs. 719, 720. Theater of Dionysus. Plans: period of Nero; latest period

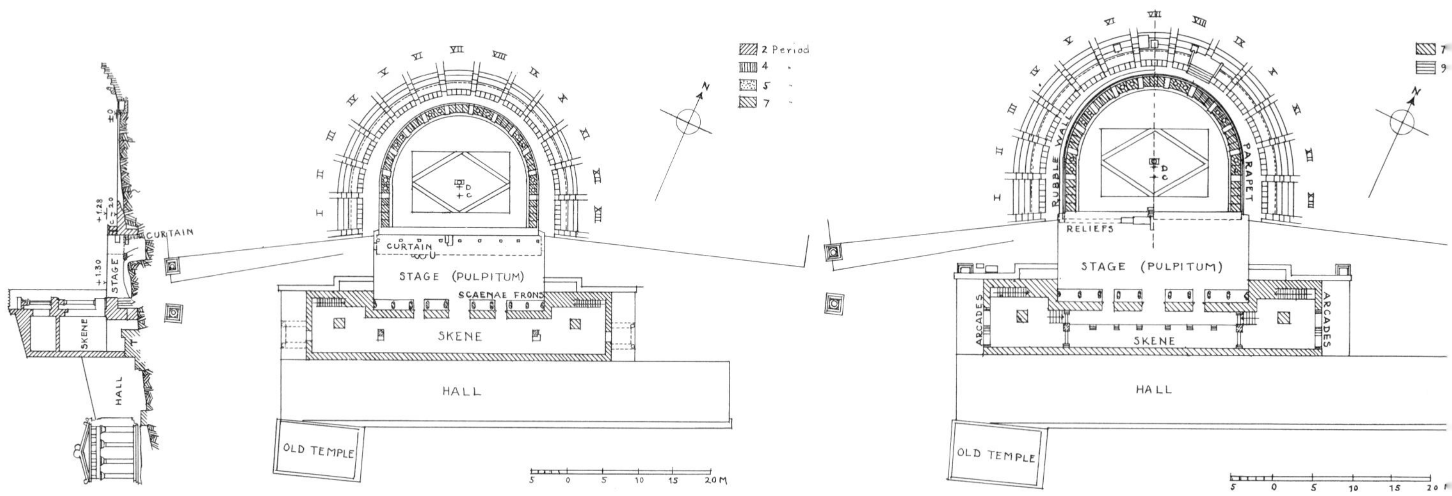

Figs. 721, 722. Theater of Dionysus. Reconstructions of the Neronic stage, Fiechter

arena, which served for gladiatorial shows and animal baitings. The orator Dio Chrysostomus in his discourse to the people of Rhodes (*Oratio*, XXXI, 121), blames the Athenians because they look on gladiatorial shows "in their theater under the very walls of the Acropolis, in the place where they put up their Dionysus in the orchestra, so that often a fighter is slaughtered among the very seats in which the hierophant and the other priests must sit." Such occurrence may have been the reason for erecting the parapet.

After the destruction of Athens by the Herulians in 267, the archon Phaedrus again remodelled the stage in about A.D. 270. The front wall of the pulpitum had the old "phlyakes" stairs in the center; a geison block of the stoa of Eumenes is reused for the uppermost step. At its right half, which is alone preserved, the well-known earlier reliefs with the story of Dionysus are reused (Ch. II, Figs. 53-55). They served, however, only as structural material, not as decoration. All the heads of the figures were broken off along with the upper part of the background, and a heavy cornice was laid over them. I believe that they were originally the four sides of an altar dedicated to Dionysus, either of the Neronic or of the Hadrianic period.[47] The ancient theater of Dionysus was desecrated and no longer required an altar, for the scenic and thymelic plays in honor of the god were transferred to the theater of Herodes Atticus (Figs. 712-716). Between the reliefs are niches in which kneeling satyrs, probably taken from the older stage, were placed, but they do not support anything. The niches as well as the reliefs were thickly covered with stucco, painted red. The front wall of this latest stage as well as the parapet around the orchestra were reinforced by a rubble wall so as to be waterproof (Figs. 717-718 and 720). The water channel was covered with marble slabs between the old bridge stones. Thus the orchestra could be transformed into a watertight basin for the aquacades or water ballets that were so popular in the late Roman period[48] (see Ch. XV, Fig. 784). The parapet and the stage wall cut off the parodoi

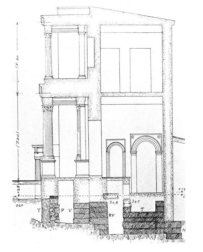

Fig. 723. Reconstruction of the Neronic stage, side view, von Gerkan

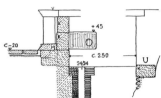

Fig. 724a. Shaft for curtain, b. cross-section

from the orchestra; and the side entrances, therefore, led behind the parapet into the lowest praecinctio to the seats of honor and to the staircases in the auditorium. In the postscaenium the dressing rooms were cancelled and one continuous hall was formed, entered by double arches from the outside on the east and west (Figs. 720 and 723).

Fig. 725. Theater of Dionysus. Seats of honor and Roman parapet

The theater of Dionysus was in continuous and intensive use for many centuries, but in the later periods the crude Roman amusements, which were ordinarily given in the amphitheaters, replaced the sacred performances.

An amphitheater was built in Corinth only in the

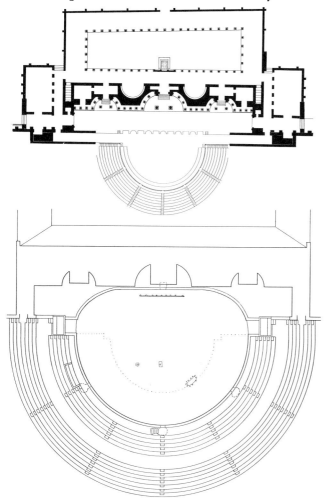

Figs. 726, 727. Corinth, restored plan of Roman theater; restored plan of arena

late Roman period. Before this was done the theater in this city, so thoroughly investigated by Stillwell, received a "phlyakes" stage in the earliest Roman period. It was rebuilt in the early first century A.D. in the Roman style with a straight scaenae frons, but then in the Hadrianic period with three hemicycle exedrae and columns standing on a podium with entablature, which follow the regia and hospitalia with their curved lines (Figs. 726-729).[49] Between them the straight friezes were probably decorated with a gigantomachy, an amazonomachy, and the deeds of Heracles. At either end are large halls instead of the modest paraskenia in Athens, with staircases to the tribunes over the side entrances at the end of the long vaulted parodoi (aditi maximi). At the back of the scaenae frons is a rectangular colonnaded peristyle, probably planted as a garden, serving as foyer or lobby behind the scaena, in accordance with the prescription of Vitruvius for such porticos (v,9,1 and v,9,5): "post scaenam porticus . . . media spatia . . . adornanda viridibus videntur. . . ." ("Colonnades must be constructed behind the scaena . . . the space in the middle between the colonnades and open to the sky, ought to be embellished with green things. . . .") From this colonnade staircases flanked by pilasters and freestanding columns led down to the stage level. The front wall of the stage was of stone and had provision for a curtain. Later, in 211-217, the theater was again remodelled into a hunting theater for an expected visit of the emperor Caracalla (Fig. 727). The first ten rows of seats were removed, the rock was cut back and three small caverns or refuges were cut into it. A high wall decorated with paintings showing animal hunting (see Ch. XV, Fig. 839) surrounded the arena. The tiers of seats now terminated at the top of a podium, leaving the orchestra in the form of a sunken pit. At the same time the lowest seats got hereby a better view of the performances on the stage. Similar changes were made in the theaters of Assos, Magnesia, Pergamum, and

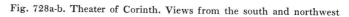

Fig. 728a-b. Theater of Corinth. Views from the south and northwest

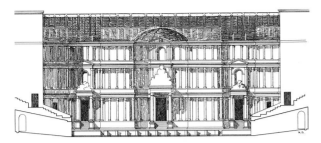

Fig. 729. Theater of Corinth. Scaenae frons, reconstruction

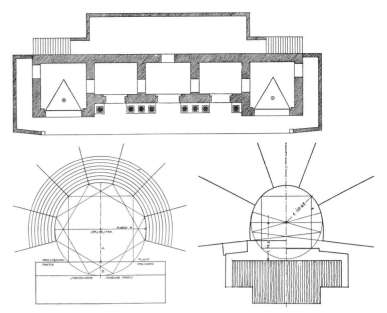

Figs. 730, 731. Theater of Magnesia. Plan of stage, and comparison with Vitruvius

Tyndaris. These changes enlarged the orchestra which was used for gladiatorial and animal combats. In the second half of the third century the orchestra level in Corinth was raised again, the lower seats were restored, the painted arena wall was partly destroyed, a gutter and a new parapet were built. The parapet was—as in Athens—reinforced and made waterproof by a masonry backing. This was probably done for the water ballets so popular in the imperial period.[50] The theater of Corinth seems to have been in use until the invasion of Alaric in A.D. 396.

The conservative city of Sparta held mostly non-scenic contests and games in honor of Leonidas and other heroes. It had a Hellenistic high stage introduced at a late date and that only in the form of a wooden rolling stage which was stored in a skenotheke, a shed in the parodos, and wheeled out over tracks on play days. This happened probably not before the first century B.C. When this wooden skene burnt down in the first century A.D. Vespasian erected the first architectural scaenae frons, decorated with columns standing on a podium, but without a permanent pulpitum. A temporary wooden stage about five feet high could have been erected. A permanent stage seems to have been built not before about A.D. 200.[51]

Stobi in Macedonia (now Jugoslavia) received a scaenae frons still later, in the Hadrianic period. It was connected with a shrine of Nemesis. It never had a stage. The five doors of the scaena led down by flights of five steps directly into the arena. Thus Stobi was a kind of half amphitheater, with a refuge for hunters, used for gladiatorial fights and venationes. The latter were still given at about A.D. 300.[52] A similar arena with a parapet was built in the theater at Philippi in Macedonia in the second century.[53]

In Asia Minor the rebuilding of Greek into Roman theaters led to many unusual forms. Magnesia, Priene, Ephesus and Miletus kept the height of the Hellenistic proskenion stage, but decorated its background with the Roman scaenae frons. Magnesia has the Greek form of the auditorium and the orchestra described by Vitruvius (Figs. 730-731).[54]

Fig. 732. Theater of Priene. Plan of Roman scaenae frons

The thyromata of the late Hellenistic stage were kept, but three columns were erected before them on each side between the doors and one each outside, next to the large paraskenia. The open side entrances over closed corridors are entered from the side rooms, from the second story of the scaena, and protected by high walls. These additions were probably made in the first century B.C. when Romaia, plays in honor of the Romans, were given here. The program included newly-written tragedies, satyr dramas, and comedies.[55] It is likely that the tragedies and satyr dramas were given in the orchestra, the comedies on the stage. Later the stage was brought farther forward, supported by pillars, at the same height as the Hellenistic proskenion. The Roman stage closed the open parodoi. Along the back of the scene building a terrace reached by side staircases led through a door into the central room opposite the regia.

Priene remained for a long time in its Hellenistic form (see Ch. IX, Figs. 416-425), but in the Antonine period it also received a modest scaenae frons (Fig. 732).[56] The thyromata wall was torn down, and farther back two semicircular niches framed by free-standing columns between the three doors were built up over the rear rooms of the scene building, which were vaulted to support the new heavy wall. The front wall of the proskenion remained standing. Between the columns thin walls of cement were erected. They were painted on yellow ground in white, black, and red to represent doors, with the exception of the three real doors of the Hellenistic proskenion (above, Fig. 424). There were no versurae and the parodoi remained open.

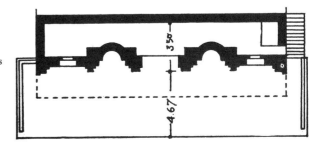

217

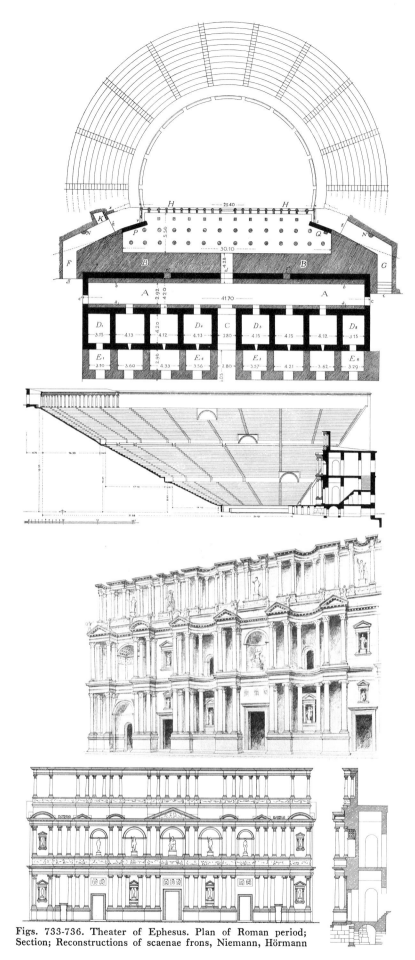

Figs. 733-736. Theater of Ephesus. Plan of Roman period; Section; Reconstructions of scaenae frons, Niemann, Hörmann

In the large theater of Ephesus, on the other hand, the front wall of the proskenion was moved forward in order to attain a deep Roman stage (Figs. 733-736).[57] Around A.D. 44 the remodelling began by moving the stage forward about 20 feet (6 m.) with the help of twenty-six columns in two rows and before them one row of ten square piers (Fig. 733). At the front, twenty-two Hellenistic pillars with engaged columns, including their threshold, were reused (cf. Figs. 441-447 in Ch. IX). This pulpitum closed off the open parodoi. Vaulted entrances led as ramps up to the stage. The main room of the stage building was vaulted. A scaenae frons dedicated in A.D. 66, reconstructed by Niemann (Fig. 735) and by Hörmann (Fig. 736), had five doors, columns on high podia, an architrave with sculptured friezes; in the second story were pediments and in both stories niches for statues. The details are not quite certain. Vaulted entrances led from arches of the outer wall to the diazomas (Fig. 734). In about 140-144 the orchestra, reduced by the pulpitum, was enlarged by cutting away the seats at the height of the pulpitum; and a parapet was laid around the orchestra, so that gladiatorial shows and animal fights could be presented. The intercolumnia of the proskenion were closed and niches added in the outermost ones. A colonnade was added at the edge of the uppermost gallery. Finally in the third century a third story was added to the scaenae frons (Figs. 734-736). There is no third story behind it in the scene building. The Romans loved façades, even if they represented an empty decoration.

The Hellenistic theater of Miletus was also rebuilt on the Roman plan (Figs. 737-739).[58] It had three galleries which could be entered from vaulted corridors by many doors. The floor of the pulpitum was laid like that in Ephesus, on three rows of pillars, but the front wall of the stage was of the height of the old proskenion with columns and three entrances to the hyposkenion. The scaenae frons behind the deep stage was laid out in the early imperial period, but it was rebuilt with richer decorations about the middle of the second century (Fig. 739). It had a deep central niche in the form of the segment of a circle, with four large columns before it, while the columns on pedestals follow the receding form of the niche. The same plan is used in three stories, and many tabernacles testify to the use of many statues. The orchestra was paved with red, violet, and bluish-white marble plaques. It was changed into an arena by cutting down the lowest seats. The parodoi were closed to the arena and became entrances to the stage (Fig. 737). A portico with cross vaulting on arches was added above the auditorium.

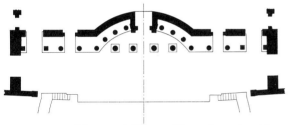

Figs. 737-739. Theater of Miletus. Views from the side and above; Plan of the scaenae frons

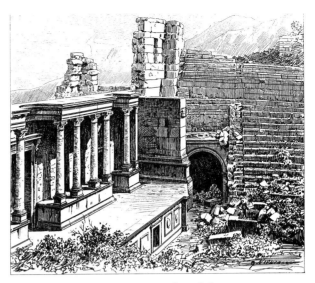

Fig. 740. Theater of Termessus. View of the stage

fights and baitings were held in the orchestra, thereby converting it into an arena. The parapet around the orchestra, which in other theaters separated the officials and guests of honor seated in the orchestra from the common folk, has here become a protection against the wild animals, as in the amphitheaters. The stage building belongs to the Antonine period.

The situation is similar in Sagalassus (Figs. 741-742).[60] The auditorium is built on a hillside in Greek fashion and extends beyond the semicircle by one wedge-shaped section on each side. But only the

Figs. 741, 742. Theater of Sagalassus. Plan; Reconstruction of the stage

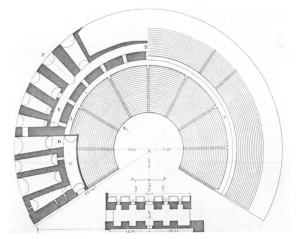

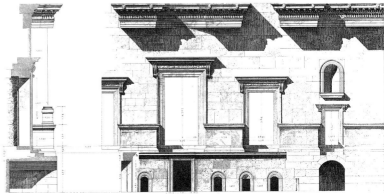

While the theaters of Priene, Ephesus, and Miletus are more Greek than Roman, the theaters in Termessus and Sagalassus in Pisidia are more Roman than Greek. Termessus (Fig. 740)[59] originally had an auditorium going beyond the half-circle and a stage building separated from it by open parodoi. Above the auditorium, however, was a Roman colonnade, closed on the outside, open to the inside. A broad staircase leads down from the colonnade to the lower gallery. The parodoi were later vaulted over and tribunals were built over their inner entrances. The stage building received a scaenae frons with five doors, before which columns with Roman composite capitals were erected on high pedestals in a straight line. Heavy side walls were erected to support a stage roof. The front wall of the podium is 2.36 meters in height, built up with square blocks and decorated with shields in framed plaques. Three doors, only 0.98 meters high, lead into the orchestra, which has a parapet 1.75 meters high to protect the spectators. It is clear that animal

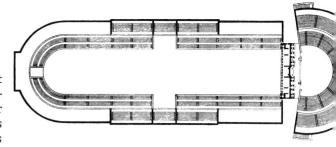

east part is built against the slope of a hill. The west portion is built up in the Roman manner on radiating walls and rising vaults. The semicircular corridor (diazoma) which separates the two galleries has behind it a concentric vaulted corridor, which opens with doors onto the open corridor. Narrow parodoi separate the auditorium and the stage building. The scaenae frons has five doors, in decreasing height, with niches for statues over the smaller doors and pairs of columns on high pedestals between the doors. The pulpitum is 2.77 meters high (9 feet), and is built with large stoneblocks. The center door is 2.09 meters high, and thus is usable by men, while the other doors are only 0.87 meters high, too small for human beings, and thus certainly meant for animals. It seems, therefore, that besides animal baiting, gladiatorial fights were also given in the orchestra.

The Greek world, with the exception of some places like Corinth, did not adopt the amphitheater from the Romans, as the formerly uncultivated provinces had done. If the masters of the ancient world did not wish to do without their beloved bloody games in the Greek provinces, they had to make provisions for them in the theater, as they did in Athens (see above, Figs. 717-720). This explains, therefore, the peculiar form of the theaters of Asia Minor. The correspondence to the Greek theater of Vitruvius is no more true for these Graeco-Roman theaters than for other Roman theaters of the Empire. One must not, therefore, conclude with Dörpfeld that Vitruvius must necessarily have known such theaters. All of them are much later than Vitruvius.[61]

In Aezani in Asia Minor an auditorium in the Greek horseshoe form was combined in the Hadrianic period with a circus or stadium in such a way that the scaenae frons of the shallow but high stage was at the same time a kind of triumphal arch serving as entrance to the circus (Figs. 743-744).[62] The scaenae frons has a central niche decorated with columns of larger size than the other columns, which stand about 6 feet from the wall. They are of composite order in the lower, of Corinthian order in the upper story. A similar combination is found in Pessinus, also in Asia Minor, only here the theater is not on an axis, but at right angles to the circus, in the middle of one flank.[63] In both cases there is no scenebuilding behind the empty façade.

Odea

The name odeion, Latin odeum, is derived from ode, song (ᾠδή). The odeum thus is a music hall for concerts and recitations which were accompanied by musical instruments (see Ch. I, pp. 3f.). The

Figs. 743, 744. Aizani, theater and circus. Plan; View of the ?

oldest known odeum was built by Pericles near the theater of Dionysus at Athens (see Ch. V, Fig. 237). It was destroyed by the army of Sulla in 86 B.C. and reconstructed in 52 B.C. at the expense of Ariobarzanes II of Cappadocia (63-52 B.C.) by two Roman architects, C. and M. Stallius (*CIA*, III,541). Just as in the case of this Periclean odeum, the music halls were often built in the vicinity of larger theaters. They are distinguished from them by the rectangular form of the outer walls which carry a roof (theatrum tectum), and they are always smaller than the open-air theaters. The oldest well-preserved Roman odeum, called theatrum tectum, is the small theater in Pompeii (Ch. XIII, Figs. 613-615). Other combinations of theater and odeum are testified for Naples and Taormina in Italy; and preserved in France at Lyon (Fig. 673) and Vienne; in

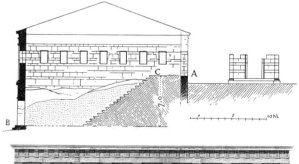

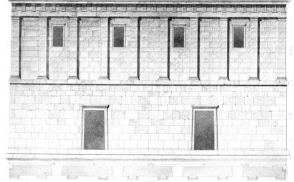

Figs. 745, 746. Odeum of Termessus. Section; Exterior

Syria at Amman (Philadelphia); in Pamphylia at Aspendus; and in Pisidia at Termessus (Figs. 745-746) and Sagalassus.[64] The finest odeum in Greece, according to Pausanias (VII,20) was the one in Patras, which was only surpassed in size and decoration by the one which Herodes Atticus had built in memory of his wife Regilla in Athens. It is generally assumed that this is the one on the southeast slope of the Acropolis (above, Figs. 712-716).

Not much later than the time when the Periclean odeum was restored, Agrippa, the general and son-in-law of Augustus, built a concert hall on the market-place of Athens, called the Agrippeion by Philostratus (*Vitae Sophistarum*, II, 5,4, and 8,4) and mentioned by Pausanias in his description of the Agora (I,8,6 and 14,1). This odeum must have been erected around 15 B.C., for Agrippa visited Athens in 16 and 14, not long before his death in 12 B.C. It has been excavated by American scholars and published in a model paper by Homer Thompson[65] (above, Figs. 617-619). It has been found in the same place where dances and songs in honor of Dionysus were performed and wooden bleachers erected, before the theater in the sanctuary of Dionysus was built. The original building had an auditorium which was square in plan, and which could seat about 1,000 persons. It had a long narrow stage and an orchestra of less than a half-circle with a small altar in the middle. The orchestra was paved with opus sectile in white Pentelic, gray-blue Hymettian, green marble from Carystus, purple and pink with white marble from the islands, red and yellow limestone, and black slate. The stage front was decorated with herms—the shafts were of green, the heads of white Pentelic marble, on a blue plinth—and crowned by a sima on which a lotus and palmette design is carved. To the north behind the scaena was a small entrance porch, to the south a long narrow lobby or foyer at the back of the auditorium. A balcony was laid around three sides. This building probably was to replace the Periclean building near the theater, whose many interior columns must have interfered with the view as well as with the acoustics, and thus was probably considered obsolete by the Romans.

The odeum in the Agora is thus a Roman building, but one developed from Hellenistic assembly halls, like the Bouleuterion of Miletus (Fig. 633),[66] built in 175-164 B.C., the ecclesiasterion in Priene,[67] and other meeting places of political bodies.[68] It is certainly the same type of rectangular building with a roof and sloping auditorium which was the model for the unified open-air theater of the Romans also (cf. the theater of Pompey, Ch. XIII, p. 181, Figs. 630-632). The walls of the upper stories of these assembly halls were strengthened by half columns or pilasters, between which windows admitted light. This is the case in the odeum of Agrippa as well as in later odea like the one in Termessus (Figs. 745-746)[69] and the one at Aosta in Piedmont (Fig. 747).[70] The latter has twelve small arched windows in the second story and four large arched openings in the uppermost story. The Roman odea improve the roofed buildings by reducing the orchestra, cutting off drastically the sides of the curved tiers, adding more windows, and eliminating the columns entirely, of which there still had been four in Miletus (Fig. 633).

Fig. 747. Odeum of Aosta. Exterior

It seems, however, that this last improvement brought disaster to the odeion of Agrippa in Athens. The span of 25 meters was too large for the construction of a room without any other support than the outer walls. It collapsed in the second century. The auditorium, therefore, was greatly reduced, by shifting the south wall to the north, so that the span was 7.66 meters less, and the auditorium could then seat not more than 500 persons. Instead of the podium and the north porch, a long open colonnade was erected, its entablature supported by six square piers decorated with colossal figures of tritons, flanked by pedestals for statues of seated philosophers (Fig. 619b). The odeum had become a lecture hall for the four great philosophical schools, for which Marcus Aurelius had created two chairs each, the incumbents to be chosen by the teacher of the Emperor, Herodes Atticus (Philostratus, II,2). I believe that this rhetor gave the celebrated roof of cedar wood which Philostratus mentions, not to the theater on the south slope of the Acropolis, which he built to replace the desecrated theater of Dionysus for scenic plays (see above, p. 211ff., Figs. 712-716), but to the odeum on the market place, which had become a university.[71] Such auditoria for

221

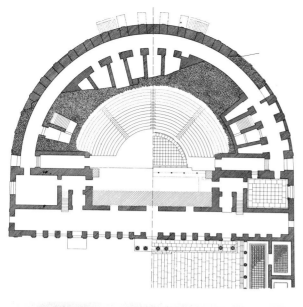

Figs. 748, 749. Odeum of Corinth. Plan; View from the north

lectures were sometimes incorporated in gymnasia as, for example, in Syracuse and in Epidaurus (Figs. 620-621)[72] and Sylleum in Pamphylia.[73]

Vitruvius (v,11,2) in his prescriptions for the Greek palaestra speaks of roomy recesses (exedrae) with seats in them, where philosophers, rhetoricians, and others who delight in learning may sit and converse. He mentions (v,11,1) that such buildings are not used in Italy. The Romans did not care for the intellectual and physical education which was the center of life for the Greeks. There seems to have been just one odeum in Rome, erected by Domitian in the Campus Martius 86 B.C. (Suetonius, *Domi-*

Fig. 750. Odeum of Butrinto. General view

tian, 5). The Romans preferred shows for the eyes, not active intellectual or bodily participation in exercises. Thus even odea, as well as many theaters, were changed into arenas for gladiatorial and animal fights, or for water ballets. This happened in Corinth, the odeum of which is mentioned by Pausanias (ii,3,6) and which has been excavated by American scholars and published in a complete way by Broneer (Figs. 748-749).[74] It was connected with the open-air theater by a colonnaded court. It had two galleries with seats for about 3,000 persons. The upper gallery was entered from higher ground by outer stairways which opened into the cavea by vomitoria. Erected toward the end of the first century, it was rebuilt by Herodes Atticus around 175 (Philostratus, *Vitae Sophistarum,* ii,2, p. 551). The floor and walls were revetted with marble. The columns of the scaenae frons were carved in different kinds of marble. About fifty years later, however, this elegant music hall was made into an arena. The stage was removed, the lowest tiers of seats cut away to erect a wall of about 2 meters, in order to enlarge the arena and to protect the spectators against the wild beasts. The rooms in the side buildings became cages for the animals or refuges for the hunters.

While the Romans built amphitheaters side by side with the theaters, the Greeks built music halls or auditoria even in remote parts of the Greek world during the imperial period. Thus a well-preserved odeum of small dimensions built in Roman brick work has been excavated in Butrinto in Albania (Fig. 750).[75] A strong wall reinforced by pilasters carried the roof. The stage building was vaulted. The auditorium and orchestra are in horseshoe form. Other odea are preserved in Gortyn in Crete,[76] Ephesus,[77] Amman in Transjordan,[78] and Cretopolis in Pisidia (Fig. 751).[79]

Fig. 751. Odeum of Cretopolis. Plan and section

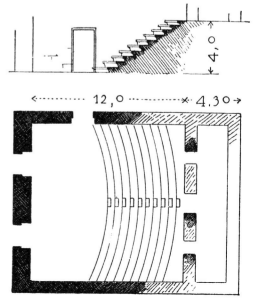

Sculptured Decorations

The Greek theater in the classical period had little sculptural ornament, except on the altar which stood in the center of the orchestra. A few portrait statues were erected to distinguished men, like Themistocles and Miltiades in the theater of Dionysus at Athens in the fifth century,[80] and the great tragic poets Aeschylus, Sophocles, and Euripides in the fourth century (see Ch. II, Figs. 64, 101, 108). In the Hellenistic period Menander was the first comic poet so honored (see Ch. VIII, Figs. 318-319). The background was not decorated with statues but was painted (Ch. IX, Figs. 446, 471-474). Even the figure of Demetrius mentioned by Athenaeus (xii,536a) was only painted (see Ch. IX, p. 124). A fine late Hellenistic example of an altar decorated in relief with satyr masks carrying full garlands of ivy, grapes, and acanthus has been found in the sanctuary of Dionysus (Fig. 752).[81] Broad fillets hang down and a rosette is carved above the center of each garland. The followers of Dionysus, satyrs and maenads, are well fitted for decoration in the sanctuary of the god. In the archaic period a relief with satyrs and maenads decorated some building. It was believed to be from the pediment of the oldest temple of Dionysus (Ch. V, Fig. 222). An altar had on its four sides the history of Dionysus. It is now used as building material in the front of the late stage of Phaedrus (Figs. 53-55; 717-720), but belongs either to the Neronic or—less likely—to the Hadrianic period.

Fig. 752. Altar found in sacred precinct of Dionysus, Athens

The same uncertainty of date is found among scholars for the kneeling figures of Sileni, used by Phaedrus in the niches between the reliefs (Figs. 53, 718).[82] They remained visible while the reliefs were covered with mortar. It is not certain what they originally carried, but it was probably an entablature. Again I believe that they are of the Neronic age, when the first Roman stage was built and dedicated to Nero and Dionysus. Herbig assumes that these and a third Silenus carried a basin for holy water. The replica in the Museo dei Conservatori on the Capitol in Rome carries a wineskin (Fig. 754);[83] the other, in the Louvre, a cushion (Fig. 753).[84] Both attributes are probably additions of the copyists. The original has been dated in the

Figs. 753, 754. Kneeling Sileni. Marble statues, Louvre; Capitoline Museum

223

third quarter of the 4th century B.C., which date I believe to be too early. The satyr in Athens probably belongs to the same Roman decoration of the theater of Dionysus as the large figures of Sileni, which have a pillar in the back and thus certainly had an architectural connection. The one with his hands at his side, his head leaning forward, his tail outlined against the pillar (Fig. 755),[85] must have had a companion; perhaps they stood as telamons at the versurae or paraskenia, like the Pans in the theaters of Segesta and of Pompey in Rome (see Ch. XIII, Figs. 603-604). The Papposileni, Father Silenus in goatskin (Figs. 756-757),[86] also originally supported some weight. Besides four small ones, there is the fragment of one colossal silenus (Fig. 756) which originally must have reached a height of about 3 meters. He also must have had a counterpart, while the smaller figures must have stood in one row somewhere in the scaenae frons. All have heavy mantles and long full beards. Only one (Fig. 757) has the head preserved. He wore a thick wreath which was originally enriched with bronze leaves, for which only the holes remain. He has pig's ears, and his head is lifted with a pathetic expression.

Figs. 755-757. Colossal Silenus; Fragment of large Silenus; Head of Silenus. Marble, Theater of Dionysus

Two women in full dresses with many folds are preserved only in their lower part.[87] The better preserved (Fig. 758) is 1.30 meters high. The right foot is missing. On the left foot there is a shoe on a high sole with ornate lacing. Both women stood on plinths about 1.30 meters high and both have pilasters at their backs. One (Fig. 758) has been found in the east, the other in the west part of the stage building. They are again companion pieces. Herbig explains them, probably rightly, as personifications of Tragedy and Comedy, comparing them to the same personifications on the relief of Archelaus (Ch. I, Fig. 2). Herbig dates the women in the Neronic-Flavian period, the sileni in the Hadrianic-Antonine period. I believe that they all belong to the Neronic stage.

It is to be regretted that these statues from the Athenian theater—and indeed most statues found in Roman theaters—cannot be seen any more in their precise architectural locations. We cannot completely visualize a Roman theater or odeum without its rich sculptural decoration. The Romans loved to assemble masses of statuary in their public places and particularly in their theaters. We learn that in 58 B.C. Marcus Aemilius Scaurus erected a wooden temporary theater with three thousand bronze statues standing between the columns. This was perhaps a kind of exhibition of the loot of Greek works of art which the Roman generals and consuls had assembled in Rome. Later copies of celebrated masterpieces were added to the originals. Thus an archaistic statue of Athena has been found in the odeum of Corinth (Fig. 759),[88] copies of classical statues in the theater of Corinth; and the Demeter and Kore, called the Herculaneum women from these statues, were found in the theater of Herculaneum. Dionysus himself, the god of the theatrical contests, was always a good choice, and we find him in the odeum of the Athenian Agora.[89] The satyrs, his followers, are used in a great number in Athens; groups of satyrs struggling with nymphs, in Daphne. The mask, his sacred symbol, is used on friezes, like the ones in Philippi and Pergamum (Ch. IX, Figs. 311-313, 380) and on oscilla, decorative marble disks, like one found in the theater at Vaison.[90] Caryatids and telamons, often in the guise of satyrs, take the place of pillars (Figs. 615, 755).[91] Since, however, many theaters in the Hellenistic and particularly in the Roman period were no longer connected with Dionysus but with other gods, statues of all kinds of gods—such as Athena, Aphrodite, and Demeter—were set up in the theaters. Portrait statues of emperors were erected in the theaters of Vaison and Orange in the central niche of the scaenae frons.[92] Statues of magistrates and deserving citizens were erected in a larger number

Fig. 758. Lower part of colossal female. Marble, Theater of Dionysus

Fig. 759. Archaistic Athena. Marble statue from Odeum in Corinth

than those of outstanding spiritual men. Personifications, like the Tyche of Antioch, Nemesis, and Nike were occasionally used according to local preference; and Muses, like the ones on the relief of San Elia (Ch. XIII, Fig. 629), or Tragedy and Comedy—if the woman in Fig. 758 and her companion are rightly interpreted—were a natural choice. The many niches and tabernacles of the Roman scaenae frontes demand filling with statues. Friezes with reliefs were often inserted in the entablatures, as in Ephesus, Side, Delphi, and Corinth. The deeds of Heracles, the battles with centaurs, Amazons, and giants are used. The rich sculptured decoration of the theater at Side includes reliefs with masks, busts of Artemis and Demeter, Nikes in the central pedi-ment, battle scenes, and the finding of Ariadne on the island of Naxos by Dionysos.[93]

The theaters of Leptis Magna and Merida are the only ones where, thanks to the careful work of the Italian and Spanish excavators who have set up the statues again in their original locations, we can get some idea of the true appearance of a Roman scaenae frons (Figs. 681-682, 698). It would be a rewarding task to collect the decorative statues and friezes which are now scattered in museums and bring them back to their architectural frames, at least in reconstructed drawings. As most theaters are dated, the statues could also be dated according to the period of the theaters where they were used.

CHAPTER XV

PLAYS OF THE ROMAN EMPIRE

See Figs.
801, 810

THE passion of the Romans for plays of every kind constantly increased. In the time of the Emperor Augustus the calendar (fasti) tells us that there were over 60 days on which public spectacles were given regularly in connection with the old religious festivals. They always began with scenic plays, followed by circus performances. The calendar lists: (1) Ludi Romani, September 4-19, of which ludi scenici 4-12; (2) Ludi Plebeii, November 4-17, of which scenici 4-12; (3) Ludi Megalenses, April 4-10, of which scenici 4-9; (4) Ludi Cereales, April 12-19, of which scenici 12-18; (5) Ludi Florales, April 28-May 3, of which scenici, mostly mimes, only on the last day, May 3; and (6) Ludi Apollinares, July 6-13, of which scenici 6-12. Thus the majority, about 40 days out of 60, were devoted to theater plays. During the Empire, however, interest in the scenic plays declined and that in the spectacles in the circus and amphitheater grew steadily. The result was that toward the end of antiquity, in the year A.D. 354, of the 175 days set aside for festivals only about 100, that is, four-sevenths were devoted to theater plays. Although the scenic plays had been more than doubled, the games in the amphitheater and in the circus had increased almost four times.

The forms of plays created during the republican period lived on, but the emphasis was shifted from the more serious to the lower classes of scenic plays. At the end of the republic, tragedy and comedy in the Graeco-Roman form, crepidata and palliata, held first place. During the Empire they were pushed more and more into the background by the lower varieties of drama. Sometimes only single scenes of tragedy were declaimed. The heir of tragedy became the pantomime with a continuous plot and the acting of a single mute actor. The heir of comedy became the mime played without masks and with subject matter taken from daily life. The heir of the Atellan farce became the Latin farce with coarse and low-class plots and characters. The theater plays, in order to compete with circus and gladiatorial entertainments, had to become steadily more sensational.[1]

While the Greeks gave definite plays different from each other in the different cults—tragedies and comedies for Dionysus in Athens; mainly athletic games and races for Zeus in Olympia; mainly musical plays for Apollo in Delphi (to which later athletic games and races modelled on those in Olympia were added, as was true also at the Panathenaic festivals for Athena in Athens)—the Romans, in contrast, gave to each god the same kinds of plays. The Romans also gave the same kinds of spectacles for funeral games, when scenes from tragedies and even comedies were presented; for birthday celebrations of emperors; on the occasion of dedications of buildings; and for triumphal games. They even gave different plays at the same festival at the same time in different places. Thus at the secular festival celebrated by Augustus in 17 B.C.—for which Horace composed his *Carmen Saeculare,* sung by a chorus of boys and girls—three day-long Greek thymelic or lyric plays were given in the theater of Pompey, Greek scenic plays in the Circus Flaminius, and Latin plays in a newly-erected temporary wooden building near the Tiber. These were followed by seven days of games in the circus. The birthday of Augustus on September 23 was also celebrated with circus games.

This mixture of plays at the same occasion explains the fact that in the monuments we often have a combination of tragedy and comedy, which were both still popular in the first century A.D. The mask reliefs in Pompeii, Ostia, and Rome often have tragic masks on one side and comic masks on the other (pp. 155, 158, Figs. 562 and 572-573). The Dionysiac masks on other reliefs (see Fig. 578) may refer as much to the connection with the Dionysiac cult—which, however, in imperial Rome was very loose—as to the satyr drama, which also remained alive in the Empire. Horace, in his poem on the art of writing poetry, not only gives rules for tragedy but also for the satyr drama (*Ars Poetica,* vv. 220-250).[2]

There are many pictures in Pompeii belonging to the first century A.D., before its destruction in 79, which prove that tragedy and comedy were as vigorous in this more and more Romanized colony as they must have been in Rome itself. Of course, the question always arises as to whether the wall paintings reproduce Greek or Roman representations, and whether they show contemporary performances or are copies of earlier votive pictures. After the earthquake of 63, many painters may have come from Rome and may have copied Greek paintings assembled in Rome by the Roman conquerors. Yet there are two features which betray contemporary representations as the source: the stage costume and details of Roman theater buildings.

760

7(

762

76

Figs. 760-764. Masks of tragedy and comedy set on movable steps; Andromeda; Youth, Woman of tragedy; Father, Youth of comedy. Wall paintings from Pompeii, Naples

Thus tragic and comic masks are on the same wall in Boscoreale. A series of masks, alternating tragic and comic, lying above little staircases, which the Romans had taken over from the popular farce (see above, Figs. 483, 485, 488, 489, 491, 518, 688), together with the very high hairdress, the onkos, for the tragic masks seem to prove that these are masks actually used on the Roman stage (Figs. 760-764).[3] One (Fig. 760) may be Andromeda, with a veil hanging from the extremely high onkos, a sea dragon below her, as we saw it in the relief and the painting with the masks of Andromeda and Perseus (Figs. 570-571). The masks of a youth beside which a spear is leaning (Fig. 761) and of a woman (Fig. 762) both have a fillet and a wreath in their highly-built-up long hair. One of the comic masks represents a father with a long beard (Fig. 763) and one

76

Fig. 765. Wall decoration with alternating tragic and comic scenes. Casa del Centenario, Pompeii

a youth with a book basket (capsa) beside him (Fig. 764), both with the rolled arrangement of the hair, the speira, used in New Comedy.

Scenes from tragedy and comedy alternate within a frieze in two houses in Pompeii, the Casa del Centenario (Fig. 765)[4] and the Casa di Casca at the crossing of Via dell'Abbondanza and Vicolo di Tesmo.[5] In both reappears a painting containing Lykos, Megara, and Amphitryon, while the one from Casa del Centenario also has at the left side Heracles (Figs. 766-767). This seems to be a revision of the *Madness of Heracles* by Euripides, reworked by Accius for the Roman stage, on which

Accius and Naevius were still presented in the first century A.D. The play of Accius was named after Amphitruo, the old father of Heracles. In both pictures he stands next to Megara, the wife of Heracles. The mischievous tyrant Lykos sits on an altar to the right, apparently filled with fear on account of the arrival of Heracles. In the Greek original he does not appear at the same time as Heracles. Amphitryon probably received greater emphasis in the Latin than in the Euripidean play. He may also have been killed by Heracles on the stage.

Among the tragic scenes from the Casa del Cen-

Fig. 766. Heracles, Amphitryo, Megara, and Lycus. Casa del Centenario, Pompeii

Fig. 767. Amphitryon, Megara, and Lycus. Casa di Casca, Pompeii

Figs. 768, 769. Priam kneeling to Achilles; Medea pointing her sword at her children. Casa del Centenario, Pompeii

tenario are Priam, seated, and Hecuba talking to him, and Priam kneeling before Achilles supplicating for the body of his son Hector (Figs. 765 and 768). These two paintings may be taken from a Latin play dealing with the Trojan saga so popular in Italy. Medea pointing the drawn sword at her children (Fig. 769), who are being brought to her by their tutor, does not agree with the *Medea* of Euripides, where the children are killed inside the house. In Seneca's *Medea* the children are killed on the stage, but the mother kills them when alone with them and not in the presence of a servant. In Seneca's tragedy, however, Medea wounds her arm with her sword before the children are brought in, and in the tragedy underlying the painting in the Casa del Centenario it is to be assumed that she killed the children on the stage. The spirit is certainly the same as in the contemporary tragedies of Seneca, and one can easily imagine the tragedies of Seneca with their rhetorical pathos and far-fetched declamations being presented in this form. The other tragic scenes in the Casa di Casca are unfortunately effaced, and it is not possible to identify them. There might have been some illustration of Seneca among them. There seem to have been twelve pictures in the atrium, probably six tragic and six comic scenes.

Among the three preserved comic scenes in the Casa di Casca most important is the one where an old slave mocks a woman and a youth, a scene also known from a replica in Herculaneum (above, Fig. 395).[6] In one painting from the Casa del Centenario we see a young man coming home accompanied by a torch-bearing slave and a little boy, on whose head he has put his hand, while a servant

looks on from behind a door (Fig. 770). On another, an older man followed by a slave stands near an altar on which a goose is lying, killed by an arrow. A priestess wearing a fillet and a wreath and holding another wreath in her hand stands to the left (Fig. 771). Neither these nor the other pictures can be explained by their subject matter.[7] There is, indeed, no comedy preserved from this period. The wall paintings, however, testify to the presentation of comedies along with tragedies during the period of the first century A.D.

In Palermo there are also one tragic and one comic painted scene which again belong together. One scene consists of a hero and a messenger, perhaps Oedipus at the moment when the messenger from Corinth tells him of the death of his adoptive father (Fig. 772).[8] The scene reminds one of Seneca's *Oedipus*, vv. 784ff. and 1042. One would like to give to this scene as a companion piece a painting from the Casa dei Dioscuri in Naples of a heroine and her serving woman (Fig. 773).[9] The heroine is carrying a baby in swaddling clothes, and she may be Auge with little Telephus. The figures in both pictures have the exaggerated tall onkos, wooden high soles under their boots, rich dresses of variegated colors, and show lively gesticulation. The messenger has disorderly hair; the serving woman has a quince-colored yellow complexion, a stump nose, and a protruding chin. But the actual companion piece in the Casa dei Dioscuri was the comedy scene in Bonn (above, Fig. 327) and the one belonging to the painting in Palermo was the comedy scene between a lady and a cook (above, Fig. 383).[10] A similar scene is in Plautus' *Menaechmi*, vv. 219-225. This testifies again to the fact that

Figs. 770, 771. Young master's return; Priestess, old man and slave near altar. Casa del Centenario, Pompeii

Fig. 772. Tragic scene, hero and messenger. Palermo

Fig. 773. Heroine with baby and nurse. Casa del Dioscuri

comedies in the style of Menander, Plautus, and Terence were still performed in the first century, but with stronger exaggerations in the costume than before. It also asserts the fact that both kinds were given and painted side by side.

Contemporary performances are certainly meant when a luxurious Roman scaenae frons is set up behind the figures. Thus the figures in the painting in the house of the goldsmith Pinarius Cerialis (Fig. 774)[11] reoccur in other paintings and they do not have theatrical dresses.[12] But in the House of the

Goldsmith they are set before an elaborate scaenae frons: Iphigenia appears above a staircase in the regia, the royal door, framed by a rich architecture with columns, pediment, and acroteria. Before the hospitalia, the side doors, on the one side Thoas is seated with a bodyguard; on the other side, Orestes and Pylades are standing. Naevius was the first to write a Latin *Iphigenia* based on Euripides' *Iphigenia in Tauris*, and there may have been other adaptations.

This picture with the story of Iphigenia and three

Fig. 774. Iphigenia in Tauris. Wall painting, House of the Goldsmith (Pinarius Cereales), Pompeii

Fig. 775. Stage with the presentation of a mime. Wall painting, Pompeii

other paintings from the Casa dei Gladiatori in Pompeii correspond remarkably to the theaters of Pompeii and Herculaneum (Figs. 775-778).[13] We find here once more in the scaenae frons the central niche flanked by rectangular niches, the columns or pilasters set upon bases, the three elevated doors from which stairs led down to the stage for an effective entrance of the actors, and in the front wall (proscenium) of the pulpitum the small rounded and rectangular niches (Figs. 777-778). The painted walls show abundant decoration: in the front niches statuettes, carved parapets between the columns, and bronze ornaments, all of which—even if more easily executed in paint than in solid material— were certainly not lacking in the theaters at Rome. There, as in Pompeii, mimes, pantomimes, and occasionally athletic games were given in the theaters before a similar rich background. The mime (Fig. 775) shows a young hero dressed in a chlamys standing in the regia, two older warriors fully armed in the hospitalia, and slaves in the background between them holding a wine jar and a torch in preparation for a banquet. The pantomime (Fig. 776) depicts the story of the contest between Apollo and Marsyas. The actor appeared first in the left hospitalium as Athena, trying out the flutes which she has invented. In the right hospitalium he ap-

pears as Marsyas who has picked up the flutes, despite the curse put on them by Athena. Marsyas challenged Apollo to a musical contest. The victor Apollo stands with his cithara in the royal door. Four members of the chorus who sang the plot are seen in the background between the three doors and in the outermost doors. The third picture (Figs. 777-778) shows a victorious athlete holding a palm branch led by Victory out of the central door, while other athletes appear in the hospitalia. Tragic masks allude to the fact that tragedies were also performed on this stage. The athletes are indeed only late intruders. They lived in the barracks above the colonnade behind the theater (Ch. XIII, G in Fig. 605), and when the games in the amphitheater were forbidden as a consequence of the riot of the year 59 (see above, Fig. 624), they were transferred to the large theater. The discus thrower and the boxer in the outer niches of the proscenium allude to the athletic games, while the poet reading from a scroll in the center reminds one of the more serious performances.

There hardly could be a better frame and more gorgeous background for the tragedies of Seneca (A.D. 5-65)[14] than this type of scaenae frons, which belongs to his period. His nine plays, the only Latin tragedies preserved for us, were written during his

Fig. 776. Stage with the presentation of a pantomime. Wall painting, Pompeii

Figs. 777, 778. Stage with victorious athletes and decorated
proscenium. Wall painting, Pompeii

banishment in Corsica (41-49) or during the time
when he was tutor and advisor to Nero (49-59). It
is the period when the wall-paintings (Figs. 765-
769 and 772-773) were painted, which are related
to the bloody and rhetorical dramas of Seneca in
subject-matter, actions, and costume. All tragedies
of Seneca are based on older plays which were
never meant for reading but only for presentation.
The *Hercules Furens, Troades, Medea,* and *Hippolytus* are Latin adaptations of Euripides' tragedies; the *Oedipus* and *Hercules Oetaeus* are based
on Sophocles, and the *Agamemnon* on Aeschylus.
The *Phoenissae* combine motifs of all three classical
Greek writers. The only play for which the original
is not preserved for us is the *Thyestes.* It might be
the *Atreus* of Accius, at the presentation of which
Seneca was present, or the *Thyestes* of Ennius, first
produced in 169 B.C., or the *Thyestes* of Varius, presented in 29 B.C. (see Ch. XI, p. 156). Seneca de-

Fig. 779. Two tragic actors threatening children (Atreus and Merope?). Lamp, Rome

Fig. 780. Portrait of Seneca. Marble bust, Berlin

scribes the fiendish revenge taken by Atreus upon his brother Thyestes because he had seduced his wife. Atreus kills his nephews and gives their flesh and blood to the unsuspecting father to eat and drink. The killing of the children of Thyestes, or in any case of children, is also represented on a lamp in the Museo Nazionale Romano delle Terme in Rome (Fig. 779).[15] A king and a queen, probably Atreus and Merope or Laodameia, hold the children who struggle to get away, because the man threatens them with a large sword. Both have diadems on their lofty onkoi and are on high stilts. This might be a still later revision of this subject which appealed to the Roman love of cruelty.

Seneca kept the dramatic and theatrical forms of the Greek models, even including the chorus, but he assimilated the borrowed material to the Roman character. Seneca's portrait in Berlin also testifies to his purely Roman personality (Fig. 780).[16] He was certainly thinking of performing his tragedies in the theater, for one of his letters (*Epist.* I,xi,7) demonstrates his interest in stage presentations. He has such effective roles for great actors that it would be unlikely for the great actors of his time to pass them by. When the *Medea* of Euripides was presented by the Morningside players of Columbia University in New York, the Broadway actress who played

Medea inserted the gruesome speech of the *Medea* of Seneca (vv. 740ff.), singing incantations to the gods of the nether world.

Seneca may also have inspired his pupil Nero to give tragic recitations on the stage. Nero appeared as god, hero, or heroine; he sang the parts of the blinded Oedipus, the insane Heracles, and Orestes as matricide. Nero even took the part of Canace and mimicked the cries of a woman in labor. His last appearance was as Oedipus in exile, a role presented in the Greek language (Suetonius, *Nero*, X, XXI, XLVII). At these occasions he must have worn the tragic costume in the form depicted in the wall-paintings of his period (above, Figs. 768-769 and 772-773). He certainly appeared in this theatrical costume when he presented himself in Athens in the theater of Dionysus, which was rebuilt for him and dedicated to him together with Dionysus (above, Ch. XIV, Figs. 717-722). Among the single scenes or speeches which he declaimed (Lucian, *Nero*, 2-3.10) there may well have been some from the tragedies of his teacher Seneca. Professional actors dared to rival him—for example, the actor Epirotes —and as Nero was proud of his skill it was an honor to compete against him (Lucian, *Nero*, 9). Another actor pretended that he was singing the songs exactly as Nero had done in Olympia (Philostratus, *Vita Apollonios Tyana*, v,ix,8). These were probably rhapsodic songs, and as rhapsode Nero may have worn the cithara player's costume. It may even be that the statue in the Vatican, occasionally attributed to Skopas, showing an Apollo with portrait features, represents Nero idealized as Apollo the cithara player (Fig. 781).[17] In a similar form Nero is represented on his coins, as Suetonius (*Nero,* xxv) has observed: "item statuas suas citharoedico habitu, qua nota etiam nummum percussit." (There were statues of Nero in the dress of a cithara player, and he issued a coin in the same guise.)[18] Nero is said to have "danced" the Turnus and Dido after Virgil.[19] We know also that other famous poetical works such as the *Medea* of Ovid and even orations were declaimed on the stage, probably in this costume of a musician.

The influence of Seneca began immediately after his death. The *Octavia* was even attributed to Seneca, but it could have been written only after the death of Nero (A.D. 68), and therefore only after the death of Seneca (A.D. 65).[20] The story is laid in 62, when Seneca was still councilor of Nero, but he retired after Nero had murdered his mother and banished and later killed his wife Octavia. As the death of Nero is predicted, it was certainly written after 68. It displays, however, a rhetorical style, misplaced erudition, hollow lamentations, and no real action—all of which are found in Seneca's tragedies. The *Octavia* is the only tragedy with a national theme, a fabula praetexta, known to us, for all the others are known only by their titles, such as the *Domitius* and the *Cato* of Curiatus Maternus, dating from the time of Nero, or the *Aeneas* of Pomponius Secundus. As these patriotic plays were given in the Roman toga with purple stripes, the dress worn by the upper classes (Fig. 550), it is not possible to distinguish them in monuments. It seems possible to me that the scene on a pulpitum before a scaenae frons from Castel S. Elia represents such a praetexta, as several persons are represented in the toga (Ch. XIII, Fig. 629).[21] This Roman dress is clearly recognizable in the tall man standing in the center before the regia below the statue of Apollo in the upper niche, and in the two men with staffs, probably the lictors, who accompany the main figure. The flute player who also has a footclapper and the player of a syrinx are at the head of a chorus, while another chorus of twelve little girls, behind whom stand four grown-up persons, has been explained by Anti as a chorus of girls who performed in honor of Juno in the ludi falisci given in Falerii in the Romanized period. This relief belongs to about the middle of the first century, in the period of Seneca. Chorus-singing with the accompaniment of the flute remained popular in the Hellenistic and Roman periods (Hyginus *Fab.* 273.) Ptolemy Auletes and Marcus Antonius favored this type in the first century B.C. (Strabo, xviii,796; Plutarch, *Ant.* 24). Seneca definitely influenced not only the age immediately following his own, but all subsequent periods.

Fig. 781. Apollo Kitharoidos, perhaps Nero. Marble, Vatican

While historical plays were seldom written and tragedies often declaimed only in detached scenes or detached roles lacking in continuity, the pantomime with its continuous plot became the real heir of tragedy.[22] The pantomime actor danced the individual roles, which means that he had to refine his gestures to such a high degree and perform his movements so expressively that in him alone one could see embodied now a god and now a goddess, now a hero and now a heroine. These characters were made more readily distinguishable by changes in the actor's masks and attributes. The text sung by the chorus (see Figs. 776, 782) was for the most part a second-rate revamping of well-known tragic scenes. We know many librettos through the book on the dance by Lucian (Lukianos) of Syria, who wrote in the time of the Antonines. In the time of Nero a pantomime "danced" the adultery of Ares and Aphrodite. He had to play Sol, Hephaestus, Aphrodite, Ares, and other gods one after the other (Lucian, *Dialogus de Saltatione,* 63). In another pantomime he had to represent Bacchus, Cadmus, Pentheus and Agave (*Anthologia Palatina Plan.* 289). But better writers also, such as Lucanus (A.D. 39-65), a nephew of Seneca, and Statius (A.D. 45-96) wrote these Fabulae Salticae. Among the titles which have been handed down to us are *Atreus and*

235

Fig. 782. Dwarf fluteplayer Myropnous. Tombstone

closed mouth (in contrast to the masks of tragedy), the tragic costume made of expensive material, and they appeared before the same gorgeous scaenae frons. The emperors particularly favored the pantomimes. Common names for them are Paris and Pylades. Thus one pantomime, Paris, was the teacher and friend of Nero. The pantomime Pylades was liked by Trajan. L. Aurelius Apolaustus was a Syrian freedman of Lucius Verus; a statue was erected to him at Tivoli as the "best of his time" (temporis sui primus), and an honorary statue base was dedicated to Aurelius Pylades in Puteoli.[24] Most of the pantomimes were Greek, many from the countries which were the homelands of the founders of this kind: Syria, the country of Pylades, and Alexandria, the home of Bathyllus (see above, p. 165). They travelled to Rome and the Roman provinces. The honorary inscription for the pantomime M. Septimius Aurelius in Leptis Magna, praising him as the best of his time, tells us that he performed also in Milan, Vicenza, and Verona.

When women appeared as pantomimes they were considered shameless (Juvenal, vi,66 and xii,62). But the Emperor Justinian of Byzantium made Theodora, a pantomime, his queen. From Trier, the capital of the Western Roman Empire, an ivory relief now in Berlin (Fig. 783)[25] depicts such a woman in about the fourth century. Her masks represent a hero, a heroine, and a youth. The attributes of the sword, crown, and lyre indicate the content of the Fabula Saltica.

Fig. 783. Pantomime. Ivory relief from Trier, Berlin

Thyestes, Ajax, Niobe, The Mad Heracles by Lucanus, and *Agave* by Statius (Juvenal, 7,87). In the latter, the roles of Bacchus, Pentheus, Cadmus, and Agave were danced successively by the same actor, Paris. In the pantomime *Achilles on the Isle of Skyros* the personages of Achilles, the spinning maidens, Odysseus, Diomedes, and others had to be characterized in succession. The music was undignified, frivolous, sensual, with loud yet enervating tunes. Double pipes, lyre, trumpets, and scabellum, a foot clapper, that is, a rattle beaten with the foot for the rhythm (see above, Fig. 629 and below, Fig. 829), formed a noisy orchestra, though at times pleasant and easy melodies and many trills accompanied the songs of the chorus. Sometimes abnormal musicians such as dwarfs were used. Thus Myropnous, the fluteplayer for a chorus, is shown on his tombstone in Florence (Fig. 782)[23] with an enormous head in contrast to his crippled short legs. The pantomime actors, on the other hand, must have been well-built men and women with supple bodies. They must have worn with the masks which had a

The ballet is related to the pantomime when a solo dance, to the mime when a group dance. In Greece it was called Pyrrhiche when danced by armed men who presented sham battles. In Rome this dance was given a dramatic content. Male and female dancers fought with each other or represented satyrs, maenads, and corybants. They were dressed in tunics embroidered with gold, wore purple mantles, and had golden wreaths. The mythological ballet dramatized such scenes as the story of Pentheus and Dionysus, and the Judgment of Paris, described by Apuleius (*Metamorph.*, x,29-34), which took place in the second century in the theater of Corinth. Luxurious scenery represented Mount Ida with animals, plants, and springs on it. The setting and the costumes were sophisticated and rich. Venus appeared naked save for a transparent silken palla round her hips. She was surrounded by dancing Cupids, Graces, and Horae. Minerva was accompanied by the demons of horror, Juno by Castor and Pollux, Paris by his herd. At the end the scenery was lowered with the aid of a sinking machine.

Water ballets and water plays, aquacades, were given in small water basins, which were built into the theaters[26] (see below, p. 253). They were choreographic mimes, tetimimes, mimes for Tethys, the wife of Okeanos. Martial (*Libellus spectaculorum*, 8 and 16f) mentions a ballet with nereids and a mime in which Leander swam to Hero. A mosaic found in the grandiose late Roman Villa at Piazza Armerina in central Sicily—built or decorated perhaps for the Emperor Maximian Herculeus, about 297-300—shows the skimpy bathing suits of ten female athletes and ballerinas (Fig. 784).[27] The undress surpasses even modern beachwear. The victorious girl in the center of the lower row holds a crown over her head and a palm branch in her left

Fig. 784. Girls dressed in bathing suits for water ballet or athletic sports. Mosaic, Piazza Armerina, Sicily

hand. Others have clappers, a tambourine, or a wreath; and one has a large fan-like flower which looks like a small umbrella. One girl with a loose palla around her body comes running with a crown in her right hand and a palm branch in her left hand.

In the second and following centuries the Roman games and plays were more and more extended to the provinces. The scenic and thymelic plays were brought to the whole Roman imperium by the guilds which developed from the Hellenistic technitae and the Roman troupes of actors.[28] Here also variety was required. On the pulpitum of the theater of Sabratha (see Ch. XIV, Figs. 694-695) a tragic scene of a hero holding a club and of a heroine, both wearing large masks and standing on high stilts—perhaps Theseus and Phaedra—has as a counterpart a mime which displaced comedy in the favor of the public (Figs. 785-786).[29] The mime enjoyed the greatest popularity of all, because of its lack of masks, its sketching of ordinary life, and its frequent use of current themes and political satire. In later centuries it reigned over the stage almost exclusively. The mockery of the gods, taken over from

Figs. 785, 786. Hero and heroine, tragic scene; Scene from a mime. Marble reliefs from pulpitum of theater at Sabratha

Fig. 787. Funeral plays. Wall painting from the necropolis of Cyrene

comedy and farce, was exaggerated to absurdity. Luna appeared as a man, Diana was whipped, and Jupiter made his last will and testament. At the time of Tiberius, Lentulus and Hostilius wrote a mime about Anubis as adulterer. Love and adultery were also popular themes for civic mimes and low-class comedy. Something similar may have been the subject of the mime in Sabratha. A seated woman seems to order two men about, one elegant and the other stupid-looking. This may be a scene like that described in Ovid (*Tristia,* II,497-514): a rich woman with her elegant lover and her stupid husband.[30] A similar subject is found in Molière's *George Dandin.* The men in Sabratha wear togas and the woman also wears an everyday dress. The background shows rich stage doors.

In other mimes the play catered to the popular morals—the rich were persecuted, the poor became rich, and lovers were discovered and driven off. As in modern motion pictures, animals were permitted to take part. Thus at the time of Vespasian, a dog— a forerunner of Rin-tin-tin and Lassie—had the chief role in a presentation at the theater of Marcel-

lus in Rome. In Corinth, after the ballet, Lucius, changed into a donkey, is to take part in a sordid mime, but runs away (Apuleius, *Metamorph.,* v,34-35). Attempts were also made to compete with the cruel games of the amphitheater. On the day when Caligula was murdered, the robber Laureolus in a mime was actually nailed to a cross and died before the eyes of the spectators (Suetonius, *Caligula,* LVII). Blows, ear-boxing, kicks, dances at suitable and unsuitable times, acrobats, and lively gesticulation with the hands were added to the mimicry. Women, who were permitted to appear here as in the pantomime, often stepped on the stage half naked, particularly at the Floralia in Rome, like Aphrodite in the ballet in Corinth and the girls in the aquacade in Sicily (Fig. 784). The result was that the profession of a female mime had a very bad reputation. Aelian (*Fragm.* 123) says that a courtesan is worse than an actress in the mime. The Christian writers, when fighting against the late, degenerate form of the theater, fought chiefly against the mime, which had occasionally ridiculed Christian religious rites.

The guilds now had their headquarters in Rome. They had become a world organization, a professional body, no longer under the patronage of Dionysus. They travelled not only to public festivals for all gods, but also to private festival celebrations including important funeral games. They were obliged to give plays as varied as possible in order to satisfy the restless and novelty-loving public of the Empire, which demanded their services in far-separated places. Thus the wall-paintings, now unfortunately destroyed, from a grave in the necropolis of Cyrene (Fig. 787)[31] shows a group of tragic actors: a cithara player and a flute player, each surrounded by a chorus of seven young men; two solo citharists; and one solo fluteplayer. Thus dramatic, lyric, and purely musical performances seem to have been combined. The tragic actors have richly-patterned sleeved robes, large masks with an onkos which is higher than their faces, and probably high buskins, crepidae, with heavy wooden block-like soles which the copyist has mistaken for little podia. The one in the center has the club of Heracles, the one to the right has a herald's staff; he may be Mercury. At his side is a table with wreaths and palm branches for the victors. The seven chorus members around the tragic actors and the cithara player, who performs in lively movement, are all of about the same height and age. The fluteplayers' chorus, in contrast, contains two little boys. Next to the solo fluteplayer and to one solo citharist is also a boy. The other citharist has at his side two boys arranging something on a table; these may be the keepers of the wardrobe for the troupe. There follows to the left a richly-decorated door and then a grown-up man talking to another boy. This may be one of the poets who were attached to the travelling troupes. The boys may be the personal servants of the poets and of the musicians particularly engaged to care for their instruments and other paraphernalia.

Dramatic and lyric performances combined are also seen on a marble relief depicting the funeral plays for the young Flavius Valerianus, given for him by his father and therefore represented on his tombstone, which is now in the garden of the Villa Doria Pamphili in Rome (Fig. 788).[32] The date is given by the form of the toga of the deceased—whose half-length portrait is sculptured at the right end—with the stiffly-pleated folded band in the fashion of the early third century. Behind the bust of Flavius Valerianus is a small shrine with primitive figures of his ancestors, as they were kept in the atria of patrician houses and exhibited at the occasion of the funerals. Three scenic and three lyric artists perform in two groups. A citharist, resembling Nero (Fig. 781) in dress and attitude, accompanies

Fig. 788. Funeral plays for Flavius Valerianus

a reciter holding a scroll, and a singer is in the background. The main tragic hero in sleeved robe, on high stilts and wearing a mask with long twisted locks, holds a club in his left hand and declaims with outstretched right arm. He may be Heracles or Theseus. The mask of a heroine is seen in the background. There follows a younger actor holding what seems to be a torch. His mask, like that of the bearded hero, has such large openings for eyes and mouth that his real eyes and lips obviously were seen. The younger man does not have either the sleeved robe or the stilts. He may be a secondary character, and his costume of daily life may be taken over from comedy. The tragic actors are accompanied not by the usual instruments but by a water organ operated by a boy. Again we see that the troupes had young children in their service. It is difficult to decide whether actors of a comedy or a lyric group with a fluteplayer are lost at the left side. In any case thymelic or lyric presentations were often combined with scenic ones, and pure musical performances, originally given in the odea as semi-dramatic concerts, seem to have been popular for funeral games.

Tragedy and even satyrplay were certainly presented in Rome as well as in the provinces during the later Empire. Lucian (Lukianos, *Dialogus de Saltatione*, 27) describes the tragic actors of his time: "As far as tragedy is concerned, let us form our opinion of its character from its outward semblance. What a repulsive and frightful spectacle is a man tricked out to disproportionate stature, mounted upon high clogs (embates), wearing a mask that reaches up above his head, with a mouth that is set in a wide yawn, as if he meant to swallow the spectators. I forbear to speak of the pads for the breast and for the paunches (prosternidia and progastridia), wherewith he puts on an artificial and counterfeit corpulence, so that the disproportion in height may not betray itself the more in a slender figure." The monuments agree with this

Figs. 789-792. Royal pair; Two women sacrificing; Mercury leading Alcestis; Hero and satyr. Mosaics from Porcareccia

statement. On a mosaic found near Porcareccia, the ancient Lorium in Etruria, now in the upper lobby of the winding entrance stair to the Vatican Museum, late Roman representations in theatrical costume are depicted (Figs. 789-792).[33] The mosaic contains twenty-two hexagonal panels with two tragic actors each; one with a tragic hero and a satyr; one with a seated poet accompanied by two muses and a boy holding a mask; eight trapezoidal panels containing one mask each. The tragic groups may mean that only single scenes were taken out for recitation, but the presence of the poet makes that unlikely. The examples here given represent a pair of rulers, perhaps Agamemnon and Clytemnestra or Theseus and Phaedra (Fig. 789); two women sacrificing a small animal on a high altar (Fig. 790); Mercury leading a veiled woman, perhaps Alcestis (Fig. 791). The satyr (Fig. 792) dances around a hero who is wearing a wreath and a fillet and carrying a scepter. As in the classical satyr drama (see Ch. I, Figs. 32, 36, 39), the satyr capers around the serious figures of Greek mythology. The costumes on the mosaic are patterned with stripes of motley colors, with broad belts. Lofty onkos and high soles in the form of blocks lengthen the body in an unnatural way. The impression is clumsy and crude, in agreement with the description of an actor who appeared in a not yet cultivated part of Spain as described by Philostratus (*Apollonios Tyana*, v, 91): "When the actor was silent walking on high stilts (okribantes) which made him over life-size,

Figs. 793, 794. Clytemnestra kneeling to Achilles and servant, tragic scene; Electra on couch and Pylades, comic scene. Cake moulds, Ostia

and with a wide open mouth, they were already fearful. But when he lifted his voice, the spectators fled from the theater as if persecuted by a demon."

Tragedies and comedies continued to be given at the same festivals as circus and amphitheatrical games in the first half of the third century, as testified by cake moulds found in Ostia (Figs. 793-794).[34] About two hundred double forms were found in a storeroom, each large enough for about one pound of cake, so that two hundred cakes could be baked at one time. The same room also contained thirty-five large storage vessels and some jugs, all of the same shape and with a capacity of about three-fourths of a quart. Near the storeroom is a large bakery. There seems to be no doubt that these are provisions for dealing out to the audience cake and wine or honey wine (crustulum and mulsum), on the occasion of the festivals represented in the moulds.[35] Perhaps these gifts were also transported to Rome for the festivals there.

On the mould with a tragic scene a weeping woman kneels before a youth, perhaps Clytemnestra supplicating Achilles to save Iphigenia (Fig. 793). She has, according to Euripides' *Iphigenia in Aulis*, brought her daughter to the harbor town, believing

that she is to be given in marriage to Achilles. The servant informs her that Iphigenia is to be killed instead, and she kneels to Achilles (v. 900). The servant does not speak any more after v. 895 and probably left the scene. He is turning away, and energetically tying his mantle around his neck. He resembles a slave of comedy with his grotesque mask, stuffed-out body, and rough dress, which seems to be made of fur. He thus is best described as the oldest slave in tragedy who does not wear an onkos and is dressed in fur (Pollux, IV,137: diphtherias, διφθερίας). We might, therefore, assume that the cake baked in this form was dealt out at the occasion of a Latin adaptation of Euripides' *Iphigenia*.

The comic scene on another mould (Fig. 794) shows a similar servant seated at the feet of a heroine who is reclining on a couch. We have three replicas: a fragment in the British Museum (Fig. 795), the upper part found in Paestum, and a mould found in 1951 on the Agora of Athens (Fig. 796).[36] This latter one has the inscriptions COMEDIA and PYLADES. This Pylades may be the friend of Orestes, who in Euripides' *Orestes*, v. 1658f., is ordered by Apollo, and also in the same author's *Electra* is

Figs. 795, 796. Replicas of Electra-Pylades moulds

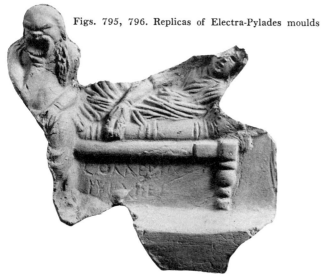

Fig. 797. Tragic scene. Lamp, Ostia   Fig. 798. Tragic actor. Lamp, Dresden

ordered by the Dioskuroi, v. 1249, to give his sister Electra in marriage to Pylades, here disregarding the fact that she had already been forced to marry a poor peasant. That is good stuff for a comedy. The low-class person on the mould may, therefore, be the discarded boorish first husband seated mournfully at the feet of Electra where, in Euripides' *Orestes*, the heroine is seated at the feet of the ailing Orestes. The possibility that Pylades is the name of a pantomime or a mime, which imitated or caricatured a tragedy, is suggested by the name of Pylades so frequently mentioned for pantomimes (see above, p. 236), but the inscription COMEDIA is against this assumption. The scene on a lamp, also found in Ostia (Fig. 797)[37] has the same grouping of a female reclining and a male figure seated on a couch, but this time both figures wear full tragic costume, and here they might be Electra and Orestes. Both are holding swords, as if to defend themselves against the Argives who have sentenced them to death. They might, however, also be Protesilaos and Laodameia.

It is rare to find a mythological comedy, as the *Pylades* must have been, among the subject matters of New Comedy. We know, however, that even Menander wrote travesties of the heroic saga. The center picture of a large floor mosaic found in Ulpia Oescus in Bulgaria shows four comic actors and above them the inscription: *The Achaioi* of Menander ([M]ENANΔΡΟΥ ΑΧΑΙΟΙ, Fig. 315 in Ch. VIII). The date is about A.D. 200. It represents the quarrel of Agamemnon and Achilles in the presence of Patroclus and an aged seated man, who may be Nestor or Phoinix, the old advisor of Achilles.

The terrifying appearance of Roman tragic actors can be seen in moulds as well as on lamps. One from the Sieglin Collection, which was assembled in Egypt, is with a comedy counterpart in Dresden (Fig. 798).[38] It shows a warrior hero with a sword at his left side. He wears the sleeved robe with broad belt and the paludamentum, the Roman chlamys, and walks on high blocks (embates, crepidae). He has an oversized onkos, to which he lifts his right hand, as he bows his head forward.

The well-known ivory statuette in the Petit Palais in Paris, painted gaily in blue, the sleeves alternately striped in blue and yellow (Figs. 799a-b),[39] has gestures which are, if possible, still more pathetic than on other monuments, and an onkos still more exaggerated, surmounting an exceedingly elongated face. The lofty stilts lengthen the body immensely. The statuette depicts, possibly, an elderly woman, perhaps Clytemnestra in a scene with one of her children, Orestes or Electra, both of whom she hates, and who in turn hate and wish

Fig. 799. Tragic actor. Ivory statuette, Paris

Figs. 800, 801. Masks of tragic hero and heroine. Marble

Fig. 802. Three tragic masks. Mosaic by Heraclitus, Lateran

to murder her. The actors who so frightened the audience that it fled from the theater in Hispalis (Sevilla) in Spain, must have appeared in a similar outfit as described around A.D. 150 by Lucian. The actor turns his head violently to the right, and holds his right hand before his breast as if to avert a blow. Eyes and mouth of the real face appear through the openings of the mask. The arm is too short and thin in comparison with the long body, which appears to have some stuffing.

The tragic masks of the later empire must indeed have been particularly frightening, as those worn by the actors represented on the monuments (Figs. 785, 793, 799) demonstrate. The same is true for a great number of single masks in marble, terracotta, and mosaic. The earlier masks are often still rather serene, for example, the mask from the House of the Large Fountain in Pompeii (Fig. 800).[40] The mask of a heroine from Tralles (Fig. 801)[41] in Constantinople has long twisted locks and a pathetic expression, but as yet no distortions. The three

tragic masks on the mosaic made by Heracleitus, in the Lateran (Fig. 802)[42] represent a woman with much jewelry on her lofty hairdress in the center, flanked by an older and younger man. They have large rounded openings for the eyes and wide irregular openings for the mouth. Like the unswept floor, to which they belong, they seem to be later distortions of an older original. A mask found in Spain in Barcelona (Fig. 803)[43] has an onkos which towers over the forehead, and from which baroque twisted long locks hang. The eyes and mouth of the actor appear through the wide openings of the mask. The same is true for a mask from Carthage in the Louvre (Fig. 804).[44] Ample space for eyes and

Figs. 803, 804. Tragic masks. Marble, Barcelona; Louvre

243

Fig. 805. Tragic masks. Marble, theater of Ostia

mouth to show is left in the masks of Heracles and several bearded heroes in the later remodelled theater of Ostia (Fig. 805, cf. Ch. XIV, Fig. 650).[45] These masks are conceived in harsh lines, with deep folds on forehead and between the eyes, protruding small cheeks, stiff arrangement of the hair with two tiers on the onkos and much play of light and shade. These masks testify that even in this late period tragedy was alive in this harbor town and therefore also in Rome. The fragment of a season sarcophagus has, above the fruit garland representing autumn, good masks of Heracles and Deianeira (Fig. 806).[46]

Fig. 806. Heracles and Deianeira. Masks from Season Sarcophagus, Berlin

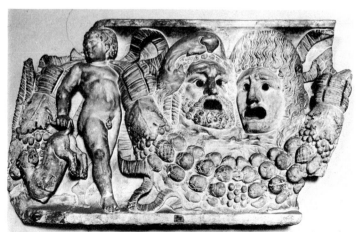

That comedy also was performed in Rome and other cities is proved by the comic and tragic scenes painted side-by-side in the wall-paintings of the Casa del Centenario and Casa di Casca in Pompeii (Figs. 765-771), and in Palermo (Figs. 383 and 772), and by the tragedy and comedy scenes on cake moulds from Ostia (Figs. 793-794), and on lamps, like Fig. 798 and its counterpart from Alexandria in Dresden. That Latin comedies were performed in the later period of the Empire is testified by the mosaic from Thracia (Fig. 315) and by the Terence manuscripts (Figs. 559-561). We even possess a late Roman original comedy in the Querolus.[47]

Tragic and comic masks are used as decorations side by side, as in Boscoreale and in the Casa del Triclinio and in a mosaic in Herculaneum.[48] The type of the comic masks is that of the father of comedy with twisted long strands in his beard. A similar mask from Minturnae in the University Museum of Philadelphia (Fig. 807)[49] was found together with another comic and two tragic masks. The same type appears also on a mosaic from the Villa of Hadrian in the Cabinetto delle Maschere of the Vatican (Fig. 808).[50] On a bench lies such a mask of the father of comedy next to one of a young man and opposite it a female mask, while the mask of another youth is on a lower base, near which two vases allude to a banquet, and a lyre alludes

Fig. 807. Father mask   Fig. 808. Group of masks

Fig. 809. Youth
of comedy

Fig. 810a-c.
Slave of comedy

to the music used in all Roman comedies. The exaggerations of the later period appear in the mask on a herm in the Galleria Geographica of an older youth with curly hair, falling in corkscrew locks on his shoulders (Fig. 809).[51] The actor's own mouth is seen in the wide opening of the mask and the wide pupils of the mask also allow for his eyes to shine through. This mask confirms the description of the mask of the serious curly-haired youth in Pollux (iv,147) who draws his eyebrows upward, and has one wrinkle on his forehead. The harsh rendering of the muscles, as in the tragic masks from Ostia (Fig. 805) is found in the colossal mask from the tomb of the Calpurni on the Via Salaria (Fig. 393 in Ch. VIII) and in the mask carved in Rosso Antico in the Villa Albani.[52] Some of these masks have mouths so wide that half of the face is swallowed by them.

The over-lifesize mask found in the Kerameikos in Athens near the Dipylon (Fig. 810a-c),[53] carved in Pentelic marble, is in the tradition of New Comedy. It exaggerates the differentiation of the two sides of the mask, which began in Middle Comedy (see Ch. III, p. 47, Figs. 196-198; Ch. VIII, p. 94, Figs. 335-337) and is described by Quintilian, xi,3,74: "The actor could change his expression by turning one or the other side of his head to the audience." Here the expression of gaiety on one, and the expression of anger on the other half is well expressed, but the means of expression are grossly distorted forms. The nose is extremely broad and flattened into a leaf pattern. The openings for the eyes have impossible shapes. The eyebrows are connected with each other in a grotesque curve. They leave only a small upper forehead into which wavy lines are cut. The hair on the speira looks like wire. It is the mask of the leading servant as described by Pollux (iv,149) who has a speira of red hair, draws his eyebrows up, and draws the skin on his forehead together.

The descriptions of Julius Pollux, *Onomastikon*, written in the time of the Emperor Commodus (A.D. 180-192), iv, 133-142 for tragic, 142 for satyric, and 143-155 for comic masks have been and can be quoted frequently for the Hellenistic as well as for the Roman periods. They prove the continued interest in the Graeco-Roman plays. They are probably based on the typical wardrobe of the travelling guilds. In practice, the masks might have been arranged on shelves in the sequence of the appearance of the dramatis personae, as they are in the Terence manuscripts (Fig. 560). Thus, when the same actor played several roles, he could quickly take up each mask as he needed it. In Pollux' catalogue, however, we have an arrangement according to classes, sex, and age. Thus there are for tragedy six old men, eight young men, three slaves, and eleven women; for the satyr play one young and one bearded satyr beside an old papposilenus; for comedy, nine older men, eleven younger men, seven slaves, three old women, five young women, seven courtesans, and two young maid servants. Thus there are 44 comic masks as against 28 tragic masks, testifying to the greater variety in comedy than in tragedy. It is difficult to say how far the sources for the catalogue of Pollux go back to the earlier periods. Pollux' description of forms and colors in stage costumes (iv,116-120) can in any case give only a small selection of those used in the different periods. Again he may be describing the typical wardrobe of the traveling troupes.

811a-b

Figs. 811-816. Roman theater tickets.
(See List of Illustrations and Sources)

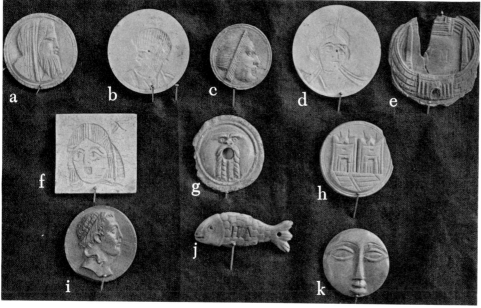

812a-k

815a-b

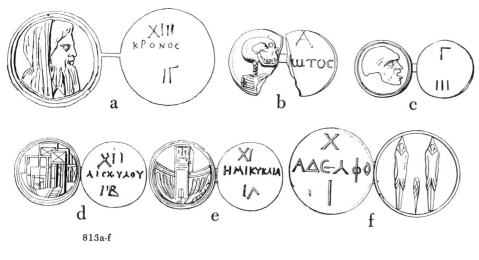

813a-f

814a-c

816a-c

The great variety of plays given during the Empire is also reflected in the theater tickets, many of which have been found in Pompeii, Rome, and in the provinces as well (Figs. 811-816).[54] Good collections are the one formerly in the Collection Froehner, now in the Cabinet des Médailles of the Bibliothèque Nationale (Figs. 812-814), and those in the Louvre (Fig. 815) and in the Museo teatrale alla Scala at Milan (Fig. 816). The tickets are usually made of bone or ivory and they have an engraved picture on one side, and inscriptions on the other (cf. p. 71, Fig. 270, p. 90 and p. 186, Fig. 320). They are mostly round, sometimes square (Figs. 811, 812f and 816a) and occasionaly have the forms of fish, of birds, or fruit (Figs. 812j, 816b-c and 814b). The engravings testify to tragedy by masks with towering onkos, wreath, and long strands of hair falling onto the shoulders and down the back (Figs. 811 and 812f). Comedy is indicated by masks with speira for a serious youth (Fig. 812c), rich headdress for a courtesan (Fig. 814c), a grotesque mask for a slave (Fig. 816a), and a baldheaded mask for the senex, the old man (Fig. 813c). In one case the representation of twins, named brothers (adelphoi, ἀδελφοί) on the other side, seems to point to the Greek original of the *Twin Brothers Menaechmi* by Plautus (Fig. 813f). The skeleton (Fig. 813b) refers to funeral games. The ticket found in Athens near the Odeion with the inscription Aischylou (Αἰσχύλου) and a complicated building on the other side (Fig. 813d) may refer to a revival of Aeschylus, but could also mean a statue like the one set up by Lycurgus in 340-330 (see Ch. II, Fig. 64). Such statues of celebrities or of gods and heroes were erected in many theaters, and their names were attached to particular sections, to which the tickets led the visitors. For the theater of Syracuse, for example, the names attached to the different sections include Zeus, Heracles, and Hieron.[55] The head of Zeus on a ticket in the Louvre (Fig. 815b), of Kronos (Figs. 812a and 813a) and of a Hellenistic ruler with diadem (Fig. 812i) both in the Cabinet des Médailles, therefore, might refer to statues or names marking definite sections of the theater. The central part of a theater, inscribed on the other side "semicircle" (hemikyklia, ΗΜΙΚΥΚΛΑΙΑ), (Fig. 813e) with a shrine above the center, agrees in the form with the theater of Pompey (see Ch. XIII, Fig. 631) and that in Leptis Magna (Ch. XIV, Fig. 696), where such little sanctuaries were built above the central sections. The outside entrances to the theaters are represented by elaborate porches, with birds seated on the wall to the right and left (Fig. 814a) or a statue above the lintel (Fig. 815a). A double gate (Fig. 812h) may lead to adjoining entrances for two different galleries. Similar tickets were also used for the circus (Fig. 812e) and amphitheater.

While the higher-class entertainments still persisted, some of the theater plays degenerated into sensational amusements for the common people. It is, therefore, not to be wondered at that the Atellan farce, from the very first created for the amusement of the people and transmitted to the Romans by the Oscans (cf. Ch. X, p. 148), should ascend to a conspicuous place in the theater of the Empire, and that it should entirely displace comedy, although even comedy had adapted itself more and more to the crude taste of the Roman populace. The following example from the time of Nero illustrates how extreme the tendency had become. A fabula togata of Afranius was given under the title of *Incendium* or the *House on Fire*. In it a house was actually burned down, and the actors had to rescue the rich furnishings, that is to say, they were permitted to plunder it. They were allowed to keep such furnishings and furniture as fell into their hands (Suetonius, *Nero*, XI,2). The actors of the Atellan farce, like the comic actors, played in masks. Therefore they could eventually dare to offer criticism of public affairs and even of the Emperor, although such boldness might become dangerous. An actor of the Atellan farce who attacked Caligula was burned to death in the amphitheater (Suetonius, *Caligula*, XXVII,4). Another actor of the farce, who ridiculed the poisoning of the Emperor Claudius and the drowning of Agrippina, was banished by Nero (Suetonius, *Nero*, XXXIX,3). Trimalchio in Petronius (*Cena Trimalchionis*, 53,15) asserts that he bought a set of comedians, but limited them to Atellan farces. The Atellana was still popular under Trajan and Hadrian (Juvenal, III,174f. *Hist. Aug. Hadrianus*, 25,4).

The fixed types of Maccus, Bucco, Pappus, and Dossenus remained typical for the Atellan farce (see Chs. X, p. 131 and XI, p. 148). A masterly Graeco-Roman bronze statuette in the Metropolitan Museum of Art—formerly in the Ficoroni Collection and probably found in Southern Italy—may be a Dossenus (Fig. 817).[56] A meagre hunchback stands

Fig. 817. Actor of farce. Bronze statuette, Metropolitan Museum

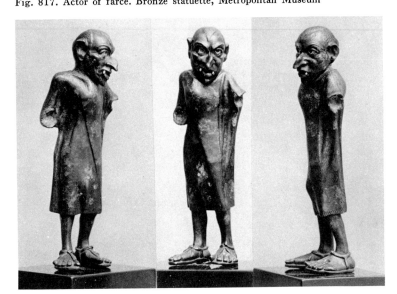

Figs. 818, 819. Actors of farce. Terracotta

Fig. 820. Actor of farce   Figs. 821-822. Manduci

Figs. 823, 824. Lamia; Fragment (of Lamia mask?)

awkwardly on his thin legs. He has a big mask with bald forehead, large ears, an enormous crooked nose, and teeth wrought in silver standing out of the corners of his mouth. The actors of the farce were often people with abnormally ugly bodies, extremely lean and small or excessively tall or fat for comic contrast. A terracotta statuette made in the factory of Vindex in Cologne, now in Bonn (Fig. 818)[57] may be a Maccus, a stupid and gluttonous rustic. The miserable cripple has drawn his mantle over his head and holds the edges together before his breast. His enormous mask has a crooked face, a gigantic nose, a much too broad mouth with puckered corners, unsymmetrical eyebrows and a wart on the forehead. The wart reappears on the fragment of a mask in Bonn.[58] A mask from Western Crete in Candia (Fig. 819)[59] has again the enormous nose and grotesque eyebrows under a bald fore-

head. The crooked nose and mouth as well as very unequal eyes appear on a mask in Tarentum (Fig. 820).[60] On a bronze head in the Metropolitan Museum of Art in New York[61] warts are everywhere: on the crown of the pointed bare head, on the nose, and on both cheeks. This must be a juggler of the farce (scurra) who was called fighting cock (Cicirrus). This name is given to Oscan performers by Horace (Sat. 1,5,vv.50ff.). They entertain him and his party on the occasion of his journey to Brindisi in a villa near Caudium with a duet of abuse.

The actor of the farce named Manducus had, in addition to the other characteristics of the farcical masks, enormous chattering teeth. Good examples are in Worms (Fig. 821), Cologne, and Bonn (Fig. 822).[62] A female addition is Lamia, a spook to frighten children. The naughty children were swallowed by her and pulled out of her body, to the delight of the childish adults and to the horror of the children. A mask of such a frightening female may be represented in a terracotta mould found in a kiln at Westheim near Augsburg (Fig. 823)[63] and in the fragment of a woman's mask, found near the theater of Heddernheim and now in the Historical Museum of Frankfurt (Fig. 824).[64] The six holes along the upper edge of this fragment are for ribbons to bind the mask to the head and were then probably covered with a peruke. The forehead, nineteen centimeters broad, fitted to the author's forehead in a perfect manner. Thus these masks of Germania Romana were certainly for practical use in the farces.

The farce remained popular in its original home in Southern Italy. It did not gain a foothold in the Greek East, but became popular in the still barbaric northern provinces, where the Roman armies had it introduced. It degenerated to a crude horseplay, particularly in Germania. But masks from Crete to Cologne bear striking resemblance to each other.

Still more important for the late period and for the continued vigorous life of ancient civilization was the mime.[65] Like the Atellan farce, it served as an entr'acte and a concluding play, especially after more serious dramas in the first centuries of the Empire (cf. above, p. 232). Later it became more and more independent, and gradually it degenerated. The mimes were wandering entertainers who gave little farce-like shows inside and outside the theater. They dived deeply into the seamy aspects of life.

The mimes did not wear masks, but actors with grotesque faces were used. It often is difficult to determine when such heads and statuettes are simple caricatures or mimes caricaturing life. Thus a head in Munich (Fig. 825)[66] has all the characteristics of a low-class mime player: stupid yet cunning expression, thick lips, large nose and ears, small eyes and a distorted long bare skull. The same type of mime player is represented in a group, probably from Egypt, in Hildesheim (Fig. 826).[67] Two men in short belted tunics seem to present a gay and lively dialogue scene, a lusus (paignion, παίγνιον). One, the main player (archimime) has almost female hanging breasts. He gesticulates with his lifted left hand, while his right hand is stretched out to the side, in a gesture imitated by the second player who has to emphasize and ridicule the jokes of the first. He has laid his left arm around the shoulders of his companion. These are genuine stupid fools (morio, moroi) with shining bald foreheads (mimus calvus, moros phalakros). They are barefooted, "planipes saltans," mimes dancing with flat feet, as described by Gellius (*Noctes atticae*, I,xi,12).

Sometimes the phallus of the old Doric farce was retained, as in a bronze statuette in Florence.[68] The mime is dancing clumsily, lifting his right hand to his mouth, which is overshadowed by a crooked and pointed nose. He and some particularly grotesque heads found on the Agora of Athens (Fig. 827) wear the peaked cap, which out of the headgear of travelers and peasants has become the fool's cap of the Roman mimes, of mediaeval buffoons, of Shakespeare's jesters, and of modern circus clowns.[69]

While some of these mimes wear only cap and loincloth, others are dressed in a kind of paenula, to which the pointed fool's cap is attached as a hood, similar to the mantle worn by the little demon Telesphorus accompanying Asclepius.[70] Many such figures have been found in Germania and in the Agora of Athens.[71] A bronze statuette in Florence[72] has a grotesque oldish face which appears framed by the edges of the mantle, which go up to the hood. Several of these mimes are used for lamps and from their opened cloaks protrudes a mighty phallus which is used as the muzzle of the lamp (Fig. 828). Perhaps this type was used for gods, for Seneca (*Epist.* CXIV,6) describes a person wearing a cloak covering his head and wrapped round both his ears as "just like fugitive gods in a mime." The gods could, however, also wear an ordinary pallium wrapped around the head.

The most characteristic costume of the mime is the centunculus, a dress composed of many different colored patches (Apuleius, *Apologia sive de magia*, p. 416). A statuette of a female mime found in Syria, from the collection of the late Professor Friend in the Art Museum in Princeton (Fig. 829a-b)[73] combines this clown's costume with the high-peaked fool's cap. She wears a jacket with a

Figs. 825, 826. Mime, profile; Two mimes

Figs. 827a-b, 828. Mimes with fools' caps; Mime in Paenula. Statuette; Roman lamps, Agora, Athens

frilled collar, scallops hanging down on hips and back, and a belt from which eight straps hang down over the tunic. The mima is at the same time dancing, gesticulating, and accompanying herself with music. She holds clappers in both lifted hands, throws back her head, beating the rhythm with the scabellum, the footclapper, under her left foot. She also accompanies her dance with bells, seven attached to her cap, three to the lowest points of the scallops of her jacket, eight to the ends of the flaps over her skirt, and four to the strips ornamenting the buskin to which the clapper is attached. Her other foot is bare.

The mimes associated themselves often with joculatores, jugglers, like the statuette of a Negro in Berlin, tossing with head, hand, knee, three balls at the same time (Fig. 830),[74] said to have come from Thebes. These merrymakers—mimes, dancers, rope dancers, jongleurs, jugglers, acrobats, and sometimes also boys leading animals like monkeys

Figs. 829a-b, 830. Female mime; Negro juggler

Fig. 831. Actor of comedy

Fig. 833. Tragic actors, *Medea* and *Oedipus*

or bears—lived on through the Middle Ages. They transmitted their skill as small wandering troupes or as individual actors (see below, Ch. XVI).

Comedy and tragedy continued, however, into at least the third century. This is proved for comedy by a late Roman relief formerly in the Villa Albani, now in the Louvre (Fig. 831).[75] An actor wearing a mask with speira and beard and a large opening for the mouth, which is clearly seen, declaims with his head turned to the left, his right arm lifted. He wears the sleeved tunic and the pallium. He stands against a curtain which hangs in bow lines (siparium). Tragedy is represented on two fragments from the Collection Campana. It decorated the cover of a sarcophagus, testified as such by the remains of a colossal mask at the corner (Fig. 832a-b).[76] There are remains of five figures. Near the right end (Fig. 832b) two heroes are conversing. They have masks with wide openings for the visible mouth, high onkos and a broad fillet over curly hair. The one to the right has a scepter in his left arm and holds his left wrist with his right hand. The other leans his head forward. A small figure, prob-

ably a slave boy, brings a casket which he carries, stooping under the weight, on his back and supports with his lifted hands. Next to the second hero is a water organ (cf. the tomb relief of Valerianus Paterculus, Fig. 788) and behind it a pillar. On the other side of the organ a man holding a curved staff in his left arm is kneeling or beginning to kneel to the two heroes, stretching out his right hand toward the knees of the second hero. Another man, probably a servant, is turning away, holding with his right hand a mantle, which hangs down from his right shoulder. All four men wear tights; the sleeves of the heroes are of smooth material, those of the kneeling man and the servant indicated as rough material, tricot, felt, or fur, by regular rows of bored holes. They appear on the legs of the second hero and the kneeling man, on the sleeves of the kneeling man and the servant and on the whole body of the last. This shows his stuffed-out stomach, similar to the servant on the cake mould from Ostia (Fig. 793). His mantle is knotted around his hips, while those of the others are draped in the usual manner. The first hero has a high belt. The slave wears a short tunic. The background has a curtain, shown to the side of the first hero, and a door, shown between the two heroes. Some trellis appears between the kneeling man and the servant. It seems possible that the scene is taken from funeral plays, during which some celebrated scene from tragedy was performed.

While all spectacles ended in Rome in 568 after the coming of the Lombards, they continued in Constantinople, that is, in the Byzantine Empire, as late as 692.[77] Here, in this Eastern Roman Empire, tragedy with its late Roman pathos and costume, the mime as a low burlesque show, alternating with jugglers, horse shows, and animal baitings lived on from the fourth into the seventh century. Ivory tablets which the consuls handed out when they gave these plays represent below the large figure of the consul throwing the mappa to open the games, all these still popular entertainments.

A fragment in the Hermitage (Fig. 833),[78] dated around 500, shows two scenes from tragedy. The upper represents Medea. The youthful actor has taken off his large mask, which has a high onkos

Fig. 832a-b. Tragic scene. Fragments from marble sarcophagus, Louvre

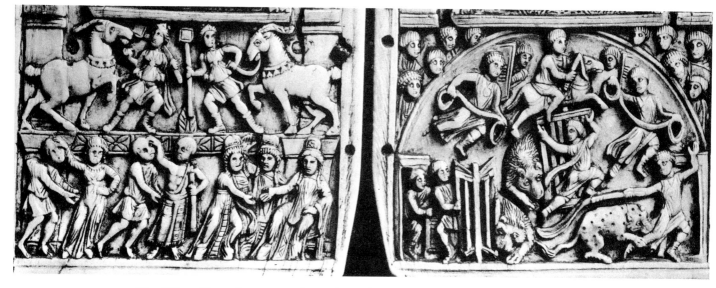

Fig. 834. a, Horse show, scenes from mime and tragedy; b, Animal baiting

covered by a Phrygian cap, and saluts the acclaiming audience with his raised right hand. The two boys at his side point with lively movements to their mother, and a man in the background also acclaims the actor. In the lower scene the actor probably represents the blind Oedipus leaning on two boys, with his two daughters in the background. The secondary persons, however, may perhaps represent members of the chorus.

In the diptych of the consul Anastasius issued in 517, now in the Cabinet des Médailles of the Bibliothèque Nationale in Paris (Fig. 834a-b),[79] a tragic scene comprising two seated and one standing person is represented in the lower register, right. On another tablet of the same consul, found in Limoges, now in Leningrad, Fig. 835,[80] there is in the same place only one tragic actor, an older man, leaning heavily on a boy and lifting his right hand. (This may be the old Tiresias from an Oedipus drama.) Next to the tragic scene (Fig. 834a) a mime is depicted. It shows a man holding a sword and a woman with a crown, both in long dresses, laying their right hands on the foreheads of two bald-headed, idiotic looking men in short dress. Both these stupidi have identical movements, with trembling knees and outstretched hands as if supplicating. Perhaps we have here a scene with magicians and charlatans healing blind men. Another mimus on a tablet of the same date, 517, found in Liége, now in the Victoria and Albert Museum at London (Fig. 836),[81] has in the center a young man who seems to deal out compensation and punishment. He lays his hand on the head of a youth who is coming forward smiling, with hands outstretched, while a man behind him lifts his left hand. On the other side two slaves, whose hands are bound behind their backs, are punished by having crabs hung from their noses. One of them tries to scrape off the torturing pincers on a table.

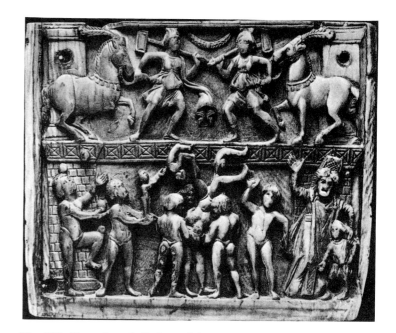

Fig. 835. Horse show, ball player, living pyramid, tragic hero

Fig. 836. Horse show and scene from mime

251

Fig. 837. Horse show, chorus, ball player. Ivory tablet, Verona

Figs. 838, 839. Animal baiting. Terracotta relief, Milan; Painting from balustrade, theater of Corinth

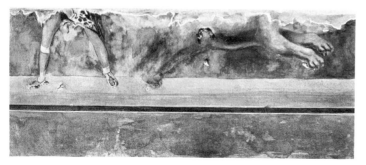

The public, hardened by bloody spectacles, must surely have laughed heartily over this torture.

Besides these theatrical plays there are race horses brought forward (Figs. 834-837). These horse shows allude to the races in the circus. Near the Tiresias in tragic costume (Fig. 835) there are seven acrobats forming a complicated living pyramid, to the apex of which a little boy is just being lifted. The counterpart to Tiresias at the other end of the register is a juggler with three balls, one each on his head, his right hand, and his bent knee (cf. the statuette, Fig. 830). Another such ball player is represented on an ivory tablet of Anastasius, dated 517, in Verona (Fig. 837).[82] Beside him is a chorus of four boys and three men, the latter perhaps the conductor, the musician with a syrinx, and the poet. Thus there are again seven men in the chorus as in the funeral games of Cyrene (Fig. 787). To the right is an organ which probably accompanied the songs or recitals of the chorus.

Animal baitings belonging in the amphitheater are also frequently represented (Fig. 834b). Lions, panthers, bears, stags and elephants are popular in these venationes.[83] Gladiators no longer fought against each other,[84] but they fought in Rome and elsewhere against the wild beasts,[85] as seen on a terracotta relief in the Museo teatrale alla Scala di Milano (Fig. 838).[86] The circus plays remained widely popular everywhere. The circus always was a separate building for chariot races, although it occasionally was brought together into an architectural unit with a theater, as in Orange, Aezani, and Pessinus (cf. Ch. XIV, Figs. 678 and 743).[87] Special amphitheaters were generally built for the gladiatorial fights and animal baitings in those lands where the Romans first introduced their culture. When, however, amphitheaters were not available, the wild games fought their way into the theater buildings. The oldest evidence is in Pompeii, where the square behind the large theater was used as barracks for gladiators and where they appeared after 63 against the same richly-decorated scaenae frons as the mimes and pantomimes, a fact evidenced by the wall paintings of the latest style in Pompeii (cf. Figs. 777-778). For Athens, gladiatorial fights are attested for the period of Augustus by Dio Chrysostomus (*Oratio*, xxxi,121). A marble parapet was later erected to protect the audience (see Ch. XIV, Figs. 717-720, 725). In the theater of Corinth gladiatorial fights and animal baitings are proved for the early third century by the paintings on the parapet around the orchestra (Fig. 839).[88] Lions, bulls, and leopards are recognizable. In other theaters the orchestra was also equipped as an arena for these popular games. The so-called Termessustype is certainly designed for animal baitings, as the small doors leading into the orchestra prove (Ch. XIV, Figs. 740-742). It is a compromise building which permitted the Romans in Asia Minor during the second century A.D. to enjoy their beloved bloody spectacles in spite of the lack of amphitheaters.

In several theaters, as in Athens, the parapet was made watertight (see Ch. XIV, Fig. 720),[89] or, as in Corinth, the lowest ten rows of seats were removed and the rock cut down so as to make a podium for the auditorium (see Fig. 727).[90] The arena, then, can hardly have served—as was formerly believed—for mock naval battles (naumachiae), for which it is too small and for which special buildings were erected.[91] They were used rather for water ballets, aquacades (see above, p. 237). Sometimes rectangular, round, or oval water basins were placed in the orchestra, as in Corinth, Pompeii, Tyndaris, and Taormina (see above, Figs. 599, 607, 616, 728). These could also be used, in addition to swimming feats, for exhibiting and baiting water beasts like crocodiles and hippopotami.[92]

The games in the theaters and amphitheaters became continually wilder and bloodier, in Rome as well as in the provinces.[93] In the time of Trajan, 10,000 pairs of gladiators, as well as 11,000 animals, were presented in the Flavian amphitheater at Rome during four months. At this time a musician, dressed as Orpheus, was torn to pieces by wild beasts. How many death sentences were carried out there for helpless and innocent persons we do not know. Finally, slaves, prisoners of war, and robbers who had to fight for their lives or be defenselessly slaughtered, were replaced by Christian martyrs (Augustine, *Confessions*, VI,8,13). This ended in the closing of all arenas, including the theaters, after the general recognition and acceptance of Christianity.

The form and content of the ancient theater, however, have lived on or have been resuscitated in later times. Our modern theater buildings and dramatic performances are incomprehensible without a knowledge of Greek and Roman antiquity.

CHAPTER XVI

THE INFLUENCE OF THE ANCIENT THEATER ON

THE MODERN THEATER

THE history of the Greek and Roman theater, like the history of the whole Greek and Roman culture, is so rich and many-sided that each later period of European civilization has found some aspect of it to use as an inspiration or model for its own time. Even the periods which resented the ancient theater and the religion which underlay its productions found something to explore and to use for their own goals. Thus the mediaeval period with its distrust of everything pagan and the romantic age of the early nineteenth century with its hatred for classicizing and its nationalistic tendency, drew occasionally on ancient sources which are still living and productive today.

Although in mediaeval times the tragedy and the theater buildings of the Greeks and Romans were unknown, the Latin comedies of Plautus and Terence remained alive. In the tenth century the nun Roswitha of Gandersheim wrote six religious and moral comedies in imitation of Terence, in which she portrayed in the Latin language the victory of Christianity over paganism.[1] In the twelfth century Vital de Blois, a French writer, adapted the *Querolus*—the only Latin comedy of the imperial period, then considered to be by Plautus—in his *Aulularia* and presented the story of Amphitruo in his *Geta*. The comedies of Plautus and Terence were copied and read all through mediaeval times, with Terence preferred and continuously illustrated.[2] This, however, was done only in the monasteries and in small intellectual circles. There were no theatrical presentations and no real continuity in the study of the Latin comedy.

For the entertainment of the people the performances of mimes, farces, jugglers, rope dancers, and jesters lived on. Such lower-class performances are always more conservative and more persistent than those of literary drama. In Europe the actors of the mime gave their third-rate entertainments in the small cities and villages, in inns and in castles.[3] They have found a permanent home in the modern circus. As frequently rather serious jesters, they play an important role in the drama of Shakespeare. The Turks also took over the mime and turned it into Karagöz.[4] The farce continues even today in both of its most important seats, in Southern Italy as Commedia dell'Arte with Pulcinella and Arlequino

(harlequin),[5] and in Western Germany as puppet shows with Kasperle. The English Punch and Judy show also has its origin here.[6] These figures inherited the patchwork costume of the later Roman mime, the centunculus (see Ch. XV, Fig. 829). The old Pappus or Senex became Pantaloon, the clever Dossenus the doctor, the greedy Maccus Pulcinella; the boasting Bucco and Manducus with his chattering teeth became the German Kasperle and the English Punch.

In the Renaissance, the reawakening of ancient civilization included the study of the Latin writers Plautus, Seneca, and Vitruvius, who were used as models for creative production.

In Italy the Latin comedies were imitated as early as the late fourteenth century, when for example Petrarch wrote his *Philologia*, said to have been in Terentian character. It is unfortunately lost. The influence of Plautus during the fifteenth century was, however, much greater than that of Terence.[7] Both were published in printed editions, first Terence in 1470, then Plautus in 1472. There followed performances of Plautus in the palaces of Cardinals, thus the *Aulularia* was presented in 1484 in the palace of the Quirinal. The *Menaechmi* was performed before the Pope in the Vatican in 1502. At Ferrara comedies by Plautus in translation were presented as early as 1486. At the wedding of Lucrezia Borgia at Ferrara in 1502 five comedies of Plautus were presented on five succeeding days. In the sixteenth century many comedies were produced in Italy which combined the motifs of Latin comedies with portrayal of contemporary Italian life, the earliest being Ariosto's *La Cassaria* and *I Suppositi*, each based on several Latin models. This comedy was called the *commedia erudita* in contrast to the *commedia dell'arte*.

During the sixteenth century the influence of the Roman comedy spread to Spain, Germany, and Holland.[8] The University of Salamanca decided in 1574 that henceforth no comedies except those of Plautus and Terence should be performed at the University.

In the seventeenth century the most famous imitator of Plautus and Terence was Molière. His *L'Étourdi ou les Contretemps* (1653) is related to Plautus' *Bacchides*; his *L'École des Maris* (1661) is adapted from Terence's *Adelphoi*; his *Amphitryon* (1668) is an imitation of Plautus' tragicomoedia with the same title; *L'Avare* (1668) is a reworking of the *Aulularia*; finally, *Les Fourberies de Scapin* (1671) is based on Terence's *Phormio*. Molière is rather Terentian in spirit, but this spirit is combined with farcical elements which were taken from Plautus.

In England during the sixteenth century Plautus and Terence were frequently presented in schools and universities.[9] The students of the St. Paul's School in London performed *The Menaechmi* by Plautus in 1527 and the *Phormio* by Terence in 1528. At Oxford the *Andria* by Terence was produced in 1559 and at Cambridge the *Aulularia* by Plautus was put on, with Queen Elizabeth present, in 1564. Plays in imitation of Latin comedies were frequent, but they show combination with influences from Italian comedies and with English settings.

Shakespeare had certainly read Plautus in his school days. In his *Comedy of Errors* (about 1591), he used the *Menaechmi* as his model, enriching it with motifs from the *Amphitruo*.[10] He doubled the number of the twins and thereby increased the confusion and the number of farcical complications. His Falstaff is a blending of the braggart warrior and the parasite in the *Miles gloriosus* and other plays by Plautus.

Shakespeare and his contemporaries considered Plautus a model for comedy and Seneca a model for tragedy (cf. Polonius in *Hamlet*, ii,ii,419f: "Seneca cannot be too heavy, nor Plautus too light").

Seneca dominated the tragic stage of the Renaissance for 300 years.[11] The first early Renaissance dramas in the Latin language and in Senecan form are the *Eccerinis* and the *Achilleis* written by Alberto Mussato of Padua in about 1314. Italian tragedies of the sixteenth century are almost purely Senecan. They emphasize the elements of horror and gruesomeness, the motif of vengeance, ghosts, and death on the stage. French tragedy down to the neo-classic tragedies of Corneille (1606-1684) and Racine (1639-1692), on the contrary, banned scenes of gruesome violence and death. They preferred to develop the characters with indomitable will in exceedingly intricate plots. Their interest in psychology, however, is closely related to Seneca.

In England the tragedies of Seneca were performed in schools and universities from as early as 1560. The first English translation appeared in 1581.[12] After this, purely Senecan tragedies were written for academic circles. But Marlowe in his plays and particularly Thomas Kyd in his *Spanish Tragedy* (1586) fused Seneca and the popular English drama. Bloody scenes, revenge, horror, and violence entered the main stream of the English drama, continued in the plays of Shakespeare and persisted well into the seventeenth century. The Elizabethan drama inherited from Seneca superhuman villains, bloodthirsty passion, but also an effective rhetorical style, sincere tragic sentiment, and good dramatic technique. The bloody scenes, murder on the stage, revenge, cruelty, and pathos in the English drama surpass even Seneca in intensity and frequency. Senecan sensationalism and rhetoric appealed to the playwrights of the Renaissance, and thus Seneca helped them to create their own dramas. Through Seneca, therefore, the subjects first given literary form by Aeschylus, Sophocles, and Euripides have taken their place in the literature of the world.

Vitruvius became the model for the theater building of the later Renaissance and the baroque period, just as Plautus and Terence had become the models for comedy and Seneca for tragedy. Vitruvius was rediscovered and printed for the first time in 1484. Up to that date there had been no special theater building. The mediaeval plays were given in the churches; the Renaissance plays in palaces, schools, and universities. The first stages built especially for classical plays were erected in schools and academies of Italy, France, England, and Germany, in a form developed from mediaeval art combined with precepts taken from Vitruvius. Such a stage is represented in late fifteenth-century manuscripts of Terence.[13] A platform four to five feet high has at the rear a façade of pillars supporting arches. The different houses needed for comedy are placed in compartments of the arcade. Curtains hide the interior, which would occasionally be revealed. Each principal character has his own house. The idea is that of a row of houses along an open street. Although the architect tried to recreate a Roman stage, it is in reality an adaptation of the mediaeval stage with forms taken from a misinterpreted description by Vitruvius. The actors wore their contemporary Renaissance costumes.

The late fifteenth, the sixteenth, and the seventeenth centuries were much interested in the machinery of the ancient theater as described by Vitruvius. A linen background was fixed on a skeleton of planks and parted in the center, so that it could be drawn away to show other scenery, like the ancient scaena ductilis. Three-sided devices revolving around a pivot could be used for different pictures on side wings or for living pictures (tableaux vivants), like the ancient scaena vertilis or the periaktoi (cf. Ch. VI, pp. 74-75). They were called telari because they were painted on linen (Fig. 840a-b) and were used from the late fifteenth century on in France. In Florence they are described and recommended by Vignola in the sixteenth cen-

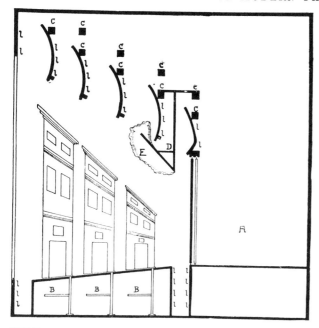

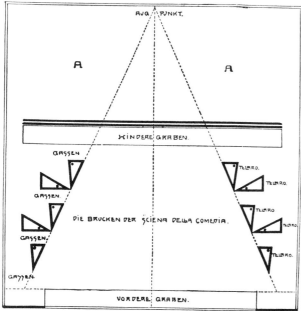

Fig. 840a-b. Telari stage by Joseph Furttenbach; Section; Plan

tury. In the early seventeenth century Inigo Jones devised a scheme following Vitruvius of turning sections around for scene changes in Christ College at Oxford (1605).[14]

In London the inn-yards were used for plays. A platform on trestles was erected at the far end of the yards with doors leading to it from inside the inn. Richer patrons used galleries around the court. Special theaters were erected in a similar form beginning in 1576; such were the Theatre (1576), the Swan (ca.1595) and the Globe (1599), the theaters used by Shakespeare and his contemporaries. Above

the large open platform were galleries divided by pillars.[15] They resemble the Assteas stage (cf. Fig. 479), the stage used in Southern Italy for the popular farce, but there is hardly any real connection. It is possible that wandering troupes of mimes may have carried this form through Europe. It is, however, more likely that similar requirements and circumstances produced similar forms.[16]

At the same time in Italy the study of Vitruvius led to a quite different form. Italian designers followed his indications for different scenery for the different kinds of plays and used his plans for arranging the auditorium, the orchestra, and the stage. Their experiments in reproducing the Roman theatrical forms culminated in the Teatro Olympico in Vicenza, designed by Palladio and erected 1580-1584 (Fig. 841).[17] The auditorium and the orchestra have the Roman semi-circular arrangement. Small staircases lead from the orchestra to the long stage, which is backed by a richly-designed façade with one large central opening and four other smaller doors and with two more doors from the side buildings for entrances. But a contemporary addition was the perspective vistas of city streets seen through the large central door. This opening served as a frame for the painted changing scenes, and from it developed the modern "proscenium arch." In the Farnese Theater at Parma built in 1618 the Roman forms are distorted.[18] The auditorium is elongated, the stage has a richly sculptured proscenium arch, and a kind of scaenae frons architecture is added above the seats. This led to our modern theaters with boxes arranged around the auditorium in several stories. As in the drama, so in the theater building; the Roman source was used as a model for the creations of the period.

Joseph Furttenbach built a theater in 1640/41 in Ulm in which he used the scaena ductilis, the scaena vertilis, and the flying machine (Fig. 840a-b).[19] In a trench at the back of the stage movable coulisses could be parted in the center and drawn to the sides and thus the scenes were changed. Three prismatic trestles at each side could be turned by a handle to show different sides with different paintings. Cranes with square hooks could carry clouds and heavenly apparitions. Such a flying machine was also used in Turin in the seventeenth century.[20]

The study of the Latin authors during the sixteenth century was supplemented by that of the Greek authors. Aristotle's *Poetics* was read but sometimes misunderstood. He was credited with the three unities of action, place, and time.[21] This induced the playwrights to restrict themselves to a single plot, to avoid a change of scenery, and to limit the action to not more than one day. This was in contrast to the taste of the late Renaissance and the baroque period, when audiences wanted rich shows and got them in the intermezzi, given between the acts of the dramas, where scenery could be changed at will, and discrepancies of time and place were disregarded.

Greek Comedy was almost non-existent during the Renaissance. Menander was unknown; he had disappeared behind his Latin imitators. Aristophanes was occasionally performed in Cambridge: *Plutus* in 1536 and *Peace* in 1546.[22] A program drawn up for Jesuit colleges in 1551 recommends readings from *Plutus* (the latest of Aristophanes' comedies) in the class for beginning Greek.[23]

The comedies of the seventeenth and eighteenth centuries continued to use the stock characters of the Latin comedy: the contrasting pairs of old men and of youths, the braggart soldier, the parasite, the miser, the servant, the maid; also the same plots: comedies of errors, mistaken identity, impersonation, disguise. While in the seventeenth century Plautus was favored as a model, Terence, who was nearer to the Greek originals, became more popular in the eighteenth.[24]

The plays by the three classical Greek tragic writers were first printed by Aldus in Venice: Sophocles was published in 1502, Euripides in 1503, and Aeschylus in 1518. From then on they were translated and adapted in Italy, France, and Germany. Sophocles' *Oedipus the King* was performed in an Italian translation at the occasion of the opening of the Teatro Olympico (see Fig. 841) in 1585.[25] Music was used as a background. In Germany, Melanchthon, the friend of Luther, translated Greek plays into Latin. The celebrated Meister Hans Sachs wrote an *Alcestis* in 1555.

Opera, the most important creation based on the Greek tragedies, originated at the end of the sixteenth century in Florence.[26] A group of scholars, poets, and musicians called the Camerata gathered in 1594 in the palazzo of the nobleman Giovanni Bardi. They discovered that music had played a predominant role in ancient tragedy. Members of this group included Vincenzo Galileo, the father of Galileo Galilei, a musician and mathematician, much interested in the revival of ancient music; Jacopo Peri and Guilio Caccini, musicians; and Ottario Rinuccini, a poet. Peri and Rinuccini collaborated in *Dafne*, performed in 1597; Caccini with both in *Euridice*, performed in 1600. They were convinced that they had recreated Greek tragedy. This mixture of drama, music, and spectacle spread through all Italy, France, Austria, Germany, and England. Claudio Monteverdi performed his *Dafne*, *Arianna*, and *Orfeo* at Mantua in 1607-1608. Mythological stories in dialogue against a musical background, thought to be reincarnated Greek tragedy, became

Fig. 841. Teatro Olympico, Vicenza

so popular that most theaters from then on were built in large scale and with overladen decorations solely for opera. Venice had one opera house in 1637, ten more in 1700, by which time some 360 operas had been produced.

The eighteenth century is a period of great actors and singers, and opera flourished. Gluck based *Orpheus und Eurydike* (1762) on principles of the Greek drama, which he attempted to recreate. His pupil Antonio Maria Gasparo Sacchini (1772-82, active in London; 1782-86 in Paris where he died) wrote an opera, *Edipo a Colono*, based on Sophocles' last tragedy. More sumptuous theaters were built for opera: San Carlo in Naples, 1737, and La Scala in Milan, 1778. The Metropolitan Opera House in New York City still follows in general the Italian pattern. Richard Wagner was the last composer to attempt to produce a drama in the nineteenth century in music, with the legendary background of his own people for subject matter, just as the Greeks had used their myths. The Festival theater in Bayreuth, built in 1876 for Wagner's operas, still has the Italian kind of stage setting, but has improved the auditorium by adopting the ancient system (see below).

In the second half of the eighteenth century Greek drama was rediscovered, reinterpreted, and revitalized in new tragedies. The leading intellectual men in Germany and Italy now read the Greek originals, not only translations. Winckelmann as a poor schoolmaster in his youth read Sophocles among other Greek writers. He certainly could find here, as later in visual art, the same essential quality of "noble simplicity and quiet grandeur."[27] Lessing, the great critic of drama, was the first to declare in 1759 that the French neoclassical tragedy is far inferior to the Greeks.[28] Goethe read Greek tragedies in 1773 and imitated the *Iphigenia in Tauris* of Euripides in his *Iphigenia*, which he wrote in 1779 in prose and recast in verse in 1787. He performed, himself, the role of Orestes in the presentation of this tragedy in Ettersburg near Weimar.[29] Schiller composed for his *Bride of Messina* (1803), beautiful—even if only pseudo-classic—choral songs and gave to this drama an excellent balanced form in the classic spirit. In Italy Alfieri gave a new development to the stories used by the Greek tragic writers. He imitated Euripides, Sophocles, and Aeschylus in his *Oreste* (1776), Sophocles in his *Antigone* (1783), and Euripides in his *Alceste seconda* (1790). He is, however, rather more Senecan than Greek.[30] This style of drama and grand opera has remained prevalent in Italy up to the present day.

The nineteenth century is a century of classical scholarship.[31] Much research was done, and Greek and Latin had the undisputed primary position in the curricula of high schools and universities in England as well as in Germany, Italy, and France. More and more people read the authors in the original. While Keats knew only translations, Shelley read the dramatic poets, of whom Aeschylus was his favorite, in Greek. He even wrote in 1816 a *Prometheus Unbound* as a sequel to Aeschylus' *Prometheus Bound*.[32] He was reading Sophocles' dramas at the time of his death. He also translated Euripides' *Cyclops*. When, however, he tried to write an Aristophanic comedy with the title *Oedipus Tyrannus* or *Swellfoot the Tyrant*, he failed. It is impossible to transfer Aristophanic comedy into any other period. Robert Browning translated three Greek dramas, among them the *Agamemnon* of Aeschylus. Nietzsche produced in 1872 a new theory for the origin of Greek tragedy.[33] In contrast to the prevailing opinion that it was impassive and stiff, he saw that it had grown out of the dithyrambic frenzy of the Dionysiac cult in combination with the beauty of the cult of Apollo. His hero was Aeschylus. His friend Wagner adopted for his new form of opera, the music drama, the conception that music is the soul of drama and drama is the body of the work.

At the end of the nineteenth and during the first half of the twentieth century, Greek and Latin lost their leading position in education. They had to yield to more practical training in modern languages, physical science, economics, and psychology. One reason for the decline was that many eminent scholars taught the classics in a way which deterred students seeking to understand the spirit of antiquity. This author remembers a class with Professor Hermann Diels in Berlin University on Plato. He used up many hours discussing the different forms of different words in different manuscripts, and we learned hardly anything about the significance of Plato's ideas.[34] Yet the interest in Greek drama reached an unusual height in the same period.

In the twentieth century the attitude of scholars and poets in reference to Greek and Latin drama has changed. In order to bring the masterpieces to a larger public than only the classicists, who became less and less interested in the languages themselves, eminent scholars translated the dramas into their native tongues. Thus Ulrich von Wilamowitz Moellendorf in Germany, Gilbert Murray at Oxford, and Moses Hadas at Columbia University, have translated the Greek tragedies and comedies on the basis of a much deeper and more scholarly knowledge than any of their predecessors.[35]

The modern poets, on the other hand, use the ancient originals as vehicles for bringing forth their own ideas of the great issues of human life: love, war, sin, tyranny, courage, fate. They preserve the outlines of the ancient myth as transmitted by the

Greek tragic poets, but they alter the values, the motifs, the significance, and the results. Their own philosophy and political creeds are brought in. Thus Eugene O'Neill in his *Mourning Becomes Electra* uses the frame given by Aeschylus' trilogy the *Oresteia*, but the scene is laid among the Puritan aristocracy of New England in the time of the Civil War, instead of in the royal house of Mycenae at the time of the Trojan War. It has been remarked that O'Neill used the severe dramatic structure of Aeschylus' masterpiece for "a grand stupendous thriller," "his most ambitious and impressive play," and "a mechanical imitation of the Attic pattern."[36] The last work by Gerhard Hauptmann (died 1946) published in 1949, *Die Atriden-Tetralogie* (*Iphigenie in Aulis; Agamemnons Tod; Elektra;* and *Iphigenie in Delphi*) is based on the *Oresteia* of Aeschylus and the *Electra, Iphigenia in Aulis* and the *Iphigenia in Tauris* by Euripides. Hauptmann uses, however, the ancient stories of the house of Atreus to describe the mood in Germany during the Nazi period and the lost war. It was performed by the Utah Players in their home state and in other places in the West.

The French and the German writers are particularly inclined to imbue the classical dramas with political allusions. Thus Jean-Paul Sartre, in *The Flies*, written in 1943 during the Nazi occupation of France, reworks the *Eumenides* of Aeschylus in such a way that the flies represent the feeling of guilt instead of being revenging furies. Orestes does not kill his mother and her paramour out of revenge for his father, but to liberate the population of Thebes from tyranny. The moral implication is that France must achieve self-reliance and assume a sense of responsibility.[37] Anouilh has reworked Sophocles' *Antigone* (1942) in a similar sense. This play was produced in Paris at the time when it was occupied by the Germans. The framework of Sophocles was retained, but the leading characters were changed. The criticism of the tyrant is so subtle that the Nazis did not grasp the significance. When this play was presented by Cedric Hardwicke

on Broadway in 1946 in the English translation of Lewis Galantière the idea of protest was not brought out. Therefore neither public nor critics understood that politics had replaced religion. The audiences were bored and the play closed rather quickly, despite the great art of Katharine Cornell as Antigone.[38] The impression of dullness was increased by the commentator who substituted in this play for the chorus, by the introduction of the nurse who is a Euripidean character, and by everyday dress, particularly the kind of housecoat for Antigone and an evening coat for Creon instead of the beautiful Greek dresses. More authentic dresses were used in another representation of the same play in the off-Broadway production of the Circle-in-the-Square Theater at Sheridan Square in Greenwich Village in 1951. Even if Creon had not worn the swastika, the veiled allusion to the problems of the Hitler era came out very well. In the German *Antigone* by Walter Hasenclever, presented in 1917, the figure of Creon bore a resemblance to the last German Emperor, Wilhelm II, but at the same time seemed to foreshadow the era of Hitler, whose Gestapo drove Hasenclever to his suicide in 1940. In a similar way the *Trojan Women* (*Die Troerinnen*) by Franz Werfel (1914), presented in the Deutsche Theater in Berlin and in many other German cities, seems to predict the defeat and survival of Germany after both world wars, as the original by Euripides predicted the defeat and survival of Athens after the Peloponnesian war.

The *Medea* of Euripides was adapted by Anouilh in 1946, translated into English by Robinson Jeffers, and staged by John Gielgud in 1947-1949 on Broadway.[39] The translation, the production, and the great art of Judith Anderson (Fig. 842a-b) all showed a tendency toward the Senecan spirit. Instead of the tragic grandeur of a deceived and humbled proud woman, only the jealousy of a disappointed loving wife was worked out. The background of a decaying Minoan palace (Fig. 842a), such as neither Corinth nor Athens could ever have known, also detracted

Fig. 842. Judith Anderson in *Medea*; a, with John Gielgud as Jason; b, with her children

from the tragic story. Great modern actresses like Judith Anderson are inclined to the more pathetic style of Seneca; recently a retired Broadway actress, playing the *Medea* of Euripides on the Columbia campus, insisted upon inserting one speech from Seneca into the Euripidean text. The idea of Medea, the fate of a foreigner in a hostile land, was also used by Maxwell Anderson in his *Wingless Victory* (1937). Hugo von Hofmannsthal's *Electra* (1903) and the music written for it by Richard Strauss develops the torrid and violent feelings only alluded to in the plays of the same name by Sophocles and Euripides. Robinson Jeffers' *The Cretan Woman*, performed 1954 at the Provincetown Theater in New York City, is a distorted version of Euripides' *Hippolytus* mixed with Senecan frenzy, calculated revenge, and modern adulterous passion. Jeffers interprets the Greek myth with ludicrous prejudices. The costumes were good, but the scenery was poor. Gabriele d'Annunzio in his *Hippolite* (1909) complicated the passionate love of Phaedra with her deep hatred of her husband, in order to make the play more exciting. Siegfried Lipiner added (in 1913) hidden love of Hippolytus for Phaedra. All these modern additions spoil the beauty of the Greek originals.

The best modern adaptation of a Latin comedy is the *Amphitryon 38* by Jean Giraudoux, adapted from the French by S. N. Behrman, and produced in New York City in 1937 and 1938 by the Theatre Guild with Alfred Lunt and Lynn Fontanne as Jupiter and Alcmene. Giraudoux—as before him Molière (1668), Kleist (1807) and other imitators—has retained the invention and the working out of the theme by Plautus (see Ch. XI, p. 151); but he reveals new ideas about love between husband and wife, and the power of women over men. He believed that he had written the 38th version of the story. If he has counted rightly, his play ought to have the number 39, as he did not know about the phlyakes farce on the same subject (see above, Ch. X, Fig. 484). In the meantime a fortieth *Amphitryon* has become a musical comedy: *Out of This World* by Cole Porter, produced on Broadway in 1950. It lays the old story in modern Athens and moves back

Fig. 843a. Aristophanes' *Birds* performed by high school students in Berlin. Painting by Eric Heckel

in the direction of the old farce. The same is true for *The Boys from Syracuse*, a musical comedy by Rodgers and Hart, with text by George Abbott, based on Plautus' *Menaechmi*.[40] In the *Menaechmi* two brothers are constantly mistaken for each other. Shakespeare took this subject for his *Comedy of Errors*. He was, however, also influenced by the theme of mistaken identity between Jupiter and Amphitryon on the one side, and Mercury, the servant of the Olympian gods, and the mortal servant Sosias on the other side. Both these plays, however, are inconceivable without the Greek and Southern Italian masked and stereotyped costume. Only with the typical disguise and complete covering of face and body is the interchange of indistinguishable brothers made possible.

While the humor and stage efficiency of Plautus is indestructible, the representative of Greek Old Comedy, Aristophanes, does not lend himself to modern adaptations and cannot be understood without a thorough study of the political, cultural, and literary circumstances under which he wrote. The *Lysistrata*, made into a farce from the Greek of Aristophanes by Gilbert Seldes, and produced by the Philadelphia Theatre Association in New York City, 1930-31, reached 252 performances. When, however, the *Lysistrata* was made into a "movie" in Vienna and announced in New York in 1948 as "The

Fig. 843b. Menander's *Samia*

Fig. 844. Performances of Plautus and Terence by German students; a-c, Cassel; d, Giessen

Battle of the Sexes," it became, despite some Viennese grace related to Aristophanes' grace, a deserved failure. The same is true of the recent attempts to rewrite and produce the *Thesmophoriazusae* and the *Ecclesiazusae* of Aristophanes. The first, in an anonymous translation edited by Whitney Oates and Eugene O'Neill, Jr., was performed at the Rooftop Theater in New York City. The latter, presented under the title *Time for a Change* by the Division of Social Philosophy of Cooper Union in New York City, used the literal translation by Benjamin Bickley Rogers in Loeb's Classical Library. Both were conceived as farces, which Aristophanes' comedies with their serious backgrounds decidedly are not. If Aristophanes is played in a more serious mood, as the *Lysistrata* was performed by Max Reinhardt in the Grosse Schauspielhaus at Berlin, or the *Frogs* in Wellesley and Reed College, Portland, Oregon in 1940, the result is more satisfactory. Students of a High School in Berlin ventured in 1935 to present Aristophanes' *Birds*. The gay, masked production amused the audience and inspired the celebrated painter Erich Heckel for a painting of the two main actors and part of the bird-chorus (Fig. 843a).

Menander, the newly-discovered representative of Greek New Comedy, in contrast to Aristophanes, lends himself beautifully to modern presentations. A successful production, under the direction of Carl Robert, of the *Arbitrants* in German translation was given in Lauchstedt, in the old theater, in 1908 by students of Halle University, among them Gerhard Rodenwalt. The *Arbitrants* in English translation was produced in 1929 at Haverford and Bryn Mawr Colleges under the direction of L. A. Post; and the same play was given in Berkeley, California, in the translation of Gilbert Murray (1948). *The Girl from Samos*, reconstructed with fragments from the *Arbitrants*, was produced by Ida Lublinski Ehrlich in Everyman's Theatre in New York City during 1954-1955. Her play is more than a mere translation; she has blended together all the preserved scenes and all important characters found in the original fragments and made them into a delightful unit. Seeing her performance one realizes that all Greek dramatic poetry was meant to be produced and not

only read (Fig. 843b). An excellent and enjoyable performance of the newly found *Dyskolos* by Menander was given by the students of Fordham University in New York, in the translation by Gilbert Highet, in 1960. I believe that the plays by Menander have a meaning for modern audiences and a great future in the theater of our time, for their human qualities appeal to human nature at all times.

The best and most successful performances of ancient drama are those which are given in good and faithful translations without trying to bring in modern ideas, but where every effort is made to bring out the ancient conceptions. Thus the modern presentations of Plautus and Terence in Cassel and Frankfurt in Germany in 1930 by high school students led by Dr. Zuntz and in Giessen by university students were a great success (Figs. 844a-d). They were given in Greek dress, as the Latin comedies as well as those of Menander were given also in antiquity. Plautus' *Amphitruo* was given in the Roman theater of Ostia in 1955.

Performances of Greek tragedies could be seen in our time in many places: in Greece, Italy, France, Germany, Holland, England, and in the United States, mostly in good translations into the respective languages, but sometimes even in the original or modern Greek. This was the case in the impressive performances produced by an American, married to a Greek poet, Madame Sikilianos, in the ancient theater in Delphi in 1927 and 1930 (Figs. 845-846).[41] The back part of the orchestra was raised and temporarily built into a kind of podium. Here Prometheus in Aeschylus' *Prometheus* was seen bound to a rock, which was supposed to blend with

Fig. 846a-b. Performance of Aeschylus' *Prometheus* in Delphi

Fig. 845. Theater of Delphi during Aeschylus' *Prometheus*

Fig. 847a-d. Performance of Aeschylus' *Suppliants* in Delphi

the mountains in the background. The chorus of the Oceanides in the orchestra was sometimes turned toward him, with their backs to the spectators, lifting their hands while singing to him. In the same place the *Suppliants*, the oldest tragedy of Aeschylus known to us, was performed in 1930 (Figs. 847a-d). The chorus, which here has the leading part, performed various movements and dances in the orchestra (Figs. 847a-c). The actors, the king of Argos, for example, or the Egyptian herald who tries to seize one of the Danaides (Fig. 847d), or occasionally even some representatives of the chorus mounted the podium (Fig. 847c). The actors wore masks and long flowing robes (Fig. 848, Io, and Fig. 849, Oceanus). Special costumes and masks for the Egyptian herald in the *Suppliants* (Fig. 850) and for Hephaestus in the *Prometheus* (Fig. 851) were very impressive. Aeschylus' *Aga-*

memnon also was performed in 1930 in Delphi (Fig. 852), and the *Prometheus* was produced by Vittorio Gassman in 1956 in the ancient theater of Syracuse.[42]

The *Persians* was performed with masks in Frankfurt and without masks by the Berlin "Sprechchor" in the ancient Theater of Herodes Atticus in Athens in 1930. *The Seven against Thebes* was given in Ostia in 1927, where also the *Antigone* by Sophocles and the *Clouds* by Aristophanes were presented.[43]

The favorite drama by Aeschylus for modern presentation is, however, the *Agamemnon*. It was given in Greek in Delphi in 1930 and in Italian in the ancient theater of Syracuse in 1914, with an excellent actress as Cassandra (Fig. 853).[44] This author saw, in 1934, an outstanding performance in Greek at Bradfield College in England. This is a school for boys, most of whom afterwards pass to the universi-

Figs. 848-853. Modern actors in ancient tragedy

848   849   850   851   852   853

Fig. 854. Performance of Aeschylus' *Agamemnon*, Bradfield College, Reading, England

ties of Oxford and Cambridge and continue to take interest in their old college. The theater building and the acting, therefore, have had the benefit of advice from eminent scholars who were formerly students at Bradfield. The stage is a low podium between the two paraskenia. The theatron has the ideal democratic form that allows every spectator an equally good view of the play. It is built as the Greek theaters always were on the slope of a hill round the orchestra, this being a perfect circle. The background is a palace in simple lines with one door and a few steps leading to the low platform. The pictures of the chorus in the orchestra or the scene of Agamemnon and Cassandra arriving in their chariots surrounded by the soldiers in the midst of the chorus in the orchestra (Fig. 854) were fascinating. All parts, male and female, were played by students about eighteen years old. It was amazing how the heroic greatness and eternal vitality of the Greek tragedy came to life again in this excellent performance. Wonderful productions of *Agamemnon*, *Prometheus*, and other Greek tragedies have been given in the Greek language since 1928 in Wellesley College.

The whole *Oresteia—Agamemnon, Choephorae, and Eumenides*—was given in 1954 in Greek in the Randolph-Macon College at Lynchburg, Virginia. This college has performed Greek plays each year

since 1909, all in the Greek language. Besides the *Oresteia*, the *Electra* of Sophocles, the *Medea* and *The Trojan Women* of Euripides, and the *Birds* of Aristophanes were performed against improvised backgrounds with great success. Fordham University in New York City also performed Greek drama in the original language prior to World War II. The whole *Oresteia* was reduced to one hour for a presentation on television in January 1959 in New York. Even in this compressed version some scenes, for example the return of Agamemnon, made a great impression.

Revivals of the tragedies of Sophocles in good and exact translations, well presented, always make a deep impression. The *Antigone* was given in 1921 in the Volksbühne (the popular stage) at Berlin, in a fine translation by Walter Amelung under the direction of Jürgen Fehling and with a stirring performance by the young Mary Dietrich.[45] The actress looked like the Iphigenia of Feuerbach and brought out the human side of the Sophoclean character with deep understanding. The author saw an excellent presentation of Sophocles' *Electra* at Cedar Crest College, Pennsylvania, in an open-air theater where it was given several times up to 1956.

The best performances of *Electra* and *Oedipus the King* that the author has seen were given in 1952 in New York. The plays were presented in

Fig. 855a-c. Performance of Sophocles' *Electra* by the Greek National Theater

modern Greek by the Greek National Theater, staged by Alexis Minotis, with Katina Paxinou as Electra and Jocasta. Electra hugging the urn supposed to contain the ashes of her brother Orestes, who is standing beside her alive (Fig. 855a); Electra embracing the feet of the old pedagogue who has brought Orestes home (Fig. 855b); Electra surrounded by the chorus, who really gave emphasis to her expression of grief (Fig. 855c)—all these scenes made the great art of Sophocles come to life again. Similarly moving was *Oedipus the King* with Alexis Minotis in the title role. When old Tiresias loomed threateningly over Oedipus who asks, "What parents?" surrounded by the chorus members, transmitting their sympathetic feelings (Fig. 856a), and when Oedipus realized the bitter truth through the testimony of the old servant, "Ah me—I am on the dreaded brink of speech," and the chorus appeared stunned by the revelation of the guilt of their venerated king (Fig. 856b), then the eternal value of Greek tragedy was brought out in full power.[46] The chorus, all too often a stumbling block in modern productions, here was excellent. The National Theater has repeated these performances in Greece: *Oedipus the King* in 1951 at Delphi, in 1955 in Athens together with Euripides' *Hecuba*, and in 1956 at Epidaurus, where Sophocles' *Antigone* and the *Medea* of Euripides were also performed. The Greek Art Theater has performed three Greek plays in Athens in the theater of Herodes Atticus, where

other plays were also given (Fig. 857):[47] in 1930 the *Persians* (see above, p. 262) and in 1955 Sophocles' *Oedipus the King*, Euripides' *Hecuba*, and the *Orfeo* by Gluck, one of the early operas based on Greek tragedy, and in 1956 the *Medea* by Euripides. *Oedipus the King* was also presented in the reconstructed theater of Sabratha (Fig. 695) in the presence of Mussolini in 1937. Max Reinhardt presented the same tragedy in his great drama theater (Grosse Schauspielhaus) where in the large orchestra the crowds of people and then the chorus were presented in a clear and integrated way. The music had a wonderful effect with the stage building serving as a sounding board.

Oedipus the King is a favorite with modern actors and stage managers. Laurence Olivier of the Old Vic in London, England, gave a truly tragic performance on Broadway in 1946 in this play. The proud behavior in the beginning, the turning from confidence to fear, the despair at the end, made this a memorable recreation of the Greek spirit. The production in Stratford, Ontario, in 1954 and 1955 by Tyrone Guthrie, despite excellent actors, and despite the attempt to imitate Greek costume, had no power to move the audience. The human characters were distorted and literally stilted, on Roman elevated boots, and wore much too stylized monstrous masks, quite different from what we know Sophocles used. The movements were rigid and stylized to the extreme. It was like a Freudian inter-

Fig. 856a-b. Performance of Sophocles' *Oedipus the King* by the Greek National Theater

Fig. 857. Performance in the Theater of Herodes Atticus, Athens

pretation, which makes the one case of a son killing his unknown father and marrying his unknown and still young mother (Greek girls married at 12-15 years of age) into a neurotic "Oedipus complex." The theater was also too small for such a severe and gigantic mounting. A film version of the production under the direction of Guthrie was presented in New York in 1957 and was better than the theater production. It was concise and serious. The play fared still better in the performance by Reinhardt in the Circus Schumann in 1910 (Fig. 858) and even better in 1919 in the Grosse Schauspielhaus, built for 3,500 spectators who were barely separated from the large orchestra, with the sky-dome above.[48] Reinhardt opened this great playhouse with Aeschylus' *Oresteia*.

The students of the Catholic University of America in Washington presented an adaptation of *Oedipus the King* by Leo Brady in many colleges in America, and in April 1959 it was performed in Carnegie Hall, New York. The chorus spoke clearly and melodiously. The deep meaning of Sophocles' masterpiece was well transmitted.

Oedipus the King, Oedipus Colonus, and *Antigone* were produced in 1955 in New York City by Milton Miltiades at the John Memorial Hall in good performances. In 1956 he made a "Theban Trilogy" of the plays, performing them for several weeks on

Fig. 858. Performance of *Oedipus the King* in the Schumann Circus. From a painting by Orlik

Fig. 859. The Hearst Greek Theater of the University of California, Berkeley

Fig. 860. The Dietrich Eckard Freilichtbühne, Berlin

three succeeding evenings in the sequence of the events, not in the order of their creation by Sophocles. An attempt to produce *Antigone* on television in 1956 failed because it was acted by glamorous actors, who did not understand the principles and emotions of the Greek drama. Of all the seven plays by Sophocles, so far as I know, only the *Philoctetes* and the *Trachinian Women* have never been performed in our time.

Euripides, although in spirit the most modern of the three great tragic poets, is less popular in modern times than the two others. His *Medea* in the adaptation of Robinson Jeffers (Fig. 842) and *The Trojan Women* in the adaptation of Franz Werfel in the Deutsche Theater in Berlin are not pure Euripides, but modernizations. *The Trojan Women*, the *Iphigenia in Tauris*, and the *Iphigenia in Aulis* presented by the Columbia Theater Associates of Columbia University in Brander Matthews Theater and in Low Library's large central hall in 1936-37, 1942, and 1950, were genuine classical revivals under the direction of Milton Smith. The *Iphigenia in Tauris* was also presented in 1938 in the theater of Sabratha. This play was also produced in 1951 in an open-air theater at the Holland Festival by the Nederlandse Comedie in a round orchestra, with masks and a highly stylized chorus of dancers.[49] The *Hippolytus*, one of the finest plays of Euripides, was more often selected.

In 1931 the Experimental Theater of Vassar College produced an impressive performance of Euripides' *Hippolytos* in Greek. The singers and chorus linked the audience to the action; they moved mainly on wide, curved steps before the low stage. It was presented in Oxford in 1920, in Giessen by Professor Bernbeck with the assistance of this author in 1922, in the theater of Epidaurus in 1954 (see Fig. 866), and in Syracuse in 1956, where the *Electra* of Sophocles was also presented.[50] Both tragedies made deep impressions on the educated audiences. The *Alcestis*, the play which Euripides tried to substitute for a satyr play, was given at William and Mary

College in Williamsburg, Virginia; at Barnard College, and at the Riverdale Country School for Girls, New York City, in 1948. The high school production, to this author, seemed the best of the three, and the play, on account of its light touch of humor, fine character delineation, and brevity (it is the shortest of all plays by Euripides), is particularly fit for presentation by young people. The *Hecuba* was presented in 1955 in the Herodes Atticus Theater at Athens and the *Medea* there in 1956 as well as in Epidaurus. Wheaton College (Massachusetts) presented the *Antigone* in 1955 and the *Trojan Women* in 1956. Wellesley College produced the *Medea*, both *Iphigeneia* tragedies and the *Trojan Women* in the Greek language, 1928-1934.

Thus, only seven of the seventeen extant plays by Euripides have found favor in modern times. The author at least has never seen or heard about presentations of the *Andromache, Bacchae, Electra, Helen, Heracles, Heracleidae, Ion, Orestes, Phoenissae* or *Suppliants*. There are still treasures to be discovered by modern stage managers. On the other hand, all of Aeschylus' and all but two of Sophocles' plays have had modern productions.

In the spring of 1957 Wayne Richardson arranged a Trojan Trilogy, consisting of Aeschylus' *Agamemnon*, Sophocles' *Electra*, and Euripides' *Trojan Women*, the first two in the translation of Richmond Lattimore, the last by Francis Fergusson. It was produced in the Theater Marquee in New York, with *The Trojan Women* as the first play. Although it was the last to be produced in antiquity, it precedes the other two in time of the action. It was an extremely interesting experiment.

Greek tragedies have been presented in our century in ancient Greek theaters—Epidaurus (festivals since 1954), (Fig. 866), Delphi (Figs. 845-852), Syracuse (Fig. 853); in ancient Roman theaters—Theater of Herodes Atticus (Fig. 857), Ostia, Sabratha (Fig. 695), Orange (see Fig. 676); modern theaters—in New York City on Broadway (Figs. 842, 855, 856) and off Broadway (Fig. 843b) and in the Brander Matthews Theater at Columbia University, in Berlin in the Grosse Schauspielhaus and the Deutsche Theater, in Frankfurt, Cassel, Mainz, Giessen (Figs. 844a-d); in modern open-air theaters—in Reading, England (Fig. 854), in Holland, in American colleges like Cedar Crest, Elizabeth, California (Fig. 859), in the Dietrich Eckart Freilicht theater, Berlin (Fig. 860);[51] in the circus (see Fig. 858); in community halls and barns. The best productions were those where chorus and actors acted together in the orchestra before a palace out of which, as in ancient times, the main actors stepped (see Figs. 854, 857, 858). When, however, the managers tried to present a scene simultaneously on the stage and in the orchestra, the attempt was not successful, or was even ridiculous, and sometimes confusing. The old mistaken idea, that the actors performed on the stage while at the same time the chorus sang and danced in the orchestra, has definitely to be discarded. The idea that one or a few speakers can be substituted for the chorus is a false one; the result is always unsatisfactory.

Aside from those already named, other American colleges and universities are also active in stage production and have done much to improve the revivals of Greek plays. A partial list might include the following: Vassar College, Reed College in Portland, Oregon; Northwestern University; the Pacific Little Theater in Stockton and several other California theaters.

Barnard College, the college for girls at Columbia University, has a specialty in the reviving of the Greek spirit. Each year they have Greek Games, in which they attempt to reproduce, as nearly as modern conditions permit, a classical festival. It is built around some story of Greek mythology, dealing with some god or hero like Athena, Apollo, Orpheus, Hephaestus. The chorus sings the story which, however, is also acted in short mimetic scenes. Story, songs, music, dances and costumes are created by the girls themselves. A contest in dance (see Fig. 861) is followed by the athlete's oath to Zeus and to the god or hero to whom the games are dedicated (Fig. 862). There follow contests in discus throwing (Fig. 863), jumping of hurdles, hoop rolling, a chariot race, and a torch race. Costumes and movements are excellent. One actress (Fig. 864) could be Antigone with the jar on her way to bury her brother Polyneices, while the choral dance (Fig. 861) reminds us of the *Bacchae* of Euripides. The poise of the discus thrower (Fig. 863) looks like a copy of the discobolus of Myron, who renders the fleeting pause between the two main movements of this sport.

The scene of action for modern presentations thus has been everything from the Greek orchestra to the

Figs. 861-864. The Greek Games at Barnard College

low Roman stage, the modern stage, or a primitive stage erected in the open air or in a hall. In most cases the modern stage is used. This is quite satisfactory, as the Romans not only produced Greek plays on their stage, but had the forms of the Greek theater building adapted to their needs. The form of the Roman theater is indeed the underlying foundation of our theater building today, and knowledge of it is necessary if one wants to understand the modern theater.

The modern auditorium has adopted more and more the practical form of the ancient theatron and cavea, instead of the ornate boxes erected for public display of socially-prominent people. This is still kept mostly for opera houses. The first theater to change to the democratic form where everybody can hear and see equally well was the Festival Theater at Bayreuth, designed by Gottfried Semper and opened in 1876 for Wagner. He was followed by Max Littmann with his Schillertheater in Berlin and his Künstlertheater in Munich with a steeply slanting floor with equally good seats for everybody.[52] The Grosse Schauspielhaus, built by Hans Poelzig in 1919 in Berlin for Max Reinhardt has the big U-shaped auditorium of the Greeks instead of the half-circle auditorium of the Romans. It surrounds the orchestra in the Greek manner and brings the audience in close contact with the actors and the chorus. The spectator becomes part of the performances; he is much more absorbed in the action than when a proscenium arch around the stage separates him from the play. He—like the chorus—becomes a sympathetic listener and spiritual partner of the proceedings. He shares the great emotions and eternal problems of humanity which the Greek tragic poets presented.[53] This is also the case in the Dietrich Eckart Freilichtbühne (Fig. 860) built recently in Berlin and the "Greek" theater at the University of California at Berkeley (Fig. 859), which, however, has a Roman stage form and uses the orchestra—as the Romans did—for spectators. Most assembly halls, playhouses, and movie theaters today use the Roman half-circle or less.

If modern contrivances are used, such as the revolving stage, this also goes back to ancient usage, although there it was in a more modest form. Inspired by the turning machines—eccyclema, hemicircle, and strophion—described by Vitruvius and Pollux,[54] the Japanese first constructed a revolving stage in 1760. From them Karl Lautenschläger took it over and used it for the Residenz-Theater in 1896 in Munich, as did Max Reinhardt for his Deutsche Theater in 1904-05 in Berlin.[55] Some Broadway theaters, and Billy Rose for his aquacade, have used the revolving stage. Light effects, so highly developed in modern technique, were restricted in Greece and Rome to natural sunlight. They could only use the dawn for scenes at daybreak, like the first scene of *Agamemnon*, or the sunset for scenes at twilight like the death of Oedipus in *Oedipus at Colonus*.

Thus the question, how can a Greek tragedy or comedy be presented in our time, has been solved by practical means in many countries. When we try to solve the question from a theoretical and ideal point of view, I would say that there are many possibilities for the presentation of a Greek drama. We must consider: A) Costume, B) Scenery, C) The Theater Building.

A. Costume

1) Imitate the costume which the Greeks used in their theater. This is a religious costume and is in harmony with the religion not only of Dionysus but with the deep ethos of Greek tragedy and the seriousness with which the Greek hero fights against fate or submits to it as sent by a god. The full costume including the mask is particularly adapted to the tragedies of Aeschylus with their monumental simplicity and grandeur. I have seen the *Persians* most successfully played with masks by Cassel High School seniors (see above, p. 262).

2) Use the beautiful, richly decorated, long-sleeved robe and the decorated boots, but not the mask. The mask is a religious symbol, which no longer has any meaning for us. It can easily become rigid or ridiculous. Particularly for the harmonious serenity of Sophocles the heroic costume without the mask is excellently suited, as I have seen it at its best in Syracuse (Fig. 853).

3) Use the ancient Greek costume of everyday life. The simple and harmonious Greek dress shows the same spirit as the tragic literary work or as the contemporary architecture, sculpture, or painting. We will bring out the spirit of the work of art best when we use for the dramas the costume which is just as well an expression of the spirit of the great classical period as the dramas themselves. Particularly for the humanist Euripides the variegated free draperies of the Greek chiton, peplos, and himation are more suitable than the rigid mask and sleeved enfolding robe. Tragedy was performed using this costume in Bradford College by the seniors, advised by Oxford scholars (Fig. 854), and by the Greek National Theater (Figs. 855-856).

4) Do not in any case use Roman costume with high stilts, exaggerated masks, white color! Greek dress was colorful, dignified, and simple.

5) Do not play in modern dress. Our spirit is not the spirit of classical Greece—just as the Renaissance spirit was not the spirit of Latin Terence—and therefore the contrast impresses us as ridiculous. It is a great mistake to play ancient tragedy in modern dress, as Katharine Cornell did in Sophocles' *Antig-*

one in 1946 in New York City. Despite her great mimetic art, the play did not make an impression, while it did succeed in 1951 in the presentation by young actors in the Circle-in-the-Square, Greenwich Village, New York City.

B. *Scenery*

As the spirit of literature and art is the same in the same period, it is permissible to copy back-drops and side-wings from contemporary Greek buildings like the temples of Aigina, Olympia, or the Parthenon. We must, however, consider that during the period of the three great tragic poets the development of art was very rapid and rich. Probably each year the architecture was built differently and in more developed form than in former years. Painting also developed quickly from simple to more and more naturalistic forms. Agatharchus began the study of perspective in the period of Aeschylus, and the Boscoreale frescoes (above, Figs. 471-474) show us the last development of perspective Greek scene painting, before the Romans replaced it with plastically built architectural backgrounds. When choosing a background setting, we have to take account of the fact that it is not always the first presentation which agrees with the intentions of the dramatic poet. Siegfried Wagner, the son of Richard Wagner, asserted fifty years after the first presentation of the *Ring* and long after the death of his father that only then did the presentation of the *Ring* agree with the ideas of the composer. It is difficult to keep the right balance in the settings. If they are too rich, they encumber the art of the actors; if they are too poor or sketchy, they distract the audience. Craig rightly said: "A vast and forbidding doorway, I often think, still remains the best background for any tragedy. . . ." He adds: "Of course it all depends whether you come to the theater for drama or literature."[56]

When the great Greek poets wrote their works, they found neither scenery nor machinery. The parodies of Aristophanes show how imperfect the flying machine, the conventions for showing interior scenes, and the machine for the appearance of gods still were at the end of the fifth century. But as these contrivances had been *invented* in the period of the poets, there is no harm in using the *perfected* machinery of our own theater for presentations of Greek drama.

C. *The Theater Building*

The Greek theater was an open-air theater. When it is possible, as in Athens, Epidaurus, Syracuse, and Delphi, to use the ancient theater, the presentation in the round orchestra with a background building will be of great value. But the theater building had only its first development in Greece, was perfected by the Romans, and still challenges our modern theater buildings. Any theater, therefore, can be used for the presentation of Greek drama. It does not make much difference whether the drama is presented in the open air, on a meadow, in a barn, in a circus, in a museum or university auditorium, in an ancient theater or in a sophisticated, modern theater building. The modern attempts at central staging, as in the theater of the Circle-in-the-Square in New York, or in a projected theater for the University of Arkansas,[57] are really a return to the original and primitive idea of the dramatic dance in religious performances. The audiences stood or sat on all sides of the Greek threshing floor and the Roman circus, which were the places of action before Aeschylus and Sophocles in Athens and Plautus in Rome needed background scenery on one side and the audience concentrated on the opposite side. Wherever a clever director and responsive actors absorb the spirit of Greek drama, the eternal value of its heroic greatness and vitality will be brought to the surface and stir the emotions of a cultivated audience regardless of the outer surroundings.

Theatrical entertainment in America today resembles very much that of the Roman Empire. Serious drama and refined comedy in the legitimate theater are rather neglected. Motion pictures, musical comedies, athletic contests, and recently all these on television, are in favor. A continuance of a largely improvisational comic tradition is found in the popular entertainments of today: in the Italian Commedia dell'Arte, in Gilbert and Sullivan and in the American musical comedy, in light farce and on the radio, in the movies, and in comic strips.[58] Mr. Milquetoast is a perfect farcical senex. A celebrated female pantomime player was Ruth Draper who died in 1956; another, Angna Enters, calls herself a dance-mime, but is really a pantomime artist who tours with her one-woman "Theater of Angna Enters" in the United States and abroad. Aquacades were given in New York by Billy Rose. In California Esther Williams performs in similar water ballets. Dances like the ones from which the dithy-

Fig. 865. Dance of Austrian school teachers in the orchestra of Epidaurus

ramb and the tragic chorus started can be seen on a restored wooden stage and in the orchestra in ancient theaters such as those presented by Austrian schoolteachers in Epidaurus (Fig. 865) and in Arles, or gymnastic performances in Taormina.[59] Bull fights like the venationes in the Roman amphitheater are practiced in Spain, Mexico, and in a mild form in the amphitheaters of Nîmes and Arles.[60] The Romans introduced their animal baiting in the provinces of Gallia and Hispania, and from Spain they were transferred to Mexico.

Modern buildings for athletic games are often imitations of the Roman amphitheaters, as in the case of New York City's Madison Square Garden, the Rose Bowl in Pasadena, California, and the Cotton Bowl in Dallas, Texas. The Lewisohn "Stadium" near City College in New York City is not a stadium, which was a race-course, but half an elliptical amphitheater. The Central Park Theater in New York, built in 1959 over the Skating Rink, is a completely round amphitheater.

A strong movement to revive the best of the world's dramatic literature in adequate productions has started, particularly in colleges and small off-Broadway theaters. To the best belongs the Greek Drama.

Fig. 866. Performance of Euripides' *Hippolytos*, August 1954, in the theater at Epidaurus

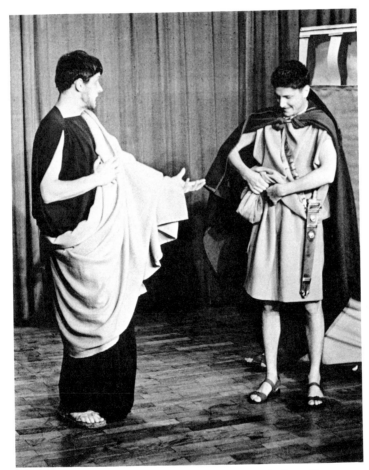

Fig. 867. Performance of Plautus, *Pseudolus*, 1964, in Jena, Germany

ABBREVIATIONS FREQUENTLY CITED

AbhBerl (Gött, Münch, Leipz, Sächs, Bayr) = Abhandlungen der Berliner (Göttinger, Münchner, Leipziger, Sächsischen, Bayrischen) Akademie (Gesellschaft) der Wissenschaften
ABSA = Annual of the British School at Athens
AdI = Annali dell'Instituto di Corrispondenza Archeologica
AJA = American Journal of Archaeology
AJP = American Journal of Philology
Ant.Denk. = Antike Denkmäler
Arch.Anz. = Archäologischer Anzeiger
ArchRW = Archiv für Religionswissenschaft
Arndt = Arndt, Griechische und römische Porträts, herausgegeben von Bruckmann
Arndt-Amelung = Arndt and Amelung, Photographische Einzelaufnahmen antiker skulpturen
Ath.Mitt. = Athenische Mitteilungen des deutschen archäologischen Institut

BCH = Bulletin de Correspondance Hellénique
BerlWPr = Berliner Winckelmannsprogramm
Bethe, *Prolegomena* = Bethe, *Prolegomena zur Geschichte des Theaters im Alterum*
Bieber, *Denkmäler* = Margarete Bieber, *Denkmäler zum Theaterwesen*
BMMA = Bulletin of the Metropolitan Museum of Art, New York
BrBr = Brunn-Bruckmann-Arndt, Denkmäler griechischer und römischer Skulptur
Bulle, *Untersuchungen* = Bulle, *Untersuchungen an griechischen Theatern*

CIL = Corpus Inscriptionum Latinarum
CJ = Classical Journal
CP = Classical Philology
CR = Classical Quarterly
CRPétersb = Compte-rendu de la Commission impériale archéologique, St. Pétersbourg
CVA = Corpus Vasorum Antiquorum

D-R = Dörpfeld and Reisch, Das Griechische Theater

Fiechter, *Baugesch.Entw.* = Fiechter, *Baugeschichtliche Entwicklung des antiken Theaters*
Fiechter, *Dionysostheater* = Fiechter, *Theaterbauten,* 5-7, 9, *Das Dionysostheater in Athen*
Fiechter, *Theaterbauten* = Fiechter, *Antike Griechische Theaterbauten*
Flickinger, *Greek Theater* = Flickinger, *The Greek Theater and Its Drama*
F-R = Furtwängler and Reichhold, *Griechische Vasenmalerei*

HallWPr = Hallisches Winckelmannsprogramm

HBr = Hermann-Bruckmann, *Denkmäler der Malerei*
Helbig[3] = Helbig-Amelung, *Führer durch die öffentlichen Sammlungen klassischer Altertümer in Rom,* 3rd edition
Hesperia = Hesperia, The Journal of the American School of Classical Studies at Athens

IG = Inscriptiones Graecae

JdAI = Jahrbuch des deutschen archäologischen Instituts
JHS = Journal of Hellenic Studies
JOAI = Jahreshefte des oesterreichischen archäologischen Instituts
JRS = Journal of Roman Studies

MAAR = Memoirs of the American Academy in Rome
MdI = Mitteilungen des deutschen archäologischen Instituts
MonInst = Monumenti Inediti Pubblicati dell'Instituto di Corrispondenza Archeologica
MonPiot = Monuments et Mémoires, Fondation Eugène Piot

NJb = Neue Jahrbucher für das klassische Altertum

PBSR = Papers of the British School at Rome
Pickard-Cambridge, *Dithyramb* = A.W. Pickard-Cambridge, *Dithyramb, Tragedy, and Comedy*
Pickard-Cambridge, *Theater of Dionysus* = A.W. Pickard-Cambridge, *The Theater of Dionysus in Athens*
Pickard-Cambridge, *Festivals* = A.W. Pickard-Cambridge, *The Dramatic Festivals of Athens*

Real-Enc. = Pauly-Wissowa, *Real-Encyclopädie der klassischen Altertumswissenschaft*
Robert, *Masken* = Robert, *Masken der Neueren Attischen Komödie,* 25. *HallWPr*
Röm.Mitt. = Mitteilungen des deutschen archäologischen Instituts, Römische Abteilung

SBBerl (Leipz, Münch, Wien) = Sitzungsberichte der Berliner (Leipziger, Münchner, Wiener) Akademie
Schefold, *Bildnisse* = K. Schefold, *Die Bildnisse der antiken Dichter, Redner und Denker*
Séchan, *Tragédie grecque* = Séchan, *Études sur la tragédie grecque*
Skulpt.Vat.Mus. = Die Skulpturen des Vaticanischen Museums

Webster, *Production* = T.B.L. Webster, *Greek Theater Production*
Wieseler, *Theatergebäude* = F. Wieseler, *Theatergebäude und Denkmäler des Bühnenwesens*

NOTES TO THE TEXT

NOTES TO CHAPTER I. THE RISE OF THE SATYR PLAY AND OF TRAGEDY

[1] Watzinger, *Das Relief des Archelaos von Priene*, 63. *BerlWPr*, 1903. Lippold in *Röm.Mitt.*, XXXIII(1918), 74ff. Schede, in *Röm.Mitt.*, XXXV(1920), 69ff. A. H. Smith, British Museum *Catalogue of Sculpture*, III(1904), 244ff., No. 2191, fig. 30. A. Levi, in *Bolletino d'Arte*, Series VI, No. 6(1926-27), p. 353, fig. 3. A. B. Cook, *Zeus*, I, 129ff., figs. 97-98, pl. XIII. Pickard-Cambridge, *Festivals*, p. 229, fig. 194. Bieber, *The Sculpture of the Hellenistic Age* (1955), p. 127f., figs. 404 and 497.

[2] Nietzsche, *The Birth of Tragedy from the Spirit of Music.*

[3] Strabo, XIII,2,4, p. C 618. Plutarch, *De Musica*, p. 1140f. Cf. Wilamowitz, "Der Timotheos-Papyrus gefunden bei Abusir," *Wissenschaftliche Veröffentlichung der deutschen Orient-Gesellschaft*, 1903, Heft 3, p. 10f. Wilamowitz, *Timotheos, Die Perser*, aus einem Papyrus von Abusir (1903), p. 27, lines 235-238 and p. 64ff. M. Wegner, *Das Musikleben der Griechen* (1949), pp. 28ff., 141f. On music in tragedy see Carlo del Grande, *Dioniso*, III(1931-32), 228-247, 346-360; IV(1933-34), 291-322 with appendix pp. i-xii. F. Behn, *Musikleben im Altertum und frühen Mittelalter*, 1955, Ch. VII, pp. 79ff., figs. 108-110.

[4] Fig. 3 in the Vatican, Museo Etrusco-Gregoriano from Phot. Alinari, No. 35726; Fig. 4 in Athens National Museum, Nos. 1183, cf. 1469. Couve-Collignon, *Vases d'Athènes*, Nos. 1260 and 1263. Bieber, *JdAI* (1917), 65f., fig. 35. Others are in the Vatican, No. 86, Helbig³, No. 491. For other citharoidoi with the large cithara see Beazley, *JHS* 42(1922), 70ff., pls. II and V; Gisela Richter, *Red-Figured Athenian Vases in the Metropolitan Museum*, Nos. 66 and 94, pl. 70 (*Pan-Painter*). Max Wegner, *Das Musikleben der Griechen* (1949), pp. 28ff., fig. 3, pls. 7a, 16b, 18, 28a, 31a, 32a. Behn, *op.cit.*, figs. 111-119.

[5] F-R, pl. 64 (Alkaios-Sappho). Orsi, in *Mon. ant. dei Lincei* XIX(1908), 102ff., figs. 9-10, pl. III; cf. p. 95, fig. 11, for the vase by Oltos in London, British Museum E 18. Hoppin, *A Handbook of Attic Redfigured Vases*, I, p. 24, No. 25 and p. 464f. Beazley, *Attic Red-Figure Vase-Painting*, p. 31, No. 2, Syracuse Mus. No. 26967.

[6] F-R, II, 183f., fig. 64. Pfuhl, *Malerei und Zeichnung*, figs. 324, 334, 338, 341, 376, 377, 409. Hoppin, *Redfig. Vases*, I,310; II,116. G. Richter, *Red-Figured Vases*, No. 15, pp. 39f., pl. 17 (Berlin Painter); No. 19, pp. 44f., pl. 21 (Eucharides Painter). Wegner, *op.cit.*, pp. 37ff., figs. 4-5, pls. 11-17, 19-22.

[7] For Auloi see Wegner, *op.cit.*, pp. 52ff., figs. 10-12, pls. 4-10. Behn, *op.cit.*, pp. 96ff., figs. 131-141. For the long dress of the fluteplayer see E. Bielefeld, "Ein böotischer Tanzchor des 6. Jh. v. Chr." in *Festschrift für Friedrich Zucker* (1954), p. 31 and p. 34, note 8. Also Beazley, *Hesperia*, XXIV(1955),308ff., pl. 87.

[8] F-R, pl. 136. Pfuhl, *op.cit.*, fig. 468. Hoppin, *op.cit.*, I,214f.

[9] Weege, *Der Tanz* (1926), pp. 31ff., 98ff. Séchan, *La Danse grecque* (1930), pp. 35ff. M. Emmanuel, *The Antique Greek Dance*, transl. from the French (2nd ed., 1927), pp. 216ff. For the importance of the dance in tragedy see H. D. F. Kitto, in *JHS*, 75, 1955, pp. 36ff. Music and dance reinforced the dramatic words.

[10] Collignon-Couve, *Vases d'Athènes*, No. 468, pl. XX. Séchan, *op.cit.*, p. 49, fig. 3. Brinckmann, "Altgriechischer Mädchenreigen," in *Bonner Jahrbücher*, 130(1925), pp. 118ff. Shear, in *Hesperia*, VII(1938), 341, fig. 23. Wegner, *Musikleben*, pl. 1a-b.

[11] F-R, pls. 1-3, 11-13. Weege, *op.cit.*, fig. 75. Séchan, *op.cit.*, p. 61, fig. 6.

[12] Aristotle, *Poetics*, IV, 1449a, 10ff. ἡ μὲν ἀπὸ τῶν ἐξαρχόντων τὸν διθύραμβον. Flickinger, *The Greek Theater and its Drama*, pp. 6ff., is right when he returns confidently to this most important source. Pickard-Cambridge, *Dithyramb*, pp. 174ff., extends to Aristotle as well as to the most important contemporary monuments the astute criticism with which he has especially well refuted the following other theories for the origin of tragedy:

a) The Eleusinian Mysteries. A. Dieterich, "Entstehung der Tragödie," in *ArchRW*, XI(1908), 163ff., and *Kleine Schriften*, pp. 414ff. Followers of this theory are Jane Harrison, Gilbert Murray, and F. M. Cornford.

b) Rites at the tombs of ancestors who had become heroes. Ridgeway, *Origin of Tragedy* (1910) and *Dramas and Dramatic Dances of Non-European Races in Reference to the Origin of Greek Tragedy* (1915).

c) Spring rites for the year's demon, a theory deduced partly from modern plays in Thrace, Thessaly, and Skyros. Dawkins, in *ABSA*, XI(1904-05),72ff., and in *JHS*, XXVI (1906), 191ff. Wace in *ABSA*, XVI(1909-10), 232ff. Murray, in Harrison, *Themis*, pp. 341ff. Cf. also Farnell, *Cults of the Greek States*, V, 107ff.

d) Rites for the dead. M. Nilsson, "Der Ursprung der Tragödie," in *NJb*, XXVII(1911), 609ff., and 673ff.

e) Rites for Zeus in Crete, where he was reborn in the form of Zagreus. Cook, *Zeus* (1914), I, 665ff., and 695ff.

It is hardly necessary to consider the modern theory of Winterstein, *Der Ursprung der Tragödie, ein psychoanalytischer Beitrag zur Geschichte des griechischen Theaters* (1925). Following the example of Freud, who transferred information gathered from insane or feeble-minded persons to normal and highly intellectual persons, Winterstein tried to demonstrate the development of the highest dramatic form of Greek literature from neurotic and infantile qualities. Freud's "Oedipus complex" shows the ignorance of this Freudian school, which completely misunderstood the celebrated masterpiece of Sophocles.

[13] Bergk, *Poetae Lyrici Graeci*, 4th ed., II, 404, Fragment 77: ὡς Διονύσου ἄνακτος καλὸν ἐξάρξαι μέλος οἶδα διθύραμβον, οἴνῳ συγκεραυνωθεὶς φρένας.

[14] Suidas, *s.v.* Arion: πρῶτος χορὸν στῆσαι καὶ διθύραμβον ᾆσαι καὶ ὀνομάσαι τὸ ᾀδόμενον ὑπὸ τοῦ χοροῦ καὶ σατύρους εἰσενεγκεῖν ἔμμετρα λέγοντας. Cf. Pickard-Cambridge, *Dithyramb*, pp. 131ff.

[15] Hydria Mus. No. 03.788. Brommer, *Satyroi*, p. 40, fig. 18, and *Satyrspiele, Bilder griech. Vasen*, pp. 12ff., fig. 6. Frances Jones, *The Theater in Ancient Art*, Princeton Exhibition, 1952, p. 2, fig. 1. Beazley, *Hesperia* XXIV(1955), 310ff., pl. 86b.

[16] British Museum, *Catalogue of Vases*, B 467. A. H. Smith, *JHS*, XI(1890), 278ff., pls. XI-XII. Bieber, *Denkmäler*, p. 100f., no. 39, fig. 104. Webster, *Niobiden-Maler*, in Beazley-Jacobsthal, *Bilder griechischer Vasen*, pls. 14-15. Pickard-Cambridge, *Dithyramb*, pp. 156f., fig. 14. Beazley, *Hesperia*, XXIV(1955), 316f., pl. 88a. Buschor, "Feldmäuse," *Sitzungsberichte Bayr. Akad. d. Wiss.*, München, 1937, Phil.-hist. Abt., pp. 1ff., figs. 4-5.

[17] G. Richter, *Red-Figured Athenian Vases in the Metro-*

politan Museum, No. 155, pp. 195f., pl. 155. Beazley, *Hesperia*, XXIV(1955), 314f.

[18] Stuart and Revett, *Antiquities of Athens* (1825), I, Ch. IV, pp. 53ff., pls. 23-30. De Cou, *AJA*, VIII(1893), 42ff. *BrBr*, pl. 488. Judeich, *Topographie von Athen*, 2nd ed. (1931), pp. 305ff., pl. 14. Dinsmoor, *The Architecture of Ancient Greece* (1950), p. 237f., pls. LIX-LX.

[19] Hartwig, *Meisterschalen*, pls. 32f. Pfuhl, *Malerei und Zeichnung*, III, figs. 426, 427, 430 (Brygos). Cf. G. Richter, *Red-Figured Vases*, No. 33, p. 55, pl. 32 (Oinokles painter). F. Brommer, *Satyroi*, Diss. Munich, 1937, has compiled much material for the representations of satyrs.

[20] G. Richter, *op.cit.*, No. 42, p. 64f., pl. 42 (Kleophrades painter). Beazley, *Der Kleophrades-Maler* (in *Bilder griech. Vasen*, ed. Beazley, and Jacobsthal, 1933), pls. 5-6. G. Richter, *op.cit.*, No. 55, pp. 77f., pls. 59-60 (Makron); No. 109, p. 140ff., pl. 109 (Methyse painter); No. 128, p. 161f., pl. 127 (Leucippid painter). F-R, pls. 44-45. Weege, *Der Tanz*, figs. 89, 91, 95, 97, 98, 125, 127-30.

[21] Frickenhaus, *Lenäenvasen*, 72. *Programm zum Winckelmannsfest* (Berlin, 1912), pp. 1ff., Nos. 1-29, pls. I-V. Weege, *Der Tanz*, figs. 101, 103, 105, 107-13. Pickard-Cambridge, *Festivals*, pp. 27ff., figs. 10-17. Nilsson, *Griechische Religion*, I(1941), p. 555, pl. 37, 1.

[22] Weege, *Der Tanz*, pp. 56ff. Séchan, *op.cit.*, pp. 159ff. Lilian Lawler, "The Menads," in *MAAR*, VI(1927), 69ff., pls. XIII-XXII.

[23] Bieber, in *JdAI*, XXXII(1917), 68ff., and above, pp. 8-9, on the Dionysiac ecstasy. Cf. Thrämer, in Roscher, I,1035ff., and Rapp, *ibid.*, II,2252ff. Farnell, *Cults of the Greek States*, V,102ff.

[24] On satyr plays see: M. Bieber, *Ath.Mitt.*, XXXVI(1911), 269ff., pl. 13-14, in Athens and Bonn (our Figs. 27-28). F. Brommer, *Satyrspiele, Bilder griechischer Vasen* (1944), with 67 illustrations. Our Fig. 26, a rhyton from Nola in the British Museum *Catalogue*, E 790, and Fig. 29, the fragment formerly in the Arndt Collection now in Amsterdam, are illustrated in Bieber, *JdAI*, XXXII(1917), 56ff., figs. 28-29. Figs. 27-28 in Brommer, *op.cit.*, pp. 12ff., figs. 4 and 6.

[25] The calyx crater now in the British Museum (Fig. 30): Séchan, *Trag.gr.*, p. 42f., fig. 11. Trendall, *Frühitaliotische Vasen*, pl. 12b. Brommer, *op.cit.*, Figs. 7-8.

[26] Frickenhaus, "Zum Ursprung von Satyrspiel und Tragödie," in *JdAI*, XXXII(1917), 1ff. Bieber, *ibid.*, "Die Herkunft des tragischen Kostüms," pp. 15ff., 48ff., fig. 19. Bieber, *Denkmäler*, pp. 91ff., No. 34, figs. 97-98, pl. 48. Buschor, in F-R, III,132-50, pls. 143-5. Pfuhl, *Malerei und Zeichnung*, II,590f., III, fig. 575. Brommer, *op.cit.*, p. 9f., fig. 1. Pickard-Cambridge, *Dithyramb*, p. 153, figs. 11-12, and *Festivals*, p. 179, fig. 28. I cannot accept the theory of Buschor, that the actors are those of tragedy, while the chorus is that of the satyr play. If this were true, there would be tragic actors surrounded by a satyr chorus and no tragic chorus, and a satyr chorus without their actors. But the leader Papposilenus is conferring with one of the actors; they therefore belong together. One might also expect representatives of comedy if the two other forms of dramatic plays were indicated.

[27] Fragments from Tarentum in Würzburg: Bulle, *Corolla Curtius*, pp. 151-160, pls. 54-56. Pickard-Cambridge, *Festivals*, p. 183, figs. 40a-c (our Figs. 34-35).

[28] HBr, pl. 14. Fiechter, *Baugesch.Entw.*, pp. 46ff., fig. 51. Bieber, *Denkmäler*, pp. 95ff., No. 35, pls. 49-50. E. Rizzo, *La Pittura Ellenistico-Romana*, p. 68, pl. CXLVI. Pickard-Cambridge, *Festivals*, p. 188, fig. 69. Spinazzola, *Le Arti decorative*, 179. Pernice, in Winter, *Die Hellenistische Kunst in Pompeji*, VI, 1938, *Pavimente und Mosaiken*, p. 171.

[29] Naples, Museo Nazionale No. 2846. Crusius, in *Festschrift für Overbeck*, pp. 103ff. Robert, *Oidipus*, I,259ff., fig. 45; II,96ff. Bieber, *Denkmäler*, p. 96, fig. 99; p. 98, No. 36. Brommer, *op.cit.*, pp. 44ff., fig. 44; cp. his fig. 45. The vase is attributed to Python by Watzinger, in F-R, III,372f., and Trendall, *Paestan Pottery*, p. 68f., No. 118, pl. XXIA; *idem*, *PBSR*, XX(1952), 10 and 34, No. 154, pl. XII a.

[30] Welcker, *Nachtrag zu der Schrift: Ueber die Aeschyleische Trilogie nebst einer Abhandlung über das Satyrspiel*, 1826. Wernicke, in Roscher, III,1409ff.; *idem*, "Bockschöre und Satyrdrama," in *Hermes*, XXXII(1897), 290ff. Fensterbusch, in *Bursians Jahresberichte*, No. 253(1936), 12ff. Wilamowitz, *Einleitung in die griechische Tragödie* (1907), pp. 81ff.; *idem*, in *NJb*, XXIX(1912), 449ff. Bethe, *Prolegomena*, pp. 37ff.; Körte, *ibid.*, pp. 339ff.

[31] Frickenhaus, in *JdAI*, XXXII(1917), 1ff. Cp. Fensterbusch in *Bursians Jahresberichte*, No. 253(1936), 16ff.

[32] Sophocles, *Ichneutae*, vv. 375ff.: ἀλλ' αἰὲν εἶ σὺ παῖς · νέος γὰρ ὢν ἀνὴρ πώγωνι θάλλων ὡς τράγος κνήκῳ χλιδᾷς. Παύου τὸ λεῖον φαλακρὸν ἡδονῇ πιτνάς. Aeschylus, Fragment 207 (*Oxford Classical Texts*, 1937) = Plutarch, *De Cap. ex Inimicis Utilitate*, p. 86f.: τοῦ δὲ σατύρου τὸ πῦρ, ὡς πρῶτον ὤφθη, βουλομένου φιλῆσαι καὶ περιβαλεῖν, ὁ Προμηθεύς: Τράγος, ἔφη, γένειον ἄρα πενθήσεις σύγε. Cp. Pickard-Cambridge, *Dithyramb*, pp. 153ff. Shorey, in Flickinger, *Greek Theater*, p. 30, note 3.

[33] For satyrs surrounding Prometheus, see Beazley, "Prometheus Fire-Lighter," in *AJA*, 43(1939), 618ff., pls. XIII-XV, figs. 1-6, 9-14, and *ibid.*, 44(1940), p. 212, fig. 1. Our Fig. 39, *ibid.* 43(1939), pl. XIV, in Gotha, Germany, No. 73. Brommer, *op.cit.*, pp. 41ff., figs. 40-43. Baur, *Catalogue of the Stoddard Collection*, p. 86, pl. 7 above. A crater in Ferrara with Prometheus, satyrs, and a fluteplayer: Beazley, *Hesperia*, XXIV(1955), 311, pl. 88b.

[34] Jahn, "Perseus, Herakles, Satyrn auf Vasenbildern und das Satyrdrama," in *Philologus*, XXVII(1868),1ff., pls. I-IV. The crater from Southern Italy, published by Jahn with Perseus and Silenus is now in Bonn, Akademisches Kunstmuseum, No. 79. Bieber, in *Ath.Mitt.*, XXXVI(1911),269ff., pls. XIII-XIV. Flickinger, *op.cit.*, pp. 25ff., figs. 5-7. G. Richter, in *BMMA*, XXX(1935),86ff.; *idem*, *AJA*, XXXIX(1935),182ff., figs. 1-4. G. Richter, *Red-Figured Athenian Vases in the Met. Mus.*, No. 88, pl. 90 (our Fig. 41). *Corpus Vasorum ant.*, Bologna, pl. 24, 1-3. *AJA*, XXXIX(1935),184, figs. 3-4 (our Fig. 42). Our Fig. 43 is now in Milan, Moretti Collection.

[35] Bieber, in *JdAI*, XXXII(1917),49ff., 80; Figs. 20-26 and 46. Trendall, *Paestan Pottery*, p. 54, fig. 39, Allard Pierson Museum, No. 2491. Athens Mus., No. 1329, Couve-Collignon, *Vases d'Athènes*, No. 1897. Mus. Nos. 12254-5. Nicole, *Cat. Vases d'Athènes*, Nos. 1113-4. Papposilenus with cothurnus before him. Our Fig. 45 is Athens, No. 12595. Vase Jatta in Ruvo, our Fig. 38, Mus. No. 1528; Robert, *Masken*; *HallWPr*, pp. 109 and 112, fig. 128.

[36] Pfuhl, *Malerei und Zeichnung*, I,480,482; III, fig. 467. Seltman, *Attic Vase-Painting*, p. 63, pl. 27b (our Fig. 40).

[37] F-R, pl. 47,2. Bieber, *Denkmäler*, pp. 9ff., figs. 4-6.

[38] Pratinas, Fragment 18, apud Athenaios, XIV, p. 617 c: τίς ὁ θόρυβος ὅδε; τί τάδε τὰ χορεύματα; τίς ὕβρις ἔμολεν ἐπὶ Διονυσιάδα πολυπάταγα θυμέλην.

[39] British Museum E 768. F-R, pl. 48. Flickinger, *op.cit.*, p. 31, fig. 10. Pickard-Cambridge, *Festivals*, p. 232, fig. 199. Brommer, *op.cit.*, pp. 60ff., fig. 66.

[40] On the tripod of victory see: Emil Reisch, *Griech. Weihgeschenke*, in *Abh. des arch. epigr. Seminars Wien*, No. 8 (1890), pp. 63ff., figs. 1-11. On animals as prize of victory see Scholion to Plato, *Republic*, p. 394 C.

[41] Vittorio Macchioro, *Zagreus*, Studi Intorno al' Orfismo, new edition, 1930, pp. 219ff. L. R. Farnell, *Cults of the Greek States* (1909), v.106,162,164ff. Frazer, *The Golden Bough*, one vol. ed., 1925, p. 391f.

[42] Later statues of Papposilenus in full goatskin chiton, besides the vases (cf. note 35), see particularly Fig. 46, the statue carrying the child Dionysus, found in the theater of Athens, Mus. No. 257. Arndt-Amelung, E. A. No. 643. Bieber, *JdAI*, xxxii(1917), 80, fig. 46. Pickard-Cambridge, *Festivals*, p. 179, fig. 29. Terracotta statuettes of Papposilenus with the infant Dionysus: from Melos, British Museum C 74, R. A. Higgins, *Catalogue of the Terracottas in the Department of Greek and Roman Antiquities*, i,197f. No. 736, pl. 97; from Halae, Hetty Goldman and Frances Jones, "Terracottas from the Necropolis of Halae," *Hesperia*, xi(1942),405f., pl. xxiii—they date the actors 390-350 b.c.; from Corinth, Results of Excavations, xii, No. 331, pl. 29. Fig. 47 from Rome in Berlin No. 218. Wieseler, *Theatergebäude*, pl. vi, 1. Terracotta statuettes of Silenus in fur tights and mantle: Winter, *Typen der figürlichen Terrakotten*, iii, 2, p. 397, figs. 1, 2, 4-6; p. 398, figs. 2, 4-8. See statues from Delos in *BCH*, xxxi(1907),517ff., pls. x-xi. An excellent marble statue of Papposilenus has been found in a Roman villa near Anzio, *Ill. London News*, Feb. 1, 1958, pp. 196f. For Maenads in sleeved dresses, see Bieber, in *JdAI*, xxxii (1917),58f., fig. 30.

[43] Good examples of satyrs in loin cloth are also on the Naples Pronomos vase (Figs. 31-33), in two craters in Deepdene (Cook, *Zeus*, i, 701f., pl. xxxix), an Attic dinos in Athens and fragments with similar satyrs dancing before a fluteplayer in Bonn (Bieber, *Ath.Mitt.*, xxxvi[1911],269f., pl. 13. Brommer, *Satyrspiele*, fig. 2. Pickard-Cambridge, *Festivals*, p. 180f., figs. 30-31). A satyr mask from Samos in the British Museum may have been actually worn in a satyr play, Higgins, *Cat. of the Terracottas*, British Mus., p. 142, no. 523, pl. 70. Webster, *Production*, p. 157, pl. 66.

[44] Bieber, *JdAI*, xxxii(1917),68ff. Pickard-Cambridge, *Dithyramb*, pp. 149ff., discusses the explanations of tragedy as chorus dressed in goatskins and as chorus dancing around a goat destined to be a prize or a sacrifice. He chooses the latter possibility.

[45] See in addition to the sources quoted in note 41: Rizzo, *Dionysos Mystes*. R. Eisler, *Orphisch-dionysische Mysteriengedanken*, in *Vorträge Bibliothek Warburg*, ii(1922-23). De Jong, *Das antike Mysterienwesen*. Vollgraff, *Over den Oorsprong der Dionys. Mysterien*, in *Mededeel. Akad. Wetenschappen* (Amsterdam, 1924), Deel 57, Ser. A, No. 2. Rostovtzeff, *Mystic Italy*, pp. 34ff. Reitzenstein, *Hellenistische Mysterienreligionen* (3rd ed., 1927), pp. 12 and 96ff. Bieber, in *JdAI*, xliii(1928),326f.; idem, "The Mystery Frescoes," in *The Review of Religion*, ii(1937),3ff. Martin Nilsson, *A History of Greek Religion* (1925), pp. 205ff. and 293; idem, *Geschichte der griechische Religion* (1950), in *Handbuch der Altertumswissenschaft Fünfte Abteilung, Zweiter Teil*, I, 216-219 and 532-568; II, 663.; idem, *The Dionysiac Mysteries of the Hellenistic and Roman Age* (1957). Farnell, *Cults of the Greek States*, v,85ff.

[46] Olivieri, *Lamelle Aureae Orphicae*, pp. 4ff. Vollgraff, *op.cit.*, p. 9. V. Macchioro, *op.cit.*, pp. 85ff. Farnell, *Greek Hero Cults* (1921), p. 376f. For the vase in Berlin (Fig. 50) see C. Blümel, *Antike Kunstwerke* (1953), p. 16f., No. 9. Bielefeld, in *Rheinisches Museum für Philologie*, vol. 97 (1954), 92ff.

[47] Gregor Krause and K. With, *Insel Bali*, ii,19ff., pls. 13-25 (our Figs. 51-52). Unfortunately the tourist trade has degenerated these religious festivals to shows, which have even been brought to London and to New York, in 1952-1953. The dancers are no more in a state of trance. They still use the old art and some of the old ornaments, but they are without inner exaltation. It is interesting to see here the transformation of a sacred performance secularized into a profane presentation. Although something similar happened in Greece, the reasons for the change there were higher and deeper ones.

[48] Aristotle, *De Arte Poetica* IV, 1449a, 9f.: γενομένης δ' οὖν ἀπ' ἀρχῆς αὐτοσχεδιαστικῆς . . . .

NOTES TO CHAPTER II. ATTIC TRAGEDY

[1] Svoronos, *Das Athener Nationalmuseum*, i,232ff., pls. 61-64. Bieber, *Denkmäler*, p. 18f., pls. 6-7. A. B. Cook, *Zeus*, i, pp. 708-711, pl. xl. Herbig, in Fiechter, *Dionysostheater*, ii,36ff., pls. 9-16. Herbig dates the reliefs in the Hadrianic period. Alice Mühsam, in *Berytus*, x(1952), 86-88, calls our Fig. 54 Hadrianic, our Fig. 55 Antonine. I do not see the difference, but as she dates both around a.d. 160, they would be Antonine. This to the author seems too late. I still believe that the time when the theater was rededicated to Nero and Dionysus was the best occasion to erect a new altar with the story of Dionysus. See our Ch. XIV, p. 213ff. and Figs. 719, 721-722.

[2] The passages relating to Thespis have been gathered and treated critically in Pickard-Cambridge, *Dithyramb*, pp. 97ff.

[3] The date is given by the Marmor Parium. See Jacoby, *Das Marmor Parium* (1904) and *Fragmenta Hist. Gr.*, ii, 239ff.

[4] Horace, *De Arte Poetica*, vv. 275-77: "dicitur et plaustris vexisse poemata Thespis." Cp. Pickard-Cambridge, *Dithyramb*, p. 114.

[5] Bethe, *Prolegomena*, p. 44f. Frickenhaus, in *JdAI*, xxvii (1912),61ff., supplementary plate I. Bieber, *Denkmäler*, pp. 87ff., No. 33, figs. 91-95. Pickard-Cambridge, *Dithyramb*, pp. 112ff., figs. 4-10, and *Festivals*, pp. 11ff., figs. 6-7. Nilsson, *Griechische Religion*, i, p. 550, pl. 36,1. Deubner, *Attische Feste*, pp. 102ff., pls. 11 and 14 gives the carrus navalis to the Anthesteria, and Pickard-Cambridge is inclined to follow him. See, however, my Ch. IV, note 12, Fig. 219 on the wedding car, which belongs to the Anthesteria.

[6] The cup of Exekias: F-R, i, pl. 42. Pfuhl, *Malerei und Zeichnung*, i, p. 268; iii, fig. 231. Technau, *Exekias*, in *Bilder griech. Vasen*, ed. Beazley and Jacobsthal, ix, p. 10, No. 21, pl. 5. Pickard-Cambridge, *Festivals*, p. 11, fig. 8.

[7] Wilamowitz, *Aeschyli Tragoediae*, p. 18f. Bieber, in *JdAI*, xxxii(1917),18f., and in *Real-Enc.*, xiv,2072ff. F. Löhrer, *Mienenspiel und Maske in der griechischen Tragödie*, p. 1f., in *Studien zur Geschichte und Kultur des Altertums*, xiv, 1927.

[8] Bieber, in *AJA*, 45, 1941, pp. 529-36, pl. xiv. G. Richter, *Redfigured Athenian Vases in the Met. Mus.*, No. 51, pls. 47-8, and *Attic Red-Figured Vases* (1946), p. 87, fig. 62.

[9] M. Pohlenz, "Das Satyrspiel und Pratinas" in *Nachrichten Gött. Ges.d.Wiss.*, 1926, pp. 298ff.

[10] Stuart Jones, *Catalogue of Sculpture in the Capitoline Museum*, p. 252, Stanza dei filosofi, No. 82, pl. 60. Arndt-Bruckmann, *Porträts*, pls. 111-112. Hekler, *Bildniskunst*, p. xii pl. 14. Bieber, *Denkmäler*, p. 81f., No. 27, pl. 43,1, and *Sculpture of the Hellenistic Age*, p. 58, fig. 179. Orsi, "Il Volto di Eschile" in *Dioniso*, i(1929),1-7, pls. i-ii. M. Squarciapino, *Archeologia Classica*, Rivista dell'Istituto di archeologia della Università di Roma, 5(1953),55-60, pl. xiii. G. Hafner, "Das Bildnis des Aischylos," *JdAI*, lxx, 1955, pp. 105-128,

figs. 6-9. The story of the baldness of Aeschylus is told by Pliny, *Natural History*, x,3; Aelian, *De Natura animalium*, VII,16; Valerianus Maximus, IX,12.

[11] T.B.L. Webster, *Diogenes* 5(1954),86, favors a date after 468 for the *Suppliants*. He bases this opinion on the fragmentary hypothesis in the *Oxyrhynchus Papyrus*, 2256, fr. 3, where a victory of Aeschylus over Sophocles with a group of plays containing the *Danaids* and *Amymone* is recorded. If the production included the *Suppliants*, it might have been a revival. The simplicity of the plot, the inactivity of the actors, and the important role of the chorus in my opinion are in favor of an early composition. Some scholars—for example, A. Lasky and A. Raubitschek—believe that the *Suppliants* is a later drama by Aeschylus. They also base this belief on the *Oxyrhynchus Papyrus*, fr. 3. But this may refer to a later revival, and the late dating has been doubted by Pohlenz and Gilbert Murray. See Lasky in *Gnomon* 28(1956),26ff.; Murray, ed., *Aeschylus*, p. vf.

[12] Suidas, *s.v.* Aischylos. Bieber in *Real-Enc.*, xiv,2073, *s.v.* Maske. K. Reinhard, *Aischylos* (1949), p. 11, asserts rightly, that the Aeschylean theater was much richer in effects than the later dramas.

[13] Amelung, *Skulpt. vat. Mus.*, i,72, Braccio nuovo, No. 53, pl. 9. Hekler, *op.cit.*, pl. 7b. Bieber, *Denkmäler*, p. 81f., No. 27, pl. 42. Pickard-Cambridge, *Festivals*, p. 185, fig. 45. The Lycurgean statues of the three tragic poets are mentioned by Plutarch, *Vita X Orat.*, Lycurgus 11 and Pausanias I,21.

[14] Head in Florence: Bieber, *Sculpture of the Hellenistic Age*, p. 58, fig. 179 (our Fig. 65). Head in Naples: Arndt, *Porträts*, pl. 401f. Others, *ibid.*, 402-410. Schefold, *Bildnisse*, p. 88, 4 and 207. Head in Copenhagen: Poulsen, *Cat. of ancient Sculpture in the Ny Carlsberg Glyptotek* (1951), p. 297, No. 421. *Billedtavler*, pl. xxx. Poulsen, *From the Collections of the Ny Carlsberg Glyptotek*, i(1931), *Iconographic Studies*, pp. 65ff., figs. 49-50. Hafner, *op.cit.*, fig. 1.

[15] Bieber, in *JdAI*, xxxii(1917),70ff., figs. 36-39. *Musées de l'Algérie et de la Tunisie*, i, Delattre, *Musée Lavigerie de Carthage*, i(1900), pp. 80ff., pl. xii; *ibid.*, *Musée Aloui*, Suppl. ii(1910), pp. 143f., pls. lxxii, lxxiii,1 and lxxiv,5. G. Perrot, *Le Musée de Bardo à Carthage*, p. 20f. Ehrenberg, *Karthago* (1927), pl. i. F. Behn, "Vorgeschichtliches Maskenbrauchtum," in *Berichte der sächsischen Akademie der Wissenschaften zu Leipzig*, Phil. hist. Klasse, Vol. 102, 1(1955), p. 9f., pl. 10. Gauckler, *Nécropole Puniques de Carthage*, i(1915), Nos. 198-200, pls. cxcviii-cc.

[16] For the masks from the shrine of Artemis Orthia see Dawkins, *ABSA*, xii(1905-06),324ff. Bosanquet, *ibid.*, pp. 338ff., pls. x-xii. Dickins in Dawkins, *The Sanctuary of Artemis Orthia at Sparta* (1929), pp. 163ff., pls., 47-62. Higgins, *Catalogue of the Terracottas* in the Department of Greek and Roman Antiquities, British Museum, pp. 285ff., pls. 143-145. Higgins assumes that these are faithful copies of masks intended to be worn at the occasion of the dances in honor of Artemis. For the masks from the shrine of Demeter see Cavvadias, *Fouilles de Lycosura*, pl. iv. Dickins, in *ABSA*, xiii(1906-07),373ff., figs. 14 and 26, pl. xiv. Bieber, *Griechische Kleidung*, p. 68, pl. xxxiv,1-2, and *s.v.* Maske in *Real-Enc.*, xiv(1930),2070f. Wace in *AJA*, xxxviii(1934),107ff., pl. x.

[17] Furtwängler, *Antike Gemmen*, i, pl. ii, Nos. 30-35. Evans, *Palace of Minos*, i,708, fig. 532; iv,2, p. 393; p. 431, fig. 354; p. 441, figs. 364-365; pp. 441ff., figs. 367-369; pp. 452ff., figs. 377-387, 390-392; p. 522, fig. 468. Nilsson, *The Minoan-Mycenean Religion and its Survival in Greek Religion*, 2nd ed. (1950), pp. 374ff.

[18] Tsountas, *Ephemeris* (1887), pp. 162ff., pl. x. Evans,

op.cit., iv,2, p. 441f., fig. 366. Nilsson, *op.cit.*, p. 377, fig. 184.

[19] Rodenwaldt, in Propyläen-Kunstgeschichte, *Kunst der Antike*, pl. 171; *idem* in *Bilderhefte antiker Kunst*, v(1938), *Altdorische Bildwerke in Korfu* (1938), pp. 16ff., pls. 10-14; *idem* in *Korkyra*, ii(1939),15ff., pls. i-viii. Kaiser Wilhelm II, *Erinnerungen an Korfu*, pp. 78ff., figs. 17-20. Picard, *Sculpture Antique*, p. 275f., fig. 71. Charbonneaux, *La Sculpture grecque archaïque*, p. 22, fig. on pp. 20-21, pls. 24-25. On Medusa in general see Thalia Phillies Howe, Diss. Columbia University, (1952), an interpretation of the *Perseus-Gorgon Myth in Greek Literature and Monuments*, pls. i-iv (pl. iii a-b: Corfu); *idem*, "The Origin and Function of the Gorgon-Head," in *AJA* 58(1954),209-221, pls. 35-36.

[20] Buschor in F-R, pl. 145. Cf. A. von Salis, in *JdAI*, xxv(1910),126ff., supplementary pl. 4.

[21] Bieber, in *JdAI*, xxxii(1917),89ff., fig. 59. Pickard-Cambridge, *Festivals*, p. 183, fig. 41. Cf. also Trendall, *Frühitaliotische Vasen*, in *Bilder griech. Vasen*, ed. Beazley and Jacobsthal, No. 12(1928), p. 25, pl. 27a.

[22] Bieber, *loc.cit.*, fig. 60.

[23] Reisch, "Griechische Weihgeschenke," in *Abh. arch.ep. Seminar Univ. Wien*, 1890, Heft viii, p. 145, figs. 13-14. Bieber, *op.cit.*, pp. 92ff., figs. 57-58, 61-65, 68-70 and in *Real-Enc.*, xiv,2071ff. Frickenhaus, *Lenäenvasen* 72. *BerlWPr* (1912), figs. No. 1, 2b, 9, 11, 18, 19, 23, 26, 27, 29, pls. i-iii, v. Weege, *Der Tanz*, figs. 101, 103, 105, 107-13. Pickard-Cambridge, *Festivals*, pp. 27ff., figs. 10-17. Deubner, in *JdAI*, xlix(1934),1ff. Farnell, *Cults of the Greek States*, v,240ff., pls. xxxii-xxxiii. Winter-Pernice, *Der Hildesheimer Silberfund*, pls. xi-xvi. G. van Hoorn, *Choes and Anthesteria* (1951), p. 97, No. 271, fig. 38.

[24] Lucy Talcott, "Kourimos Parthenos," *Hesperia*, viii (1939),267f., fig. 1. Pickard-Cambridge, *Festivals*, p. 178f., fig. 25.

[25] Bieber, *op.cit.*, pp. 81ff., figs. 47-56. Terracotta head from Olympia (Fig. 75): *Ausgrabungen Olympia*, iii, p. 35f., fig. 37, pl. vii. Head from Delos in Athens (Fig. 76): National Museum, No. 49 and fragmentary head *ibid.*, No. 46. Hermes of Alcamenes from Pergamon in *Ausgrabungen in Pergamon*, vii. Winter, *Die Skulpturen*, i,48ff., No. 27, Beiblatt 5, pl. ix. Double herm in the Stadion of Athens (Fig. 77): Altmann in *Ath.Mitt.*, xxix(1904),179ff. and 185. Double herm in the Louvre, from Collection Campana, No. 198. Head from Pompeii in Naples (Fig. 78): Bieber, *op.cit.*, p. 85f., fig. 56.

[26] Lobeck, *Aglaophamos*, i,84. Albert Müller, *Bühnenaltertümer*, p. 229. The former belief has been refuted by Pringsheim, *Archäologische Beiträge zur Geschichte des Eleusinischen Kults*, pp. 7ff.

[27] Hydria from Cumae in Leningrad: *Comptes rendus Pétersbourg* (1862), pl. iii; *Journal Int. d'Arch. Numis.*, iv (1901),400ff., pl. 15. Hydria from S. Maria di Capua in Lyons (Fig. 79): Schefold, *Kertscher Vasen*, p. 126, pl. 35, No. 368. F-R, pl. 70. Pfuhl, *Malerei und Zeichnung*, ii, p. 707; iii, fig. 596.

[28] *Ephemeris Arch.* (1901), 1ff., pl. i. *Journal Int. d'Arch.*, iv(1901),169ff., pl. x. Pringsheim, *op.cit.*, pp. 64ff.

[29] Lovatelli, *Ant. Monumenti*, pp. 25ff., pls. ii-iii. Helbig³, No. 1325. Rizzo, in *Röm.Mitt.*, xxv(1910),130, fig. 9, pl. vii. Moebius, in *Ath.Mitt.*, 60-61(1935-6),235f. and 250.

[30] Rizzo, *op.cit.*, pp. 89ff., pl. ii. Moebius, *op.cit.*

[31] Pringsheim, *op.cit.*, p. 7. Foucart, *Les Grands Mystères*, p. 32.

[32] Pringsheim, *op.cit.*, p. 14. Cf. Körte in *Festschrift zur 49. Versammlung deutscher Philologen* (Basel, 1907), p. 202.

[33] F-R, pls. 1-3, 11-13. Pfuhl, *Malerei und Zeichnung*,

1,255ff., III, figs. 215, 217. See particularly the fragments by the painter Sophilos, *ibid.*, 1,246ff., III, fig. 202. Graef, *Vasen von der Akropolis*, I, No. 587, pl. 26.

34 See Bieber, in *Real-Enc.*, second series, IV A *s.v.* Syrma, p. 1786f.

35 Bieber, "Herkunft des tragischen Kostüms," *JdAI*, XXXII(1917),19ff., fig. 1 and pl. I; *idem, Denkmäler*, pp. 88 and 90, fig. 90. Pickard-Cambridge, *Festivals*, p. 213f., fig. 162.

36 Bieber, *JdAI*, XXXII(1917),22ff., figs. 2-6.

37 Svoronos, *Athener National Museum*, pp. 154ff., No. 1463, pl. XXIX. Benndorf, *JOAI*, II(1899),255ff., pls. V-VII. Bieber, *op.cit.*, p. 26, fig. 5, and p. 32, fig. 9.

38 Bieber, *op.cit.*, p. 41, fig. 15. Athens Nat. Mus., No. 1362. Couve-Collignon, *Vases d'Athènes*, No. 1889.

39 Bieber, *op.cit.*, p. 33, fig. 10. Bieber, *The Sculpture of the Hellenistic Age*, p. 154, fig. 655.

40 Naples. Mus. No. 9276 and 112286. Bieber, *JdAI*, XXXII (1917), pp. 28ff., figs. 7-8, 12, 14.

41 Bieber, *op.cit.*, pp. 36ff., fig. 13.

42 On the cothurnus see Alfred Körte, *Festschrift zur 49. Versammlung deutscher Philologen* (Basel, 1907), pp. 203ff. Bieber, *Dresdener Schauspielerrelief*, pp. 48ff. S. P. Karouzou, *JHS*, LXV(1945), p. 38ff., fig. 1, believes that the earliest representation of an actor wearing cothurni in a satyr drama is on a lekythos, Athens Inv. No. 17612.

43 Beazley, *Vases in American Museums*, p. 168, fig. 104. Buschor in F-R, III, text to pl. 145, p. 134f., fig. 62. Hoppin, *Handbook of Attic Red-figured Vases*, 1,83, No. 6. Caskey and Beazley, *Attic Vase-Paintings in the Museum of Fine Arts*, I, No. 63, pl. 29. Pickard-Cambridge, *Festivals*, p. 182, fig. 39. T.B.L. Webster, *Greek Art and Literature*, pl. 18, facing p. 144.

44 Bieber, *op.cit.*, p. 43f. Vita ed. Wilamowitz in *Aeschyli Tragoediae*, p. 5, part 14.

45 Kendall K. Smith, "The Use of the High-Soled Shoe or Buskin in the Greek Tragedy of the Fifth and Fourth Century, B.C.," in *Harvard Studies in Classical Philology*, XVI(1905),123ff. A. Körte, *op.cit.*, pp. 198ff. Bieber, *op.cit.*, pp. 42ff. Other literature, *ibid.*, and C. Fensterbusch in *Bursians Jahresberichte*, No. 253, 1936, pp. 8ff.

46 Bieber, *op.cit.*, p. 28f., fig. 7; p. 32f., fig. 10; p. 41f., fig. 15; p. 49f., fig. 20; pp. 53ff., 25-27. Studniczka, *Kalamis, Abh. sächs. Ges.*, IV(1907),78, pl. 7a (our Fig. 91). Bulle, *Schöner Mensch*, pl. 45. De Ridder, *Bronzes du Louvre*, No. 154, pl. 17. Schreiber, *Hellenistische Reliefbilder*, pls. 37-39. F-R, pl. 120,2. Trendall, *Frühitaliotische Vasen*, pp. 24f., B 36, pl. 24. Volute crater in Tarentum, No. 4358, attributed to the Karnaea painter. Wuilleumier, in *Revue arch.*, II(1933),1ff. A relief from Koropi shows 15 chorus members standing before an altar of Dionysus behind which a statue of Dionysus in short chiton with a cantharus has high cothurni. Reisch, *Weihgeschenke, Abh. arch.ep. Seminar Univ. Wien* (1890), Heft VIII, pp. 123ff., fig. 12.

47 Bieber, *op.cit.*, pp. 15ff., headband (our Fig. 92). Curtius, in *JOAI*, 36 (1946), 62ff., figs. 7-9.

48 Trendall, *op.cit.*, p. 13, No. 101, pl. 4 d, p. 15f., No. 144, pls. 10a and 11a, Copenhagen, No. 3635; Bari, No. 4409, volute crater from Ruvo. Bieber, *op.cit.*, p. 43f., fig. 16, vase from Ruvo in Naples, p. 53f., fig. 26, cover of the amphora, Naples, No. 3249, with Orestes in Delphi: F-R, III, pl. 362ff., fig. 172.

49 Bieber, in *Real-Enc.*, XIV,2082. Girard. *L'Expression des Masques chez Eschyle*, 1895.

50 F-R, pl. 120-23 and 179. Huddilston, *Griech. Tragödie im Licht der Vasenmalerei*, pp. 71ff. and 47. *Greek Tragedy in the Light of Vase-Painting*, pp. 55ff., figs. 5-9. Séchan,

Tragédie grecque, pp. 93ff., figs. 30-300, pl. 1,2 and II. Trendall, *Paestan Pottery*, pp. 60ff., pl. XVII. W. Miller, *Daedalus and Thespis*, III(1932),648f., fig. 34. Pickard-Cambridge, *Theater of Dionysus*, p. 83f., fig. 11; *idem, Festivals*, p. 220, figs. 175-77. Webster, in *Classical Quarterly* 42(1948),15.

51 James T. Allen, "On the Costume of the Greek Tragic Actor in the Fifth Century," *Classical Quarterly*, I(1907), 226ff.

52 Fig. 98: Head in the Museo archeologico in Florence, found in the sea near Livorno together with the head of Aeschylus, Fig. 65. Katherine McDowell in *JHS*, XXXIV (1904),81ff., herm in the garden of Villa Colonna, originally in one piece with a head of Aeschylus: W. Amelung, *Atti Ponteficia Academia Romana*, Series III, Memorie I, part 2 (1924), pp. 120ff. M. Bieber, *Sculpture of the Hellenistic Age*, p. 59f., figs. 180-81.

53 Arndt, *Porträts*, pls. 113-115. BrBr, pl. 427. Delbrück, *Antike Porträts*, plate 16 B. Hekler, *Bildniskunst*, p. XIV, pls. 52 and 54. Paribeni, *Il ritratto nell'arte antica*, pl. XXVI. Schefold, *Bildnisse*, pp. 90-93, 107. Bieber, *Denkmäler*, p. 82, fig. 85, pls. 44-45; and *Sculpture of the Hellenistic Age*, p. 59, fig. 183.

54 Poulsen, *Iconographic Studies*, I, fig. 71. Bieber, *Sculpture of the Hellenistic Age*, p. 59, fig. 182.

55 Aristotle, *Poetics*, pp. 1452a, 1453a-b, 1454b, 1455a. F. Fergusson, *The Idea of a Theater. A study of ten plays. The art of drama in changing perspective* (1949). Fergusson gives an excellent analysis of the *Oedipus Rex*, and he uses this drama as basis for the understanding of all tragedies, from Racine to Eliot.

56 Hauser in *JOAI*, VIII(1905),37ff., fig. 5. Gardner, in *JHS*, XXV(1905),67f., pl. I,1. B. Schröder, in *JdAI*, XXX (1915),113, fig. 11. Studniczka, *ibid.*, XXXI(1916),205, fig. 20. Beazley, *Corpus Vas. Ant. Oxford*, I, No. 530, pl. XXXII, fig. 1. Pickard-Cambridge, *Festivals*, p. 232, fig. 204.

57 Bieber, in *Ath.Mitt.*, L(1925),11ff., pl. II. Pickard-Cambridge, *Festivals*, p. 221, fig. 181. Trendall, *Paestan Pottery*, p. 88, fig. 53.

58 Gilbert Murray, rec., *Euripides, Fabulae* (1902-09); *idem, Euripides and His Age*, 2nd ed. (1946). Wilamowitz, *Euripides, Herakles*, I, 2nd ed. (1897), pp. 108ff.; *idem, Einleitung in die griechische Tragödie* (1907), pp. 1ff.

59 Arndt, *Porträts*, pls. 35-36. Hekler, *Bildniskunst*, pls. 10 and 89. Delbrück, *Porträts*, p. XXXIII, pl. 17. Arndt-Amelung, Nos. 1982-83. Paribeni, *Ritratti*, pl. XXII. Poulsen, *Iconographic Studies*, I, figs. 55-56; *idem, Cat. of Ancient Sculpture in the Ny-Carlsberg Glyptothek* (1951), No. 414b. Hinks, *Greek and Roman Portrait Sculpture in the British Museum* (1935), p. 8, pl. 4b. Mus. No. 1833. Schefold, *Bildnisse*, p. 88f., No. 3. Bieber, *Denkmäler*, p. 82f., No. 29, pl. 43,2; and *Sculpture of the Hellenistic Age* (1954), p. 60, figs. 185-187. Lost statuette drawing by Orsini (Fig. 108): *JHS*, 43(1923),64, fig. 8.

60 Bieber, *Denkmäler*, p. 82f., No. 29, pl. 46. Pickard-Cambridge, *Festivals*, p. 185, fig. 48.

61 Berlin Mus. No. 3237. Bethe, in *JdAI*, XI(1896),292ff., pl. 2. Séchan, *Tragédie grecque*, pp. 256ff., fig. 76. Bieber, *Denkmäler*, p. 103f., No. 40, fig. 105, pl. 52. Pickard-Cambridge, *Festivals*, p. 217, figs. 164-165.

62 Bethe, in *JdAI*, XI(1896),295ff.

63 Robert, in *Arch. Zeitung*, XXXVI(1878),13ff.

64 See Pottier, *Catalogue des Vases antiques du Louvre*, III,2 (2nd ed., 1929), pp. 1053ff.

65 Lucanian hydria in the British Museum No. F185; *British Mus. Cat. of Vases*, IV, p. 95f., pl. VII. Séchan, *op.cit.*, p. 261f., fig. 81.

66 Studniczka, in *Mélanges Perrot*, pp. 307ff. Svoronos, *Das*

Athener National-Museum, II, pp. 512ff., pl. LXXXII. Bieber, *Denkmäler*, p. 104f., No. 41, pl. 53. Buschor in F-R, III, text to pls. 143-145, p. 134f., fig. 61. Pickard-Cambridge, *Festivals*, p. 179, fig. 26.

[67] HBr, p. 54, pl. 42. Pfuhl, *Malerei und Zeichnung der Griechen*, II, p. 621f., III, fig. 641. W. Miller, *Daedalus and Thespis*, The Contributions of the Ancient Dramatic Poets to our Knowledge of the Arts and the Crafts of Greece, III, Painting and Allied Arts (1932), pp. 630ff., fig. 28. I cannot share the opinion of Pfuhl (*op.cit.*) and von Salis (in *JdAI* xxv[1910],144, and *Kunst der Griechen*, p. 172) that this wallpainting is copied from a picture of the classical period. The pathetic movement is thoroughly Hellenistic.

[68] Carcopino, *La Basilique Pythagoricienne*, pp. 135ff., pl. xv. Cumont, in *Rassegna d'Arte*, VIII(1921),37-44 with plate. Jolliffe and Strong, in *JHS*, XLIV(1924),65f.,91ff., fig. 15. Emily Wadsworth, in *MAAR*, IV(1924),85, pl. XLVII,2.

[69] Vogel, *Szenen Euripideischer Tragödien in griech. Vasengemälden*, 1886; Huddilston, *Greek Tragedy in the Light of Vase-Painting*, 1898, trans. by Maria Hense, *Griechische Tragödie in Licht der Vasenmalerei*, 1900. Séchan, *op.cit.*, pp. 231-518. C. Fensterbusch, in *Bursians Jahresberichte*, No. 253, 1936, pp. 2ff. W. Miller, *op.cit.*, I(1929), p. 74 with plate. For our Figs. 34-35 above, see: Bulle, in *Corolla Curtius*, pp. 151-160, pls. 54-56. Buschor, "Zwei Theaterkratere" in *Studies Presented to David Robinson* (1953), II, pp. 90-95, pl. 32a. Pickard-Cambridge, *Festivals*, p. 183, figs. 40a-c. Buschor thinks that the chorus, poet, chorodidiaskalos, and the musicians of Euripides' *Hippolytus* are represented. The fluteplayer and one actor have the sleeved robe. Four white masks are preserved. The style is similar to the Pronomos vase (Figs. 31-33) and the date is around 400 B.C.

[70] Vogel, *op.cit.*, pp. 68ff. Huddilston, *op.cit.*, pp. 121ff. Séchan, *op.cit.*, pp. 379ff., figs. 109-114. Philippart, "Iconog-

raphie de l'Iphigénie en Tauride d'Euripide" in *Revue Belge de Philol. et d'Histoire*, IV(1925),5ff. F-R, pl. 148. Pickard-Cambridge, *Theatre of Dionysus*, pp. 86ff., figs. 14-16 and 19. Ippel, in *Studies Presented to D. M. Robinson* (1951), I,809ff., pls. 105-6. Webster, *Greek Theatre Production* (1956), pp. 15 and 102f., pl. 7.

[71] D-R, pp. 307ff. The idea of Frickenhaus (*Altgriech. Bühne*, p. 7f.) that these halls were wooden structures on the eccyclema (see Ch. VI) and rolled out with it, seems to me absurd.

[72] Robert, *Oedipus*, pp. 381ff., figs. 51-52. Pickard-Cambridge, *Theater of Dionysus*, p. 85f., fig. 13.

[73] Séchan, *op.cit.*, p. 490, fig. 144. Pace, in *Mon. ant.*, 1922, pp. 524ff., figs. 1-3, pl. I. Trendall, *Paestan Pottery*, p. 7f., pl. I,b. Early Paestan crater in Syracuse, No. 36319. Fig. 118: formerly Collection Castellani and Hearst, now in the Metropolitan Museum of Art, New York, No. 56.171.58. D. von Bothmer, *BMMA* (1957), p. 179, fig. 2. I owe the new photograph for Fig. 118 to his kindness.

[74] Schaal, *De Euripid. Antiopa*, Diss. Berlin, 1914. Séchan, *op.cit.*, pp. 291ff.

[75] Berlin Mus. No. 3296. Found in Palazzuolo. Schaal, *op.cit.*, pl. I. Séchan, *op.cit.*, pp. 305ff., fig. 88. Trendall, *op.cit.*, p. 7f., pl. IIa.

[76] Munich, Mus. No. 810. Found in Canosa. F-R, pl. 90. Bieber, *Denkmäler*, pp. 105ff., No. 42, fig. 106, pl. 54. A. B. Cook, *Zeus* I,251f., pl. XXII. Séchan, *op.cit.*, pp. 405ff., pl. VIII. Pickard-Cambridge, *Theatre of Dionysus*, p. 92, fig. 21. Robert, *Archäologische Hermeneutik*, pp. 159ff., fig. 130. Robert believes that the vase painter had himself arbitrarily changed the Euripidean drama. The changes, however, are not in the form but in the substance of the plot, thus literary, not artistic deviations from Euripides.

NOTES TO CHAPTER III. OLD COMEDY AND MIDDLE COMEDY · ARISTOPHANES

[1] Bethe, *Prolegomena*, pp. 48ff. F. M. Cornford, *The Origin of the Attic Comedy* (1914), pp. 35ff. Romagnoli, *Nel Regno di Dioniso. Studi sul teatro comico greco* (1923). Pickard-Cambridge, *Dithyramb*, pp. 221ff. and 244ff.; idem, *Festivals*, p. 194f. H. Herter, *Vom dionysischen Tanz zum komischen Spiel. Die Anfänge der attischen Komödie* (1947).

[2] Wilhelm, *Urkunden dramatischer Aufführungen*, pp. 10 and 18. Pickard-Cambridge, *Festivals*, pp. 83, 106, 119.

[3] British Mus. No. B 509 (our Fig. 123): Cecil Smith in *JHS*, II(1881), 309ff., pl. XIV. Berlin Mus. No. F 1830 (our Fig. 124): Bieber, *Denkmäler*, p. 127f., No. 71b-c, figs. 119-121. Pickard-Cambridge, *Dithyramb*, pp. 244ff., figs. 16-17.

[4] Boston Mus. No. 20,18. Flickinger, *Greek Theater*, p. 40, figs. 15-16. F. Brommer in *Arch. Anz.*, LVII(1942),65ff., figs. 1-2. He gives parallels for the dolphin riders in his figs. 3-9. For other animal dances in comedy see Pickard-Cambridge, *Dithyramb*, p. 247, and *Festivals*, p. 195, note 1. Bielefeld, "Ein Delphinreiter-Chor," *Arch. Anz.*, LXI/II (1946/47),48-54.

[5] Berlin Inv. No. F.16 97. Gerhard, *Trinkschalen und Gefässe*, II, pl. XXI. Bieber, *Denkmäler*, p. 127, No. 71a, pl. 66. Pickard-Cambridge, *Dithyramb*, p. 246f., fig. 18.

[6] Th. Zielinski, *Gliederung der attischen Komödie* (1885) pp. 175ff. Bethe, *Prolegomena*, p. 55. Pickard-Cambridge, *Dithyramb*, pp. 292ff.

[7] Gregor Krause and Karl With, *Insel Bali* (1920), I, pls. 20-21; II, p. 23.

[8] Poppelreuter, *De Comoediae Atticae Primordiis* (1892), pp. 23ff. G. Körte in *Real-Enc.*, XI, *s.v.* Komödie, pp. 1242ff., especially p. 1251.

[9] Pickard-Cambridge, *Dithyramb*, pp. 274ff.

[10] G. Körte in *JdAI*, VIII(1893),89ff., and *Ath.Mitt.*, XIX (1894),346ff. G. Loeschcke, *ibid.*, pp. 510ff., pl. VIII. Bieber, *Denkmäler*, p. 129, No. 72a, fig. 122. Payne, *Necrocorinthia*, p. 118f., fig. 44 G., and p. 314, No. 1073.

[11] Pickard-Cambridge, *Dithyramb*, p. 265f., figs. 33-41. A. Greifenhagen, *Darstellung des Komos im VI Jahrhundert* (1929), pp. 59, 66f. and 102f. note 128, pl. I; idem, "Ein böotischer Tanzchor des 6. Jh. v. Chr.," in *Festschrift für Friedrich Zucker* (1954), pp. 27ff. Padded dancers on Corinthian plaques: *Ant.Denk.*, I, pl. 7, 14a; II, pl. 39,9. Vases: Payne, *Necrocorinthia*, pp. 118ff., fig. 44A-F., pl. 33, No. 2, 9-10; pp. 194ff., figs. 88a and 89, pl. 51, 1-7 and 52, 1-3. Buschor, *Satyrtänze*, pp. 18ff. T. B. L. Webster, "Greek Comic Costume: its History and Diffusion," *Bulletin of the Rylands Library* 36(1954),579ff. Our Fig. 131 in the Metropolitan Museum of Art, No. 22, 139, 22 is an Attic imitation. Payne, p. 194, No. 8, pl. 51,6. G. Richter, *Handbook of the Greek Collection* (1953), p. 57, pl. 37b., dated 590-570 B.C.

[12] Charlotte Fränkel, *Rheinisches Museum für Philologie* (1912), pp. 94ff. Bieber, *Denkmäler*, p. 129f., No. 72b, fig. 123a-b. Flickinger, *Greek Theater*, p. 47f., fig. 20. Payne, *Necrocorinthia*, pp. 122 and 317, No. 1178. Pickard-Cambridge, *Dithyramb*, pp. 263ff. Pottier, *Album Vases ant. du Louvre*, I,55, E 632. A. B. Cook, *Zeus*, III,559f., fig. 381.

[13] Kaibel, *Comicorum Graecorum Fragmenta*, in *Fragmenta Poetarum Graecorum*, VI,1 (1899), 91-133, Nos. 1-239. Idem in *Real-Enc.*, VI(1909),34-41. Olivieri, *Frammenti della Commedia greca e del Mimo nella Sicilia e nella Mag-*

na Grecia, Testo e Commento (1930; second ed. 1947), pp. 183ff.

[14] Heracles: Kaibel, *op.cit.*, p. 104f., Nos. 76-78. Odysseus: p. 108ff., Nos. 99-108.

[15] Hetty Goldman and Frances Jones, "Terracottas from the Necropolis of Halae," *Hesperia*, XI(1942),405f., pl. XXIII. The actors are dated 390-350 B.C. David Robinson, *Excavations at Olynthos*, IV(1931),70 and 86f.; VII(1933), 78ff.; X(1941),1ff. Text to pl. I, bronze statuette of actor; XIV(1952),263f.,272ff. The destruction of Olynthos. 348 B.C., gives a *terminus ante quem*. Dorothy Thompson, *Hesperia*, XXI(1952),141ff., Nos. 43-47, pl. 38: "the terracottas [of actors] are not popular until Old Comedy had died out." Statuettes, heads, and moulds for similar heads of actors have been found in Corinth: Agnes Stillwell, *Corinth*, XV,1 (1948), Nos. 43-50, pp. 102-4, pls. 35-36; XV,2(1952), p. 143f., pl. 29, Nos. XIX 10-12, dated first half of fourth century. R. A. Higgins, *Catalogue of the Terracottas in the Department of Greek and Roman Antiquities*, British Museum, I(1954),171,197-202, Nos. 736-748. Higgins dates these early to mid fourth century.

[16] Berlin, Mus. Nos. 8823 and 8405. Bieber, *Denkmäler*, p. 132, Nos. 79-80, pl. 69. Pickard-Cambridge, *Festivals*, p. 204, figs. 103 and 109.

[17] Fig. 135 and 137: in the Boston Museum of Fine Arts, No. 01.8013, Fat Man. Traces of red in the face and on the feet, blue on the wreath; No. 01.7758, bought in Athens, said to be from the Kabeirion in Thebes, Thin Man. Fig. 138: Walters, *British Museum Catalogue of Terracottas*, C. 239; Higgins, *op.cit.*, p. 198, No. 737, pl. 97. Fig. 136 is found in Megara Hyblaea, now in the Archaeological Collection of the University of Rostock.

[18] Fig. 139 in Boston, Fine Arts Museum, No. 01.7838. Found in Greece. Hair and beard red. Mantle light violet. Basket yellow with traces of gold at the rims. Fig. 140 Louvre, Mus. No. 300, found in Greece. Beard and hair dark reddish-brown. Mantle blue. Fig. 142, Boston, Mus. No. 13.99. Traces of light red on the face, blue-black on the iris, grayish-black on the mouth. Fig. 143 in the Louvre, Mus. No. S 1682. Fig. 141 from a mould for an actor carrying a broad and low basket on his head, found in Olynthus. D. Robinson, *Olynthos*, XIV(1952),263f., No. 364, pl. 108.

[19] Fig. 145, Berlin, Mus. No. 8265. A similar fig. in the Louvre, Mus. No. 295: Pickard-Cambridge, *Festivals*, p. 208, fig. 139. Fig. 144: Princeton University, The Art Museum, No. 48-50. Frances Jones, in *The Record of the Art Museum*, X, 1(1951), 1-4. Frances Jones, *The Theater in Ancient Art: An Exhibition*, The Art Museum, Princeton University (1952), p. 5, No. 13. Fig. 146 in Munich Antikensammlungen, Mus. No. 5390. See also, Winter, *Typen der figürlichen Terrakotten* in Kekule, *Antike Terrakotten*, III, part II, p. 414, figs. 2-3.

[20] Fig. 147, Munich Antikensammlungen, Inv. No. 5389. Bieber, *Denkmäler*, p. 133, No. 83, pl. 71. Pickard-Cambridge, *Festivals*, p. 204, fig. 111. See also: Dorothy Thompson, *Hesperia*, XXI(1952), pl. 38. Walters, *British Mus. Cat. of Terracottas*, C 238. Higgins, *op.cit.*, p. 198, No. 738, pl. 98.

[21] Walters, *British Mus. Cat. of Terracottas*, C 90. Higgins, *op.cit.*, p. 200, No. 743, pl. 98 (our Fig. 148). Luschey, *Ganymed*, Heidelberger Beiträge zur antiken Kunstgeschichte (1942), p. 71f., fig. 1. Pickard-Cambridge, *Festivals*, p. 207f., figs. 130-134. Dorothy Thompson, *Hesperia*, XXI (1952), 142f., Nos. 44-47, pl. 38. Winter, *Typen der figürlichen Terrakotten*, in Kekule, *Antike Terrakotten*, III, 2, p. 418,9 and p. 419,2-4.

[22] Louvre No. CA 6816.

[23] Our Fig. 150: Louvre No. 294. Good technique. Cf. below, Fig. 196 in the Metropolitan Museum from Middle Comedy. As this figure in the Louvre has already the differentiation of the eyebrows, it may also, like others listed, already belong to the Middle Comedy. A related figure in the British Museum: Walters, *op.cit.*, C 62. Higgins, *op.cit.*, p. 200, No. 742, pl. 99. Higgins explains this as a thief who has found sanctuary on an altar.

[24] Fig. 151 in Rostock, Archeological Collection of the University. Bought in Naples. A similar figure, complete, is in the Museo Teatrale in Milano, No. 208.

[25] Fig. 152 in Bonn, Akademisches Kunstmuseum, Inv. No. D 5. An excellent figure of a slave with red hair and beard, who offers food to the baby in his arm is in the British Museum, Walters, *op.cit.*, C 237. Higgins, *op.cit.*, p. 199, No. 740, pl. 97.

[26] Fig. 153: Berlin Mus. No. 6892. Bieber, *Denkmäler*, p. 133, No. 84, pl. 70,3. Fig. 154: Berlin No. 7820. Bieber, *Denkmäler*, p. 133f., No. 85, pl. 72,3. Tights yellow, chiton blue, chlamys white, shoes dark blue, scabbard yellow. Robert, *Masken*, p. 21, fig. 17. Zahn, "Maison" in *Die Antike*, II(1926),328ff., pl. 23. Pickard-Cambridge, *Festivals*, p. 204, fig. 110.

[27] Fig. 155: Tarentum: *Notizie degli Scavi* (1897), p. 216, fig. 36. Fig. 156: Berlin, Mus. No. 7042a. Found in Megara. Robert, *Masken*, p. 12f., fig. 24. Bieber, *Denkmäler*, p. 134, Nos. 86-87, pl. 72,1-2. Hair white. Eyebrows and iris black. Face, arms, legs lively red. Chiton white. Mantle light blue.

[28] Berlin, Mus. Nos. 7603-4. Bieber, *Denkmäler*, p. 135, Nos. 90-91, pl. 74,1 and 3. In both, hair, face, beard, arms, legs red. Fig. 158 carries a yellow caldron; his lips are violet. Fig. 157 has a yellow metal ring over his bald pate. On the skillet over his left shoulder are yellow cakes with red points. The bundle on his back is red and yellow. Fig. 159: David Robinson, *Olynthos*, X(1941),1ff., pl. I.

[29] Fig. 160: Boston, Museum of Fine Arts, No. 01.7762. Cf. Pottier, *Les statues de terres cuites*, 120, fig. 42. Fig. 161: British Museum, Higgins, *op.cit.*, No. 745, p. 201, pl. 99; Pickard-Cambridge, *Festivals*, p. 209, fig. 142. Fig. 162: Athens, Nat. Mus. No. 13015; Pickard-Cambridge, *Festivals*, p. 209, fig. 143. Fig. 163: Berlin Museum, No. 7089. Fig. 164: Metropolitan Museum of Art, No. 07.286.8. Fig. 165: Archaeological Collection of the University of Rostock. Bought in Naples. Cf. *Fouilles de Delphes*, V, pl. XXIII,5.

[30] Fig. 166 in Würzburg. The left leg and right foot of the man are restored. Bieber, *Denkmäler*, p. 136, No. 92, pl. 74,4. Pickard-Cambridge, *Festivals*, p. 204, fig. 108. Fig. 167: Louvre, said to be found in Cyprus. A group of an actor holding a woman in his arm is in the Museo teatrale of Milano, No. 310. Another comic actor in a group with a dancing woman, from Centuripe in Karlsruhe: Kekule, *Figürliche Terrakotten*, II, *Terrakotten von Sizilien*, p. 74, pl. XLIV,2; Winter, *ibid.*, III, 2, p. 423,7. I owe the excellent photographs of the delightful pair (Figs. 166a-e) to the kindness of Professor Hans Moebius.

[31] W. Beare, "Actors' Costumes, in Aristophanes Comedy," *CQ*, IV(1954),64-75, denies that padding and phallus were used otherwise than occasionally. I believe that these contrivances were only occasionally hidden under the dress of everyday life for women and dignified persons. See also T. B. L. Webster, "Attic Comic Costume: A Reexamination," *Ephemeris* (1953-4, appeared 1957), 192ff.

[32] Fig. 168: Statuette in Vienna, Austria, formerly in the possession of Hartwig, Mus. No. 161, Inv. No. 1844.

[33] Carapanos, *Dodone*, pl. XIII, No. 5. Bieber, *Denkmäler*, p. 131f., No. 78, pl. 68. Pickard-Cambridge, *Festivals*, p. 202f., fig. 102.

34 Heracles: Figs. 170-171: Boston Museum of Fine Arts, from Greece. Mus. No. 01.8014. Berlin Mus. Nos. 8838, cf. head No. 4781. Bieber, *Denkmäler*, p. 130f., Nos. 73-74, pl. 67, face, hands, and lion skin dark red. Jersey reddish-yellow, chiton red. Quiver reddish yellow. Munich Mus. No. 382, formerly collection Arndt. Walters, *British Museum Cat. of Terracottas*, C 80. Higgins, *op.cit.*, p. 199, No. 741, pl. 98. Webster in *Bulletin of the Ryland Library*, XXXII (1949),97f., fig. 7. Pickard-Cambridge, *Festivals*, p. 199, figs. 82. Odysseus: Fig. 172: Louvre, No. 485. Fig. 173: Munich Mus. No. 383a, Inv. No. 6926, formerly collection Arndt. Cf. *Fouilles de Delphes*, V, pl. XXII,2. A mould for part of this type has been found on the Agora of Athens: Davidson and Thompson, *Small Objects from the Pnyx*, I, 147, No. 65, fig. 61. Kadmos: Figs. 174-175: Louvre, from Cyprus? Both are sphenopogons. Hero with pestle (Ares) in Munich (Fig. 176). Replica in the Museo teatrale in Milano, No. 142. Hero: Fig. 177; Louvre, No. 298. Face red, hair and beard brown, eyebrows black. Mantle yellowish-green. Crown red.

35 Bieber, *Denkmäler*, p. 131, No. 76, pl. 67,4.

36 Fig. 179: statuette of a tympanon player in costume of Old Comedy in the Louvre, No. 297. For clapper (krotalon) and tympanon see Wegner, *Das Musikleben der Griechen*, pp. 62ff.

37 Schnabel, *Kordax*, 1910. Vincenzo Festa, *Memorie dell' Accademia di Archeologia di Napoli*, IV(1919),35ff. Weege, *Der Tanz in der Antike* (1926), pp. 98ff., 105ff. Séchan, *La dance grècque antique* (1930), pp. 187ff.

38 Schnabel, *op.cit.*, pp. 17ff., pl. I. Bieber, *Denkmäler*, p. 175f., No. 186, fig. 141. Olivieri, *Frammenti della Commedia*, p. 220, fig. 16. For satyr dances out of which the kordax can have developed, see Weege, *op.cit.*, pp. 105ff., figs. 138-146, 159, 171.

39 Agora Museum, Athens, Nos. S 1025a-c. I owe the photographs to the kindness of Alison Frantz and Evelyn Harrison, who will publish the marble base in her Catalogue of Sculptures from the Agora. For dedications of choregi see Reisch, *Griechische Weihgeschenke*, in *Abh. epigr. arch. Seminar der Universität Wien*, Heft VIII(1890), pp. 116ff. For such of agonotheti, who replaced the choregi in lean periods, *ibid.*, pp. 90ff.

40 Mercklin, *Röm.Mitt.*, 38/9(1923/4),82f., fig. 7. T.B.L. Webster, in *Bulletin of the John Rylands Library*, 36(1954), 585, fig. 3. Brommer, "Kopf über Kopf" in *Antike und Abendland*, IV,42ff., figs. 2-3, note 3. Beazley, in *Attic Vase Paintings in the Museum of Fine Arts, Boston*, II,83f., text to pl. LXII. He believes the heads on top of the real heads to be a token disguise rather than masks.

41 Louis Lord, *Aristophanes, His Plays and Influence* (1931). Gilbert Murray, *Aristophanes, A Study* (1933).

42 Kaibel, *Comicorum Graec. Fragmenta*, p. 5, Platonius. Dorothy Thompson in *Hesperia*, XXI(1952),144: "The change of mask type may also probably be associated with the enlargement of the auditorium of the theatre under Lykurgus."

43 Bibliography in Bieber, *The Sculpture of the Hellenistic Age*, p. 143, note 63. To be added: David M. Robinson, *AJA*, 59(1955),25-27, pl. 17, figs. 30-33 (our Figs. 183a-c). Lippold in Arndt, pls. 1211-1219. Felletti-Maj, *Museo Nazionale Romano, I Ritratti*, p. 22f., Nos. 23-25. B. Strandman, "The Pseudo-Seneca," *Opuscula Academica, Kunsthistorics Tidskrift*, 19 (Stockholm, 1950), pp. 53-82, with 6 plates. Cf. Ch. VIII, n. 10.

44 Körte in *JdAI*, VIII(1893), p. 69, fig. 1. Bieber, *Denkmäler*, p. 136f., No. 97, fig. 124. Flickinger, *Greek Theater*, p. 47, fig. 17. Bethe, *Griechische Dichtung*, pl. VIII. Pickard-Cambridge, *Festivals*, p. 195f., fig. 80.

45 Metropolitan Museum of Art, Inv. Nos. 13.225.13-28. G. Richter, in *BMMA*, IX(1914),235f. Webster in *CQ*, XLIII(1948),20ff. *Idem, Studies in Later Greek Comedy*, pp. 76 and 85. Pickard-Cambridge, *Festivals*, p. 199f., figs. 84-88. Dorothy Thompson in *Hesperia*, XXI(1952),143. F. Jones in *The Theater in Ancient Art, An Exhibition* (The Art Museum, Princeton University), 1952, Nos. 14-27. G. Richter, *Handbook of the Greek Collection* (1953), 112f., pl. 93a-f.

46 Parallels from Olynthus, dated before 348, in David M. Robinson, *Excavations at Olynthos, The Terracottas*, Vol. IV(1931), p. 70, No. 364, pl. 38, veiled young lady (see our Fig. 192); p. 86f., No. 404, pl. 46, nude man (our Fig. 195); Vol. VII(1933), p. 81, No. 308, pl. 38, seated man with finger in mouth (our Fig. 197); Vol. XIV(1952), pp. 272ff., No. 378, pl. 113 and No. 380G, pl. 116, weeping man (our Figs. 188 and 199); pp. 276ff., No. 380, pl. 115, man with punch bowl (our Figs. 190 and 200) and pl. 116, old woman (our Figs. 185 and 193). Other parallels to our Figs. 185-186 are in the British Museum. Both old nurse and giggling young woman in the Brit. Mus.: Pickard-Cambridge, *Festivals*, p. 209, figs. 140-141. Walters, *op.cit.*, C.4; Higgins, *op.cit.*, p. 200ff., Nos. 744 and 747, pl. 99. For others see Winter, in Kekule, *Terrakotten*, III. *Typen der figürlichen Terrakotten*, II, p. 414, Nos. 7-8; 417, No. 3; 418, Nos. 4,10,11; 421, No. 8; 424, No. 9; 462, Nos. 1, 7, 8; 463, No. 1. Cf. also above, Fig. 165, note 29.

47 Bieber, *Denkmäler*, p. 132f., No. 82, pl. 70,2.

48 An excellent example of the young woman is in Heidelberg: H. Luschey, "Komödien-Masken," in *Ganymed*, Heidelberger Beiträge zur antiken Kunstgeschichte (1949), pp. 72ff., figs. 2-3. Other replicas: David Robinson. *Olynthos*, IV(1931), The Johns Hopkins Studies in Archaeology, No. 12, p. 70, text to No. 364, pl. 38.

49 D. Robinson, *op.cit.*, IV, p. 86f., believes this fat man to be a hermaphrodite. But the flabby breast is that of an older man, not of a woman.

50 See our notes 15, 46, 49. For the seated slave see Winter, *Typen der figürlichen Terrakotten*, Part II, p. 419, figs. 6-7, and p. 424, fig. 9. See also Higgins, *op.cit.*, p. 200, Nos. 742-743, pls. 98 and 99.

51 Platonius, *On the Different Comedies* (Περὶ διαφορᾶς κωμῳδιῶν), Kaibel, p. 5, ¶11: "The comedy of the middle period made a business of ridiculing the stories told by the poets." List of extant titles of mythological plays written between 400 and 300 in Meinecke, *Comicorum Fragmenta*, pp. 283-284.

52 E. Strong, in *JHS*, XXIII(1903),356ff. Webster in *Studies . . . David Robinson*, I, p. 590f., pl. 55; *idem, Studies in Later Greek Comedy*, p. 10f., pl. I; *idem, Production*, 56, 62, 69, 119, pl. 16. Pickard-Cambridge, *Festivals*, p. 200, fig. 89. I owe the photograph for Fig. 201 to the generosity of Professor Webster.

53 Bulle, *Das Theater zu Sparta, SBMünch* (1937), Heft 5, pp. 51ff., pl. V. Dugas, *Revue Études anciennes*, 49(1936), 226, pl. III,1. Beazley, in *JHS*, LIX(1939), p. 10f., fig. 30. Papaspyridi-Karouzou, *ibid.*, LXV(1945),40,42, pl. 5 (drawing by Gilliéron). Brommer, *Satyrspiele*, pp. 25ff., figs. 17-19. Pickard-Cambridge, *Theatre of Dionysus*, p. 74; *idem, Festivals*, p. 237. Webster, in *CQ*, 42(1948), 18f.; *idem, Ephemeris*, 1957, (1953-54), 199f., fig. 4; *idem, Production*, 7, 20, 109, pl. 14.

54 Athens, No. 5815 (1931). Körte, in *Ath.Mitt.*, XIX (1894),346ff., and *NJb*, XLVII(1921),311f. Bieber, *Denkmäler*, p. 153, No. 126, pl. 87, 1. Pickard-Cambridge, *Dithyramb*, p. 269f. Zahn in text to F-R, III,180, note 5, believes the vase, Fig. 203, to be southern Italian and to represent a phlyakes farce. A. D. Trendall kindly informs me

that it is not Boeotian but Corinthian red-figure, and takes with it the fragment from Corinth published by Luce, *AJA* xxxiv,(1930), p. 342, fig. 6.

[55] Percy Gardner, *Catalogue of Greek Vases in the Ashmolean Museum*, p. 18f., No. 262, pl. 26. Bieber, *Denkmäler*, p. 154, No. 128, figs. 134-135. W. Miller, *Daedalus and Thespis*, Vol. III, p. 657f., fig. 39. P. Wolters and Gerda Bruns, *Das Kabeironheiligtum bei Theben*, I(1940),95ff., p. 99 K 19, p. 100 K 21, pl. 27,3. *JHS*, XIII(1893), 77ff., pl. 4. A. B. Cook, *Zeus*, III, 160, fig. 70.

[56] Berlin Ms. No. 3284. Bieber, *Denkmäler*, p. 153f., No. 127, pl. 87,2. Wolters and Bruns, *op.cit.*, p. 100 K 22, pl. 27,1.

[57] Heidelberg Mus. No. B 134. Luschey, *Die Welt der Griechen* (1948), p. 62, No. 16; *idem* in *Ganymed*, ed. Herbig (1949), p. 75, fig. 4. Webster, in *Festschrift Bernhard Schweitzer*, p. 261f., pl. 57,1; *idem, Studies in Later Greek Comedy*, p. 11f., pl. II,1; *idem, Production*, 61, 65, 67, pl. 15a. Kraiker, *Kat. d. Vasen Heidelberg*, p. 239, pl. 48.

[58] Margaret Crosby, *Hesperia*, XXIV(1955),76-84, pls. 34-37.

[59] Athens, Mus. No. 12683. Nicole, *Vases d'Athènes*, No.

1119. Heydemann, *Vasensammlung Neapel*, No. 3232. Bieber, "Die Herkunft des tragischen Kostüms" in *JdAI*, XXXII (1917),62f., figs. 32-33. Beazley, in *JHS*, LIX(1939),23ff., fig. 60; 30ff., No. 82-83, on Persian dances, performed on a table by men in Oriental dress and by girls. *Idem* in *Hesperia*, XXIV(1955),304ff., pl. 85, on Orientals with fluteplayer.

[60] Bulle, *Festschrift für Loeb*, p. 28, figs. 14-16.

[61] *Exploration arch. de Delos*, XII, 38f., pls. 22 and 24. Rumpf in *Studies presented to David Robinson* (1953), II,84-89, pl. 30 (Robinson Collection), pl. 31 (Cleveland) No. 26549=our Fig. 214. For other representations of men in women's clothing see Buschor, in *JdAI*, 38/9(1923/4),128-132, fig. 1. Buschor's idea, that these are men celebrating the skirophoria has been refuted by Deubner, *Attische Feste*, p. 49f., 132f., pl. 21,3. Beazley, *Attic Red-Figure Vases*, Boston, II,55ff., No. 99, pl. LI. He believes that it means some sacred rite, not a komos. Cf. also Beazley, *Attic Red-Figure Vase-Painting*, p. 123, No. 29; p. 173, No. 11; p. 379, No. 30. The vase in the Robinson Collection, formerly in Baltimore, now in Oxford, University of Mississippi: *CVA*, Baltimore, pls. 28 and 28a. Another example in Madrid: Leroux, *Vases Grecs de Madrid*, p. 82f., No. 155, pl. XIX.

NOTES TO CHAPTER IV. THE DIONYSIAC FESTIVALS

[1] Mommsen, *Feste der Stadt Athen*, pp. 349ff., 372ff., 384ff., 428ff. Thraemer, in Roscher, I,1071ff. Nilsson, in *JdAI*, XXXI(1916, 323ff. Navarre, *Théâtre Grec* (1925) pp. 101ff. Allen, *Stage Antiquities* (1927), pp. 31ff. Deubner, *Attische Feste* (1933), pp. 93ff. Pickard-Cambridge, *Festivals*, pp. 1-126 includes all literary and epigraphical sources.

[2] Aristotle, *Poetics*, III-V, pp. 1448a-1449a. Deubner, *op.cit.*, pp. 134ff.

[3] *IG*² 3090. Pickard-Cambridge, *Festivals*, pp. 43f. and 54.

[4] *IG*² 3094-5, 3098. Pickard-Cambridge, *Festivals*, p. 45.

[5] N. Kyparissis and W. Peck, in *Ath.Mitt.*, 66(1941),218ff., pl. 73. Pickard-Cambridge, *Festivals*, p. 44f., fig. 18. Webster, "Greek Comic Costume," in *Bull. Ryland Library* 36 (1954), pl. 3; Webster, *Production*, pp. 56, 62, 64-66, 73, 117, pl. 19; Webster, *Studies in Later Greek Comedy*, p. 75f., pl. III.

[6] Bieber, "Eros and Dionysos on Kerch Vases," in Studies in Honor of T. Leslie Shear, *Hesperia*, Supplement VII (1949),31ff.

[7] Körte in *Real-Enc.*, XI,1207ff., and 1228ff. Deubner, *Attische Feste*, pp. 123ff. Dittmer, *The Fragments of Athenian Comic Didascaliae found in Rome*, 1923. Wilhelm, *Urkunden dramatischer Aufführungen*, pp. 43ff. E. Capps, "The Roman Fragments of Athenian Comic Didascaliae," *CP*, II(1907),201ff. Pickard-Cambridge, *Festivals*, pp. 22ff.

[8] Dörpfeld, *Ath.Mitt.*, XX(1895),161ff.,368ff., pl. IV; and XLVI(1921),81ff. *Ant.Denk.*, II, pls. 37-38. Frickenhaus, in *JdAI*, XXVII(1912),80ff.; *idem*, 72.*BerlWPr*, 1912. Judeich, *Topographie von Athen*, 2nd ed., 1931, pp. 290ff., figs. 36-37. E. Capps, *CP*, II(1907), 25ff. Anti, *Teatri Greci arcaici* (1947), pp. 202ff., pl. V. Bieber, in *AJA*, 58(1954),280, pl. 52, fig. 7. C. F. Russo, "I due teatri di Aristofane," *Rendiconti*, Academia dei Lincei, Serie VIII, Vol. XI(1956),14-27.

[9] Photius, *s.v.* Ληναῖον. *Etym.Mag.*, *s.v.* ἐπὶ Ληναίῳ. Bekker, *Anecdot.* 1, 278. Dörpfeld, in *Ath.Mitt.*, XX(1895),182ff. Judeich, *op.cit.*, p. 294f., footnotes.

[10] See for the Anthesteria: Deubner, *JdAI*, XLII(1927), 172ff., and *Attische Feste*, pp. 93ff. Children's Choes: Deubner, *op.cit.*, p. 115f., pls. 13, 16, 17, 28-31. Pickard-Cambridge, *Festivals*, p. 10, figs. 1a-c, 2a-c. P. Karouzou in *AJA*, 50(1946), 123ff., figs. 1-10. G. van Hoorn, *Choes and An-*

thesteria (1951), pp. 15ff. G. Richter, *Handbook of the Greek Collection* (1953), p. 103, pl. 84c-f.

[11] Deubner, *JdAI*, 42(1927),177, figs. 7-9; *idem, Attische Feste*, pp. 104ff., pl. 11, 2-4. He explains the object carried behind the wedding car wrongly as a stylis. See M. Bieber in *Hesperia*, v, Supplement VII(1949),31ff., pls. 4-5. Pickard-Cambridge, *Festivals*, p. 14f. G. Richter, *Handbook of the Greek Collection*, p. 103f., pl. 84e, "Children imitating the ceremonial wedding of Dionysos." G. van Hoorn, *op.cit.*, p. 159, No. 757.

[12] Black-figured lekythos in Giessen, now on loan in the Oberhessischen Museum of the city, formerly in the collection of the Department of Archaeology of the (destroyed) University. A fine lekythos with a bridal procession by the Amasis painter has been recently acquired by the Metropolitan Museum.

[13] Albert Müller, *Bühnenaltertümer*, pp. 330ff. Reisch, in *Real-Enc.*, III, *s.v.* Choregia, pp. 2409ff. Allen, *Stage Antiquities*, pp. 44f. Deubner, *Attische Feste*, pp. 138ff. Pickard-Cambridge, *Festivals*, pp. 77ff. T.B.L. Webster, *Greek Theatre Production*, 29ff.

[14] Adolf Wilhelm, *Urkunden dramatischer Aufführungen*, pp. 13ff., especially list on p. 18. Flickinger, *Greek Theater*, pp. 318ff., with list, fig. 75, *IG*², No. 2318-2325. Pickard-Cambridge, *Festivals*, pp. 75ff., 103ff.

[15] James Turney Allen, "On the Program of the City Dionysia during the Peloponnesian War," in *University of California Publications in Classical Philology*, XII, No. 3 (1938),35-42.

[16] The odeum has been excavated by the Greek Archaeological Society. Kastriotes in *Arch.-Ephemeris* (1914), pp. 143ff.; (1915), pp. 145ff.; (1922), pp. 25ff. Orlandos, *PraktikaArch.*, 86(1931),25ff.; 87(1932),27f., with ill. Walter Miller, *Daedalus and Thespis*, I,289ff. James Turney Allen, "On the Odeum of Pericles and the Periclean reconstruction," *University of California Publ. in Classical Archaeology*, I, No. 7 (1941), pp. 173ff. Pickard-Cambridge, *Theater of Dionysus*, p. 1f., figs. 1-2; *Festivals*, p. 65f. Dilke in *ABSA*, XLIII(1948),185f. Dinsmoor, in *Studies Presented to David Moore Robinson* (1951), II,309ff., fig. 2.

[17] See for Figs. 56-58 above, Ch. II, n. 5.

[18] *IG*, II², No. 1368. Dinsmoor, *Hesperia*, XXIII(1954),306f.

[1] Bequignon, in *MonPiot*, xxxiii(1933),44ff., fig. 1, pl. vi (our Fig. 220). On bleachers see Frickenhaus, in *Real-Enc.*, ix(1914), *s.v.* Ikria. For the collapse of the ikria happening not in the sacred precinct, but on the agora see Judeich, *Topographie von Athen* (2nd ed., 1931), p. 69 and A. von Gerkan, in his review of Fiechter, *Dionysostheater, Gnomon,* xiv(1938),238.

[2] B. H. Stricken, "The Origin of the Greek Theater," *Journal of Egyptian Archeology* 41(1955),34-47. A. D. Ure, "Threshing Floor and Vineyard," *CQ,* xlix (new series v, 1955), 225-230.

[3] See Ch. IV, p. 51. Fig. 221 from Bieber, "The Entrances and Exits of Actors and Chorus in Greek Plays," *AJA,* 58(1954),280f., pl. 52, fig. 8.

[4] D-R, pp. 7ff. Wiegand, *Archaische Porosarchitektur,* p. 51. Heberdey, *Altattische Porosskulptur,* pp. 75ff., fig. 53. Fiechter, *Dionysostheater,* 1, p. 11f., pl. 2; 3, p. 66f. Svoronos, *Das Athener National-Museum,* iii,673, No. 3131, pl. ccxxxvi. Svoronos says that it was found in the old temple. Pickard-Cambridge, *Theatre of Dionysus,* pp. 3ff., fig. 3. Dinsmoor, *The Architecture of Ancient Greece,* p. 89. Dinsmoor does not believe that the relief belongs to the temple, as the style is not of the same period and the slope of the tympanon too low.

[5] Fiechter, *Dionysostheater,* 1 (Heft 5), pp. 38ff., figs. 27-30; 3 (Heft 7), p. 67, fig. 29, pl. 16; 4 (Heft 9), pp. 7ff., figs. 1-12, pls. 1-5. Flickinger, "The Theater of Aeschylus," in *Transactions and Proceedings of the American Philological Association,* lxi(1930),80ff., fig. 8. Anti, *Teatri Greci arcaici* (1947), pp. 55ff., fig. 17, pl. ii. Dinsmoor, *The Architecture of Ancient Greece,* p. 119f.; *idem* in *Studies Presented to David Robinson,* pp. 310ff. Pickard-Cambridge, *Theater of Dionysus,* pp. 5ff., figs. 4-6. Ida Thallon Hill, *The Ancient City of Athens* (1953), "The Theatre of Dionysus," pp. 113-124.

[6] Rizzo, *Il teatro Greco di Siracusa,* pp. 33ff., figs. 10-11, 13-14, pls. i-ii. Bieber, *Denkmäler,* p. 49f., pl. 21. Bulle, *Untersuchungen,* pp. 152ff., dates the koilon in the period of Hieron II (270-215), which would mean that the oldest form built by the architect Damocopus for Hieron I (478-467) has disappeared. Anti, *Teatri arcaici,* pp. 85ff., pls. iii-iv reconstructs for Syracuse—as he does for Athens—straight seats on three sides of a rectangular orchestra (see Figs. 228-229).

[7] D-R, pp. 25ff. Bieber, *Denkmäler,* p. 7, fig. 2. James T. Allen, "The Greek Theater of the Fifth Century," in *The University of California Publications in Classical Philology,* vii, No. 1 (1920), 20ff., fig. 16 (our Fig. 227, the auditorium is drawn too regularly); cf. pp. 1-119, "The Greek Theater of the Fifth Century B.C." *ibid.,* No. 2, pp. 121-128; "The Orchestra Terrace of the Aeschylaean Theater"; *ibid.,* v (1918),55ff., "The Key to the Reconstruction of the Fifth Century Theater of Athens." *Idem,* in *The University of California Publications in Classical Archaeology,* i, No. 6 (1937),169ff., "On the Athenian Theater Before 441 B.C." Frickenhaus, *Die altgriechische Bühne,* pp. 74, 84, fig. 25. Bulle, *Untersuchungen,* pp. 75ff., 211f. Fiechter, *Dionysostheater,* 3, pp. 66ff., fig. 29 and pl. 16 (our Figs. 224 and 226). Mahr, *Origin of the Greek Tragic Form,* pp. 18ff., 65ff., figs. 3-5, 8-10. Anti, *op.cit.,* pp. 55ff., figs. 17-18, pl. ii (our Figs. 228-229).

[8] See the cross section: D-R, pl. v,2 (our Fig. 230), Noack, *Skene tragike,* p. 3, fig. 2. Frickenhaus, *op.cit.,* p. 121, fig.

24. Bieber, *Denkmäler,* p. 12, fig. 7. Flickinger, *Greek Theater,* p. 65, fig. 32a.

[9] D-R, pp. 109ff., fig. 43. Bieber, *Denkmäler,* p. 20, fig. 13 (our Fig. 231). Flickinger, *op.cit.,* p. 227, figs. 70-71. Bulle, *Untersuchungen,* pp. 9ff., pls. 1-2. P.E. Arias, *Il teatro Greco fuori di Atene,* pp. 24ff., figs. 6-10. Anti, *Teatri Greci arcaici,* pp. 45ff. Pickard-Cambridge, *Festivals,* p. 50f., figs. 19-20. A. B. Cook, *Zeus,* i, 479f., fig. 346. Cook compares Thorikos to the theatrical area and the dancing ground built by Daidalos for Ariadne in Cnossus (*Iliad* 18, 591f.).

[10] See D-R, p. 32f.: the skene is outside of the orchestra before the old temple. Noack, *op.cit.,* pp. 6ff., fig. 3: the oldest wooden scene buildings are inside the orchestra. James T. Allen, "The Greek Theater of the Fifth Century B.C.," *op.cit.,* pp. 28ff., fig. 19 (our Fig. 232), illustrates the different theories regarding the position of the early scene building. Bulle, *Untersuchungen,* pp. 64ff., believes to have found remains of an old stone skene, but is refuted by Fiechter, *Dionysostheater,* Part 1, p. 90f.

[11] Fiechter, *Dionysostheater,* Part 1, pp. 12ff., 55, 89f., 91, No. 2, figs. 6-7, pl. 1,3-4; iii, p. 68f., pls. 17-18, figs. 30-31 (our Figs. 233-236). Allen, *op.cit.,* pp. 31ff.

[12] Pfuhl, *Malerei und Zeichnung der Griechen,* pp. 665f., 674, paragraphs 723 and 733. Bulle, *Untersuchungen,* pp. 215ff. G. Richter, "Perspective" in *Scritti in onore di Nogara* (1937), p. 386, pls. l,1 and liii.

[13] This has been pointed out by Noack, *op.cit.,* pp. 29ff. Bulle, *Szenenbilder zum griechischen Theater des fünften Jahrhunderts v. Chr.* (1950), therefore, is absolutely wrong when he puts a frame consisting of two turrets and a big pediment around most of his scenes for the poets of the fifth century. His source is the southern Italian terracotta model of a stage, our Fig. 480 in Ch. X.

[14] Dinsmoor, in *Studies Presented to David Moore Robinson* (1951), i,313ff., fig. 2 (our Fig. 237). For the odeum see Ch. IV, note 16.

[15] Bieber, in *AJA,* 58(1954), 277f., figs. 1-3 on pl. 51 and fig. 4 on pl. 52. For a good description of a presentation of King Oedipus in ancient Athens, see Navarre, *Les représentations dramatiques en Grèce* (Paris, Les Belles Lettres, 1929), pp. 34ff. A good reconstruction of a classic Greek scenebuilding (our Fig. 239) in D-R, p. 273, fig. 93.

[16] E. Capps, "The Stage in the Greek Theater According to Extant Dramas" in *Transactions of the American Philological Association,* xxii(1891),1ff. John White, "The Stage in Aristophanes" in *Harvard Studies in Classical Philology,* ii(1891),159ff.,173ff. Sandford, *The Stage in the Attic Theater of the Fifth Century* (1895), pp. 70ff., 94ff. D-R, pp. 176ff. Pickard-Cambridge, *Theater of Dionysus,* pp. 30ff. Bulle, *Szenenbilder,* makes another great mistake when he places most of the action of the classical plays on a low stage between the paraskenia.

[17] Pickard-Cambridge, *Theatre of Dionysus,* pp. 15ff., fig. 7. Dinsmoor, *The Architecture of Ancient Greece,* pp. 208ff., fig. 77. *Idem, Studies Presented to David Moore Robinson,* pp. 315ff., figs. 1 and 2.

[18] Fiechter, *Dionysostheater,* Part 1, pp. 16ff; 3, pp. 69ff., figs. 32-34; from these are taken our Figs. 241-242. Mahr, *The Origin of the Greek Tragic Form,* pp. 87ff., fig. 22. From him is taken our Fig. 240.

[19] Broneer, "The Tent of Xerxes and the Greek Theater" in *University of California Publications in Classical Archaeology,* i, No. 12 (1944), pp. 305ff.

20 *Altertümer von Pergamon*, IV,3ff., pls. 4-12. D-R, p. 151, fig. 61. Dörpfeld in *Ath.Mitt.*, XXXII(1907),220ff., figs. 12-14. Bieber, *Denkmäler*, pp. 37ff., fig. 39, pls. 14-18. Bulle, *Untersuchungen*, p. 256f.

21 Dinsmoor in *Studies . . . Robinson*, p. 328f. G. Caputo in *Dioniso*, XIII(1950), 30.

22 Krause and With, *Insel Bali*, II, pl. 16 (our Fig. 249). Bieber, *Denkmäler*, p. 13, fig. 8. Hielscher, *Roumanie* (1933), figs. 188-189.

23 Lehmann-Hartleben in Bulle, *Untersuchungen*, p. 61f., pls. 6-7. Dinsmoor, in *Studies . . . Robinson*, p. 328f., fig. 3. Pickard-Cambridge, *Theatre of Dionysus*, p. 191f., fig. 8.

24 D-R, pp. 40ff., pls. I-II. Judeich, *Topographie von Athen²*, pp. 308ff., fig. 39, cf. p. 315. Bieber, *Denkmäler*, pp. 14ff., fig. 9. Flickinger, *Greek Theater*, figs. 32, 36, 37. Fiechter, *Dionysostheater*, Part 1, pp. 76ff., figs. 67-74, pls. 1, 10-11. A. von Gerkan in *Gnomon*, 14(1938),232ff.

25 Bieber, *Denkmäler*, pl. I. Judeich, *op.cit.*, p. 311f. Fiechter, *Dionysostheater*, part 1, pp. 62ff., figs. 53-54; 3, fig. 2, pl. 25.

26 A. von Salis, *JdAI*, XXV(1910),134ff. Bieber, *Denkmäler*, p. 15. Fiechter, *Dionysostheater*, Part 3, p. 76. Buschor, in F-R, III, 144f., text to pl. 145 does not believe the vase painters copied the murals. Our Fig. 252 in *Ant.Denk.*, I, pl. 36. Pfuhl, *Malerei und Zeichnung*, II,586f., §§632f.; III, fig. 581.

27 D-R, p. 373, fig. 93 (our Fig. 239); cf. also pp. 307ff., figs. 72-73. Color reproduction in Cybulski, *Tabulae quibus antiquitates Graecae et Romanae illustrantur*, fig. 12. Durm, *Baukunst der Griechen*, p. 470. Allen, "The Greek Theater of the Fifth Century B.C.," pp. 95ff., fig. 23; cf. above note 7. Pickard-Cambridge, *Theater of Dionysus*, pp. 75ff., "The Prothyron," figs. 9-29.

28 Lehmann-Hartleben in *JdAI*, XLII(1927),30f., figs. 1-2. Bulle, *Untersuchungen*, pp. 230ff., fig. 4a; *idem*, "Eine Skenographie," 94th *BerlWPr* (1934), pp. 13ff., fig. 6 (our Fig. 253). Flickinger in *Mélanges offerts à Octave Navarre*, p. 196, fig. 2; *idem*, in *Transactions and Proceedings of the American Philological Association*, LXI, p. 99f., fig. 10. Pickard-Cambridge, *Theatre of Dionysus*, p. 171, fig. 58. Webster, *CQ*, 42(1948),16.

29 Pottier, *Catalogue des vases antiques du Louvre*, III, pp. 1053ff. Séchan, *Tragédie grècque*, pp. 38ff. J. T. Allen, "The Greek Theater of the Fifth Century B.C.," pp. 43ff.

30 D-R, pp. 59ff., pls. III-IV. Frickenhaus, *op.cit.*, fig. 27. Bulle, *Untersuchungen*, pp. 47ff., pls. 3-5. Judeich, *op.cit.* (2nd ed.), p. 312f., fig. 40. Fiechter, *Dionysostheater*, Part 1, pp. 20ff., figs. 11-20, pls. 1-7; Part 3, pp. 72ff., figs. 36-37, pls. 19-20. Ida Thallon Hill, *The Ancient City of Athens: Its Topography and Monuments* (1953), Ch. XII, "The Theatre of Dionysos," pp. 113ff. Pickard-Cambridge, *Theatre of Dionysus*, p. 155, fig. 52. Schleif, in *Arch.Anz.* 52(1937), gives a good survey of the classical period of the theater of Dionysus, based on the actual remains.

31 D-R, p. 61f., and Reisch, *ibid.*, p. 301. Bulle, *Untersuchungen*, pp. 50ff., is of the opinion that these posts were not supports for an upper story, but for shelves, where rolls of painted canvases used for scenery were stored.

32 Reisch, in D-R, p. 298f. Pickard-Cambridge, *Theatre of Dionysus*, pp. 148ff., figs. 46-52.

33 D-R, pp. 62ff., figs. 19-22. Allen, "Problems of the Proskenion," in *University of California Publications in Classical Philology*, VII(1919-1924),206f., fig. 4. Mahr, *op.cit.*, pp. 90ff., figs. 23-24. The design by Dinsmoor, unpublished, I owe to his generosity (Fig. 258).

34 Fiechter, *Baugesch.Entw.*, pp. 9ff., figs. 11-13 and 15; *idem*, *Dionysostheater*, Part 1, pp. 26ff.; Part 3, figs. 36-37, pls. 19-20.

35 Bulle, *Untersuchungen*, pp. 27f., and 338, fig. 31. Fiechter, *Dionysostheater*, Part 3, fig. 44. Bulle, *Szenenbilder*, fig. on p. 21 and pls. 2-12.

36 Frickenhaus, *op.cit.*, pls. II-III. Fiechter, *Baugesch.Entw.*, fig. 63; *idem*, in *Dionysostheater*, Part 3, figs. 37 and 42.

37 Fiechter, *Dionysostheater*, Part 3, fig. 36. This figure, and his fig. 37, in their upper parts look more Hellenistic than classical.

38 The inscription belongs to the year 274 B.C. *IG*, XI, 2, No. 199 A, 93-94. The reconstruction of Vallois, in *Nouvelles Archives des Missions scientifiques*, XXII(1921),213ff., repeated in Navarre, *Le théâtre Grec* (1925), p. 73, fig. 17, is based on the inscriptions, not on the actual remains. Cf. Bulle, *Untersuchungen*, pp. 174ff., for the inscription.

39 D-R, pp. 112ff., fig. 44. Fiechter, *Baugesch.Entw.*, pp. 4ff., figs. 6-7. Bieber, *Denkmäler*, p. 20f., pls. 14-15. Frickenhaus, *op.cit.*, p. 111, fig. 14. Bulle, *Untersuchungen*, pp. 81ff., pl. 11. P. E. Arias, *Il Teatro greco fuori di Atene*, pp. 115ff., figs. 77-79. Fiechter, *Theaterbauten*, VIII(1937), figs. 34-35, pl. 7. Pickard-Cambridge, *Theatre of Dionysus*, p. 198f., figs. 64-65. Cf. below, Ch. VI, Figs. 284-288 and Ch. IX, Figs. 452-454.

40 Rizzo, *Il Teatro Greco di Siracusa*, pp. 72ff., fig. 31. Bulle, *Untersuchungen*, pp. 152ff. C. Anti, *Il Teatro antico di Siracusa* (1948), fig. 9 does not assume that there were paraskenia.

41 O. Puchstein, *Die griechische Bühne*, p. 110f., figs. 31-33. Bieber, *Denkmäler*, p. 50f., figs. 54-55, pl. 22. Bulle, *Untersuchungen*, pp. 110ff., pls. 19, 26, 28-29. Arias, *op.cit.*, pp. 143ff., figs. 95-98. A. von Gerkan, "Zu den Theatern von Segesta und Tyndaris," in *Festschrift Andreas Rumpf*, pp. 82ff., figs. 5-6.

42 Puchstein, *op.cit.*, p. 117f., figs. 34 and 36. Bulle, *Untersuchungen*, pp. 131ff., pls. 33-34, 38-40. Arias, *op.cit.*, p. 149f., fig. 99.

43 A. Mau, in *Röm.Mitt.*, XXI(1906),1ff., pl. I. Bieber, *Denkmäler*, pp. 52ff., No. 13., figs. 56-57. Bulle, *Untersuchungen*, pp. 165ff.

44 Bulle, *Eine Skenographie*, pp. 3ff., figs. 1-5, pls. I-II. Pickard-Cambridge, *Theatre of Dionysus*, pp. 170ff., figs. 55-57. Ippel, in *Studies Presented to David Moore Robinson*, I,809f., fig. 1. Webster, in *CQ*, 42(1948), p. 15f.; *idem*, *Production*, 105, pl. 10.

45 Fiechter, *Baugesch.Entw.*, pp. 9ff., *idem.*, *Dionysostheater*, Part 1, p. 23f., figs. 14-15; Part 3, pls. 18-19. Mahr, *The Origin of the Greek Tragic Form*, pp. 88ff., figs. 22-24.

46 Cf. Hesychius and Suidas *s.v.* Aulaia (αὐλαία: τὸ τῆς σκηνῆς παραπέτασμα). Bethe, *Prolegomena*, pp. 186ff. Bulle, *Untersuchungen*, p. 159f., note 2. Fiechter, *Baugesch.Entw.*, p. 54.

47 Anti, *Teatri arcaici*, pp. 202ff., figs. 61-63, pl. v. Bieber, *AJA*, 58(1954),280f., figs. 7-8 on pl. 52.

48 Flickinger, *CP*, XXXV(1940),71f. His drawing in *The Greek Theater and its Drama*, p. 89, fig. 44, indicating the movements of the actors in the *Frogs*, is mistaken, because he tries to adapt them to the large theater of Dionysus Eleuthereus and disregards the paraskenia, laying the house of Heracles behind the side door of the palace.

49 Fiechter, *Dionysostheater*, Part 1, pp. 62ff.; Part 3, pp. 52f., fig. 37, pl. 25. Pickard-Cambridge, *Theatre of Dionysus*, pp. 134ff., figs. 34-38. Mahr, *The Origin of the Greek Tragic Form*, pp. 87ff., figs. 22-24.

50 *IG*, II2², No. 3056. Stuart and Revett, *Antiquities of Athens* (1787), II, Ch. IV, pp. 29ff., pls. 1-6. G. Welter, in *Arch.Anz.*, LIII(1938), pp. 33ff. Pickard-Cambridge, *Theater of Dionysus*, p. 169, figs. 53-54. A. H. Smith, *British Museum Catalogue of Sculpture*, I, 257ff., No. 432. BrBr, pl. 119. G. Becatti, "Attikà. Saggio sulla scultura del el-

lenismo," in *Rivista del Instituto archeologico*, VII(1940), 20f., fig. 5. Bieber, *Sculpture of the Hellenistic Age*, p. 66, fig. 213.

[51] D-R, pp. 45ff., figs. 14-15. Bieber, *Denkmäler*, p. 17, pls. 4-5. Flickinger, *Greek Theater*, p. 90, fig. 45. Fiechter, *Dionysostheater*, Part 1, pp. 62ff., figs. 54-59; Part 3, p. 51, fig. 35. Sven Risom, in *Mélanges Holleaux* (1913), pp. 257ff., pls. VIII-XI. Möbius in *Ath.Mitt.*, LI(1926),120, pl. XX,1. Pickard-Cambridge, *Theatre of Dionysus*, pp. 141ff., figs. 39-41. Theodor Kraus, *JdAI*, 69(1954), 32-48, figs. 1-6.

[52] Pickard-Cambridge, *Festivals*, p. 273f., fig. 206, No. 7.

[53] Pickard-Cambridge, *op.cit.*, pp. 270ff., fig. 205. Benndorf, *Archäologische Beiträge zur Kenntnis des attischen Theaters*, pp. 36ff. Svoronos, *Journal internationale d'archéologie numismatique*, I(1898),37ff., pls. A'-Z'; III(1900), 197ff., 322ff., pls. I' and IZ'-IK'; VIII(1905),323ff. *Idem*,

Les Monnaies d'Athènes, pls. 100-102. Bieber, *Denkmäler*, p. 84f., fig. 87.

[54] D-R, pp. 120ff., fig. 50, pls. VI,2, VII and IX. Noack, *Die Baukunst des Altertums*, p. 61f., pls. 81-82. Bieber, *Denkmäler*, pp. 24ff., No. 5, figs. 19-20, pls. 9-11. A. Fossum, *AJA*, XXX(1926),70f., fig. 1. Bulle, *Untersuchungen*, pp. 167ff. Arias, *Teatro greco fuori di Atene*, pp. 88ff., figs. 58-63. Dinsmoor, *The Architecture of Ancient Greece*, pp. 244ff., fig. 90, pl. LXII. Pickard-Cambridge, *Theatre of Dionysus*, p. 204, figs. 70-71. Bieber, "A Free Theater for a Free People," *Theater Arts* (1941), pp. 908ff. Professor A. von Gerkan informs me, that he is preparing a monograph on the theater of Epidauros. He dates it not before 300, when the skene, the proskenion with grooves for the pinakes, the ramps, the parodos-pylons and the lower part of the auditorium were erected.

NOTES TO CHAPTER VI. SCENERY AND MECHANICAL DEVICES

[1] Vitruvius and Pollux, as well as the extant dramas, are used for the problems regarding decorations in the classical dramas by: Albert Müller, *Bühnenaltertümer*, pp. 113ff. Haigh, *The Attic Theater*, pp. 179ff. Flickinger, *Greek Theater*, pp. 97ff., 284ff. Allen, "The Greek Theater of the Fifth Century B.C.," in *University of California Publications in Classical Philology*, VII(1919),69ff., and *Stage Antiquities*, pp. 100ff. Bulle, *Untersuchungen*, pp. 212ff., 294ff. Pickard-Cambridge, *Theatre of Dionysus*, pp. 122ff., 234ff. Webster, *Production*, pp. 13f., 27f., 162f.

[2] D-R, p. 204ff.

[3] Anti, *Teatri archaici*, pp. 85ff., pls. III-IV; *idem, Il Teatro antico di Siracusa*, pp. 37ff., figs. 6-8.

[4] Kaibel, *Comicorum Graec. Fragmenta*, p. 148, No. 3. Olivieri, *Frammenti della Commedia greca*, p. 114. Suidas, *s.v.* Phormos Syracusios. Aristotle, *De Arte Poetica*, v, p. 1449b 6, mentions Phormis together with Epicharmus as a comic poet.

[5] Pfuhl, *Malerei und Zeichnung*, II,665f., §723 and p. 674 §733. Flickinger, *Greek Theater*, p. 66. Mary Swindler, *Ancient Painting*, pp. 225f., 335. Bulle, *Untersuchungen*, pp. 215ff. Gisela Richter, in *Scritti in onore di Nogara* (1937), pp. 383ff., pls. LI-LIII. Curtius, *Pompejanische Malerei*, pp. 121f., 182f. Beyen, *Die Pompejanische Wanddekoration*, I, 96ff., 352ff. Little, in *Art Bulletin*, XIX(1917),485ff.

[6] Albert Müller, *Bühnenaltertümer*, pp. 116ff. D-R, pp. 210ff. Bulle, *Untersuchungen*, pp. 214ff. Pickard-Cambridge, *Theatre of Dionysus*, pp. 122ff.

[7] Beside Athenaeus, XIII, 587b see Harpokration *s.v.* Nannion, and Servius, note to Vergil, *Georgica*, III, 24. Cf. D-R, p. 214f. Puchstein, *Die griech. Bühne*, p. 88. Bulle, *Untersuchungen*, p. 290f. Pickard-Cambridge, *Theatre of Dionysus*, p. 157f.

[8] Anti, *Teatri archaici*, pl. VI.

[9] D-R, pp. 133ff., figs. 54-55. Bieber, *Denkmäler*, p. 27f., figs. 22-23. Fiechter, *Antike griechische Theaterbauten*, IV, *Das Theater von Megalopolis*, 1931. Bulle, *Untersuchungen*, pp. 97ff., pls. 17-18. P. E. Arias, *Il Teatro Greco fuori di Atene*, pp. 100ff. Dinsmoor, *The Architecture of Ancient Greece*, pp. 249f., and 307. Pickard-Cambridge, *The Theatre of Dionysus*, pp. 199ff., figs. 66-67.

[10] Albert Müller, *Bühnenaltertümer*, pp. 122f., 161. D-R, pp. 210 and 255. Fiechter, *Baugesch.Entw.*, p. 116f. Frickenhaus, *Die altgriech. Bühne*, pp. 50 and 95, as well as Bulle, *Untersuchungen*, p. 286f., consider the periaktoi to be from the Hellenistic period. Cf. also: Beyen, *Die pompejanische Wanddekoration*, I,145f., note 4, and p. 279f. W. Miller, *Daedalus and Thespis*, I, Architecture (1929), p. 325. Pickard-Cambridge, *Theater of Dionysus*, pp. 126 and 234-238 considers the evidence skeptically.

[11] Albert Müller, *op.cit.*, pp. 157ff. D-R, pp. 255f. Flickinger, *Greek Theater*, pp. 208, 233f. Kelley Rees, "The Significance of the Parodoi in the Greek Theater," *AJP*, XXXII (1911),377ff. Fensterbusch, in *Philologus*, LXXXI(1925), 480ff. Warnecke, *ibid.*, LXXXIV(1928),118f. Mary Johnston, *Exits and Entrances in Roman Comedy* (1933) accepts the view that the Greeks assumed the right entrance to lead to the market and the harbor, the left to the country. W. Beare, in *CQ*, XXXII(1938),205ff., discusses the same conventional significance to be attached to the side entrances prevailing in the theaters of Magna Graecia. M. Bieber, "Entrances and Exits of Actors and Chorus in Greek Plays," *AJA*, 58(1954), 278ff.

[12] O. Walter, *JOAI*, XVIII(1915), Beiblatt, 68ff. Frickenhaus, *op.cit.*, pp. 91ff., fig. 9b. A. von Gerkan, *Theater von Priene*, p. 103. Bieber, *Denkmäler*, pp. 26, 28, fig. 21. Walter, *op.cit.*, and Bulle, *Untersuchungen*, p. 90 explain these devices as being for the erection of poles.

[13] D-R, pp. 150ff., figs. 61-62. Bohn, *Altertümer von Pergamon*, IV,3ff., pl. IV. Dörpfeld, *Ath. Mitt.*, XXXII(1907),215ff. Bieber, *Denkmäler*, p. 37f., fig. 30, pls. XIV-XVIII. Bulle, *Untersuchungen*, p. 256f. explains these holes in Pergamon as well as those in Elis as contrivances for poles; A. von Gerkan, *Theater von Priene*, p. 101f., for wing decorations arranged obliquely as side closings of the logeion.

[14] Bulle, *Untersuchungen*, p. 77f., pl. 6, figs. 12-14. Fiechter, *Dionysostheater*, III,23f., fig. 12. Both believe the stones to have been used for turning masts. Bulle thinks this might have been the crane or the flying machine.

[15] Furttenbach, *Mannhafter Kunstspiegel* (1663). Hammitzsch, *Der moderne Theaterbau* (1906), p. 30, fig. 13. Michael, *Deutsches Theater* (Jedermanns Bücherei, 1923), p. 18, fig. 75.

[16] D-R, pp. 234ff. Bethe, *Prolegomena*, pp. 100ff. Flickinger, *Greek Theater*, pp. 284ff. Mahr, *The Origin of the Greek Tragic Form*, pp. 101ff., fig. 27 a-b (our Fig. 280 a-b). His simple designs are better than the attempts by Frickenhaus, *Die altgriechische Bühne*, pp. 7ff., pl. III, to give an idea of the appearance of the eccyclema. W. Miller, *Daedalus and Thespis*, I, 315ff. Flickinger, in *Mélanges Navarre* (1935), pp. 196-206. Pickard-Cambridge, *Theater of Dionysus*, pp. 100-122, gives all the ancient sources.

[17] D-R, p. 247f. Kelley Rees, "The Function of the Prothyron ($\pi\rho\delta\theta\nu\rho\sigma\nu$) in the Production of the Greek Plays," *CP*, X(1915),117ff. C. Fensterbusch, *Die Bühne des Aristophanes* (1912); *idem* in *Bursians Jahresberichte*, 1930, p. 81. M. Bieber, "The Entrances and Exits of Actors and Chorus in Greek Plays," *AJA*, 58(1954),279f., pl. 52, figs. 5-6.

[18] D-R, pp. 227ff. Bethe, *Prolegomena*, pp. 142ff. W. Miller, *Daedalus and Thespis*, I,326ff. Bulle, *Untersuchungen*, p. 291f.; *idem, Szenenbilder zum griechischen Theater des 5. Jahrhunderts v. Chr.* (1950), pp. 47ff., pls. 10, 12, 14, 15. Pickard-Cambridge, *Theatre of Dionysus*, pp. 41, 55f., 61f., 68, 127f.

[19] M. Bieber, in *AJA*, 58(1954),279ff., pl. 52, figs. 5-6.

[20] See above, Fig. 237, and Dinsmoor, in *Studies Presented to David M. Robinson* (1951)I,329ff., fig. 2.

[21] Messerschmidt, in *Röm. Mitt.*, 47(1932),138ff., figs. 5-7. Curtius, in *Scritti in onore di Nogara* (1937), pp. 105ff., note 1. Pickard-Cambridge, *Theatre of Dionysus*, p. 100, figs. 30-31. Gisela Richter, The Met. Mus. of Art, *Handbook of the Greek Collection*, p. 116, pl. 96c.

[22] Fossum in *AJA*, 2nd series, II(1898),187ff. D-R, pp. 113ff., figs. 44-45. Bieber, *Denkmäler*, p. 20f., No. 3, figs. 14-15. Bulle, *Untersuchungen*, pp. 81ff., 226ff. Fiechter, *Baugesch. Entw.*, pp. 4ff., 70f., figs. 6-8. *Idem in Antike griechische Theaterbauten*, VIII, *Das Theater in Eretria* (1937), p. 38, pl. 8. Flickinger, *Greek Theater*, pp. 104ff., figs. 53-55, 72. Pickard-Cambridge, *Theatre of Dionysus*, p. 198f., figs. 64-65.

[23] Fiechter, *Das Theater in Eretria*, pp. 25ff., figs. 21 and 25.

[24] Flickinger, in *CJ*, XXXIV(1939),355ff.

[25] R. Stillwell, *Corinth*, II, *The Theatre* (1952), p. 10f., 39f., 134f., figs. 26, 33-34.

[26] E. Buschor, "Feldmäuse," in *SBMünch* (1937), pp. 22-34.

[27] Fiechter, *Dionysostheater*, III,69f., figs. 33-34.

[28] Against Wilamowitz, *Aeschylus-Interpretationen*, pp. 6ff., and Noack, *Skene Tragike, Eine Studie über die scenischen Anlagen auf der Orchestra des Aischylos und der anderen Tragiker* (1915), rightly Bethe, *Prolegomena*, pp. 89ff., and Bulle, *Untersuchungen*, pp. 214 and 222.

[29] Hedwig Kenner, *Das Theater und der Realismus in der griechischen Kunst* (Wien, 1954), pp. 65-188, makes a valiant attempt to collect all the material for the scenery and properties used in plays acted in the classical period. Her main source, the Pompeian wall paintings, can, however, be used only with great caution. Consequently I have used them mostly in my later chapters. See my review in *Gnomon*, 28(1956),127-134.

NOTES TO CHAPTER VII. THE EVOLUTION OF THE ART OF ACTING

[1] Bacchylides, *The Poems and Fragments*, ed. R. C. Jebb, pp. 230ff., No. XVII. Comparetti, *Mélanges Weil*, p. 23. Pickard-Cambridge, *Dithyramb*, p. 43f., and *Festivals*, pp. 127ff.

[2] Flickinger, *Greek Theater*, p. 165f. Cf. Ch. V, figs. 224, 238, 281.

[3] Vita Aeschylus 3; Vita Euripides; Scholion to Aristophanes, *Nubes*, line 1266. Aristotle, *Rhetor.*, III,1, p. 1403f.

[4] Haigh, *The Attic Theatre*, pp. 57ff. Flickinger, *Greek Theater*, pp. 162ff., 183ff. O'Connor, *Chapters in the History of Actors and Acting in Ancient Greece* (1908), p. 111, No. 292; p. 117f., No. 351; p. 135, No. 467.

[5] J. T. Allen, "Greek Acting in the Fifth Century," in *University of California Publications in Classical Philology*, II,No.15(1916),279-289. Anna Spitzbarth, *Untersuchungen zur Spieltechnik der griechischen Tragödie* (Zurich, 1946). Famec Lorene Shister, "The Portrayal of Emotion in Tragedy," *AJP*, LXVI(1945),377-397; *ibid.*, LXIX(1948),229-231. Pickard-Cambridge, *Festivals*, pp. 153ff.

[6] Wilhelm, *Urkunden dramatischer Aufführungen*, pp. 34ff., 52ff., 187ff. *IG*, II,2², Nos. 2319-2325. O'Connor, *op.cit.*, pp. 26f., 45ff.; 107ff., No. 274; 114, No. 321.

[7] Wilhelm, *op.cit.*, pp. 137ff., 147f., 170f. O'Connor, *op.cit.*, pp. 27, 46f., 61f. Flickinger, *Greek Theater*, p. 183. Pickard-Cambridge, *Festivals*, pp. 114.ff.

[8] Haigh, *op.cit.*, p. 57. Flickinger, *op.cit.*, p. 184f. Wilhelm, *op.cit.*, p. 26, 28, 40ff. O'Connor, *op.cit.*, p. 73f., No. 13; p. 103, No. 239; p. 119f., No. 359; p. 141, No. 535.

[9] Haigh, *The Attic Theatre*, pp. 234ff. Flickinger, *Greek Theater*, pp. 174ff., 182, 186f. Kelley Rees, "The Meaning of Parachoregema," *CP*, II(1907),387ff.

[10] Devrient, *Das Kind auf der antiken Bühne* (1904). William Nickerson Bates, *Euripides, Student of Human Nature* (1930), pp. 42ff.

[11] Haigh, *op.cit.*, pp. 230ff. Rees, *The So-called Rule of the Three Actors in the Classical Greek Drama* (1908). Listmann, *Die Technik des Dreigesprächs in der griechischen Tragödie* (1910). Kaffenberger, *Das Dreischauspielergesetz in der griechischen Tragödie* (1911). Flickinger, *Greek Theater*, pp. 173ff., 180, fig. 67. C. Fensterbusch, in *Bursians Jahresberichte über die Fortschritte der klassischen Altertums-* *wissenschaft*, Vol. 253(1936),36ff. Todd, in *CQ*, XXXII (1938),30ff., reaffirms the rule of the three actors. See for the number of actors and the distribution of parts (roles): Pickard-Cambridge, *Festivals*, pp. 137ff.

[12] O'Connor, *Chapters in the History of Actors and Acting in Greece*, p. 113, No. 307.

[13] Aristotle, *Poet.* 1449b,5. Second Argument to Aristophanes, *Peace*. Suidas, *s.v.* Chionides. *IG*, II,2², No. 2319. Wilhelm, *Urkunden dramatischer Aufführungen*, pp. 147ff., 168f., 187f., 252ff. Haigh, *op.cit.*, pp. 6f., 26f., 355f. Flickinger, *Greek Theater*, p. 54f. O'Connor, *op.cit.*, pp. 47ff., 51f., 64-66. Bulle, *Festschrift für James Loeb*, p. 7. Pickard-Cambridge, *Festivals*, p. 125f.

[14] M. Bieber, *Skenika*, p. 11f., fig. 6. A. Rumpf, "Mimus und Logos," *Festgabe Niessen*, pl. VII, figs. 1 and 3. Neugebauer, *Die griech. Bronzen der klassischen Zeit und des Hellenismus*, Staatliche Museen Berlin (1951), No. 71. Pickard-Cambridge, *Festivals*, pp. 153ff., 185, figs. 49-52. Fig. 290 from Amisus (Samsun) at the Black Sea in the Louvre, CA 1784. Fig. 291 in Vienna, Austria, Mus. No. Terracottas 175, Inv. No. 1564 from Myrina, and Fig. 292 from Asia Minor in Athens: Bieber, *Denkmäler*, p. 121f., Nos. 56 and 58, pl. 61, 1 and 3. The Viennese terracotta has traces of light violet on the chiton and red on the border of the mantle. Fig. 293 from Rheneia in the Museum of Athens. Fig. 294 said to be from Pergamon in the Berlin Mus. No. 7635, Rayet, *Monuments de l'art*, II, pl. 43. Winter, *Typen der Terrakotten*, II,426, No. 3.

[15] Fig. 295: bronze statuette in Florence, Museo Archeologico, No. 2327, L. A. Milani, *Museo archeologico di Firenze*, II, Tav. CXXXIX,3. Procacci, in *Dioniso*, V(1935),1ff., fig. 2. Fragment of a similar figure in terracotta in Boston, found in Smyrna, head, arms, legs missing. Fig. 296: Terracotta statuette from Tarentum. Fig. 297: Boston, No. 01.7679, found in Myrina. Dorothy Burr, *Terracottas from Myrina in Boston Museum of Fine Arts*, No. 113, pp. 76f., pl. XLII,2; left arm and fingers of the right hand are missing. The object attached to the left breast seems to be a wineskin which was carried on the left shoulder. Traces of red on the face and neck, yellow on hair and beard, orange-red on the tights, light yellow on the chiton. Fig. 298: Athens, National Mu-

seum, No. 5055. Probably from Myrina. Robert, *Masken*, p. 70f., fig. 89. Fig. 299: Vienna, Austria, Mus. No. 176, Inv. No. 1567. Found in Smyrna. Good work. For other figures of comic actors see Ch. III, figs. 133-179. Bieber, *Denkmäler*, pls. 67-74, 89-102.

[16] See Pottier et Reinach, *La Nécropole de Myrina*, pp. 468-472, pl. xlv, figs. 1, 4, 7-9.

[17] Wallpainting in Naples: Mus. No. 9036; Helbig, *Wandgemälde*, No. 1457; Curtius, *Die Wandmalerei Pompejis*, p. 273, fig. 162; Pickard-Cambridge, *Festivals*, p. 85, fig. 44. Relief in Lyme Park: Webster, *Studies . . . Robinson*, pp. 590ff., pl. 55; Pickard-Cambridge, *Festivals*, p. 200, fig. 89. Relief in Vienna: Kunsthistorisches Museum. Relief in Naples: Nat. Mus. No. 6700. For poets studying their masks, see Krüger, *Ath. Mitt.*, xxvi(1901),126ff., pl. vi.

[17a] A colossal bronze tragic mask was found in 1959, in the remains of a warehouse at the Piraeus which was probably burnt at the time of Sulla's attack in 86 b.c. I owe the photograph to the kindness of Professor J. Papademetriou, the ephor of Attica and the head of the Department of Antiquities.

[18] Bieber, *Denkmäler*, p. 110, No. 44, pl. 55,2. Mus. No. 9019. Helbig, *op.cit.*, No. 1460. Bulle, *Festschrift für Loeb*, pp. 10ff., figs. 2-5. Wiegand, *Antike Fresken* (1943), pl. ix, in color. Other colored reproductions in *Enciclopedia dello Spettacolo*, Vol. I, and Maiuri, *Roman Painting* (Skira, 1953), p. 92f. Pickard-Cambridge, *Festivals*, p. 184, fig. 43. Herrmann-Bruckmann, *Denkmäler der Malerei des Altertums*, pl. 3.

[19] Alda Levi, *Le Sculture nel Palazzo ducale di Mantova* (1931), p. 21f., No. 11, pl. xxvi. Arndt-Amelung, No. 9. Bieber, *JdAI*, xxxii(1917), 79f., fig. 45.

[20] Lippold, *Skulpturen des Vatikanischen Museums*, iii,21ff. Sala delle Muse, pl. 4, No. 499. Bieber, *Denkmäler*, p. 122, No. 60, pl. 62,1.

[21] Bulle, *Festschrift für James Loeb*, pp. 6ff., figs. 1, 1a, 2, 6, pl. 11. E. Langlotz, *Griechische Vasen in Würzburg*, p. 148f., No. 832, pl. 240. Pickard-Cambridge, *Festivals*, p. 181, figs. 34-35. Webster, *Art and Literature*, p. 19, pl. 3a.

[22] F. Poulsen, *Catalogue of Ancient Sculpture in the Ny Carlsberg Glyptotek* (1951), p. 173, No. 233. *Billedtavler*, pl. xvii. Not a muse, but an actor.

[23] J. T. Allen, "Greek Acting in the Fifth Century B.C.," in *University of California Publications in Classical Philology*, ii(1916),279ff. Flickinger, *Greek Theater*, p. 190. Bulle, *Festschrift für Loeb*, pp. 8ff.

[24] Haigh, *The Attic Theater*, pp. 281ff. O'Connor, *op.cit.*, pp. 82ff., No. 62 and p. 103, No. 239. Bulle, *op.cit.*, p. 9. Pickard-Cambridge, *Festivals*, pp. 286ff.

[25] Haigh, *op.cit.*, p. 42f. Bulle, *Festschrift für Loeb*, p. 9f.

[26] O'Connor, *op.cit.*, p. 5f., p. 46. Pickard-Cambridge, *Festivals*, p. 294.

[27] Wilhelm, *Urkunden dramatischer Aufführungen*, p. 40. Haigh, *op.cit.*, pp. 96ff. O'Connor, *op.cit.*, p. 119. *IG*, ii,2², No. 2320.

[28] Haigh, *op.cit.*, p. 256f. O'Connor, *op.cit.*, pp. 128ff.,

No. 421. Schede, in *Ath. Mitt.*, 44 (1919), pp. 16ff., and in *Amtliche Berichte aus den Kunstsammlungen* (Berlin, 1919), pp. 121ff. Pickard-Cambridge, *Festivals*, pp. 167 and 174.

[29] Haigh, *op.cit.*, pp. 74ff. O'Connor, *op.cit.*, p. 114, No. 319. Flickinger, *Greek Theater*, p. 191. D. L. Page, *Actors' Interpolations in Greek Tragedy* (1934).

[30] Lüders, *Die Dionysischen Künstler* (1873). P. Foucart, *Les Associations réligieuses chez les Grecs: Thiases, Erames, Orgeoni* (1873); idem, *De collegiis scenicorum artificium* (1873). F. Poland, *Geschichte des griechischen Vereinswesens* (1909), pp. 129ff.; idem in *Real-Enc.*, second series, v,2473ff., *s.v.* Technitai. Farnell, *Cults of the Greek States*, v,146ff., note 104. C. Fensterbusch, *Bursians Jahresberichte*, Vol. 253(1936),22ff. Pickard-Cambridge, *Festivals*, pp. 286ff. Daux, *Delphes au II.-I. Siècle* (1936), pp. 350ff.

[31] See above, note 18.

[32] Bieber, *Das Dresdner Schauspielerrelief* (with plate); idem, *Denkmäler*, p. 110f., No. 45, pl. 55,1. Sieveking in BrBr, Pl. 628. Pickard-Cambridge, *Festivals*, pp. 226ff., fig. 193. Bulle, *Festschrift für Loeb*, pp. 13ff., 37f., figs. 27 and 27a-b. Bulle and Schweitzer, *Die Bildniskunst der römischen Republik* (1948), p. 64, see in the portrait that of a Roman actor like Quintus Roscius Gallus, whose portrait was made by Pasiteles in the period of Sulla. Old drawing by Pietro Santi Bartoli in Buonarroti, *Medaglioni antichi*, p. 446f.

[33] Schreiber, in *Abh. sächs. Ges. d. Wiss.*, xxii(1909), 761ff., pls. i-iii; *Hellenistische Reliefbilder*, pls. xlvi-xlviii. Copies in Naples, Museo Nazionale, and in Rome. Stuart Jones, *Sculptures of the Municipal Collections of Rome*, Museo Capitolino, p. 270, Sala dei Filosofi, No. 118, p. 61; *Palazzo dei Conservatori*, p. 89f. Galleria No. 26a, pl. 31. Bulle, *Das Theater zu Sparta*, pp. 91ff., fig. 4, pls. vi-vii. Pickard-Cambridge, *Theater of Dionysus*, p. 196, fig. 62.

[34] Haigh, *op.cit.*, pp. 278ff.

[35] Lüders, *op.cit.*, pp. 65ff., 74ff. Pickard-Cambridge, *Festivals*, pp. 298ff., and Appendix, pp. 315ff., for the inscriptions related to the guild of Teos.

[36] Rudolf Herzog, in *Philologus*, lx(1901),440ff. O'Connor, *op.cit.*, p. 80, No. 40. Flickinger, *Greek Theater*, p. 191f.

[37] See note 14.

[38] See note 15.

[39] O'Connor, *op.cit.*, pp. 39ff. On the mimic art of the actors see B. Wernicke, article "Mimik," in *Real-Enc.*, 15 (1932), pp. 1715-1725.

[40] Berlin, Inv. No. 8328. Furtwängler, *Arch. Anz.*, viii (1893),95, No. 24 (with fig.).

[41] Altmann, *Ath. Mitt.*, xxix(1904),179, fig. 18 and pp. 192ff., figs. 27-28. Bieber, *Denkmäler*, p. 124f., No. 69, fig. 118. The mask of the cook of comedy (Fig. 380), *ibid.*, p. 169, No. 166, pl. civ, fig. 3. Winter, *Die Skulpturen von Pergamon*, vii, 2, pp. 314ff., figs. 404a-e.

[42] Hermann Reich, *Der Mimus*, pp. 19ff., 231ff., 331, 360ff. Herzog-Crusius, *Die Mimiamben des Herondas* (1926) pp. 40ff., 51ff. Cf. below, Ch. VIII, fig. 414-415 and Ch. XV, Figs. 783, 786, 825-829.

NOTES TO CHAPTER VIII. NEW COMEDY · MENANDER

[1] Legrand, "*Daos*, Tableau de la Comédie Grecque pendant la Période dite nouvelle" in *Annales de l'Université de Lyon*, ii, Droit et Lettres, Nouvelle Série, Fasc. 22(1910), translated into English and rightly shortened to about two-thirds of the original length by James Loeb, *The New Greek Comedy* (1917). Bieber, *Denkmäler*, pp. 155ff. Alfred Körte in *Real-Enc.*, xi, pp. 1266ff. Robert, *Masken*. Antonia K. H.

Simon, *Comicae Tabellae*, *Die Szenenbilder zur griechischen Neuen Komödie*, in Schaubühne, Quellen und Forschungen zur Theatergeschichte, ed., C. Niessen and A. Kutscher, Vol. 25(1938). T.B.L. Webster, "The Masks of Greek Comedy," *Bulletin of the John Rylands Library*, Vol. 32(1949-50),97-133, figs. 1-8; idem, *Studies in Later Greek Comedy* (Manchester University Press, 1953). A useful list of masks of

New Comedy in *idem, Production,* 186-192. Before the original Menander was known, most authors had attributed many features belonging to Latin comedy to the unknown Greek models.

2 See Körte in *Real-Enc.,* XI, p. 1268f. Maidemont, in *CQ,* XXIX (1935),1-24.

3 Menander, *The Principal Fragments,* with an English translation by Francis G. Allison, The Loeb Classical Library (1921). C. R. Post, *Three Plays by Menander* (1929); reprinted in Oates and O'Neill, *The Complete Greek Drama,* II (1938). Gilbert Murray, *Two Plays of Menander* (1945). Ida L. Ehrlich, *The Girl from Samos,* reconstructed from the fragments of Menander (1955). She has blended together the preserved scenes and important characters found in the fragments and made them into a fine New Comedy. The manuscript of the *Dyskolos* of Menander recently was found and is now in a private collection in Geneva, Switzerland. Published in *Papyrus Bodmer,* IV, *Ménandre, Le Dyscolos,* Geneva, 1958. Translated under the name of *Curmudgeon* by Gilbert Highet, in *Horizon* I, 1959, pp. 78-89.

4 Ursinus, *Imagines* (1570), p. 33. G. Kaibel, *Epigrammata Graeca ex Lapidibus conlecta,* p. 490, No. 1085. A. Körte, "Homer und Menander," *Hermes,* 71(1936),221f. F. Poulsen, *Coll. Ny Carlsberg,* III(1942),98f. The translation is by A. M. Friend, in *Antioch-on-the-Orontes,* III,251.

5 Teofil Ivanov, *Une Mosaïque Romaine de Ulpia Oescus,* Monuments de l'Art en Bulgarie, II (Sofia, 1954). In Bulgarian with French résumé. Bieber, *AJA,* LX, 1956, p. 80f.

6 Nauck, *Tragicorum Graecorum Fragmenta,* pp. 161-164, Nos. 138-152.

7 E. Loewy, *Inschriften griechischer Bildhauer,* No. 108. *IG,* ed. min.; III,1, No. 3777. F. Studniczka, *Das Bildnis Menanders,* reprinted from *NJb,* XLI(1918),3f., fig. 1.

8 Reisch, *Griechische Weihgeschenke,* Abh. des arch.-epigr. Seminars der Universität Wien, Heft VIII(1890), p. 54f. Sieveking in BrBr, pl. 626. Schreiber, *Hellenistische Reliefbilder,* pl. 84. Bernoulli, *Griechische Ikonographie,* pl. XV. Hekler, *Bildniskunst,* pl. 108. Bieber, *Denkmäler,* p. 156f., No. 129, pl. 88; *idem, Sculpture of the Hellenistic Age,* p. 53; *idem, Festschrift Rumpf* (1951), pp. 14-17, pl. V. Webster, in *Bulletin of the John Rylands Library,* XXXII(1949),102ff. Pickard-Cambridge, *Festivals,* p. 201, fig. 93.

9 Studniczka, *Das Bildnis Menanders,* reprint from *NJb,* XLI(1918),1ff. Bernoulli, *Griechische Ikonographie,* II,103ff., pl. XIV. Hekler, *Bildniskunst,* pls. 105-8. Delbrück, *Antike Porträts,* XXXIVf., pl. 20. Bieber, *Denkmäler,* p. 83f., No. 30, fig. 86, pl. 47; *idem, Sculpture of the Hellenistic Age,* pp. 51ff., figs. 150-157. Arndt, pls. 1217-1221. Felletti Maj, Museo nazionale Romano. *I Ritratti,* Nos. 21, 26-28. Vagn Poulsen, *Les Portraits Grecques* (Copenhagen 1954), No. 41. J. F. Crome, in *Atti e Memorie, Reale Accademia Virgiliana di Mantova,* XXIV(1935),28ff., figs. 2-47. Crome's attempt to interpret this portrait as Vergil has been refuted by Poulsen, in *Gnomon,* XII(1936),90-95; and David Robinson in *Proceedings of the American Philosophical Society,* 83(1940), No. 3, pp. 465ff. pls. I-III, figs. 1-4, 10-13. The interpretation of Menander is accepted by Schefold, *Bildnisse,* p. 114f., fig. 3 and p. 216; L. Laurenzi, in *La Critica d'Arte,* XIX-XX (1939)28ff., pls. XVI-XIX; *idem, Ritratti greci* (1941), pl. XLVII, fig. 5. David M. Robinson, "A New Marble Bust of Menander, Wrongly Called Vergil," *Proceedings of the American Philosophical Society,* 83(1940),465ff. *The Theater in Ancient Art, An Exhibition,* The Art Museum, Princeton University, 1952, figs. 57-61. The interpretation of Vergil is accepted by Lippold, *Porträtstatuen,* pp. 89ff.; *idem* in *Röm. Mitt.,* XXXII(1918),96ff., pl. 30; Herbig, "Zum Menander-

Vergil-Problem," in *Röm. Mitt.,* LIX(1944),78ff., fig. 1, pls. 13-14; Rhys Carpenter, in *MAAR* (1941), pp. 96ff.; G. Hafner, *Späthellenistische Bildnisplastik* (1954), pp. 93ff., pls. 33-34, A 30. G. Richter, *Greek and Roman Antiquities in the Dumbarton Oaks Collection,* presents all the evidence for both sides and remains undecided.

10 R. Kekule, *Akademisches Kunstmuseum Bonn,* p. 144, No. 688, pl. 2. Bernoulli, *op.cit.* I,174f., figs. 34-35. Arndt, *Porträts,* pl. 124. R. Paribeni, *Notizie degli Scavi* (1929), pp. 351ff., pl. 16-17; *idem, Ritratto,* pl. LXIV. M. Bieber, in *Röm. Mitt.,* 32(1917),129, pl. 7, and *Sculpture of the Hell. Age,* p. 142, figs. 596-597. F. Poulsen, "Iconographic Studies," *Coll. Ny Carlsberg,* I(1931),26ff., fig. 21; III(1942), 98f. Crome, *op.cit.,* pp. 14, 21ff., figs. 1-4. R. and E. Boehringer, *Homer, Bildnisse und Nachweise,* pp. 68ff., Nos. XIII-XVI, pls. 37-42. Laurenzi, *Ritratti,* p. 139, pl. XLVII B,4. Pace, *Dioniso,* VIII(1940),50-87 and fig. to p. 4; and *Arte e Civiltà della Sicilia,* III(1945),339ff., figs. 70-71, calls the head Epicharmos. G. Richter, "Greek Portraits," *Coll. Latumus,* XX(1955),31ff., doubts that the "Pseudo-Seneca" is Aristophanes. Cf. Ch. III, no. 43.

11 A. Michaelis, *Ancient Marbles,* p. 557, No. 66. Crome, *op.cit.,* p. 19, figs. 41-43; Restored: eyebrows, left part of forehead, nose, mouth, bust. Crome, fig. 43 shows the head without the restoration, but with the modern bust.

12 A. E. Kontoleon, in *Ath. Mitt.,* XIV(1889),130. Ernest Noir, in *Société Royale d'Archéologie d'Alexandrie, Bulletin,* 32-33(1938), N.S. 10, p. 157, fig. 1. Herbig, *op.cit.,* p. 87, fig. 4.

13 The mosaic in Trier (Treves): *Ant. Denk.,* I, pl. 48. Crome, *op.cit.,* p. 57f., fig. 61. The mosaic in Princeton: Stillwell, *Antioch-on-the-Orontes,* III, The Excavations, 1937-1939, p. 185f. No. 131, pl. 63. A. M. Friend, *ibid.,* "Menander and Glykera in the Mosaics of Antioch," p. 248ff. The upper part of both heads, also with the wreaths, are preserved in another mosaic, *ibid.,* p. 176, No. 110, pl. 50. Doro Levi, *Antioch Mosaic Pavements,* pp. 201ff.

14 A. Maiuri, *Casa di Menandro,* pp. 106ff., figs. 50, 52, 53, pl. XII in color. Schefold, *op.cit.,* p. 164f., No. 1. Herbig, *op.cit.,* p. 79, fig. 3. The height of the figure is 1.08 m.

15 T. Campanile in *Bolletino communale,* LIV(1928),187ff., pls. I-II. Crome, *op.cit.,* 15f., 18, 21, 35, figs. 5-15, 22-24, 44. Buckler, in *Journal of the Royal Society,* XIV(1924),46, pl. VII. Schefold, *op.cit.,* pp. 114, 116f., fig. 2. Laurenzi, *op.cit.,* p. 139f., pl. XLVII, fig. 1.

16 Studniczka, *op.cit.,* pp. 6, 9, 11f., 14, pl. 4, figs. 1-3; pl. 7, fig. 2; pl. 8, fig. 2. Bernoulli, *op.cit.,* II,105f., fig. 8. Poulsen, in Arndt-Amelung, Nos. 3113-4. Crome, *op.cit.,* pp. 29ff., 34f., pl. 20, figs. 45-47. Herbig, *op.cit.,* pp. 80ff., pl. 13. Bieber, *Sculpture of the Hellenistic Age,* pp. 51ff., figs. 150 and 152.

17 Héron de Villefosse, *MonPiot,* V(1899),64ff.,224ff., pl. VII. Crome, *op.cit.,* pp. 166f., 216.

18 Robert, *Masken.* Bieber, article, "Maske" in *Real-Enc.,* XIV,2076ff.,2093ff. O. Navarre, "Les masques et les rôles de la comédie nouvelle," *Revue des études anciennes,* XVI (1914),1-40. T.B.L. Webster, "The Masks of Greek Comedy," *Bulletin of the John Rylands Library,* 32(1949),3ff.; Webster, "Note on Pollux List of Tragic Actors," *Festschrift Andreas Rumpf* (1951), pp. 141-150. Webster, *Production,* pp. 73-96, 186-192. Pickard-Cambridge, *Festivals,* pp. 177ff., 194ff.

19 Ruesch, *Guida del Museo di Napoli,* No. 575, Sandrart, *Teutsche Academie,* II(1679), second part, p. 14, pl. 113. Schreiber, *Hellenistische Reliefbilder,* pl. 83. Sieveking, in BrBr, pl. 630a. Robert, *Masken,* p. 61f., fig. 85. Bieber, *Skenika,* 75. *Programm zum Winckelmannsfest* (Berlin,

1915), p. 9f., fig. 4; *idem, Denkmäler*, p. 157, No. 130, pl. 89. Spinazzola, *Arti decorative in Pompei*, pl. 74. Pickard-Cambridge, *Theater of Dionysus*, p. 219, fig. 77; *idem, Festivals*, p. 201, fig. 94.

20 Cabinet des Médailles, No. 122. Bieber, *Denkmäler*, p. 163, No. 140, pl. 95,1. Jean Babelon, *Choix de Bronzes et Terres cuites des Collections Janzé et Oppermann* (1929), p. 23, No. 10, pl. IX. Height ca. 40cm. The hair of the excited man is red, his mantle has traces of pink.

21 *Museo Borbonico*, I, pl. 20. Wieseler, *Bühnengebäude*, pl. 11, No. 3 (with an inexact drawing). Helbig, *Wandgemälde Campaniens*, No. 1470. Bulle, *op.cit.*, p. 280f., fig. 13. Simon, *Comicae Tabellae*, pp. 11ff., No. 7, pl. II and pp. 166ff. Bieber, *Denkmäler*, pl. 91,1. Pickard-Cambridge, *Festivals*, p. 202, fig. 101. L. Richardson, *MAAR*, XXIII(1955),153, pl. LI,2.

22 Naples, Museo Nazionale, No. 9035. Helbig, *Wandgemälde*, No. 1471. Bieber, *Denkmäler*, p. 158f., pl. 91.1. Simon, *Comicae Tabellae*, pp. 7ff., No. 5, and pp. 145ff. Rizzo, *La Pittura Ellenistico-Romana*, p. 68, pl. CXLVIII,2. Richardson, *op.cit.*, p. 155, pl. LII,2.

23 Found on the Aventine. Fine technique. Stuart Jones, *Sculptures of the Museo Capitolino*, p. 134, Sala delle Colombe, No. 37A, pl. 35. Bieber, *Denkmäler*, p. 162, No. 137, pl. 91,2. Pickard-Cambridge, *Festivals*, p. 210, fig. 158.

24 Found in Pompeii. Now in Dresden, Staatliche Museen. P. Herrmann, *Skulpturensammlung Dresden, Verzeichnis der Bildwerke*, No. 224. Treu, in *Mitteilungen aus den sächsischen Kunstsammlungen* (1911), p. 164f., fig. 5.

25 Athens, Nat. Mus. Bieber, *Denkmäler*, p. 168, No. 162, pl. 103,1. Robert, *Masken*, p. 18, fig. 37. Pickard-Cambridge, *Festivals*, p. 204, fig. 107.

26 Robert, *op.cit.*, p. 20, figs. 43-45. Pickard-Cambridge, *op.cit.*, p. 204, fig. 105, in Dresden, found in Boeotia.

27 This mask, together with the whole collection of Greek minor arts, was given in 1933 by the author to the dealer Bernhard Wohlgemut in Berlin, who is said to have sold it in Berlin, but never paid the owner. He is said to have been deported in 1943 to Theresienstadt, and has not returned. The name of the buyer is not known to me.

28 Alda Levi, *Catalogo delle Sculture Greche e Romane del Palazzo Ducale di Mantova*, p. 47, No. 80, pl. LIB. Traces of yellow in hair, brows, and beard.

29 In the storerooms of the National Museum at Athens, No. 1754. Bieber, *Denkmäler*, p. 169, No. 168, pl. 105,3.

30 Athens, National Museum, No. 5045. Robert, *Masken*, p. 80, fig. 98. Bieber, *Denkmäler*, p. 163, No. 141, pl. 95,2. Cf. also Pottier et Reinach, *Nécropole de Myrina*, pp. 468ff., pl. XLV,1. Pickard-Cambridge, *Festivals*, p. 205, fig. 113.

31 Bieber, in Arndt-Amelung, No. 4746.

32 Berlin, Altes Museum, Antiquarium, No. 6623. Bieber, *Denkmäler*, p. 124, No. 67, pl. 65,2. There wrongly used for the tragic delicate youth. Webster, in *Bulletin Rylands Library*, 32(1949),34, No. 12, has rightly interpreted it as comic, probably the curly (οὖλος) youth of Pollux, IV,147. Some traces of red in face, light blue in eyes, black on onkos.

33 Berlin, Altes Museum, No. 7969. Bieber, *Denkmäler*, p. 163, No. 142, pl. 96,1. Robert, *Masken*, p. 66f., fig. 87. Lietzmann, *Bilderanhang zu Wendland, Hellenistische-römische Kultur*, p. 420, pl. III,3. Pickard-Cambridge, *Festivals*, p. 205, fig. 114.

34 Athens, National Museum, No. 5060. Bieber, *Denkmäler*, p. 167, No. 155, pl. 100,3.

35 Bieber, *Denkmäler*, p. 169, No. 164, pl. 103,3-4. Pickard-Cambridge, *Festivals*, p. 205, fig. 115.

36 Louvre, Salle B, No. CA, 1958.

37 Boston Museum of Fine Arts, No. 01.7752. Dorothy

Burr, *Terracottas from Myrina in the Museum of Fine Arts, Boston*, p. 77, No. 114, pl. XLII. Face orange-red, hair dark red, wreath green. The marble mask, British Mus. No. 2440: Webster, *Bulletin Rylands Library*, XXXII(1949), fig. 1; Webster, *Studies in Later Greek Comedy*, p. 119, pl. IVA. Pickard-Cambridge, *op.cit.*, p. 205, fig. 116.

38 Bieber and Rodenwaldt, in *JdAI*, XXVI(1911),1ff., figs. 1-2. Ruesch, *Guida del Museo di Napoli*, Nos. 167 and 169. Mus. Nos. 9985 and 9987. Hermann-Bruckmann, *Denkmäler der Malerei*, pp. 30ff., pls. 106-7. Rodenwaldt, *Die Kunst der Antike*, p. 490, pl. XXXIV and Curtius, *Pompejanische Wandmalerei*, pl. IX-X, have colored reproductions. Bieber, *Denkmäler*, pp. 159ff., Nos. 135-6, pls. 92-93. Fiechter, *Baugesch. Entw.*, figs. 52-53. Pfuhl, *Malerei und Zeichnung*, II,848ff.; III, figs. 684-5. Rizzo, *La Pittura Ellenistico-Romana*, p. 67f., pls. CXLIV-V. Spinazzola, *Arti decorative in Pompei*, pl. 198. Simon, *Comicae Tabellae*, pp. 14ff., No. 8; 20ff., No. 10; pp. 157ff., 169f. Pickard-Cambridge, *Theater of Dionysus*, p. 223f., figs. 85-86; *idem, Festivals*, p. 201, fig. 95. Maiuri, *Roman Painting* (Skira, 1953), pp. 94ff. (street scene in color). Pernice and Winter, *Hellenistische Kunst in Pompeji, Pavimente und figürliche Mosaiken*, p. 169ff., pls. 70-71 (colored). Lippold, *Antike Gemäldekopien, Abh. Münchener Akademie der Wiss.*, N.F. 33(1951),139ff. Webster, *Production*, pp. 23, 87, 90, 162; pls. 21-22. Against his interpretation of Fig. 347 as Menander's *Women at Breakfast*, see Bieber, in *AJP* 78(1957), 209.

39 Museo Nazionale, Naples, No. 9034. *Guida Ruesch*, No. 1805. Bieber and Rodenwaldt, *JdAI*, XXVI(1911),13, fig. 5, and p. 19. Herrmann-Bruckmann, *Denkmäler der Malerei*, pp. 134ff., fig. 36 in text to pl. 106. Bieber, *Denkmäler*, p. 161.

40 Cf. note 38. Colored photographs made for me by Joseph Young of Los Angeles, California, bring out the lively colors of the two mosaics which have been recently cleaned. They will be published in the Encyclopedia Hebraica, Jerusalem.

41 Robert, *Masken*, p. 46, fig. 82. Bieber, *Denkmäler*, p. 169, No. 171, pl. 107,3. Pickard-Cambridge, *Festivals*, p. 209, fig. 146.

42 Bieber, *Denkmäler*, p. 168, No. 159, pl. 101,3-4.

43 Bieber, *Denkmäler*, p. 169f., No. 172, pl. 107,4.

44 Robert, *Masken*, p. 46f., figs. 83-4. Pickard-Cambridge, *Festivals*, p. 210, fig. 147. Another good example in the British Museum: Webster, *Studies in Later Greek Comedy*, p. 119, pl. IVC.

45 Berlin, Altes Museum, Antiquarium, No. 7401. Bieber, *Denkmäler*, p. 167, No. 156, pl. 100,4.

46 British Museum Terracottas, E 31. Pickard-Cambridge, *Festivals*, p. 209, fig. 144.

47 Bieber, *Denkmäler*, p. 167, No. 158, pl. 101,1. Berlin, Altes Museum, Antiquarium, No. 6901.

48 Robert, *Masken*, p. 70, fig. 88.

49 Bieber, *Denkmäler*, p. 170, No. 175, pl. 106,3. Robert, *Masken*, p. 37, fig. 63. Naples, Museo Nazionale, No. 6612. Pickard-Cambridge, *Festivals*, p. 210, fig. 152.

50 Bieber, *Denkmäler*, p. 168, No. 160, pl. 102,1. Cf. Robert, *Masken*, p. 39f., fig. 68, and p. 74f.

51 Bieber, *Denkmäler*, p. 170, No. 173, pl. 106,1. Robert, *Masken*, p. 81, fig. 99. Pickard-Cambridge, *Festivals*, p. 210, fig. 148.

52 Munich, Glyptothek No. A 357, formerly Collection Paul Arndt. Bieber, *Denkmäler*, p. 168, No. 161, pl. 102,2.

53 Athens, National Museum No. 5032. Robert, *Masken*, pp. 37ff., figs. 64-65, wrongly interpreted as the gossiping

wife of a burgher. Bieber, *Denkmäler*, p. 167, No. 157, pl. 101,2.

54 Bieber, *Denkmäler*, p. 170, No. 174, pl. 106,2, Naples, Museo Nazionale, No. 6625. Pickard-Cambridge, *Festivals*, p. 210, fig. 153.

55 Bieber, *Denkmäler*, p. 170, No. 176, pl. 106,4. Naples, Museo Nazionale, No. 6616. Pickard-Cambridge, *Festivals*, p. 210, fig. 154.

56 See note 32. Berlin, Altes Museum, Antiquarium, No. 6622. Simon, *op.cit.*, p. 113, pl. vi,2.

57 Boston Museum of Fine Arts, No. 01.7753. Dorothy Burr, *Terracottas from Myrina in the Museum of Fine Arts*, Boston, p. 77f., No. 115, pl. xlii,3.

58 Amelung, ii,512, Galleria dei Busti, No. 313, pl. 72. Robert, *Masken*, p. 37, pl. i. Bieber, *Denkmäler*, p. 170, No. 177, pl. 107,1-2. Pickard-Cambridge, *Festivals*, p. 210, fig. 156.

59 Louvre, Salle B, CA. 1958.

60 Bieber, *Denkmäler*, p. 170, No. 178, pl. 107,5-6. Pickard-Cambridge, *Festivals*, p. 207, fig. 126. München, Antiquarium. Sieveking, *Münchener Jahrbuch* (1916),153, No. 5 (Ill.); *Arch. Anz.*, xxxii(1917),30f. Nos. 5-6.

61 Bieber, *Denkmäler*, p. 164f., No. 147-8, pl. 98,1-2. A replica of the soldier was formerly in the possession of Hartwig, said to be from Tarentum.

62 Bronze from the Agora: Shear, *Hesperia*, vi(1937),351, fig. 15. Pickard-Cambridge, *Festivals*, p. 210, fig. 161.

63 Walters, *Cat. Terracottas British Museum*, C 827: Webster, "The Masks of Greek Comedy," *Bulletin of the John Rylands Library*, 32(1949),8f.,37, No. 27, i c. He explains the mask as that of a servant. Pickard-Cambridge, *Festivals*, p. 208, fig. 138, names him a soldier slave(?). Bieber, *AJA*, 60(1956), 172, fig. 8, explains him as a warrior.

64 Helbig, *Wandgemälde*, No. 1468. *Museo Borbonico*, iv, pl. 18. Robert, *Masken*, pp. 5, 22f., figs. 7-9. Bieber, *Denkmäler*, p. 159f., No. 134, fig. 136. Simon, *Comicae Tabellae*, pp. 28ff., No. 14 and pp. 165f. Rumpf, "Mimus and Logos," *Eine Festgabe für Carl Niessen*, pp. 163-170. Pickard-Cambridge, *Festivals*, p. 202, fig. 98. Mrs. Simon and Rumpf have interpreted the two main figures of this wall-painting as slaves, but a slave would not hold a spear, and the fawning attitude of the bowing man is that of a parasite. Bieber, *AJA*, 60(1956),172, fig. 6, returns to the explanation as a braggart warrior.

65 Robert, *Masken*, pp. 22ff., figs. 48-52; p. 95, fig. 110. Bieber, *Denkmäler*, p. 164, No. 144, pl. 97,1-2. Pickard-Cambridge, *Festivals*, p. 206, fig. 120.

66 Bieber, *Denkmäler*, p. 169, No. 165, pl. 104,1-2.

67 Bieber, *Denkmäler*, p. 164, No. 145, pl. 97,3. Berlin, Antiquarium, No. 7395. Pickard-Cambridge, *Festivals*, p. 206, fig. 119.

68 Replica in Munich, Antiquarium, No. 5395. Another replica was formerly in the possession of Hartwig, perhaps from Tarentum. Another replica said to be from Megara, now in the Louvre. Froehner, *Terres cuites d'Asie Mineure de la Collection Gréaux*, p. 85, pl. 110,1. Cf. Robert, *Masken*, p. 68f.

69 Berlin, No. 7397. Replica formerly Hartwig said to be from Tarentum.

70 Formerly Collection Jandolo in Palazzo Borghese. Messerschmidt in *Röm.Mitt.*, 46(1931),56ff., fig. 5.

71 Fig. 376 kindly given to me by Professor Seyrig of Beirut. Fig. 377 I owe to Professor Dinsmoor.

72 Berlin, Altes Museum, Antiquarium, No. 7953. Robert, *Masken*, p. 14, fig. 26. Bieber, *Denkmäler*, p. 163, No. 143, pl. 96,2. Lietzmann, *Bilderanhang zu Wendland, Hellenis-*

tisch-römische Kultur, p. 420, pl. iii,2. Pickard-Cambridge, *Dithyramb*, fig. 44; *Festivals*, p. 207, fig. 124.

73 Altmann, in *Ath.Mitt.*, xxix(1904),192ff., fig. 28. Winter, *Altertümer von Pergamon*, vii,2, p. 315, fig. 404d. Robert, *Masken*, p. 15, fig. 28. Bieber, *Denkmäler*, p. 169, No. 166, pl. 104,3. Pickard-Cambridge, *Festivals*, p. 186, fig. 53.

74 Formerly Collection Lecuyer. Cartault, *Coll. Lecuyer*, pl. l,2. Robert, *Masken*, p. 15, fig. 29. Pickard-Cambridge, *Dithyramb*, p. 279, fig. 46; *Festivals*, p. 200, fig. 92.

75 Munich: Antikensammlungen, Inv. No. 6928. Palermo: Bieber, *Skenika*, p. 19ff., fig. 13; *Denkmäler*, p. 158, No. 131, pl. xc,1. Simon, *Comicae Tabellae*, p. 9ff., No. 6, p. 147ff., pl. i.

76 Bieber, *Denkmäler*, p. 168, No. 163, pl. 103,2. Robert, *Masken*, p. 27, fig. 55.

77 Leipzig, Kunstgewerbemuseum. Bielefeld in *Wiss. Zeitschrift Univ. Greifswald*, 'Analecta arch.' (1954/5), pp. 100f., figs. 11-12.

78 Louvre, No. 199. Bieber, *Denkmäler*, p. 164, No. 146, pl. 97,4. Robert, *op.cit.*, p. 16, fig. 33. Pottier et Reinach, *Nécropole de Myrina*, p. 475, pl. 46,4. Pickard-Cambridge, *Festivals*, p. 203f., fig. 106. Mask found in Priene, now in Berlin: Robert, *Masken*, p. 16f., fig. 30. Zahn in Wiegand-Schrader, *Priene*, p. 361, fig. 447.

79 Boston, No. 87 399. Said to be from Myrina or Southern Italy. Messerschmidt, in *Röm.Mitt.*, 46(1931),60, fig. 6a; cf. p. 64. Similar mask on fragmentary statuette bought in Myrina, now in Heidelberg: Luschey, *Ganymed*, p. 78f., figs. 9-10.

80 Conze, *Altertümer von Pergamon*, i,2, p. 260f., No. 20. Bieber, *Denkmäler*, p. 169, Nos. 168-169, pl. 105, Nos. 2-3.

81 Bieber, *JdAI*, 32(1917),76f., fig. 43. For the loss of this mask, together with the whole collection of Greek minor arts of the author, see note 27.

82 Brückner and Bieber, *Skenika*, p. 9f., pl. ii.

83 Berlin, Altes Museum, Antiquarium No. 6957. Robert, *Masken*, p. 27f., fig. 57. Pickard-Cambridge, *Festivals*, p. 207, fig. 127.

84 The replica from Herculaneum has been found together with the slave and fluteplayer (our Fig. 328). *Pitture d'Ercolano*, iv,159, pl. 33. *Museo Borbonico*, iv, pl. 33. Ruesch, *Guida di Napoli*, p. 388, No. 1803, Mus. No. 9037. Bieber-Rodenwaldt, *JdAI*, 26(1911),11, fig. 4. Robert, *Masken*, p. 42f., fig. 72. Bieber, *Denkmäler*, p. 158, No. 132, pl. 90,2. Pickard-Cambridge, *Festivals*, p. 202, fig. 97. The painting in Pompeii, our Fig. 395: Maiuri, *Pompeii, Musei e Mon. d'Italia*, No. 3, p. 63.119, pl. xxxiv, fig. 63; *idem*, in *Notizie degli Scavi* (1929), pp. 410ff., pl. xxiv. Rizzo, *Pittura Ellenistico-Romana*, p. 68, pl. cxlvii. Maiuri, *Les Fresques de Pompéi*, Encyclopédie Alpina, pl. xxxvii; *idem*, *Roman Painting* (Skira, 1953), pp. 94ff. in color.

85 Athens Museum, No. 5057. Robert, *Masken*, p. 71, fig. 90. Bieber, *Denkmäler*, p. 167, No. 153, pl. 100.1.

86 See Ch. VII, p. 81.

87 Athens, National Museum, No. 5058. Robert, *Masken*, p. 14, fig. 27. Cf. Pottier et Reinach, *La Nécropole de Myrina*, p. 471f., pl. xlv, fig. 1. Bieber, *Denkmäler*, p. 166, No. 154, pl. 100,2. Pickard-Cambridge, *Festivals*, p. 207, fig. 129. See also Figs. 297 and 299.

88 Berlin, Altes Museum, No. 7078. Kekule and Pernice, *Ausgewählte Terrakotten*, p. 27, pl. 36,3. Bieber, *Denkmäler*, p. 134, No. 88, pl. 73,3. Replicas are in Vienna, Austria: Robert von Schneider, in *Arch.Anz.*, vii(1892),119, No. 153, and in the South Kensington Museum of London, No. 617.84.

89 Robert, *Masken*, pp. 10ff., fig. 23. Bieber, *Denkmäler*, p. 166, No. 150, pl. 98,4. Pottier et Reinach, *Nécropole de Myrina*, p. 471f., pl. xlv,8.

90 Athens, National Museum, No. 5055. Probably also,

like Fig. 399, from Myrina. Robert, *Masken*, p. 70f., fig. 89.

⁹¹ Bieber, *Denkmäler*, p. 135, No. 89d., pl. 73,4. Found in a tomb near the armory of Tarentum. *Notizie degli Scavi* (1897), p. 216, fig. 37.

⁹² Ruesch, *Guida del Museo di Napoli*, p. 495, No. 2041. Mus. No. 6146. Simon, *Comicae Tabellae*, p. 24f., No. 11, pl. III and p. 152f. Pernice in Winter, *Hell. Kunst in Pompeii*, VI(1938),172, pl. 72,1.

⁹³ Munich, Antikensammlungen, formerly collection Arndt, A379. Bieber, *Denkmäler*, p. 165f., No. 149, pl. 98,3.

⁹⁴ *Catalogo del Museo Teatrale alla Scala* (Milano, 1914), p. 49, No. 18. Bieber, in *Bulletin of the Princeton Museum of Historical Art*, IX(1951),4-12, fig. 4.

⁹⁵ I owe the photographs to the kindness of Professor Seyrig. They were made in the Bibliothèque Nationale at Paris, numbers A7633-7635.

⁹⁶ *British Museum Catalogue of Bronzes*, No. 1626.

⁹⁷ Museo archeologico, No. 2325. L. A. Milani, *Il Museo archeologico di Firenze*, II,30, pl. 140,1.

⁹⁸ Berlin, Altes Museum, Antiquarium, No. 323. Robert, *Masken*, p. 10, fig. 20. *Arch. Zeitung*, XII(1854), pl. 69, figs. 21-22. Pickard-Cambridge, *Festivals*, p. 207, fig. 126. He follows Robert's identification as the curly-haired slave.

⁹⁹ Louvre, No. 293. Bieber, "The Statuette of an Actor of New Comedy," *Bulletin of the Princeton Museum of Historical Art*, IX(1951),4-12, fig. 5.

¹⁰⁰ Bieber, in *Bulletin of the Princeton Museum of Historical Art*, IX(1951),4-12, figs. 1-2.

¹⁰¹ Cf. British Museum Terracottas, D 322. Pickard-Cambridge, *Festivals*, p. 207, fig. 130; and for the crossed hands, *ibid.*, fig. 133, Copenhagen Mus. No. 1067. Pottier-Reinach, *Nécropole de Myrina*, p. 475f., pl. XLVI,5.

¹⁰² Robert, *Masken*, p. 10, fig. 21. Athens, National Museum, No. 5030. Pickard-Cambridge, *Festivals*, p. 207, fig. 125.

¹⁰³ Hartford, *Wadsworth Athenaeum Museum Bulletin* (1924), p. 10. Formerly in the Morgan Collection. Salomon Reinach, *Répertoire de la Statuaire*, v,1, p. 537,6.

¹⁰⁴ Berlin Bronzen, Inv. No. 8937. Pernice, *Arch. Anz.* (1904), p. 37, No. 13. Robert, *Masken*, p. 82f., fig. 103. Neugebauer, *Bronzen der klassischen und hellenistischen Zeit* (Berlin, 1951), No. 71. A. Rumpf in "Mimus und Lo-

gos," *Eine Festgabe für Carl Niessen* (1952), p. 167f., pl. VII. Particularly lively is the seated slave in the terracotta: *Nécropole de Myrina*, p. 471f., pl. XLV,8.

¹⁰⁵ Robert, *Masken*. M. Bieber, article, 'Maske,' in *Real-Enc.*, XIV(1930),2093ff. O. Navarre, *Revue des Études anciennes*, XVI(1914),1ff. T.B.L. Webster, "The Masks of Greek Comedy," *Bulletin of the John Rylands Library*, XXXII(1949),126ff. Pickard-Cambridge, *Festivals*, pp. 190-193, 202-212. Gisela Krien, "Der Ausdruck der antiken Theatermasken nach Angaben im Polluxkatalog und in der pseudoaristotelischen Physiognomik," *JOAI*, XLII(1956),84-117.

¹⁰⁶ M. Bieber, in *Festschrift Andreas Rumpf* (1952), pp. 14ff.; *AJP*, LXXV(1954),311.

¹⁰⁷ Hermann Reich, *Die ältesten berufsmässigen Darsteller des griechisch-italischen Mimus*, Programm des Königsberger Gymnasiums, 1896/7. *Idem*, *Der Mimus, ein literarisch-entwicklungsgeschichtlicher Versuch* (1903). J. Horowitz, *Spuren griechischer Mimen im Orient* (1905). M. Bieber, in *JdAI*, 32(1917), 61-64, fig. 31-33; *idem*, *Denkmäler*, pp. 175ff. Saglio in Daremberg-Saglio, *Dictionnaire des Antiquités*, 1,1078ff. Wüst in *Real-Enc.*, XV(1932), 1727-43, *s.v.* Mimus. Olivieri, *Frammenti della Commedia greca e del Mimo nella Sicilia e nella Magna Grecia* (1930), pp. 167ff. Herzog-Crusius, *Die Mimiamben des Herondas* (1926). Pace, in *Dioniso*, I(1929),224-230. Kaibel, *Comicorum Graecorum Fragmenta*, pp. 154-181 (Sophron).

¹⁰⁸ Olivieri, *op.cit.*, p. 197f., fig. 15. Rizzo, in *Dedalo*, VII,1926, pp. 402-417. Pace, *Arte e Civiltà della Sicilia*, III, p. 344f., fig. 72; *idem*, *Dioniso* I(1929), 224-230.

¹⁰⁹ See Ch. III, note 53.

¹¹⁰ Grenfell, *Alexandrian Erotic Fragment and other Greek Papyri* (Oxford, 1896). Crusius, *Die Mimiamben des Herondas*, 5. ed., 1914, pp. 124ff. U. von Wilamowitz, "Des Mädchens Klage" in *Göttinger Nachrichten*, phil.-hist.-Klasse 1896, pp. 209ff. Beare, *The Roman Stage*, 2nd. ed. 1955, p. 229 and Appendix L, text and translation.

¹¹¹ Watzinger, *Ath.Mitt.*, XXVI(1901),1ff., pl. I. Crusius, *Festschrift für Gomperz* (1902), pp. 381ff. R. Herzog in *Philologus*, LXII(1903),35ff. Bieber, *Denkmäler*, p. 176f., No. 187, fig. 142. Olivieri, *op.cit.*, p. 184f., fig. 14.

¹¹² Translation of Herondas, *Mime 2*, in Higham and Bowra, *The Oxford Book of Greek Verse*, p. 556.

NOTES TO CHAPTER IX. THE HELLENISTIC THEATER BUILDING

¹ Shaw, ed. Tauchnitz, vol. 4555, p. 121f.; ed. Brentano (New York, 1919), "The Author's Apology for *Great Catherine*," p. 129.

² Cf. Bieber, *Gnomon*, VIII(1932),478ff.

³ A. von Gerkan, *Das Theater von Priene*, als Einzelanlage und in seiner Bedeutung für das hellenistische Bühnenwesen (1921). Bieber, *Denkmäler*, pp. 29ff., No. 8, pl. XIII, figs. 27-38. Bulle, *Untersuchungen*, pp. 250ff. Fensterbusch, *Bursians Jahresber.*, 227(1930),35ff. Dinsmoor, *The Architecture of Ancient Greece* (1950), pp. 301ff., fig. 111, pl. LXIX. Pickard-Cambridge, *Theatre of Dionysus*, pp. 202ff., figs. 68-69. Bieber, *AJA* 58(1954),280, pl. 53, fig. 11a.

⁴ The instructive reconstruction of the undecorated theater by Fiechter, published by Frickenhaus, in *Bonner Jahrbücher*, 125(1919),200, pl. XXXVII,1. Bieber, *Denkmäler*, p. 35, fig. 35. From it is taken Fig. 424.

⁵ Von Gerkan, *op.cit.*, p. 70, pls. XXXI and XXXVI.

⁶ Bulle, *Untersuchungen*, p. 251f.

⁷ Homolle, *BCH*, XVIII(1894),162ff.; Chamonard, *BCH* XX(1896),281ff. Dürrbach, *Choix d'Inscriptions de Délos* (1921), p. 110f. Bulle, *op.cit.*, pp. 174-192. *IG*, XI,2, Nos.

105-133, 142-291. Vallois, *Revue des études anciennes* (1928), pp. 171-179. Pickard-Cambridge, *Theatre of Dionysus*, pp. 241ff., 169f., 206-209. Dilke, *ABSA*, 45(1950),59f. Dinsmoor, *op.cit.*, pp. 298ff. Webster, *Production*, pp. 146-155. Vallois, *L'Architecture hellénique à Délos*, I(1944), 220-246.

⁸ *IG*, XI,2, No. 161. Dürrbach, *op.cit.*, No. 125, p. 249f. Bulle, *op.cit.*, p. 175.

⁹ *IG*, XI,2, 199 A. Bulle, *op.cit.*, p. 176f., pp. 182ff. The expressions "skene" and "paraskenion" are used sometimes in the singular, sometimes in the plural, and often in an inexact manner either for a part of the building or for the paintings on the pinakes or canvases.

¹⁰ Chamonard, *BCH*, XX(1896),279ff. Bulle, *op.cit.*, pp. 177ff., 186ff.

¹¹ Homolle, *BCH*, XVIII(1894),165, No. 11. Bulle, *op.cit.*, p. 180, VII and p. 191.

¹² *IG*, VII,423; D-R, pp. 100ff., figs. 35-42, pl. VI,1. Fiechter, *Baugesch.Entw.*, pp. 1ff., figs. 1-5, 64a-b. From his figs. 1-2a and 64 are taken our Figs. 427 and 429. Fiechter, *Theaterbauten, I, Das Theater von Oropos*, pp. 15ff., figs. 4-11.

From fig. 11 and pl. 8 are taken our Figs. 426 and 428. The remodeled drawing for Fig. 427 has been made by Miss Elizabeth Wadhams.

[13] Bulle, *Untersuchungen*, pp. 303ff. He sees the same spirit which created the proskenion with engaged columns as merely decorative supporting wall, in the wooden sarcophagi from Abukir and in the house sarcophagi from the Crimea related to the Saitic wooden sarcophagi. It seems to me possible, however, that the sarcophagi from the Crimea may follow a tradition from Asia Minor living on in Miletus, the mother city of the colonies in Southern Russia. Studniczka (*Abh. Sächs. Akad.*, xxx(1914),66ff., No. 2, pls. 1-2) was right when he supposed the symposium tent of Ptolemy II, as described by Callixenus, to have had low colonnades attached as porches on three sides before the central main building.

[14] Berlin, *Vorderasiatisches Museum*, Room 13. Walter Andrae, *Archaischer Ischtar Tempel in Assur* (39. Wissenschaftliche Veröffentlichung der deutschen Orientgesellschaft, 1922), pp. 34ff., figs. 5-6. Andrae, *Das Gotteshaus und die Urformen des Bauens im Alten Orient* (1930), pp. 67ff., pl. IV.

[15] Franz Oelman, "Hilani und Liwanhaus," *Bonner Jahrbücher*, 127(1922),189ff.; Figs. 432a-g are taken from his figs. 9b-c, 15-17.

[16] Oelman, *op.cit.*, p. 211f., fig. 21. The late Professor Herzfeld, of Princeton University, kindly confirmed this fact.

[17] Flinders-Petrie, *Gizeh and Rifeh*, British School of Archaeology in Egypt and Egyptian Research Account, thirteenth year, 1907, pp. 14ff., especially p. 17f., pls. xv-xviii; particularly good is pl. xviii A. Baldwin Smith, *Egyptian Architecture*, p. 199, pl. lxiv, 8-9. Our Figs. 433-434 correspond to Nos. 21 and 93 therein.

[18] Cf. Oelman, *op.cit.*, pp. 192ff., figs. 1-2. From it is taken Fig. 432a. Here also are open terraces in front of the upper story between the side wings which are built like turrets.

[19] Olympia, Leonidaeum: Dörpfeld, *Olympia* II, *Die Baudenkmäler von Olympia*, pp. 83ff., pls. 62-63. Dinsmoor, *The Architecture of Ancient Greece*, p. 251, fig. 44L on p. 114.

[20] Southeast building in Olympia: Dörpfeld, *op.cit.*, pp. 73ff., figs. 55-56, pls. 52-54.

[21] Maiuri, *La villa dei Misteri*, pp. 46ff., fig. 13, pls. B,D, and E. Bieber, in *Review of Religion*, ii(1937),4, fig. i. Maiuri, *Pompeii*, fig. 93 (our Fig. 435).

[22] Swoboda, *Römische Paläste*, p. 14f., figs. 6-7; p. 24, fig. 13; pp. 29ff., pls. i-vii. M. Rostovtzeff, in *JdAI*, xix (1904),103ff., pls. v-vi. Rostovtzeff, *Röm.Mitt.*, xxvi(1911), figs. 56-57, pls. vi,1, vii,2. Herrmann-Bruckmann, *Malerei*, pl. 163. Swindler, *Ancient Painting*, fig. 548. Mau, *Pompeji*, pp. 350ff., figs. 187-188. Mau-Kelsey, *Pompeii*, p. 358f., fig. 177 (our Fig. 436). Thédenat, *Pompéi*, p. 163, fig. 121. Cf. Noack and Lehmann-Hartleben, *Baugeschichtliche Untersuchungen am Stadtrand von Pompeji* (1936), pp. 193ff., pls. 1, 4, 7, 10, 21, 22, 24.

[23] Wallpainting in Naples from Stabiae, Inv. No. 9409. Swoboda, *op.cit.*, p. 53, pl. iiia. Rostovtzeff, in *Röm.Mitt.*, xxvi(1911), pl. viii,2.

[24] D-R, pp. 379ff. Dörpfeld in *Ath.Mitt.*, xxviii(1903), 383, 411ff.; and xlix(1924),50ff.

[25] A. von Gerkan, *Theater von Priene*, pp. 73ff. Frickenhaus in *Real-Enc.*, iii A, pp. 484 and 492, agrees with him. Cf. the critical remarks of James T. Allen, "Problems of the Proskenion," in *University of California Publications in Classical Philology*, vii(1923),197ff. His attempt to date the form of the proskenion as an independent building (fig. 4) back to the fifth century is not acceptable.

[26] Bethe, *Prolegomena*, pp. 230ff. Fiechter, *Baugesch.*

Entw., pp. 28ff. Fiechter, *Dionysostheater*, iii, pp. 76ff., fig. 38, pl. 21; Cf. note 51. Bulle, *op.cit.*, pp. 234ff. Bulle, as always, dates the new form too early, into the fourth century B.C. Cf. Chamonard, *BCH*, xx(1896),256ff., especially 291ff., "La question du Logeion." Bieber, *Denkmäler*, pp. 29, 33ff., 73f. Dinsmoor, *The Architecture of Ancient Greece*, pp. 298ff.

[27] Cf. Vitruvius, V, 5, 7, and the tale in Plutarch, *Moralia*, 1906 B (Disputatio qua docetur ne suaviter quidem vivi posse secundum Epicuri decreta, Ὅτι οὐδὲ ζῆν ἐστιν ἡδέως κατ' Ἐπικοῦρον). When Alexander the Great wanted a bronze proskenion in Pella, the architect did not allow it, because it would spoil the sound of the actor's voice.

[28] Athenaeus, xiii,587b. See Ch. VI, note 7.

[29] Von Gerkan supposes that there was but one door. Bulle, *op.cit.*, p. 251f., on the other hand, assumes that there were three doors from the very beginning.

[30] Clarke-Bacon-Koldewey, *Investigations at Assos*, pp. 121ff. Puchstein, *op.cit.*, pp. 57ff., fig. 12. D-R, pp. 148ff., fig. 60. Frickenhaus, *Altgriech. Bühne*, pp. 36, 99, figs. 1-3. Bulle, *Untersuchungen*, p. 253.

[31] Heberdey-Niemann-Wilberg, *Forschungen in Ephesos*, ii(1912), pp. 1ff. Bieber, *Denkmäler*, pp. 38ff., No. 10, figs. 40-51, pls. xix-xx and *AJA* 58(1954), 281, pl. 53, fig. 11b. von Gerkan, *op.cit.*, p. 90f. Bulle, *Untersuchungen*, p. 253ff.

[32] Bulle, *Untersuchungen*, p. 247: "Flachwandtypus."

[33] Wiegand, *Priene*, fig. 229. A. von Gerkan, *op.cit.*, p. 75f., pls. vii,3; viii, xxxii, xxxiii,2. Bieber, *Denkmäler*, p. 31, fig. 27. Frickenhaus, *Altgriech. Bühne*, pp. 36, 99, fig. 1.

[34] Chamonard, *BCH*, xx(1896),281ff., pls. xix-xx. D-R, pp. 144ff., figs. 58-59. Dörpfeld's design of the upper story with only one door in the front is probably wrong. Puchstein, *Die griech. Bühne*, pp. 53ff., figs. 10-11. Frickenhaus, *op.cit.*, fig. 3. Bieber, *Denkmäler*, p. 28f., No. 7, figs. 24-26, pl. 12. Pickard-Cambridge, *Theatre of Dionysus*, pp. 206ff., figs. 74-75.

[35] For Leonidaeum see note 19. For the ship of Ptolemy IV see note 13. The tent of Ptolemy: Caspari, in *JdAI*, xxxi (1916),1ff., figs. 10-14.

[36] Fossum-Capps, *Papers of the American School at Athens*, vi(1897),76ff.,135ff., pls. 4, 12-15, D-R, pp. 113ff., figs. 44-45, pl. 12. Puchstein, *op.cit.*, p. 94ff., fig. 25. Fiechter, *Baugesch.Entw.*, pp. 4ff., 70ff., figs. 6-8. Frickenhaus, *op.cit.*, pp. 40, 43, 48, figs. 10, 14. Flickinger, *Greek Theater*, pp. 104ff. Bieber, *Denkmäler*, p. 20f., No. 3, figs. 14-15, pl. viii. Bulle, *op.cit.*, pp. 81ff., pl. 11. Fiechter, *Das Theater in Eretria*, in *Theaterbauten*, viii(1937), pp. 34ff., figs. 32-35, pls. 7-9. Dinsmoor, *The Architecture of Ancient Greece*, p. 300, fig. 110, p. 305f. See above, Ch. V, Figs. 263-265 and Ch. VI, Figs. 284-288.

[37] Fossum, *AJA*, ix(1905),263ff., pls. 8-9. Bulle, *op.cit.*, pp. 192ff. Fiechter, *Das Theater von Sikyon*, in *Theaterbauten*, iii(1931). Pickard-Cambridge, *Theatre of Dionysus*, pp. 204ff., fig. 73.

[38] Puchstein, *Die griechische Bühne*, frontispiece. Cf. above, Ch. V, Figs. 271-274.

[39] Powell in *AJA*, viii(1904),174-201. Flickinger, *Greek Theater*, p. 61, fig. 25. Bulle, *op.cit.*, pp. 91ff., 255f., pls. 14-16. Fiechter, *Die Theater von Oiniadai und Neu-Pleuron*, *Theaterbauten*, ii(1931), pp. 7ff., figs. 1-4, pls. 1-6. Arias, *Il teatro greco fuori di Atene*, pp. 46-57. Pickard-Cambridge, *Theatre of Dionysus*, p. 209.

[40] Stillwell, *Corinth*, ii, *The Theater*, pp. 15ff., 133ff., pl. iii (plan), pl. viiia (restoration of the proskenion with ramps).

[41] A. von Gerkan, *Das Theater von Priene*, p. 93f. Dörpfeld, in *Ath.Mitt.*, 47(1922), p. 28 and 49; (1924), p. 90f. Bieber, *Denkmäler*, pp. 21ff., No. 4, figs. 16-18. Pickard-

Cambridge, *Theatre of Dionysus*, p. 204, fig. 72. Dinsmoor, *The Architecture of Ancient Greece*, p. 305, fig. 112.

[42] Ch. V, Figs. 243-247, note 20. Dinsmoor, *The Architecture of Ancient Greece*, pp. 307, 316, 331, fig. 121, pl. LXXI.

[43] Koldewey, *Das wiedererstehende Babylon⁴* (1925), pp. 293ff., figs. 248-254. Frickenhaus, *op.cit.*, p. 44, fig. 17. Bulle, *Untersuchungen*, p. 246.

[44] Herzog and Ziebarth, in *Ath.Mitt.*, XXIII(1898),314ff., pls. XII and XII A. Bulle, *op.cit.*, pp. 242ff., fig. 5. Fiechter, *Die Theater von Oiniadae und Neu Pleuron*, in *Theaterbauten*, II(1931), pp. 19ff., figs. 5-6, pls. 7-12.

[45] D-R, pp. 97ff., fig. 34 (from here is taken Fig. 463). Puchstein, *Die griech. Bühne*, pp. 105ff., figs. 27-28. Bulle, *op.cit.*, p. 203f. Frickenhaus, *op.cit.*, pp. 43, 113, fig. 16. Fiechter, *Das Theater im Piraeus, Theaterbauten*, IX(1950), pp. 35ff., Figs. 15-17, pl. 6. Arias in *Dioniso*, IV(1934),93-99, figs. 1-3, compares the theater of Thera (Dörpfeld in Hiller von Gaertringen, *Thera*, III,249) with the theater in the Piraeus. It was also built in the 2nd century B.C.

[46] Pausanias, VIII,32,1. D-R, pp. 133ff., figs. 54-55. Bieber, *Denkmäler*, p. 27f., figs. 22-23. Fiechter, *Das Theater von Megalopolis*, in *Theaterbauten*, IV(1931). Bulle, *Untersuchungen*, pp. 97ff., pls. 17-18. Arias, *Il teatro fuori Atene*, pp. 100ff., figs. 67-68. Dinsmoor, *The Architecture of Ancient Greece*, p. 249f. and 307. Pickard-Cambridge, *Theatre of Dionysus*, pp. 199ff., figs. 66-67.

[47] Woodward, in *ABSA*, 26(1923/4), 119ff.; 27(1925), 175f., pls. XXVII-XXX; 28(1926), 3ff.; 30(1928/30), 151ff. Bulle, *Untersuchungen*, pp. 108ff. Bulle, "Das Theater zu Sparta" in *Sitzungsber. Bayer. Akad.* (1937), Heft 5, pp. 1ff. pls. I-VII. Dinsmoor, *op.cit.*, pp. 307f., 310.

[48] A. von Gerkan, *Das Theater von Priene*, pp. 49 and 85.

[49] Picard, *BCH*, 45(1921),108ff., fig. 9; and 47(1923), 336f., pls. 7-8. Bulle, *Untersuchungen*, p. 205f.

[50] See note 45.

[51] Lehmann-Hartleben and Bulle, *op.cit.*, pp. 24ff. and 45ff., pl. 5, Map 5, pls. 8-10. Fiechter, *Dionysostheater*, I (1935), pp. 20ff., 28f., pls. I, V, VI, and VII; III(1936), pp. 15, 41, 76ff., fig. 38 and pls. 4,21; IV(1950), p. 28, fig. 10; p. 45, fig. 19. A. von Gerkan, in *Gnomon*, 14(1938),241f. Pickard-Cambridge, *Theatre of Dionysus*, pp. 175ff., fig. 59. Dinsmoor, *The Architecture of Ancient Greece*, pp. 298ff.

[52] Fiechter, *Dionysostheater*, IV(1950), pp. 11ff., figs. 3-4. See Ch. V, note 51.

[53] A. Lesky, *Hermes*, 72(1937),123ff. Bieber, *AJA* 58 (1954), 281, pls. 52-53, figs. 9-10. The sketches Figs. 468-469 were drawn for me by Penelope Dimitriou and redrawn by Elizabeth Wadhams.

[54] Wiegand-Schrader, *Priene*, fig. 257. A. von Gerkan, *Das Theater von Priene*, p. 85, pl. XXVI,6. Bieber, *Denkmäler*, fig. 33.

[55] Bulle, *Untersuchungen*, pp. 175, 181, 186.

[56] See Ch. V, note 46.

[57] Bulle, *Untersuchungen*, pp. 277ff., figs. 11-15. Our Fig.

470 is based on his fig. 12. Cf. Bieber-Rodenwaldt, in *JdAI*, XXVI(1911),3ff.

[58] A.M.G. Little, "Scaenographia," *The Art Bulletin*, XVIII (1936), 407ff., figs. I-VIII; XIX(1937), pp. 487ff., figs. 3-12. Beyen, *Die pompejanische Wanddekoration vom zweiten bis zum vierten Stil*, I(1938), pp. 89ff. and 352ff. Little, "A Roman Sourcebook for the Stage" *AJA*, 60(1956),27ff., pl. 20.

[59] Barnabei, *La Villa di Boscoreale*, pp. 71ff., pls. 9-10. Fiechter, *Die Baugesch.Entw.*, pp. 42ff., figs. 43-45. Bulle, *Untersuchungen*, pp. 273ff., figs. 9-10. Swindler, *Ancient Painting*, p. 327. Pfuhl, *Malerei und Zeichnung der Griechen*, II, pp. 810ff., 868f., §953; III, fig. 707. Curtius, *Pompejanische Malerei*, pp. 114ff. Friend, *Art Studies*, VII(1929),9ff., pl. V, fig. 10; pl. VI, fig. 13. Beyen, *op.cit.*, pp. 141ff., figs. 56-65. Little, *AJA*, 39(1935), 370ff., and 49(1945),135ff. *Art Bulletin*, 18(1936),411ff., and 19(1937), 491. Spinazzola, *Arti decorative in Pompei*, pl. 93. Gisela Richter, *Handbook of the Classical Collection* (1930), pp. 218ff., fig. 155 and in *Scritti in onore di Bartolomeo Nogara* (1937), pp. 382ff., pls. LI-LII. Pickard-Cambridge, *Theatre of Dionysus*, pp. 227ff., figs. 89-92, 94. Phyllis Williams Lehmann, *Roman Wall Paintings from Boscoreale in the Metropolitan Museum of Art*, Monograph on Archaeology and Fine Arts, V (1953),82ff., pls. X-XXXIII. Bieber, *AJA*, 57(1953),239.

[60] The translations of Vitruvius are those by M. H. Morgan in *Vitruvius, The Ten Books on Architecture*, pp. 150ff., 211.

[61] Fiechter, in Frickenhaus, *Altgriechische Bühne*, pl. I. Bieber, *Denkmäler*, p. 44, fig. 47. Friend, in *Art Studies*, VII (1929),21, pl. VIII, fig. 17.

[62] See for the programs of the festivals in the Hellenistic period, Bethe, *Prolegomena*, pp. 244ff. Pickard-Cambridge, *Theatre of Dionysus*, pp. 240ff.; Pickard-Cambridge, *Dithyramb*, pp. 61ff. Dinsmoor, *Hesperia*, XXXIII(1954),306f.

[63] Cf. Dörpfeld, "Das griechische Theater Vitruvs," in *Ath.Mitt.*, XXII(1897),439ff.; XXIII(1898),326ff.; XXVIII (1903),383ff. Bethe, "Das griechische Theater Vitruvs," *Hermes*, XXXIII(1898),313ff. Flickinger, *Greek Theater*, pp. 75ff. Fensterbusch, in *Bursians Jahresberichte*, 227(1930), 58ff. Dinsmoor, *The Architecture of Ancient Greece*, p. 313, fig. 114.

[64] Bethe, in *Hermes*, XXXVI(1901),597ff. Fensterbusch, "Σκηνή bei Pollux" in *Hermes*, LX(1925), 112ff.

[65] Puchstein, *Altgriechische Bühne*, p. 46f., was the first to recognize that Vitruvius is in accord with the Hellenistic stage buildings, D-R, pp. 158ff., figs. 67-71. Choisy, *Vitruve*, I, pp. 197ff.; IV, pls. 48-52. Prestel, *Architektur des Vitruv*, V, pls. XLVIII-IX. Capps, "Vitruvius and the Greek Stage," in *University of Chicago Studies in Classical Philology*, I(1895),93ff. Flickinger, *Greek Theater*, pp. 75ff., fig. 43. Fiechter, *Baugesch.Entw.*, pp. 59ff., figs. 54-57. From him are taken our Figs. 475-476.

[66] O.A.W. Dilke, "The Greek Theater Cavea," *ABSA*, 43(1948),125ff.; "Details and Chronology of Greek Theater Caveas," *ibid.*, 45(1950),56ff., figs. 15-16, pls. 1-5.

NOTES TO CHAPTER X. ITALIAN POPULAR COMEDY (THE PHLYAKES)

[1] Rizzo, *Il teatro Greco di Siracusa* (1923), p. 5f. Anti, *Teatri Greci archaici* (1947), pp. 85ff., pls. III-IV; *Guida del Teatro antico di Siracusa* (1948), pp. 37ff., figs. 4-8. Pace, *Arte e Civiltà della Sicilia*, II(1938), pp. 303ff., pl. VI, figs. 271-274.

[2] Kaibel, *Comic. Graec. Fragm.*, p. 148. Kaibel has drawn from the ancient sources the conclusion that Phormis had invented the coulisses; cf. Ch. VI, note 4. Phormis was also

a writer. One of his plays was named *Kepheus or Perseus*; cf. Fig. 202 in Ch. III.

[3] Vogel, *Szenen Euripideischer Tragödien in griechischen Vasengemälden* (1886). Huddilston, *Greek Tragedy in the Light of Vase Paintings* (1898). Séchan, *Tragédie grecque*, pp. 231ff. Bulle, *Skenographie*, 94. *Berliner Winckelmannsprogramm* (1934). Trendall, *Paestan Pottery*, p. 32. Pickard-Cambridge, *Festivals*, pp. 218ff., figs. 169-189.

⁴ Cf. Ch. II, pp. 31ff. and Ch. V, pp. 66ff.; especially the Medea vase in Munich with the central hall (figs. 121-122), F-R, pl. 90; the crater in the Louvre with scenes from the *Iphigenia in Tauris*, after Euripides (Fig. 115). Lehmann-Hartleben, in *JdAI*, xlii(1927),30f., figs. 1-2. Bulle, *Untersuchungen*, p. 230f., fig. 4a; Bulle, *Skenographie*, pp. 13ff., fig. 6, and the fragment in Würzburg with a scene from a drama of the daughters of Pelias (Fig. 266). Bulle, *Skenographie*, figs. 1-4, pls. i-ii for paraskenia. Webster, *Production*, pp. 97ff.

⁵ The fragments have been collected by Kaibel, *op.cit.*, pp. 183-197. Olivieri, *Frammenti della commedia greca e del mimo nella Sicilia e nella Magna Grecia* (1930; second edition 1947). Olivieri, E. della Valle, e A. Colonna, in *Dioniso*, viii (1940), 3-39 with bibl.

⁶ The phlyakes vases have been collected by: Heydemann, in *JdAI*, i(1886)260ff. Bieber, *Denkmäler*, pp. 138ff., Nos. 101-125, pls. 76-86. Wüst, article "Φλύακες" (Phlyakes) in *Real-Enc.*, xx(1940), pp. 392ff. (88 numbers). Bieber, *ibid.*, s.v. Maske, pp. 2088-2593. Catteruccia, *Pitture vascolari italiote di soggetto teatrale comico* (1951). His list, which is closely based on that by Wüst with a few additions comprises over 100 vases. Cf. also for the phlyakes vases: Bethe, *Prolegomena*, pp. 278ff. Romagnoli, *Nel regno di Dioniso*² (1923). O. Navarre, in Daremberg-Saglio, *Dictionnaire des Antiquités*, iv,435ff. Zahn, in F-R, iii,180f., to pl. 150,2; Zahn in *Die Antike*, 7 (1931), 70ff. Bulle, in *Festschrift für Loeb* (1930), pp. 29ff., figs. 17-20 (Gnathia vases). Allardyce Nicoll, *Masks, Mimes and Miracles*, pp. 50ff. Pace, *Arte e Civiltà della Sicilia antica*, iii(1945), pp. 313ff. Chapter on "Epicharmo e il teatro Siceliota." D'Amico, *Storia del Teatro dramatico*, i, Chs. 6-9. T.B.L. Webster, "South Italian Vases and Attic Drama," in *CQ*, 42(1948), 15-27. Webster, "Masks on Gnathia Vases," *JHS*, 71(1951), 222-232. Webster tries to explain the phlyakes vases from Attic comedy. Trendall, *Paestan Pottery*, pp. 14f., 26, 36ff., 63, 65, 69f., 92f., 111. Trendall, *PBSR*, xx(1952),1-53. Trendall, *Catalogue of Phlyax Vases*, Institute of Classical Studies, London (1959), discusses about 165 vases.

⁷ British Museum, F 157 (237). F-R, ii, p. 263, pl. 110. Trendall, *Frühitaliotische Vasen* in Beazley-Jacobsthal, *Bilder griechischer Vasen*, Vol. 12, No. 237, p. 18, pl. 14a.

⁸ Körte, in *Real-Enc.*, i A, p. 843f., article "Rhinthon." Kaibel, *ibid.*, vi, article "Epicharmos," pp. 34-41; Kaibel, *Comicorum Graec Fragm.*, pp. 183-189. Olivieri, *op.cit.*, pp. 122-137.

⁹ Alvarez-Ossorio, *Vasos griegos en el Museo arch. Madrid*, pp. 22 and 41f., No. 11094, pl. xxii. Leroux, *Vases grecs et italo-grec du Musée archéol. de Madrid*, pp. 205ff., No. 369, pl. xlv. Bethe, in *JdAI*, xv (1900),59ff., fig. 1; *Arch.Anz.*, *ibid.*, p. 224. Bieber, *Denkmäler*, pp. 107ff., No. 43, figs. 107-108. Hoppin, *Handbook of Greek Blackfigured Vases*, p. 438f. Patroni, *Ceramica antica nell'Italia meridionale*, in *Memorie della real Accademia di archeologia di Napoli*, xix(1897/98), pp. 37ff., fig. 30. Pickard-Cambridge, *Theatre of Dionysus*, p. 221f., figs. 83-84. Trendall, *Paestan Pottery*, pp. 31ff., pl. vii, H. Kenner, *Das Theater und der Realismus in der griechischen Kunst*, pp. 150-152, fig. 28.

¹⁰ Petersen, *Röm.Mitt.*, xii(1897),140ff., fig. 11. Bethe, in *JdAI*, xv(1900),59ff., figs. 2 and 8. Fiechter, *Baugesch. Entw.*, pp. 102 and 110, fig. 98. Bieber, *Denkmäler*, p. 76f., No. 23, fig. 80. Alda Levi, *Le Terracotte Figurate del Museo Nazionale di Napoli* (1926), pp. 173ff., No. 773, fig. 134. Pickard-Cambridge, *Theatre of Dionysus*, p. 220f., fig. 82. Trendall, *Paestan Pottery*, p. 32 with note 41, fig. 12.

¹¹ See Hauser, in F-R, iii, 62. Sieger, *Shakespeare und seine Zeit*, p. 40. M. Hammitzsch, *Der moderne Theaterbau*, pp. 56ff., figs. 32-33. A. H. Thorndike, *Shakespeare's Thea-*

ter, pp. 50ff., illustrations on pp. 51, 71, 164. Joseph Quincy Adams, *Shakespearean Playhouses*, pp. 166ff. (The Swan Playhouse in London, 1596).

¹² Bethe, *JdAI*, xv(1900),59ff. Dörpfeld, *ibid.*, xvi(1901), 22ff., opposes this opinion. Cf. C. Fensterbusch, *Bursians Jahresberichte*, 227(1930),65f. Trendall will discuss the different forms of the stage in Sicily and southern Italy in his forthcoming book on the phlyakes vases.

¹³ HBr, pl. 14. Fiechter, *Baugesch.Entw.*, p. 46f., fig. 51. Bieber, *Denkmäler*, p. 95f., No. 35, pls. 49-50.

¹⁴ *British Museum Cat. of Vases*, iv, p. 72, F 149; cf. p. 99, F103. *CVA*, iv,Ea, pls. 6-7. Hauser in F-R, iii, pp. 58ff., figs. 27-28. Patroni, *Ceramica antica nell'Italia meridionale*, pp. 65ff., fig. 40. Murray in *JHS*, xi(1890),225ff., pls. 6-7. Hoppin, *Handbook of Blackfigured Vases*, p. 452f. Swindler, *Ancient Painting*, p. 295, fig. 473. Zahn, in *Antike*, 7(1931), 88, fig. 10. Trendall, *Paestan Pottery*, pp. 56ff., pl. xv. Zahn and Trendall date Assteas and Python to the middle and third quarter of the fourth century, thus earlier than Rhinthon.

¹⁵ See Fig. 540, note 90 at the end of this chapter.

¹⁶ Overbeck-Mau, *Pompeji*, pp. 266 and 476.

¹⁷ Overbeck-Mau, *Pompeji*, pp. 249, 265-266. Della Corte, in *Notizie degli Scavi* (1929), p. 395f., fig. 23. Mau, *Pompeji*, pp. 255ff., figs. 129-130. Maiuri, in *Bolletino d'Arte*, ser. 2, viii(1928/9), 512f. (Fullonica Stephani). Maiuri, *Pompeii*, in *Musei e Monum. d'Italia*, No. 3, p. 125, pl. xv, fig. 72 (Via dell' Abbondanza). Maiuri, *Ercolano*, p. 56 (Casa del Tramezzo di Legno) and 68 (Casa dei Cervi); Maiuri, *Herculaneum*, Guide Book, n.d., p. 86, pl. xiv, fig. 24 (Casa del Tramezzo di Legno); *ibid.*, p. 94, pl. xxii, figs. 39-40 (Samnitic House); Maiuri, *Herculaneum* (1932), p. 56, fig. and pl. (Casa del Tramezzo di Legno), and p. 59, fig. (Samnitic House).

¹⁸ See the House on Abbondanza Street: Ippel, *Pompeji*, p. 51, fig. 47. Maiuri, *Pompeii* (1929), figs. pp. 98-99; Maiuri, *Pompeji* (1940), figs. on pp. 104, 105, and 107.

¹⁹ Bulle, *Untersuchungen*, pp. 110ff., pls. 23-25. Cf. Ch. XIII, Figs. 601-602.

²⁰ Leningrad, Hermitage, No. 1115 (1777). Romagnoli, *Nel Regno di Dioniso*, p. 23f., Fig. 26. Olivieri, *op.cit.*, p. 127f., fig. 3. Bieber, *Denkmäler*, p. 141f., No. 105, pl. lxxix. Trendall, *Paestan Pottery*, p. 37f., fig. 16. Hauser in F-R, ii, p. 261f., pl. 110,3. Catteruccia, *op.cit.*, p. 25f., No. 10, pl. ii.

²¹ On Atellan masks see Marx, in *Real-Enc.*, ii, s.v. Atellanae Fabulae, p. 1918f. Bethe, *Prolegomena*, pp. 297ff. Wüst, *op.cit.*, in *Real-Enc.*, xx(1941), p. 294f., has misunderstood my assertion, that we have here the forerunners of the typical Atellan masks, as if I had explained the Leningrad vase as an Atellan farce.

²² Leningrad, Hermitage, No. 1775. Bieber, *Denkmäler*, p. 140f., No. 102, pl. 77. Catteruccia, *op.cit.*, p. 19f., No. 2. Romagnoli, *Nel Regno di Dioniso*, p. 22, fig. 24. Radermacher, "Zur Geschichte der griechischen Komödie," in *Sitzungsberichte der Akad. d. Wiss. Wien*, Vol. 202 (1924/ 5), 17-19.

²³ Found in Bitonto, in Bari, No. 2970. Romagnoli, *Ausonia*, ii(1907),245ff. Bieber, *Denkmäler*, p. 141, No. 103, pl. 78. Catteruccia, *op.cit.*, p. 21, No. 4, pl. ii. Romagnoli, *Nel Regno di Dioniso*, p. 17f., fig. 18. A. B. Cook, *Zeus*, iii,1078f., fig. 864.

²⁴ Vatican Mus. No. 121. Gabrici, *Ausonia*, v(1910), p. 59f., fig. 1. Bieber, *Denkmäler*, p. 140, No. 101, pl. 76. Romagnoli, *Nel Regno di Dioniso*, p. 21., fig. 23. Zahn, in *Die Antike*, viii(1931),82ff., fig. 17; Zahn, in F-R, iii, pp. 182, 189-190, fig. 95. Catteruccia, *op.cit.*, p. 18f., No. 1, pl. i. Trendall, *Paestan Pottery*, p. 39, pl. ixc; Trendall, *Vasi Ita-*

lioti ed Etruschi a figure rosse, in *Vasi Antichi Dipinti del Vaticano*, I, Vasi Proto-Italioti, Pestani e Campani. Vasi Apuli fino a circa il 375 A.C., p. 27f., No. U19, pl. VII,6. Beare, *Roman Stage*, 2nd ed., 1955, pl. to p. 46. Rumpf, *Malerei und Zeichnung*, in *Handbuch der Archaeologie*, IV (1953),140f., pl. 45,5. A. B. Cook, *Zeus*, III,734f., fig. 534.

[25] *British Museum Catalogue of Vases*, IV,122, F 269. *British Museum Guide to the Exhibitions Illustrating Greek and Roman Life* (1908), pp. 52ff., fig. 33; 3rd ed. (1929), pp. 186ff., fig. 206. Bieber, *Denkmäler*, p. 141f., No. 104, fig. 126. Olivieri, *op.cit.*, p. 135, fig. 5. Pace, *Arte e civiltà della Sicilia antica*, III,328f., fig. 68. Pace, in *Dioniso*, VIII (1940), 72ff., fig. 3. Catteruccia, *op.cit.*, p. 26f., No. 11, pl. III.

[26] Rizzo, in *Röm.Mitt.*, XV(1900),268f., fig. 2. Bieber, *Denkmäler*, p. 143, No. 107, fig. 127. Catteruccia, *op.cit.*, p. 22f., No. 6, pl. I (ill. from photograph). Pace, *Arte e Civiltà della Sicilia*, II,472, fig. 342. Libertini, *Il Museo Biscari*, p. 175, No. 735, pl. 83.

[27] Tillyard, *The Hope Vases*, p. 117, No. 220, pl. 31. Catteruccia, *op.cit.*, p. 69, No. A, pl. V.

[28] Berlin No. 3046. Bieber, *Denkmäler*, p. 143, No. 106, pl. LXXX,1. Olivieri, *Frammenti della Commedia*, p. 156, fig. 7. Catteruccia, *op.cit.*, p. 23f., No. 7, pl. V. Romagnoli, *Nel Regno di Dioniso*, p. 29f., fig. 38.

[29] Lentini (Leontini), Palazzo comunale. Stephani, *Mon. Inst.*, IV(1844-48), pl. 12. *AdI* (1844), pp. 245ff. Rizzo, *Röm.Mitt.*, XV(1900),261ff. Bethe, *JdAI*, XV(1900),67f., figs. 6-7. Olivieri, *Frammenti della Commedia*, p. 158, fig. 8. Bieber, *Denkmäler*, p. 144f., No. 108, fig. 128. Webster, *CQ*, 42(1948),21. Catteruccia, *op.cit.*, p. 21f., No. 5, pl. III. Elena Zevi Fiorentini, in *Memorie della Pontificia Accademia Romana di Archeologia*, Serie III, Vol. VI, No. II (1942),39-52, pls. I-II, figs. 1-5. I owe the photograph (Fig. 488a) to Professor Rizzo.

[30] Museo teatrale della Scala in Milano, No. 12. Rizzo, *loc.cit.*, pl. VI; he suggested the Alcestis story. *Catalogue des antiquités de la Collection Théâtrale de Jules Sambon* (1911), p. 6, No. 33, pl. II. Bieber, *Denkmäler*, p. 144, No. 108, pl. 81. Catteruccia, *op.cit.*, p. 24f., No. 9, pl. II. Pace, *op.cit.*, II, 473, fig. 343. Fiorentini, *op.cit.*, p. 46 fig. 6.

[31] Found probably in Sant'Agata dei Goti, formerly in Coll. Raimone. Gerhard, *Antike Bildwerke*, I (1827-37), pl. 73. Romagnoli, *Nel regno di Dioniso*, p. 28f., fig. 36. Bieber, *Denkmäler*, p. 147f., No. 113, fig. 130. Catteruccia, *op.cit.*, p. 36f., No. 29, pl. XIV.

[32] *British Museum Catalogue of Vases*, IV, p. 74f., F 151. Romagnoli, in *Ausonia*, II(1907-8),166,172, fig. 24. Buschor, *Griechische Vasenmalerei* (second edition 1914), p. 215f., fig. 159. Bieber, *Denkmäler*, p. 145, No. 109, pl. 82. Romagnoli, *Nel regno di Dioniso*, p. 27f., fig. 35. Catteruccia, *op.cit.*, p. 38f., No. 25, pl. VI. Ch. Picard, in *Comptes rendus de l'Acad. des Inscr.* (1950), 273-276; he suggests the interpretation of Chiron departing for the hereafter (l'audelà).

[33] Bari, Museo Provinciale. Romagnoli, *Ausonia*, II(1907/8),251ff., figs. 6, 8-10. Bieber, *Denkmäler*, p. 145, No. 110, pl. 80,2. Pfuhl, *Malerei und Zeichnung*, II, p. 718; III, p. 361, fig. 805. Romagnoli, *Nel regno di Dioniso*, p. 24f., figs. 27-29. Catteruccia, *op.cit.*, p. 38f., No. 31, pl. VI. A. B. Cook, *Zeus*, III,738, fig. 535. Beazley, *Etruscan Vase-Painting*, pp. 39ff., discusses the many vases with the birth of Helen. See particularly the vase in Naples: Trendall, in *PBSR*, 20(1952), p. 17, No. 363, pl. XVIb.

[34] Berlin No. 3045, bought in Naples. Studniczka, in *JdAI*, XXVI(1911),93, fig. 28. Bieber, *Denkmäler*, p. 145f., No. 111, pl. 83,1. Romagnoli, *Nel regno di Dioniso*, p. 26, fig. 32. Catteruccia, *op.cit.*, p. 33, No. 24, pl. V.

[35] Museo di Villa Giulia, No. 50279. Gabrici, in *Ausonia*, V(1910),56-68, pl. III. Bieber, *Denkmäler*, p. 146f., No. 112, fig. 129. Rizzo, in *Röm.Mitt.*, XL(1925),217-239, pl. XV and supplementary pls. V-VII. Romagnoli, *Nel regno di Dioniso*, p. 26, fig. 33. Olivieri, *Frammenti della Commedia*, p. 155, fig. 6. Zahn, in F-R, III,194f., fig. 98, pl. 150,2; Zahn, in *Die Antike*, VII(1931),84ff., fig. 8. Hoppin, *A Handbook of Greek Blackfigured Vases*, p. 440f. Pfuhl, *Malerei und Zeichnung*, II,718f.; III,360, fig. 803. Trendall, *Paestan Pottery*, fig. 13, pl. VIa. CVA, Villa Giulia, III-IV, pl. 12; II, 1-4. Catteruccia, *op.cit.*, p. 37f., No. 30, pl. VII.

[36] Louvre, Salle K No. 523. *Encyclopédie Phot.*, III, fig. 37d. Wieseler, *AdI* (1859), p. 384f. *Mon.Inst.*, VI, pl. XXXV,2. Romagnoli, *Nel regno di Dioniso*, p. 25f., fig. 31. Pace, *Arte e civiltà della Sicilia ant.*, III, p. 324f., fig. 64. Pace, in *Dioniso*, VIII, 1940, pp. 73ff., fig. 5. Catteruccia, *op.cit.*, p. 35, No. 27, pl. VI. A. B. Cook, *Zeus*, III, pp. 291ff.

[37] Tischbein, *Vases du Cabinet Hamilton*, IV, pl. 57. Wieseler, *Theatergebäude*, pl. IX,4. Bieber, *Denkmäler*, p. 148, No. 114, fig. 131. Olivieri, *Frammenti della Commedia*, p. 166, fig. 12. Catteruccia, *op.cit.*, p. 64, No. 75, pl. XIV. Margaret Crosby, *Hesperia*, XXIV(1955),82f., fig. 2. She doubts my interpretation, because on an Attic vase of about 400 (her pl. 37) a man seated on a fish is rowing, and thus the story must be Athenian.

[38] Bulle, in *Festschrift für Loeb*, p. 37. Ducati, *Storia della Ceramica Graeca*, p. 450.

[39] Naples Mus. No. 3368. Romagnoli, *Nel Regno di Dioniso*, p. 18f., fig. 19. Catteruccia, *op.cit.*, p. 42, no. 35.

[40] Bari, Museo Provinciale, No. 4073. Zahn in *Die Antike*, VII(1931), p. 90f., figs. 12-13. Catteruccia, *op.cit.*, p. 55, No. 59, pl. X.

[41] Syracuse, Mus. No. 47039. Cultrera in *Dioniso*, V (1935-36),199ff., figs. 1-5. Horn in *Arch.Anz.* (1936), pp. 536ff., figs. 34-37. CVA, Siracusa, I, IV E, pl. 3,4. Libertini, *Bolletino d'Arte* (1950), p. 107, fig. 13. Catteruccia, *op.cit.*, p. 48f., No. 46, pl. XI.

[42] G. van Hoorn, *Choes and Anthesteria*, p. 183, No. 920 bis, fig. 411. Giglioli, *Archeologia Classica* 4(1952),98f., pl. XXVIII,2.

[43] *British Museum Catalogue of Vases*, IV,64, F 124.

[44] *British Museum Catalogue of Vases*, IV,73f. F 150. Rizzo, in *Dedalo*, VII(1926/7),411f. Trendall, *Paestan Pottery*, p. 39f., pl. IXd. CVA, British Museum, IV Ea, pl. 11, 1, a-b.

[45] Formerly Forman Collection, now in Boston, Museum of Fine Arts, No. 00.363. Bulle, in *Festschrift Loeb*, p. 31, fig. 19b. Catteruccia, *op.cit.*, p. 64f., No. 77, pl. XII. These authors did not realize that the vase is in Boston. Frances F. Jones, *The Theater in Ancient Art*, An Exhibition in the Art Museum, Princeton, 1952, No. 33.

[46] The fragment has a white wash. The lips are painted red.

[47] Collection Jatta in Ruvo, No. 901. Hauser, in F-R, II,261, pl. 110,2. Bieber, *Denkmäler*, p. 150, No. 120, pl. 84,2. Romagnoli, *Nel Regno di Dioniso*, p. 29, fig. 37. Catteruccia, *op.cit.*, p. 32, No. 23, pl. V. The explanation by Hauser as Kirke threatened by Odysseus and Elpenor is impossible, as Elpenor was still a pig, before Odysseus forced the sorceress to give him back his human form.

[48] Moscow, Mus. No. 735. Romagnoli, *Nel Regno di Dioniso*, p. 26f., fig. 34. Blavatski, *Moscow Museum Bulletin* (1930), p. 45, fig. 1. Blavatski, *History of Ancient Figured Pottery* (in Russian), p. 234 (ill.). Trendall, *Paestan Pottery*, p. 92, fig. 57. Catteruccia, *op.cit.*, p. 36, No. 28, pl. VI. The explanation by Blavatski of the slaves as warriors with shields or luggage and the return of Briseis to Agamemnon does not fit the picture.

[49] Crater in the Kunsthistorische Museum Vienna, Austria, No. 466 (formerly 714). Jahn, *Arch. Zeitung* (1855), p. 54f., and Wieseler, *ibid.*, pp. 88ff., pl. 78,3. Catteruccia, *op.cit.*, p. 53f., No. 54, pl. x.

[50] Jacobsthal, *Göttinger Vasen*, p. 26, No. 48, pl. xviii, Fig. 51. Catteruccia, *op.cit.*, p. 58f., No. 65, pl. xviii.

[51] Naples Mus., No. 118 333. D-R, p. 323, fig. 79. Fiechter, *Baugesch. Entw.*, p. 37, fig. 35. Catteruccia, *op.cit.*, p. 48, No. 45, pl. xiv. Webster, *CQ*, 42(1948),22.

[52] Berlin No. V. 3044. Bieber, *Denkmäler*, p. 148f., No. 116, pl. 84,1. Patroni, *Ceramica antica*, pp. 38ff., figs. 32-33. Rizzo, *Teatro di Siracusa*, p. 85f., fig. 36; Rizzo, in *Röm.Mitt.*, xl(1925),224f., figs. 4-5. Zahn in F-R, iii,178ff., figs. 93-94, pl. 150,2; Zahn, in *Die Antike*, vii(1931),70ff., figs. 1-3, excellent colored Plate 6. Olivieri, *Frammenti della Commedia*, pp. 160f., fig. 9. Trendall, *Paestan Pottery*, p. 26, pl. vb. Catteruccia, *op.cit.*, p. 43f., No. 38, pl. vii. On the reverse of this vase is the scene of Dionysus followed by a satyr.

[53] Overbeck-Mau, *Pompeji*, pp. 248, 334, 425. Thédenat, *Pompéi*, p. 71, fig. 17. Mau, *Pompeji*, p. 238, fig. 121. Mau-Kelsey, *Pompeii*, p. 255, fig. 120. Gisela Richter, *Ancient Furniture*, p. 143f., fig. 341. Pernice and Winter, *Die Hellenistische Kunst in Pompeji*, 5. *Tische . . . Altäre und Truhen* (1932), pp. 70ff., figs. 33-35, pls. 50-58.

[54] Formerly in the Collection Caputi in Ruvo. Heydemann, *Vase Caputi*, in 9. *Hallisches Winckelmanns-Program* (1884), pp. 3ff., pls. i-ii. Bieber, *Denkmäler*, p. 150f., No. 121, fig. 132. Romagnoli, *Nel Regno di Dioniso*, p. 16, fig. 16. Catteruccia, *op.cit.*, p. 41, No. 34, pl. xiv. The reverse of this vase has the scene of Heracles carrying the world, mocked by satyrs (above Fig. 43).

[55] Berlin No. F 3047. Romagnoli, in *Ausonia*, ii(1907), 164 and 169, fig. 21; Romagnoli, in *Nel Regno di Dioniso*, p. 16, fig. 17. Bieber, *Denkmäler*, p. 151, No. 122, pl. 86,1. Catteruccia, *op.cit.*, p. 51f., No. 50, pl. viii. G. von Lücken, *Greek Vase Paintings* (1921), pl. 59.

[56] Leningrad, Hermitage. Inv. No. 2074. Bieber, *Denkmäler*, p. 151f., No. 123, pl. 86,2. Catteruccia, *op.cit.*, p. 49f., No. 47, pl. viii. Margaret Crosby, *Hesperia*, xxiv(1955), 80f., pl. 36c. She compares it to an Attic vase (our Fig. 209) and explains it as men carrying a large cake baked on a spit.

[57] G. Richter, in *BMMA*, xxii(1927),56ff., fig. 1. Messerschmidt in *Röm.Mitt.*, 47(1932), pp. 134ff., fig. 4. His interpretation of the picture as a scene from Middle Comedy seems impossible to me, for the latter was already a comedy of manners, not a tragicomoedia. Trendall, *Frühitaliotische Vasen*, in *Bilder griechischer Vasen*, ed. Beazley and Jacobsthal, p. 25f., No. B 75, pl. 28b. Catteruccia, *op.cit.*, p. 50f., No. 48, pl. viii. Webster in *Festschrift Bernhard Schweitzer*, p. 260f. For the inscriptions see Beazley, *AJA* 56(1952),193ff., figs. 1-2, pl. 32.

[58] Berlin No. 3043. Bieber, *Denkmäler*, p. 152, No. 124, pl. 85,4. Olivieri, *Frammenti della Commedia*, p. 164f., fig. 11. Catteruccia, *op.cit.*, p. 43, No. 37, pl. ix.

[59] Leningrad, Hermitage, No. 1779. Hauser, in F-R, ii, 261, pl. 110,1. Bieber, *Denkmäler*, p. 148, No. 115, pl. 83,2. Pfuhl, *Malerei und Zeichnung*, ii,718; iii,361, fig. 804. Romagnoli, *Nel Regno di Dioniso*, p. 19, fig. 20. Pace, *Arte e civiltà della Sicilia antica*, iii, p. 329f., fig. 69. Catteruccia, *op.cit.*, p. 46f., No. 41, pl. viii.

[60] Louvre Room K No. 18. Wieseler, in *Arch. Zeitung* (1885), pp. 48ff., pl. 5,1. Catteruccia, *op.cit.*, p. 52f., No. 52. Webster, *CQ*, 42(1948),24, gives a different interpretation: marketing with a big basket.

[61] Boston, Museum of Fine Arts, AP 486, No. 03.831. Catteruccia, *op.cit.*, p. 59, No. 66 bis, pl. xi. Frances F. Jones, *op.cit.*, No. 31.

[62] *British Museum Catalogue of Vases*, iv, p. 97f., F 189.

Bethe, *JdAI*, xv(1900),73, fig. 11. Bieber, *Denkmäler*, p. 150, No. 119, pl. 85,2. Romagnoli, *Nel Regno di Dioniso*, p. 13, fig. 12. Trendall, *Paestan Pottery*, p. 70, pl. xxiid. *CVA*, British Museum, ii, iv, Ea, pl. 11,2. Catteruccia, *op.cit.*, p. 53, No. 53, pl. ix. Webster, *CQ*, 42(1948),24; he interprets it as a master leading his slave.

[63] Heidelberg Mus. No. U 8. Bieber, *Denkmäler*, p. 149, No. 117, pl. 85,3. Olivieri, *Frammenti della Commedia*, p. 162, fig. 10. Neutsch in *Die Welt der Griechen* (Heidelberg, 1948), p. 61, No. 13, fig. 32. Catteruccia, *op. cit.*, p. 57, No. 62, pl. ix.

[64] Bari, Museo Provinciale No. 2795. Romagnoli, in *Ausonia*, ii(1907/8),243ff., fig. 2; Romagnoli, *Nel Regno di Dioniso*, p. 11f., fig. 11. Bieber, *Denkmäler*, p. 149, No. 118, pl. 85,1. Catteruccia, *op.cit.*, p. 56, No. 60, pl. ix. Old men are excellently rendered and contrasted with their servants on fragmentary vases found near Gela and Manfria: Orlandini, *Bolletino d'Arte*, 4th Series, 38(1953), 155ff., figs. 1-4.

[65] This crater with gossiping women in Heidelberg U 6 was acquired in 1900 from Hartwig. Catteruccia, *op.cit.*, p. 59, No. 66. Neutsch, *Die Welt der Griechen* (1948), p. 61, No. 12.

[66] Vienna, Austria, Mus. No. 928. Very colorful: chiton white; mantle yellow with brown shading; face, arms, and legs flesh colored. Zahn, *Arch. Zeitung* (1855), p. 55, pl. 77,2. Laborde, *Coll. Lambert*, i,67. G. von Lücken, *Griechische Vasen*, pl. 120. Bulle, in *Festschrift für Loeb*, p. 34, fig. 24. Webster, *JHS*, 71(1951),224, No. 42.

[67] Langlotz, *Griechische Vasen in Würzburg* (1932), p. 147, No. 283a, pl. 239. Catteruccia, *op.cit.*, p. 66, No. 81. Zahn, in *Die Antike*, vii(1931),94f., fig. 14.

[68] Naples, Museo Nazionale, No. 1782. Romagnoli, *Nel Regno di Dioniso*, p. 7f., fig. 6. Bulle, *Festschrift Loeb*, p. 31f., fig. 20. Catteruccia, *op.cit.*, p. 60f. No. 68, pl. xii. Webster, *loc.cit.*, No. 43.

[69] Drago in *Iapigia*, vii(1936),377ff. Catteruccia, *op.cit.*, p. 66f., No. 85, pl. xii. Horn, in *Arch. Anz.*, 52(1937),443ff., fig. 34. Webster, *loc.cit.*, p. 223, No. 41.

[70] Bulle, *Festschrift Loeb*, p. 29f., fig. 18. Romagnoli, *Nel Regno di Dioniso*, p. 10, fig. 10. Catteruccia, *op.cit.*, p. 62, No. 71. Hedwig Kenner, in *CVA*, Vienna, Sammlung Matsch, pp. 25ff., pl. 18. Metropolitan Museum, No. 51.11.2. *BMMA* (October 1954), p. 64. Webster, *loc.cit.*, p. 223, No. 39, and p. 232. Very colorful; tights fleshcolored, tunic bluish white, mantle purple red.

[71] Boston Museum of Fine Arts, No. 13.93.

[72] *British Museum Catalogue of Vases*, iv, 225, F 543. Bulle, *Festschrift Loeb*, p. 29, figs. 11 and 17. *CVA*, British Mus., i, iv D c, pl. 2,2. Catteruccia, *op.cit.*, p. 63, No. 73. Webster, *loc.cit.*, No. 38. Mingazzini, *Archeologia Classica* 6(1954),294, pl. cxv,2.

[73] Louvre, Salle K, No. 244. Trendall, *Paestan Pottery*, p. 69, pl. xxii c. Catteruccia, *op.cit.*, p. 30, No. 17. On the other side of the crater are Dionysus and another small altar.

[74] See Bulle, *Festschrift Loeb*, p. 26, figs. 11a and 12. Webster, "Masks on Gnathia Vases," *JHS*, lxxi(1951), 222ff., figs. 1-5, pl. xlv.

[75] Bieber, *Denkmäler*, p. 139f., Nos. 98-100, pls. 75, 3-7; cf. p. 192, bibl. Catteruccia, *op.cit.*, pp. 75ff., pl. xiii, 1-3.

[76] Webster, *CQ*, xlii(1948),19ff.; Webster, *JHS*, lxxi (1951),229ff.; Webster, *Bulletin of the John Rylands Library*, xxxii(1949),111ff., and xxxvi(1954),563ff.

[77] Trendall, *Vasi Italioti . . . del Vaticano*, p. 64f., U. 49, pl. xix d-f. Trendall, *PBSR*, xx(1952),7 and 31f., No. 78, pl. ix b.

[78] Frances Jones, *Record of the Art Museum*, Princeton University, xi(1952),29ff., fig. 1; Jones, *The Theater in An-*

cient Art, An Exhibition, Princeton University, 1951-52, fig. 32.

[79] Trendall, *Paestan Pottery*, pl. xxib (Los Angeles) and c (Louvre).

[80] Trendall, *Vasi italioti . . . del Vaticano*, p. 33, U 18, pl. x. Trendall, *Paestan Pottery*, pls. xxiia-b and xxiiia. Catteruccia, *op.cit.*, p. 29, no. 15, illus. on title-page. See for a similar vase with a phlyax standing before Dionysus: Leroux, *Vases de Madrid*, p. 222, no. 386, pl. xlix.

[80a] Crater in Museo Eoliano, Lipari, Sicily, Inv. No. 927. Dionysus and two phlyakes watch a female tumbler; in two windows women (wearing white masks?) look down. Attributed to Assteas, ca. 350 B.C. Bernabo Brea, *Il Castello di Lipari*, pl. 79 (in color). Trendall, *Catalogue of Phlyakes Vases*, London (1959), No. 74, pl. iiie.

[81] *British Museum Catalogue of Vases*, iv,97, F 188. Trendall, *Paestan Pottery*, p. 38, fig. 15. *CVA*, British Museum 2, iv Ea, pls. 2-3. Catteruccia, *op.cit.*, p. 29, No. 15, pl. iv. A. B. Cook, *Zeus*, iii,2, p. 1000, fig. 810.

[82] Trendall, *PBSR*, p. 5 and 27f., No. 43, pl. v c. Ruvo, Collection Jatta No. 1402. Romagnoli, *Nel Regno di Dioniso*, p. 1, fig. in frontispiece, cf. p. 20. Jatta, in *Iapigia*, iii(1932), 253ff., figs. 36-37. Catteruccia, *op.cit.*, p. 28, No. 13, pl. iv. Next to the satyr dances a nude old woman with grotesque features.

[83] Cf. the pictures from the back of the Assteas vase in Madrid, Alvarez-Ossorio, *op.cit.*, pl. xxii,2 and in Berlin, Hoppin, *Handbook of Blackfigured Vases*, 347b and 439b: Dionysus riding on a panther among his thiasus. Picture from the back of the Assteas crater in Berlin (Fig. 508), see note 52. Patroni, *op.cit.*, p. 43, fig. 33. Hoppin, *op.cit.*, p. 436f. Rizzo, in *Röm.Mitt.*, xl(1925),225, fig. 5. Zahn, in F-R, iii,178f., fig. 94; Zahn, in *Die Antike*, vii(1931),73, fig. 3: Dionysus and satyr. Trendall, *Paestan Pottery*, p. 39f., fig. ixa, Madrid; ixb, Oxford, Ashmolean Museum. A phlyax mask hangs over Papposilenus playing the flute for Dionysus

on a vase in Sydney: Nicholson, collection in the University Museum, *Handbook*, sec. ed., pl. 11. Trendall, *op.cit.*, p. 68, pl. xxd. See also Trendall, p. 69f., pls. xxiia-b and xxiiia; and next note.

[84] Trendall, *Paestan Pottery*, p. 62, No. 113, pls. xviii and xixc, Supplement No. 148; Trendall, *Vasi italioti . . . del Vaticano*, p. 29f., No. ADl, pl. viii. Greifenhagen, *Griech. Vasen auf Bildnissen*, p. 205f., pls. i-ii. Zahn, in F-R, iii, pp. 183 and 192f., figs. 96-97.

[85] Pickard-Cambridge, *Festivals*, p. 200, fig. 91a.

[86] Marx, in *Real-Enc.*, ii, 1914-1921, s.v. Atellanae fabulae. Dieterich, *Pulcinella*, pp. 84ff. Cornford, *The Origin of Attic Comedy*, p. 183f. Little, *AJA*, xlii(1938),129f.

[87] *British Museum Catalogue of Vases*, iv,113, F 233. Bieber, *Denkmäler*, p. 152f., No. 125, fig. 133. Anti, *Monumenti dei Lincei* 26(1920),527ff., fig. 12. Anti considers the statuette of Heracles to be a copy of the Heracles of Polyclitus. Catteruccia, *op.cit.*, p. 62, No. 72, pl. x. *CVA*, iv, Ea, pl. xi,17, fig. 18a-b. Romagnoli, *Nel Regno di Dioniso*, p. 7, fig. 5.

[88] Bieber, *Denkmäler*, p. 142 text to No. 105; Bieber, in *Real-Enc.*, xiv,2088ff. Zahn, in F-R, iii,183f. and 191, text to pl. 150,2.

[89] D-R, pp. 311ff. Fiechter, *Baugesch.Entw.*, pp. 37ff., figs. 28-41. Trendall, *Paestan Pottery*, p. 26f., pls. 6-7, and in his forthcoming book on the phlyakes vases.

[90] Drerup, in *Ath.Mitt.*, xxvi(1901),9ff.,25ff. Bulle, *Untersuchungen*, pp. 159ff., pl. 47, figs. 3-4. Rizzo, *Il teatro di Siracusa*, pp. 77ff. Anti, *Teatro antico di Siracusa* (1948), pp. 73ff., fig. 11. Rizzo and Anti do not believe that this wooden stage was built especially for the Syracusan Rhinthon, but agree that his hilarotragedies were performed on it.

[91] Stillwell, *Corinth*, II, *The Theater*, pp. 78ff., 135, pl. va.

[92] Bethe, *Prolegomena*, pp. 293ff., was the first to emphasize this importance of the wooden southern Italian stage.

NOTES TO CHAPTER XI. THE ROMAN PLAYS AT THE TIME OF THE REPUBLIC

[1] Cf. for this chapter in general: J. W. Duff, *A Literary History of Rome from the Origins to the Close of the Golden Age²* (1910), pp. 156ff. Teuffel-Kroll, *Geschichte der römischen Literatur⁷* (1920). Schanz, *Geschichte der römischen Literatur⁸* (1927). Bayet, *Littérature latine* (1934). W. Beare, "The Italian Origin of Latin Drama," *Hermathena*, xxiv(1939),30-53; Beare, *The Roman Stage, A Short History of Latin Drama in the Time of the Republic* (1950; second edn., 1955). Habel in *Real-Enc.*, Supplement, Vol. v, pp. 608ff., s.v. Ludi publici. M. Hadas, *A History of Latin Literature* (1952), pp. 15ff., Chs. ii, iii. Ribbeck, *Scaenicae Romanorum poesis Fragmenta³* (1897-98). E. Paratore, *Storia del Teatro Latino* (1957).

[2] Bayet, *op.cit.*, pp. 30ff., 40ff. Wissowa, in *Real-Enc.*, vi, p. 2222, s.v., Fescennini versus.

[3] Weege, *Etruskische Malerei*, supplementary, pl. i; pls. 3-6, 14, 19, 21, 27, 31-33, 36-39, 45, 68, 74-75, 86-90; Weege, *JdAI*, xxxi(1916),105ff., figs. 5, 7-9, pls. 11-12. Ducati, *Storia dell'Arte etrusca*, ii, pls. 77, 86-87, 89; cf. i, pp. 224 and 235f. Ducati in *Dioniso*, i(1929),170-171, figs. 1-2. Prentice Duell, "The Tomba del Triclinio at Tarquinia," *MAAR*, vi(1927),19ff., pls. 2-3. Pallottino, *Etruscan Painting* (1952), pp. 38f., 43ff., 65f., 68f., 73ff. (colored reproductions). For athletic games see Weege, *Etruskische Malerei*, pls. 91-97, and supplementary pl. ii; Weege, *JdAI*, xxxi(1916),122ff., supplementary plates 1-2 and pl. 8. Ducati, *op.cit.*, pls. 78, 84-85, 133-134. Pallottino, *op.cit.*, p. 38f. Dances on cinerary urns: Ducati, *op.cit.*, pl. 24, fig. 79,

pls. 114-115. Stryk, *Etruskische Kammergräber*, p. 132f. Gladiators: Körte, *Urne etrusche*, iii, pl. 128.

[4] Weege, *op.cit.*, pls. 90, 94-95. Ducati, *op.cit.*, i,225f.; ii, pl. 79. F. Poulsen, *Etruscan Tomb Painting*, p. 12f., figs. 4-6. Altheim, *Archiv für Religious-Wissenschaft*, xxvii (1929),35ff., pl. i. Pallattino, *op.cit.*, p. 40f. G. Becatti e F. Magi, *La Pittura Etrusca, Tarquinii*, 1-42, figs. 10-12, pls. i, v, vii, viii, x, xi, xv, xvi.

[5] Ducati, *op.cit.*, pp. 415ff., pls. 184, No. 467; p. 435f., pl. 200, No. 503 (terracotta mask from Orvieto). Messerschmidt, *Röm.Mitt.* 45(1930), pl. 57f. Giglioli, *L'Arte Etrusca*, pls. 258, 1, 2, 4 and 330. Pallottino, *op.cit.*, pp. 115ff. Our Fig. 545 is in Rome, Villa Giulia.

[6] Lafaye, in Daremberg-Saglio, *Dictionnaire des Antiquités grecques et romaines*, s.v. Satura. Kroll in *Real-Enc.*, s.v. Satura, second series, Vol. ii, A, pp. 192ff. He denies the existence of a dramatic satura. W. Beare, *The Roman Stage*, p. 13f., with note on Livy, vii,2.

[7] Weege, *Etruskische Malerei*, supplementary pl. ii, and in *JdAI*, xxxi(1916),122ff., supplementary pls. 1-2. Poulsen, *Etruscan Tomb Painting*, p. 24f., fig. 19. Beare, *op.cit.*, fig. opposite p. 10.

[8] E. Marx, in *Real-Enc.*, ii,2, pp. 1914-1921, s.v. Atellanae fabulae, especially p. 1918f.

[9] Ch. X, note 87.

[10] Ch. X, note 21.

[11] Berlin No. 4715. Robert, *Masken*, p. 83f., figs. 104-105. Bieber, *Skenika*, 75. *BerlWPr*, p. 22f., fig. 15. Verpus is a

castrated man in Juvenal and Martial, thus a *virgus* or male *virgo*. See Beare, *op.cit.*, p. 20. A similar statuette with youthful mask on the seat: Breccia, *Alexandrea at Aegyptum*, p. 252, fig. 153.

[12] Terracotta statuettes in Naples, Nos. 22248-9, found in Pompeii. Ruesch, *Guida del Museo di Napoli*, Nos. 446-7. Rohden, *Terrakotten von Pompeji*, pp. 22, 46f., pl. XXXV. Déonna, *Les Statues de Terre cuites dans l'Antiquité*, p. 203, figs. 18-19. Alda Levi, *Catalogo delle terrecotte del Museo di Napoli*, p. 202f., No. 872, pl. XIV; 2/3 lifesize, H. 1.13 m. For the arrangement of the pallium see L. Wilson, *The Clothing of the Ancient Romans* (1938), pp. 78ff., figs. 49-51 and 148ff., Fig. 102.

[13] Fig. 550: Vagn Poulsen, *Les portraits romaines* I, no. 77, pls. 135-137. Arndt-Bruckman, *Porträts*, pls. 698-700. Wilson, *Toga*, fig. 29. West, *op.cit.*, I, p. 197, pl. 51, fig. 225.

[14] Terracotta statuettes from Canino in the British Museum, *Catalogue of Terracottas*, p. 342f., D 223-227. The *Catalogue* calls them actors of the palliata and explains them as being a parasite, a miser, and a thief or money lender. Allardyce Nicoll, *The Development of the Theater*, p. 78, figs. 68-69; Nicoll, *Masks, Mimes, and Miracles* (1931), p. 49, fig. 36, names British Museum D 224 a "mimic fool." Similar in Ficoroni, *De Larvis Scenicis*, pl. IX. *cis*, pl. IX.

[15] Cf. Wilson, *op.cit.*, pp. 36ff., and 87ff.

[16] George E. Duckworth, *The Nature of Roman Comedy, A Study in Popular Entertainment* (1952), pp. 40ff. W. Beare, *The Roman Stage, A Short History of Latin Drama in the Time of the Republic* (1955), pp. 23ff.

[17] Cf. Leo, *Plautinische Forschungen*, 2nd ed. (1912), pp. 82ff. Little, "Plautus and Popular Drama," in *Harvard Studies in Classical Philology*, XLIX(1938),209ff. Beare, *The Roman Stage*, pp. 35ff. Duckworth, *op.cit.*, pp. 49ff.

[18] The bronze statuettes of master and slave were bought in 1917, Metropolitan Museum, Inv. Nos. 17.229.28 and 17.230.28. The bronze statuette in Cassel: Bieber, *Skulpturen und Bronzen in Cassel*, p. 74, No. 238, pl. 45. The statuette in Baltimore: Inv. 54.746. Dorothy Hill, *Catalogue of Classical Bronze Sculpture in the Walters Art Gallery*, p. 71, No. 150, pl. 32.

[19] Vatican, Galleria dei Candelabri, Nos. 60, 71. Lippold, *Skulpturen des Vaticans*, III,2, pp. 322f., 329f., pl. 148. British Museum, *Catalogue of Sculpture*, III, p. 166, No. 1767. Both in Bieber, *Denkmäler*, p. 166, Nos. 151-152, pl. 99. See our Figs. 406-413 in Ch. VIII.

[20] See Ch. X, Fig. 504, note 47.

[21] Ch. X, note 24. T. B. L. Webster, *Studies in Greek Comedy*, pp. 87-97, assumes as the original of *Amphitruo* an unknown Greek Middle Comedy written soon after 330 B.C., thus before the time of Menander as well as of Rhinthon. The originality of Plautus is underestimated by Webster. See in contrast: Beare, *The Roman Stage*, pp. 56-59, and Duckworth, *op.cit.*, p. 394: "Plautus' own contributions to the genre . . . should not be underestimated."

[22] Cf. Eduard Fränkel, *Plautinisches in Plautus* (1922). The *Captivi* was produced in 189 B.C. at the Ludi Romani. Wellesley, "The Production Date of Plautus' *Captivi*," *AJP*, LXXVI(1955), 298-305.

[23] Beare, *op.cit.*, pp. 209-222.

[24] On dramatic performances in the time of Plautus and Terence, see Lily Ross Taylor, in *Transactions of the American Philological Association*, LXVIII(1937),284ff. Beare, *op.cit.*, p. 152f.

[25] For Terence see Gilbert Norwood, *The Art of Terence* (1923) and recently Duckworth, *op.cit.*, pp. 56ff., and Beare, *op.cit.*, pp. 81ff., with a good explanation of contaminatio on pp. 300-303.

[26] K. E. Weston, "The Illustrated Terence Manuscripts," in *Harvard Studies of Classical Philology*, XIV(1903),37ff. *Terenti Codex Ambrosianus* H. 75, Praefatus E. Bethe, ed., de Vries, 1903. Codex Parisinus 7899, Manuscrit Latin de la Bibliothèque nationale. Omont, *Comédies de Terence*, Bibliothèque nationale (1907). J. von Wageningen, *Album Terentianum* (1790). *Codex Vaticanus Latinus* 3868, praef. G. Jachmus, ed. Ehrle (1908). G. Jachmann, *Geschichte des Terenztextes* (1923/24), p. 12f. (Rektoratsprogramm). Robert, *Masken*, pp. 87ff., figs. 107-124. Bieber, *Denkmäler*, pp. 170ff., Nos. 179-182, figs. 137-140. L. Webber Jones, "The Archetypes of the Terence Miniature" in *Art Bulletin*, X(1927),103ff. L. W. Jones and C. R. Morey, *The Miniatures of the Manuscripts of Terence Prior to the Thirteenth Century* (1931). Jones and Morey give reasons against the dependence of the miniatures on actual stage representations, pp. 42ff., 113ff., 195ff., 203ff. I cannot see, however, how a purely literary creation based on reading could give to all characters, in most cases, the right theatrical masks, garments, and outfits. See particularly Robert, *Masken*. Cf. also C. Fensterbusch in *Bursians Jahresberichte*, No. 253, 1936, pp. 44ff. Duckworth, *The Nature of Roman Comedy* illustrates his book with Terentian miniatures.

[27] *Terentius Afer Codex Vaticanus Latinus*, 3868, pls. 35 and 65. K. Weitzmann, *Illustrations in Roll and Codex, A Study of the Origin and Method of Text Illustrations* (1947), pp. 73, 87, 109f., 158f., figs. 59, 69, 95. Cf. also *Codex Latinus*, Paris 7899, figs. 150 and 153.

[28] C. Saunders, *Costume in Roman Comedy* (1909). Beare, *op.cit.*, pp. 173ff. A good example of a comic actor in a pallium is a marble statuette in Herculaneum, found in Insula IV 1-2 (plan in Maiuri *Ercolano*, p. 27, fig. 3), in glass case of the Atrium. An old man with bald pate is holding a scroll, like the advocati (lawyers) in Terence's *Phormio*, vv. 446ff. See also Bieber, "Romani Palliati," *Proceedings, American Philosophical Society* 103, 1959, pp. 381ff., figs. 7-8.

[29] Donatus, *De Comoedia*, VI, 3. Kaibel, *Gr. Com. Fragm.*, I, p. 68f. Saunders, "The Introduction of Masks on the Roman Stage," *AJP*, XXXII(1911),58-73. Gow, "The Use of Masks in Roman Comedy," in *Journal of Roman Studies*, II(1912),65ff. Beare, *op.cit.*, pp. 182ff. and 293ff. Duckworth, *The Nature of Roman Comedy*, pp. 92ff.

[30] Naples, Nos. 6619 and 6633. Cf. Ruesch, *Guida di Napoli*, p. 166, No. 559. Schreiber, *Hellenistische Reliefbilder*, pl. 99 (our Figs. 562 and 563). Pl. 98 has a similar combination of comic masks in high relief on one, and tragic masks in low relief on the other side. The preference for comedy shows in the fact that the comic masks are in high relief on the front, the tragic in low relief in the back. Amelung, *Skulpturen des vatikanischen Museums*, I, p. 376, Museo Chiaramonti, No. 106, pl. 39. Robert, *Masken*, p. 7f., fig. 14. Bieber, *Denkmäler*, p. 162, Nos. 138-139, pl. 94. Pickard-Cambridge, *Festivals*, p. 210, figs. 159-160. Webster, in *Bulletin of the John Ryland Library*, 32(1949/50), p. 15. He sees in the mask behind the delicate youth not a satyr but a "wavy-haired boy." For the decoration with such masks in the Casa degli Amorini Dorati see Sogliano, *Notizie degli Scavi* (1907), pp. 549ff., figs. 1-5, 8, 10-12, 19, 21, 22, 25, 26, 28, 29.

[31] Beare, *The Roman Stage*, pp. 89f., 94f.

[32] Bieber, *Skulpturen und Bronzen in Cassel*, p. 45, No. 88, pl. XXVIII.

[33] Mus. No. 9991. Ruesch, *Guida*, p. 57, No. 179. Bieber-Rodenwaldt, in *JdAI*, XXVI(1911),14, fig. 6. Pernice in Winter, *Hellenistische Kunst in Pompeji*, VI(1938), *Pavimente und Mosaiken*, p. 158f., pl. 59. See also the similar garland with masks around the mosaic with doves, *ibid.*, p. 164, pl. 64.

[34] Naples, No. 6634. Ruesch, *Guida*, p. 168, Nos. 571-574; p. 166 on similar oscilli. Bieber, *Skenika*, p. 10, fig. 5.

[35] Niccolini, *Le Case ed i Monumenti di Pompei*, IV,1, pl. XXXV,3-4. Bieber, *Skenika*, p. 13, Fig. 8; Bieber, *Denkmäler*, p. 12, Nos. 65-66, pl. 65. Pickard-Cambridge, *Festivals*, p. 187, figs. 58-59, 62-63.

[36] Found in Pompeii, in Naples, No. 6621. Ruesch, *Guida*, p. 551, No. 560. Bieber, *Denkmäler*, p. 122f., No. 61, pl. 63,1. Pickard-Cambridge, *Festivals*, p. 187, fig. 60.

[37] Bieber, *Denkmäler*, p. 123, No. 62, pl. 64,1. Pickard-Cambridge, *Festivals*, p. 187, fig. 61.

[38] Robert, in *Archäologische Zeitung*, XXVI(1878),13ff., pl. 3; Robert, *Archäologische Hermeneutik*, p. 196f., fig. 152. Pickard-Cambridge, *Festivals*, p. 189, fig. 71. Other painted mask groups in Robert, *Arch. Zeitung*, *loc.cit.*, pls. 4-5.

[39] Naples, Mus. Nos. 6631 and 6638 (our Fig. 572). Ruesch, *Guida*, p. 166f., Nos. 562 and 564.

[40] Mariani, in *Bulletino comunale Romano* (1902), pp. 20ff. Mustilli, *Il Museo Mussolini*, p. 51f., Nos. 8-11, pls. XXXV,146; XXXVI,148.

[41] Museo di Napoli, No. 9994. Ruesch, *Guida*, No. 182.

Mau, *Pompeji*, p. 275, fig. 142; sec. ed., p. 303, fig. 158. Leonhard, *Mosaikstudien zur Casa del Fauno* in Pompeji, p. 3. Bieber, *Denkmäler*, p. 112, fig. 117; p. 124, No. 68. Bieber, in *Röm.Mitt.*, 60/61(1953/54), pp. 102, pl. 35,1.

[42] Curtius, *Die Wandmalerei Pompejis*, p. 83, fig. 57; cp. the whole walls, figs. 56, 58, 59. Phillies Williams Lehmann, *Wallpaintings from Boscoreale*, pp. 19ff., figs. 17-18.

[43] Ruesch, *Guida*, p. 167, Nos. 564-565.

[44] Mus., No. 6637. Cf. Ruesch, *Guida*, p. 168, Nos. 571-574.

[45] British Museum, *Catalogue of Sculpture*, III, p. 375, No. 2454, fig. 58.

[46] Cf. Ch. VIII, notes 107-112. Beare, *op.cit.*, pp. 139ff.

[47] Bulle, *Festschrift für Loeb*, p. 28, figs. 14-16. Cf. Leroux, *Vases Grecques et Italo-Grecs du Musée archéologique de Madrid*, p. 308f., No. 596, pl. LIV; here another woman, walking on her arms, is holding a small ball in her hand.

[48] Beare, *op.cit.*, pp. 133ff.

[49] Beare, *op.cit.*, pp. 118ff., 254ff.

NOTES TO CHAPTER XII. THE ART OF ACTING AT ROME

[1] B. Warnecke, "Gebärdenspiel und Mimik der römischen Schauspieler," in *NJb*, XXV(1910),580ff. *Idem* in *Real-Enc.*, VIII,2116ff., *s.v.* Histrio. Navarre, in Daremberg-Saglio, *Dictionnaire des antiquités*, III,210ff., *s.v.* Histrio. Gow, in *JRS*, II(1912),72.

[2] Warnecke, "Die bürgerliche Stellung der Schauspieler im alten Rom" in *NJb*, XXXIII(1914),95ff.

[3] Catherine Saunders, *Costume in Roman Comedy*, 1909. G. E. Duckworth, *The Nature of Roman Comedy*, pp. 88-94, "Costume and Mask."

[4] Bronze statuette in the Boston Museum of Fine Arts M 1704.H. without base, 0.09; with base 0.105. Bluish color like many bronzes from Herculaneum.

[5] I owe the photograph for Fig. 581 to Eduard Schmidt, who took the photograph when the statuette was offered for sale in Munich.

[6] Terracotta lamp in the Antiquario of the Museo Nazionale Romano delle Terme in Rome, Inv. No. 62462. Messerschmidt in *Röm.Mitt.*, 45(1930),182ff., pls. 63-4. The lamp has black varnish, and details of the figures are in red.

[7] Marble statuette in Villa Albani, No. 647. Arndt-Amelung, No. 4135. The head does not belong and the hand with mask is modern.

[8] Constantinople (Istanbul) Museum, No. 1768. Mendel, *Catalogue des Sculptures*, Constantinople, II,283, No. 560. Traces of red on face and mantle, blue for the beard on the mouthpiece of the mask.

[9] British Museum, Catalogue of Bronzes, p. 130, No. 742. Cf. for similarly constructed handles: Ducati, *Storia del Arte Etrusca*, I, 440ff.; II, pls. 207, 238, 240, Nos. 513, 583, 585. A. della Seta, *Museo di Villa Giulia*, I,399ff., pl. LX. Gisela Richter, Metropolitan Museum of Art, *Catalogue of Bronzes*, pp. 77f. Nos. 122-124; figs. on p. 79, and *Handbook of the Etruscan Collection*, p. 51f., figs. 155-6. Dorothy Hill in *Studi etruschi*, XI(1937),121ff., pls. XIV, XVI, 3. The name Etruscan cistae ought to be dropped for these receptacles found in Latin territory, probably freed from Etruscan domination at the same time as Rome, although in both Rome and Praeneste Etruscan influence continued for a long time. The date of all cistae to me seems later than the fifth, and of most, later than the fourth centuries.

[10] Verona, Museo lapidaria. Dütschke, *Antike Bildwerke in Oberitalien*, IV,203, No. 462. Reisch, *Griechische Weih-*

geschenke, p. 142. Arndt-Amelung, No. 3. Schreiber, *Brunnenreliefs Grimani*, p. 96, No. 66; and *Hellenistische Reliefbilder*, pl. LXXXV.

[11] D-R, pp. 328ff., figs. 82-3. Puchstein, *Die griech. Bühne*, p. 26f., fig. 4. Rhoden-Winnefeld, *Architektonische Tonreliefs der Kaiserzeit*, p. 143f., figs. 266-267. Fiechter, *Baugesch.Entw.*, p. 101, fig. 96. Pickard-Cambridge, *Theatre of Dionysos*, p. 219f., figs. 78-79.

[12] Lippold, *Die Skulpturen des Vat. Mus.*, III,2, pp. 322f., No. 60; 329f., No. 71, pl. 148.

[13] Rizzo, in *JOAI*, VIII(1905),203ff., pl. v. Rhoden-Winnefeld, *op.cit.*, pp. 143ff., 280, pl. 81. Bieber, *Skenika*, *BerlWPr* (75), pp. 15ff., fig. 9; and *Denkmäler*, pp. 111ff., No. 46, fig. 109, pl. 56. Fiechter, *Baugesch.Entw.*, p. 101, fig. 97. Pickard-Cambridge, *Theatre of Dionysos*, p. 220, fig. 80; and *Festivals*, p. 186, fig. 57.

[14] Otto Jahn, in *Abh. Münchener Akad.*, VIII(1858),231ff., pl. IV. Samter, in *Röm.Mitt.*, VIII(1893),105ff.,119f., No. 4. Hülsen, *ibid.*, pp. 145ff. Bendinelli, in Rizzo, *Monumenti della Pittura in Italia* (Roma, Sezione III), Fasc. v, p. 15f., pl. VIII,3. Length of the frieze 0.95, height, 0.18 m. The date is probably the late first century B.C.

[15] Lateran, Mus. No. 1063. Visconti, *AdI* (1866), pp. 312ff. *Mon.Inst.*, VIII,28,3. Maximilian Mayer in Roscher, II,1570f., fig. 18. A. B. Cook, *Zeus*, III,934f., fig. 779. Nogara, *Le Nozze Aldobrandini e altre Pitture antiche*, p. 63ff., fig. 2, pl. XLVA, Amelung-Helbig. *Führer durch Rom*, 3rd ed., No. 1239. Bieber, *Skenika*, pp. 17ff., fig. 11.

[16] Mus. No. 9563. Ruesch, *Guida del Museo di Napoli*, p. 307, No. 1306. Carl Robert, *Kentaurenkampf und Tragödienszene*, 22. *HallWPr* (1898), pp. 14ff., pl. II. Robert believed the original of the painting to be a votive tablet of the choregus for the victory with Euripides *Hippolytus* in 428 B.C. This is, for reasons of style and costume, quite impossible. Bieber, *Skenika*, pp. 14ff. and *Denkmäler*, p. 112f., fig. 110, No. 47. Pickard-Cambridge, *Festivals*, p. 189, fig. 70.

[17] Bulle in *Festschrift für Loeb*, pp. 37ff., figs. 27 and 27 a-b. Bieber, in *Real-Enc.*, XIV, *s.v.* Maske, p. 2082f. Cf. Ch. VII, p. 84.

[18] Ruesch, *Guida del Museo di Napoli*, No. 929. Arndt, pls. 457-458. Hekler, *Bildniskunst*, p. XXIXf., No. 130. Kluge

and Lehmann-Hartleben, *Antike Grossbronzen*, II,4, fig. 1. Bieber, *Denkmäler*, p. 177f. No. 190, pl. 109. Goethert, *Zur Kunst der römischen Republik*, p. 23f. Brendel, in *Die Antike* (1933),p. 138f. Curtius, in *Röm.Mit.*, 50(1935), p. 302, note 2. Eugenie Sellers Strong, in *Cambridge Ancient History*, vol. of plates, IV,162b. F. Poulsen, "Probleme der römischen Ikonographie" in *Archaeologisk-Kunsthistorische Meddelelser*, II,1(1937), p. 22, No. 4, fig. 49. Vessberg, *Studien zur Kunstgeschichte der römischen Republik*, p. 228f. West, *Römische Porträtplastik*, I, 44f., pl. IX, fig. 30. Schweitzer, *Bildniskunst der römischen Republik*, pp. 79ff., figs. 99 and 103. Paribeni, *Il Ritratto nell'Arte Antica*, pl. 98.

[19] Cf. Robert, "Pantomimen im griechischen Orient," in *Hermes*, 45(1930),106ff. Wüst, in *Real-Enc.*, XV,2(1938), 1727ff., and *ibid.*, XVIII,3(1949), ed. Kroll-Ziegler, pp. 833-869.

[20] Mus. No. 1128. Two of four small pictures on the upper left wall. Lessing-Mau, *Wand und Deckenschmuck eines Hauses bei der Farnesina*, pl. 7. *Mon.Inst.*, XII,8, Nos. 4-5 and 22, Nos. 2-3; our Fig. 593 is the same as 22, No. 2. Helbig-Amelung, *Führer durch Rom*, 3rd ed., p. 209, No. 1479. Birt, *Buchrolle*, p. 141, fig. 78.

[21] Naples, Mus. No. 12733. I owe the photograph for Fig. 594 to the kindness of Professor Amadeo Maiuri.

[22] U. von Wilamowitz-Möllendorf, "Der Timotheos-Papyrus, gefunden bei Abusir, 1902," in *Wissenschaftliche Veröffentlichungen der deutschen Orientgesellschaft*, Heft 3 (1903), p. 10f. and *idem, Timotheos, Die Perser*, p. 27, lines 241-248, pp. 55ff.

NOTES TO CHAPTER XIII. THE DEVELOPMENT OF THE THEATER BUILDING
DURING THE REPUBLICAN PERIOD

[1] See Ch. XI, note 7.

[2] The mistaken idea that the public had to listen to the plays standing, has been refuted by Beare, *The Roman Stage* (1955), pp. 231-237; and A. Rumpf, in *Mitteilungen des Deutschen Archaeologischen Instituts*, III(1950),40ff.

[3] The phlyakes stage of Syracuse discovered by Drerup (*Ath.Mitt.*, XXVI[1902],9ff,26ff.) was denied by Rizzo (*Il Teatro Greco di Siracusa*, pp. 77ff.) who considered the traces to be a channel for the curtain. Bulle (*Untersuchungen*, pp. 152, 159ff., pl. 47, figs. 3-4) has, however, proved that there was a stage for the phlyakes plays. He dates it in the same period as the proskenion, after 238 B.C. See Anti, *Guida del Teatro antico di Siracusa* (1948), pp. 79ff.

[4] Puchstein, *Die griechische Bühne*, pp. 110ff., figs. 31-33. Hittorf and Zanth, *Recueil des monuments de Ségeste*, pls. 7-10. Strack, *Theatergebäude*, pls. 1 and VI,6. Bulle, *Untersuchungen*, pp. 110ff., pls. 19-32. Bieber, *Denkmäler*, p. 50f., No. 12, figs. 54-55, pl. 22. Arias, *Il Teatro Greco fuori di Atene*, pp. 143ff., figs. 95-98. Pace, *Arte e artisti della Sicilia antica*, II,314ff., figs. 275-277. Pierro Marconi, *Dioniso*, I(1929),8-14. A. von Gerkan, *Theater von Priene*, p. 106; and in *Festschrift Andreas Rumpf* (1950), pp. 82-92, fig. 5.

[5] Strack, *op.cit.*, pl. VI. Puchstein, *op.cit.*, pp. 117ff., figs. 34-36. Bulle, *op.cit.*, pp. 131ff., pls. 33-41. Pace, *op.cit.*, II, 318ff., fig. 279. Gerkan, in *Festschrift Rumpf*, pp. 88ff., fig. 6. Arias, *op.cit.*, p. 149f.

[6] Bulle, *op.cit.*, p. 130f. Marconi, *Notizie degli Scavi*, 1929, pp. 295ff., pls. XIV-XV. Bieber in *Gnomon*, 8(1932),474. Professor Meritt and Professor Rudolf Herzog gave me their opinions orally.

[7] Bulle, *op.cit.*, pp. 126f., 147ff. Gerkan, *Festschrift Andreas Rumpf*, p. 86f.

[8] Stuart Jones, *Catalogue of Sculptures of the Museo Capitolino*, pp. 22 and 25, Cortile Nos. 5 and 23, pl. 2, Phot. Anderson 1776-1777.

[9] Mazois, *Les Ruines de Pompéi*, IV,61-70, pls. XXX-XXXIV. Overbeck-Mau, *Pompeji*, 4th ed., pp. 156ff., figs. 88-94. Mau, *Pompeji*, 2nd ed. (1908), pp. 129ff., figs. 64-65. Mau-Kelsey, *Pompeii*, pp. 141ff., map III, figs. 64-71. Mau, in *Röm.Mitt.*, XXI(1906),1ff., figs. 1-10, pl. I. Thédenat, *Pompéi*, pp. 78ff., fig. 42. Puchstein, *Die griech. Bühne*, pp. 75ff., fig. 19; and in *Arch.Anz.*, XXI(1906),301ff. Byvank, in *Röm.-Mitt.*, XL(1925),107ff., figs. 1-6, Beilage II. Bieber, *Denkmäler*, pp. 52ff., No. 13, figs. 56-57, pls. 23-25. Bulle, *Untersuchungen*, pp. 165ff., pl. 13. Fiechter, *Baugesch.Entw.*, pp. 76ff., figs. 66-69. Fensterbusch, in *Bursians Jahresbe-richte*, 227(1930),48ff. Anderson-Spiers-Ashby, *The Architecture of Rome*, p. 91, pl. XLVII. Maiuri, "L'ultima fase edilizia di Pompei" in *Instituto di Studi Romani*, Sezione Campana 1942, XX, pp. 77-80; Maiuri, *Introduzione allo studio di Pompei* (1943), pp. 34ff.; Maiuri in *Notizie degli Scavi*, V (Serie VIII, 1951), pp. 126-134, figs. 1-6; Maiuri, *Pompei* (1951), p. 26, figs. 36-37.

[10] Mazois and Gau, *Les Ruines de Pompéi*, IV,55-60, pls. XXVII-XXIX. Niccolini, *Le Case ed i Monumenti di Pompei*, IV,2, pl. XIX (restoration), XX (view). See pls. XXI and K for a view of the theatrical area. Overbeck-Mau, *op.cit.*, pp. 171ff., figs. 97-101. Mau, *op.cit.*, pp. 140ff., figs. 66-70. Mau-Kelsey, *op.cit.*, pp. 153ff., figs. 66-71. Thédenat, *op.cit.*, pp. 82ff., fig. 43. Bieber, *Denkmäler*, pp. 52ff., No. 13, fig. 56, pl. 25. Fiechter, *Baugesch.Entw.*, p. 78, fig. 66. Bulle, *Untersuchungen*, p. 205f., pl. 46. Robertson, *Greek and Roman Architecture* (2nd ed., 1943), p. 273f., fig. 114. Anderson-Spiers-Ashby, *op.cit.*, p. 91, pls. XLVI-VII. Maiuri, *Pompei*, p. 26f., fig. 38-39, 41. Spano, "Osservazioni intorno al theatrum tectum di Pompei," in *Annali del Ist. Sup. S. Chiara*, I(1949). Homer Thompson, in *Hesperia*, XIX(1950), 90f.

[11] For odea see Durm, *Baukunst der Griechen*, pp. 487ff., fig. 433. Cagnat et Chapot, *Manuel d'archéologie romaine*, pp. 190ff., figs. 101-102.

[12] Odeum of Taormina: Bieber, *Denkmäler*, p. 62, pl. 28,2.

[13] Gabrici, "Contributo archeologico alla topografia di Napoli," in *Monumenti Antichi* (1951), pp. 656 and 674, pl. IV.

[14] Homer Thompson, in *Hesperia*, XIX(1950),31ff., pls. 16-60.

[15] O. Broneer, *The Odeum, Corinth*, Results of the Excavations by the American School of Classical Studies at Athens, II(1932).

[16] Kavvadias, *Praktika* (1904), pp. 49-51, pl. A. Durm, *op.cit.*, p. 489f., fig. 434. Hanson, *Roman Theater-Temples*, p. 97, fig. 48.

[17] Mazois, *op.cit.*, pp. 77-86, pls. XLIII-XLVIII. Niccolini, *op.cit.*, pls. XVII (restoration), XVIII and I (views). Overbeck-Mau, *op.cit.*, pp. 176ff., figs. 102-114. Mau, *op.cit.*, pp. 196-209, figs. 96-102, pl. VI. Mau-Kelsey, *op.cit.*, pp. 212ff. Thédenat, *op.cit.*, pp. 94ff., figs. 52-54. Maiuri, *Pompei*, pp. 27-30, figs. 42-43. Ippel, *Pompeji*, pp. 62ff., figs. 58-61. Colin, "Nouveaux graffites de Pompéi," in *L'Antiquité classique*, XX(1951),136-139. Girosi, "L'anfiteatro di Pom-

pei," in *Memorie R. Accad. di Archeologia di Napoli*, v (1936),34f.

[18] See for the amphitheaters of Capua and Puteoli: Durm, *Handbuch der Architektur*, ii,685f., figs. 752-753. Drexel, in Friedländer, *Sittengeschichte*, iv(9th ed., 1921), p. 209f. List of about 80 other amphitheaters, *ibid.*, pp. 205-240. Friedländer, *Roman Life and Manners*, trans. by Gough (1913), iv,193-255.

[19] Naples, Mus. No. 112222. A. Sogliani, *Pitture Murali*, No. 604. Niccolini, *op.cit.*, pl. xxxi (in color). Mau, *op.cit.*, fig. 101. Ippel, *op.cit.*, p. 4, fig. 4. Durm, *Handbuch der Architektur*, ii,2, second ed. *Die Baukunst der Römer*, p. 681, fig. 749.

[20] A. Maiuri, *Gli Scavi di Pompei* (1951), pp. 22-25, pl. iii.

[21] C. Robertson, *Greek and Roman Architecture*, pp. 279ff., on the contrivance for supporting awnings in theaters, and 283ff., in amphitheaters. For the awnings in the theater at Pompeii, cf. Mazois, *Ruines de Pompéi*, iv, pl. xx. Overbeck, *Pompeji*, p. 164, fig. 89. Mau, *op.cit.*, p. 132f., fig. 65. Mau-Kelsey, *op.cit.*, p. 145, fig. 65. Lily Ross Taylor, "Lucretius on the Roman Theatre," in *Studies in Honour of Gilbert Norwood*, ed. Mary White (1952), pp. 147-155.

[22] *Forschungen in Ephesos*, ii, p. 162, No. 39, line 4 and No. 40, line 6.

[23] Mazois, *Ruines de Pompéi*, iv,64, pls. 33 and 36. Overbeck, *Pompeji* (3d ed., 1875), p. 140f., figs. 89-90. Mau, *Pompeji*, p. 134. Fiechter, *Baugesch.Entw.*, p. 120f., figs. 119-120. Noack, *Die Baukunst des Altertums*, p. 64, pl. 86a. Maiuri, *Pompei* (1951), fig. 37.

[24] Drerup in *Ath.Mitt.*, xxvi(1901),29ff. Rizzo, *Il Teatro di Siracusa*, p. 64, fig. 27, p. 73, fig. 30, No. 3; p. 78, fig. 32c; pp. 49ff. Anti, *Guida del Teatro di Siracusa*, pp. 98-101, 104.

[25] On aulaeum see: Formigé, *Mémoires présentés à l'Académie des Inscriptions et Belles Lettres*, 1st series, xiii (1914),34(58)ff., and xiii, 2 (1923), 35ff. Boeswillwald, *Timgad*, p. 117f. Daremberg-Saglio *s.v.* Aulaeum. Stillwell, in *Corinth*, ii, *The Theater*, p. 78, fig. 67. Beare, *The Roman Stage*, Appendix E, pp. 257-264, reprinted from *Hermathena*, lviii, pp. 104-115. See also Ch. XIV, note 23.

[26] Umberto Ciotto, "Relievo Romano e plutei medievali retrovati a Castel S. Elia," in *Bolletino d'Arte*, Serie iv, Vol. 35(1950), pp. 1ff., figs. 1.5-6. C. Anti in *Festschrift Rudolf Egger* (1952), pp. 189-205, figs. 1-2, from Beiträge zur älteren europäischen Kulturgeschichte I. G. Traversari, "Monete Commemorative dei Ludi saeculares Septimi con Scena Teatrale a Siparia," in *Revista Italiana di Numismatica*, iv, serie quinta, lviii(1956),1-10, pl. ix,4. He compares with the relief of S. Elia coins of Septimius Severus with siparia above the scene for the secular plays given by the Emperor, pl. ix,1-3.

[27] Jordan, *Forma Urbis Romae*, pp. 22ff., 30, pl. iv. Jordan-Hülsen, *Topographie der Stadt Rom im Altertum*, i,3, pp. 524ff. Streit, *Das Theater*, pp. 46ff., pl. vi. Fiechter, *Baugesch.Entw.*, pp. 79ff., fig. 70a. Bieber, *Denkmäler*, pp. 56ff., figs. 58-59. Bulle, *Untersuchungen*, p. 271f. Platner-Ashby, *Topographic Dictionary of Rome*, pp. 515ff., *s.v.* theatrum Pompei. A. Rumpf, in *Mitteilungen des Deutschen archäologischen Instituts*, iii(1950),40-50. Caputo, in *Dioniso*, xvii(1954),11-17 (an excellent summary of the article of Rumpf). Hanson, *op.cit.*, pp. 43-55, figs. 15-19.

[28] Rumpf, *op.cit.*, pp. 48ff.

[29] Noack, *Baukunst des Altertums*, pp. 68ff., pl. 94. Dinsmoor, *The Architecture of Ancient Greece*, pp. 295ff., figs. 108-109. See Ch. XIV, note 66.

[30] Caputo, *op.cit.*, p. 16.

[31] D-R, pp. 333f., fig. 84. Benndorf, in *JOAI*, v(1902), 188ff., figs. 53-55. Fiechter, *Baugesch.Entw.*, p. 102, fig. 99. Bieber, *Denkmäler*, p. 76, No. 22, pl. 40, No. 1. Pickard-Cambridge, *Theatre of Dionysus*, p. 220, fig. 81.

[32] Serradifalco, *Antichità della Sicilia*, v, pp. 36ff., pls. xxi-xxii. Noack, *Baukunst des Altertums*, p. 66, pl. 90. Fiechter, *Baugesch.Entw.*, pp. 86 and 115, fig. 76. Bieber, *Denkmäler*, p. 61f., No. 15, figs. 63-64, pls. 27-28a. Pace, *Arte e Civiltà della Sicilia*, ii, pp. 323ff., figs. 282-285. Caristie, *Monuments antiques à Orange*, p. 56, pl. xxxiv, fig. vi, and pl. xli. Guido Libertini in *Dioniso*, ii(1930),111-121, figs. 1-3. M. Santangelo, *Taormina e Dintorni* (1950), pp. 34-57. A. W. van Buren, *AJA* 60(1956),397, pl. 134, figs. 28-29 (new reconstruction).

[33] Inscriptions on the Acti ludorum saecularum in 17 B.C. and A.D. 204: Mommsen and Hülsen, in *Ephemeris Epigraphica*, viii(1891),225ff.,274ff. Dörpfeld in *Ath.Mitt.*, xxii(1897),446f. D-R, p. 279. Fiechter, *Baugesch.Entw.*, p. 81. Dessau, *Inscriptiones Lat. sel.*, No. 5050. CIL, vi, No. 32323, 32326-32334. Romanelli, *Notizie degli Scavi*, vii(1931),313ff.,325ff. Lily Ross Taylor in *AJP*, lv(1934), 101ff.

[34] Lanciani, *Ruins and Excavations of Ancient Rome*, pp. 493. Jordan-Hülsen, *Topographie*, i,3, p. 519. Platner-Ashby, *Topographic Dictionary of Rome*, p. 513, *s.v.* theatrum Balbi.

[35] Serlio, *Architettura*, iii,47, after Peruzzi; *ibid.* (1566), p. 69f., and *Tutte le opera d'Architettura* (1584), p. 70f. Jordan-Hülsen, *op.cit.*, i,3, pp. 515ff. Streit, *Das Theater*, pp. 52ff., fig. 12, pl. vii. Bieber, *Denkmäler*, p. 58f., fig. 61, pl. 26. Durm, *Baukunst der Römer*, p. 653, fig. 729. Noack, *Baukunst*, p. 102, pl. 135. Platner-Ashby, *op.cit.*, pp. 513ff., *s.v.* theatrum Marcelli. G. Lugli, *Roma Antica. Il centro monumentale* (1946), pl. ix. Our Fig. 641 is a drawing by Miss E. Wadhams, remodelled from Streit.

[36] Piranesi, *Il teatro di Ercolano* (1783). Mazois, *Les Ruines de Pompéi*, iv(1812),71-76, pls. 35-41. Walston, *Herculaneum*, pls. 12-13. Mau, *Pompeji*, pp. 540ff., figs. 297-8. Fiechter, *Baugesch.Entw.*, p. 85, fig. 73, Maiuri, *Ercolano*, pp. 27ff.; Maiuri, *Herculaneum*, English and French editions (1932), pp. 27-29; Maiuri, *Herculaneum*, trans. by Priestley (1937), pp. 61-65, fig. 6, pl. xl; figs. 71-72; Maiuri, *Pompei e Ercolano* (1950), p. 240, pl. xix; Maiuri, *Ercolano* (1946), pp. 69ff., fig. 6; p. 120, pl. xl, figs. 71-72. Hanson, *op.cit.*, p. 74f., fig. 41.

[37] Prestel, *Architektur des Marcus Vitruvius Pollio*, pp. 218ff., pls. xlv-l. Choisy, *Vitruve*, i,197-208, iv, pls. 48-52. Morris H. Morgan, *Vitruvius' Ten Books on Architecture*, pp. 137ff. Bulle, *Untersuchungen*, pp. 270ff. Durm, *Baukunst der Römer*, p. 646f., figs. 724-726. Flickinger, *Greek Theater*, p. 75f., fig. 42. Dinsmoor, *The Architecture of Ancient Greece*, p. 316, fig. 113.

[38] C. Anti, "L'acustica fattore determinante della storia dei teatri greci e romani," *Atti della Accademia Patavina di Scienze, Lettere ed Arti*, lxiv(1951-52), 5-27.

[39] D-R, pp. 386ff., figs. 96-99, pl. viii.

[40] Fiechter, *Baugesch.Entw.*, pp. 100ff., especially 104 and 108f.

[41] Bulle, *Untersuchungen*, pp. 260ff.

[1] See the lists in Drexel, Vol. IV(1921) of Friedländer, *Sittengeschichte*, 9-10. edition, Appendix XVI, pp. 205-240, amphitheaters; pp. 240-242, circus buildings; pp. 243-257, theater buildings. I can, of course, illustrate and discuss only the most important ones.

[2] Ostia: Fiorelli, in *Notizie degli Scavi* (1881), pp. 109ff., pl. I. D'Espouy-Joseph, *Architektonische Einzelheiten*, pl. 100. Bieber, *Denkmäler*, p. 58, figs. 60-61. Vaglieri, *Ostia* (1914), pp. 72ff., No. 28. G. Calza, *Ostia, Guida storico monumentale*, pp. 102ff., fig. 31; cf. p. 23, fig. 5; Calza, *Ostia, Historical Guide to the Monuments* (trans. by R. Weeden-Cook), pp. 110ff., fig. 31; cf. p. 23, fig. 5; Calza, *Il Teatro Romano di Ostia* (1927); Calza in *Capitolium*, V(1927), 74-84. Gismondi in *Anthemon, Scritti in onore di Carlo Anti*, pp. 293-308, pls. XXVIII-XXXI. I owe the photographs, Figs. 648-649 of the newly-reconstructed theater to the kindness of Raissa Calza. Hanson, *op.cit.*, p. 95f., fig. 45.

[3] E. Strong, *Roman Sculpture*, pp. 24ff., pls. LXXIII-LXXIV.

[4] Minturnae: Jotham Johnson, *Excavations at Minturnae*, I(1935), p. 2, fig. 1 (plan); pp. 6ff., fig. 2 (aerial photo); pp. 57ff., fig. 29 (view). Johnson in *Real-Enc.*, Suppl. Vol. VII, *s.v.* Minturnae. S. Aurigemma and A. de Sanctis, *Gaeta, Formia, Minturno*, Itinerari dei Musei e Mon. d'Italia, No. 92(1955), pp. 38ff., figs. 6-8, pl. XXVIII.

[5] See Ch. XIII, note 26.

[6] Fiesole: Galli, "Fiesole, Gli Scavi," in *Piccolo Cicerone moderno*, II, 32ff., figs. 16-27; pp. 123ff., figs. 109-119. A. J. Rusconi, *Italia Artistica*, No. 109, "Fiesole," pp. 23ff., with 5 figs. Broneer, in *Corinth*, X, *The Odeum*, p. 26, fig. 17. Pericle Ducati in *Dioniso*, I(1929),188-190, fig. 6. Minto in *Dioniso*, VI(1937),4-7, figs. 5-12. Hanson, *op.cit.*, pp. 76, 99, figs. 43, 53. A similar early theater on Etruscan soil is in Ferento near Viterbo. Pietro Romanelli, in *Dioniso*, I(1929),260-266, with 4 figs. Fiechter, *Baugesch.Entw.*, p. 86, fig. 75.

[7] Scipione Maffei, *Verona Illustrata*, IV(1826),63ff. S. Ricci, in *Notizie degli Scavi* (1894), pp. 223ff. and *Il Teatro Romano di Verona*, I(1895). G. Ghorardini, in *Notizie degli Scavi* (1905), pp. 259ff. Giani, *L'antico teatro di Verona* (1908), with 19 plates. G. Biadego, *Verona* (1914), pp. 17-28.

[8] Maffei, *Degli amfiteatri e singolarimente del Veronese* (1728), trans. by Gordon as *Complete History of the Ancient Amphitheaters*, more particularly regarding the architecture of those buildings, and in particular that of Verona, 1730, pp. 74ff., 138ff., 190ff., pls. III, V-XIII (1730). Drexel, in Friedländer, *Sittengeschichte*, IV(9-10. ed., 1921), 216; cf. II, 109f. G. Biadego, *Verona* (1914), pp. 13-17. A. Guérinet, *Vérone, Padoue, Milan, Vicence*, pl. I.

[9] Colosseum: Maffei, *op.cit.*, trans. by Gordon (1730), pp. 57ff., 202ff., pl. IV. Desgodetz, *Les édifices antiques de Rome mesurés et dessinés* (1682), p. 246. Canina, *Edifizi*, IV, pls. 164-177. Duc, *Monuments antiques*, II,2. Jordan-Hülsen, *Topographie von Rom*, 1,3, pp. 282ff. Kiepert-Hülsen, *Formae Urbis Romae*, 2nd ed., p. 48f. O. Richter, *Topographie der Stadt Rom*, in Iwan Müllers *Handbuch der Altertums-Wissenschaft*, pp. 167ff., figs. 15-16. Durm, *Baukunst der Römer*, in *Handbuch der Architektur*, II,2, pp. 669ff., figs. 742-747. Cagnat et Chapot, *Manuel d'Archéologie romaine*, I(1916),196ff., figs. 104-105. Noack, *Baukunst des Altertums*, pp. 103ff., pls. 136-138. Lugli, *La Zona archeologica di Roma* (1924), pp. 119ff., fig. 27. Gall, in *Real-Enc.*, VII, pp. 2516ff. Friedländer, *Sittengeschichte*, II, 110ff.

[10] For the coins see Maffei, *op.cit.*, pp. 41ff., pl. I and Appendix, pp. 410-412. Mattingly, *Coins of the Roman Empire* in the British Museum, II, Vespasian to Domitian, pp. LXXVI and 262, pl. 50,2, No. 190.

[11] Maffei, *op.cit.*, p. 372.

[12] Maffei, *op.cit.*, transl. by Gordon, 1730, pp. 315ff., pls. XIV-XV. Gnirs, in *JOAI*, XV(1912), Beiblatt, pp. 239ff.; XVIII (1915), Beiblatt, pp. 163ff.; Gnirs, *Führer durch Pola*, pp. 33ff., 104f., 111f.

[13] R. Peyre, *Nîmes, Arles, Orange, Saint-Rémy* (nouvelle éd., 1910), pp. 6ff. A. Halleys and R. Peyre, *Le Midi de France et ses villes d'Art*, pp. 6ff. J. Sautel, *Les Villes Romaines de la Vallée du Rhône* (1926), pp. 122ff.

[14] Peyre, *op.cit.*, and Halleys-Peyre, *op.cit.*, pp. 74ff. Durm, *Baukunst*, pp. 696ff. Sautel, *Les Villes Romaines de la Vallée du Rhône*, pp. 20ff.

[15] Arles: Caristie, *Notice sur l'état actuel des théâtres antiques d'Orange et d'Arles*, pp. 21ff., pls. VI-IX; Caristie, *Monuments antiques à Orange*, p. 47, pl. XXXIV, No. 2, and pl. XLI, No. 3. Fiechter, *Baugesch.Entw.*, p. 86f., fig. 77, and p. 121f., fig. 121. Peyre, *op.cit.*, pp. 78ff., with 2 figs. Formigé, "Remarques diverses sur les Théâtres Romains à propos de ceux d'Arles et d'Oranges," in *Mémoires présentés par divers savants à l'Académie des Inscriptions et Belles Lettres*, XIII,1(1923), pp. 25ff., pl. I and XIII,2; pp. 40ff., figs. 6-7 and 9; pp. 58ff., figs. 11, 14-16. Sautel, *Les Villes Romaines de la Vallée du Rhône*, pp. 26ff.

[16] E. Strong, *Roman Sculpture*, p. 62f., pl. XIX. Gonse, *Les Chefs-d'oeuvre des Musées de France*, p. 68. Formigé, "L'autel aux cygnes d'Arles et la thymele dans les théâtres greco-romaines." *Revue arch.*, XXI(1944),21-34.

[17] Formigé, *Le Théâtre Romain de Vienne* (1950). See the restored plan, fig. 30, and for the temples on top of the cavea pp. 9-11. Wuilleumier, *Les Théâtres de la Gaule. Le Théâtre de Vienne*. Wuilleumier, "Les Théâtres Romains de la Région Lyonnaise," *Revue d'Histoire du Théâtre*, I (1948), 49f. Formigé, *Mélanges Picard*, I(1949),382-386.

[18] Sautel, *Les Villes Romaines de la Vallée du Rhône*, p. 104f. Sautel, "Le Théâtre de Vaison et les Théâtres Romains de la Vallée du Rhône," in *Études et Documents sur Vaison-la-Romaine*, III(1946),37-47; and XI(1951),44-47 (bibliography for theaters in the Rhone Valley). *Dioniso*, VI(1937-38),176f., fig. 3 (model). Sautel, *Vaison la Romaine* (10th ed., 1951), pp. 6-8. Sautel, *Vaison dans l'Antiquité*, I, pp. 253-254; III, pls. 89-93.

[19] Wuilleumier, in *Gallia*, VII (1948),225-227. Wuilleumier, *Les Fouilles de Fourvière à Lyon* (11th ed., 1952), pp. 6-10, figs. 1-10. Wuilleumier, *Lyon, Métropole des Gaules* (1953), pp. 1-117, figs. 1-12.

[20] Orange: Caristie, *Notice sur l'état actuel des théâtres ant. d'Orange et d'Arles*, pp. 10ff., pls. I-V. Caristie, *Monuments antiques d'Orange, Arc de Triomphe et théâtre* (1856), pp. 33-86, pls. XXX-LI. Peyre, *Nîmes, Arles, Orange* (nouvelle éd., 1910), pp. 149ff. Hallays and Peyre, *Le Midi de la France et ses villes d'art* (1931), pp. 115ff. Formigé, "Remarques diverses sur les théâtres romaines," in *Mémoires présentés par divers savants à l'Académie des Inscriptions et Belles Lettres*, 1st series, XIII(1923),25-90, figs. 1-18, pls. I-IV. "Note sur la scène du théâtre d'Orange," *ibid.*, XII, 2(1933),697-712. Durm, *Baukunst der Römer*, p. 651f., fig. 727; p. 656, fig. 732; p. 659, fig. 735. Fiechter, *Baugesch. Entw.*, p. 87, fig. 78. Bieber, *Denkmäler*, p. 65f., No. 17, fig. 69, pls. 32-33. Noack, *Baukunst des Altertums*, p. 65f., pls. 88-89. Sautel, *Les Villes Romaines de la Vallée du*

Rhône, pp. 95-100. D. S. Robertson, *A Handbook of Greek and Roman Architecture* (1929, second ed. 1943), p. 279f., pl. x. Bachy, "Un théâtre romain, Orange," in *Phoibos*, III-IV(1948-1950),97-109, figs. 1-15.

[21] Caristie, *Monuments antiques à Orange*, pls. XLIV and LI, p. 66f., and p. 79f., fig. 32.

[22] Caristie, *op.cit.*, reconstruction on pl. L.

[23] On the Roman curtain, see Formigé, *op.cit.*, XIII(1932), 40ff., figs. 6-7 and 9; pp. 58ff., figs. 11, 14-16. Wuilleumier, "Théâtres et Amphithéâtres romains de Lyon," in *Annales de Gand*, I(1937),151ff. Beare, *op.cit.*, 5th edn., pp. 257ff. See also Ch. XIII, n. 25.

[24] Drexel, *op.cit.*, pp. 222ff.

[25] Drexel, *op.cit.*, p. 253f.

[26] Merida: José Ramón Mélida, *Monumentos romanos di España*, pp. 17ff., pls. 24-26; Mélida, *Il Teatro Romano de Merida* (1915). Cf. *Arch.Anz.*, 1912, p. 456f., and 1914, pp. 317ff. Mélida in *Art and Archeology*, XXV(1928),30ff. Bieber, "Wurden die Tragödien des Seneca aufgeführt?" in *Röm.Mitt.*, 60/61(1953/54), pp. 100ff., pl. 40,1-2; the illustrations used there and our Figs. 681-684 were given to me by Emeline Hill Richardson.

[27] Drexel, *op.cit.*, pp. 227 and 254f.

[28] Drexel, p. 228f. Cagnat et Chapot, *Manuel d'Archéologie Romaine*, I(1916),193ff., fig. 103. Cagnat, *Les Villes d'Art célèbres, Carthage, Timgad, Tébessa*, p. 31.

[29] Timgad: Gsell, *Monuments antiques de l'Algérie*, I, 197ff., fig. 65, pl. L. Ballu, *Les Ruines de Timgad* (1891), pp. 153ff.; *Les Ruines de Timgad Découvertes* (1903-1910), p. 16f.; (1911), p. 17f. Cf. plan on Map No. 18. Boeswillwald-Cagnat-Ballu, *Timgad. Une cité Africaine* (1905), pp. 93-120, figs. 42-52, pls. XIII-XV. Cagnat, *Carthage, Timgad, Thebessa*, pp. 88-90. Bieber, *Denkmäler*, pp. 62ff., figs. 65-68, pl. 29. Durm, *Die Baukunst der Römer*, p. 660f., fig. 736. Fiechter, *Entwicklungsgeschichte*, pp. 88 and 122, figs. 82 and 84. Frézouls, *Dioniso*, XV(1952),90-94, pl. I,1.

[30] Djemila: Gsell, *op.cit.*, I,186-189, figs. 61-62, pls. XLIV-V. Boeswillwald-Cagnat-Ballu, *op.cit.*, p. 105f., fig. 45. Ballu, *Guide illustré de Djemila* (1926), pp. 42 and 46. Fiechter, *op.cit.*, p. 87, figs. 79 and 83. Bieber, *Denkmäler*, pp. 62ff., fig. 67. Allais, *Djemila* (1938), pp. 15f., 52-54. Leschi, *Djemila* (1938), p. 22. Frézouls, *op.cit.*, pl. I,2.

[31] Dugga: Carton, "Le Théâtre romain de Dougga," in *Mémoires présentés à L'Académie des Inscriptions et Belles Lettres*, XI,1(1902),1-117 and XI,2(1904),79-191, pls. I-XVIII. Carton, *Dougga* (2nd éd., 1922). Boissier, *L'Afrique romaine* (1909, 4th éd.), p. 230. Fiechter, *op.cit.*, pp. 87 and 122, figs. 80 and 122. Cagnat, *Carthage, Timgad, Thebessa*, pp. 90ff. Noack, *Baukunst des Altertums*, p. 64f., pl. 86,b. Homer F. Pfeiffer, in *MAAR*, IX(1931),145-156, frontispiece and pls. 11-15. Bieber, *Denkmäler*, pp. 62-64, fig. 66, pls. 30-31. Caputo, in *Dioniso*, n.s., IX(1942), 12; X(1947),5-23.

[32] Sabratha: Giacomo Guidi, in *Africa Italiana*, III(1930), 1-52, figs. 1-42, pls. I-II; VI(1935),30ff. Giuseppe Caputo, in *Dioniso*, I, No. 2, 1937 (publ. 1939), pp. 3ff., pls. I-VIII. Giuseppe Gullini, in *Bulletino della Commisione archeologico, Bulletino del Museo dell Impero Romano*, LXXI (1945),21-34. Cf. also Mariani, "Del teatro Romano di Sabratha al teatro Olympico di Vicenza," in *Rivista Italiana del Dramma*, I,3, pp. 294-302. Caputo, *Il teatro di Sabratha*. Monografie di Archeologia libica III, Rome, L'Erma di Bretschneider, in the Press.

[33] Christian Hülsen, *Das Septizonium des Septimius Severus*, 46th *BerlWPr* (1886). Giuseppe Spano, in *Memorie della Accademia dei Lincei*, CCCXLVI(1950), Serie VIII, Vol. III,3, pp. 179ff., fig. 3.

[34] Leptis Magna: G. Caputo and Giorgio Levi della Vida, "Il teatro augusteo di Leptis Magna secondo le ultime scoperte," in *Africa Italiana*, VI(1935),92-103. "Il teatro di Leptis Magna," in *Rivista Italiana del Dramma* (1940), pp. 202-212. "Architettura del teatro di Leptis Magna," in *Dioniso*, XIII(1950),164-178, figs. 1-6. For some details, cf. *ibid.*, XII(1949),83-91 and 214f; XX(1957),3-7. "Principali restauri monumentali e lavori di protezione nel triennio 1946-8 in Sabratha e Leptis Magna," in *Reports and Monographs, Department of Antiquities in Tripolitania*, II(1949),15-19. Cf. also Caputo in *Arch.Anz.* (1939-1941), pp. 717 and 726, note 2. Bieber in *Röm.Mitt.*, 60/61(1953/54), pp. 104f., pl. 41, fig. 1. I owe the photographs published there and those for our Figs. 696-699 to the great kindness and generosity of Professor Caputo. Hanson, *op.cit.*, pp. 59f., 90, 95, figs. 21-22. Caputo, *Il teatro di Leptis Magna*. Monografie di Archeologia libica VI, Rome, l'Erma di Bretschneider, in the press.

[35] A. Reifenberg, "Caesarea," in *The Israel Exploration Journal*, I,i(1950-51),24ff. Drexel, in Friedländer, *Sittengeschichte*, IV,237. Other amphitheaters in Asia, *ibid.*, pp. 232-238.

[36] Texier, *Description d'Asie mineure* (1849), I, p. 168, pl. 62; III, pls. 232-241. Lanckoronski, *Städte Pamphyliens und Pisidiens* (1890), I, 85, 91, 102-120, 144f., figs. 74, 81-120, pls. XVI, XX-XXVII. Durm, *Baukunst der Griechen*, p. 468f., fig. 421a-b; Durm, *Baukunst der Römer*, p. 654, fig. 730. Noack, *Baukunst des Altertums*, p. 106f., pl. 142. Fiechter, *Baugesch.Entw.*, pp. 95, 123ff., figs. 91-92, 123. Bieber, *Denkmäler*, pp. 68ff., No. 19, figs. 73-74, pls. 36-39. Bulle, *Untersuchungen*, pp. 267f. D. S. Robertson, *A Handbook of Greek and Roman Architecture* (2nd ed., 1943), pp. 276ff., figs. 116-117. Pickard-Cambridge, *Theatre of Dionysus*, p. 254, note 1, fig. 131. Dinsmoor, *The Architecture of Ancient Greece*, p. 310f.

[37] Puchstein, in Wiegand, *Palmyra*, Ergebnisse der Expeditionen von 1902 und 1917 (1932), pp. 41ff., pls. 11, 19-23.

[38] A. Schenk, Graf von Stauffenberg, *Die römische Kaisergeschichte bei Malalas* (1931), p. 46. I owe the reference and information to the late Professor Friend of Princeton.

[39] Lanckoronski, *op.cit.*, I,98-102, figs. 77-80, pls. XVIII-XIX.

[40] Amman: Howard Crosby Butler, *Syria*, Princeton University Expedition to Syria, Sect. II A, Southern Syria (1919), pp. 34f., 47f., 275, figs. 31-33, pl. IV. See also Baalbeck in Syria, Th. Wiegand, *Baalbek, Ergebnisse der Ausgrabungen und Untersuchungen, 1898-1905* (1921-1925), I,42, fig. 20.

[41] Donald N. Wilber, in *Antioch-on-the-Orontes*, ed. Stillwell, II(1938),57-94, pls. V-VII. Schenk, *op.cit.*, p. 260.

[42] Bosra: De Vogüé, *Syre centrale*, pl. 5. Brünnow and Domaszewski, *Provincia Arabia*, III,47ff., pls. 50-51, figs. 928-982. Fiechter, *Baugesch.Entw.*, p. 95f., fig. 93. Durm, *Baukunst der Römer*, p. 652, fig. 728; pp. 661ff., figs. 737-739. H. C. Butler, *op.cit.*, p. 274f., figs. 241-242, pls. XIV-XV.

[43] Eš-Šuhba: Brünnow und Domaszewski, *op.cit.*, pp. 169ff., pl. 52, figs. 1059-1067. Butler, *Architecture and other Arts*, pp. 390ff., fig. 135. Fiechter, *op.cit.*, p. 96, fig. 94. Cf. also, *ibid.*, fig. 95, Gerasa, with a similar straight scaenae frons. P. Coupel et E. Frézouls, *Le théâtre de Philippopolis en Arabie* (1956).

[44] Theater of Herodes Atticus: Stuart and Revett, *Antiquities of Athens*, II, pls. I-II; III, pl. II; IV, pl. IV. Judeich, *Topographie von Athen*, 2nd ed., pp. 326ff. Versakis, *Ephemeris arch.* (1912), pp. 161ff., pls. 8-12. Fiechter, *Baugesch. Entw.*, pp. 88f., 122, 124, fig. 85; Fiechter, *Dionysostheater*, III,80f., note 2, fig. 50. Bieber, *Denkmäler*, pp. 67f., No. 18, fig. 72, pls. 34-35. Picard, *L'Acropole d'Athènes*, p. 82, fig. 75, pls. 83-85. Broneer, *AJA*, XXXII(1928),447ff.

⁴⁵ D-R, pp. 82ff., figs. 27-32. Bieber, *Denkmäler*, p. 18f., fig. 12, pls. 6-7. Bulle, *Untersuchungen*, pp. 16f., 19 and 80. Fiechter, *Theaterbauten*, Hefte 5-7 and 9, *Das Dionysostheater*, I, pp. 32ff., 41ff., figs. 31-42; pp. 62ff., figs. 53-55; p. 73f., figs. 61-63; III, pp. 25ff., figs. 13-16, pl. 11; pp. 56f., 78ff., figs. 45-49, pls. 22-23; IV, Nachträge, pp. 17ff., fig. 5, pls. 3-5. Schleif, in *Arch.Anz.*, 52(1937), p. 26f., figs. 4-5. A. von Gerkan, "Die neronische Scaenae Frons des Dionysostheaters in Athen," in *JdAI*, 56(1941),163ff., figs. 1-5. Dinsmoor, *Architecture of Ancient Greece*, p. 309f. Flickinger, *Greek Theater*, p. 72f., figs. 39-41. Pickard-Cambridge, *Theater of Dionysus*, pp. 247ff., figs. 122-129. Ida Thallon Hill, *The Ancient City of Athens* (1953), pp. 113-124. A general view of the Graeco-Roman Athenian theater can be seen on a coin of the second century A.D.: British Museum *Cat. of Greek Coins, Attica*, pl. XIX, fig. 8.

⁴⁶ Bulle in Fiechter, *Dionysostheater*, III,60ff., figs. 41-43. IG, II.III², No. 3182.

⁴⁷ Svoronos, *Das Athener Nationalmuseum* (1908), pp. 232ff., pls. 61-64 was the first to recognize the reliefs as those from an altar dedicated to Dionysus. Cook, *Zeus*, I (1914),708ff., annexed pl. XL. Quilling, *Die Jupitersäule des Samus und Severus*, pp. 44, 143f., note 10, fig. on p. 144. Picard, *L'Acropole*, pp. 75ff., pl. 74. Graindor, *Athènes sous Hadrien*, p. 277; Graindor, *Athènes de Tibère à Trajan*, pp. 199ff. Herbig, in Fiechter, *Dionysostheater*, II, *Die Skulpturen*, pp. 36ff., pls. 9-16. Josephine Shear, *Hesperia*, V(1936), 324. These three authors date the reliefs in the period of Hadrian. Pickard-Cambridge, *Theatre of Dionysus*, pp. 261ff., figs. 135-138; his figs. 133 and 134 do not belong to the bema reliefs, but to a big series of fragments found by me in the storerooms of the Museum and recently by the American excavators on the Agora.

⁴⁸ G. Traversari, "Tetimimo e Colimbètra," in *Dioniso*, XIII(1950),3-20. Gismondi, "Colimbètra di Ostia, in *Anthemon, Sritti in onore di Carlo Anti*, pp. 293-308, pls. XXVIII-XXXI.

⁴⁹ Th. L. Shear, *AJA*, 32(1928),447ff. Richard Stillwell, *Corinth, The Theatre*, Results of Excavations conducted by the American School of Classical Studies at Athens, II(1952), 41-105, figs. 2, 4, 76-94, pls. I, VII, VIIIb.

⁵⁰ Traversari, *op.cit.* in *Dioniso*, XIII(1950). Cf. Ch. XV, Fig. 784.

⁵¹ Sparta: Woodward, *ABSA*, 26(1923-25),119ff.; 27 (1925-26),175f., pls. XXVII-XXX; 30(1928-30),151ff. Bulle, *Untersuchungen*, pp. 108ff.; Bulle, "Das Theater in Sparta," in *Sitzungsberichte der Bayr. Akad. d. Wiss.* (1934, Heft 5), pp. 1ff., pls. 1-3. Dinsmoor, *The Architecture of Ancient Greece*, pp. 307f., 310.

⁵² Stobi: E. Weigand, *Arch. Jahrb.*, XXIX (1914),37ff.; Weigand, *Wiener Jahrb. für Kunstgeschichte*, V(1928),71ff. Saria, in *Arch. Anz.*, LIII(1938),71ff. Dinsmoor, *op.cit.*, p. 310. Bulle, *Das Theater in Sparta*, p. 46f., note 2.

⁵³ Collard, "Le Théâtre de Philippes," *BCH*, LII(1928), 74ff., pls. II-V; Collard, *Philippes. Villes de Macédoine* (1937).

⁵⁴ Magnesia: Dörpfeld, *Ath.Mitt.*, XIX(1894),65ff., pls. 1-4. D-R, pp. 153ff. Puchstein, *Griech. Bühne*, pp. 59ff., figs. 13-14. Bulle, *Untersuchungen*, pp. 261ff., fig. 6a-b. (Our Fig. 730 is his fig. 6b). Fiechter, *Baugesch.Entw.*, pp. 21, 60, 72f., 91, figs. 25 and 58. Dinsmoor, *Architecture of Ancient Greece*, p. 250.

⁵⁵ Kern, in *Ath.Mitt.*, XIX(1894),96ff.; Kern, *Inschriften von Magnesia*, No. 88. Pickard-Cambridge, *Theater of Dionysus*, p. 243f.

⁵⁶ Th. Wiegand, in Wiegand-Schrader, *Priene, Ergebnisse der Ausgrabungen*, pp. 253ff., figs. 254-257. A. von Gerkan, *Das Theater von Priene*, pp. 50, 57f., 83ff., figs. 9-10, pl.

XXVI,6. Fiechter, *op.cit.*, p. 91f., fig. 87. Bieber, *Denkmäler*, pp. 34 and 36, fig. 36.

⁵⁷ Niemann, Heberdey, and Wilberg, *Forschungen in Ephesos*, II, *Das Theater in Ephesos*, pp. 30ff., figs. 3-4, 6-9, 15, 31, 57-99, pls. I-II, IV-IX. Fiechter, *Baugesch.Entw.*, p. 90f., fig. 86 and p. 113f. Dinsmoor, *The Architecture of Ancient Greece* (1951), pp. 308 and 311, fig. 113, pl. LXIX,2. Pickard-Cambridge, *Theatre of Dionysus*, p. 254, note 1, fig. 130. Hörmann, in *JdAI*, 38/9(1923/4),275ff. Beilage VI-VIII (reconstruction of the scaenae frons).

⁵⁸ Th. Wiegand, "Dritter vorläufiger Bericht über Milet," in *Sitzungsberichte, Berliner Akademie der Wissenschaften* (1904), pp. 76-85, figs. 2-6. A. von Gerkan, in Wiegand, *Milet*, II,3, *Die Stadtmauern* (1935), p. 88f., fig. 57. Noack, *Baukunst*, p. 65, pl. 87. F. Kraus, in *Bericht über den VI. Internationalen Kongress für Archäologie* (Berlin, 1939), pp. 387ff., pls. 36-37. Kraus is preparing a full publication.

⁵⁹ Termessus: Texier, *Description d'Asie mineure*, III, pls. 173-179. Lanckoronski, *op.cit.*, II,92ff., figs. 50-55, pls. X-XIII. Chamonard, *BCH*, XXX(1896),304ff. Dörpfeld, *Ath. Mitt.*, XXII(1897),442ff., pl. X. Fiechter, *Baugesch.Entw.*, pp. 60, 92f., figs. 59, 89. Bieber, *Denkmäler*, p. 70f., fig. 75, pl. 40,2. Bulle, *Untersuchungen*, p. 262, fig. 7, and pp. 267ff. Dinsmoor, *Architecture of Ancient Greece*, p. 309.

⁶⁰ Sagalassus: Lanckoronski, *op.cit.*, II,152ff., figs. 127-137, pls. XXVI-XXX. Fiechter, *op.cit.*, pp. 31, 60, 93f., 114, figs. 60 and 90. Bieber, *Denkmäler*, p. 71, figs. 76-77. Bulle, *op.cit.*, p. 267f.

⁶¹ Dörpfeld, *Ath.Mitt.*, XXII(1897),439ff., especially pp. 442ff., figs. 1-2, pl. X. Against his theory see Dinsmoor, *The Architecture of Ancient Greece*, p. 308, note 1, and p. 310, note 4.

⁶² Aezani: Texier, *op.cit.*, I, pls. 40-45. Caristie, *Mon. ant. à Orange*, pp. 55 and 66f., pl. XXXI and XLIV, No. 5, fig. 4. Durm, *Baukunst der Griechen*, p. 466f., fig. 420. Fiechter, *Baugesch.Entw.*, p. 91f., fig. 88. Bieber, *Denkmäler*, p. 66f., figs. 70-71. Dinsmoor, *Architecture of Ancient Greece*, pp. 311 and 320.

⁶³ Pessinus: Caristie, *op.cit.*, p. 66f., pl. XLIV, fig. 3. Texier, *op.cit.*, I, 168, pl. 62. Durm, *Baukunst der Griechen*, p. 494f., fig. 439. Dinsmoor, *op.cit.*, p. 320.

⁶⁴ Butler, *Syria*, II,50ff., figs. 34-35. Lanckoronski, *op.cit.*, I,135 (L in plan of Aspendus, facing p. 128); II,43, 98-100, figs. 56-62, pl. XIV (Termessus); p. 134 (Sagalassus). Wuilleumier, *Les Fouilles de Fourvière* (1952), pp. 6-10, figs. 7-12. Formigé, *Le Théâtre de Vienne*, p. 10f., figs. 1 and 7.

⁶⁵ Homer A. Thompson, "The Odeion in the Athenian Agora," *Hesperia*, XIX(1950),31-141, figs. 1-21, pls. 16-80.

⁶⁶ Wiegand, *Milet*, I,2, Knackfuss, *Das Rathaus von Milet* (1908), pp. 25ff., figs. 1-88, pls. I-XIV. Corrections in I, 7(1924), 279f. Durm, *Die Baukunst der Griechen*, p. 544f., fig. 494. Dinsmoor, *Architecture of Ancient Greece*, p. 296f., fig. 109. Thompson, *op.cit.*, p. 90, pl. 41. D. S. Robertson, *A Handbook of Greek and Roman Architecture* (2nd ed., 1943), pp. 178ff., figs. 79-80.

⁶⁷ Wiegand and Schrader, *Priene*, pp. 219ff., figs. 210-223. Schede, *Ruinen von Priene*, pp. 63ff., fig. 76. Dinsmoor, *op.cit.*, p. 295f., fig. 108. D. S. Robertson, *op.cit.*, p. 176f., figs. 78 and 84, pl. VII.

⁶⁸ W. A. McDonald, *The Political Meeting Places of the Greeks* (1943). The Johns Hopkins University Studies in Archeology, No. 34(1942), pp. 170ff., pl. IV (Athens); pp. 87ff., figs. 9-10, pl. VI (Priene); pp. 211ff., figs. 22-23, pl. XIV (Miletus). C. Caputo, *Anthemon, Scritti in onore di Carlo Anti*, pp. 280ff., p. 289, fig. 1 (bouleuterion of Ptolemais), pl. XXVII (ecclesiasterion of Cyrene).

⁶⁹ Lanckoronski, *op.cit.*, II,98ff., figs. 56-62, pl. XIV.

⁷⁰ Durm, *Baukunst der Römer*, p. 665f., figs. 740-741.

Fiechter, *Baugesch.Entw.*, p. 85f., fig. 74. Carducci, "Teatri del Piemonte Romano," in *Dioniso*, vi(1937-38), 297-303, with 8 figures. Rosi, "Il teatro di Aosta," in *Rivista Italiana del Dramma*, i(1937),1ff. Raissa de Chirico (Calza) in *Arch. Anz.*, 52(1937),350ff., fig. 1. It has about 3500 seats. Lugli, in *Archeologia classica*, i(1949),158, pl. xlvi,2.

[71] Walden, *The Universities of Ancient Greece*, pp. 83ff. Oliver, in *Hesperia*, iii(1934),191ff.

[72] Kavvadias in *Praktika of the Arch. Society* (1904), pl. A′. Durm, *Baukunst der Griechen*, p. 489f., fig. 434; cf. p. 498f., figs. 441-442.

[73] Lanckoronski, *op.cit.*, i,70f., p. 90, plan of Sylleum, fig. 51K.

[74] Oscar Broneer, in *AJA*, 32(1928),447ff., pls. vi-vii; Broneer, *Corinth*, x, *The Odeum*.

[75] Luigi M. Ugolini, in *Dioniso*, iii(1931-32),7-12, figs. 1-4; Ugolini, *Il teatro di Butrinto*, in *Albania antica*, Vol. iv. I owe the photograph for Fig. 750 to the kindness of Signor Ugolini.

[76] Pernier, in *Annuario della R. Scuola di Archeologia di Atene*, viii-ix(1925-26),1ff., pl. 5.

[77] Heberdey, *JOAI*, xv(1912), Beiblatt, pp. 167ff., figs. 132-133. Keil, *Führer durch Ephesos*, p. 92f., figs. 53-54.

[78] Butler, *Syria*, ii, A, p. 50f., figs. 34-35.

[79] Lanckoronski, *op.cit.*, ii, 99, 101, and 125, fig. 59. Cf. for other Odea in Pamphilia and Pisidia, *ibid.* see above, Figs. 745-746, note 64.

[80] Bieber, in *AJA*, 58(1954), 280ff., pl. 54, figs. 12-15.

[81] Rodenwaldt, *Die Kunst der Antike*, pl. 482. Napp, *Bukranion und Guirlande*, Diss., Heidelberg (1930), p. 6. Cf. the altar from Ostia, above, note 3, and from Arles, Strong, *Roman Sculpture*, pl. xix.

[82] Herbig, in Fiechter, *Theaterbauten, Das Dionysostheater in Athen*, ii,14f., pl. 5, 1-2. Bieber, *Denkmäler*, p. 18f., pls. 6-7.

[83] Stuart Jones, *Sculptures of the Palazzo dei Conservatori*, p. 104, Giardino, No. 104, pl. 87.

[84] Greifenhagen, in *Röm.Mitt.*, 45(1930),156f., fig. 8.

[85] Herbig, *op.cit.*, p. 9f., fig. 1, pl. i.

[86] Herbig, *op.cit.*, pp. 10ff., figs. 3-9, pls. 2-4. Pickard-Cambridge, *Theater of Dionysus*, p. 263f., fig. 141.

[87] Herbig, *op.cit.*, p. 16, figs. 13-14, pl. 6. Pickard-Cambridge, *op.cit.*, p. 263, figs. 139-140.

[88] Broneer, *Corinth, The Odeum*, pp. 117-123, figs. 111-113, pls. xv-xvi. Broneer, *AJA*, 32(1928), 466-468, fig. 8, pl. vi.

[89] Homer Thompson, *op.cit.*, p. 78, S 531, pl. 51.

[90] Stillwell, *Antioch-on-the-Orontes*, ii(1938),173f., Nos. 161-168, pls. 13-14; cf. BrBr, pls. 731-732. Joseph Sautel, *Vaison dans l'Antiquité* (1926), ii,198, No. 412 iii, pl. xlix, masks of a tragic hero and a heroine. Paul Collart, *BCH*, 52(1928),92ff., figs. 9-10, masks as decorations in Philippi and other theaters.

[91] See above, notes 82-84 for satyrs. Picard, in *Anthemon*, pp. 273-280, pl. xxiv for caryatids.

[92] J. Sautel, *Le théâtre de Vaison* (1951), p. 4ff., figs. 1, 4, 7, 8, 23.

[93] Bulle, *Untersuchungen*, p. 259. Lévêque, *BCH*, 75 (1951),247ff., pls. xxvii-xxix; *Fouilles de Delphes*, iv, pl. lxxii. These friezes in Delphi, formerly dated in the Hellenistic period, now are rightly put in the early second century A.D. The friezes in Corinth will be published by Edward Capps, Jr. Arid Müfid Mansel, *Die Ruine von Side*, Figs. 110-117.

NOTES TO CHAPTER XV. PLAYS OF THE ROMAN EMPIRE · SENECA

[1] Friedländer, *Sittengeschichte* (9th ed.), ii,1ff.,10ff.,21ff., 50ff.,77ff.,92ff.,112ff.; Drexel, *ibid.* (10th ed.), iv,205ff., 268ff.; A. B. Gough, *Roman Life and Manners under the Early Empire* (1913), translated from Friedländer, *Sittengeschichte*, in 4 vols., Freese and Magnus in 3 vols., ii,1ff. (circus, 19ff.; amphitheater, 40ff.; gladiatorial games, 41ff.; animal baitings, 62ff.; naumachiae, 74ff.; theater, 90ff.; Cf. also Appendix, pp. 148ff.; 255). Albert Müller, "Das Bühnenwesen in der Zeit von Constantin dem Grossen bis Justinian," in *NJb*, 12(1909),36ff. J. W. Duff, *A Literary History of Rome in the Silver Age, from Tiberius to Hadrian* (1927), pp. 157ff., 247ff. Habel, in *Real-Enc. s.v.* Ludi publici, Supplement, Vol. v, pp. 608ff.

[2] Birt in Dieterich, *Pulcinella*, pp. 290-301.

[3] Beyen, *Pompejanische Wanddekoration*, p. 141, fig. 23 (Boscoreale). Naples, Museo nazionale, Nos. 9804-6, 9838, 9850, 9898.

[4] *Mon. Inst.*, xi, pls. 30-32; Maas, *AdI* (1881), pp. 109ff. Bieber, *Denkmäler*, pp. 115ff., No. 49, figs. 112-114; and *Skenika*, p. 8, fig. 3. Pickard-Cambridge, *Festivals*, p. 189f., figs. 72-75. Dieterich, *Pulcinella*, pls. i-iii. M. Bieber, "Wurden die Tragödien des Seneca in Rom aufgeführt?" in *Röm. Mitt.*, 60/61(1953/54), 103, pls. 37,2 and 38.1.

[5] Maiuri, *Notizie degli Scavi* (1929), p. 404ff., figs. 29 and 31, pls. xxiii-xxiv. Rizzo, *La Pittura Ellenistico-Romana*, p. 68, pl. cxlvii. Bieber, *op.cit.*, pl. 37,1.

[6] See Ch. VIII, Fig. 395. Replica from Herculaneum in Naples, Museo Nazionale, Inv. No. 9037, Ruesch, *Guida*, No. 1803.

[7] Dieterich, *Pulcinella*, pp. 1ff., 182ff., pls. ii-iii. Robert, *Masken*, pp. 18f., 24f., 36, 63, 70, figs. 39, 53-54, 61, 86, 88.

[8] Helbig, *Wandgemälde Campaniens*, No. 1467. Bieber, *Skenika*, pp. 18ff., fig. 12; and *Denkmäler*, p. 117, No. 50, pl. 57. Pickard-Cambridge, *Festivals*, p. 190, fig. 76. Bieber in *Röm.Mitt.* 60/61(1953/54), p. 102f., pl. 35,2.

[9] Helbig, *op.cit.*, No. 1465. Naples, No. 9039. Ruesch, *Guida*, No. 1802. Bieber, *Skenika*, p. 20f., fig. 14; and *Denkmäler*, p. 117, No. 51, pl. 58. Pickard-Cambridge, *Festivals*, fig. 77. Rizzo, *op.cit.*, pl. cxlviii. Richardson, in *MAAR*, xxxiii(1955),153f., pl. li,1.

[10] See Ch. VIII, fig. 383. Bieber, *Skenika*, p. 19f., fig. 13; and *Denkmäler*, p. 158, No. 131, pl. 90.1. Pickard-Cambridge, *Festivals*, p. 201f., fig. 96.

[11] E. Loewy, in *JdAI*, xxxxiv(1929),102f., pl. i. Rizzo, *La Pittura Ellenistico-Romano* (1929), p. 15, pl. xxv, F. Wirth, *Römische Wandmalerei* (1934), p. 33, pls. 4-5. Spinazzola, *Arti decorative in Pompei*, pl. 119. Pickard-Cambridge, *Theatre of Dionysus*, p. 232, fig. 115.

[12] Helbig, *Wandgemälde*, No. 1333. Herrmann, *Denkmäler der Malerei*, pls. 115-116. Rizzo, *op.cit.*, pls. 77-78. O. Elia, *Le Pitture della Casa del Citarista*, in *Monumenti della pittura antica scoperti in Italia*, iii, *Pompeii*, i, pls. A and vi. M. Gabriel, *Masters of Pompeian Painting*, pls. 25-26. Richardson, "The Casa dei Dioscuri and its Painters," in *MAAR*, xxiii(1955), 136, pl. xxxiv.

[13] Cube, "Römische Scaenae frons in den pompejanischen Wandbildern IV. Stils," in *Beiträge zur Bauwissenschaft*, vi(1906),28ff., pls. ii-vii. Fiechter, *Baugesch.Entw.*, pp. 106ff., figs. 104-106. Bieber, *Denkmäler*, pp. 77ff., Nos. 24-26, figs. 81-83, pl. 41. Friend, in *Art Studies*, vii(1929),9, 17ff.,27f., pl. xii, fig. 39. Beyen, *Die pompejanische Wanddekoration*, i(1938),126f., figs. 44-45. A.M.G. Little, "A Roman Sourcebook for the Stage," *AJA*, 60(1956),28ff., pls. 21-22.

[14] J. W. Duff, *A Literary History of Rome in the Silver Age, from Tiberius to Hadrian* (1937), pp. 247ff. Best English prose translation by F. J. Miller, The Loeb Classical Library (1929), 2 vols., with useful comparative analysis of the difference in plot and structure between the Greek plays and their Senecan descendants. Duckworth, *The Complete Roman Drama*, 2 vols. (1943), Introduction, I, xxxviff. T. S. Eliot, Introduction to Seneca, His Tenne Tragedies, Tudor translations (1927). M. Hadas, *A History of Latin Literature* (1952), pp. 248ff. Bieber, *Röm.Mitt.*, 60/61(1953/4), pp. 100-106, pls. 35-41. Mendell, *Our Seneca*, p. 88, and Beare, *The Roman Stage*, pp. 226f., believe that Seneca wrote his tragedies for recitation only, not for production on the stage.

[15] Ficoroni, *De Larvis Scenicis*, p. 102, pl. LXXIX. Wieseler, *Theatergebäude und Denkmäler des Bühnenwesens*, p. 110, No. 24, suppl. pl. A, No. 24. Messerschmidt, "Tragödienszenen auf römischen Lampen." *Röm.Mitt.* 44(1929), 40-42, pl. 7b. Fig. 779 from Phot. Faraglia with the permission of the directors of the Museo Nazionale Romano. Bieber, *Röm.Mitt.*, 60/61(1953/4), p. 103f., pl. 86,2.

[16] Arndt, *Porträts*, pl. 1200. Blümel, *Katalog Berlin, Römische Bildnisse*, p. 44, R 106.

[17] Sala delle Muse No. 516. Helbig-Amelung, *Führer durch Rom*, 3rd ed., No. 263. Lippold, *Skulpturen des Vaticanischen Museums*, III,i, pp. 60ff., pls. 6-7.

[18] Cohen, *Médailles impérials*, 2nd ed., I, No. 197. Rizzo, in *Bulletino comunale di Roma*, LX(1933),59.

[19] Suetonius, *Nero*, LIV; Macrobius, *Sat.*, v, 17.5.

[20] Duff, *op.cit.*, p. 273f. Miller, *op.cit.*, II,401ff.

[21] U. Ciotti, "Rilievo romano a plutei medioevali ritrovati a Castel S. Elia," in *Bolletino d'Arte*, Serie IV, Vol. 35 (1950),1ff., figs. 1,5. C. Anti, "Rilievo teatrale Romano de Castel S. Elia," in *Beiträge zur älteren europäischen Kulturgeschichte*, I, *Festschrift für Egger*, (1952), pp. 189-205, figs. 1-2.

[22] Cf. for the pantomime: Albizzati, "Pantomimus" in *Rendiconti della Pontificia Accademia Romana*, V(1926/27: 1928), pp. 27ff., pl. I c. Butler, *Post-Augustan Poetry*, pp. 26ff. Weege, *Der Tanz*, pp. 104f., 156ff. Louis Robert, "Pantomimen im griechischen Orient," *Hermes*, LXV(1930),106ff. Robert deals with inscriptions of pantomimes in Greece and Asia Minor, which, in his opinion, prove that the pantomime is of Greek origin. I interpret them as a proof of the Roman influence penetrating the Greek East as early as the period of Sulla. E. Wüst, *s.v.* "Pantomimus" in *Real-Enc.*, XVIII,3(1949),847ff.

[23] Sandrart, *Teutsche Academie*, II,1679, second part, p. 14, pl. II,1. Dütschke, *Antike Bildwerke in Oberitalien*, III, 166f., No. 335. It belongs to the late Antonine period. The tombstone of another choraules with the name of Ruphus, of the third century, born in Mylasa in Asia Minor, found in Cologne, has been erected by his relative Dionysius Asclepiades from Alexandria. Klinkenberg, *Kunstdenkmäler der Stadt Köln*, I, parts 1-2. *Das römische Köln*, p. 285.

[24] Base for Aurelius Apolaustus in the garden court of the Museo Nazionale Romano delle Terme. R. Paribeni, *Le Terme di Diocleziano* (4th ed., 1922), No. 439. Base for Aurelius Pylades in Naples, Museo Nazionale No. 121523. *New Guida Ruesch*, No. 8.

[25] Strygowski, "Hellenistische und Koptische Kunst in Alexandrien," *Bulletin de la Société d'Alexandrie*, V(1902), 53f. Bieber, *Denkmäler*, p. 125f., No. 70, pl. 63,2. Delbrück, *Consular-Diptychen*, pp. 29, 36ff., 67ff. Allardyce Nicoll, *Masks, Mimes and Miracles* (1931), p. 132, fig. 97.

[26] Traversari in *Dioniso*, N.S., XIII(1950),18ff., XV(1952), 3ff.

[27] G. V. Gentili in *Notizie degli Scavi* (1950), pp. 291ff.,

figs. 2ff.; pp. 323ff., fig. 26. Pace in *Anthemon*, pp. 312-317, pl. XXXII. A. W. van Buren, *AJA*, 56(1952),139, pl. 23B. G. Falzoni in *Le Vie d'Italia* (1951), pp. 88-93. B. Pace, *I Mosaici di Piazza Armerina* (1955), pp. 77-91, pls. XIV-XVI (in color). Gentili, *The Imperial Villa of Piazza Amerina* (1956). Traversari, *Memorie della Accademia Patavina*, LXIX (1956-7), 3-14, figs. 1-6. Traversari explains the girls as athletes, the "umbrella" as the wheel of a circus chariot.

[28] Pickard-Cambridge, *Festivals*, pp. 306-315.

[29] Giacomo Guidi, *Africa Italiana*, III(1930),29ff., figs. 25-26 and 40; cf. pp. 2ff., fig. 1.

[30] See also Juvenal, *Satire* VI, vv. 41-44. R. W. Reynolds, "Adultery Mime," *CQ*, XL(1946),77-84.

[31] Pacho, *Relations d'un voyage dans la Marmarique, La Cyrénaïque*, etc., pls. 49-50. Wieseler, *Theatergebäude*, p. 99f., pl. XIII,2. Pickard-Cambridge, *Theatre of Dionysus*, p. 245, fig. 120.

[32] Lippold in Arndt-Amelung, *Einzelaufnahmen ant. Skulpturen*, No. 2366. Bieber, *Denkmäler*, p. 120f., No. 55, pl. 59,3.

[33] Vatican, Ambulacro superiore del Nuovo Ingresso. A. L. Millin, *Description d'une mosaïque du Musée Pio-Clémentine à Rome, représentant des scènes de tragédies* (1829). Wieseler, *Denkmäler*, pp. 48ff., pls. VII-VIII. Nogara, *Mosaici del Vaticano*, pp. 27ff., pls. 56-66. Amelung, *Skulpt. Vat. Mus.*, II, 401ff. Helbig, *Führer durch Rom*, 3rd ed., by Amelung, I,116. Bieber, *Denkmäler*, pp. 118ff., No. 54, figs. 115-116, pl. 60. Pickard-Cambridge, *Festivals*, p. 190, figs. 78a-h.

[34] A. Pasqui, in *Notizie degli Scavi* (1906), pp. 357ff., 368f., figs. 10-11. Bieber, *Skenika*, 75. *BerlWPr* (1915), pp. 3ff., pl. I, and *Denkmäler*, p. 118, No. 52, pl. 59,1. Pickard-Cambridge, *Festivals*, p. 187, fig. 65. Raissa Calza, *Il Museo di Ostia*, p. 17. Maria Squarciapino, "Forme Ostienes," *Archaeologica classica*, VI(1954),83-99, pl. XVIII. The moulds with circus plays: *Notizie* (1906), pp. 359ff., figs. 1-3; Squarciapino, pl. XVIII,6, XIX,1-2. Animal baitings: *Notizie*, pp. 362ff., figs. 4-8; Squarciapino, pl. XIX,3-6. Single animals: *Notizie*, p. 370f., figs. 12-15; Squarciapino, pl. XX,1-6. I cannot accept her assumption that the moulds served for wax ex-votos.

[35] Drexel, "Crustulum et mulsum," *Römisch-germanisches Korrespondenzblatt*, IX(1916),17ff.

[36] *British Museum Catalogue of Terracottas*, E70. Athens, Agora Excavations, Inv. No. T 2404, L. 0.08. Found in a burnt layer in front of the Middle Stoa. Clairève Grandjouan, *The Athenian Agora. Terracottas and Plastic Lamps*, No. 502.

[37] Bieber, *Skenika*, pl. 1b; and *Denkmäler*, p. 118, No. 53, pl. 59,2. Messerschmidt, *Röm.Mitt.* 44 (1929),39, pl. 7a. Squarciapino, *op.cit.*, p. 118, pl. 59b.

[38] Dresden, formerly Museum Albertinum, *Katalog der Skulpturen*, p. 2600. Mus. No. L 373. Stamped AVCEND, see CIL, XV, 6326. Cf. for the same potter Walters, *Catalogue of Lamps in the British Museum*, No. 527, which was found in the harbor of Alexandria.

[39] *Mon.Inst.*, XI, pl. XIII. *Collection Dutuit* (1897), No. 126, pl. 114. Bieber, *Denkmäler*, p. 122, No. 59, pl. 62,2. Petit Palais Mus. No. 181. Pickard-Cambridge, *Festivals*, p. 187, fig. 66. For the fact that this costume is by no means that of the actors of the fifth century, see James Turney Allen, *CQ*, I(1907),226-228.

[40] Casa della Gran Fontana. Maiuri, *Pompeji*, p. 64. Ippel, *Pompeji*, pp. 109 and 111, fig. 102. Spinazzola, *Arti decorative in Pompei*, pl. 194 (illustration of the fountain).

[41] Mendel, *Sculptures du Musée de Constantinople*, II,87f., No. 328; *BCH*, XXVIII (1904),71, pl. VI.

[42] Nogara, *Mosaici del Vaticano e Laterano*, pp. 3ff., pls.

5-6. Helbig (3rd ed., by Amelung), *Führer durch Rom*, II, 49f., No. 1231.

[43] Bieber, *Röm.Mitt.*, 60/61(1953/54), 102, pl. 36, 1.

[44] Louvre, Salle d'Afrique, No. 1836. Héron de Villefosse, *Musée Africain du Louvre*, p. 6, pl. X,4. *Musée de l'Algérie et de la Tunisie*, p. 14.

[45] Calza, *Il teatro Romano di Ostia*, fig. on p. 32; Calza, *Capitolium*, V(1927),81ff., fig. on p. 84.

[46] Berlin, *Beschreibung der antiken Skulpturen* (1891), p. 342, No. 857. Cf. masks over garlands: J. Toynbee, *The Hadrianic School*, pp. 205-210, pls. XLIII,2-3; XLV,1-3.

[47] Duckworth, *The Complete Roman Drama*, II,891ff.

[48] Maiuri, *Ercolano*, p. 43f., pl. XX, fig. 35.

[49] A. Adriani, "Minturno. Catalogo delle sculture negli anni 1931-1933," *Notizie degli Scavi*, (1938), p. 193, No. 39, fig. 23.

[50] Amelung, *Skulpt. Vat. Mus.*, II,725a. Helbig, *op.cit.*, p. 158f. Nogara, *Mosaici*, pp. 16ff., pl. 28.

[51] Vatican, Galleria Geographica, No. 890. Pistolesi, *Il Vaticano*, VI, pl. CII. Lippold, *Skulpt. Vat. Mus.*, III,2, pp. 478f., No. 47, pl. 213. Gisela Krien, "Die Angleichung der tragischen und komischen Theatermasken in der spätrömischen Zeit," in *Maske und Kothurn*, Vierteljahrsschrift für Theaterwissenschaft, Universität Wien, I(1955),82f., fig. 4. G. Krien emphasizes the fact that, in the late Roman period, tragic as well as comic masks were adapted to the Roman inclination for pathos, exaggerated stylization and decorative usage. Therefore, the sharp division between tragic and comic masks of the classical Greek period was disregarded.

[52] Bieber, *Skenika*, 75th *BerlWPr* (1915), 9f., pl. II.

[53] Brückner, in *Skenika*, 75th *BerlWPr* (1915), pp. 32ff., pls. IV-VI.

[54] Benndorf, *Archäologische Beiträge zur Kenntnis des Theaters*, pp. 36ff. Bieber, *Denkmäler*, p. 85f., figs. 89-90. Pickard-Cambridge, *Festivals*, p. 274f., fig. 206, Nos. 9-10.

[55] Rizzo, *Il teatro greco di Siracusa*, pp. 46ff. Anti, *Teatro antico di Siracusa*, p. 88. *IG*, XIV, 3.

[56] Dieterich, *Pulcinella*, pp. 150ff. Gisela Richter, *Bronzes of the Metropolitan Museum of Art*, pp. 81ff., No. 127; Richter, *AJA*, XVII(1913),149ff., pls. V-VI; Richter, *Handbook of the Classical Collection* (1930), p. 196f., fig. 135; *Handbook of the Greek Collection* (1953), p. 126, fig. 105a. A. Nicoll, *Masks, Mimes, and Miracles*, p. 48, fig. 32.

[57] Bonn, Rheinisches Landesmuseum No. 15752. Lehner, *Führer durch das Provinzialmuseum* (1915), p. 68. Bieber, *Denkmäler*, p. 174, No. 183, pl. 108,3. Nicoll, *op.cit.*, p. 72, fig. 70.

[58] Dütschke, in *Bonner Jahrbücher*, 78(1884),126ff.

[59] Bieber, *JdAI*, 32(1917),72ff.

[60] Bieber, *JdAI*, 32(1917),76, fig. 42.

[61] G. Richter, The Metropolitan Museum of Art, *Greek, Etruscan, and Roman Bronzes* (1915), p. 138, No. 276.

[62] Landesmuseum Bonn No. 2877. Museum Wallraf-Richartz, Cologne, No. 3851. Dütschke, *Bonner Jahrbücher*, 78(1884),126f., pl. II. Lehner, *Führer durch das Provinzialmuseum* (1915), p. 67f. Klinkenberg, *Die Kunstdenkmäler der Stadt Köln*, I,1, p. 371f., fig. 180, pl. CXIIa; cf. p. 259. Bieber, *JdAI*, 32(1917),72ff., figs. 40-41; Bieber, *Denkmäler*, p. 174f., Nos. 184-185, pl. 108,1-2. Nicoll, *Masks, Mimes and Miracles*, p. 70, figs. 66-67.

[63] The reconstruction, Fig. 823 has been made in the Museum of Mainz. I owe the photograph to Professor Behn, now in Leipzig.

[64] Historical Museum in Frankfurt, No. 83. The theater in Heddernheim was destroyed in A.D. 120.

[65] Ribbeck, *Comicorum Romanorum Fragmenta* (3rd ed., 1898), pp. 339-385. R. Herzog, "Zur Geschichte des Mi-

mus," *Philologus* (1903), pp. 35ff. E. Wüst, *s.v.* "Mimos" in *Real-Enc.*, XV,2(1932),1727ff. Warnecke, *ibid.*, pp. 1749ff. Boissier, in Daremberg-Saglio, *s.v.* "Mimus," III,1903ff. Friedländer, *Sittengeschichte*, II,113ff. Friedländer, translated by Gough-Freese-Magnus, *Roman Life and Manners*, II,91ff. Nicoll, *Masks, Mimes and Miracles*, pp. 47ff., 83ff., 136f. Beare, *op.cit.*, pp. 138ff., 229, and 304ff. The Oxyrhynchus mime printed and translated in his Appendix L is particularly sordid in subject-matter and indecent in language.

[66] Bieber, *Denkmäler*, p. 177, No. 189, pl. 108,4. Nicoll, *op.cit.*, p. 47, fig. 33. Other similar figures wearing loincloth and cap only, see Dieterich figures on pp. 143, 160f., and 181. Nicoll, *op.cit.*, p. 19, fig. 2, and p. 79, fig. 77. Zahn, *Kto-Chro, Glasierter Tonbecher im Berliner Antiquarium*, 81. *Winckelmanns-Programm*, Berlin (1923), pp. 6 and 9, fig. 2, pls. II-III. Weege, *Der Tanz*, p. 11, fig. 9, and pp. 168ff., fig. 238. T. L. Shear, *AJA*, 42(1938),7f., fig. 8b; Lehmann, *ibid.*, p. 83, pl. XV B. Hetty Goldman, *AJA*, XLVII (1943),22ff., and *Tarsus*, I,349, No. 318, pl. 237. Bendinelli, *Le Pitture del Colombario di Villa Pamphili*, in *Monumenti della Pittura antico in Italia*, III, fasc. V. Maiuri, in *Röm.Mitt.*, 60-61(1953-54),92-99, pls. 31,2-3; 32-33.

[67] Bieber, *Denkmäler*, p. 177, No. 188, pl. 108,5. Nicoll, *op.cit.*, p. 47, fig. 31.

[68] Milani, *Museo archeologico di Firenze*, II,30, pl. 140,3. Dieterich, *Pulcinella*, p. 169. Reisch, *Mimus*, I,258. Nicoll, *op.cit.*, p. 91.

[69] See Reisch, *Mimus*, pp. 448 and 579. Dieterich, *op.cit.*, pp. 153ff. Nicoll, *op.cit.*, p. 88.

[70] Lillian M. Wilson, *The Clothing of the Ancient Romans*, pp. 87-92, figs. 52-54, pls. XLVI-XLVII.

[71] Our Fig. 827: Shear, *Hesperia*, VIII(1939),243, fig. 45. See Johannes Schmidt *s.v.* Telesphoros I in Roscher, *Lexikon der Mythologie*, Vol. V, pp. 309ff., figs. 1-10. The mimes from the Agora will be published by Clairève Grandjouan in the Agora Publication *Roman Terracottas*. I owe the photographs for our Figs. 827-828 to Miss Lucy Talcott.

[72] Mus. No. 2321. A. Milani, *op.cit.*, 30, pl. 140, 2. Dieterich, *op.cit.*, fig. on p. 166; cf. p. 171f.

[73] Bieber, "Mima saltatricula," *AJA*, 43(1939),640-644, fig. 1. Now in the Art Museum, Princeton University.

[74] Berlin, Mus. No. 8327. Furtwängler, in *Arch. Anz.*, VIII(1893),95, No. 23. Köster, *Die griechischen Terrakotten*, p. 89f., pl. 101.

[75] Louvre Ma 501. Clarac pl. 113, 3 = S. Reinach, *Répertoire de la Statuaire*, I,3, fig. 3. Large parts of the curtain are restored.

[76] Louvre Ma 3192-3. I owe the photographs for Figs. 831-832 to the kindness of the Director of Antiquities in the Louvre, Professor Charbonneaux.

[77] R. Delbrück, *Die Consular-Diptychen* (1929), pp. 78ff.; Dieterich, *Pulcinella*, p. 220f. Nicoll, *Masks, Mimes and Miracles*, pp. 135ff.

[78] Inventory No. Byzanz 85/11. Delbrück, *op.cit.*, p. 280f., pl. N53.

[79] Dieterich, *op.cit.*, fig. on p. 221. Delbrück, *op.cit.*, pp. 78f., 131f., No. 21.

[80] Delbrück, *op.cit.*, pp. 79 and 125f., N. 18. Nicoll, *Masks*, pp. 142ff., fig. 99. H. Peirce and R. Tyler, *L'Art Byzantine* (1934), II, pl. 13c.

[81] Delbrück, *op.cit.*, pp. 127ff., figs. 1-2 N 20. Peirce-Tyler, *op.cit.*, II, pl. 30a. A. Nicoll, *op.cit.*, frontispiece.

[82] Delbrück, *op.cit.*, pp. 79 and 126f. N 19.

[83] Delbrück, *op.cit.*, pp. 75-78, N 9-12, 20, 21, 58, 60.

[84] On gladiatorial fights, see Friedländer, *Sittengeschichte*, II, 9th ed., pp. 50ff.; IV, 9th ed., pp. 258ff.; translated by Gough and Freese-Magnus, *Roman Life and Manners*, II, 41ff.; IV,166ff.

[85] On animal baiting, see: Friedländer, *op.cit.*, II,77ff.; IV,268ff., trans. by Gough and Freese-Magnus, II,62ff.; IV, 181ff. Delbrück, *op.cit.*, pp. 75ff., 110ff., pls. N 9-12, 20, 21, 37, 57-8, 60.

[86] Museo teatrale alla Scala in Milano, Mus. No. 123. Formerly in the Collection théâtrale de Jules Sambon. Cf. Rohden-Winnefeld, *Terrakotta-Reliefs der römischen Kaiserzeit*, p. 312; others, *ibid.*, p. 141f., and 276f., pl. LXXIV. Cf. also the marble relief, Torlonia, *Mon. Inst.*, III, pl. XXXVIII.

[87] On circus races, cf. Saglio in Daremberg-Saglio, *Dictionnaire des Antiquités*, I,2(1887),1187-1201. Friedländer, *op.cit.*, II,21-50. F. G. Moore, *The Roman's World*, pp. 138-143. Delbrück, *op.cit.*, p. 74f. N 6 and 56.

[88] Shear, *AJA*, XXIX(1925),382f., figs. 1-4; *ibid.*, XXX (1926),440ff., figs. 4-7. Stillwell, *Corinth*, II; *The Theater*, pp. 87ff., figs. 76-83. The drawings of the now destroyed paintings were made by Josephine Shear-Harwood.

[89] Cf. D-R, pls. III and X. Bulle, *Untersuchungen*, pp. 19 and 80. Fiechter, *Dionysostheater*, I,61; III,82.

[90] Stillwell, *Corinth*, II, *The Theater*, pp. 84-98, pl. VIIB. C. W. Blegen, *Troy*, I(1950), fig. 122. For other theaters the orchestra of which was made into an arena: Stobi, Philippi, and Kourion on the island of Cyprus, see Stillwell, *op.cit.*, p. 96.

[91] On naval show battles (naumachiae), see Friedländer, *Sittengeschichte*, II,92ff., trans. by Gough and Freese-Magnus, II,74ff.

[92] G. Traversari, *Dioniso*, XIII(1950),18ff., and XV(1952), 3ff., figs. 2-3. Traversari, "Venationes con bestie di terra e d'acqua in bacini occasionali e teatrali," *Atti della Academia Patavina di scienze, Lettere et Arti*, LXV(1952-53),3ff. For the water basin in Corinth, see Stillwell, *op.cit.*, p. 98, fig. 84, pl. IV.

[93] Cf. Friedländer and Gough, *op.cit.*, *passim*. Delbrück, *op.cit.*, pls. N 9, 37, 58, 60.

NOTES TO CHAPTER XVI. THE INFLUENCE OF THE ANCIENT THEATER ON THE
MODERN THEATER

[1] C. C. Coulter, the "Terentian Comedies of a Tenth Century Nun," *Classical Journal*, 24(1928-29), 515-529.

[2] For mediaeval Terence manuscripts see Ch. XI, Figs. 559-561, note 27.

[3] J. S. Tunison, *Dramatic Traditions in the Dark Ages*, Chicago, 1907. Chambers, *The Mediaeval Stage*, Oxford, 1903. Hermann Reisch, *Die ältesten berufsmässigen Darsteller des griechisch-italischen Mimus*, 1897; *idem, Der Mimus*, 1903. Horowitz, *Spuren griechischer Mimen im Orient*, Berlin, 1903.

[4] G. Jacob, *Geschichte des Schattentheaters*, 2nd ed., Hanover, 1924; Jacob, *Karagöz, Türkische Schattenspiele*, edited, translated, and explained by Hellmut Ritter (1924), I, pls. 1-8.

[5] W. Smith, *The Commedia dell'Arte*, New York, 1912. P. L. Duchartre, *La comédie italienne*, Paris, 1924; Constant Mic, *La Commedia dell'Arte*, Paris, 1927. Dieterich, *Pulcinella*, pp. 233ff. Allardyce Nicoll, *Masks, Mimes and Miracles*, pp. 83ff., 135ff., 290ff.; *idem, World Drama from Aeschylus to Anouilh*, p. 197f. Mario Apollonia, "Arlechino," in *Enciclopedia dello Spettacolo* (Roma, 1954), I,3-9, pls. 15-16. Here good colored illustrations of the patchwork costume, which Pulcinella and Harlequin have inherited from the centunculus of the late Roman mime; cf. above Ch. XI, Figs. 542-543, and Ch. XV, Fig. 829. The Etruscan-Roman Charun, Ch. XI, Figs. 544-545, became the mediaeval devil.

[6] Dieterich, *Pulcinella*, pp. 266ff.

[7] K. von Reinhardstoettner, *Plautus. Spätere Bearbeitungen plautinischer Lustspiele*. Duckworth, *The Nature of Roman Comedy*, pp. 397ff.

[8] Duckworth, *op.cit.*, pp. 402ff.

[9] Duckworth, *op.cit.*, pp. 408ff.

[10] Gilbert Highet, *The Classical Tradition*, pp. 197ff., 214. Duckworth, *op.cit.*, pp. 412ff. J. W. Draper, "Falstaff and the Plautine Parasite," *Classical Journal*, 33(1937/8), 390-401.

[11] J. W. Cunliffe, *The Influence of Seneca on Elizabethan Tragedy* (London, 1893). F. L. Lucas, *Seneca and Elizabethan Tragedy* (Cambridge, 1922). Duckworth, *The Complete Roman Drama*, I,xli-xlvi. T. S. Eliot, *Selected Essays, 1917-1932* (New York, 1932), pp. 51-88, 107-112. Mendell, *Our Seneca* (Yale University Press, 1941), pp. 189-200. Highet, *op.cit.*, pp. 207-209. Bieber, *Röm.Mitt.*, 60/61(1953/ 54), 106. Sheldon Cheney, *The Theatre* (New York, 1935), p. 181f.

[12] Newton, *The Tenne Tragedies*, 1581, republished by T. S. Eliot, *Seneca, His Tenne Tragedies*, with an introduction (London, 1927).

[13] Kernodle, *From Art to Theater*, pp. 160ff., fig. 48. Nicoll, *World Drama*, p. 178f.

[14] Furttenbach, *Architectura recreationes* (1640), pp. 64-70, pls. 22-23. Hammitzsch, *Der moderne Theaterbau I. Der höfische Theaterbau* (Berlin, 1907), p. 30, fig. 13. Kernodle, *op.cit.*, pp. 107f., 183f. Vignola, *Le due regole della prospettiva pratica* (1583).

[15] Highet, *op.cit.*, p. 129f. Allardyce Nicoll, *World Drama from Aeschylus to Anouilh*, pp. 254ff. Hammitzsch, *Der moderne Theaterbau I. Der höfische Theaterbau*, pp. 57ff., fig. 32 (Swan Theater); fig. 33 (Red Bull, 1662).

[16] Kernodle in a letter of 1943 pointed out to me the possibility that the façade and rear balcony of the type of the Assteas stage was taken over from the theater by artists and handed down through both the Byzantine and Carolingian traditions. Late mediaeval and early Renaissance paintings and sculpture have upper balconies on the scene of the same basic pattern as Assteas and the stages he copied. Cf. also, Kernodle, *From Art to Theater*, p. 141f. See above, Ch. X, Figs. 479-480, note 14 on the Assteas stage.

[17] Nicoll, *op.cit.*, p. 179, plate facing p. 193. Mariani, "Del Teatro Romano di Sabratha al teatro Olympico di Vicenza," *Rivista Italiana del Drama*, I,3, pp. 294-302. Martin Hammitzsch, *Der moderne Theaterbau* (1906), pp. 15ff., figs. 5-6. For the scenes painted by Serlio according to Vitruvius in 1545 see Kernodle, *From Art to Theater*, p. 181, fig. 52. Lukomski, *I Maestri della Architettura classica da Vitruvio allo Scamazzi*, translated by Lino Cappuccio (Milano, 1933), pp. 113, 119, 121, designs of 1521-1556. Hammitzsch, *op.cit.*, pp. 23ff., figs. 9-10.

[18] Nicoll, *op.cit.*, plate facing p. 224. Hammitzsch, *op.cit.*, p. 36f., figs. 15-16.

[19] Joseph Furttenbach, *Architectura recreationis* (1640), pp. 64ff., figs. 22-23. *Mannhafter Kunstspiegel* (1663), fig.

12a-b (our Fig. 840a-b). Hammitzsch, *Der moderne Thea-terbau*, p. 30, fig. 13. Michael, *Deutsches Theater* (Jeder-manns Bücherei, 1923), p. 18, fig. 75. Cf. above, Ch. VI.

[20] Furttenbach, *op.cit.*, fig. 12a. Nicoll, *op.cit.*, p. 178f., plate facing p. 256.

[21] Highet, *op.cit.*, pp. 142f., 298f. Nicoll, *op.cit.*, p. 180.

[22] Katherine Lever, "Greek Comedy in the Sixteenth Cen-tury English Stage," *Classical Journal*, 42(1946-47), pp. 169-174.

[23] R. R. Bolgar, *The Classical Heritage* (Cambridge, 1954), p. 495f.

[24] Duckworth, *op.cit.*, pp. 423-431.

[25] Kernodle, *op.cit.*, p. 168.

[26] Curt Sachs, *Our Musical Heritage. A Short History of Music*, pp. 196ff., 207ff. P. H. Láng, *Music in Western Civilization*, pp. 334-344. E. Dickinson, *The Study of the History of Music*, p. 67. Allen, *op.cit.*, p. 181f.

[27] Justi, *Winckelmann und sein Jahrhundert*, i(1898),202f. Highet, *op.cit.*, pp. 356ff.

[28] Lessing, *Briefe die neueste Literatur betreffend* No. 17, February 1759.

[29] W. J. Keller, *Goethe's Estimate of the Greek and Ro-man Writers* (Madison, Wisconsin, 1916). Gassner, *Masters of the Drama* (1954), pp. 317ff. Goethe as Orestes with Corona Schröter as Iphigenia: cut by G. M. Kraus, *Goethe-Gedenkblätter*, ed. Goethe National Museum in Weimar (3rd ed., 1925), p. 82 and fig. on p. 86.

[30] Highet, *op.cit.*, p. 425f.

[31] Highet, *ibid.*, pp. 466ff.

[32] Highet, *ibid.*, p. 419. N. I. White, *Portrait of Shelley* (New York, 1945), p. 465.

[33] Nietzsche, *Die Geburt der Tragödie aus dem Geist der Musik* (The Birth of Tragedy from the Spirit of Music).

[34] See similar stories in Highet, *op.cit.*, pp. 491ff.

[35] See Bibliography, XI. English Translations.

[36] Gassner, *Masters of the Drama*, pp. 643, 655, 657ff. Highet, *op.cit.*, p. 526.

[37] Gassner, *op.cit.*, p. 715f. Highet, *ibid.*, p. 538f.

[38] Allardyce Nicoll, *World Drama from Aeschylus to Anouilh*, pp. 914-918. Highet, *op.cit.*, p. 527. Gassner, *op.cit.*, p. 711f. Katharine Cornell misinterpreted the tragic conflict of Antigone as one between "the spirit and the flesh."

[39] Nicoll, *op.cit.*, pp. 916ff. Highet, *op.cit.*, p. 524. Gass-ner, *op.cit.*, p. 739f., pl. 14. Randolf Goodman, *Drama on Stage*, New York, 1961, pp. 13-28.

[40] See the introduction to the plays of Plautus by Duck-worth, *The Complete Roman Drama*, i,6f., Amphitruo; p. 118, Aulularia; p. 438f., *The Twin Brothers Menaechmi*. Allen, *Stage Antiquities*, pp. 166ff. Highet, *op.cit.*, p. 353. Duckworth, *The Nature of Roman Comedy*, p. 431f.

[41] Oates-O'Neill, *The Complete Greek Drama*, frontis-piece, production of *Prometheus Bound* at Delphi, 1930.

[42] *Prometheus* in Syracuse: see *Holiday* magazine, May 1956, p. 49.

[43] Guido Calza, *Capitolium*. v(1927),81ff., figs. on p. 84f.

[44] Sapori, *Rassegna d'Arte*, viii(1921),101ff., report on presentations in Syracuse.

[45] Mary Dietrich played the parts of heroines in the Max Reinhardt presentations in Berlin. Unfortunately she died young.

[46] Bieber, *AJA*, lviii(1954),277f., pl. 51, figs. 1-3.

[47] I owe the photograph for Fig. 857 to the photographer Hermann Landshoff. It is reprinted from *Mademoiselle*, Street and Smith Publications, Inc., 1955.

[48] Herald, *Das grosse Schauspielhaus; Heinz Reinhardt und seine Bühne* (1919). Oskar Fischel, *Das Moderne Büh-nenbild*, p. 25, fig. 11. Kenneth Macgowan, *Theater of To-morrow*, pp. 191-200. Macgowan and Melnitz, *The Living Stage*, fig. on p. 446. Cf. M. L. Barstow, " 'Oedipus Rex': A Typical Greek Tragedy," *The Greek Genius and Its Influence*, ed. Lane Cooper. Sheldon Cheney, *The Theatre*, pl. opposite p. 519 (Oedipus in a circus by Orlik). Hamlin, *Forms and Functions* (1952), iii,412ff., figs. 278-281 (similar theaters in New York).

[49] See *Theatre Arts*, October 1951, p. 30f.

[50] *Dionisio*, xix (1956), 172-185, with illustrations.

[51] See on open air theaters: Sheldon Cheney, *The Open Air Theatre*, 1918.

[52] For the Festival Theater at Bayreuth see Hamlin and Lee Simonson, *Forms and Functions*, iii,409, fig. 274. For the Munich Art Theater (Künstlertheater), *ibid.*, p. 410, fig. 275; cf. also Littmann's theater in Stuttgart, *ibid.*, p. 411f., fig. 276. For the Munich Theater see also Sheldon Cheney, *The Theatre*, fig. opposite p. 457.

[53] See note 48.

[54] See above Ch. VI. Bulle, *Untersuchungen*, p. 288f., fig. 18.

[55] Alexander Bézanet, *Le Théâtre au Japon* (Paris, 1901), p. 268. Macgowan and Melnitz, *op.cit.*, pp. 319, 442, 444, 451, 495. Walter Renée Fuerst and Samuel J. Hume, *Twentieth Century Stage Decoration*, pp. 87ff., figs. 17-22.

[56] Edward Gordon Craig, *On the Art of the Theatre* (Chi-cago 1911), plate facing p. xiv. It is a very impressive back-ground indeed.

[57] Hamlin, *op.cit.*, iii,436f., fig. 288. Burris-Meyer and Edward Cole, *Theatres and Auditories*. Progressive Architec-ture Library (New York, 1949), p. 212.

[58] Allardyce Nicoll, *Masks, Mimes and Miracles*, p. 348.

[59] See *National Geographic Magazine* (May 1956), pp. 666ff. The commentator Eugene D. Kammerman, manages to make three mistakes in one sentence: "Where togaed Romans once played the farces of Terence and Plautus." 1) Terence and Plautus wrote comedies, not farces; 2) these republican playwrights were not performed in the imperial theaters of the provinces; 3) they were played in the Greek pallium, not in the Roman toga. For Taormina see *Holiday* magazine (May, 1956), p. 48.

[60] See *National Geographic Magazine* (May 1956), pp. 672ff. for the bloodless bullfights.

LIST OF ILLUSTRATIONS AND SOURCES

Fig. A, *frontispiece*. Colossal Tragic Mask, Bronze, Hellenistic Period. Found, 1959, in a warehouse in the Piraeus, probably burnt during Sulla's attack in 86 B.C., *see Fig. 301*
Fig. B, *pp. iv-v.* Theater at Taormina, *see Fig. 636*
Fig. C, *p. xi.* Aristophanes' *The Birds*, Berlin, 1935, *see Fig. 843a*
Fig. D, *p. xvi.* Actors celebrating, *see Fig. 538*

CHAPTER I. THE RISE OF THE SATYR PLAY AND OF TRAGEDY

CHAPTER II. ATTIC TRAGEDY

310

CHAPTER III. OLD COMEDY AND MIDDLE COMEDY

311

CHAPTER IV. THE DIONYSIAC FESTIVALS

CHAPTER V. THE DEVELOPMENT OF THE THEATER BUILDING IN THE CLASSICAL PERIOD

CHAPTER VI. SCENERY AND MECHANICAL DEVICES

CHAPTER VII. THE EVOLUTION OF THE ART OF ACTING

313

CHAPTER VIII. NEW COMEDY

CHAPTER X. ITALIAN POPULAR COMEDY (THE PHLYAKES)

317

CHAPTER XI. THE ROMAN PLAYS AT THE TIME OF THE REPUBLIC

CHAPTER XII. THE ART OF ACTING IN ROME

CHAPTER XIII. THE DEVELOPMENT OF THE ROMAN THEATER
BUILDING DURING THE REPUBLICAN PERIOD

CHAPTER XIV. ROMAN THEATER BUILDINGS IN ITALY AND THE PROVINCES DURING THE EMPIRE

CHAPTER XV. PLAYS OF THE ROMAN EMPIRE

CHAPTER XVI. THE INFLUENCE OF THE ANCIENT THEATER ON THE MODERN THEATER

BIBLIOGRAPHY

Note: The bibliography has been arranged according to subject, so that in this many-sided field the reader can find more easily the books and papers which interest him especially. Inside each division the arrangement is alphabetical. The divisions on literature and epigraphy are far from complete, as they can easily be found elsewhere.

HANDBOOKS AND HISTORIES OF THE THEATER

Allen, James Turney. *Stage Antiquities of the Greeks and Romans and Their Influence*. New York, 1927.
———. "On the Odeum of Pericles and the Periclean Reconstruction of the Theater," *University of California Publications in Classical Archaeology*, I, No. 7 (1941), pp. 173-177.
Bethe, Erich. *Prolegomena zur Geschichte des Theaters im Altertum*. Leipzig, 1896.
Bieber, Margarete. *Die Denkmäler zum Theaterwesen im Altertum*. Berlin, 1920.
———. *The History of the Greek and Roman Theater*. Princeton University Press, 1939.
d'Amico, Silvio. *Storia del Teatro drammatico*, I. Rome, 1939-1940.
Fensterbusch, Curt. "Bericht über die Literatur zur Geschichte des Theaters der Griechen und Römer," *Jahresberichte der Klassischen Altertums Wissenschaft*, 227 (1930), III, 4-12; 253 (1936), III, 1-57.
Flickinger, Roy C. *The Greek Theater and its Drama*. The University of Chicago Press, 1918; 4th edition, 1936.
Haigh, A. E. *The Attic Theatre*, 3rd edition by Pickard-Cambridge. Oxford, 1907.

Körting, G. *Geschichte des griechischen und römischen Theaters*. Paderborn, 1897.
Little, Alan M. G. *Myth and Society in Attic Drama*. Columbia University Press, New York, 1942.
Müller, Albert. *Lehrbuch der griechischen Bühnenaltertümer*. Freiburg, 1886.
———. *Das attische Bühnenwesen*, 2nd edition, Gütersloh, 1916.
Navarre, Octave. *Le Théâtre Grec*. Paris, 1925.
Nicoll, Allardyce. *The Development of the Theater. A Study of Theatrical Art from the Beginnings to the Present Day*. 3rd ed. New York, 1946, pp. 17-62, figs. 1-51.
Oehmichen, Gustav. *Griechischer Theaterbau. Nach Vitruv und den Ueberresten*. Berlin, 1886.
———, and Paul Stengel. "Das Bühnenwesen der Griechen und Römer," in Iwan Müller, *Handbuch der klassischen Altertumswissenschaften*. Vol. V, part 3. München, 1890.
Schneider, G.C.W. *Das Attische Theaterwesen. Zum besseren Verstehen der griechischen Dramatiker nach den Quellen dargestellt*. Weimar, 1835.
Wieseler, Friedrich. *Theatergebäude und Denkmäler des Bühnenwesens bei den Griechen und Römern*. Göttingen, 1851.

ORIGINS OF THE THEATER

Bieber, Margarete. Review of Hedwig Kenner, *Das Theater und der Realismus in der griechischen Kunst* (1954) in *Gnomon* (1956), 127-134.
Brommer, F. "Satyroi." Dissertation, Würzburg, 1937.
Cornford, F. Macdonald. *The Origin of Attic Comedy*. Cambridge, 1934.
Dieterich, Albrecht. "Die Entstehung der Tragödie," *Archiv für Religionswissenschaft*, XI (1908), 163ff.; reprinted in *Kleine Schriften*, pp. 414ff.
Ducati, Pericle. *Storia dell'Arte etrusca*, II. Pls. 77, 79, 84-87, 89. Florence, 1927.
Grande, C. del. *Tragodia. Essenza e genesi della tragedia*. Napoli, 1952.
Herter, Hans. *Vom dionysischen Tanz zum komischen Spiel, Darstellung und Deutung*, I. Iserlohn, 1942.
Kenner, Hedwig. *Das Theater und der Realismus in der griechischen Kunst*. Wien, 1954.

Mahr, August C. *The Origin of the Greek Tragic Form*. New York, 1938.
Nilsson, M. "Der Ursprung der Tragödie," *Neue Jahrbücher für das klassische Altertum*, 1911, pp. 609 and 673f.
———. *Geschichte der griechischen Religion*, Iwan Müller, *Handbuch der klassischen Altertumswissenschaften*. Abt. V, Teil II. Vol. 1. ed. W. Otto. Munich, 1941. Pp. 215-219 (Satyrn und Silene); pp. 532-568 (Dionysos).
Pallottino, M. *Etruskische Malerei*. Geneva, 1952. *Etruscan Painting*. New York, 1952, pp. 38ff., 65f., 73ff.
Pickard-Cambridge, Arthur Wallace. *Dithyramb, Tragedy and Comedy*. Oxford, 1927.
Pohlenz, M. "Das Satyrspiel und Pratinas von Phlius," *Nachrichten der Göttinger Gesellschaft der Wissenschaften*, 1926, pp. 298ff.
Poulsen, F. *Etruscan Tomb Paintings*. Oxford, 1922. Pp. 12f., figs. 4-6.

Radermacher, L. *Beiträge zur Volkskunde aus dem Gebiet der Antike.* Sitzungsberichte der Akademie der Wissenschaften. Wien. Philologisch-historische Klasse. Band 187, Abh. 3, 1918, pp. 18ff., 32ff.: "Menschen und Tiere" (Karikatur).

Reisch, E. "Zur Vorgeschichte der attischen Tragödie," *Festschrift Th. Gomperz,* 1902, pp. 451ff.

Ridgeway, William. *The Origin of Tragedy with Special Reference to the Greek Tragedians.* Cambridge, Eng., 1910.

————. *The Dramas and Dramatic Dances of Non-European Races in Special Reference to the Origin of Greek Tragedy*; with an Appendix on the Origin of Greek Comedy. Cambridge, Eng., 1915.

————. *Dramatic Dances of Non-European Races.* Cambridge, Eng., 1925.

Winterstein, Alfred. *Der Ursprung der Tragödie. Psychoanalytischer Beitrag zur Geschichte des Griechischen Theaters.* Imago-Bücher, VIII. Leipzig, 1925.

THEATER BUILDING

1. Greek

Allen, James Turney. "The Key to the Reconstruction of the Fifth-Century Theater at Athens," *University of California Publications in Classical Philology,* V, No. 2, 1918; "The Greek Theater of the Fifth Century Before Christ." *ibid.,* VII, No. 1, 1920; "The Orchestra Terrace of the Aeschylean Theater," *ibid.,* No. 2, 1922; "Problems of the Proskenion," *ibid.,* No. 5, 1923. "On the Program of the City Dionysia during the Peloponnesian War," *ibid.,* XII, No. 3, 1938.

Anti, Carlo. *Teatri Greci arcaici da Minosse a Pericle.* Padua, 1947.

————. *Guida del Teatro antico di Siracusa,* Firenze, 1948.

————. "L'acustica fattore determinante della storia dei teatri greci e romani," *Atti della Accademia Patavina di Scienze, Lettere, ed Arti* (Padova), LXIV (1951-52), 1-27.

Arias, Paolo Enrico. *Il Teatro greco fuori di Atene.* Firenze, 1934.

Bieber, Margarete. "A Free Theater for a Free People," *Theater Arts,* 1941, pp. 908-916.

Broneer, Oscar. "The Tent of Xerxes and the Greek Theater," *University of California Publications in Classical Archaeology,* I, No. 12, 1944, pp. 305-12.

Bulle, Heinrich. "Untersuchungen an griechischen Theatern," *Abhandlungen Bayer. Akad. Wissenschaften,* phil.-hist. Klasse, Vol. XXXIII, München, 1928.

Capps, E. "The Stage in the Greek Theatre According to the Extant Dramas," *Transactions of the American Philological Association,* XXII, 1891. Reprinted Berlin, 1893.

Dinsmoor, William Bell. *The Architecture of Ancient Greece. An Account of Its Historic Development.* Revised and enlarged edition based on the first part of *The Architecture of Greece and Rome* by William J. Anderson and R. Phené Spiers (1927). London-New York, 1950. Theater: Archaic, p. 119f.; Fifth Century, 207-211; Fourth Century, 244-251; Hellenistic and Graeco-Roman, 297-330.

————. "The Athenian Theater of the Fifth Century," *Studies Presented to David Moore Robinson.* Saint Louis, Washington University, I, 1951, pp. 309-330.

Dörpfeld, Wilhelm, and Emil Reisch. *Das Griechische Theater.* Athens, 1896.

Fensterbusch, Curt. In Pauly-Wissowa, *Real-Encyclopädie der Classischen Altertumswissenschaft,* zweite Reihe, Vol. V, 1934. Pp. 1384ff. *s.v.* "Theatron" and p. 2030f. *s.v.* "Theologeion."

Fiechter, Ernst Robert. *Die baugeschichtliche Entwicklung des antiken Theaters.* München, 1914.

————. *Antike griechische Theaterbauten.* 9 vols. Stuttgart, 1930-37. Leipzig. Sächsische staatliche Forschungsinstitute. Forschungsinstitut für klassische Philologie und Archaeologie. Vol. 1. *Das Theater in Oropos,* 1930. Vol. 2. *Die Theater von Oiniadai und Neupleuron,* 1931. Vol. 3. *Das Theater in Sikyon,* 1931. Vol. 4. *Das Theater in Megalopolis,* 1931. Vols. 5-7. *Das Dionysos-Theater in Athen.* I. *Die Ruine.* II. *Die Skulpturen vom Bühnenhaus* (Herbig). III. *Einzelheiten und Baugeschichte* (mit Bulle und Kübler), 1935-36. Vol. 8. *Das Theater in Eretria,* 1937. Vol. 9. *Das Dionysos-Theater in Athen,* IV. *Nachträge* (supplement to Vols. 5-7). *Das Theater im Piraieus, Das Theater auf Thera.* Stuttgart und Köln, 1950.

Frickenhaus, August. *Die altgriechische Bühne.* Strassburg, 1917.

————. "Antike Bühnenkunst," *Bonner Jahrbücher,* Heft 125, 1919, pp. 195-210, pl. XXXVII.

Gerkan, Arnim von. *Das Theater von Priene.* München, 1921.

Heberdey, Niemann, Wilberg. *Das Theater in Ephesos,* in *Forschungen in Ephesos,* II. Oester. arch. Inst., Wien, 1912.

Hill, Ida Thallon. *The Ancient City of Athens. Its Topography and Monuments.* London, 1953. Ch. XII, "The Theatre of Dionysos," pp. 113-124.

Libertini, Guido. *Il Teatro antico e la sua Evoluzione.* Catania, 1933.

Noack, Ferdinand. *Skene Tragike. Eine Studie über die scenischen Anlagen auf der Orchestra des Aischylos und der anderen Tragiker.* Tübingen, 1915.

Pickard-Cambridge, Arthur Wallace. *The Theatre of Dionysus in Athens.* Oxford, 1946.

Puchstein, Otto. *Die griechische Bühne. Eine architektonische Untersuchung.* Berlin, 1901.

Rizzo, G. Emanuele. *Il Teatro Greco di Siracusa.* Milano-Roma, 1923.

Robertson, D. S. *A Handbook of Greek and Roman Architecture,* Cambridge, 1929, sec. ed. 1954. Pp. 164-169, figs. 71 (Epidauros), 72-73; Priene, pp. 271-283.

Romagnoli, Ettore. *Il Teatro Greco.* Milano, 5th ed., 1924.

Stillwell, R. *Corinth, The Theater, The Results of Excavations Conducted by the American School of Classical Studies at Athens,* II. Harvard University Press, 1952.

2. Roman

Anderson, W. J. and R. P. Spiers (revised and rewritten by Thomas Ashby). *The Architecture of Ancient Rome.* New York and London, 1927. Pp. 87-98, figs. 21-26, pls. LXVI-XLVIII.

Bachy, Victor. "Un théâtre Romain, Orange," *Phoibos,* III-IV (1948-1950), 97-109, figs. 3-14.

Boeswillwald, E., Cagnat, B., Ballu, A. *Timgad, une cité africaine sous l'empire romain.* Pp. 93ff., figs. 42-52, pls. XIII-XV and 105f., fig. 45. Paris, 1905.

Broneer, O. *Corinth, The Odeum, Results of Excavations Conducted by the American School of Classical Studies at Athens,* X. Harvard University Press, 1932.

Calza, Guido. *Il teatro Romano di Ostia.* Rome, 1927.

————. *Ostia.* Pp. 8f., 26f., figs. 19-21, 25. Milan, 1925.

Caputo, G. In *Dioniso* (Bolletino dell' Istituto Nazionale del Dramma antico), x (1947), 5-23 (Leptis Magna).

———. "Architettura del teatro di Leptis Magna," *Dioniso*, XIII (1950), 164-178.

Il Teatro di Leptis Magna; Il Teatro di Sabratha, Monografie di Archeologia libica III and VI, Rome, l'Erma di Bretschneider, in the press.

Carton, L.B.Ch. *Le théâtre Romain de Dougga*. 2nd ed. Tunis, 1922.

Cube, G. von. "Römische Scaenae Frons in den Pompejanischen Wandbildern IV. Stils," *Beiträge zur Bauwissenschaft*, VI, 1906. Pp. 28ff., pls. II-VII.

Drexel, F., in L. Friedländer, *Darstellungen aus der Sittengeschichte Roms in der Zeit von Augustus bis zum Ausgang der Antonine* 9-10th. ed. IV (Anhänge), ed. G. Wissowa, 1921. "Gebäude für die öffentlichen Schauspiele in Italien und den Provinzen," pp. 205-257. "Kostüm und Bewaffnung der Gladiatoren," pp. 258-267, "Ueber die bei den röm. Venationen verwandten Tiere," pp. 268-275.

Fiechter, Ernst Robert. *Antike griechische Theaterbauten*, vol. 9, *Das Dionysostheater* IV (time of Nero), pp. 17-21, fig. 5, pls. 3-5. Stuttgart, 1950.

Formigé, Jules. "Remarques diverses sur les théâtres Romains d'Arles et d'Orange," *Mémoires présentés à l'Académie des Inscriptions et Belles-Lettres*, XIII, Part 1, Paris, 1923, pp. 25-90, figs. 1-19, pls. I-V. "Notes sur la scène du théâtre d'Orange, *ibid.*, XIII, Part 2, 1933, pp. 697-712, pls. XVI-XVII.

———. *Le théâtre romain de Vienne*. Vienne, 1950.

Frézouls, Eduard. "Teatri Romani dell'Africa francese," *Dionisio*, XV (1952), 90-103, pls. I-II.

———. "Les théâtres romains de Syrie," *Annales archéologiques de Syrie*, II (1952), 46-100.

———. *Le Théâtre de Philippopolis en Arabie*, Paris, 1956.

Gerkan, Arnim von. "Zu den Theatern von Segesta und Tyndaris," *Festschrift Andreas Rumpf*, Krefeld, 1952, pp. 82-92, figs. 5-6.

Guidi, Giacomo. In *Africa Italiana*, III (1930), 36ff. (Sabratha).

Gullini, Giuseppe. "Sabratha," *Bulletino della Commissione archeologica, Bull. del Museo del Impero Romano*, LXXI (1943-1945), 21-34, figs. 1-2, 10.

Hanson, John Arthur. *Roman Theater-Temples*. Princeton Monographs in Art and Archaeology, 33. Princeton University Press, 1959.

Hörmann, Hans. "Die römische Bühnenfront zu Ephesos" *Jahrbuch des deutschen arch. Instituts*, 38/9, 1923/4, pp. 275ff. Beilage VI-VIII.

Lanckoronski, K. *Städte Pamphyliens und Pisidiens*, I-II. Vienna, 1890-92.

Lugli, Giuseppe. "L'Origine del teatro stabile in Roma antica," *Dioniso*, IX (1942), 2-3, 55-64.

Maiuri, Amedeo. *Introduzione allo studio di Pompei* (1943), pp. 34ff.

———. "Saggi nella Cavea del "Teatro grande," *Notizie degli Scavi*, Serie VIII, vol. V, 1951, pp. 126-134.

———. *Pompei*. Novara, 1951, pp. 26-30, pls. 36-45.

———. *Pompei*, in *Musei e Monumenti d'Italia*, No. 3., pp. 23ff., fig. 3, pl. XIII, figs. 23-24, pl. XIV, figs. 25-26.

———. *Ercolano*. Novara, 1932, pp. 27ff. *Herculaneum*, Paris, 1932, figs. on pp. 27-29. *Herculaneum*, tr. by V. Priestley, Rome, 1937, pp. 61-65, fig. 6, pl. XL, figs. 71-72

Marconi, P. *Verona Romana*. Bergamo, 1937, pp. 131ff.

Mau, August. *Pompeji in Leben und Kunst*. Leipzig, 1900, pp. 129-150 (Theater); 196-209 (Amphitheater).

Mélida, José Ramon. *Il Teatro Romano di Merida*. Madrid, 1915.

Paratore, Ettore, *Storia del Teatro Latino*. Milano, 1957.

Paribeni, R. "Il teatro durante l'impero romano," *Dioniso*, VI (1937), 45ff., 209-216.

Peyre, R. *Nîmes, Arles, Orange*. Paris, 1910, pp. 78ff.

———. *Le midi de la France et ses villes d'art: Avignon, Nîmes, Arles, Orange*. Paris, 1931.

Pfeiffer, Homer. *Memoirs of the American Academy*, IX (1931), 145-156, pls. 11-15, and frontispiece (Dugga).

Platner, Samuel B. and Ashby, T. *Topographical Dictionary of Ancient Rome, s.v.* "theatrum Balbi, Marcelli, Pompeii," pp. 513ff. London, 1929.

Puchstein, Otto, in Wiegand, Theodor, *Palmyra. Ergebnisse der Expeditionen von 1902 und 1917*. Berlin, 1932, pp. 41ff., pls. 11, 19-23.

Robertson, D. S. *Handbook of Greek and Roman Architecture*. Cambridge, 1929, 2d ed., 1954, pp. 271-283, figs. 114-118, Pompeii; pl. XX, Orange; figs. 115-118, Aspendus.

Rumpf, Andreas. "Die Entstehung des römischen Theaters," *Mitteilungen des Deutschen archäologischen Instituts*, III (1950), 40-50.

Sautel, J. *Le théâtre de Vaison et les théâtres Romains de la Vallée du Rhône. Etudes et Documents sur Vaison-La Romaine*, XI, 1951. Avignon, new ed. Bibliography on the theaters in the Rhone Valley, pp. 44-47.

Thompson, Homer A. "The Odeion in the Athenian Agora," *Hesperia*, Journal of the American School of Classical Studies at Athens, XIX (1950), 31-141, pls. 16-60.

Wuilleumier, P. "Théâtres et amphithéâtres Romains de Lyon," *Annales de Gand*, I (1937), 131ff.

———. *Lyon, Métropole des Gaules*. Le monde romain Collection publiée sous le patronage de l'Association Guillaume Budé. Paris, 1953.

———. "Fouilles de Fourvière, à Lyon," in *Suppléments à Gallia*, éd. du Centre National de la Recherche Scientifique, 1951.

———. *Les Fouilles de Fourvière*, 11th ed., Lyon, 1952.

PRODUCTION AND REPRODUCTIONS OF THEATER PERFORMANCES

Anti, Carlo. "Rilievo teatrale Romano da Castel S. Elia," *Beiträge zur älteren Kulturgeschichte*. Band I, *Festschrift für Rudolf Egger*, pp. 189-205, figs. 1-2. Klagenfurt, 1952.

Beyen, H. G. *Die pompejanische Wanddekoration vom zweiten bis zum vierten Stil*, I. Haag, 1938, Pp. 97-207, figs. 22-33, 44-61.

Bieber, Margarete, and Alfred Brückner, "Kuchenform mit Tragödienszene," *Skenika*, 75. Programm zum Winckelmanns-Feste der archäologischen Gesellschaft zu Berlin, 1915.

———. "A Tragic Chorus on a Vase in the Metropolitan Museum," *AJA*, 45 (1941), 529-536.

———. "Wurden die Dramen des Seneca in Rom aufgeführt?" *Mitteilungen des deutschen Instituts in Rom*, 60/61 (1953-54), 100-106.

———. "The Entrances and Exits of Actors and Chorus in Greek Plays, with Appendix: The Statues of Miltiades and Themistokles in the Theater at Athens," *AJA*, 58 (1954), 277-284, pls. 51-54.

———. Articles in *Enciclopedia dello Spettacolo, s.v.* Frickenhaus, Fiechter, Ludi, Scenotecnica, Scenografia, Spettacoli Greci, Spettacoli in Roma, Theologeion, Thyroma, Velum, Rome, 1956-.

327

Brommer, F. *Satyrspiele. Bilder griechischer Vasen.* Berlin, 1944.

Bulle, Heinrich, *Eine Skenographie.* 94. Winckelmanns-Programm. Berlin, 1934.

———, and Wirsing, Heinrich. *Szenenbilder zum griechischen Theater des 5. Jahrhunderts v. Chr.* Berlin, 1950.

Buschor, Ernst. "Feldmäuse," *Sitzungsberichte Bayrische Akademie der Wissenschaften,* München, Philosophisch-historische Klasse, 1937, Heft 1, pp. 1-34.

Capps, E. *The Introduction of Comedy into the City Dionysia.* Decennial Publications of the University of Chicago, 1903.

———. "The Chorus in the Later Greek Drama," *AJA,* XI (1895), 287ff., 325ff.

Delbrück, Richard. *Die Consular-Diptychen, in Studien zur spätantiken Kunstgeschichte im Auftrag des Deutschen archäologischen Instituts,* ed. R. Delbrück und H. Lietzmann. Berlin und Leipzig, 1929, pp. 78ff.

Dieterich, Albrecht. *Pulcinella. Pompejanische Wandbilder und römische Satyrspiele.* Leipzig, 1897.

Fensterbusch, Curt. *Die Bühne des Aristophanes.* Leipzig, 1912.

Formigé, Jules. "Notes complémentaires sur les théâtres romains," *Bulletin des Antiquaires de France,* 1913, pp. 111-114. "Les representations dans les théâtres romains," *ibid.,* 1921, pp. 88-93, 315-317.

Friedländer, Ludwig. *Darstellungen aus der Sittengeschichte Roms, in der Zeit von Augustus bis zum Ausgang der Antonine,* 9th ed., besorgt von Georg Wissowa, II. Leipzig, 1920, pp. 1-160, "Die Schauspiele."

Harsh, P. W. *Studies in Dramatic "Preparation" in Roman Comedy.* Chicago, 1935.

Hook, La Rue Van. *Greek Life and Thought.* Chaps. XII-XV, pp. 172-216. Columbia University Press, revised ed., 1933.

Ivanov, Teofil. "Une mosaïque Romaine de Ulpia Oescus," *Monuments de l'Art en Bulgarie,* II, 1954. Académie des Sciences, Sofia (Scene from Menander, Achaioi).

Johnston, Mary. *Exits and Entrances in Roman Comedy.* Geneva, N.Y., 1933.

Jones, W. and Morey, C. R. *The Miniatures of the Manuscripts of Terence Prior to the Thirteenth Century.* Princeton, 1931.

Little, Alan M. G. "Scaenographia," *Art Bulletin,* XVIII (1936), 407ff., figs. I-VIII.

———. "Perspective and Scene Painting," *ibid.,* XIX (1937), 485-495.

———. "A Roman Source Book for the Stage," *AJA,* 60 (1956), 27-33, pls. 20-27.

Moore, Frank Gardner. *The Roman's World.* New York, 1936. Ch. VI, "Festivals and Diversions," pp. 135-153.

Musenides, Takis. "Aischylos und sein Theater," *Die Bühnenkunst der Antike,* I. Berlin, 1937.

Pasqui, A. in *Notizie degli Scavi,* 1906, pp. 357ff. (Kuchenformen).

Petersen, E. *Die Attische Tragödie als Bild- und Bühnenkunst.* Bonn. 1915.

Pickard-Cambridge, A. W. *The Dramatic Festivals of Athens.* Oxford, 1953.

Séchan, Louis. *Études sur la Tragédie grecque dans ses rapports avec la Céramique.* Paris, 1926.

Simon, Antonia, Katharina, Henriette (Antonia Goethert). *Comicae Tabellae. Die Szenenbilder zur griechischen 'Neuen Komödie,'* in *Die Schaubühne, Quellen und Forschungen zur Theatergeschichte.* Band 25. Emsdetten, 1938.

Taylor, Lily Ross. "The Opportunities for Dramatic Performances in the Time of Plautus and Terence," *Transactions American Philological Association,* LXVIII (1937), 284-304.

Terentius Codex Ambrosianus. Phototype editus, praefatus est Ericus Bethe. Lugduni Batavorum (Leyden), 1903.

Vogel, Julius. "Scenen Euripideischer Tragödien in griechischen Vasengemälden," *Archäologische Beiträge zur Geschichte des griechischen Dramas.* Leipzig, 1886.

Webster, T. B. L. *Greek Theatre Production.* London, 1956. (Review by M. Bieber, *AJP* 78 (1957), 206-213.)

Weitzmann, Kurt. "Three Bactrian Silver Vessels, with Illustrations from Euripides," *Art Bulletin* 25 (1943), 289-324.

———. "Euripides Scenes in Byzantine Art," *Hesperia* 18 (1949), 159-210.

Weston, Karl E. "The Illustrated Terence Manuscripts," *Harvard Studies in Classical Philology,* XIV (1903), 37-54, with 90 plates.

———. *Terence Illustrated. An Exhibition.* Williams College, Williamstown, Mass., 1955.

MUSIC AND DANCE

Behn, Friedrich. *Die Musik des Altertums.* Mainz, 1925.

———. *Musikleben im Altertum und frühen Mittelalter.* Stuttgart, 1954.

Bethe, E. "Die griechische Tragödie und die Musik," *Neue Jahrbücher für das klassische Altertum,* XIX (1907), 81-95.

Emanuel, Maurice. *La Dance grecque antique.* Paris, 1896.

———. *The Antique Greek Dance.* Translated from the French by Harriet Jean Beauley. 2nd ed. London, 1927.

Georgiades, Thrasybulos. *Musik und Rhythmus bei den Griechen,* Hamburg, 1958.

———. *Greek Music, Verse and Dance,* Merlin Music Books V, New York.

Kitto, H. D. F. "The Dance in Greek Tragedy," *Journal of Hellenic Studies,* LXXV (1955), 36-41.

Lawler, Lillian M. *The Dance of the Ancient Greek Theater,* University of Iowa Press, 1964.

Mountford, J. F. "Greek Music in the Papyri and Inscriptions" in *New Chapters in Greek Literature,* II, 1929, pp. 146-183.

——— and R. P. Winnington-Ingram, "Music" in *Oxford Classical Dictionary,* 1949.

Roos, Ervin. *Die tragische Orchestrik im Zerrbild der altattischen Komödie.* Lund, 1951.

Sachs, Curt. *Die Musikinstrumente,* Breslau, 1923.

———. *Die Musik des Altertums,* Breslau, 1924.

———. "Die Musik der Antike," in *Handbuch der Musikwissenschaft,* ed. E. Bücken. Potsdam, 1930.

———. *The History of Musical Instruments.* New York, 1940.

———. *The Rise of Music in the Ancient World, East and West.* New York, 1943.

Schnabel, Heinz. *Kordax. Archäologische Studien zur Geschichte eines antiken Tanzes und zum Ursprung der griechischen Komödie.* München, 1910.

Séchan, Louis. *La Danse grecque antique.* Paris, 1930.

Thierfelder, A. *Altgriechische Musik. Sammlung von Gesängen aus dem klassischen Altertum vom 5. bis 1. Jahrhundert v. Chr.* Leipzig, 1899.

Vetter, W. "Musik" in Pauly-Wissowa, *Real-Encyclopädie,* XVI, 1, 1933, pp. 823ff.

Weege, Fritz. *Der Tanz in der Antike.* Halle, 1926.

Wegner, Max. *Das Musikleben der Griechen.* Berlin, 1949.

POPULAR THEATER

Bieber, Margarete. "Mima Saltatricula," *AJA*, 43 (1939), 640-644.

Catteruccia, Luigi M. *Pitture vascolari italiote di soggetto teatrale comico.* Roma, 1951.

Daremberg-Saglio, *Dictionnaire des Antiquités*: G. Boissier, s.v. "Mimus," III,2 (1904), pp. 1899-1907; O. Navarre, s.v. "Persona," IV,1 (1906), pp. 406-416; Navarre, s.v. "Phlyakes," IV,1 (1906), pp. 435-438; G. Lafaye, s.v. "Satura," IV,2 (1906), pp. 1078-1080.

Heydemann, H. "Die Phlyakendarstellungen auf bemalten Vasen," *Jahrbuch des deutschen archäologischen Instituts*, I, 1886, pp. 260ff.

Horovitz, J. *Spuren griechischer Mimen im Orient.* Berlin, 1905.

Körte, Alfred. "Archäologische Studien zur alten Komödie," *Jahrbuch des deutschen archäologischen Instituts*, VIII, 1893, pp. 61ff.

Nicoll, Allardyce. *Masks, Mimes and Miracles. Studies in the Popular Theatre.* London and New York, 1931.

Pauly-Wissowa. *Real-Encyclopädie des klassischen Altertums.* Marx, "Atellanae Fabulae," II,2 (1892), pp. 1914-1821. Kroll, "Satura," sec. series, II,1 (1921), pp. 192-200. Wüst, "Mimus," XV (1932), pp. 1727-43. Wüst, "Phlyakes," XX,2 (1941), pp. 292-306. Wüst, "Pantomimus," XVIII,3 (1949), pp. 833-869.

Reich, Hermann. *Der Mimus. Ein litterar-entwickelungsge-schichtlicher Versuch.* 1. *Theorie des Mimus*; 2. *Entwickelungsgeschichte des Mimus.* Berlin, 1903.

———. *Der Mann mit dem Eselskopf. Ein Mimodrama vom klassischen Altertum verfolgt bis auf Shakespeares Sommernachtstraum.* Weimar, 1904.

Traversari, Gustave. "Colombètra e Tetimimo," *Dioniso* (Bolletino dell'Instituto Nazionale del Dramma Antico), N.S., XIII (1950), 18-35, and XV (1952), 3-12.

———. "Venationes con bestie di terra e d'acqua in bacini occasionali e teatrali," *Atti della Academia Patavina di Scienze Lettere ed Arti*, LXV (1952-53), 3-16.

Trendall, A. D. *Paestan Pottery. A Study of the red-figured Vases of Paestum.* The British School at Rome. London, 1936. Pp. 21ff., 60ff.; figs. 19-31.

———. *Paestan Pottery* (revision and supplement). *Papers of the British School at Rome*, 20 (New Series, VII) 1952, pp. 1-53, pls. I-XIX.

———. "Vasi italioti ed etruschi a figure rosse," *Monumenti Musei e Gallerie Pontificie del Vaticano*, I (1953), 24ff., pls. VII-VIII.

———. *Catalogue of Phlyakes Vases*, London Institute of Classical Studies (1959).

Zahn, R. "Vom Maler Assteas und der griechischen Posse Unteritaliens," *Die Antike*, VII (1931), 70ff.

———. "Krater des Assteas," in Furtwängler-Reichhold, *Griechische Vasenmalerei*, III (1932), pp. 178ff. to pl. 150.

ACTORS AND ACTING

Allen, James Turney. "Greek Acting in the Fifth Century," *University of California Publications in Classical Philology*, II, No. 15 (1916), pp. 279-289.

Bieber, Margarete. "The Statuette of an Actor of New Comedy," *Bulletin of the Art Museum*, Princeton University, 1951, pp. 4-12.

Bulle, H. "Von griechischen Schauspielern und Vasenmalern," *Festschrift für James Loeb*, pp. 5ff. München, 1930.

———. "Weihebild eines tragischen Dichters," *Corolla Curtius*, pp. 150-160, pls. 54-57. Stuttgart, 1937.

Goldman, Hetty, and Jones, Frances. "Terracottas from the Acropolis of Halai," *Hesperia*, XI (1942), 365-421.

Hunningher, B. "Acoustics and Acting in the Theater of Dionysus Eleuthereus," *Mededelingen der Nederlandse Akademie van Wetenschappen*, No. 9, 1956.

Kaffenberger, M. "Das Dreischauspielergesetz in der griechischen Tragödie." Diss. Giessen, 1911.

Lüders, O. *Die Dionysischen Künstler.* Berlin, 1873.

O'Connor, J. B. *Chapters in the History of Actors and Acting in Ancient Greece together with a Prosopographia Histrionum Graecorum.* Chicago, 1908.

Rees, K. *The So-Called Rule of Three Actors in the Classical Greek Drama*, Chicago, 1908.

———. "The Three-Actor Rule in Menander," *Classical Philology*, V (1910), 291-302.

———. "The Meaning of Parachoregema," *Classical Philology*, II (1907), 387-400.

Romagnoli, Ettore. *Nel Regno di Dionise.* Bologna, sec. ed. 1923.

Shister, Famic Lorine. "The Portrayal of Emotion in Tragedy," *American Journal of Philology*, LXVI (1945), 377-397 and LXIX (1948), 229-231.

Sittl, K. *Die Gebärden der Griechen und Römer.* Leipzig, 1890.

Spitzbarth, Anna. *Untersuchungen zur Spieltechnik der griechischen Tragödie.* Winterthur, 1945.

Warnecke. "Die bürgerliche Stellung der Schauspieler im alten Rom," *Neue Jahrbücher für das klassische Altertum*, XXXIII (1914), 95ff.

COSTUMES

Abrahams, Ethel B. *Greek Dress.* London, 1908.

Beare, W. "Masks on the Roman Stage," *Classical Quarterly*, XXXIII (1939), 139-146.

Bieber, Margarete. "Die Herkunft des tragischen Kostüms," *Arch. Jahrb.*, XXXII (1917), 15-104.

———. Article "Kothurn," XI (1922), 1520; article "Maske," XIV,2 (1930), 2070-2105, in Pauly-Wissowa, *Real-Encyclopädie*.

———. *Griechische Kleidung.* Berlin, 1928.

———. *Entwicklungsgeschichte der griechischen Tracht von der vorgriechischen Zeit bis zur römischen Kaiserzeit.* Berlin, 1934.

———. Articles in *Enciclopedia dello Spettacolo* s.v. Costume, Onkos, Somation.

———. "Roman Men in Greek Himation" (Romani Palliati). *Proceedings of the American Philosophical Society*, 103, 1959, 374-417.

———. "Das Menander-Relief der Sammlung Stroganoff," *Festschrift Andreas Rumpf*, pp. 14-17. Krefeld, 1952.

Hense, Otto, *Die Modifizierung der Maske in der griechischen Tragödie*, 2nd. ed. Freiburg, 1905.

Heuzey, L. *Histoire du Costume antique, d'après des Études sur le modèle vivant.* Paris, 1922.

Higgins, R. A. *Catalogue of the Terracottas in the Department of the Greek and Roman Antiquities, British Museum.* London, 1954. Pp. 198-202, Nos. 737-802, pls. 97-99.

Körte, A. "Der Kothurn im fünften Jahrhundert," *Festschrift zur 49. Versammlung deutscher Philologen und Schulmänner.* Basel, 1907. Pp. 203ff.

———. "Archäologische Studien zur alten Komödie," *Arch. Jahrb.*, VIII (1893), 61ff.

Krien, Gisela. "Die Angleichung der tragischen und komischen Theatermasken in der spätantiken Zeit," in *Maske und Kothurn, Vierteljahrsschrift für Theaterwissenschaften*, I, 1955, pp. 79-87. Ed. Institut für Theaterwissenschaft an der Universität Wien, Hermann Böhlaus Nachf. Graz-Köln.

———. "Der Ausdruck der antiken Theatermasken nach Angaben im Polluxkatalog und in der pseudoaristotelischen Physiognomik," *JOAI*, XLII (1956), 84-117, figs. 45-59.

Luschey, Heinz. "Komödien-Masken" in *Ganymed, Heidelberger Beiträge zur antiken Kunstgeschichte*, pp. 70-84, Figs. 1-9. Heidelberg, 1949.

Reisch, Emil. *Griechische Weihgeschenke.* University Wien. Abhandlungen des archäologisch-epigraphischen Seminars No. 8, 1890.

Repond, Jules. *Les Secrets de la Draperie antique, de l'Himation Grec au Pallium Romain*, in *Studi di Antichità Cristiana del Pontificio Instituto di Archeologia Cristiana*, III. Rome-Paris, 1931.

Robert, Carl. *Die Masken der neueren attischen Komödie.* 25th Hallisches Winckelmanns-Programm. Halle, 1911.

Rumpf, Andreas. "Einige komische Masken" in *Mimus und Logos, Eine Festgabe für Carl Niessen*, pp. 163-170, pls. VI-VII. Emsdetten, Westfalen, 1952.

Saunders, C. *Costume in Roman Comedy.* Columbia University Press, 1909.

———. "The Introduction of Masks on the Roman Stage," *AJA*, XXXII (1911), 58ff.

Smith, K. K. "The Use of the High-heeled Shoe or Buskin in Greek Tragedy," *Harvard Studies in Classical Philology*, XVI (1905), 123.

Webster, T.B.L. "South Italian Vases and Attic Drama," *Classical Quarterly*, XLIII (1948), 15ff.

———. "The Masks of Greek Comedy," *Bulletin of John Rylands Library*, XXXII (1949), 97-133, figs. 1-8.

———. "Masks on Gnathia Vases," *Journal Hellenic Studies*, LXXI (1951), 222ff., pl. XLV.

———. "The Costume of the Actors in Aristophanic Comedy," *Classical Quarterly*, new series, V (1955), 94f.

———. "Notes on Pollux' List of Tragic Masks," *Festschrift Andreas Rumpf*, pp. 141-150, Krefeld, 1952.

DRAMATIC LITERATURE

1. ANCIENT WRITERS

Aristotle. *De arte poetica. The Poetics.* Ed. W. H. Fyfe. Loeb Classical Library, 1927.

Donatus, Aelius. *Commentum de Comoedia*

Donati in Commenta Terentiana Praefationes, ex recensione Augusti Reifferscheidii. Breslau, 1875. *Idem*, rec. P. Wessner. Leipzig, 1902-08.

Hunt, A. S. *Tragicorum Graecorum Fragmenta papyracea nuper reperta.* Oxford, 1912.

Kaibel, K. *Comicorum Graecorum Fragmenta.* Berlin, 1899.

Nauck, August. *Tragicorum Graecorum Fragmenta.* Leipzig, 1889.

Olivieri, A. *Frammenti della Commedia greca e del mimo nella Sicilia e nella Magna Grecia.* Naples, 2nd ed. 1946-1947.

Pollux, *Onomasticon.* ed. E. Bethe. Leipzig, 1931-1937.

Ribbeck, Otto. *Tragicorum Latinorum Fragmenta*, 3rd ed. Leipzig, 1897.

———. *Comicorum Romanorum Fragmenta*, 3rd ed. Leipzig, 1898.

Vitruvius. *The Ten Books on Architecture*, trans. by Morgan, Harvard University Press, Cambridge, 1926, pp. 137ff.

2. MODERN WRITERS

Beare, W. "The Italian Origin of Latin Drama," *Hermathena*, XXIV (1939), 30-53, 88f.

———. *The Roman Stage. A Short History of Latin Drama in the Time of the Republic.* London, 1950; 2nd. ed., 1955.

Blumenthal, A. von. *Sophokles. Entstehung und Vollendung der griechischen Tragödie.* Stuttgart, 1936.

Bowra, C. M. *Sophoclean Tragedy.* Oxford, 1945.

Duckworth, George E. *The Nature of Roman Comedy. A Study in Popular Entertainment.* Princeton University Press, 1952.

Duff, J. Wight. *A Literary History of Rome from the Origins to the Close of the Golden Age*, 3rd. ed. London, 1953, Chapters IV-V.

Ehrenberg, Victor. *The People of Aristophanes. A Sociology of Old Attic Comedy.* Oxford, 1943.

Fergusson, Francis, *The Idea of a Theater.* Princeton 1949. Pocket ed., Doubleday Anchor Books, New York, 1953.

Fränkel, E. *Plautinisches In Plautus.* Berlin, 1922.

Harsh, P. W. *Handbook of Classical Drama*, 2nd ed., Stanford, 1948.

Jahresberichte über die Fortschritte der klassischen Altertumswissenschaft.

Aeschylus: Morel, W. Vol. 234 (1932), pp. 67-106 and vol. 259 (1938), pp. 1-34.

Sophocles: Blumenthal, A. von. Vol. 261 (1938), pp. 67-139 and vol. 277 (1942), pp. 1-72.

Euripides: vol. 259 (1938), pp. 35-66

Griechischen Komödie: Wüst, vol. 263 (1939), pp. 1-99. (Comprehensive critical bibliographies.)

Kitto, H. D. F. *Greek Tragedy: A Literary Study.* 2d ed., rev. London, Methuen, 1950.

Idem, a Doubleday Anchor Book, A 38, 1954.

Körte, G. *Die griechische Komödie. Aus Natur und Geisteswelt*, 1914.

Idem in Pauly-Wissowa, *s.v.* Komödie, XI, pp. 1207ff.

Kroll, Wilhelm, *s.v.* "Satura" in Pauly-Wissowa, second series, zweite Serie, II, 1, 1921, pp. 192-200.

Legrand, Ph. E., "Daos, Tableau de la Comédie Grecque pendant la Période dite Nouvelle" in *Annales de l'Université de Lyon*, II, Droit et Lettres, Nouvelle Série, Fasc. 22, 1910. Translated and shortened to two-thirds of the original by James Loeb in *The New Greek Comedy*, 1917.

Leski, A. *Die Griechische Tragödie.* Leipzig, 1938.

Leski, A. *Die tragische Dichtung der Hellenen*. Göttingen, 1956 (Studien zur Altertumswissenschaft, 2).

Little, A. M. G. "Plautus and Popular Drama," *Harvard Studies in Classical Philology*, XLIX (1938), 205-228.

Lord, L. E. *Aristophanes, His Plays and His Influence*. Boston, 1925.

Lucas, D. W. *The Greek Tragic Poets*. London, 1950.

———. *Greek Drama for Everyman*. New York, 1953.

Miller, H. W. "A Survey of Recent Euripidean Scholarship, 1940-1954," *Classical Weekly*, 49 (1956), 81-92.

Miller, Walter. *Daedalus and Thespis. The Contribution of the Ancient Dramatic Poets to Our Knowledge of the Arts and Crafts of Greece*. I. Architecture, II. Sculpture, III. *Painting and Allied Arts*. I: New York, 1929. II-III: University of Missouri Publications, VI and VII, 1931-1932.

Murphy, Charles T. "A Survey of Recent Work on Aristophanes and Old Comedy," *Classical Weekly* 49 (1956), 201-211.

Murray, Gilbert. *Aristophanes. A Study*. Oxford, 1933.

———. *Euripides and His Age*. New York, 2nd ed., 1946.

Navarre, Octave. *La comédie des mœurs chez Aristophane*. Toulouse, 1931.

Norwood, Gilbert. *Greek Tragedy*. 2nd ed. London, 1928.

———. *Essays on Euripidean Drama*. Berkeley, 1954.

———. *Greek Comedy*. London, 1931.

———. *The Art of Terence*. Oxford, 1923.

Petersen, E. *Die attische Tragödie als Bild- und Bühnenkunst*. Bonn, 1915.

Pohlenz, M. *Die griechische Tragödie*. 2nd ed., Göttingen, 1954.

Post, L. A. *From Homer to Menander: Forces in Greek Poetic Fiction*. Berkeley, 1951.

Radermacher, L. "Zur Geschichte der griechischen Komödie," *Akademie der Wissenschaften*. Wien, vol. 202, 1. Abh. 1924, pp. 1-44. I. Phlyakes; II. Stoffgeschichtliches.

Reinhardt, Karl. *Aischylos als Regisseur und Theologe*. Bern, 1949.

———. *Sophokles*. 3rd ed. Frankfurt a.M., 1947.

Sheppard, J. T. in *Cambridge Ancient History*, V, 1927, Chapter V.

Webster, T.B.L. An Introduction to Sophocles. Oxford, 1936.

———. Greek Art and Literature, Oxford, The Clarendon Press, 1939, passim, particularly: pp. 57ff. Aeschylus; 87ff. Sophocles; 150ff. Euripides.

———. *Studies in Menander*. Manchester University Press, 1950.

———. *Studies in Later Greek Comedy*, Manchester University Press, 1953.

———. *Art and Literature in Fourth-Century Athens*. University of London, Athlone Press, 1956.

Wilamowitz-Möllendorff, U. von. *Einleitung in die griechische Tragödie*. Berlin, 1907.

———. *Euripides, Herakles*, I. Berlin, 1895. Chapters I-IV.

Wissowa, G. *Religion und Kultus der Römer*. 2nd ed. München, 1912, pp. 449-467.

INSCRIPTIONS

Capps, E. "A New Fragment of the List of Victors at the City Dionysia," *Hesperia*, XII (1943), 1ff.

Corpus Inscriptionum Graecarum (CIG), 4 vols. Berlin, Akademie der Wissenschaften, ed., Boeck, 1828-1877. *Inscriptiones Graecae*. (IG), 14 vols. *ibid*., 1873-1890, ed., Kirchoff, Kaibel et alii.

Corpus Inscriptionum Latinarum (CIL). Berlin, Akademie der Wissenschaften, 1862-1943 (1862-1936, 14 vols. 1893-1943, editio altera).

Dittenberger, W. *Sylloge Inscriptionum graecarum*. 3 vols. Leipzig, 1898-1901.

Durrbach, F. *Choix d'Inscriptions de Délos*. Paris, 1921.

Homolle, M. *Bulletin de Correspondance Hellénique*, 1894, pp. 162ff. (Delos)

Inscriptiones Graecae. (IG). Akademie der Wissenschaften. Berlin, 1873-1915. Editio minor 1913-1940.

Inscriptiones Atticae. IG, II-III, ed. J. Kirchner. Berlin, 1913.

Inscriptiones Argolides, IG, IV, ed. F. Hiller von Gaertringen. Berlin, 1929.

Jacoby, F. *Das Marmor Parium*, 1904. IG, XII,5, No. 444.

Meritt, B. "Greek Inscriptions," *Hesperia*, VII (1938), 116f.

Wilhelm, A. *Urkunden dramatischer Aufführungen in Athen*. Mit einem Beitrag von Georg Kaibel. Wien, 1906.

ENGLISH TRANSLATIONS

Aristophanes. *The Eleven Comedies*. Tudor Publishing Co., 1936.

Banks, Theodore Howard. *Sophokles. Three Theban Plays (Antigone, Oedipus the King, Oedipus at Colonus)*. Oxford University Press, 1956.

Cooper, Lane. *Fifteen Greek Plays*. Oxford University Press, 1943.

Duckworth, G. E. *The Complete Roman Drama*, 2 vols. New York: Random House, 1942.

Eliot, Charles W., ed. *Nine Greek Dramas*. The Harvard Classics, 8. New York, 1900.

Everyman's Library, Vol. 62, *Aeschylus, Lyrical Dramas*; Vol. 114, *Sophocles, Dramas*; Vols. 63 and 271; *Euripides, Plays*.

Fitts, Dudley. *Greek Plays in Modern Translation*. New York: The Dial Press, 5th ed., 1953.

Grene, David, and Richmond Lattimore, eds. *The Complete Greek Tragedies*. The University of Chicago Press, 1953-1959.

Hadas, Moses, and J. H. McLean, eds. *The Plays of Euripides*. New York: The Dial Press, 1936.

Hamilton, Edith. *Three Greek Plays*. New York: W. W. Norton and Co., 4th ed., 1956.

Loeb Classical Library (Greek and English): H. W. Smyth, *Aeschylus*, 2 vols.; F. Storr, *Sophocles*, 2 vols.; A. S. Way, *Euripides*, 4 vols.; B. B. Rogers, *Aristophanes*, 3 vols.; F. G. Allinson, *Menander*; (Latin and English): P. Nixon, *Plautus*, 5 vols.; J. Sargeaunt, *Terence*, 2 vols.; F. J. Miller, *Seneca*, 2 vols.

Murray, Gilbert, tr. *The Plays of Euripides*. London: Longmans, Green and Co., 1931.

Oates, Whitney J. and Eugene O'Neill, Jr. *The Complete Greek Drama*, 2 vols. New York: Random House, 1938.

———. *Seven Famous Greek Plays*. New York: The Modern Library, 1950.

Post, L. A. *Menander. Three Plays*, translated and interpreted. London and New York: E. P. Dutton and Co., 1929.

Robinson, C. A. *An Anthology of Greek Drama.* New York: Rinehart and Co. Vol. I, 1949; Vol. II, 1954.

Vellacott, P., tr. *Euripides. Alcestis and Other Plays* (*Hippolytus, Iphigenia in Tauris*). The Penguin Classics, 1953.

————. *Euripides. The Bacchae and Other Plays* (*Ion, The Women of Troy, Helen*). The Penguin Classics, 1954.

Watling, E. F. tr. *Sophocles. The Theban Plays.* The Penguin Classics, 5th ed., 1953.

————. *Sophocles. Electra and Other Plays* (*Philoctetes, Women of Trachis, Ajax*). The Penguin Classics, 2nd ed., 1954.

THE INFLUENCE OF THE ANCIENT THEATER ON THE MODERN THEATER

Allen, James Turney. *Stage Antiquities of the Greeks and Romans and Their Influence.* New York, 1927. pp. 149-182.

Cheney, Sheldon. *The Theatre. Three Thousand Years of Drama, Acting, and Stagecraft.* New York, 1935.

Duckworth, G. E. *The Nature of Roman Comedy. A Study in Popular Entertainment.* Princeton University Press, 1952, Chapter 15, "The Influence of Plautus and Terence upon English Comedy," pp. 396-433. Extensive bibliography on pp. 462-464.

Gassner, John. *Masters of the Drama.* New York, 1940, 3rd revised ed., 1954.

Hamlin, Talbot. *Forms and Functions of Twentieth-Century Architecture*, Columbia University Press, 1952. III. Building Types, pp. 396-477, theaters by Hamlin and Lee Simonson; pp. 478-520, auditoriums by A. L. Harmon.

Hammitzsch, Martin. *Der moderne Theaterbau I, Der höfische Theaterbau.* Berlin, 1906.

Highet, G. *The Classical Tradition. Greek and Roman Influences on Western Literature.* New York, 1949.

Kernodle, George R. *From Art to Theatre. Form and Convention in the Renaissance.* University of Chicago Press, 1944.

Lang, Paul Henry. *Music in Western Civilization.* New York, 1941.

MacGowan, Kenneth and William Melnitz. *The Living Stage. A History of the World Theater.* New York, Prentice Hall, 1955. Good bibliography on pp. 509-518.

Nicoll, Allardyce. *Masks, Mimes and Miracles. Studies in the Popular Theatre.* London, 1931.

————. *The Development of the Theater. A Study to the Present Day.* 3rd ed. New York, 1952.

————. *World Drama from Aeschylus to Anouilh.* London, 1949.

Sachs, Curt. *Our Musical Heritage. A Short History of Music.* 2nd edition, New York, 1955.